Writings
of the
Revolution

Writings of the Revolution

Selected Readings on Software Engineering

Edited by
Edward Yourdon

6308

YOURDON Press
1133 Avenue of the Americas
New York, New York 10036

Copyright © 1982 by YOURDON inc., New York, N.Y.

Printed in the United States of America

Library of Congress Catalog Number 81-71933

ISBN: 0-917072-25-1

This book was set in Times Roman by YOURDON Press, using a PDP-11/45 running under the UNIX† operating system.

---

†UNIX is a registered trademark of Bell Laboratories.

CONTENTS

ACKNOWLEDGMENTS

We gratefully acknowledge the following organizations for their permission to reprint the articles in this volume:

1. "A Technique for Software Module Specification with Examples," by D.L. Parnas, originally appeared in *Communications of the ACM*, Vol. 15, No. 5 (May 1972), pp. 330-36. Copyright © 1972 by the Association for Computing Machinery, Inc. Reprinted by permission.

2. "Cost/Benefit Analysis of Information Systems," by J.C. Emery, originally published by The Society for Management Information Systems (Chicago: Society for Management Information Systems, 1971); current excerpt reprinted from *System Analysis Techniques*, J.D. Couger and R.W. Knapp, eds. (New York: John Wiley & Sons, Inc., 1974), pp. 395-425. Copyright © 1971 by J.C. Emery. Reprinted by permission.

3. "Evolution of Business System Analysis Techniques," by J.D. Couger, originally appeared in *ACM Computing Surveys*, Vol. 5, No. 3 (September 1973), pp. 167-98. Copyright © 1973 by the Association for Computing Machinery, Inc. Reprinted by permission.

4. "Structure of the 'THE'-Multiprogramming System," by E.W. Dijkstra, originally appeared in *Communications of the ACM*, Vol. 11, No. 5 (May 1968), pp. 341-46. Copyright © 1968 by the Association for Computing Machinery, Inc. Reprinted by permission.

5. "Program Development by Stepwise Refinement," by N. Wirth, originally appeared in *Communications of the ACM*, Vol. 14, No. 4 (April 1971), pp. 221-27. Copyright © 1971 by the Association for Computing Machinery, Inc. Reprinted by permission.

6. "A Software Design and Evaluation System," by R.M. Graham, G.J. Clancy, and D.B. DeVaney, originally appeared in *Communications of the ACM*, Vol. 16, No. 2 (February 1973), pp. 110-16. Copyright © 1973 by the Association for Computing Machinery, Inc. Reprinted by permission.

7. "Design and Code Inspections to Reduce Errors in Program Development," by M.E. Fagan, originally appeared in *IBM Systems Journal*, Vol. 15, No. 3 (July 1976), pp. 182-211. Reprinted by permission from *IBM Systems Journal*, Copyright © 1976 by International Business Machines Corporation.

8. "Notes on Avoiding 'GO TO' Statements," by D.E. Knuth and R.W. Floyd, originally appeared in *Information Processing Letters*, Vol. 1 (1971), pp. 23-31. Copyright © 1971 by North-Holland Publishing Co. Reprinted by permission.

9. "Better Manpower Utilization Using Automatic Restructuring," by G. DeBalbine, originally appeared in *AFIPS Proceedings of the 1975 National Computer Conference,* Vol. 44 (Montvale, N.J.: AFIPS Press, 1975), pp. 319-27. Copyright © 1975 by the American Federation of Information Processing Societies, Inc. Reprinted by permission.

10. "PDL — A Tool for Software Design," by S.H. Caine and E.K. Gordon, originally appeared in *AFIPS Proceedings of the 1975 National Computer Conference,* Vol. 44 (Montvale, N.J.: AFIPS Press, 1975), pp. 271-76. Copyright © 1975 by the American Federation of Information Processing Societies, Inc. Reprinted by permission.

11. "The Emperor's Old Clothes," by C.A.R. Hoare, given as the 1980 Turing Award Lecture, originally appeared in *Communications of the ACM,* Vol. 24, No. 2 (February 1981), pp. 75-83. Copyright © 1981 by the Association for Computing Machinery, Inc. Reprinted by permission.

12. "Böhm and Jacopini's Reduction of Flow Charts," by D.C. Cooper, originally appeared in *Communications of the ACM,* Vol. 10, No. 8 (August 1967), pp. 463, 473. Copyright © 1967 by the Association for Computing Machinery, Inc. Reprinted by permission.

13. "Proof of a Program: FIND," by C.A.R. Hoare, originally appeared in *Communications of the ACM,* Vol. 14, No. 1 (January 1971), pp. 39-45. Copyright © 1971 by the Association for Computing Machinery, Inc. Reprinted by permission.

14. "Mathematical Foundations for Structured Programming," by H.D. Mills, originally appeared as IBM Corp. Report No. FSC 72-6012 (Gaithersburg, Md.: IBM Federal Systems Division, 1972). Reprinted by permission of IBM Federal Systems Division, Copyright © 1972 International Business Machines Corporation.

15. "Software and Its Impact: A Quantitative Assessment," by B.W. Boehm, originally appeared in *Datamation,* Vol. 19, No. 5 (May 1973), pp. 48-59. Reprinted With Permission of DATAMATION® magazine, © Copyright by TECHNICAL PUBLISHING COMPANY, A DUN & BRADSTREET COMPANY, 1973 — all rights reserved.

16. "A Model of Large Program Development," by L.A. Belady and M.M. Lehman, originally appeared in *IBM Systems Journal,* Vol. 15, No. 3 (1976), pp. 225-52. Reprinted by permission from *IBM Systems Journal,* Copyright © 1976 by International Business Machines Corporation.

17. "Project Planning and Control," by W.S. Donelson, originally appeared in *Datamation,* Vol. 22, No. 6 (June 1976), pp. 73-75, 78, 80. Reprinted With Permission of DATAMATION® magazine, © Copyright by TECHNICAL PUBLISHING COMPANY, A DUN & BRADSTREET COMPANY, 1976 — all rights reserved.

18. "Estimating Software Costs," by L.H. Putnam and A. Fitzsimmons, originally appeared as a three-part series in *Datamation,* Vol. 25, No. 9 (September 1979), pp. 189-98; Vol. 25, No. 10 (October 1979), pp. 171-78; and Vol. 25, No. 11 (November 1979), pp. 137-40. Reprinted With Permission of DATAMATION® magazine, © Copyright by TECHNICAL PUBLISHING COMPANY, A DUN & BRADSTREET COMPANY, 1979 — all rights reserved.

19. "Models of Computations and Systems — Evaluation of Vertex Probabilities in Graph Models of Computations," by D. Martin and G. Estrin, originally appeared in *Journal of the ACM,* Vol. 14, No. 2 (April 1967), pp. 281-99. Copyright © 1967 by the Association for Computing Machinery, Inc. Reprinted by permission.

20. "Exploratory Experimental Studies Comparing Online and Offline Programming Performance," by H. Sackman, W.J. Erikson, and E.E. Grant, originally appeared in *Communications of the ACM,* Vol. 11, No. 1 (January 1968), pp. 3-11. Copyright © 1968 by the Association for Computing Machinery, Inc. Reprinted by permission.

21. "Toward a Theoretical Basis for Estimating Programming Effort," by M.H. Halstead, originally appeared in *Proceedings of the ACM Conference* (October 1975), pp. 222-24. Copyright © 1975 by the Association for Computing Machinery, Inc. Reprinted by permission.

22. "A Method of Programming Measurement and Estimation," by C.E. Walston and C.P. Felix, originally appeared in *IBM Systems Journal,* Vol. 16, No. 1 (January 1977), pp. 54-73. Reprinted by permission from *IBM Systems Journal,* Copyright © 1977 by International Business Machines Corporation.

23. "Measuring Programming Quality and Productivity," by T.C. Jones, originally appeared in *IBM Systems Journal,* Vol. 17, No. 1 (January 1978), pp. 39-63. Reprinted by permission from *IBM Systems Journal,* Copyright © 1978 by International Business Machines Corporation.

24. "A Measure of Control Flow Complexity in Program Text," by M.R. Woodward, M.A. Hennell, and D. Hedley, originally appeared in *IEEE Transactions on Software Engineering,* Vol. SE-5, No. 1 (January 1979), pp. 45-50. © 1979 IEEE. Reprinted, with permission, from IEEE TRANSACTIONS ON SOFTWARE ENGINEERING, Volume SE-5, Number 1, pp. 45-50, January 1979.

25. "The Magical Number Seven, Plus or Minus Two: Some Limits on Our Capacity for Processing Information," by G.A. Miller, originally appeared in *The Psychological Review,* Vol. 63, No. 2 (March 1956), pp. 81-97. Copyright © 1956 by the American Psychological Association. Reprinted by permission of the publisher and author.

Section 1
ANALYSIS TECHNIQUES

More than a dozen years ago, a group of the world's leading computer scientists gathered in Garmisch, Germany, to participate in a now-famous software engineering conference sponsored by NATO. In the midst of their discussions, one participant — Dr. Edward David, who later became an advisor to President Nixon — remarked:

> There is no theory which enables us to calculate limits on the size, performance, or complexity of software. There is, in many instances, no way even to specify in a logically tight way what the software product is supposed to do or how it is supposed to do it.*

Throughout the computer field in the late 1960s and early 1970s, there was a growing awareness of the various problems involved in developing computer software; one of the most fundamental problems was simply figuring out what the user intended the software to do.

The task of determining what the user or customer wants from a computer system is generally known as *systems analysis,* and that is the subject of the first three papers in this collection. Originally published between 1971 and 1973, the writings of Parnas, Emery, and Couger give us a great deal of insight into the state of the art a decade ago, and provide clear evidence of the beginnings of a movement toward the more rigorous, formal methods of systems analysis that have come into common use in the 1980s.

Parnas: A Technique for Software Module Specification with Examples

Parnas' paper, "A Technique for Software Module Specification with Examples," written in 1971, shows early recognition of the problems of developing proper functional specifications for software. As Parnas points out at the beginning of the paper, "The specification must provide to the intended user *all* the information that he will need to use the program correctly, *and nothing more.*" Nearly a dozen years later, many systems analysts have still not learned that simple truth; their functional specifications are filled with extraneous information (such as thinly disguised sales pitches intended to persuade the user that the proposed system will be the most glamorous thing since the invention of television) and horrendous amounts of redundancy.

---

*E.E. David, *Software Engineering: Report on a Conference Sponsored by the NATO Science Committee,* eds. P. Naur and B. Randell (Garmisch, Germany: October 7-11, 1968), p. 69.

1

Parnas also emphasizes the crucial distinction between the *specification* of a system, and the *implementation* of the specification. As he says, "The specification must provide to the implementer, *all* the information about the intended use that he needs to complete the program, and *no additional information. . . .*" While many modern practitioners of systems analysis have taken this message to heart, it still has not been heard by many — they continue to write functional specifications that not only describe *what* the system must do, but also *how* the system will be implemented.

A third important point Parnas raises is the need for *formal* specifications — sufficiently formal to be conceivably tested in some *mechanical* way for completeness and consistency. Although many of today's functional specifications are still notoriously informal and imprecise, often because they are written in narrative English, we have at least come to appreciate the importance of testing the specification long before we test the code. Numerous studies in the past five years have confirmed that an error detected in the specification during the analysis phase of a project is approximately ten times cheaper to correct than if the same error is detected at the design phase.

Parnas proposes a specific technique for developing functional specifications that will avoid the problems mentioned above; the notation he uses is an ALGOL-like precursor to what many people now call pseudocode or structured English. It is questionable whether a user really would read through the specifications that Parnas uses as examples (I have to admit that my own eyes began to glaze over after the second example), but that depends on what one means by "user." It is evident from Parnas' examples that his specifications are *module* specifications, and that his user is probably a programmer — that is, someone who intends to use one of Parnas' modules as part of some other system. Interestingly, Parnas' emphasis here on separating the description of a function from the description of its implementation is embodied also in the concept of "information hiding" that Parnas popularized in the early 1970s.*

Today's systems analyst is often a person who has never written a line of code; too, he is more likely to be concerned with payroll systems and banking systems than systems that deal with symbol tables and pushdown stacks. Nevertheless, Parnas' ideas are important, have general application, and should be read carefully.

Emery: Cost/Benefit Analysis of Information Systems

The same can be said for Emery's "Cost/Benefit Analysis of Information Systems," published in 1971. In the 1980s, much emphasis has been placed on the *tools* of systems analysis — particularly graphic tools that the analyst can use to better portray a proposed system to the user. But the fundamental question still is that of deciding whether the system is worth building at all; the techniques that Emery describes for determining the costs and benefits of a system are as valid today as they were in 1971.

Emery points out that the early data processing systems developed in the 1950s and 1960s tended to serve the needs of bottom-level workers and supervisors in an organization; they replaced manual record-keeping and computation with faster, more reliable, more economical methods. However, most modern systems are more concerned with information: how to capture, analyze, organize, and present it to middle- and upper-level managers who need the information to make business decisions.

---

*D.L. Parnas, "On the Criteria to Be Used in Decomposing Systems into Modules," *Communications of the ACM*, Vol. 5, No. 12 (December 1972), pp. 1053-58. Reprinted in *Classics in Software Engineering*, ed. E.N. Yourdon (New York: YOURDON Press, 1979), pp. 141-50.

Information, as Emery points out, has both a value and a cost. His paper nicely summarizes a number of factors that affect the value and cost of information: response time, accuracy of data, amount of available detail, and the length of time the information is retained, to name a few. The last several pages of the paper deal with a variety of techniques for defining costs and benefits of a proposed system; in addition, the paper addresses the user's role in the cost/benefit study, and the need for users and analysts to cooperate throughout the effort.

In many cases, users identify "intangible" costs and benefits when discussing a proposed system with an analyst. Emery warns that identification of cost/benefit traditionally has been poorly handled by many systems analysts, and cautions that the primary difference between a "tangible" and an "intangible" benefit is the difficulty of estimating monetary value for a benefit. However, even if a benefit can't be assigned a monetary value — as when the user can only say, "We want to get our accounting data more quickly" without saying how much money that's worth — it's important to be as specific as possible. Emery's point is that the above statement would be far more useful if it were phrased, "The system would be of great benefit to me if the accounting data were produced three days earlier than they are currently."

Perhaps the most important suggestion made by Emery is reserved for the last two pages: Cost/benefit analysis should continue throughout a systems development project. There are two obvious reasons for this: The initial cost/benefit study is often based on extremely sketchy information, estimates that can be refined substantially during latter stages of the project; and, second, the environment surrounding the project may change drastically during design and implementation of a system — for example, the economy may suddenly worsen, or the organization's prime competitor might alter in such a way as to render useless a system that had initially seemed justifiable.

Couger: Evolution of Business System Analysis Techniques

The third paper is Couger's "Evolution of Business System Analysis Techniques." It is the best overall tutorial on that subject that I have seen, and it is supplemented by a bibliography of forty-four books and papers. Published in the fall of 1973, Couger's article predates such current techniques as DeMarco's structured analysis, or SofTech's SADT.* The early development of PSL/PSA and ISDOS at the University of Michigan has since been well documented.[†]

Many of the analysis approaches are known by cryptic abbreviations — TAG, SOP, ADS, and MAP, for example — and a complete description would have filled several volumes of text. Couger's tutorial gives enough information for a general idea of what each vendor's analysis technique was trying to accomplish, although I found it far more interesting to see how the techniques evolved over a period of ten or twenty years than to see the seventeen different forms and charts that accompanied a particular technique. Also worth noting are analysis techniques that appeared to have a good

---

*For explanations of these techniques, see T. DeMarco, *Structured Analysis and System Specification* (New York: YOURDON Press, 1978); and *An Introduction to SADT® Structured Analysis and Design Technique,* SofTech Inc., Document No. 9022-78R (Waltham, Mass.: November 1976).

[†]See D. Teichroew and E.A. Hershey, III, "PSL/PSA: A Computer-Aided Technique for Structured Documentation and Analysis of Information Processing Systems," *IEEE Transactions on Software Engineering,* Vol. SE-3, No. 1 (January 1977), pp. 41-48. Reprinted in *Classics in Software Engineering,* ed. E.N. Yourdon (New York, YOURDON Press, 1979), pp. 389-407.

foundation — for example, Accurately Defined Systems (ADS) from NCR in 1968 — but that did not evolve and that gradually fell into disuse.

Couger defines a fourth generation of analysis techniques that will be characterized by a high degree of automation — those primarily consisting of the mechanical checking for completeness and consistency that Parnas mentioned in his paper. In addition, Couger predicts that such fourth-generation analysis techniques will lead to completely automated generation of code from the functional specification; he cites some of the decision table generators as precursors of this idea, and suggests that ISDOS is a good example of the coming world of automated systems development.

In his conclusion, Couger writes, "It is simply amazing that the systems profession delayed so long in using the computer as an aid in systems analysis. . . . The foregoing descriptions demonstrate that this deficiency is rapidly being corrected. Within the next year there should be sufficient results in each of these research efforts to evaluate their impact upon the computing community."

Well, we've had more than a year; indeed, we've had almost a decade. And yet the impact of so-called fourth-generation analysis techniques with their high degree of automation is still very slight. A few of the very large, very complex, very high-risk systems projects have been actively using automated analysis techniques since the late 1970s; for the vast majority of business data processing projects, though, Couger's optimistic conclusions are about ten years ahead of their time.

As a result, the paper continues to be excellent reading. Now that vendor-supplied analysis packages are beginning to come out of the laboratory, and cheap graphics terminals are available to help augment and support the analysis techniques, perhaps we will actually see these dreams realized in the 1980s.

Additional References on Analysis

The articles selected for this volume supplement those previously reprinted in *Classics in Software Engineering.* For a more complete picture of important papers on analysis techniques, see the following:

1.   D.T. Ross and K.E. Schoman, Jr., "Structured Analysis for Requirements Definition," *IEEE Transactions on Software Engineering,* Vol. SE-3, No. 1 (January 1977), pp. 6-15. Reprinted in *Classics in Software Engineering,* ed. E.N. Yourdon (New York: YOURDON Press, 1979), pp. 365-86.

2.   D. Teichroew and E.A. Hershey, III, "PSL/PSA: A Computer-Aided Technique for Structured Documentation and Analysis of Information Processing Systems," *IEEE Transactions on Software Engineering,* Vol. SE-3, No. 1 (January 1977), pp. 41-48. Reprinted in *Classics in Software Engineering,* pp. 389-407.

3.   T. DeMarco, "Structured Analysis and System Specification," *Proceedings of the GUIDE 47 Conference* (Chicago: GUIDE International Corp., 1978). Reprinted in *Classics in Software Engineering,* pp. 411-24.

A Technique for Software Module Specification with Examples

Because of the growing recognition that a major contributing factor in the so-called "software engineering" problem is our lack of techniques for precisely specifying program segments without revealing too much information [1, 2], I would like to report on a technique for module specification which has proven moderately successful in a number of test situations.

Without taking the space to justify them [2] I would like to list the goals of the specification scheme to be described:

1. The specification must provide to the intended user *all* the information that he will need to use the program correctly, *and nothing more.*

2. The specification must provide to the implementer, *all* the information about the intended use that he needs to complete the program, and *no additional information;* in particular, no information about the structure of the calling program should be conveyed.

3. The specification must be sufficiently formal that it can conceivably be machine tested for consistency, completeness (in the sense of defining the outcome of all possible uses) and other desirable properties of a specification. Note that we do not insist that machine testing be done, only that it could conceivably be done.

SOURCE: D.L. Parnas
Communications of the ACM, 1972.

By this requirement we intend to rule out all natural language specifications.*

4. The specification should discuss the program in the terms normally used by user and implementer alike rather than some other area of discourse. By this we intend to exclude the specification of programs in terms of the mappings they provide between large input domains and large output domains or their specification in terms of mappings onto small automata, etc.

The basis of the technique is a view of a program module as a device with a set of switch inputs and readout indicators. The technique specifies the possible positions of the input switches and the effect of moving the switches on the values of the readout indicators. We insist that the values of the readout indicators be completely determined by the previous values of those indicators and the positions of the input switches.

[*Aside:* The notation allows for some of the pushbuttons to be combined with indicator lights or readouts (with the result that we must push a button in order to read), but we have not yet found occasion to use that facility. A simple extension of the notation allows the specification of mechanisms in which the values of the readout indicators are not determined by the above factors, but can be predicted only by knowing the values of certain "hidden" readout indicators which cannot actually be read by the user of the device. We have considerable doubts about the advisability of building devices which must be specified using this feature, but the ability to specify such devices is inexpensively gained.]

In software terms we consider each module as providing a number of subroutines or functions which can cause changes in state, and other functions or procedures which can give to a user program the values of the variables making up that state. We refer to these all as *functions*.

We distinguish two classes of readout functions: the most important class provides information which cannot be determined without calling that function unless the user maintains duplicate information in his own program's data structures. A second class, termed *mapping functions,* provides redundant information, in that the value of these functions is completely predictable from the *current values* of other readout functions. The mapping functions are provided as a notational convenience to keep the specifications and the user programs smaller.

---

*It should be clear that while we cannot afford to use natural language specifications we cannot manage to do without natural language explanations. Any formal structure is a hollow shell to most of us without a description of its intended interpretation. The formal specifications given in this paper would be meaningless without a natural language description of the intended usage of the various functions and parameters. On the other hand, we insist that once the reader is familiar with the intended interpretation the specifications should answer all of his questions about the behavior of the programs without reference to the natural language text.

The experience of the author has shown that if one makes use of names with a high mnemonic value, both reader and writer tend to become sloppy and use the intended interpretation implied by the mnemonic name to answer questions which should be answered from the formal statements. For that reason the function names have not been designed to be highly mnemonic but are instead rather obscure. The functions will only be completely understood after the reader studies the text which follows. The use of obscure mnemonics is clearly a matter of personal taste, and should not be considered essential to the technique being described.

For each function we specify:

1. The set of possible values: (integers, reals, truth values, etc.)

2. Initial values: (either "undefined" or a member of the set specified in item 1). "Undefined" is considered a special value, rather than an unpredictable value.

3. Parameters: each parameter is specified as belonging to one of the sets named in item 1.

4. Effect: with the exception of mapping functions, almost all the information in the specification is contained in section 4. Under "effect": we place two distinct types of items which require a more detailed discussion.

First, we state that if the "effect" section is empty, then there is absolutely no way to detect that the function has been called. One may call it arbitrarily often and observe no effect other than the passage of time.

The modules that we have specified have "traps" built in. There is a sequence of statements in the "effect" section which specifies the conditions under which certain "error" handling routines will be called. These conditions are treated as incorrect usage of the module and response is considered to be the responsibility of the calling program. For that reason it is assumed that the "error" handling routine's body will not be considered part of the module specified, but will be written by the users of the module. If such a condition occurs, there is to be no observable result of the call of the routine except the transfer of control. When there is a sequence of error statements, the first one in the list which applies is the only one which is invoked. In some cases, the calling program will correct its error and return to have the function try again; in others, it will not. If it does return, the function is to behave as if this were the first call. There is no memory of the erroneous call.

This approach to error handling is motivated by two considerations which are peripheral to this paper. First, we wish to make it possible to write the code for the "normal" cases without checking for the occurrence of unusual or erroneous situations. The "trap" approach facilitates this. Second, we wish to encourage the proper handling of errors in many-leveled software. In our opinion this implies that each routine receives all messages from the routines that it uses and either (1) hides the trap from its user or (2) passes to its user an error indication which is meaningful to a program which knows only the specification of the routine that it called and does not know of the existence of routines called by that routine. The reader will find that our insistence that (1) response to errors is the responsibility of any routine which called another routine in an "incorrect" way and (2) that when such an error call is made, there is no record of the previous call, places quite a demand on the implementers of each module. They must not make irreversible changes unless they are certain that they can complete the changes to be made without calling any "error" routines. The reader will note that we generally specify a separate routine for each case which might be handled separately. The user may make several routines have identical bodies, if the distinction between those cases is not important to him.

The remaining statements are sequence independent. They can be "shuffled" without changing their meaning. These statements are equations describing the values (after the function call) of the other functions in the module. It is specified that no changes in any functions (other than mapping functions) occur unless they are implied by the effect section. The effect section can refer only to values of the function parameters and values of readout functions. The value change of the mapping functions are not mentioned; those changes can be derived from the changes in the functions used in the definitions of the mapping functions. All of this will become much clearer as we discuss the following examples.

In some cases we may specify the effect of a sequence to be null. By this we imply that that sequence may be inserted in any other sequence without changing the effect of the other sequence.

Notation*

The notation is mainly ALGOL-like and requires little explanation. To distinguish references to the value of a function before calling the specified function from references to its value after the call, we enclose the old or previous value in single quotes (e.g. 'VAL'). If the value does not change, the quotes are optional. Brackets ("[" and "]") are used to indicate the scope of quantifiers. "=" is the relation "equals" and *not* the assignment operator as in FORTRAN.

We propose that the definition of a stack shown in Example 1 should replace the usual pictures of implementations (e.g. the array with pointer or the linked list implementations). All that you need to know about a stack in order to use it is specified there. There are countless possible implementations (including a large number of sensible ones). The implementation should be free to vary without changing the using programs. If the using programs assume no more about a stack than is stated above, that will be true.

Example 1.

Function PUSH (a)

possible values: none
integer: a
effect: call ERR1 if $a > p2 \lor a < 0 \lor \text{'DEPTH'} = p1$
      else [VAL = a; DEPTH = 'DEPTH' + 1;]

Function POP

possible values: none
parameters: none
effect: call ERR2 if 'DEPTH' = 0
   the sequence "PUSH(a); POP" has no net effect if no error calls occur.

Function VAL

possible values: integer initial; value undefined
parameters: none
effect: error call if 'DEPTH' = 0

Function DEPTH

possible values: integer; initial value 0
parameters: none
effect: none
p1 and p2 are parameters. p1 is intended to represent the maximum depth of the stack and p2 the maximum width or maximum size for each item.

---

*Although this paper introduces a new notation it must be emphasized that the notation is not intended to be a contribution of this paper. In making a specification we include some information about a module and omit some. We are concerned primarily with the choice of the information to be supplied. We introduce notation only as needed to make that choice clear. Although we have made some attempt to adhere to a consistent notation, this paper is not a proposal that this notation be considered a language to be adopted for specification writing. We are not yet at a point where that is an important issue.

Example 2 shows a "binary tree." This example is of interest because we have provided the user with sufficient information that he may search the tree, yet we have *not* defined the values of the main functions, only properties of those values. Thus, those values might well be links in a linked list implementation, array indices in a TREESORT [3] style implementation or a number of other possibilities. The important fact is that if we implement the functions *as defined* by any method, any usage which assumes only what is specified will work.

Example 2. In the following module all function values and parameters are integers except where stated otherwise. In the interest of brevity we shall not state this repeatedly. For some values the values are *not* predicted by the definition. They are chosen arbitrarily by the system. This is done because the user should not make use of any regularity which might exist in the values assigned. The necessary relations between the values of those functions and the values of other functions are stated explicitly. Such incompletely defined functions are noted with an *. The user may store the values of those functions and use them to avoid repeated nested function calls.

Intended Interpretation:

FA = *fa*ther, LS = *l*eft*s*on, RS = *r*ight*s*on
SLS = *s*et *l*s, SRS = *s*et *r*s, SVA = *s*et *va*l
VAL = *va*lue, DEL = *del*ete, ELS = *e*xists *l*s,
ERS = *e*xists *r*s.

Function FA(i)*

possible values: integers
initial value: FA(0) = 0; otherwise undefined
effect: error call *if* 'FA'(i) undefined

Function LS(i)*

possible values: integers
initial value: undefined
effect: error call *if* 'ELS'(i) = *false*

Function RS(i)*

possible values: integers
initial value: undefined
effect: error call *if* 'ERS'(i) = *false*

Function SLS(i)

possible values: none
initial value: not applicable
effect: error call *if* 'FA'(i) is undefined
    error call *if* 'ELS'(i) = *true*

LS(i) and FA(LS(i)) are given values such that
[FA(LS(i)) = i and 'FA'(LS(i)) was undefined]
ELS(i) = *true*;

Function SRS(i)

possible values: none
initial value: not applicable
effect: error call *if* 'FA'(i) is undefined
  error call *if* 'ERS'(i) = *true*
RS(i) and FA(RS(i)) are assigned values such that
[FA(RS(i)) = i and 'FA'(RS(i)) was not defined]
ERS(i) = *true*;

Function SVA(i,v)

possible values: none
initial value: not applicable
effect: error call *if* 'FA'(i) is undefined
VAL(i) = v

Function VAL(i)

possible values: integers
initial value: undefined
effect: error call *if* 'VAL'(i) is undefined

Function DEL(i)

possible values: none
initial value: not applicable
effect: error call if 'FA'(i) is undefined
  error call if 'ELS'(i) or 'ERS'(i) = *true*
FA(i), VAL(i) are undefined
  if i = 'LS'('FA'(i)) then [LS('FA'(i)) is undefined and ELS('FA'(i)) =
    false]
  if i = 'RS'('FA'(i)) then [RS('FA'(i)) is undefined and ERS ('FA' (i)) =
    false]

Function ELS(i)

possible values: *true, false*
initial value: *false*
effect: error call if 'FA'(i) undefined

Function ERS(i)

possible values: *true, false*
initial value: *false*
effect: error call if 'FA'(i) undefined

To make this specification complete the names of the error routines must be supplied.

Example 3 shows a more specialized piece of software. It is a storage module intended for use in such applications as producing KWIC indexes. It is designed to hold "lines," which are ordered sets of "words," which are ordered sets of characters, to be dealt with by an integer representation. For this example there are some restrictions on the way that material may be inserted (only at the end of the last line) which reflect the intended use. That might well be a design error, but for our purposes the important thing to note is that the restrictions are completely and precisely specified without revealing any of the internal reasons for making such restrictions.

Example 3. Definition of a "Line Holder" Mechanism. This definition specifies a mechanism which may be used to hold up to p1 lines, each line consisting of up to p2 words, and each word may be up to p3 characters.

Function WORD

possible values: integers
initial values: undefined
parameters: *l*,w,c all integers
effect:
   call ERLWEL *if* $l < 1$ or $l > $ p1
   call ERLWNL *if* $l > $ LINES
   call ERLWEW *if* $w < 1$ or $w > $ p2
   call ERLWNW *if* $w > $ WORDS(*l*)
   call ERLWEC *if* $c < 1$ or $c > $ p3
   call ERLWNC *if* $c > $ CHARS(*l*,w)

Function SETWRD

possible values: none
initial values: not applicable
parameters: *l*,w,c,d all integers
effect:
   call ERLSLE *if* $l < 1$ or $l > $ pl
   call ERLSBL *if* $l > $ 'LINES' + 1
   call ERLSBL *if* $l < $ 'LINES'
   call ERLSWE *if* $w < 1$ or $w > $ p2
   call ERLSBW *if* $w > $ 'WORDS'(*l*) + 1
   call ERLSBW *if* $w < $ 'WORDS'(*l*)
   call ERLSCE *if* $c < 1$ or $c > $ p3
   call ERLSBC *if* c .noteq. 'CHARS' (*l*,w) + 1 call ERLSWD if $l < $ o or
   $l > $ p4 LINES = 'LINES' + 1
   then WORDS(l) =
   CHARS(*l*,w) = c
   WORD(*l*,w,c) = d

Function WORDS

possible values: integers
initial values: 0
parameters: *l* an integer
effect:
   call ERLWSL *if* $l < 1$ or $l > $ pl
   call ERLWSL *if* $l > $ LINES
   call ERLWSL *if* $l > $ LINES

Function LINES

possible values: integers
initial value: 0
parameters: none
effect: none

Function DELWRD

possible values: none
initial values: not applicable
parameters: l,w both integers
effect:
   call ERLDLE *if* l < 1 or l > LINES
   call ERLDWE *if* w < 1 or w > 'WORDS'(l)
   call ERLDLD *if* 'WORDS'(l) = 1
   WORDS(l) = 'WORDS'(l) − 1
   for all c WORD(l,v,c) = 'WORD'(l,v+1,c) if v ≥ w
   for all v > w or v = w CHARS(l,v) = 'CHARS'(l,v+1)

Function DELINE

possible values: none
initial values: not applicable
parameters: l an integer
effect:
   call ERLDLL *if* l < 0 or l > 'LINES'
   LINES = 'LINES' - 1
   if r = 1 or r > 1 then for all w, for all c
      (WORDS(r) = 'WORDS'(r+1)
      CHARS(r,w) = 'CHARS'(r+1,w)
      WORD(r,w,c) = 'WORD'(r+1,w,c))

Function CHARS

possible values: integer
initial value: 0
parameters: l, w both integers
effect:
   call ERLCNL *if* l < 1 or l > LINES
   call ERLCNW *if* w < 1 or w > WORDS(l)

Some readers may feel that the specification reveals an obvious implementation in terms of arrays. In fact, the module was implemented several times in tutorial projects and this obvious implementation was never used. Such an implementation would be impractical in most cases and a much more complex implementation was needed. The details of that implementation are hidden by this description of the module.

The limitations of the modules ($p1$, $p2$, $p3$) were expressed in terms of the array model for several reasons, among them ease of use and the fact that it permits the array implementation. The decision to use those three parameters rather than one "space" parameter is a questionable one because in some cases we may exceed the apparent capacity without exceeding the real capacity. In our experience this has not been a problem.

In making the line holder of Example 3 it may prove advantageous to (1) separate out the problem of storing the individual characters that make up a word from the problem of storing the makeup of lines out of words, and (2) avoid duplicate storing of identical words. Both can be accomplished by use of the mechanism defined in

Example 4 as a submodule for that described in Example 3. The implementer of the "line holder" would pass the individual characters of the "words" to the symbol table whose definition guarantees him that he will receive a unique encoding of every symbol. Note that the specification in Example 4 does not rule out an implementation which stores duplicate copies of words, but it does require that all receive the same encoding.

Example 4. Symbol Table Definition.

$p1$ = maximum number of symbols
$p2$ = maximum number of characters
    per symbol
$p3$ = maximum value of character

       } intended interpretation

Function STRTSM

possible values: none
initial values: not applicable
parameters: none
effects: call ERFAST if 'MAYIN' = *true*
            MAYIN = *true*

Function MAYIN

possible values: *true, false*
initial values: *false*
parameters: none
effects: none

Function CHARIN
possible values: none
initial values: not applicable
parameters: call ERCHIL if c < 0 or c > p3
          call ERMNIN if 'MAYIN' = *false*
          call ERBUFX if 'BUFFERCNT' = p2
          BUFFER('BUFFERCNT' + 1) = c
          BUFFERCNT = 'BUFFERCNT' + 1

Function BUFFER

possible values: integers
initial values: not applicable
parameters: c, an integer
effects: call ERBUFE if c < 1 or c > 'BUFFERCNT'

Function BUFFERCNT

possible values: integers 0 < BUFFERCNT $\leq$ p2
initial values: 0
parameters: none
effects: none

SYMEND

possible values: integers $0 < \text{SYMEND} \leq \text{'SMCNT'}) + 1$
initial values: not applicable
parameters: none
effects: call ERNOIN if 'MAYIN' = false
       call ERNUTN if 'BUFFERCNT' = 0
       MAYIN = false
       if there is an s $(0 < s \leq \text{'SMCNT'})$ such that
       'BUFFERCNT' = 'CHCNT' (s) and
       [if for all c $(0 < c < \text{'BUFFERCNT'})$
         BUFFER(c) = 'CHAR'(s,c)] then
         SYMEND = s
       else [call ERSYL if 'SMCNT' = pl
         for all c $(0 < c < \text{'BUFFERCNT'})$
          [CHAR('SMCNT' + 1,c) = 'BUFFER'(c)
          CHCNT ('SMCNT' + 1) = 'BUFFERCNT']
          SMCNT = 'SMCNT' + 1]
       BUFFERCNT = 0

Function CHAR

possible values: integers $0 < \text{CHAR} \leq \text{p3}$
initial values: not applicable
parameters: s and c, both integers
effects: call ERNOSY if $a < 1$ or $s > \text{H'MSCN}$
      call ERNOCH if $c < 1$ or $c > (s)\text{'TC'TN'C}$

Function SMCNT

possible values: integers $0 \leq \text{SMCNT} \leq \text{pl}$
initial values: 0
parameters: none
effects: none

Function CHCNT

possible values: integers $0 < \text{CHCNT} < \text{p2}$
initial values: not applicable
parameters: s, an integer
effects: call ERNOSY if $s < 1$ or $s > \text{'SMCNT'}$

It is important to note that the user of the "line holder" will never know or need to know of the existence of the symbol table inner mechanism.

Example 5 is intended to exhibit the situations in which mapping functions are useful in specifications. This module is an alphabetizer, intended to work with the "line holder" shown earlier. It determines values for ITH in such a way that (1) every integer between 1 and the number of lines is a value of ITH and if $i < j$ then the line numbered ITH(i) does not come before the line numbered ITH(j) in the alphabetic ordering.

Example 5. Alphabetizer for line holder. This module accomplishes the alphabetization of the contents of the modules referred to above by producing a pointer function, ITH, which gives the index of the ith line in the alphabetized sequence.

Function ITH:

possible values: integers
initial values: undefined
parameters: i an integer
effect:
   call ERAIND *if* value of function undefined for parameter given

Function ALPHC:

possible values: integers
initial value: ALPHC(l) = index of l in alphabet used
              ALPHC(l) infinite if character not in alphabet
parameter: l an integer
effect:
   call ERAABL if l not in alphabet being used, i.e. *if* ALPHC(l) = ∞

Mapping Function EQW:
possible values: *true, false*
parameters: $l1, l2, w1, w2$ all integers
values:
  EQW ($l1, w1, l2, w2$) = for all c('WORD'($l1, w1, c$) = 'WORD'($l2, w2, c$))
effect:
  call ERAEBL   *if* $l1 < 1$ or $l1 >$ 'LINES'
  call ERAEBL   *if* $l2 < 1$ of $l2 >$ 'LINES'
  call ERAEBW *if* $w1 < 1$ or $w1 >$ 'WORDS'(l)
  call ERAEBW *if* $w2 < 1$ or $w2 >$ 'WORDS' ($l2$)

Mapping Function ALPHW:
possible values: *true, false*
parameters: $l1, l2, w1, w2$ all integers
values:
  ALPHW($l1, w1, l2, w2$) = *if* ¬ 'EQW' ($l1, w1, l2, w2$) and
    k = min c such that ('WORD'($l, w1, c$) ¬ eq. 'WORD' ($l2, w2, c$))
    then 'ALPHC' ('WORD' ($l1, w1, k$)) < 'ALPHC' ('WORD' ($l2, w2, k$))
  else *false*
effect:
  call ERAWBL *if* $l1 < 1$ or $l1 >$ 'LINES'
  call ERAWBL *if* $l2 < 1$ or $l2 >$ 'LINES'
  call ERAWBW *if* $w1 < l$ or $w1 >$ 'WORDS'($l1$)
  call ERAWBW *if* $w2 < l$ or $w2 >$ 'WORDS'($l2$)

Mapping Function EQL:
possible values: *true, false*
parameters; $l1, l2$ both integers
values:
  EQL ($l1, l2$) = for all k ('EQW' ($l1, k, l2, k$))
effect:
  call ERALEL *if* $l1 < 1$ or $l1 >$ 'LINES'
  call ERALEL *if* $l2 < 1$ or $l2 >$ 'LINES'

Mapping Function ALPHL:
possible values: *true, false*
parameters: $l1, l2$ both integers
value:
   ALPHL $(l1, l2) = if \neg$ 'EQL' $(l1, l2)$ then
   (let k = min c such that 'EQW'$(l1, k, l2, k)$)
   'ALPHW'$(l1, k, l2, k)$ else true
effect:
   call ERAALB *if* $l1 < 1$ or $l1 >$ 'LINES'
   call ERAALB *if* $l2 < 1$ or $l2 >$ 'LINES'

Function ALPH:
possible values: none
initial values: not applicable
effect:
   for all i $\neg < l$ and i $\neg >$ 'LINES'
   ITH(i) is given values such that
     for all j $\neg < 1$ and j $\neg >$ LINES
      there exists a k such that ITH(k) = j
   for i ≥ -1 and $<$ 'LINES' [that 'ALPHL' (ITH(i), ITH(i + 1))]

Note that ITH as defined might be an array in which the values specified are stored by the routine ALPH, or it might be a routine which searches for the appropriate line each time called. An interesting alternative would be to make use of FIND [4] within ITH so that the computation is distributed over the calls of ITH and so that in some situations unnecessary work may be avoided. We repeat that the important feature of this specification is that it provides sufficient information to use a module which is correctly implemented according to any of these methods, *without the user having any knowledge of the method.*

Using the specifications

The specifications will be of maximum usefulness only if we adopt methods that make full use of them. Our aim has been to produce specifications which are in a real sense just as testable as programs. We will gain the most in our system building abilities if we have a technique for usage of the specifications which involves testing the specifications *long before* the programs specified are produced. The statements being made at this level are precise enough that we should not have to wait for a lower level representation in order to find the errors.

Such specifications are at least as demanding of precision as are programs; they may well be as complex as some programs. Thus they are as likely to be in error. Because specifications cannot be "run," we may be tempted to postpone their testing until we have programs and can run them. For many reasons such an approach is wrong.

We are able to test such specifications because they provide us with a set of axioms for a formal deductive scheme. As a result, we may be able to prove certain "theorems" about our specifications. Example "theorems" might be:

1.   The specification never refers to F1(p) unless it is certain that p is less than 9.

2.   Whenever F3(x) is true F4(x) is defined and conversely.

3.   It is not possible for F5(x) to take on values greater than $p3$.

4.   Error routine ERRX will never be called.

5.   There exists a sequence of function calls which will set F2(x) = F5(x) = 0.

6.   There will never exist distinct integers i and j such that F1(i) = F2(j).

By asking the proper set of such questions, the "correctness" of a set of specifications may be verified. The choice of the questions, therefore the meaning of "correctness," is dependent on the nature of the object being specified.

Using the same approach of taking the specifications as axioms and attempting to prove theorems, one may ask questions about possible changes in system structure. For example, one may ask which modules will have to be changed, if certain restrictions assumed before were removed.

It would be obviously useful if there were a support system which would input the specifications and provide question answering or theorem proving ability above the specifications. That, however, is not essential. What is essential is that system builders develop the habit of verifying the specifications whether by machine or by hand before building and debugging the programs.

Incidentally, the theorem proving approach might also be considered as a basis for a program which searches automatically for implementations of a specified module. We see this as more difficult and perhaps less urgently needed than the above.

Hesitations

To date the technique has received only limited evaluation. It has been used with reasonable success in the construction of small systems with simple modules in an undergraduate class. The largest completed specification is a description of a simplified man/machine interface for a graphics based editor system [6]. However, any attempt to use this on a larger project (where the probability of failure without the technique is high) is in a very early stage. Clearly the idea needs further practical use before its usefulness can be evaluated. I hope that some of my readers will be in a position to do this.

There appears to be a weak limitation on the technique in that it makes it easy to describe objects which receive data in small units, and where the calling program must be aware of the period between receipt of such small units. So far we have not found a way to follow the technique for such objects as a compiler where the user sends one very large unit and does not want to know of internal steps in the processing of individual characters, phrases, etc. For such situations we have been forced to make use of techniques similar to that of Wirth and Weber [5]. We did, however, combine the two techniques with some success.

In usage of these techniques it has become clear that there is a great initial resistance to their use. This approach to the description of programs as somewhat static objects, rather than sequential decision makers, is unfamiliar to men with lots of programming experience. The first few attempts always fail and require the patient guidance of an instructor. The idea is, however, simple and is eventually mastered by almost everyone.

References: Parnas

1. Buxton, J.N. and Randell, B. (Eds.), *Software Engineering Methods.* Report of a conference sponsored by the NATO Science Committee, Rome, Italy, 27-31 October 1969.

2. Parnas, D.L. Information Distribution Aspects of Design Methodology. Technical Report, Depart. of Comput. Science, Carnegie-Mellon U., Feb., 1971. Presented at the IFIP Congress, 1971, Ljubljana, Yugoslavia, and included in the proceedings.

3. Floyd, R.W. Treesort 3 Algorithm 245. *Comm. ACM 7,* 12 (Dec. 1964), 701.

4. Hoare, C.A.R. Proof of a program, FIND. *Comm. ACM 14,* 1 (Jan. 1971), 39-45. [Ed. note: Reprinted in this volume, paper 13.]

5. Wirth, N. and H. Weber. Euler: A generalization of ALGOL and its formal definition. *Comm. ACM 9,* 1 (Jan. 1966), 13-23.

6. Parnas, D.L., Sample Specification for the Man Machine Interface. Presented at the NATO Advanced Study Institute on Graphics and the Man Machine Interface, April 1971, Erlangen, West Germany (to be included in the proceedings of that institute).

Cost/Benefit Analysis of Information Systems

Value and cost as a function of information quality

A system can be perfectly efficient (in the sense of meeting specifications at the lowest possible cost) and still be a very bad one. Efficiency is not enough; the desirability of a system depends on both the cost of meeting the specifications and the value derived from the information.

Thus, any attempt to define an optimum system must consider alternative specifications. Each specification defines information in terms of such characteristics as content, age, accuracy, and so on. For the time being, however, we can enormously simplify the discussion if we artificially think of information as having only a single characteristic, which we will call its *quality*.

In effect this assumes that it is possible to trade off all of the detailed characteristics of information into a single, overall index. The justification for this totally unrealistic assumption is that it permits us to discuss some important conceptual issues without the burden of unnecessary detail. Our immediate goal is to determine the relationship between the quality of information and its value and cost. This will in turn allow us to consider the optimum balance between value and cost.

Let us first consider value as a function of quality. As we have already seen, it is usually not possible to determine this relationship. Nevertheless, we can still discuss its general characteristics. The most important one is the declining incremental value of information as its quality increases.

The gross value of information continues to increase as quality goes up. Beyond a certain point, however, increased quality may add very little to value. For example, increasing the accuracy of invoices issued to customers from 98 to 99 per-

SOURCE: J.C. Emery, *Society for Management Information Systems,* 1971.

cent reduces the number of errors by half. This may be viewed as a highly worthwhile improvement. A further reduction by a half, to 99.5 percent, is of less value. Eventually the point will be reached at which continued improvement provides very little benefit. The same thing can be said of increases in level of detail, timeliness, or any other desirable characteristic of information. Figure 1 shows this general phenomenon.

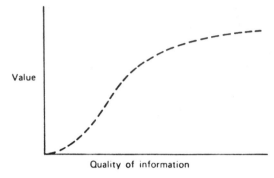

Figure 1. Value as a function of information quality. The value of information goes up as its quality increases. At high levels of quality further improvements yield relatively small incremental benefits.

We need a similar relationship between cost and quality. Each level of quality represents a different set of detailed specifications. For each set we are interested in finding the efficient system. The curve connecting the efficient points shows the trade-off between cost and quality provided by current technology. In the terminology of the economist, this curve is the *efficiency frontier*. It is shown in Figure 2.

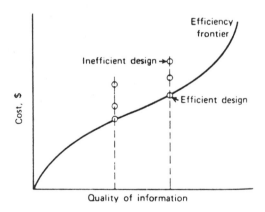

Figure 2. Cost as a function of information quality. Information is obtained from a specific system. Alternative systems vary in their efficiency, and so the cost of a given quality of information depends on the efficiency of the design used. The *efficiency frontier* represents the set of systems that provide each level of quality at the lowest cost. For a given level of efficiency, cost rises with increased quality.

Of course, we do not actually prepare curves of this sort. At most we may look at a few alternative levels of quality — a "real-time" versus a batch processing system, for example. For each level of quality we may then evaluate a few alternative designs. The smooth curve shown in Figure 2 thus represents a considerable abstraction from reality.

It is difficult to defend any particular cost curve. Nevertheless, certain characteristics are probably fairly general. For example, over a considerable portion of the curve, economies of scale are common — that is, as quality goes up, costs go up less than proportionally. Eventually, however, quality increases to the point that costs start to rise very rapidly as the limits of current technology are approached.

Balance between value and cost of information

Finding the optimum system

Having discussed (abstract) curves relating value and cost to the quality of information, we are now in a position to consider the design of the optimal system. We should aim at finding the design that maximizes the *net* benefits — that is, the difference between gross benefits and cost. Equivalently, the optimum occurs at the point where incremental value just matches incremental cost. This is shown in Figure 3.

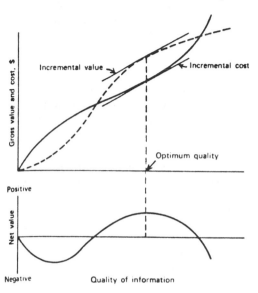

Figure 3. Determining the optimum system. The optimum level of quality occurs at the point at which net value (i.e., gross value minus cost) is maximum. This can also be viewed as the point at which incremental value equals incremental cost. Obviously, the optimum system does not provide all useful information; there will always remain unfulfilled information "requirements" that cost more to satisfy than they contribute in benefits.

Since in practice such curves rarely exist, it is not possible to actually find the optimum design. Even if the curves were known, the optimum would tend to shift during the time span required to implement the system.

Nevertheless, an important and valid conclusion emerges from this simplified view of reality. The optimum system does not supply all useful information, since some information costs more than it is worth. Therefore, the specifications of systems requirements must simultaneously consider both cost and value of information.

Effects of an advance in information technology

The (gross) value of information does not depend on the technical means of obtaining it, but costs do. Suppose that an advance takes place in the technology of processing information, such as occurred, for example, between the early 1950's (when punched card technology prevailed) and the current computer era. The advance may come from either hardware or software improvements. The effect is to drop the current cost curve below the earlier one, as shown in Figure 4.

The organization can respond in different ways to a technological advance. It can, as one alternative, choose to exploit the new technology primarily by lowering the cost of producing information. This presumably is the motivation behind projects that merely convert an old system to the new technology, without making any basic changes in information outputs. If outputs remain essentially constant, so must value; the justification must therefore come solely from the lower cost of information.

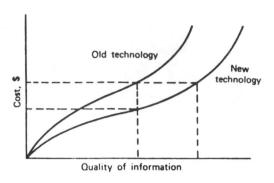

Figure 4. Lowering the cost curve with an advance in technology. As information processing technology advances, it becomes possible to obtain a given quality of information at lower cost than before. Alternatively, higher quality can be obtained at the same cost. The heavy line represents *dominant* systems that provide some combination of both higher quality and lower cost.

Alternatively, the system can be redesigned in a more fundamental way that enhances information value. Benefits in this case might come from lower operating costs, improved service, or better decision-making information. Figure 5 shows the alternatives available.

Figure 5. Effect of an advance in information processing technology on the optimum information quality. The optimum quality of information changes when an advance in technology lowers the cost of information processing. The new optimum is almost always at a higher level of quality. In this illustration the new optimum dominates the old (i.e., gives higher quality information at lower cost). In other cases, the new optimum could result in a higher cost than before but give benefits that more than offset the higher cost.

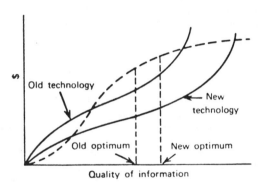

It is difficult to lay down hard and fast rules about the best strategy to follow. Clearly, however, an advance in information technology tends to shift the optimum design toward higher quality information. This is simply a manifestation of the general economic principle that a reduction in the price of a resource (relative to other resources) should normally lead to its greater use.

But even if the best long-run strategy is to upgrade the quality of information through a redesign of the system, attractive short-run benefits may also be possible through a relatively straightforward conversion of the existing system. The two approaches are not necessarily in conflict; they may proceed more or less concurrently. By the time the fundamental redesign is ready for implementation, an earlier short-term conversion may have already paid for itself handsomely through cost reductions. Unfortunately, too many organizations appear to pursue short-term savings at the exclusion of any long-term benefits.

Important characteristics of an information system that govern its value and cost

In discussing the balance between value and cost, we found it convenient to use a composite characteristic of information called quality. In practice we cannot deal with information in this way; instead we must consider each of its individual characteristics.

Although there are tradeoffs among the characteristics — between detail and timeliness, for example — it is useful to consider their separate effects on the overall value and cost of a system.

Allocation of tasks between man and machine

An information system includes both human and automatic components. A critical characteristic of a system is the way in which these tasks are divided between human and computer. Certain tasks clearly belong to one or the other, but this is by no means always the case.

Complex decision making that deals with ill-structured goals and relationships is typically best handled by man. So are tasks that occur rarely and do not involve major risks. It is exceedingly difficult (or impossible) for a computer to duplicate man's flexibility and ability to generalize, recognize complex patterns, and deal with unexpected or unusual situations. On the other hand, the computer enjoys an obvious edge over man in a number of respects — in speed, accuracy, volume of data, and the ability to draw inferences from complex models.

A system designer faces the job of allocating tasks between man and machine in the way that leads to the best overall performance. Problems of allocation arise at all levels in the system. At the operating level the designer must determine the extent to which clerical tasks should be replaced by the computer. Typical examples of such questions are:

- Should freight or passenger rates be calculated automatically within an airline information system?
- Should premiums be calculated automatically within an insurance system?
- Should detected errors be corrected automatically?
- Should a rare combination of circumstances be handled automatically (or as an "exception" dealt with by a clerk)?

Similar types of issues arise in connection with the design of decision-making systems:

- Should inventory order points and order quantities be calculated automatically?
- Should buy and sell orders be generated automatically in a trust management system?
- What thresholds should be set to require automatic decisions to be reviewed by a human?
- What tasks can the computer perform to aid human decision making?

It is difficult to provide many hard and fast generalizations about such questions. One generalization, however, is inescapable: the optimal system falls far short of complete automation. Insofar as possible, each task should be dealt with on its own merits, considering both the value and cost of performing it automatically.*

---

*The interdependencies among tasks make this approach difficult to apply in practice. For example, an on-line system for printing railroad passenger tickets would probably not be feasible if rates were calculated manually. We can broaden the definition of a "task" to include both printing and rate calculation, and then decide whether the combined task should be automated. When a task is defined too broadly, however, the designer may overlook some subtasks that could be better handled independently as a manual operation.

Content of the data base

The data base provides an organization with an image or analogue of itself and its environment. The more detailed the image, the greater its realism. This may improve the decisions that rely on the data base as a source of information, but it also increases costs.

The content of the data base depends on the data that enter the system and how long they are retained. High-volume data are usually captured in the form of transactions that feed some operational system. Sales data, for instance, are collected as part of order processing. Once immediate needs have been met — after an order has been shipped, for example — transaction data can be retained in detailed form in an accessible storage medium, or they can be retained only in aggregate form.* The level of aggregation and the length of retention are important system characteristics.

Let us examine this issue in more detail. Suppose we are designing an order processing system for a supermarket chain. Replenishment orders for each store are processed daily at a central location. The system generates shipping schedules and thus has access to data about the current day's shipments of each stocked item to each store (three cases of Campbell's tomato soup shipped to Store 53, say).

Now, it is highly unlikely that each individual replenishment order will be worth saving after it has been processed. The real issue is the level of aggregation to be retained. One alternative is to retain individual item data aggregated across all stores within a given week. Shipments to each individual store could be aggregated across all items.

Aggregation of this degree washes out information about the movement of a given item at a given store. Suppose the buying department wishes to analyze the sales of each product to determine if it generates enough gross margin to justify its use of shelf space. If only total figures are known, the decision must be based on an item's *average* sales per store. But an average can be very misleading because it hides all variation among the stores.

Sales of some items may vary greatly among stores. One supermarket firm found, for example, that virtually all of the movement of 25-pound sacks of flour occurred in a small number of rural stores serving women who were accustomed to baking their own bread. For these few stores it was essential to carry the item. However, if the decision to stock it were based solely on average sales per store, large sacks of flour would not be retained. Only a data base that retains item-store data would lead to the proper conclusion. See Figure 6.

Even if detailed data find little direct use, their retention may still be very desirable in order to allow aggregation in unanticipated ways. Suppose, for example, that an analyst performing a distribution study wishes to find the total weight of products shipped to each store. Unless item-store shipment data are maintained (as well as the unit weight of each product), it would be very difficult to retain reliable estimates of shipments. To be sure, this information could be accumulated as part of the periodic reporting scheme, but it is impossible to anticipate all possible aggregations of detailed data. The retention of relatively disaggregated data is the best way to overcome this difficulty. See Figure 7.

---

*Detailed transactions may also be retained in an inexpensive but relatively inaccessible form for archival purposes (such as microfilm). We are concerned here with data stored in a way that permits easy access for further processing.

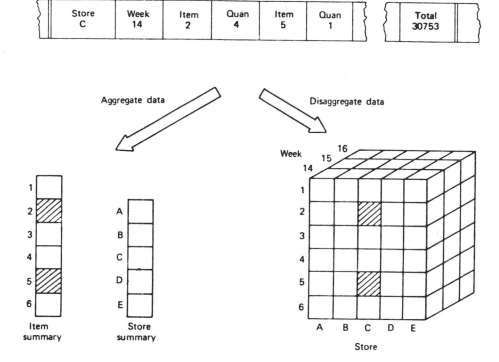

Figure 6. Retention of aggregate versus disaggregate data. Transaction data, such as the shipment transactions shown above, are rarely kept very long in complete detail; the question is, how much detail should be retained (and for how long). Maintaining only aggregate data — for example, total units shipped of each item and total dollar shipments to each store — greatly reduced storage requirements. Retaining item store shipment by week, say, drastically increases the size of the file, but allows a much greater variety of information to be obtained.

The incremental value of information diminishes as detail grows. This is so because it becomes increasingly likely that information needs can be satisfied without resorting to still finer detail. In the supermarket example, storage of item-store data by *week*, say, would probably meet most information needs; it would not be necessary to retain *daily* item-store shipments.

The incremental value of data declines with age as well as with detail. Retention of complete transaction data may be justified for a short time following a shipment to a store. After a few months, however, the details should be summarized into, say, item-store data by week; the transaction data can then be discarded (or stored in a low-cost medium for archival purposes). When older than a year, the data might be further summarized into sales by product groups (canned soups, for instance) and month. This process of increasing the degree of aggregation might continue for several years. Usually only highly aggregated data are retained permanently.

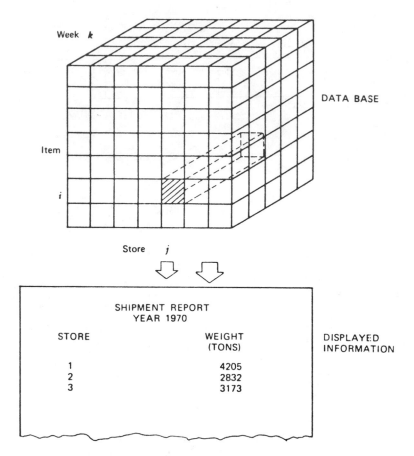

Figure 7. Aggregation of data from a disaggregated data base. A detailed data base allows great flexibility in calculating specific aggregations. For example, the total weight of product shipped to a store can be calculated if item-store shipment data are available. The item-store shipment data may, in turn, be aggregated from weekly shipment data. Thus, total weight shipped to store

$$j = \sum_i W_i S_{ij} = \sum_i W_i \sum_k S_{ijk}$$

where

W_i = unit weight of ith item
S_{ij} = total unit shipments of ith item to jth store
S_{ijk} = total unit shipments of ith item to jth store during kth week

The size of the data base obviously grows as the level of detail and length of retention increase. In fact, it can grow explosively. For example, if sales data are maintained on a daily instead of a weekly basis, the size of the file may increase by a factor of six (assuming a six-day week). A similar factorial growth occurs as other dimensions of classification are added. Differentiating between credit and noncredit sales, for example, potentially doubles the size of the file. The length of retention also has an important effect on size. The data base can grow very rapidly if steps are not taken to cull out old data.

The cost of storing data naturally increases as the size of the data base grows. The cost of the storage medium increases, but usually less than proportionately (i.e., some economies of scale are exhibited, at least over a considerable range of volume).

Far more significant is the cost of retrieving desired information. This cost depends on the way in which data are organized and accessed. Retrieval may require a sequential scan of a portion of the data base or, alternatively, relatively direct access by means of indices or linked records. In either case cost of retrieval may increase more than proportionately as the size of the data base grows.

The decision regarding the proper level of detail and length of retention should be based on the expected value of stored data. The expected value of a given data element equals its value, if it is required, multiplied by the probability that it will be required. Thus, the storing of information may be justified on the grounds that (1) it will be extremely useful if asked for, even if this is fairly unlikely (such as a cancelled check); or (2) it is very likely to be needed and its value upon retrieval exceeds the cost of retaining it. In practice one must usually rely on subjective (and somewhat vague) estimates of value and probabilities, but the person making these judgments should at least have his objective clearly in mind.

We may summarize this discussion in the following way:

- Increasing the degree of detail and the length of retention of data may drastically increase the size of the data base.

- The value of the data base tends to increase with its size, but at a diminishing rate.

- The cost of maintaining and retrieving from the data base grows rapidly as its size increases.

- The optimum size occurs at the point where incremental value equals incremental cost. Typically this point falls considerably short of retaining (for very long, at least) complete transaction data.

Selectivity of displayed data

It is not enough merely to keep useful information in the data base; the information must be displayed if it is to be used for human decision making. As the size of the data base grows, it becomes all the more critical to display only highly selective information. Ideally, the information displayed should always have some surprise content and lead to a better decision than would otherwise be made. In practice we can only approach this ideal.

Let us consider the total variety of ways information can potentially be obtained from the data base. This includes all of the individual data elements, as well as any arbitrary transformation performed on these elements. The transformations include simple aggregations, standard statistical analyses, preparation of graphical output, and even calculations using complex decision models.

Now, let us look at the information needs of a given user. The very large (in fact, infinite) set of potential information available from the data base can be partitioned in two independent ways: displayed versus nondisplayed information, and relevant versus irrelevant information.

Displayed information is that portion presented to the user. It may be displayed either in hard copy form or as a transient display on a CRT or some similar device.

The relevance of information is not as easy to define; it is a matter of degree. We will define information to be relevant if its value exceeds the incremental cost of using it — in short, if the user would benefit by having it displayed. This means that relevant information offers some surprise, leads to a decision that would otherwise not be taken, and improves payoff.

The total set of potential information can be broken down into four subsets:*

1.   Relevant and displayed.
2.   Irrelevant and not displayed.
3.   Relevant and not displayed.
4.   Irrelevant and displayed.

The designer of a system would naturally like to limit the information included in the third and fourth categories, since they represent "errors" of omission or commission. When relevant information is not displayed, decisions will not be good as they otherwise would be. When irrelevant information is displayed, the user himself must select the useful information from the useless. The greater the proportion of irrelevant information, the greater the effort on the user's part to cull it out and the greater the risk that he will overlook valuable information. Like the gold in the ocean, relevant information too diluted with useless information ceases to have any value.

Errors in information selection are unavoidable. In order to display *all* relevant information, and *only* relevant information, the system would have to determine what each user already knows and what his decision process is. This is clearly impossible, and so the choice of information to display must be a compromise between displaying too much or too little. The probability of displaying relevant information goes down as the degree of filtering increases, but this is accomplished by an increase in the probability of overlooking relevant information.

The optimum degree of selection depends on the relative penalties of the two types of errors. If failure to display critical information carries a very high penalty relative to the cost of displaying irrelevant data, then it is advantageous to err on the side of displaying too much. This is the implied motivation behind many existing information systems.

Both types of errors can be reduced simultaneously if sufficient resources are spent in implementing more effective selection.† It is primarily the cost of design effort and information processing that imposes an upper limit on the extent to which selection errors should be avoided.

Increased selectivity can be achieved through a variety of means. Some of the techniques have been used for many years, while others have become feasible only with relatively recent advances in information technology. Let us examine the more important techniques.

Appropriate aggregation of details. Virtually no one needs transaction data in complete detail (except for handling the transaction itself, of course); it is almost always necessary to aggregate the details before they can be used. The aggregation may be by product group, organizational unit, cost category, time period, or some similar dimension. The intent is to aggregate in a way that washes out irrelevant dimensions and preserves the relevant ones. For example, sales data used by the marketing vice president may

---

*The four-way breakdown is analogous to that faced in quality control, in which one is concerned with whether a product should be accepted as good or rejected as bad. The possibilities are: (1) satisfactory quality and accepted, (2) unsatisfactory and rejected, (3) unsatisfactory and accepted (the so called "buyer's risk"), and (4) satisfactory and rejected (the "producer's risk"). This analogy is worth pointing out because the issues are much the same in the two contexts.

†This is analogous to taking a larger sample in quality control applications in order to simultaneously reduce both the producer's and buyer's risks.

be aggregated by major product groups and sales regions. Finer detail (sales of a specific product, say) or some alternative aggregation (sales classified by industry, perhaps) would probably not be particularly useful in assessing the performance of regional sales managers (although obviously such information might be entirely relevant for other purposes).

Simple aggregation, in which each data element is added to its appropriate category, implies that each element carries the same relative value. A summary sales report, for example, implicitly assumes that a dollar of sales for Product X is equivalent to a dollar of sales for Product Y if they both fall within the same product group. This is often valid, but it need not be. A production report that shows delivery performance may give quite misleading information if it merely provides a count of late jobs. A much more meaningful figure would be one that weights each late job by a measure of its lateness and importance (man-hours of labor applied, for instance).

Although aggregation is essential to reduce the volume of displayed information, it always carries some risk of washing out relevant information. A sales report may hide significant trends within a product group or sales territory, for example. Similarly, an inventory report that aggregates across all items may cancel out a serious imbalance in which some items are in critically short supply while an offsetting group has a large surplus. The remedy for this is to aggregate within finer (and hopefully more relevant) categories. For example, the inventory report can aggregate according to the current status of each item, using the three categories "in control," "short," or "surplus." See Figure 8. Unfortunately, increasing the fineness of aggregation also increases the likelihood of displaying irrelevant information.

INVENTORY ANALYSIS

STATUS	NUMBER OF ITEMS	BALANCE ($000)	STANDARD ($000)	PERCENT OF STANDARD
IN CONTROL	9242	2530	2400	105
SHORT	1025	135	420	32
SURPLUS	779	832	205	406
TOTAL	11046	3497	3025	116

Figure 8. Aggregation of displayed information to reduce detail while preserving essential information. Aggregations are necessary to increase selectivity, but run the risk of washing out significant details. A complete aggregation of the above inventory information would give the misleading impression that inventory is in control (only 16 percent above standard). Aggregating the inventory items into three categories according to their current status gives a much more realistic picture at little increase in the amount of information displayed.

The risk of overlooking relevant information can be reduced by providing the user with backup details that explain each aggregation. For example, a report giving sales by product group and region might be supported with more detailed reports by sales office and product subgroups. Each detailed report may, in turn, be supported with still more detailed reports that show sales by individual salesmen and product. A detailed report should clearly show the relation between its data and the next higher aggregation. See Figure 9. Similar backup can be provided to support aggregations across cost categories, multiple time periods, and the like.

MONTHLY SUMMARY SALES REPORT ($ MILLIONS)							
		REGION					
		NORTH EAST	SOUTH EAST	CENTRAL	SOUTH WEST	WEST	TOTAL
PRODUCT GROUP	A	25	12	32	8	10	87
	B	17	9	35	4	12	77
	C	12	5	22	2	3	44
	D	(20)	7	15	15	18	75
	TOTAL	74	33	(104)	29	43	(283)

MONTHLY REGIONAL SALES REPORT ($ MILLIONS) PRODUCT GROUP D NORTHEAST REGION				
		OFFICE		
		NY	BOS	PHIL	TOTAL
	D1	4.2	1.5	2.1	7.8
PRODUCT	D2	1.8	.8	2.6	5.2
SUBGROUP	D3	1.1	1.7	.3	3.1
	D4	3.0	.3	.8	4.1
	TOTAL	10.1	4.3	5.8	(20.2)

**Figure 9. Hierarchic relationship among reports. It is desirable to provide de-
tailed backup reports for all aggregate data. A figure on a high-level report should
appear as a total on the next lower level report.**

This hierarchical linking of reports provides an effective means of reducing unnecessary detail while still allowing the user to penetrate into the details when this appears to be warranted. An obvious requirement of a complete hierarchical linking of
reports is the proper nesting of data elements in terms of data definitions, reporting
periods, and classifications. In other words, a lower level data element must be
identified uniquely with a higher level aggregation for a given classification scheme.*

Good human factors in the design of display formats. Information must be perceived before it can have value for human decision making. The effectiveness with which a user
perceives information is largely governed by the way in which it is displayed. The interface between the system and user is one of the more critical design factors.

Some of the general principles of good display are as follows:

- Use standard report formats, headings, and definitions whenever possible. This permits a user to scan a display without having to interpret
each item.

---

*Geographical boundaries provide a useful analogy. An example of proper nesting is the aggregation of Unit-
ed States counties to form states and the aggregation of states to form the United States. On the other hand,
metropolitan areas do not nest within state boundaries. Proper nesting for a given classification does not pre-
clude alternate nesting for other classifications. For example, the sales of a given item can be aggregated by
geographical boundaries, product groupings, or industries.

- Each item displayed should be labeled or have an obvious interpretation.

- Avoid unnecessary precision. Since an aggregation inevitably represents an approximation of reality, excess precision adds little value while it clutters up the display.

- Use graphical display when feasible. A graphical display reduces unneeded precision while often revealing relationships among variables much more perceptibly than a tabular display.

- Provide a basis for interpreting information. A given piece of information seldom has value by itself; it must be assessed relative to some standard or anticipated result. It is therefore important that a user be provided sufficient information to comprehend the significance or surprise content of new information. This can be done by displaying the new information (e.g., actual current results) in juxtaposition with the existing plan, standard, or past results.

- Provide links among separate displays. Each display should contain relatively little information in order not to swamp the user. It is therefore necessary to use multiple displays if much information is to be conveyed. The user should be able to relate one display to another. Hierarchical relationships among displays, as discussed in the previous section, provide one of the basic means of doing this.

Use of the exception principle. The exception principle is by no means a new idea. Its intent is to identify "exceptions" that require human attention. Information about exceptional conditions is displayed while all other information is filtered out. An exception is deemed to have occurred when actual results deviate from a standard by more than an established threshold value. See Figure 10.

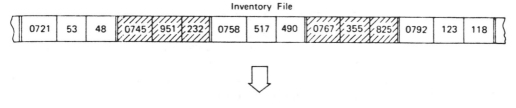

Figure 10. Exception reporting. An exception report displays only the conditions that fall outside of defined control limits. An inventory status report, for example, may show only the items that are over 200 or less than 50 percent of their standard. The system should readily handle changes in control limits in order to allow users to redefine their information requirements. The inventory standard used in the report may be set externally by management, or it could be computed periodically from an inventory model.

Threshold values are ideally set at a level that correctly distinguishes between relevant and irrelevant information. This means that information about conditions outside control limits should lead to a new decision, such as altering an existing plan. The deviation from the plan may be either favorable or unfavorable. A favorable deviation opens new opportunities that would be lost if the current plan were not revised — an increase in sales, for example, may call for increased output. An unfavorable deviation may require a change in plan in order to minimize the cost of the deviation — a renegotiation of delivery schedules when difficulties are detected in an engineering development program, for instance.

The effectiveness of an exception reporting system obviously hinges on its ability to distinguish between relevant and irrelevant information. The ideal system cannot generally be achieved in practice, since this requires complete formalization of the decision process. Suppose, for example, that we wish to report inventory status according to the exception principle. In order to identify items of inventory requiring attention (to change the existing production schedule or the order point and order quantity, say), the system must be capable of comparing the existing plan with the new optimum based on the latest known conditions. Only when there exists a significant disparity between the two is it necessary to signal an exception.

Thus, the identification of a true exception requires (1) a prediction of the likely outcome if no change in plan is made, and (2) the penalty that this outcome would entail in comparison with the current optimum plan. Only if the penalty exceeds the cost of changing the plan should the situation be labeled an exception. Such formalization rarely exists, and so it is necessary to strike a balance between the risk of displaying too much or too little information.

The control limits used to identify exceptions can be based on any (or all) of the variables used in a plan. In the case of an operating budget, for example, manufacturing overhead might be monitored in order to signal an alarm when costs become excessive. The deviation allowed each variable should be set according to its relative importance and its normal random fluctuations. Thus, a variation of 50 percent from standard may be allowed for a minor variable subject to considerable routine fluctuation, while a 5-percent variation in a well-behaved aggregate variable may be deemed worthy of management attention.

An exception can be defined in terms of trends as well as deviations. For example, an unfavorable deviation in raw material costs of, say, 8 percent may normally be considered unexceptional; but if it follows a month with a favorable variance of 6 percent, the unfavorable trend could be tagged as an exception.

Because of the imprecise nature of control limits, they should be viewed as parameters subject to change as users see fit. If too many exceptions are currently being displayed, a user may wish to broaden the limits in order to display only the most severe exceptions. If only a few exceptions occur, a user should be able to tighten limits in order to reveal the situations that may most benefit from his attention. The extreme case of zero limits should be allowed when an exhaustive display is desired, as well as "infinite" limits when no information is wanted.

A well-designed exception reporting scheme can add greatly to the value of an information system. To be sure, it carries some risk of overlooking important information. It is a profound mistake, however, to assume that this is a risk unique to formal exception reporting; a user may stand a much greater risk of overlooking significant information if it is immersed in a huge report containing mostly irrelevant data. Selection of relevant from irrelevant information must be performed either by the user himself or within the system. The capability of the computer to apply sophisticated selection criteria often gives it a tremendous advantage over the user in identifying likely candidates for closer inspection.

There are obvious costs of providing exception reporting services. The design and maintenance of a sophisticated system is by no means trivial. Users must be trained to use the system well. Some additional processing costs are usually incurred to filter out irrelevant data (although savings in display costs may in some cases more than offset this). However, when these costs are compared to the (largely hidden) costs of having users perform their own selection, the economies almost always favor formal exception reporting.

Use of Ad Hoc Inquiries. The typical periodic report is based on the anticipated recurring needs of a group of users. It therefore necessarily contains a great deal of information that is not relevant to a given user at a given point in time.*

An alternative to periodic reports is an ad hoc inquiry system that provides a response (within a reasonable time lag) to each specific request for information. See Figure 11. If information is supplied only on demand and is tailored to a specific user's needs, it stands a much higher probability of being useful.

The capabilities offered by inquiry systems vary widely. Some systems only allow data to be extracted from the data base, without any further manipulation. Of much greater use is a system that can perform appropriate aggregation of detailed data. Some systems also have built-in standard transformations of data, such as the calculation of an average, range, or standard deviation. A still more advanced capability is the ability to handle transformations defined by the user in the retrieval language of the system. Finally, in the most sophisticated systems the user can define transformations with any available language (such as FORTRAN, COBOL, or PL/1); these are properly termed data base management systems, since they serve as the basic interface with the data base. Olle (1970) discusses some of these issues.

The costs of handling ad hoc inquiries depend greatly on the particular system used, the size of the data base, and response time requirements. Costs include the effort required by the user to specify requested information, as well as the processing of the inquiries. A sophisticated system providing a powerful retrieval language and fast response may be quite expensive indeed. On the other hand, handling batch-processed inquiries of a standard nature may be quite inexpensive, particularly if the processing is combined with routine file updating.

It is sometimes feasible to maintain certain commonly used information, such as standard financial data, as a separate subset of the total data base. Relatively standard inquiries can then be handled by retrieving data from this subset. Its size may be very much smaller than the entire data base, permitting substantial economies.

---

*A specialized example of a periodic report is the standard telephone directory. It contains a very low density of useful information for any given subscriber. Nevertheless, economies favor such an approach because the cost of providing each subscriber with selected information (through a directory assistance operator or a tailor-made directory) would be prohibitive with existing technology. Besides, the cost of selection from the telephone book is relatively small (if one knows the name of the person whose number he is seeking) and is borne by the subscriber.

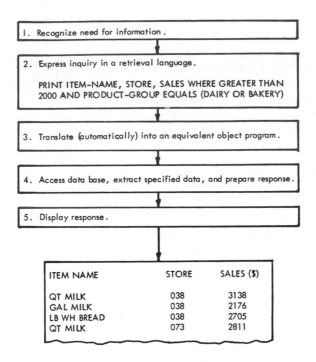

1. Recognize need for information.

2. Express inquiry in a retrieval language.

   PRINT ITEM-NAME, STORE, SALES WHERE GREATER THAN
   2000 AND PRODUCT-GROUP EQUALS (DAIRY OR BAKERY)

3. Translate (automatically) into an equivalent object program.

4. Access data base, extract specified data, and prepare response.

5. Display response.

ITEM NAME	STORE	SALES ($)
QT MILK	038	3138
GAL MILK	038	2176
LB WH BREAD	038	2705
QT MILK	073	2811

Figure 11. Processing of an ad hoc inquiry. A specific display is prepared in response to an ad hoc inquiry. The resulting information can therefore be highly selective.

Use of a Decision Model. A decision model can be viewed as a particularly effective information filter. The user of a model is presented with the output of the model, rather than its detailed inputs. Output normally is very much less voluminous than input, which drastically reduces the amount of information displayed.

The degree of filtering depends greatly on the type of model used. A decision model fully embedded within the information system, in which all input data are obtained automatically from the data base and all decisions are fed automatically into operations, provides the most extreme example. In this case only aggregate results need to be displayed for human monitoring.

This is obviously not the common situation. In most cases even "optimizing" models require human intervention in providing inputs and in reviewing and modifying outputs. Simulation models usually require active human participation in proposing alternatives and selecting the best one among them. Nevertheless, the amount of information presented to the user is usually much less than would be required if he made the decision unaided by a model.

A decision model can be combined effectively with exception reporting. The model can be run periodically to test if the latest conditions — e.g., sales, costs, etc. — should cause a revision in existing plans. If so, this fact can be displayed for human review; otherwise, nothing is reported (except perhaps aggregate performance).

Response time

The response time of an information system is the time it takes to respond to a significant stimulus. The stimulus may be the occurrence of an event that is to be reflected in the data base, such as the arrival of a sales order from a customer. Alternatively, the stimulus may be a request for information already stored in the data base. Thus, in discussing response time we are concerned with two aspects of time lag: (1) the time it takes to update the data base, and (2) the time it takes to retrieve desired information from the data base.

It is useful to break down response time in this way because value and cost may depend heavily on which aspect is being considered. Some applications may benefit significantly from quick updating and retrieval, while still others may require neither quick update nor retrieval.

Value of Short Update Time. Let us first consider the value of information as a function of its recency. The timeliness of the data base depends on the update response time. In an environment that changes both rapidly and unpredictably, the data base must be updated quickly in order to keep a faithful representation of current reality. If decisions are highly sensitive to changes in the environment, substantial penalties may be suffered if the update time is not kept short relative to the rate of these changes.

Some applications clearly benefit from on-line updating. These are nearly always found at the operating level of the organization. It is only here that events are likely to take place frequently enough to justify very short update lags. Such "real-time" applications as air traffic control, industrial process control, and stock quotation services would scarcely be feasible without a data base kept current within a matter of seconds. Airline reservation systems begin to incur significant penalties (in the form of underbooking or overbooking, for example) as updating lags exceed an hour or so. High-volume production and inventory control systems similarly benefit from rapid file updating. All of these examples exhibit the same essential characteristic: the average time interval between (unpredictable) events is short, and so effective control demands a correspondingly short update lag. Failure to revise current plans in the face of unanticipated events may lead to significant loss. See Figure 12.

Figure 12. Loss due to use of old information. A plan, once made, begins to decay with time when unexpected events occur. Replanning brings the plan back to the new optimum based on current information. The more frequent the planning and current the information, the less the loss due to use of obsolete plans. The shaded area shows the incremental loss when response time is doubled; it therefore represents the incremental value of the shorter response time.

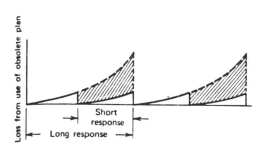

This is not a common characteristic of higher level decision processes. Individual events have little relevance at this level; all that usually matters is aggregate behavior. Aggregate variables, such as total sales and total capacity, exhibit significant change only slowly and often in a fairly predictable way. It is not necessary to provide rapid updating of the data base in order to track sluggish and well-behaved changes. Furthermore, the accuracy of predictions over the relatively long planning horizon typically associated with higher level decisions would not be significantly reduced by update lags of days or even a few weeks. We can therefore conclude that quick updating of the data base usually adds little value to higher level decision making. See Figure 13.

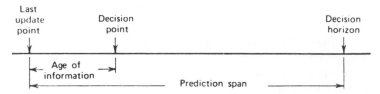

Figure 13. Effect of age of information on decisions. Decision making — whether at the operational or strategic level — requires a prediction for each of the input variables used in the decision process (e.g., sales forecasts, inventory levels, aircraft positions, etc.). The prediction span for a given variable extends to the decision horizon from the point in time at which the data base was last updated. The quality of a decision depends in part on the accuracy of the predictions. Accuracy, in turn, depends on the length of the prediction span and the inherent variability of events within the span. A rapidly changing and unpredictable environment requires a short prediction span in order to maintain control; accordingly, information must be very current in order to provide suitable accuracy. Strategic decisions, on the other hand, tend to have long-term effects; and so the decision horizon is well into the future. In this case reducing the age of information adds little to predictability over the long span.

Value of Quick Retrieval Time. The value of quick retrieval is often quite independent of the age of information obtained. Thus, under some circumstances we may want fast access to relatively old information. A short retrieval time enhances value under two circumstances: (1) a decision (and the resulting action) must be made quickly, or (2) the decision process benefits from a series of accesses performed in "browsing" fashion.

The typical real-time system requires fast action (as well as fast file updating) in order to control a dynamically changing environment. Air traffic control, to use this example again, must deal with the problem of collision avoidance. A speedy decision is warranted when two aircraft on a collision path approach one another at Mach 2. The information on which the decision is based must therefore be both current and rapidly accessible. See Figure 13.

In less dynamic cases it may be important to make a fairly quick decision even if the information supplied is not particularly current. In an order entry application, for example, it may be quite valuable to respond immediately to a customer's inquiry concerning stock availability (while the customer waits on the telephone, say). In most cases there would be no great value in having an up-to-the-minute picture of inventory status; normally it would be sufficient to base the decision on status as of some earlier cut-off point* (e.g., at the end of the previous day). This allows file updating to be handled on an economical batch basis. Inquiries between file updates can be processed through an online system or a manual operation that uses a daily status report (the choice depending on speed and cost of processing an inquiry). Most on-line reservation systems are motivated much more by the requirement for fast confirmation than by the need to keep files current within a few seconds.

---

*If inventory levels change rapidly, but fairly predictably, the system can adjust the inventory balance by the predicted withdrawals from the cut-off point up to the time of the decision. In any case, one can always increase the probability of having an item in stock by simply maintaining a larger safety stock.

Data entry applications can also benefit substantially from quick access to the data base. An interactive system can perform validity checks while a clerk remains at a remote terminal. A detected error usually can be corrected immediately, thus avoiding the serious complications involved in off-line error correction (as well as speeding up the updating process). Data accepted as valid may then be used for on-line file updating (if a short update lag is required), or may simply be stored temporarily for later batch updating.

Although the above examples are representative of important quick response applications, it certainly is true that the bulk of decision making within an organization cannot justify quick retrieval on the grounds that hasty action is called for. On the contrary, a delay in reaching a decision of days or weeks may not carry a serious penalty, especially at the strategic level. Nevertheless, even in these cases there may still be considerable value in providing information within a short response time.

Quick response tends to be especially valuable when one deals with an ill-structured problem. Typically one cannot specify in advance all required information. Instead the problem is best approached through a sequential examination of responses. Each response may suggest new information that would shed additional light on the task at hand. This "browsing" process can continue until the problem solver feels that further probes are not justified.

A quick response allows more alternatives to be examined, which normally results in an improved decision. Even though there may be no great urgency in reaching a decision, there is always some upper limit on the time available. The number of sequential probes is therefore limited by response time.

If the response is fast enough, in the order of seconds or perhaps at most a minute,* the decision can be reached through the uninterrupted participation of the human problem solver. This allows him to retain a grasp of the problem that would otherwise be lost if he were forced to switch to some other activity while he waits for a response. Although the evidence is by no means overwhelming, it appears reasonably certain that interactive man-machine problem solving of this sort can be very effective in dealing with many types of complex tasks.

A capability of this sort may be particularly useful when a decision is reached through group cooperation. For example, setting a quarterly production schedule may require the participation of the managers of marketing, manufacturing, purchasing, and personnel. The value of a man-machine model may be fairly limited unless it allows the group as a whole to explore alternative schedules. This probably is feasible only if the model provides a response quick enough to make a decision in a relatively short meeting among all participants.

Cost of Short Response Times. Having discussed the value of information as a function of response time, we can now turn our attention to the matter of costs. Cost is governed largely by the frequency with which the data base is accessed for updating or retrieval.

Consider first the case of batch processing. Response time is clearly a function of the interval between successive batches. Suppose that this interval is I, and that there is a processing lag L between the cut-off point at the end of the batch cycle and the

---

*Humans become extraordinarily impatient in an interactive environment if they have to wait very long for a response.

availability of output.

Update time depends on the timing of an event. If the event occurs just before the end of the cycle, update time is the processing lag L; if it occurs just after the cut-off point, update time is I + L. The average time, assuming that events are spaced uniformly over the processing cycle, is I/2 + L. This is shown in Figure 14. The same minimum, average, and maximum response times apply to retrieval, whether information is obtained from a periodic report or through an ad hoc inquiry.*

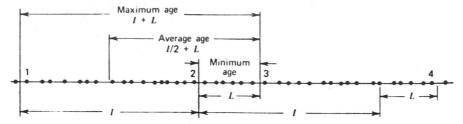

Figure 14. Response time as a function of the batch processing interval and processing lag. The time required to update a sequential file depends on the processing interval *I* and the processing lag *L*. All events that occur during a given interval are processed together in a batch. The first event within the interval (at time 1 in the figure) is not reflected in the file until *I* + *L* time units later (at time 3). Information about the last event (at time 2) enters the file in only *L* units. The average, assuming a uniform distribution of events, is *I/2* + *L*. The minimum, maximum, and average *retrieval* times are the same as the *update* times. The information retrieved from a periodic report or through batch processing of ad hoc inquiries is *L* time units old immediately upon completion of the processing cycle (at time 3); it is *I* + *L* units old at the end of the cycle (at time 4). In some applications the minimum response time may be the most important design consideration (e.g., in the case of a financial statement reviewed by management only when it first becomes available); in others, the maximum (e.g., the handling of customer orders); and in still others, the average (e.g., inventory updating).

Thus, response time is a function of the processing cycle and processing lag. The processing lag can be reduced primarily through the use of more rapid means of collecting and transmitting data, such as an on-line data collection system tied directly to a central processor. The lag can also be reduced somewhat by reducing the average time a batch must wait in queue prior to processing. This is achieved by increasing surplus capacity to absorb fluctuations in demand. The actual run time taken to process a batch is rarely a significant portion of overall response time.

The most significant component of response time is typically the processing interval I. The number of runs is, of course, inversely proportional to this interval — e.g., twice as many runs are required if the interval is cut in half. Sequential processing runs tend to be input/output bound; this tendency increases all the more as the in-

---

*These times apply only to *status* information, which gives the value of a particular variable, such as inventory level, at the cut-off point. *Operating* information deals with the series of events that occur over a reporting interval, such as the orders shipped during the past month. Immediately before an operating report is produced, the latest information available covers events that occurred as long as R + I + L time units earlier, where R is the reporting interval (usually, but not always, the same as I). The average age of operating information is R/2 + I/2 + L. Gregory and Van Horn (1963) discuss these matters in some detail (pp. 576-580).

terval shrinks (since the number of transactions goes down when they are accumulated over a shorter interval). Therefore, processing time — and hence cost — is inversely related to response time.

As the processing interval shrinks, costs of conventional sequential processing begin to grow very rapidly. Eventually the point is reached where it becomes less expensive to use indexed sequential file organization, since this allows inactive portions of the file to be skipped. As the batch interval goes down still further, random processing — i.e., handling each transaction separately — eventually becomes the least expensive method. Figure 15 illustrates how cost varies as a function of response time.

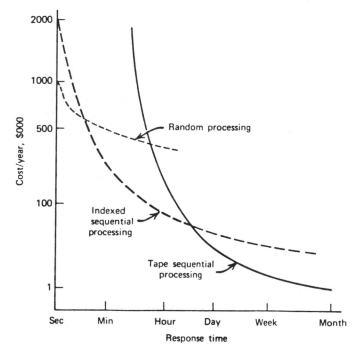

Figure 15. Cost as a function of response time. Economical batch processing with magnetic tape can be used when response time is not critical. As response time is reduced — and hence run frequency is increased — total input/output time grows rapidly. Eventually batch processing with an indexed sequential file becomes less expensive, since it allows skipping over inactive portions of the file and thus reduces input/output time. If response times are reduced still further, eventually random processing of a randomly organized file becomes the least expensive approach.

Because of the dominant nature of input/output time for batch processing, it is usually advantageous to perform both file updating and retrieval during the same run. Retrieval may consist of handling ad hoc inquiries as well as preparing periodic reports. Since all records have to be accessed with each run, the only incremental cost of combining file updating and retrieval is the added size and complexity of the combining program.

Only active portions of the file need to be accessed with either indexed sequential or random file organization. Therefore, the number of active records becomes a principal determinant of cost (and not just the number of processing runs). It may be possible to substantially reduce the number of random accesses if updating is separated from retrieval. For example, all updating can be handled in batch fashion, while ad hoc inquiries are processed randomly. Batch updating can not only lower processing costs, but it can also significantly reduce the problems of file security and reliability that always attend on-line file updating.

Accuracy

Information is accurate if the image it provides conforms closely with reality. Thus, an inventory report is accurate if the stated levels agree with actual inventory status. A sales forecast is accurate if it correctly estimates future sales.

The value of accuracy is derived from the improvements it brings in decisions or operating actions. Any decision or action is based on the information available. To the extent that this information does not accurately portray reality, outcomes will be less desirable than would otherwise have occurred.

The most stringent requirements for accuracy generally come from operational activities. A considerable loss may ensue from an error in a paycheck, purchase order, invoice, or bank balance. A good deal of effort is justified to avoid the unrecoverable losses, the confusion, and the loss of goodwill usually associated with errors of this type.

Higher level decision making generally imposes relatively mild requirements for accuracy. Most decisions and payoffs are fairly insensitive to moderate errors, and so great accuracy adds little value.

Decision-making information that comes from the aggregation of transaction data usually is accurate by virtue of operational needs. Any errors that exist in the details tend to cancel out in the aggregation process.

Some data are collected specifically for decision-making purposes — for example, demographic data used in store location studies, consumer survey data used in marketing, business intelligence data used in competitive evaluations, and economic indicators used in forecasting. It usually is not necessary to subject these data to the same close control applied in collecting operational data.

Accuracy, like all desirable characteristics of information, has a cost. It is achieved by collecting error-free data that are then processed by suitable routines. Accuracy in data collection comes from error control procedures that both discourage creation of errors and provide the means for detecting and correcting any errors that enter the system. A great deal of sophistication and ingenuity can go into these procedures. Almost any desired degree of accuracy in data collection can be attained, but at an increasingly high cost as perfection is approached. Cost is incurred in the form of collecting and maintaining redundant data for error detection and correction purposes, as well as in the implementation and operation of the routines for performing error control functions.

Accuracy depends not only on the quality of data inputs, but also on the routines used in processing information. An obvious requirement for assured accuracy is that the routines be bug free. It virtually is impossible to eliminate all bugs from a large program, but careful (and expensive) testing and maintenance procedures can reduce the probability of an error to a manageable level.

A less obvious way to increase accuracy is to apply improved estimating procedures. Decision making is concerned with predicted future conditions rather than historical accuracy. Sales data used in forecasting may be perfectly accurate; but if the estimating procedures are not suitable, the resulting errors may cause substantial penalties of stockouts or excessive inventory.

Any prediction has inherent errors, but the average size of error can be reduced through the use of appropriate estimating procedures. Accuracy is governed to some extent by the type of input data available for calculating predictions. Inputs include data about past transactions, past forecasts, economic indices, and the like. These inputs may be subjected to relatively simple procedures, such as exponential smoothing or other averaging techniques. On the other hand, accuracy may be improved significantly by using some of the more elaborate forecasting methods. Cost of such accuracy includes the maintenance of data inputs and the design and operation of the forecasting routines.

Techniques for making cost/benefit analyses

We have seen that cost/benefit analysis of information systems faces some extremely complex issues. We are a long way from developing fully satisfactory approaches. Nevertheless, an organization that sinks vast sums of money into the development and operation of an information system cannot ignore the complexities; it must deal with them in the best way it can.

Analysis of tangible cost reductions

Tangible costs and benefits are those that can be expressed in *monetary* terms. This clearly is possible in the case of projects aimed at clear-cut cost reductions in information processing. Elimination of clerical operations or lowering the cost of equipment rental (through greater efficiency or use of a later generation computer, say) are common examples of such projects. They are often accompanied by little or no change in information quality, essentially the same information is provided (hopefully) at lower cost. Under these circumstances the analysis need not concern itself with determining benefits, since they remain the same as before.

A cost reduction project thus can be viewed as a straightforward investment. As such, traditional methods of analysis can be applied. Certain expenditures must be made to implement the modified system. These are then followed (if all goes well) by reduced future operating expenditures. See Figure 16. One can analyze the investment in terms of net present value, internal rate of return, or payback period. Project selection can be dealt with in the same way used to set priorities on other forms of investment.

Figure 16. Analysis of tangible savings from an investment in an information system project. Tangible costs and benefits can be handled using traditional methods of investment analysis. The net cash flows that occur in different time periods can be translated into a single index by calculating the present value of the investment, its rate of return, or its payback period.

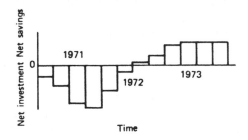

There lurks a hazard in this: it is too easy. Because cost reduction projects can be analyzed in traditional ways, the organization is often tempted to concentrate on them. This avoids the problem of having to assess benefits of improved information but runs the risk of misdirecting efforts away from projects that can make more fundamental improvements in organizational performance. This is not to say that worthwhile cost reductions should not be pursued, but the bias is often too heavily weighted in their favor.

Analysis of tangible benefits

Really significant contributions normally come through enhanced information quality. Many of the benefits from improved quality may be perfectly tangible. The benefits are certainly tangible, for example, when faster customer billing reduces cash requirements. The translation into a monetary savings requires an estimate of both an annual rate of return and the total expected cash reduction. If the rate of return is estimated to be, say, 20 percent (based perhaps on the opportunity cost of internal investments), a $100,000 reduction in cash is worth $20,000 per year.

The principal difficulty in assessing benefits of this sort is the estimation of the effects of improved information. In the above example the analyst must estimate the relation between cash requirements and billing time. If it can be assumed that faster billing will not change the distribution of time lags between the receipt of an invoice by a customer and the receipt of his payment, then the relation can be estimated quite easily. For instance, a two-day reduction in billing, with average daily sales of $50,000, will result in a $100,000 reduction in cash requirements.

The use of a formal decision model often greatly facilitates the estimation of benefits. Suppose, for example, that we would like to estimate the inventory reduction stemming from more frequent order processing. The reduction comes from lower inventory safety stocks made possible by the shorter reorder lead time (since more frequent order processing reduces the time from the breaking of an order point to the preparation of a replenishment order). The relation between processing cycle and inventory level is a very complex one, but it can be estimated easily if a suitable inventory model exists. Sensitivity studies of this sort can be used to consider the effects of altering any of the model's input data. Such studies should be an important part of implementing any decision model.

In the absence of a formal model, it becomes considerably more difficult to estimate the effects of changes in information quality. Formal models often do not exist, of course. In particular, they do not exist when the information project under consideration is the implementation of such a model.

One way to deal with this situation is to develop a "quick and dirty" model that gives a gross estimate of possible savings. For example, in estimating the benefits of more frequent order processing, we might analyze a typical inventory item using a standard inventory model. This will not give the same accuracy as an analysis of all items using a tailor made model, but when used with discretion this approach gives a satisfactory first-order approximation. Often even a cursory study allows management to reject or accept clear-cut cases. Attention can then be focused on projects that appear to be borderline cases.

Sometimes a simple model can be used to provide boundary estimates of benefits — i.e., an upper or lower limit on possible benefits. An upper limit can be used to reject unworthy projects, while a lower limit can identify worthwhile projects. For example, in considering the implementation of an improved forecasting system one can establish an upper limit by assuming that the system will give *perfect* forecasts. In a similar fashion an upper limit on the improvement in production scheduling can be obtained by assuming 100 percent capacity utilization and no interference among jobs. A proposed system could be rejected out of hand if the estimated cost of implementation exceeds the upper limit on benefits. If this is not the case, more refined analysis can often lower the upper limit in order to bring it closer to the actual value.

Lower limits can be estimated in a variety of ways. One means is to put a value on only the most easily determined benefits. In analyzing a customer billing project, for example, estimating savings from a reduction in cash requirements gives a lower limit on total benefits. Actual benefits might exceed this limit by the (unknown) value of fewer errors in billing, better by-product information for market analysis, and the like. Another technique is to calculate benefits by using *worst case* estimates for probabilistic variables. If a project is acceptable using the most pessimistic estimates, actual benefits are highly likely to prove even more attractive. See Figure 17.

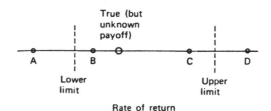

Figure 17. **Use of upper and lower limits in analyzing benefits. Suppose that the upper and lower limits shown in the diagram have been estimated for a given project. The project must provide sufficient benefits to justify its estimated cost. If point A represents the minimum acceptable payoff, the project is worthwhile by virtue of the fact that the lower limit on benefits exceeds the acceptable payoff. Similarly, the project can be rejected if point D is the minimum acceptable payoff, since this value exceeds the upper limit on benefits. The acceptance of point B and the rejection of point C require further analysis to refine the estimated upper and lower limits to bring them closer to the true payoff.**

A similar approach is to estimate the break-even improvement necessary to balance the cost of implementing a project. Suppose, for example, that a firm spends $1 million per year on advertising in magazines and newspapers. The cost of obtaining and analyzing readership data is estimated to be, say, $10,000. Thus, a one-percent reduction in advertising expenditures (while holding exposure constant) would justify the cost of the analysis. Similarly, a supermarket firm might determine that the cost of maintaining detailed sales statistics could be balanced by an increase in sales of 0.3 percent. Given such an analysis, an experienced manager can often judge whether or not the likely improvement exceeds the break-even point.

Analysis of intangible benefits

The benefits discussed so far are tangible enough, even though they may be difficult to estimate. Some benefits, however, are especially difficult to translate into a monetary value. For example, it would be very difficult indeed for General Motors to put a dollar value on the customer goodwill brought about by a reduction from 10 percent to 5 percent in the probability that a dealer will have a stockout of a needed repair part. It would be equally difficult for the Southern Railway System to attach a dollar benefit to the improved service achieved by a one-day reduction in average delivery time of freight shipments.

Almost any benefit can be assigned a tangible value if sufficient effort is devoted to the task; the difference between a "tangible" and an "intangible" benefit thus lies in the difficulty of estimating monetary value. Even a benefit such as customer goodwill could be translated into a reasonable estimate of monetary value if the effort were justified. If this is not the case, however, we must deal with the problem in other ways.

At the outset it should be pointed out that difficulty in expressing a benefit in *monetary terms* does not imply that the benefit cannot be *quantified*. Failure to appreciate this fact has often resulted in an unnecessary lack of specificity in describing intangible benefits. Thus, in the above examples it was possible to quantify benefits (e.g., stockout probability reduced from .10 to .05), even if no dollar value was attributed to them. In some cases very little quantification may be possible (and so a narrative description must suffice), but this is the exception.

Under some circumstances the analysis of intangible benefits becomes fairly straightforward. This is the case when a proposed system can be justified on tangible grounds alone (i.e., through some combination of cost reductions and tangible benefits), while also contributing significant intangible benefits. The proposed system is said to *dominate* the existing one, since it is superior in terms of both its tangible and intangible characteristics.

Opportunities of this sort are not as uncommon as one might suppose. Existing systems are rarely as efficient as they could be, and therefore offer considerable potential for cost reductions. Such savings are made all the greater when technical advances permit new economies. Rather than concentrating solely on tangible effects, however, an organization usually finds it worthwhile to take some of its gains in intangible form.

Advanced "real-time" systems often provide a variety of benefits of this sort. For example, a comprehensive airlines reservation system may be justified on such tangible grounds as reduction in the salaries of reservation and ticketing clerks, higher seat bookings, and more efficient routing and scheduling of flights. Improved customer service may be as valuable as any of these, but it is probably not possible to assign a dollar estimate to it.

If a formal model exists, it may be possible to establish an explicit tradeoff between an intangible benefit and a tangible one. Suppose, for example, that an improved inventory model is implemented. Benefits can be taken in the form of lower inventory cost, lower stockout probability, or some combination of both. Even if a monetary value cannot be placed on fewer stockouts, its cost can be expressed in terms of foregone opportunity to reduce inventory costs. See Figure 18. An experienced manager presumably can resolve questions of this sort when he is presented with explicit tradeoff information.

Figure 18. Tradeoff possibilities offered by increased efficiency. Changes in technology (or simply discovery of more efficient ways to exploit existing technology) allow new alternatives that provide tangible or intangible benefits. Such changes might permit, for example, the replacement of inventory system A by system B or C. All the benefits of system B are in the form of a tangible cost reduction. The selection of system C in preference to B implies that the intangible benefit of fewer stockouts is worth *at least* as much as the resulting reduction in cost savings.

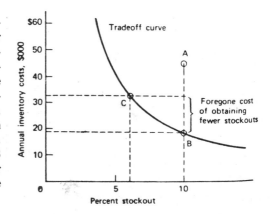

Users' role in cost/benefit analysis

As information systems become more comprehensive and integrated, formal methods of analysis become increasingly difficult to apply. Joint costs and joint benefits often make it possible to determine the payoff from any one subsystem. As the system begins to pervade day-to-day operations and higher level decision making, benefits become increasingly difficult to evaluate in monetary terms. Inevitably, then, we must rely on experienced judgment, as well as technical analysis, to make cost/benefit decisions.

Communication between user and technical staff

One of the complications of making a cost/benefit decision is that it requires close coordination between two disparate groups, the users and the technicians. A rational decision requires knowledge of both cost and benefits. Information acquires value only through use, and so it is the users who are in the best position to judge the value of information. On the other hand, users very often have only a hazy idea of the cost of information. As a result, they may specify an information "requirement" that is very expensive to satisfy, or they may fail to ask for useful information that could be provided at very little extra cost. To get costs into the picture, the technical manager and his staff must play the vital role of (1) analyzing costs and benefits to the extent possible, and (2) providing users with tradeoff information so that they will know the cost implications of their specifications.

The knowledge necessary to strike a reasonable balance between the cost and value of information is thus split between users and technicians. Clearly, then, this knowledge should be shared in some way. The dialogue between user and technicians may take several forms. One important way is by means of an iterative revision of requirements.

This process can begin by having the users specify desired characteristics of information outputs. A user might, for example, request that the system provide a response time of ten seconds in handling a given type of inquiry.*

With this and other specifications as a starting point, the technicians can then design, in gross terms, a system that meets (most of) the stated requirements. The designers may find that some few of the requirements are wholly infeasible; in these cases an alternative should be proposed. Even when a specification is perfectly feasible, the designers should provide tradeoff information so that users have some indication of the cost consequences of their specifications. For example, users may be given the following tradeoffs:

Response time	Incremental annual cost
10 seconds, 90% confidence	$50,000
10 seconds, 75% confidence	45,000
60 seconds, 75% confidence	30,000
2 hours	10,000
overnight	5,000

*Since the load on the system varies minute by minute, response time must be specified in probabilistic terms. The user may, for instance, specify that at least 90 percent of the transactions receive a response within ten seconds.

The great value of such tradeoff information is that it gives users a basis for balancing benefits against costs. A user may very well choose to alter his initial specification in light of its cost implications; at least he should be presented with this option.

Let us continue with the example of the inquiry system. Suppose that benefits are estimated as shown below. The *net* value of information can then be determined. Overnight service turns out to be the optimal response time in this example, and so the original specification should be changed.

Response time	Incremental benefit	Incremental cost	Net incremental value
10 seconds, 90% confidence	$100,000	$50,000	$50,000
10 seconds, 75% confidence	98,000	45,000	53,000
60 seconds, 75% confidence	75,000	30,000	45,000
2 hours	72,000	10,000	62,000
overnight	70,000	5,000	65,000

Tradeoffs should be expressed in monetary terms whenever feasible. Ultimately, however, the final judgment usually involves considerable subjective evaluation of intangible benefits. This should not be viewed as a serious limitation — after all, managers are paid to exercise judgment. When presented with sufficient tradeoff information, a user is probably able to strike a satisfactory balance between cost and value.

An important question remains, however: Is the user motivated to choose what he considers to be the proper balance between cost and value? He may well not be if he receives benefits while not bearing the incremental cost of obtaining them. Question: In the above example if the user does not pay incremental costs, what response time is he likely to specify? A policy of charging users for incremental costs raises all sorts of costing problems, but it is very difficult otherwise to motivate users to make wise judgments.

Determination of tradeoffs

The preparation of tradeoff information is obviously expensive. Each tradeoff point represents an alternative design in terms, say, of different capacities of main or auxiliary storage, number of I/O channels, or communication network configurations. The designers should therefore limit their consideration to a relatively few alternatives that stand some chance of being acceptable to users. For example, it serves no useful purpose for the designer to determine the cost of an order processing system that provides invoices of 95 percent accuracy if the marketing vice president insists on a minimum of 99 percent accuracy.

Some alternatives can be dismissed out of hand by having technical personnel work with users in preparing initial specifications. This will better insure that the alternatives considered will be limited to those that are reasonable from a technical point of view. An experienced designer can establish, without much analysis, fairly good boundaries on the range of feasible alternatives.

It is quite unlikely that users will be able to supply explicit estimates of value for alternative levels of information quality. A user may be willing to choose an alternative when presented with tradeoffs, and thereby establish an implicit estimate of relative values, but this is a considerably easier matter than giving explicit values. Nevertheless, the user should at least be able to provide *qualitative* tradeoff information in order that the designers can confine their attention to acceptable alternatives. In the case of the inquiry system, for example, users might be able to state in advance that overnight service is fully acceptable, interactive response is marginally useful, and any response time in between contributes very little extra benefit compared with overnight response. Designers then need only consider overnight batch processing and an interactive system.

Hierarchical nature of cost/benefit analysis

Any cost/benefit analysis takes money to perform. The more money spent, the better the estimates that can be provided. In other words, one can reduce uncertainty about the economic payoff of a project by devoting resources to the task of analysis.

The organization thus faces a typical resource allocation problem in trying to decide how much to spend on cost/benefit studies. Like other information expenditures, resources used for analysis should be spent where the results have the greatest surprise content, will lead to the most significant modifications in decisions, and offer the greatest potential payoff from improved decision making. These conditions are not met if the payoff from a project is fairly obvious, if the level of benefits expected from a project cannot justify an elaborate study, or if the benefits are intangible enough so that trying to place a monetary value on them is not worth the effort.

Very often a project can be dismissed without a great deal of analysis. Although a superficial analysis may be subject to considerable uncertainty, the estimated cost/benefit performance for a given project may be unattractive enough that further refinement is not necessary. An experienced information specialist can be very effective in identifying these marginal projects.

The remaining projects require further study. Uncertainty is reduced as implementation proceeds through gross design, detailed design, and programming. Periodically during this process management should review the project to determine if it should be abandoned, accepted, or subjected to still further analysis. See Figure 19.

Thus, cost/benefit analysis should continue throughout the life of a project. During the early, uncertain stages of a project, the amount of money spent is relatively modest. The ante goes up significantly when it reaches the stages of detailed design and programming, but by this point most of the uncertainty concerning payoff should have been eliminated.

Subjective estimation of benefits

Since it is usually necessary to rely at least partially on subjective evaluation of information benefits, it is important that users have a good conceptual grasp of the factors that contribute to value. The evidence is that these concepts are not at all universally understood. More than a few systems have been implemented in which there is an obvious imbalance between cost and value; either the system falls far short of providing the information quality that it should, or it supplies information at a cost drastically exceeding any possible value. Even a primitive understanding of the issues involved would have avoided many of the problems of this sort.

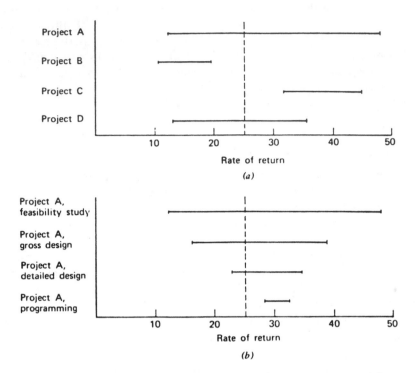

Figure 19. Uncertainty in estimating return from different projects. (a) **shows the estimated return from different projects, based on preliminary feasibility studies. Such estimates are subject to a considerable range because they are made without detailed information about the proposed systems. Nevertheless, even a superficial analysis can identify projects that appear worth pursuing in greater detail (e.g., Project A). It can also screen out projects that clearly fail to meet the minimum acceptable return of, say, 25 percent (e.g., Project B). Uncertainty is reduced as the analysis proceeds through the various stages of implementation, as is shown for Project A in** (b). **More detailed analysis and design narrows the range of estimated payoff. The estimate may stay within the acceptable region, or it may fall below the limit and call for the project to be modified substantially or even abandoned.**

Surprise content

A user, along with the technicians who aid him, should ask himself questions of the following sort:

- Does the contemplated information tell me something that I did not already know or strongly suspect?

- How frequently will I obtain a significant surprise?

- Is the information selective enough that I am likely to perceive significant facts?

- Would less detailed, accurate, timely, or reliable sources provide essentially the same surprise content?

Effect on decisions

- Will any surprise information cause me to take an action that I would otherwise not take?
- Would my decisions be significantly altered by less accurate or timely information?

Effect on performance

- What are the benefits from any change in action that results from receiving surprise information?
- Are the benefits sensitive to moderate deviations from "optimal" actions?
- Do benefits decrease significantly with delays in taking actions?

References: Emery

1. James C. Emery. 1969. *Organizational Planning & Control Systems.* Macmillan, New York. Chapter 4 discusses the economics of information, relying heavily on a theoretical model.

2. Robert H. Gregory and Richard L. Van Horn. 1963. *Automatic Data-Processing Systems,* second edition. Wadsworth Publishing Co., Belmont, California. A classical treatment of the technical and managerial issues of information systems. Chapters 14 and 15 deal with economic questions.

3. E. Gerald Hurst, Jr. 1969. "Analysis for Management Decisions." *Wharton Quarterly,* Winter, 1969. This paper presents some simple examples of Bayesian decision making and shows how the value of information can be calculated.

4. Börje Langefors. 1970. *Theoretical Analysis of Information Systems,* Volumes 1 and 2. Studentlitteratur Lund. Available from Barnes and Noble, New York. A valuable reference for anyone willing to wade through fairly heavy theory. Chapter 3 deals with the economics of information. Volume 2 is devoted mostly to questions of file organization.

5. Jacob Marschak. 1959. "Remarks on the Economics of Information." In *Contributions to Scientific Research in Management.* Graduate School of Business Administration, U.C.L.A., pp. 79-98. One of the fundamental theoretical contributions to an understanding of information economics.

6. Norman R. Nielsen. 1970. "The Allocation of Computer Resources — Is Pricing the Answer?" *Communications of the ACM,* 13,8 (August 1970), pp. 467-474. An excellent general discussion of pricing for computer services. It contains useful references to other papers on the subject.

7. T. William Olle. 1970. "MIS: Data Bases." *Datamation,* November 1970. A survey article on data base management systems.

8. Howard Raiffa. 1968. *Decision Analysis — Introductory Lectures on Choices Under Uncertainty.* Addison-Wesley, Reading, Massachusetts. A very readable discussion of Bayesian decision making by one of the leading authorities in the field.

9. William F. Sharpe. 1969. *The Economics of Computers.* Columbia University Press, New York. The most complete discussion of economic issues connected with the use of computers. Chapters 2, 5, and 9 are particularly relevant to a discussion of cost/benefit analysis of information systems.

Evolution of Business System Analysis Techniques

Introduction

Systems analysis consists of collecting, organizing, and evaluating facts about a system and the environment in which it operates.

The objective of systems analysis is to examine all aspects of the system — equipment, personnel, operating conditions, and its internal and external demands — to establish a basis for designing and implementing a better system.

Understanding the role of the systems analyst is facilitated by reference to the steps in the system development cycle. For the purposes of this paper, seven phases in system development are distinguished:

Phase I — Documentation of the existing system
Phase II — Analysis of the system to establish requirements for an improved system (the logical design)
Phase III — Design of a computerized system (the physical design)
Phase IV — Programming and procedure development
Phase V — Implementation
Phase VI — Operation
Phase VII — Maintenance and modification

Systems analysis, then, is concerned with Phase I and II of the system development cycle. The product of systems analysis is the logical design of the new system: the specifications for input and output of the system and the decision criteria and processing rules. Phase III, the physical design phase, determines the organization of files and the devices to be used.

SOURCE: J.D. Couger, *ACM Computing Surveys,* 1973.

Today's systems are complex in development. In the 1950s only subsystems were computerized, such as the payroll system. Today, in the era of integrated systems, the scope of the system is enlarged many times. Payroll is a module in the accounting sub-system, which is only one of several subsystems in the finance system.

In the 1950s *in*dependent subsystems were designed for *inter*dependent activities. The payroll application was designed as an entity when it, in reality, was a part of both the finance system and the personnel system of the firm. The payroll module of this era is redesigned to feed both of these major systems.

The systems of the 1950s were largely operational-level systems. They provided the information needed by first-level supervisors and their subordinates. Today's systems include the tactical (control) and strategic (planning) levels, as well. The thrust of system analysis/design effort in the 1970s has been to expand systems horizontally and vertically.

The expansion in scope and sophistication of systems increases the complexity of system analysis and design. There are more "front-end" costs in designing for integration.

Figure 1 shows the change in the development costs from first to third generation systems. Both the amount of cost and the distribution of resources have changed. In first generation systems, Phases I and II absorbed approximately five percent of system development cost. The expanded scope and sophistication of third generation systems has increased overall development cost, with approximately twenty percent absorbed by Phases I and II.*

However, another reason for the increase in cost of Phases I and II is the lag in development of improved system analysis techniques.

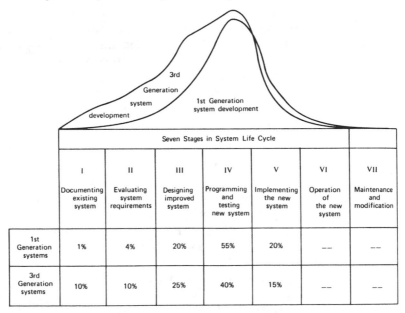

Seven Stages in System Life Cycle							
	I	II	III	IV	V	VI	VII
	Documenting existing system	Evaluating system requirements	Designing improved system	Programming and testing new system	Implementing the new system	Operation of the new system	Maintenance and modification
1st Generation systems	1%	4%	20%	55%	20%	--	--
3rd Generation systems	10%	10%	25%	40%	15%	--	--

Figure 1. Comparative costs of 1st and 3rd generation system development.

*Figures based on the author's surveys of 50 organizations, taken first in 1965 and updated in 1972.

Lag in systems analysis technique development

Concomitant with the increase in complexity of systems is the need for increased capability of system analysis techniques. Nevertheless, evolution of system analysis techniques has lagged hardware evolution by almost one full generation. Systems analysts continued to use techniques developed for unit-record systems during the era of first generation computers. Computer-oriented techniques were originated in the 1950s, lagging hardware evolution by one generation, as shown in Figure 2. The lag diminished only slightly from 1960 to 1970. However, new techniques have been developed in the last two years which reduce the gap significantly. The remainder of the paper will deal with the evolution of systems analysis techniques from the first to the third generation. Also, predictions will be provided on fourth generation systems analysis approaches.

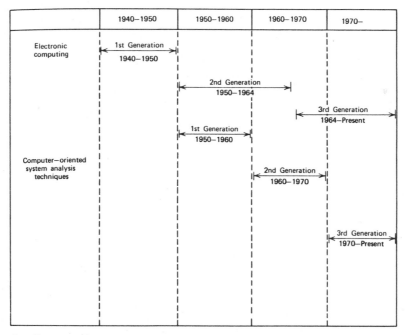

Figure 2. Comparison of evolution of hardware and system analysis techniques. (For consistency, the dates of each generation are taken from P.J. Denning's paper "Third Generation Computer Systems," *Computing Surveys,* **Vol. 3, No. 4, Dec. 1971, p. 175.)**

Schematic on the evolution of systems analysis techniques

Figure 3 provides a schematic of the evolution of systems analysis techniques through 1970. Another chart (Figure 18) will portray the third generation of techniques. Three major categories are distinguished in Figure 3. The top portion of the schematic depicts the evolution of techniques for portraying and analyzing the *flow of information* through an organization. The central portion depicts the evolution of *mathematical and statistical* techniques for system analysis. The lower portion depicts the evolution of techniques for *recording and analyzing resources.* The number in the small circle provides an index to references on the technique. References for each technique are provided in Appendix I. Sources are listed in the bibliography.

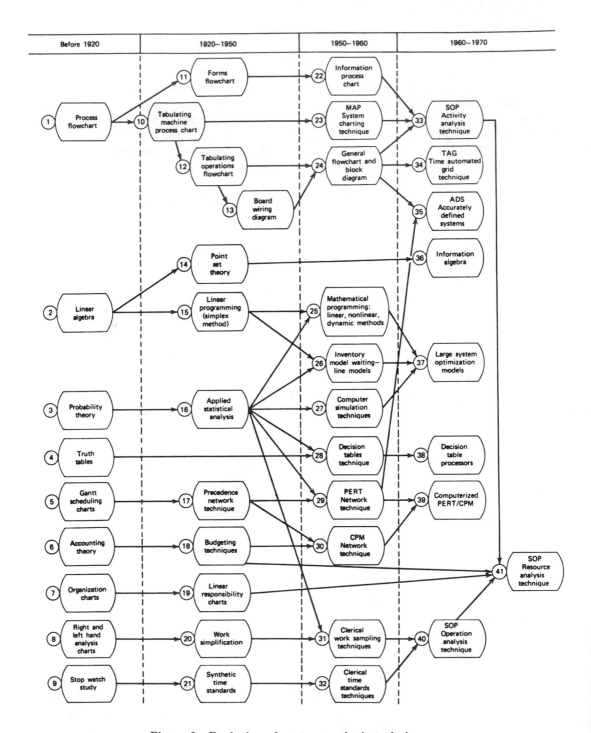

Figure 3. Evolution of system analysis techniques.

Only the top chain will be discussed in this paper because the literature is rich with descriptive material on mathematical/statistical systems analysis techniques and on resource analysis techniques. The references in the bibliography provide an opportunity for further study of these areas.

Although this paper will concentrate on the top path, techniques for analysis of information flow and system logic, it will also emphasize the convergence of the three paths into the set of third generation systems analysis techniques.

To clearly identify the evolution of computer-oriented systems analysis techniques, Figure 3 also depicts precomputer techniques.

Prior to 1920

The process flowchart was used by the industrial engineers in the early 1900s to show the flow of materials (Figure 4). Frederick W. Taylor and the Gilbreths are recognized as leaders in developing techniques for process flow analysis.

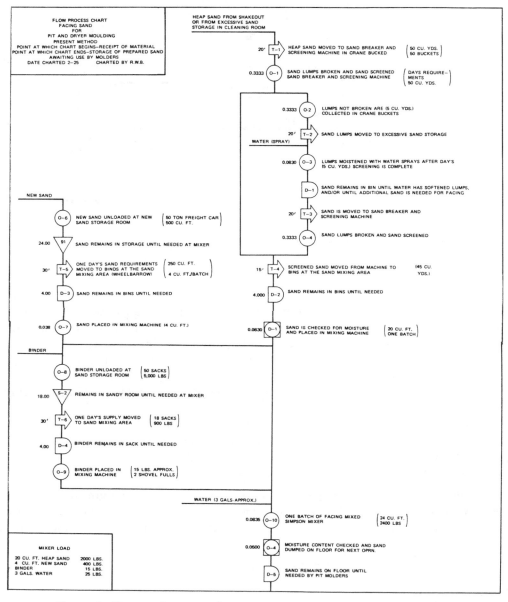

Figure 4. Process flowchart (Courtesy McGraw-Hill Book Company).

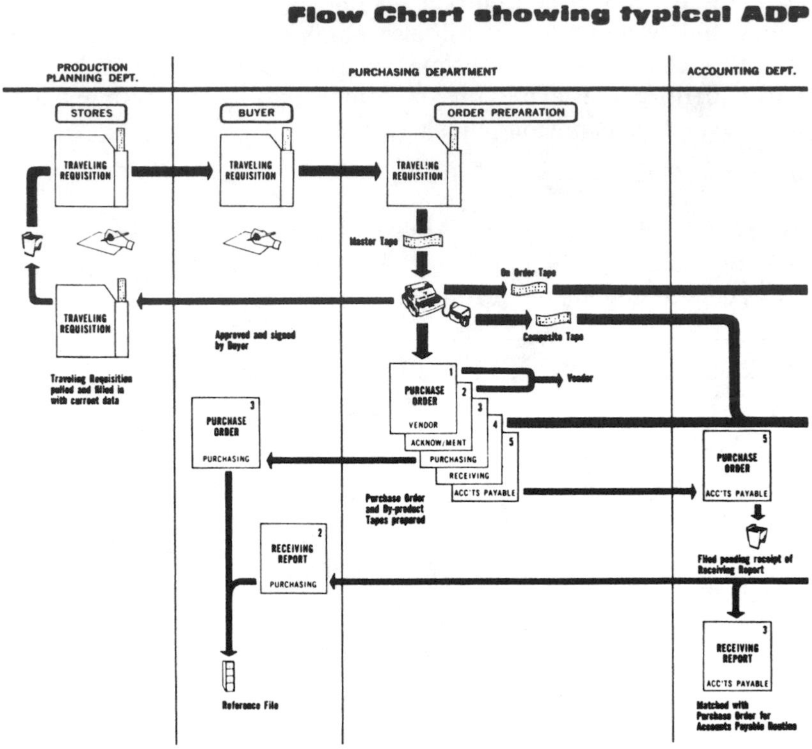

Flow Chart showing typical ADP

Figure 5a. Forms flowchart (Courtesy Moore Business Forms, Inc.).

The period 1920-1950

As organizations grew and paperwork began to be a problem, the process flowchart was modified to depict forms flow. Figure 5a illustrates the shortcomings of this approach: lack of identification of data elements and volumes. With the advent of mechanical processing of information, process flowcharts were modified to portray the devices involved in data processing, shown in Figure 5b. Later in that period the tasks of processing became complicated enough to justify a system documentation package, which included tabulating procedures, process diagrams, and board wiring diagrams, shown in Figure 6.

When computers were introduced, during the latter part of this period, systems analysts continued to use unit record-oriented techniques.

The period 1951-1960

In the 1950s, techniques especially suited for analysis of computer-based systems began to emerge. Figure 3 shows the sources through which these techniques evolved. General flowcharts and block diagrams evolved from the tabulating operation flow diagram.

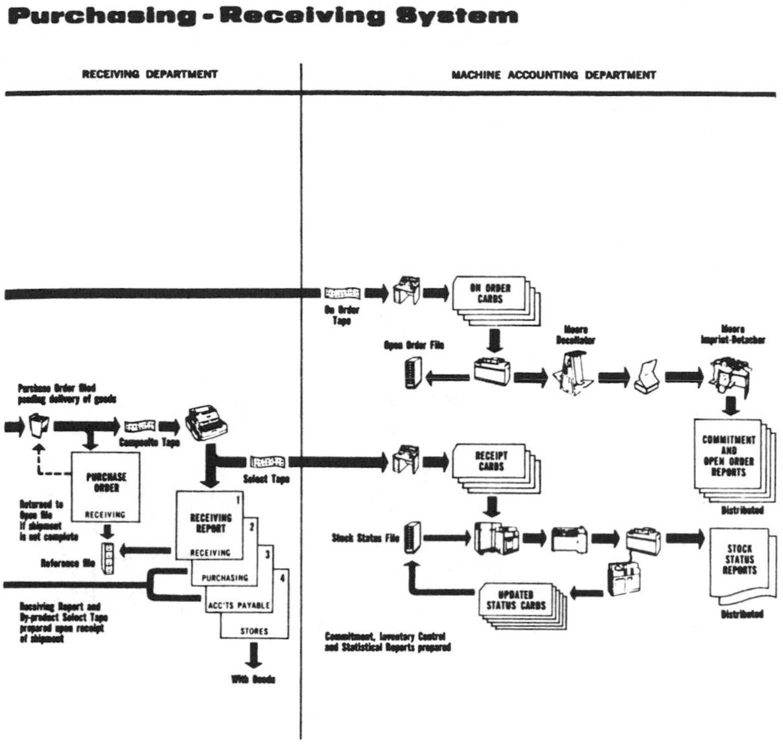

Purchasing - Receiving System

Figure 5a. Continued.

Information process charts (IPC) were a combination of forms flowcharts and block diagrams (Figure 7). One line was used for each operation, with columns provided for indicating the fields of information on which the operations were performed. Certain verbs were specified and carefully defined, to insure consistent understanding among all users of the charts. Although not widely used, the technique recognized the need for formal annotation which is necessary for computerized analysis.

MAP permitted a better overview of the flow of information, at the sacrifice of some detail provided in the annotation of IPC. In MAP, each horizontal level identified a type of document or file (Figure 8). A "transcription break" was used to show interrelationships between files. (The direction of the arrow shows the flow from one file to another.) Verbs were not as well defined as those used in IPC, therefore MAP contributed little in providing a foundation for computerized analysis.

The period 1961-1970

ADS

After several years of internal use, NCR published the manual on ADS (Accurately Defined System), in 1968. ADS was an improvement over prior techniques because it provided a well-organized and correlated approach to system definition and specification.

ADS used five interrelated forms to provide the system (application) definition, shown in Figure 9. The process began with the definition of output. Next, inputs were defined — on the second form. The third form provided the definition of computations

to be performed and the rules of logic governing the computation. The interrelationship of computations were also defined on this form, as were the sources of information
used in the computation. The fourth form, the history definition, specified information
to be retained beyond the processing cycle for subsequent use. The fifth form provided
the logic definitions, in the form of a decision table.

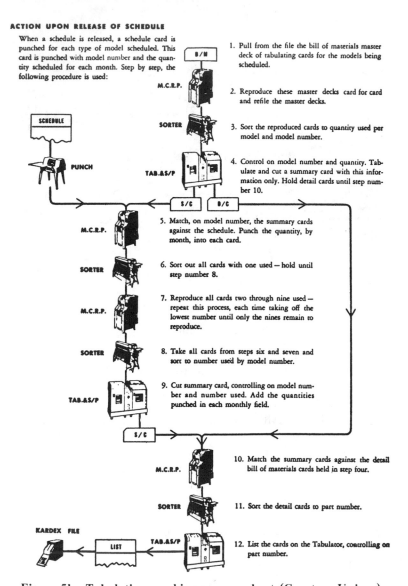

ACTION UPON RELEASE OF SCHEDULE

When a schedule is released, a schedule card is punched for each type of model scheduled. This card is punched with model number and the quantity scheduled for each month. Step by step, the following procedure is used:

1. Pull from the file the bill of materials master deck of tabulating cards for the models being scheduled.

2. Reproduce these master decks card for card and refile the master decks.

3. Sort the reproduced cards to quantity used per model and model number.

4. Control on model number and quantity. Tabulate and cut a summary card with this information only. Hold detail cards until step number 10.

5. Match, on model number, the summary cards against the schedule. Punch the quantity, by month, into each card.

6. Sort out all cards with one used — hold until step number 8.

7. Reproduce all cards two through nine used — repeat this process, each time taking off the lowest number until only the nines remain to reproduce.

8. Take all cards from steps six and seven and sort to number used by model number.

9. Cut summary card, controlling on model number and number used. Add the quantities punched in each monthly field.

10. Match the summary cards against the detail bill of materials cards held in step four.

11. Sort the detail cards to part number.

12. List the cards on the Tabulator, controlling on part number.

Figure 5b. Tabulating machine process chart (Courtesy Univac).

Within ADS information linkage was accomplished in two ways. First, each data
element was assigned a specific tag or reference. Next, each time the tag was used in
the system, it was linked back to the previous link in the chain. All elements of data
were chained from input to output, accomplished through the use of page and line
numbers.

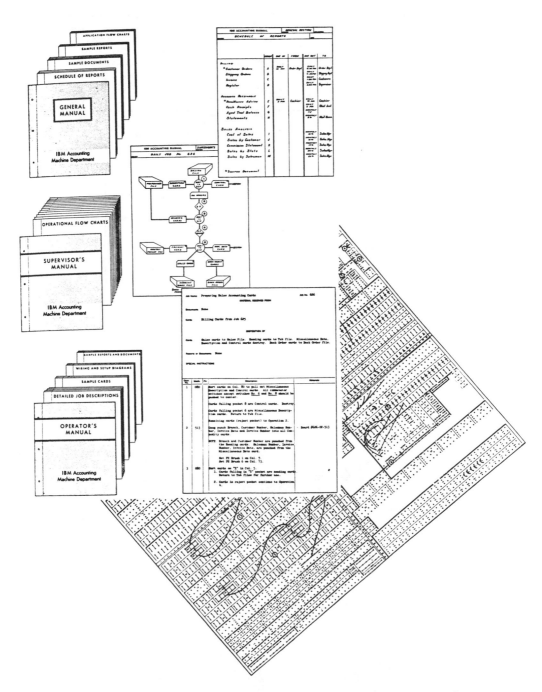

Figure 6. Tabulating operations documentation package (Courtesy IBM).

INFORMATION PROCESS CHART

ENTRIES	MAIN LINE FLOW	EXITS	SECONDARY FLOW		RECORDS	RECORD OR FIELD		FIELDS	REMARKS
▽ 2					Tool crib attendant received copy of purchase order for any tool crib rooted item being ordered.				
	(AM) 2			M e r g e	Copy of purchase order	in Purchase order book	by	Purchase order number	
▽ B 3					Material with one copy of receiving report arrives at tool crib.				
	◇ SR find 4	No find △ 6		S e a r c h	Purchase order book	by Purchase order number	f r o m	Receiving report	
	+ 5			I n s e r t	Quantity received, date received	on Purchase order			
	(CB) = 6	≠ △ 3		C o m p a r e	Destination on purchase order	w i t h Tool crib number			
▽ 5 7				C o m p a r e	Material destined for a planner, engineer or foreman				
	(CB) = 8	≠ △ 4		C o m p a r e	Material	w i t h Special purpose tool, gauge, or fixture which has assigned tool number			
	◇ SR No find 9	Find △ 7		S e a r c h	Tool number file	by Tool number	for	Location	
	≠ 10			C r e a t e	3 copies of tool card	f r o m Purchase order, dimension card		Insert all fields	

Figure 7. Information process charting.

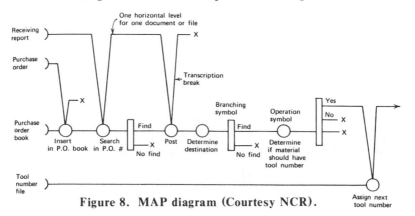

Figure 8. MAP diagram (Courtesy NCR).

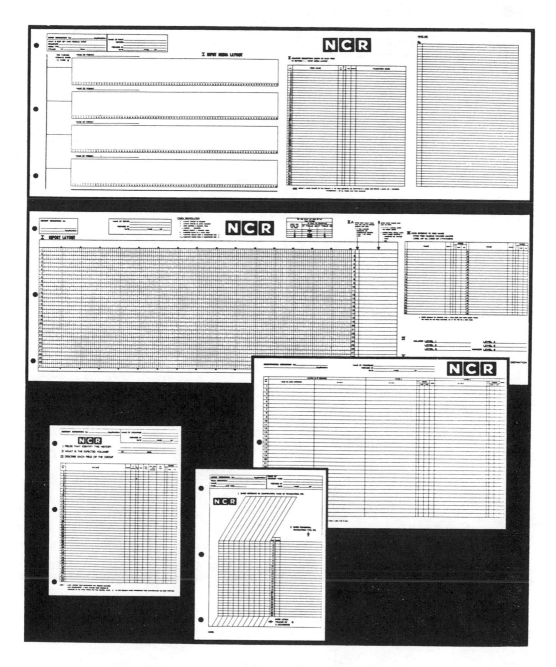

Figure 9. ADS interrelated forms (Courtesy NCR).

The process of chaining facilitated identification of omissions and contradictions in the system. Once the information requirements were established, the system design phase determined the appropriate hardware mix to effect the system.

Although NCR did not provide the means for computer processing of ADS, the technique paved the way for such use through its systematic approach to system definition.

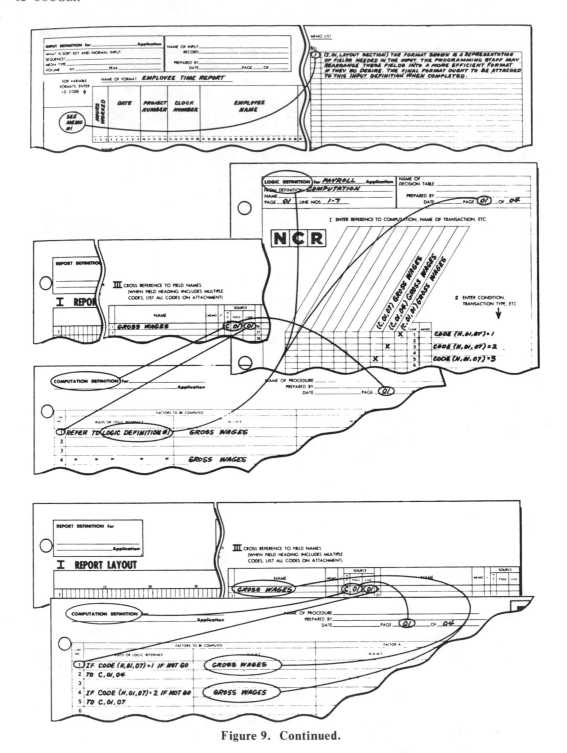

Figure 9. Continued.

Information algebra

Information algebra was an important development because it provided a *theoretical* basis for automatic processing of system specifications.

Reference to Figure 3 shows information algebra evolving from the path of mathematical/statistical analysis techniques. The approach was developed by the

Language Structure Group (LSG) of the CODASYL Development Committee.*
Formed in July, 1959, the LSG's goal was to arrive at a proper structure for a ma-
chine-independent problem-defining language, at the systems level of data processing.

An earlier approach involving the use of matrix representation was abandoned
when rigid restrictions in form were encountered. In seeking a more general representation, the LSG drew upon the work of Robert Bosak of the System Development Corporation. Bosak's unpublished paper, entitled "An Information Algebra," utilized the
concepts of modern algebra and point set theory. After many months of work and
study the language structure group expanded Bosak's work into a basic operational algebra which serves as a theoretical basis for an automatic processing of system
specifications.

The underlying concepts of the Algebra have been implicitly understood for years
by the business systems analyst. An information system deals with those objects and
events in the real world that are relevant to the task at hand. Real objects and events,
called "entities," are represented in the system by data. The information system contains information from which the desired outputs can be extracted through processing.
Information about a particular entity is in the form of "values" which describe quantitatively or qualitatively a set of attributes or "properties" that have significance in the
system.

"Existing programming languages are inherently procedural in nature, but there
are some examples in which relationships rather than procedures are specified. In particular, report writers and sort generators are of the latter type. The primary intent of
the Information Algebra is to extend the concept of stating the relationships among
data to all aspects of data processing. This will require the introduction of increased capability into compilers for translating this type of relational expression into procedural
terms. Specification of such functions as READ, WRITE, OPEN, MOVE, and much of the
procedure control definition will be left to the compiler, thereby reducing the work of
the systems analyst. The analyst will specify the various relevant sets of data and the
relationships and rules of association by which these data are manipulated and classed
into new and different sets of data, including the desired output."

Figure 10 illustrates the Information Algebra on a sample payroll problem. The
problem is to create a New Pay File from the information given in an Old Pay File, a
Daily Work File, and a New Employee File. The Daily Work File contains the daily
hours worked records for each employee for the week. The Old and New Pay Files
contain other information about the employees including the year-to-date totals of
salary earned. The New Employee File provides rate-of-pay information about new employees for incorporation in the New Pay File. The solution is based on collecting and
summarizing each employee's daily work records and on the matching of records in the
Old Pay File, the summarized Work File, and the New Employee File to create the up-
to-date records for the New Pay File for both old and new employees.

*CODASYL (Conference on Data Systems Languages). ACM, 1133 Avenue of the Americas, New York,
N.Y. 10036.

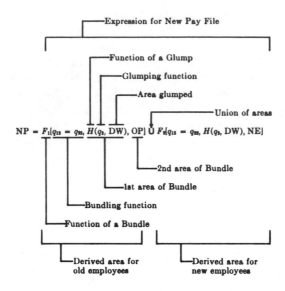

Figure 10. Illustrative payroll problems expressed in information algebra notation (excerpt from *Comm. ACM,* **Vol. 5, No. 4, Apr. 1962, p. 203).**

A property space of sufficient size to contain all the information is constructed on nine properties. Four areas corresponding to the four files are defined in this space. The properties, their value sets, and the relevance of each property to each area are shown in Table 1 where an "X" denotes relevant information and "Ω" denotes non-relevant data for that file.

Table 1
Information Algebra Payroll Problem — System Information

Properties	Value set	Old Pay File OP	Daily Work File DW	New Employee File NE	New Pay File NP
			Areas		
q_1 = File ID	PF, DW, NE	X (always PF)	X (always DW)	X (always NE)	X (always PF)
q_2 = Man ID	00000 . . . 99999	X	X	X	X
q_3 = Name	20 alphabetic characters	X	Ω	X	X
q_4 = Rate	00.00 . . . 99.99	X	Ω	X	X
q_5 = Hours	00 . . . 24	Ω	X	Ω	Ω
q_6 = Day #	0 . . . 7	Ω	X	Ω	Ω
q_7 = total salary	00000.00 . . . 99999.99	X	Ω	Ω	X
q_8 = pay period #	00 . . . 52	X	Ω	X	X
q_9 = Salary	000.00 . . . 999.00	X	Ω	Ω	X

The solution to this Payroll Problem is fully expressed by the following relationships. The New Pay File is expressed as the union of two areas, one derived for the old employees and the other for the new employees. Each of these areas in turn is a function of a "bundle" of two areas. The first area of each bundle is the same and is a function of a "glump" of the daily work file.* The second area of one bundle is the Old Pay File and the second area of the other bundle is the New Employee File.

The LSG hoped that Information Algebra, being machine independent, would foster and guide the development of more universal programming languages. The group felt, also, that Information Algebra could provide a step toward the goal of overall system optimization by making it possible to manipulate the notation in which the fundamental statement of the problem is expressed. "With current programming languages, the problem definition is buried in the rigid structure of an algorithmic statement of the solution, and such a statement cannot readily be manipulated."

The LSG did not produce a user-oriented language for defining problems, nor specify the algorithm for translating Information Algebra statements into machine-language programs. The group expected that the formalism of the approach taken in developing the Information Algebra would assist in providing a foundation for future practical and theoretical studies in the structure of data processing languages. These expectations have been fulfilled, as will be shown in the section on third generation techniques.

SOP

ADS and Information Algebra concentrate on specifying system requirements, that is, the final part of Phase II of the system development cycle. They presume completion of Phase I, the study of the organization and its information needs.

Several approaches have been developed for Phase I. Philips, the Netherlands based company, produced ARDI (Analysis, Requirements Determination, Design and Development, Implementation and Evaluation) through the work of Hartman, Matthes and Proeme [25]. IBM produced SOP (Study Organization Plan), through the work of Burton, Grad, Holstein, Meyers and Schmidt.

ARDI is not shown in Figure 3 because it was a handbook of techniques. SOP was a more significant contribution to the field, because it pulled various techniques together into an integrated approach. Its integrative quality is evidenced by the three SOP components shown in Figure 3.

SOP was designed to gather data with which to analyze the information needs of the entire organization. Information was gathered and organized into a report containing three sections, shown on the left-hand side of Figure 11.

The *General* section included a history of the enterprise, industry background, goals and objectives, major policies and practices, and government regulations.

The *Structural* section contained a schematic model of the business, describing it in terms of products and markets, materials and suppliers, finances, personnel, facilities, inventories, and information.

The *Operational* section included flow diagrams and a distribution of total resources to represent the operating activities of the business. These charts showed how the resources of a business respond to inputs, perform operations, and produce outputs.

---

*One of the distinctions which may be made between a bundle and a glump is that a glumping function partitions strictly on the basis of its assigned values for points, whereas discrimination by bundling functions is contingent on the truth of some statement. (Clearly, they coincide at times.) A second distinction is that bundles can involve many areas whereas glumps are concerned with only one. A third difference is that the elements of bundles are lines (which means that the points are ordered) whereas the elements of glumps are sets of unordered points.

The appendix included the detailed working documents needed to explain operations, identify documents, and define the files in which the organization's information is stored. These documents were organized into four levels of hierarchy, depicted on the right-hand side of Figure 11.

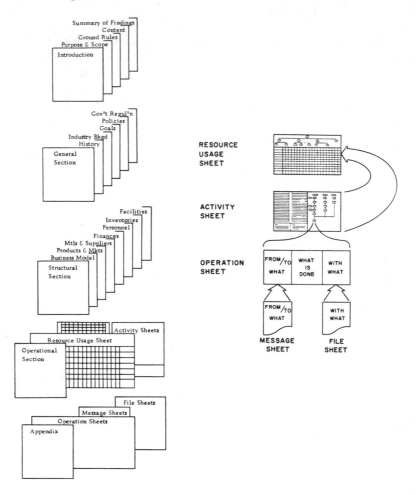

Figure 11. Contents of SOP documentation package (left) and documentation levels (right) (Courtesy IBM).

The organizational structure comprising an activity, and a cost analysis of the activity were recorded on the Resource Usage Sheet, and the flow of the activity itself was displayed on the Activity Sheet. Operations within the activity are further described on Operation Sheets, with detailed information inputs and outputs, and information resources provided on Message and File Sheets, respectively. These forms permitted the analyst to describe the flow of incoming materials or information through the internal workings of the system to output products, services, or information. The relationship of these forms is more readily understandable through the use of actual data, as shown in Figure 12.

The Resource Usage Sheet fit each system under study into its larger context. It showed the organization and structure of the business environment. It also provided a rapid analysis of costs for the organizational components being surveyed and showed the cost impact for each activity or system.

The Activity Sheet traced the flow of a single activity, breaking it down into its major operations. Each Activity Sheet presented as large a group of related operations as could be handled conveniently. It included a flow diagram of the activity with individual blocks representing various operations (each of which could be more minutely described on Operation Sheets). Key characteristics such as volumes and times were recorded in tabular form.

The Resource Usage Sheet and Activity Sheet worked together to provide a quick look at a business system. For a closer look at the operation of a system, the analyst used forms that permit a more detailed documentation: the Operation Sheet and the Message and File Sheets.

Usually an Operation Sheet existed for each block on the Activity Sheet. It was used for recording the related processing steps that form a logical operation. It described what is done, with what resources, under what conditions, how often, and to produce what specific results. Its primary purpose was to show relationships between inputs, processes, resources, and outputs.

The Message Sheet was one of two forms that supported the Operation Sheet. It described the inputs and outputs.

The File Sheet described a collection of messages, an information file. It identified the stored information the operation utilized. When describing what was done (on the Operation Sheet), the analyst could choose from several levels of detail by exercising a choice of descriptive verbs.

It is readily seen that the comprehensiveness of SOP, and the interrelated documentation techniques, enhanced the possibilities for integration of systems. However, a significant activity was missing. The relationship of the information system to the firm's master plan was not clearly distinguished.

Third generation systems analysis techniques

The first and second generation systems analysis approaches concentrated on individual systems. Although steering committees were organized to oversee feasibility studies, a computer was justified typically on one or two systems. Tangible and immediate savings could be produced by converting unit record applications to the computer. The accounting system, therefore, was one of the principal systems to justify a computer.

Emphasis, in the third generation systems concept, is on those activities which initiate actions, such as the market forecasting system. The forecast is automatically fed to all the other systems, insuring that all systems are working on the same forecast. Accordingly, the accounting system is designed to insure that the other systems are producing according to managerial performance standards.

Third generation systems philosophy concentrates on studying the organization as a whole, to avoid suboptimization. Third generation systems priority is on computerization of "lifestream" information systems. The computerization of lifestream operations of a firm produces considerably more benefit to the firm than applications in the administrative functions. Examples of lifestream information systems are order entry systems, production control systems, and inventory and distribution systems. The advantages of computerizing administrative applications usually are insignificant compared to lifestream applications. For example, a 1% decrease in the cost of a $10 million inventory, resulting in a savings of $100,000, is far easier to achieve than a comparable savings in the accounting department. Lifestream projects have significant impact on the success or failure of the enterprise.

Increases in the scope and sophistication of systems required a concomitant improvement in system development techniques. The third generation approach to refining systems techniques employed the computer as an integral component in system development. Therefore, we refer to the third generation as the era of computer-aided system analysis.

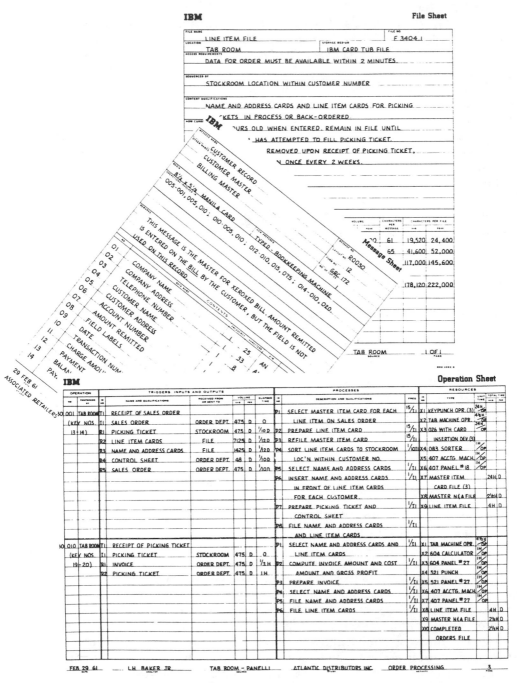

Figure 12. Illustration of the documentation levels of SOP (Courtesy IBM).

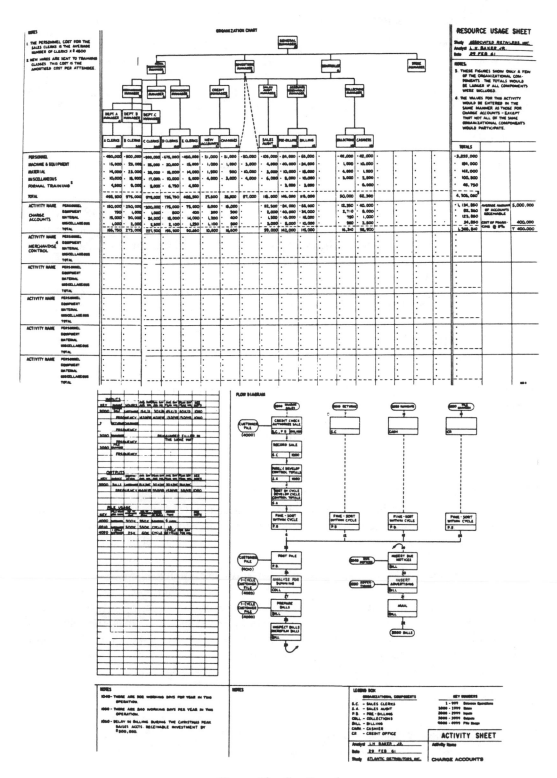

Figure 12. Continued.

Automating existing techniques

The early approach was to computerize existing techniques. Decision table processors were developed in the mid-1960s. ADS processors were developed in the late 1960s. TAG (Time Automated Grid) was developed in 1962 and automated in 1966. These three approaches will be described before proceeding to a discussion of techniques designed specifically for computer-aided system analysis.

Decision table processors

The logical approach inherent in a decision table made this technique readily adaptable for computer processing. In May, 1959, CODASYL began a project to enable computer processing of decision tables. In September, 1962, the product of this effort, DETAB-X, was made public. It consisted of a language supplement to COBOL-61, for use within the framework of decision tables. However, little use was made of the product. Finally, in 1965 the Special Interest Group for Programming Languages (SIG-PLAN) of the Los Angeles Chapter of the Association for Computing Machinery appointed a working group to develop a decision table processor. Written in a subset of COBOL, the processor (DETAB/65) accepted decision tables coded in COBOL and converted them to COBOL source code. It was implemented on a variety of CDC and IBM computers.

However, the conversion algorithm was inefficient and the technique was not widely used until the next generation of processors evolved. The principal present-day approach consists of a preprocessor, written in COBOL, which converts decision tables containing COBOL components to code acceptable to the compiler. A few processors are written in FORTRAN.

This use of the computer did not facilitate the work of the systems analyst, but it accelerated the total system development process and facilitated modification of the system.

Automated ADS

Although ADS provides a well-organized approach to cross-referencing system definition documents, modifications to the system are laborious to incorporate. Also, it is difficult to assess the consequences of a modification because ADS is based on backward referencing (i.e., from output back through intermediate processing to input). The logical sequence in designing a system is forward referencing.

In automating ADS, the documentation medium is punched cards instead of paper forms. Each line of the original ADS forms is represented by one to three punched cards. The card file is analyzed by programs which 1) check for consistency and completeness, 2) check back references, 3) generate back references that have been omitted, 4) produce a dictionary of names, 5) generate incidence and precedence matrices, 6) flag errors, and 7) produce diagnostics.

The inevitable system modifications can readily be incorporated. Cards for individual lines in the ADS definition can be revised and replaced and the effects assessed by computer analysis. The automated dictionary gives forward as well as backward referencing to aid the systems analyst in redesigning the system instead of serving primarily as a documentation tool. Incidence and precedence matrices permit analysis of the structure of the system and facilitate planning of implementation.

TAG

Developed in 1962 by D.H. Meyers, of IBM's System Research Institute, TAG was automated in 1966. To use the Time Automated Grid system, the analyst first recorded the system output requirements. Inputs were examined during later iterations of the program.

Once the output data requirements were fed into the system, TAG worked backward to determine what inputs were necessary and at what point in time. The result was the definition of the minimum data base for the system. With the aid of the reports generated by TAG, the analyst systematically resolved the question of how the required inputs were to be entered into the data flow. This approach enabled him to concentrate on pertinent input elements and to bring them into the system at the proper place. Superfluous or repetitious data were identified and eliminated from the system. Discrepancies in the use of any data element were corrected.

When both inputs and outputs were defined to TAG, the next iteration of the program produced file format and systems flow descriptions. File contents and data flow were both based upon time − the time at which data elements entered the system and the time at which they were required to produce output.

To TAG, the elapsed time between these two moments created the need for files. The files defined by TAG indicated what data must be available in each time period to enable the system to function. The job definition depicted the flow of these files, as well as that of the inputs and outputs, within and between time cycles. This approach provided an overview of the system, showing the interrelationship of all data in the system.

Knowing these interrelationships made it possible for the systems analyst to determine whether the outputs desired were quickly and easily obtained, and thus economically justified. With knowledge of the availability of data elements in given time periods, the analyst determined where additional useful outputs might be obtained.

The upper portion of Figure 13 shows the principal form used for TAG. The form was divided into two horizontal sections, one for requirement titles, the other for data names. The characteristics of the input, output, or file being described were recorded in the requirements title section. Comments on the data requirements of the input, output, or file were detailed in the data name section.

The output of the TAG system was a series of ten reports that documented input, analyzed data requirements, and provided file and data flow definition. The key report was the time-grid analysis, which traced the appearance of each data element, by time, through all the requirements in the system (shown in the lower portion of Figure 13). The grid indicated those data elements that must be carried in files, enabling the analyst to identify the minimum data base requirements.

The other nine reports were: time/key analysis, user data, glossary of data names, document analysis, sorted list of data names, summary of unresolved conditions, serial file records, direct access records, and job definition.

The development of this semi-automated technique was significant in the evolution of systems analysis techniques.

72 COUGER

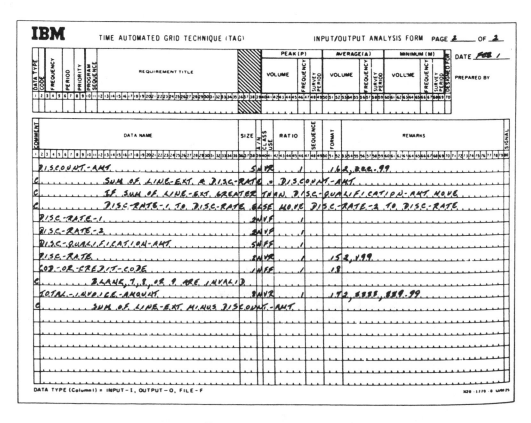

**Figure 13. TAG input form and three out of ten outputs
(Courtesy IBM).**

```
RESULTS OF ANALYSIS BY TIME-GRID TECHNIQUE


DATA                                              DATA
NUMBER DATA NAME                SIZE A/N USE       NUMBER DATA NAME                SIZE A/N USE
    21 QUANTITY-ORDERED           3   N   FI          22 SHIPPING-INSTRUCTIONS   100   A   FI
    23 SOLD-TO-ADDRESS           75   A   FI          24 TOTAL-INVOICE-AMOUNT      8   N   VR


DATA NUMBER                     21   22   23   24

CYCLE


  1 CUSTOMER-ORDER               5    1    1    0
    (   1) 8300...   1 X D
  1 WAREHOUSE-ORDER              5    1    0    0
    (   2) 8300...   1 X D
  2 INVOICE                      5    0    1    1
    (   3)10300...   1 X D

SUMMARY CODES                    1    0    1    2


MEANING OF SUMMARY CODES

0 - RATIO OF INPUT = RATIO OF OUTPUT, INPUT AVAILABLE AT TIME OF OUTPUT
1 - PLURAL CYCLES - FILES
2 - SYSTEM GENERATED (VARIABLE RESULT)
3 - NO INPUT BUT OUTPUT, NOT VARIABLE RESULT
4 - NO OUTPUT BUT INPUT
5 - RATIOS NOT EQUAL
6 - OUTPUT REQUIRED BEFORE INPUT IS AVAILABLE
```

```
DATA NO.   DATA NAME              CODE   PAGE NO.


   2       CUSTOMER-NAME            15       3
   5       DATE-OF-ORDER             4       3
   6       DISC-QUALIFICATION-AMT    3       3
   8       DISC-RATE-1               3       3
   9       DISC-RATE-2               3       3
  12       INVOICE-NO                3       3
  13       LINE-EXT                152       3
  16       PART-NAME                13       3
  18       PRICE                     3       3
  20       QTY-SHIPPED             153       3
```

```
 1     1 I CUSTOMER-ORDER              8300
                   14    0    0    0    0    0    0    0
 1     2 O WAREHOUSE-ORDER             8300
                   14   15   17    0    0    0    0    0
 2     3 O INVOICE                    10300
                   14   15   17    0    0    0    0    0
 3     4 O WEEKLY-SHIPMENT-REPORT      5000
                   15   17    0    0    0    0    0    0
```

Figure 13. Continued.

Designing computer-aided techniques

As could be expected, automating existing techniques proved to be a workable, but suboptimal approach. As a consequence, several organizations began research on problem statement languages designed to make optimal use of the computer's capabilities. Two principal efforts were going on concurrently, at Xerox and at the University of Michigan. The Michigan research produced a problem statement language (PSL) which was, in the words of Project Director Dr. Daniel Teichroew, "a generalization of Information Algebra, TAG and ADS."

After developing an automated version of ADS, the Xerox group decided to design its own problem statement language, SSP. However, SSP is not operational so this paper will confine its analysis to PSL, which is operational in several organizations affiliated with the Michigan project.

PSL & PSA

Using the Michigan approach the systems analyst concentrates on *what* he wants without saying *how* these needs should be met. The Problem Statement Language (PSL) is designed to express desired system outputs, what data elements these outputs comprise, and formulas to compute their values. The user specifies the parameters which determine the volume of inputs, and the outputs and the conditions (particularly those related to time) which govern the production of outputs and the acceptance of inputs.

The Problem Statement Analyzer (PSA) accepts inputs in PSL and analyzes them for correct syntax, then:

1) produces comprehensive data and function dictionaries,

2) performs static network analysis to insure completeness of derived relationships,

3) performs dynamic analysis to indicate time-dependent relationships of data, and

4) analyzes volume specifications.

The results of these analyses is an error-free problem statement in machine-readable format. The second output is a coded statement for use in the physical system design process.

Five classes of users received output from the PSA, as depicted in Figure 14. The system building process is a task undertaken under the direction of Problem Definition Management. This individual or group has the prime responsibility for defining the overall framework and structure of the problem. Problem Definition Management is aided in this task by a team of Problem Definers who perform the more detailed aspects of problem definition: stating the details of individual outputs, and inputs, and insuring that problem descriptions are accurate. The Data and Functional Administration group coordinates the activities of individual Problem Definers and monitors all data definitions. Another aspect of coordination is insuring that items common to many inputs and outputs are defined for the whole system. When this refers to data elements, it is done by DFA. When it refers to other items such as "total system requirements," it is carried out by a group called System Definers.

Once the problem has been defined and specified, the physical system design can begin. The Michigan research has produced an operational PSL/PSA system, used in several organizations which are affiliates in the Michigan research program.

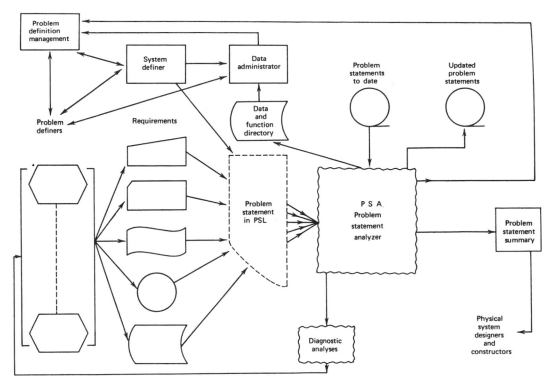

Figure 14. Problem statement language and analyzer.

Hoskyns System

Separation of the system life cycle into seven distinct phases was appropriate for three generations of system development. It is no longer appropriate. The thrust of the fourth generation is integration of the activities in system development, to more effectively utilize the computer as an aid in system development. Phase II and Phase III of the system life cycle are being merged into one activity. This situation is aptly characterized by Professor Teichroew, "Information needs interact with the characteristics of the mechanism (speed, cost, capabilities, etc.) that will be used to satisfy them. Consequently, there must be iterative cycles between the analysis and design" [33]. Therefore, the output of the combined Phase II and III is a set of automated program specifications. An intermediate step is already operational. The Hoskyns System permits automatic translation of systems specifications into computer programs.

Figure 15 illustrates the Hoskyns System approach. A preprocessor automatically translates system specification matrices into COBOL programming statements, permitting program elements to be built, then consolidated into programs. Using the Hoskyns approach [34] the system is described in terms of programs and files, and the programs are described in terms of records and data elements. These sets of relationships are recorded in the form of matrices, as shown in the figure.

The first matrix provides the program file relationships in the system, completely defining the system flow. The second matrix states the keys by which the files may be accessed and defines which record types exist in which file. These matrices also contain such information as file organization approach (i.e., index-sequential).

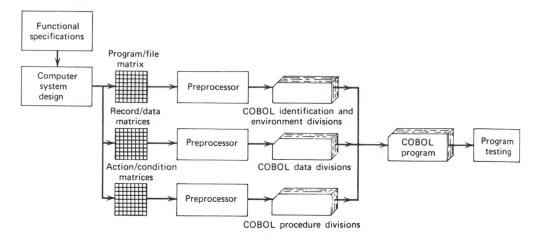

Figure 15. Hoskyns System.

Taken together, these matrices provide the information necessary to generate the identification and environment divisions for all COBOL programs in the system, as well as the File Descriptions, with record layout COPY statements for the data division. These divisions represent the envelope within which the programmer must write his procedure coding. This envelope is generated automatically from the matrices by the COBOL generating processors.

The second matrix also provides the record specification. These record descriptions are held in a library, to be called into the File Descriptions of the programs by the previously described processor.

The remaining COBOL element is the procedure division. Decision tables, prepared by the system designer, list the conditions and actions of the procedure. The decision tables are input to the COBOL procedure division processor and are incorporated into the source program.

In summary, the Hoskyns System accepts system specifications and converts them to COBOL programs without manual intervention. The system was developed and implemented in three British corporations by Hoskyns Systems Research Incorporated. It was introduced in the U.S. in 1972 and is in use at Xerox, General Foods, and Allied Chemicals.

Impact of computer-aided systems analysis

While a majority of practitioners continue to use manual systems analysis techniques, use of computer-aided techniques is growing. Some 30 organizations are affiliated with the Michigan project. ADS/PSA is operational in several organizations. TAG is used more internally by IBM than by its customers; however, several organizations are using it. A Swedish group, headed by Professor Borge Langefors, has also developed a problem statement language and analyzer, IA/1, which is close to the operational stage [35].

Despite the slowness in adoption of third generation systems analysis techniques, the fourth generation is beyond the drawing board stage and will be discussed next.

Fourth generation systems analysis techniques

Fortunately, it is not necessary to prognosticate approaches to fourth generation systems analysis. Enough research has transpired to recognize the direction of the next step in the evolution of systems analysis techniques.

As computer applications are being integrated, techniques for each of the phases of system development are being integrated. A natural extension of computerized problem statements is translation of those statements into programming language statements. However, to produce a complete system, not just portions of a system, a system optimizer must be included in the process. Optimizers of this type are already operational, but only as independent modules [28]. The fourth generation approach links these subsystems into an integrated whole.

The ISDOS project at the University of Michigan is designed to produce such a system. ISDOS is an acronym for Information System Design and Optimization System. While completion of the ISDOS project is some time away, a sufficient number of modules have been designed and tested to prove the validity of the approach.

The ISDOS project is formalizing the design process along the lines of the mathematical approaches pioneered by Langefors, Cross, Turnburke, and Martin [29-32]. Use of a multilevel approach, where the decision variables at one level become constraints at the next level, makes feasible evaluation of a large variety of design strategies.

Reference to Figure 16 shows the interaction of the four ISDOS modules. The Data Reorganizer accepts: 1) specifications for the desired storage structures from the physical systems design process, 2) definition of data as summarized by the Problem Statement Analyzer, 3) the specifications of the hardware to be used, and 4) the data as it currently exists and its storage structure. It then stores the data on the selected devices in the form specified. The third module, the Code Generator, accepts specifications from the physical design process and organizes the problem statements into programs recognizing the data interface as specified by the Data Reorganizer. The code produced may be either machine code, statements in a higher-level language (e.g., COBOL), or parameters to a software package. These two modules perform, automatically, the functioning of programming and file construction.

The final module of the ISDOS system is the Systems Director. It accepts the code generated, the timing specification as determined by the physical design algorithm, and the specifications from the Data Reorganizer, and produces the target information system. This system is now ready to accept inputs from the environment and produce the necessary outputs according to the requirements expressed in the problem statement.

PLAN/SOP

Although the objectives, policies, and practices of the organization were documented in the SOP approach, little emphasis was placed on the Master Plan for the organization — that is, the acquisition and allocation of future resources required to meet the organization's objectives.

For example, the firm may seek to become much more capital-intensive, thus drastically affecting the priority of development of subsystems. The financial subsystem would take priority over many of the labor-control subsystems for such an organization. Future plans for allocation of resources affect both priorities and contents of systems.

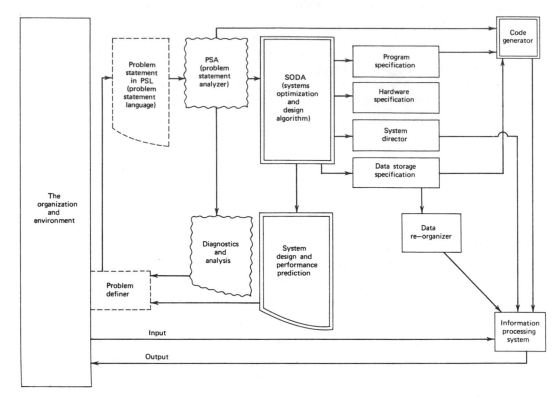

Figure 16. ISDOS — the fourth generation.

Also, the implication in the literature describing SOP is that the approach is used once, at the time the company decides to move from the fragmented, independent subsystem approach to the integrated systems approach. In actuality, it is a continuing process, with updating dependent upon the dynamic characteristics of the organization.

Therefore, a need for Phase I of the fourth generation is the coupling of the planning model to the SOP, as shown in Figure 17.

Figure 18 shows the evolution of system analysis techniques from a different perspective, with emphasis on the integration of techniques for all phases of the system development cycle. (The appendix provides references for each of the techniques, shown in the figure by the number in the small circle above each technique.) Figure 18 illustrates how the ISDOS objective is integration of all phases of the system development cycle, utilizing the computer as an integral tool in optimizing the process. The approach has great promise.

Conclusion

It is simply amazing that the systems profession delayed so long in using the computer as an aid in systems analysis. The situation was summed up appropriately by Richard Thall, one of the University of Michigan researchers, who suggested that "it is shameful that the shoemaker's children are the last to have shoes."

The foregoing descriptions demonstrate that this deficiency is rapidly being corrected. Within the next year there should be sufficient results in each of these research efforts to evaluate their impact upon the computing community.

Progress to date suggests that the gap between development of hardware and system analysis/design techniques will be substantially narrowed by the advent of the fourth generation of computers.

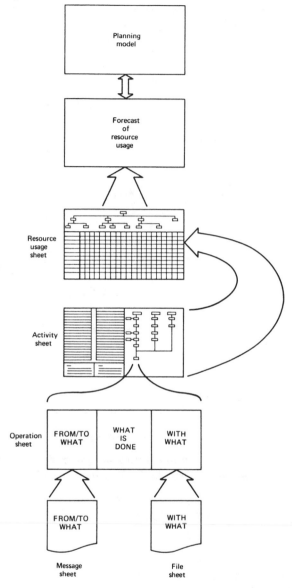

Figure 17. PLAN/SOP.

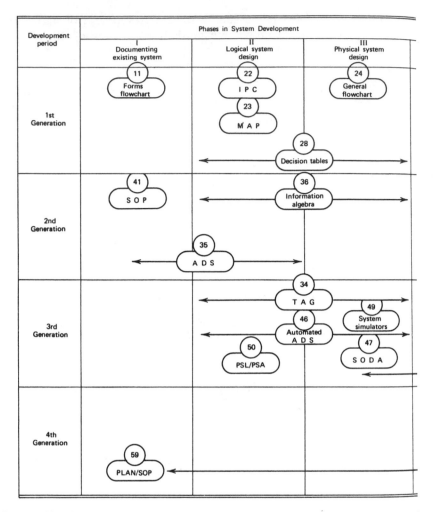

Figure 18. Evolution toward integration of system development techniques. Adapted from a chart by D. Teichroew and D. Carlson.

Appendix I

References

In anticipation that readers would want to assemble references on the techniques listed in Figures 3 and 18, the author attempted to reduce the number of sources required for reference. Therefore several handbooks are cited to enable readers to find information on the techniques. The number following each technique refers to the reference in the bibliography.

1.	process flow chart:	1, 2, 3, 4
2.	linear algebra:	3, 5, 6
3.	probability theory:	1, 3, 4, 5
4.	truth tables:	3, 6

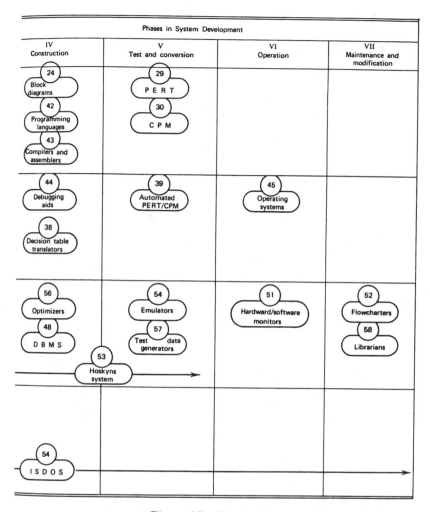

Figure 18. Continued.

5.	gantt scheduling technique:		2, 3, 4
6.	accounting theory:		4, 7
7.	organization charts:		2, 4, 10
8.	simultaneous motion charts:		1, 2, 3
9.	time study (stopwatch):		1, 2, 3, 4, 10
10.	tabulating machine process chart:		2, 15
11.	forms flow chart:		2, 10, 25
12.	tabulating operations flow chart:		2, 15
13.	board wiring diagram:		2, 15
14.	point and set theory:		3, 6
15.	linear programming (simplex method):		2, 3, 4, 5
16.	applied statistical analysis:		1, 3, 4, 5, 10
17.	precedence network technique:		3, 5, 25
18.	budgeting techniques:		1, 3, 4

19.	linear responsibility charts:	2
20.	work simplification analysis:	2, 3
21.	synthetic time standards:	2, 3, 4
22.	information process chart:	8
23.	MAP-system charting technique:	9
24.	general flowchart/block diagram:	2, 10, 14, 15, 25
25.	mathematical programming (linear, non-linear, dynamic):	3, 5
26.	inventory, waiting line models:	3, 4, 5
27.	computer simulation techniques:	3, 4, 5
28.	decision tables:	11, 12, 25
29.	PERT (program evaluation reporting technique):	2, 3, 4, 5, 10, 25
30.	CPM (critical path method):	2, 3, 4, 5, 25
31.	clerical work sampling:	2, 3
32.	clerical time standards:	2, 3, 4
33.	SOP (study organization plan) activity analysis:	16, 17
34.	TAG (time automated grid):	18, 26
35.	ADS (accurately defined systems):	19
36.	information algebra:	20
37.	large system optimization models:	5, 21
38.	decision table processor:	11, 13, 43
39.	computerized production planning:	22, 23
40.	SOP-operation analysis:	16, 17
41.	SOP-resource analysis:	16, 17
42.	programming languages:	37, 38, 39
43.	compilers and assemblers:	38, 39, 42
44.	automated debugging aids:	37, 40, 42, 43
45.	operating systems:	38, 39, 42
46.	automated ADS:	27, 33
47.	(SODA) systems optimization and design algorithm:	28
48.	(DBMS) data base management systems:	36, 42
49.	system simulators:	41, 42
50.	(PSL/PSA) problem statement language and analyzer:	24, 33
51.	hardware/software monitors:	42
52.	flowcharters:	42, 43
53.	hoskyns system:	34
54.	emulators:	37
55.	(ISDOS) information systems design and optimization:	24
56.	optimizers:	24, 43
57.	test data generators:	43
58.	librarians:	43
59.	PLAN/SOP:	44

Bibliography: Couger

1. Ireson, W., and E. Grant (Eds.), *Handbook of Industrial Engineering and Management.* Prentice-Hall, Englewood Cliffs, N.J., 1955.

2. Lazzaro, V. (Ed.), *Systems and Procedures: A Handbook for Business and Industry,* 2nd Edition, Prentice-Hall, Englewood Cliffs, N.J., 1968.

3. Maynard, H.B. (Ed.), *Industrial Engineering Handbook,* 3rd Edition, McGraw-Hill, New York, N.Y., 1971.

4. Maynard, H.B. (Ed.), *Handbook of Business Administration,* McGraw-Hill, New York, N.Y. 1967.

5. Wagner, H., *Principles of Operations Research,* Prentice-Hall, Englewood Cliffs, N.J., 1969.

6. Kattsoff, L.O., and A.J. Simone, *Foundations of Contemporary Mathematics,* McGraw-Hill, New York, N.Y., 1967.

7. Garner, P., and K.B. Berg, *Readings in Accounting Theory,* Houghton Mifflin, Boston, Mass., 1966.

8. Grad, B., and R. Canning, "Information process analysis," *Journal of Industrial Engineering* (November-December, 1969), pp. 470-474.

9. *MAP-System Charting Technique,* National Cash Register Co., Dayton, Ohio, 1961.

10. *Business Systems,* Association for Systems Management, Cleveland, Ohio, 1970.

11. Pollac, S., H. Hicks, and W.J. Harrison, *Decision Tables: Theory and Practice,* John Wiley & Sons, New York, N.Y., 1971.

12. McDaniel, H. *An Introduction to Decision Logic Tables,* John Wiley & Sons, New York, N.Y., 1968.

13. McDaniel, H., *Decision Table Software,* Auerbach, Princeton, N.J., 1970.

14. Chapin, N., *Flowcharts,* Auerbach, Princeton, N.J., 1971.

15. Feingold, C., *Fundamentals of Punched Card Data Processing,* Wm. C. Brown Co., Dubuque, Iowa, 1969.

16. Glans, T., et al., *Management Systems,* Holt, Rinehart and Winston, New York, N.Y., 1968.

17. *Study Organization Plan,* IBM (Form No. C20-8075), White Plains, N.Y., 1961.

18. *Time Automated Grid System,* IBM (Form No. GY 20-0358), 2nd Edition, White Plains, N.Y., 1971.

19. *A Study Guide for Accurately Defined Systems,* National Cash Register Co., Dayton, Ohio, 1968.

20. CODASYL Development Committee, "An information algebra," *Comm. ACM,* Vol. 5, No. 4 (April 1962), pp. 190-204.

21. Lasdon, L.S., *Optimization Theory for Large Systems,* Macmillan, New York, N.Y., 1970.

22. Miller, R.W., *Schedule, Cost and Profit Control with PERT,* McGraw-Hill, New York, N.Y., 1963.

23. Barnetson, P., *Critical Path Planning,* Auerbach, Princeton, N.J., 1970.

24. Teichroew, D., and H. Sayani, "Automation of System Building," *Datamation,* Aug. 15, 1971, pp. 25-30.

25. Hartman, W., et al., *Management Information Systems Handbook,* McGraw-Hill, New York, N.Y., 1968.

26. Kelley, J.F., *Computerized Management Information Systems,* Macmillan, New York, N.Y., 1970, pp. 364-400.

27. Thall, R.M., *A Manual for PSA/ADS: A Machine-Aided Approach to Analysis of ADS,* ISDOS Working Paper No. 35, Dept. of Industrial Engineering, University of Michigan, Ann Arbor, Mich., 1971.

28. Nunamaker, J.F., Jr., "A methodology for the design and optimization of information processing systems," *Proceedings SJCC,* AFIPS Press, Montvale, N.J., 1971, pp. 283-294.

29. Langefors, B., *Theoretical analysis of information systems,* Vol. 2, Student Litteratur, Lund, Sweden, 1966.

30. Gross, M.H., "Systems generation output decomposition method," Standard Oil Co. of New Jersey, July, 1963.

31. Turnburke, V.P., Jr., "Sequential data processing design," *IBM Systems Journal,* March, 1963.

32. Martin, J., *Design of real time computer systems,* Prentice-Hall, Englewood Cliffs, N.J., 1967.

33. Teichroew, D., "Problem statement languages in MIS," *Proceedings, International Symposium of BIFOA,* Cologne, July, 1970, pp. 253-279.

34. Rhodes, J., "A step beyond programming," *Systems Analysis Techniques,* J.D. Couger and R.W. Knapp, (Eds.), John Wiley & Sons, New York, 1973, p. 14.

35. Lundeberg, M., "IA/1 — an interactive system for computer-aided information analysis," Working Report No. 14E, ISAC, University of Stockholm, Stockholm, Sweden, 1972.

36. CODASYL, *Feature Analysis of Generalized Database Management Systems,* ACM, New York, N.Y., 1971.

37. Sammet, J.E., *Programming Languages: History and Fundamentals,* Prentice-Hall, Englewood Cliffs, N.J., 1969.

38. Rosen, S., *Programming Systems and Languages,* McGraw-Hill, New York, N.Y. 1967.

39. Donovan, J.J., *Systems Programming,* McGraw-Hill, New York, N.Y., 1972.

40. Rustin, R. (Ed.), *Debugging Techniques in Large Systems,* Prentice-Hall, Englewood Cliffs, N.J., 1971.

41. Joslin, E., *Computer Selection,* Addison-Wesley, Reading, Mass., 1968.

42. *Software Reports,* Auerbach Computer Technology Reports, Philadelphia, Pa.

43. Canning, R.D., "Cobol aid packages," *EDP Analyzer,* May, 1972.

44. Couger, J.D., "PLAN/SOP," unpublished paper.

Section 2
DESIGN TECHNIQUES

The next group of papers in this book is concerned with the subject of *design*. Dijkstra, Wirth, Graham et al., and Fagan address various aspects of design, often concerning themselves with the design of very different types of computer systems — ranging from chess-playing programs to operating systems. However, the authors all share one common view: They assume that a proper statement of requirements has already been developed, and that there is much constructive work to be done before the actual coding begins.

Dijkstra: The Structure of the "THE"- Multiprogramming System

Edsger W. Dijkstra's "The Structure of the 'THE'-Multiprogramming System" is the oldest of the four papers in this section. It was first presented at an ACM conference on operating systems in the fall of 1967, and then reprinted in May of 1968 in the *Communications of the ACM* as part of a special issue on operating systems.

At the time, I was a systems programmer specializing in the development of on-line, real-time, operating systems. I can well remember the impact Dijkstra's paper had on me in 1968 — I had always thought that one could go about the business of designing operating systems in a more or less organized way, but I had no idea that it could be done as elegantly as Dijkstra's design team had done.

Although the vast majority of designers are not interested in designing operating systems, some of the general design concepts discussed by Dijkstra apply equally well to the design of application programs and other types of systems. Probably the most important concept is that of building a system as a set of hierarchical levels, with each level hiding some of the physical details of the computer hardware from higher levels. This has been described by others as "top-down design," "levels of abstraction," and a variety of other phrases — but the significant point is that the approach can be applied equally well to the design of payroll systems as to operating systems. In the case of operating systems, Dijkstra's concept of levels has been adopted enthusiastically by design teams all over the world: There is hardly a major operating system in existence today that does not have one or more kernels or shells or rings that function in the same way as do Dijkstra's levels.

Wirth: Program Development by Stepwise Refinement

Niklaus Wirth's paper continues this theme of building a system as a series of levels. Wirth uses the eight-queens problem as an example of the concept — and while it may not seem a real-world application, it nevertheless serves to illustrate concepts that *do* apply to all software development activities.

While Dijkstra's paper was read primarily by the systems programming community, Wirth's paper and his subsequent book* had a much broader audience. Indeed, Wirth's work, and this paper in particular, is widely credited for beginning the movement toward top-down design in the early 1970s. Though it seems obvious to us today that we should decompose large systems into smaller pieces, and decompose those pieces into even smaller pieces, it was a revolutionary idea at the time.

Indeed, so *much* attention was focussed on this revolutionary divide-and-conquer concept that many of the other messages in Wirth's paper were lost. For example, he stresses the fact that at each level of the design, there are *several* possible ways of partitioning the problem into smaller pieces. Many of today's designers still make the mistake of assuming either that there is only one way of partitioning a problem into pieces, or that all partitionings are equally good. Similarly, Wirth emphasizes the need for refining *both function and data, in parallel.* Yet, many people still argue today that only the data, or that only the functions, need to be partitioned.

Wirth closes with five major conclusions concerning refinement, modularity, design notation, design decisions, and the need to take the whole design process seriously. Although this summary occupies only a page, it captures much of the wisdom of the design field during the past ten years. Indeed, I think Wirth's five concluding points might better be labeled "Wirth's Laws" and posted on the bulletin boards of all aspiring software designers.

Graham et al.: A Software Design and Evaluation System

The third paper in this section is by Robert M. Graham, Gerald J. Clancy Jr., and David B. DeVaney. It discusses the subject of design from an entirely different perspective from that of Wirth and Dijkstra: Rather than discussing how one should develop a design, it discusses the need for developing a *model* of a design — a model that can be used to test the design for completeness, consistency, and performance.

While their primary concern seems to be evaluating the efficiency and performance of the eventual system, the authors' emphasis on models is enormously informative. As they point out, ". . . the model used must faithfully represent the system actually being implemented." Many designers have learned the hard way that there is nothing worse than a false or misleading model!

Fagan: Design and Code Inspections to Reduce Errors in Program Development

This last selection also has a different approach to the topic of design. Michael Fagan does not purport to teach anyone how to design, or how to distinguish between a good and a bad design. Rather, he concentrates on how to examine a design in an organized fashion, so as to detect the greatest number of errors as quickly as possible.

---

*N. Wirth, *Systematic Programming* (Englewood Cliffs, N.J.: Prentice-Hall, 1973).

To many people, "inspection" is IBM's word for a review or walkthrough, but Fagan shows a number of important differences between the organized, formal, well-structured inspection process, and the typically informal (if not anarchistic) peer-group walkthrough process practiced in many companies. Also, many people associate inspections and walkthroughs with *coding,* but my reason for including Fagan's paper with other design papers is that although Fagan does indeed discuss code inspections, he repeatedly stresses the need for inspecting the design of a system as early as possible.

The primary reason for early inspections — in particular, for inspections of the design before the coding process commences — is that it is enormously more expensive to correct design errors if discovery is delayed until the coding phase of the project. This message appears in several papers in this book, but Fagan states it in very specific terms: He claims that it is ten to one hundred times less expensive to find and correct errors in the early phase of a project than to delay their discovery.

There are other specific facts and figures that make this paper interesting to read. Drawing on experiments within IBM, for example, Fagan states that the use of inspections increased productivity by twenty-three percent — thus demolishing the common argument that inspections and walkthroughs take too much time. He also points out that software examined with the inspection method had thirty-eight percent fewer bugs than did software examined by the informal walkthrough process.

Much of the paper is taken up with very practical guidelines and suggestions for organizing, managing, and conducting an inspection; there are charts, tables, checklists, and sample forms that can be used to put the concept into practice in your own organization immediately. It is evident throughout that the guidelines and suggestions are based on enormous practical experience — a comforting thought for the manager who is concerned about introducing untested, academic ideas into a business environment.

Summary

There is one significant shortcoming about the four papers presented in this section: They make little or no attempt to discuss the bridge between analysis and design. Fagan, for example, assumes that an "external specification" will be developed to describe the required function of the system — but he indicates that the first inspection should take place after the "internal specification" (which I interpret to mean high-level design) has been completed. Why not an inspection of the external specification? Similarly, Wirth assumes in his paper that the requirements of the eight-queens problem are easily stated, but what if the requirements themselves are enormously complex? Why not use the same concept of stepwise refinement to gradually develop a statement of requirements?

This notion that analysis and design have similar complexities, and that techniques of modeling, representation, and partitioning could be applied to both areas, has gained popularity only in the past few years. But the basic concepts of stepwise refinement, inspections, and modeling have all come from a few papers like the ones in this section. They are indeed well worth reading.

Additional Reference on Design

The articles selected for this volume supplement the design-oriented articles previously reprinted in *Classics in Software Engineering.* For a particularly relevant paper establishing the origin of structured design, see the following:

1.   W.P. Stevens, G.J. Myers, and L.L. Constantine, "Structured Design," *IBM Systems Journal,* Vol. 13, No. 2 (May 1974), pp. 115-39. Reprinted in *Classics in Software Engineering,* ed. E.N. Yourdon (New York: YOURDON Press, 1979), pp. 207-32.

The Structure
of the "THE"-
Multiprogramming System

Introduction

In response to a call explicitly asking for papers "on timely research and development efforts," I present a progress report on the multiprogramming effort at the Department of Mathematics at the Technological University in Eindhoven.

Having very limited resources (viz. a group of six people of, on the average, half-time availability) and wishing to contribute to the art of system design — including all the stages of conception, construction, and verification, we were faced with the problem of how to get the necessary experience. To solve this problem we adopted the following three guiding principles:

(1) Select a project as advanced as you can conceive, as ambitious as you can justify, in the hope that routine work can be kept to a minimum; hold out against all pressure to incorporate such system expansion that would only result into a purely quantitative increase of the total amount of work to be done.

(2) Select a machine with sound basic characteristics (e.g. an interrupt system to fall in love with is certainly an inspiring feature); from then on try to keep the specific properties of the configuration for which you are preparing the system out of your considerations as long as possible.

(3) Be aware of the fact that experience does by no means automatically lead to wisdom and understanding; in other words, make a conscious effort to learn as much as possible from your previous experiences.

SOURCE: E.W. Dijkstra, *Communications of the ACM*, 1968.

Accordingly, I shall try to go beyond just reporting what we have done and how, and I shall try to formulate as well what we have learned.

I should like to end the introduction with two short remarks on working conditions, which I make for the sake of completeness. I shall not stress these points any further.

One remark is that production speed is severely slowed down if one works with half-time people who have other obligations as well. This is at least a factor of four; probably it is worse. The people themselves lose time and energy in switching over; the group as a whole loses decision speed as discussions, when needed, have often to be postponed until all people concerned are available.

The other remark is that the members of the group (mostly mathematicians) have previously enjoyed as good students a university training of five to eight years and are of Master's or Ph.D level. I mention this explicitly because at least in my country the intellectual level needed for system design is in general grossly underestimated. I am convinced more than ever that this type of work is very difficult, and that every effort to do it with other than the best people is doomed to either failure or moderate success at enormous expense.

The tool and the goal

The system has been designed for a Dutch machine, the EL X8 (N.V. Electrologica, Rijswijk (ZH)). Characteristics of our configuration are:

(1) core memory cycle time 2.5μsec, 27 bits; at present 32K;

(2) drum of 512K words, 1024 words per track, rev. time 40msec;

(3) an indirect addressing mechanism very well suited for stack implementation;

(4) a sound system for commanding peripherals and controlling of interrupts;

(5) a potentially great number of low capacity channels; ten of them are used (3 paper tape readers at 1000char/sec; 3 paper tape punches at 150char/sec; 2 teleprinters; a plotter; a line printer);

(6) absence of a number of not unusual, awkward features.

The primary goal of the system is to process smoothly a continuous flow of user programs as a service to the University. A multiprogramming system has been chosen with the following objectives in mind: (1) a reduction of turn-around time for programs of short duration, (2) economic use of peripheral devices, (3) automatic control of backing store to be combined with economic use of the central processor, and (4) the economic feasibility to use the machine for those applications for which only the flexibility of a general purpose computer is needed, but (as a rule) not the capacity nor the processing power.

The system is not intended as a multiaccess system. There is no common data base via which independent users can communicate with each other: they only share the configuration and a procedure library (that includes a translator for ALGOL 60 extended with complex numbers). The system does not cater for user programs written in machine language.

Compared with larger efforts one can state that quantitatively speaking the goals have been set as modest as the equipment and our other resources. Qualitatively speaking, I am afraid, we became more and more immodest as the work progressed.

A progress report

We have made some minor mistakes of the usual type (such as paying too much attention to eliminating what was not the real bottleneck) and two major ones.

Our first major mistake was that for too long a time we confined our attention to "a perfect installation"; by the time we considered how to make the best of it, one of the peripherals broke down, we were faced with nasty problems. Taking care of the "pathology" took more energy than we had expected, and some of our troubles were a direct consequence of our earlier ingenuity, i.e. the complexity of the situation into which the system could have maneuvered itself. Had we paid attention to the pathology at an earlier stage of the design, our management rules would certainly have been less refined.

The second major mistake has been that we conceived and programmed the major part of the system without giving more than scanty thought to the problem of debugging it. I must decline all credit for the fact that this mistake had no serious consequences — on the contrary! one might argue as an afterthought.

As captain of the crew I had had extensive experience (dating back to 1958) in making basic software dealing with real-time interrupts, and I knew by bitter experience that as a result of the irreproducibility of the interrupt moments a program error could present itself misleadingly like an occasional machine malfunctioning. As a result I was terribly afraid. Having fears regarding the possibility of debugging, we decided to be as careful as possible and, prevention being better than cure, to try to prevent nasty bugs from entering the construction.

This decision, inspired by fear, is at the bottom of what I regard as the group's main contribution to the art of system design. We have found that it is possible to design a refined multiprogramming system in such a way that its logical soundness can be proved a priori and its implementation can admit exhaustive testing. The only errors that showed up during testing were trivial coding errors (occurring with a density of one error per 500 instructions), each of them located within 10 minutes (classical) inspection by the machine and each of them correspondingly easy to remedy. At the time this was written the testing had not yet been completed, but the resulting system is guaranteed to be flawless. When the system is delivered we shall not live in the perpetual fear that a system derailment may still occur in an unlikely situation, such as might result from an unhappy "coincidence" of two or more critical occurrences, for we shall have proved the correctness of the system with a rigor and explicitness that is unusual for the great majority of mathematical proofs.

A survey of the system structure

Storage Allocation. In the classical von Neumann machine, information is identified by the address of the memory location containing the information. When we started to think about the automatic control of secondary storage we were familiar with a system (viz. GIER ALGOL) in which all information was identified by its drum address (as in the classical von Neumann machine) and in which the function of the core memory was nothing more than to make the information "page-wise" accessible.

We have followed another approach and, as it turned out, to great advantage. In our terminology we made a strict distinction between memory units (we called them "pages" and had "core pages" and "drum pages") and corresponding information units (for lack of a better word we called them "segments"), a segment just fitting in a page. For segments we created a completely independent identification mechanism in which the number of possible segment identifiers is much larger than the total number of pages in primary and secondary store. The segment identifier gives fast access to a so-called "segment variable" in core whose value denotes whether the segment is still empty or not, and if not empty, in which page (or pages) it can be found.

As a consequence of this approach, if a segment of information, residing in a core page, has to be dumped onto the drum in order to make the core page available for other use, there is no need to return the segment to the same drum page from which it originally came. In fact, this freedom is exploited: among the free drum pages the one with minimum latency time is selected.

A next consequence is the total absence of a drum allocation problem: there is not the slightest reason why, say, a program should occupy consecutive drum pages. In a multiprogramming environment this is very convenient.

Processor Allocation. We have given full recognition to the fact that in a single sequential process (such as can be performed by a sequential automaton) only the time succession of the various states has a logical meaning, but not the actual speed with which the sequential process is performed. Therefore we have arranged the whole system as a society of sequential processes, progressing with undefined speed ratios. To each user program accepted by the system corresponds a sequential process, to each input peripheral corresponds a sequential process (buffering input streams in synchronism with the execution of the input commands), to each output peripheral corresponds a sequential process (unbuffering output streams in synchronism with the execution of the output commands); furthermore, we have the "segment controller" associated with the drum and the "message interpreter" associated with the console keyboard.

This enabled us to design the whole system in terms of these abstract "sequential processes." Their harmonious cooperation is regulated by means of explicit mutual synchronization statements. On the one hand, this explicit mutual synchronization is necessary, as we do not make any assumption about speed ratios; on the other hand, this mutual synchronization is possible because "delaying the progress of a process temporarily" can never be harmful to the interior logic of the process delayed. The fundamental consequence of this approach — viz. the explicit mutual synchronization — is that the harmonious cooperation of a set of such sequential processes can be established by discrete reasoning; as a further consequence the whole harmonious society of cooperating sequential processes is independent of the actual number of processors available to carry out these processes, provided the processors available can switch from process to process.

System Hierarchy. The total system admits a strict hierarchical structure.

At level 0 we find the responsibility for processor allocation to one of the processes whose dynamic progress is logically permissible (i.e. in view of the explicit mutual synchronization). At this level the interrupt of the realtime clock is processed and introduced to prevent any process to monopolize processing power. At this level a priority rule is incorporated to achieve quick response of the system where this is needed. Our first abstraction has been achieved; above level 0 the number of processors actually shared is no longer relevant. At higher levels we find the activity of the different sequential processes, the actual processor that had lost its identity having disappeared from the picture.

At level 1 we have the so-called "segment controller," a sequential process synchronized with respect to the drum interrupt and the sequential processes on higher levels. At level 1 we find the responsibility to cater to the bookkeeping resulting from the automatic backing store. At this level our next abstraction has been achieved; at all higher levels identification of information takes place in terms of segments, the actual storage pages that had lost their identity having disappeared from the picture.

At level 2 we find the "message interpreter" taking care of the allocation of the console keyboard via which conversations between the operator and any of the higher level processes can be carried out. The message interpreter works in close synchronism with the operator. When the operator presses a key, a character is sent to the machine together with an interrupt signal to announce the next keyboard character, whereas the actual printing is done through an output command generated by the machine under control of the message interpreter. (As far as the hardware is concerned the console teleprinter is regarded as two independent peripherals: an input keyboard and an output printer.) If one of the processes opens a conversation, it identifies itself in the opening sentence of the conversation for the benefit of the operator. If, however, the operator opens a conversation, he must identify the process he is addressing, in the opening sentence of the conversation, i.e. this opening sentence must be interpreted before it is known to which of the processes the conversation is addressed! Here lies the logical reason for the introduction of a separate sequential process for the console teleprinter, a reason that is reflected in its name, "message interpreter."

Above level 2 it is as if each process had its private conversational console. The fact that they share the same physical console is translated into a resource restriction of the form "only one conversation at a time," a restriction that is satisfied via mutual synchronization. At this level the next abstraction has been implemented; at higher levels the actual console teleprinter loses its identity. (If the message interpreter had not been on a higher level than the segment controller, then the only way to implement it would have been to make a permanent reservation in core for it; as the conversational vocabulary might become large (as soon as our operators wish to be addressed in fancy messages), this would result in too heavy a permanent demand upon core storage. Therefore, the vocabulary in which the messages are expressed is stored on segments, i.e. as information units that can reside on the drum as well. For this reason the message interpreter is one level higher than the segment controller.)

At level 3 we find the sequential processes associated with buffering of input streams and unbuffering of output streams. At this level the next abstraction is effected, viz. the abstraction of the actual peripherals used that are allocated at this level to the "logical communication units" in terms of which are worked in the still higher levels. The sequential processes associated with the peripherals are of a level above the message interpreter, because they must be able to converse with the operator (e.g. in the case of detected malfunctioning). The limited number of peripherals again acts as a resource restriction for the processes at higher levels to be satisfied by mutual synchronization between them.

At level 4 we find the independent-user programs and at level 5 the operator (not implemented by us).

The system structure has been described at length in order to make the next section intelligible.

Design experience

The conception stage took a long time. During that period of time the concepts have been born in terms of which we sketched the system in the previous section. Furthermore, we learned the art of reasoning by which we could deduce from our requirements the way in which the processes should influence each other by their mutual synchronization so that these requirements would be met. (The requirements being that no information can be used before it has been produced, that no peripheral can be set to two tasks simultaneously, etc.). Finally we learned the art of reasoning by which we could prove that the society composed of processes thus mutually synchronized by each other would indeed in its time behavior satisfy all requirements.

The construction stage has been rather traditional, perhaps even old-fashioned, that is, plain machine code. Reprogramming on account of a change of specifications has been rare, a circumstance that must have contributed greatly to the feasibility of the "steam method." That the first two stages took more time than planned was somewhat compensated by a delay in the delivery of the machine.

In the verification stage we had the machine, during short shots, completely at our disposal; these were shots during which we worked with a virgin machine without any software aids for debugging. Starting at level 0 the system was tested, each time adding (a portion of) the next level only after the previous level had been thoroughly tested. Each test shot itself contained, on top of the (partial) system to be tested, a number of testing processes with a double function. First, they had to force the system into all different relevant states; second, they had to verify that the system continued to react according to specification.

I shall not deny that the construction of these testing programs has been a major intellectual effort: to convince oneself that one has not overlooked "a relevant state" and to convince oneself that the testing programs generate them all is no simple matter. The encouraging thing is that (as far as we know!) it could be done.

This fact was one of the happy consequences of the hierarchical structure.

Testing level 0 (the real-time clock and processor allocation) implied a number of testing sequential processes on top of it, inspecting together that under all circumstances processor time was divided among them according to the rules. This being established, sequential processes as such were implemented.

Testing the segment controller at level 1 meant that all "relevant states" could be formulated in terms of sequential processes making (in various combinations) demands on core pages, situations that could be provoked by explicit synchronization among the testing programs. At this stage the existence of the real-time clock — although interrupting all the time — was so immaterial that one of the testers indeed forgot its existence!

By that time we had implemented the correct reaction upon the (mutually unsynchronized) interrupts from the real-time clock and the drum. If we had not introduced the separate levels 0 and 1, and if we had not created a terminology (viz. that of the rather abstract sequential processes) in which the existence of the clock interrupt could be discarded, but had instead tried in a nonhierarchical construction, to make the central processor react directly upon any weird time succession of these two interrupts, the number of "relevant states" would have exploded to such a height that exhaustive testing would have been an illusion. (Apart from that it is doubtful whether we would have had the means to generate them all, drum and clock speed being outside our control.)

For the sake of completeness I must mention a further happy consequence. As stated before, above level 1, core and drum pages have lost their identity, and buffering of input and output streams (at level 3) therefore occurs in terms of segments. While testing at level 2 or 3 the drum channel hardware broke down for some time, but testing proceeded by restricting the number of segments to the number that could be held in core. If building up the line printer output streams had been implemented as "dumping onto the drum" and the actual printing as "printing from the drum," this advantage would have been denied to us.

Conclusion

As far as program verification is concerned I present nothing essentially new. In testing a general purpose object (be it a piece of hardware, a program, a machine, or a system), one cannot subject it to all possible cases: For a computer this would imply that one feeds it with all possible programs! Therefore one must test it with a set of relevant test cases. What is, or is not, relevant cannot be decided as long as one regards the mechanism as a black box; in other words, the decision has to be based upon the internal structure of the mechanism to be tested. It seems to be the designer's responsibility to construct his mechanism in such a way — i.e. so effectively structured — that at each stage of the testing procedure the number of relevant test cases will be so small that he can try them all and that what is being tested will be so perspicuous that he will not have overlooked any situation. I have presented a survey of our system because I think it a nice example of the form that such a structure might take.

In my experience, I am sorry to say, industrial software makers tend to react to the system with mixed feelings. On the one hand, they are inclined to think that we have done a kind of model job; on the other hand, they express doubts whether the techniques used are applicable outside the sheltered atmosphere of a University and express the opinion that we were successful only because of the modest scope of the whole project. It is not my intention to underestimate the organizing ability needed to handle a much bigger job, with a lot more people, but I should like to venture the opinion that the larger the project, the more essential the structuring! A hierarchy of five logical levels might then very well turn out to be of modest depth, especially when one designs the system more consciously than we have done, with the aim that the software can be smoothly adapted to (perhaps drastic) configuration expansions.

Acknowledgments. I express my indebtedness to my five collaborators, C. Bron, A.N. Habermann, F.J.A. Hendriks, C. Ligtmans, and P.A. Voorhoeve. They have contributed to all stages of the design, and together we learned the art of reasoning needed. The construction and verification was entirely their effort; if my dreams have come true, it is due to their faith, their talents, and their persistent loyalty to the whole project.

Finally I should like to thank the members of the program committee, who asked for more information on the synchronizing primitives and some justification of my claim to be able to prove logical soundness a priori. In answer to this request an appendix has been added, which I hope will give the desired information and justification.

APPENDIX

Synchronizing primitives

Explicit mutual synchronization of parallel sequential processes is implemented via so-called "semaphores." They are special purpose integer variables allocated in the universe in which the processes are embedded; they are initialized (with the value 0 or 1) before the parallel processes themselves are started. After this initialization the parallel processes will access the semaphores only via two very specific operations, the so-called synchronizing primitives. For historical reasons they are called the *P*-operation and the *V*-operation.

A process, *"Q"* say, that performs the operation *"P* (sem)" decreases the value of the semaphore called "sem" by 1. If the resulting value of the semaphore concerned is nonnegative, process Q can continue with the execution of its next statement; if however, the resulting value is negative, process Q is stopped and booked on a waiting list associated with the semaphore concerned. Until further notice (i.e. a *V*-operation on this very same semaphore), dynamic progress of process Q is not logically permissible and no processor will be allocated to it (see above "System Hierarchy," at level 0).

A process, *"R"* say, that performs the operation *"V* (sem)" increases the value of the semaphore called "sem" by 1. If the resulting value of the semaphore concerned is positive, the *V*-operation in question has no further effect; if, however, the resulting value of the semaphore concerned is nonpositive, one of the processes booked on its waiting list is removed from this waiting list, i.e. its dynamic progress is again logically permissible and in due time a processor will be allocated to it (again, see above "System Hierarchy," at level 0).

COROLLARY 1. *If a semaphore value is nonpositive its absolute value equals the number of processes booked on its waiting list.*

COROLLARY 2. *The P-operation represents the potential delay, the complementary V-operation represents the removal of a barrier.*

Note 1. *P*- and *V*-operations are "indivisible actions"; i.e. if they occur "simultaneously" in parallel processes they are noninterfering in the sense that they can be regarded as being performed one after the other.

Note 2. If the semaphore value resulting from a *V*-operation is negative, its waiting list originally contained more than one process. It is undefined — i.e. logically immaterial — which of the waiting processes is then removed from the waiting list.

Note 3. A consequence of the mechanisms described above is that a process whose dynamic progress is permissible can only lose this status by actually progressing, i.e. by performance of a *P*-operation on a semaphore with a value that is initially nonpositive.

During system conception it transpired that we used the semaphores in two completely different ways. The difference is so marked that, looking back, one wonders whether it was really fair to present the two ways as uses of the very same primitives. On the one hand, we have the semaphores used for mutual exclusion, on the other hand, the private semaphores.

Mutual exclusion

In the following program we indicate two parallel, cyclic processes (between the brackets **"parbegin"** and **"parend"**) that come into action after the surrounding universe has been introduced and initialized.

```
begin semaphore mutex;  mutex := 1;
    parbegin
        begin L1:  P(mutex); critical section 1;  V (mutex);
            remainder of cycle 1; go to L1
        end;
        begin L2:  P(mutex); critical section 2;  V (mutex);
            remainder of cycle 2; go to L2
        end
    parend
end
```

As a result of the P- and V-operations on "mutex" the actions, marked as "critical sections" exclude each other mutually in time; the scheme given allows straightforward extension to more than two parallel processes, the maximum value of mutex equals 1, the minimum value equals $-(n-1)$ if we have n parallel processes.

Critical sections are used always, and only for the purpose of unambiguous inspection and modification of the state variables (allocated in the surrounding universe) that describe the current state of the system (as far as needed for the regulation of the harmonious cooperation between the various processes).

Private semaphores

Each sequential process has associated with it a number of private semaphores and no other process will ever perform a P-operation on them. The universe initializes them with the value equal to 0, their maximum value equals 1, and their minimum value equals -1.

Whenever a process reaches a stage where the permission for dynamic progress depends on current values of state variables, it follows the pattern:

> P(mutex);
> "inspection and modification of state variables including
>   a conditional V (private semaphore)";
> V(mutex);
> P(private semaphore).

If the inspection learns that the process in question should continue, it performs the operation "V (private semaphore)" — the semaphore value then changes from 0 to 1 — otherwise, this V-operation is skipped, leaving to the other processes the obligation to perform this V-operation at a suitable moment. The absence or presence of this obligation is reflected in the final values of the state variables upon leaving the critical section.

Whenever a process reaches a stage where as a result of its progress possibly one (or more) blocked processes should now get permission to continue, it follows the pattern:

> P(mutex);
> "modification and inspection of state variables including zero
>   or more V-operations on private semaphores of other processes";
> V(mutex).

By the introduction of suitable state variables and appropriate programming of the critical sections any strategy assigning peripherals, buffer areas, etc. can be implemented.

The amount of coding and reasoning can be greatly reduced by the observation that in the two complementary critical sections sketched above the same inspection can be performed by the introduction of the notion of "an unstable situation," such as a free reader and a process needing a reader. Whenever an unstable situation emerges it is removed (including one or more V-operations on private semaphores) in the very same critical section in which it has been created.

Proving the harmonious cooperation

The sequential processes in the system can all be regarded as cyclic processes in which a certain neutral point can be marked, the so-called "homing position," in which all processes are when the system is at rest.

When a cyclic process leaves its homing position "it accepts a task"; when the task has been performed and not earlier, the process returns to its homing position. Each cyclic process has a specific task processing power (e.g. the execution of a user program or unbuffering a portion of printer output, etc.).

The harmonious cooperation is mainly proved in roughly three stages.

(1) It is proved that although a process performing a task may in so doing generate a finite number of tasks for other processes, a single initial task cannot give rise to an infinite number of task generations. The proof is simple as processes can only generate tasks for processes at lower levels of the hierarchy so that circularity is excluded. (If a process needing a segment from the drum has generated a task for the segment controller, special precautions have been taken to ensure that the segment asked for remains in core at least until the requesting process has effectively accessed the segment concerned. Without this precaution finite tasks could be forced to generate an infinite number of tasks for the segment controller, and the system could get stuck in an unproductive page flutter.)

(2) It is proved that it is impossible that all processes have returned to their homing position while somewhere in the system there is still pending a generated but unaccepted task. (This is proved via instability of the situation just described.)

(3) It is proved that after the acceptance of an initial task all processes eventually will be (again) in their homing position. Each process blocked in the course of task execution relies on the other processes for removal of the barrier. Essentially, the proof in question is a demonstration of the absence of "circular waits": process P waiting for process Q waiting for process R waiting for process P. (Our usual term for the circular wait is "the Deadly Embrace.") In a more general society than our system this proof turned out to be proof by induction (on the level of hierarchy, starting at the lowest level), as A.N. Habermann has shown in his doctoral thesis.

Program Development by Stepwise Refinement

1. Introduction

Programming is usually taught by examples. Experience shows that the success of a programming course critically depends on the choice of these examples. Unfortunately, they are too often selected with the prime intent to demonstrate what a computer can do. Instead, a main criterion for selection should be their suitability to exhibit certain widely applicable *techniques*. Furthermore, examples of programs are commonly presented as finished "products" followed by explanations of their purpose and their linguistic details. But active programming consists of the design of *new* programs, rather than contemplation of old programs. As a consequence of these teaching methods, the student obtains the impression that programming consists mainly of mastering a language (with all the peculiarities and intricacies so abundant in modern PL's) and relying on one's intuition to somehow transform ideas into finished programs. Clearly, programming courses should teach methods of design and construction, and the selected examples should be such that a gradual *development* can be nicely demonstrated.

This paper deals with a single example chosen with these two purposes in mind. Some well-known techniques are briefly demonstrated and motivated (strategy of preselection, stepwise construction of trial solutions, introduction of auxiliary data, recursion), and the program is gradually developed in a sequence of *refinement steps*.

In each step, one or several instructions of the given program are decomposed into more detailed instructions. This successive decomposition or refinement of specifications terminates when all instructions are expressed in terms of an underlying

SOURCE: N. Wirth, *Communications of the ACM*, 1971.

computer or programming language, and must therefore be guided by the facilities available on that computer or language. The result of the execution of a program is expressed in terms of data, and it may be necessary to introduce further data for communication between the obtained subtasks or instructions. As tasks are refined, so the data may have to be refined, decomposed, or structured, and it is natural to *refine program and data specifications in parallel.*

Every refinement step implies some design decisions. It is important that these decisions be made explicit, and that the programmer be aware of the underlying criteria and of the existence of alternative solutions. The possible solutions to a given problem emerge as the leaves of a tree, each node representing a point of deliberation and decision. Subtrees may be considered as *families of solutions* with certain common characteristics and structures. The notion of such a tree may be particularly helpful in the situation of changing purpose and environment to which a program may sometime have to be adapted.

A guideline in the process of stepwise refinement should be the principle to decompose decisions as much as possible, to untangle aspects which are only seemingly interdependent, and to defer those decisions which concern details of representation as long as possible. This will result in programs which are easier to adapt to different environments (languages and computers), where different representations may be required.

The chosen sample problem is formulated at the beginning of section 3. The reader is strongly urged to try to find a solution by himself before embarking on the paper which − of course − presents only one of many possible solutions.

2. Notation

For the description of programs, a slightly augmented *Algol 60* notation will be used. In order to express repetition of statements in a more lucid way than by use of labels and jumps, a statement of the form

> **repeat** ⟨statement sequence⟩
> **until** ⟨Boolean expression⟩

is introduced, meaning that the statement sequence is to be repeated until the Boolean expression has obtained the value **true.**

3. The 8-queens problem and an approach to its solution*

Given are an 8 × 8 chessboard and 8 queens which are hostile to each other. Find a position for each queen (a configuration) such that no queen may be taken by any other queen (i.e. such that every row, column, and diagonal contains at most one queen).

This problem is characteristic for the rather frequent situation where an analytical solution is not known, and where one has to resort to the method of trial and error. Typically, there exists a set A of candidates for solutions, among which one is to be selected which satisfies a certain condition p. Thus a solution is characterized as an x such that $(x \in A) \; \wedge \; p(x)$.

---

*This problem was investigated by C.F. Gauss in 1850.

A straightforward program to find a solution is:

> **repeat** Generate the next element of A and call it x
> **until** $p(x) \lor$ (no more elements in A);
> **if** $p(x)$ **then** $x =$ solution

The difficulty with this sort of problem usually is the sheer size of A, which forbids an exhaustive generation of candidates on the grounds of efficiency considerations. In the present example, A consists of $64!/(56! \times 8!) \doteq 2^{32}$ elements (board configurations). Under the assumption that generation and test of each configuration consumes 100 μs, it would roughly take 7 hours to find a solution. It is obviously necessary to invent a "shortcut," a method which eliminates a large number of "obviously" disqualified contenders. This *strategy of preselection* is characterized as follows: Find a representation of p in the form $p = q \land r$. Then let $B_r = \{x \mid (x \in A) \land r(x)\}$. Obviously $B_r \subseteq A$. Instead of generating elements of A, only elements of B are produced and tested on condition q instead of p. Suitable candidates for a condition r are those which satisfy the following requirements:

1. B_r is much smaller than A.

2. Elements of B_r are easily generated.

3. Condition q is easier to test than condition p.

The corresponding program then is:

> **repeat** Generate the next element of B and call it x
> **until** $q(x) \lor$ (no more elements in B);
> **if** $q(x)$ **then** $x =$ solution

A suitable condition r in the 8-queens problem is the rule that in every column of the board there must be exactly one queen. Condition q then merely specifies that there be at most one queen in every row and in every diagonal, which is evidently somewhat easier to test than p. The set B_r (configurations with one queen in every column) contains "only" $8^8 = 2^{24}$ elements. They are generated by restricting the movement of queens to columns. Thus all of the above conditions are satisfied.

Assuming again a time of 100 μs for the generation and test of a potential solution, finding a solution would now consume only 100 seconds. Having a powerful computer at one's disposal, one might easily be content with this gain in performance. If one is less fortunate and is forced to, say, solve the problem by hand, it would take 280 hours of generating and testing configurations at the rate of one per second. In this case it might pay to spend some time finding further shortcuts. Instead of applying the same method as before, another one is advocated here which is characterized as follows: Find a representation of trial solutions x of the form $[x_1, x_2, \ldots, x_n]$, such that every trial solution can be generated in steps which produce $[x_1], [x_1, x_2], \ldots, [x_1, x_2, \ldots, x_n]$ respectively. The decomposition must be such that:

1. Every step (generating x_j) must be considerably simpler to compute than the entire candidate x.

2. $q(x) \supset q(x_1 \ldots x_j)$ for all $j \leq n$.

Thus a full solution can never be obtained by extending a partial trial solution which does not satisfy the predicate q. On the other hand, however, a partial trial solution satisfying q may not be extensible into a complete solution. This method of *stepwise construction of trial solutions* therefore requires that trial solutions failing at step j may have to be "shortened" again in order to try different extensions. This technique is called *backtracking* and may generally be characterized by the program:

```
j := 1;
repeat trystep j;
  if successful then advance else regress
until (j < 1) ∨ (j > n)
```

In the 8-queens example, a solution can be constructed by positioning queens in successive columns starting with column 1 and adding a queen in the next column in each step. Obviously, a partial configuration not satisfying the mutual nonaggression condition may never be extended by this method into a full solution. Also, since during the *j*th step only *j* queens have to be considered and tested for mutual nonaggression, finding a partial solution at step *j* requires less effort of inspection than finding a complete solution under the condition that all 8 queens are on the board all the time. Both stated criteria are therefore satisfied by the decomposition in which step *j* consists of finding a safe position for the queen in the *j*th column.

The program subsequently to be developed is based on this method; it generates and tests 876 partial configurations before finding a complete solution. Assuming again that each generation and test (which is now more easily accomplished than before) consumes one second, the solution is found in 15 minutes, and with the computer taking 100 μs per step, in 0.09 seconds.

4. Development of the program

We now formulate the stepwise generation of partial solutions to the 8-queens problem by the following first version of a program:

```
variable board, pointer, safe;
considerfirstcolumn;
repeat trycolumn;
  if safe then
  begin setqueen; considernextcolumn
  end else regress
until lastcoldone ∨ regressoutoffirstcol
```

This program is composed of a set of more primitive instructions (or procedures) whose actions may be described as follows:

considerfirstcolumn. The problem essentially consists of inspecting the safety of squares. A pointer variable designates the currently inspected square. The column in which this square lies is called the currently inspected column. This procedure initializes the pointer to denote the first column.

trycolumn. Starting at the current square of inspection in the currently considered column, move down the column either until a safe square is found, in which case the Boolean variable *safe* is set to **true**, or until the last square is reached and is also unsafe, in which case the variable *safe* is set to **false**.

setqueen. A queen is positioned onto the last inspected square.

considernextcolumn. Advance to the next column and initialize its pointer of inspection.

regress. Regress to a column where it is possible to move the positioned queen further down, and remove the queens positioned in the columns over which regression takes place. (Note that we may have to regress over at most two columns. Why?)

The next step of program development was chosen to refine the descriptions of the instructions *trycolumn* and *regress* as follows:

```
procedure trycolumn;
repeat advancepointer; testsquare
until safe ∨ lastsquare

procedure regress;
  begin reconsiderpriorcolumn
    if ¬ regressoutoffirstcol then
    begin removequeen;
      if lastsquare then
    begin reconsiderpriorcolumn;
      if ¬ regressoutoffirstcol then
        removequeen
    end
  end
end
```

The program is expressed in terms of the instructions:

> *considerfirstcolumn*
> *considernextcolumn*
> *reconsiderpriorcolumn*
> *advancepointer*
> *testsquare*   (sets the variable *safe*)
> *setqueen*
> *removequeen*

and of the predicates:

> *lastsquare*
> *lastcoldone*
> *regressoutoffirstcol*

In order to refine these instructions and predicates further in the direction of instructions and predicates available in common programming languages, it becomes necessary to express them in terms of data representable in those languages. A decision on how to represent the relevant facts in terms of data can therefore no longer be postponed. First priority in decision making is given to the problem of how to represent the positions of the queens and of the square being currently inspected.

The most straightforward solution (i.e. the one most closely reflecting a wooden chessboard occupied by marble pieces) is to introduce a Boolean square matrix with $B[i,j] = $ **true** denoting that square (i,j) is occupied. The success of an algorithm, however, depends almost always on a suitable choice of its data representation in the light of the ease in which this representation allows the necessary operations to be expressed. Apart from this, consideration regarding storage requirements may be of prime importance (although hardly in this case). A common difficulty in program design lies in the unfortunate fact that at the stage where decisions about data representations have to be made, it often is still difficult to foresee the details of the necessary instructions operating on the data, and often quite impossible to estimate the advantages of one possible representation over another. In general, it is therefore advisable to delay decisions about data representation as long as possible (but not until it becomes obvious that no realizable solution will suit the chosen algorithm).

In the problem presented here, it is fairly evident even at this stage that the following choice is more suitable than a Boolean matrix in terms of simplicity of later instructions as well as of storage economy.

j is the index of the currently inspected column. (x_j, j) is the coordinate of the last inspected square and the position of the queen in column $k < j$ is given by the coordinate pair (x_k, k) of the board. Now the variable declarations for pointer and board are refined into:

> **integer** j $(0 \leq j \leq 9)$
> **integer array** $x[1:8]$ $(0 \leq x_i \leq 8)$

and the further refinements of some of the above instructions and predicates are expressed as:

> **procedure** *considerfirstcolumn*;
>   **begin** $j := 1$; $x[1] := 0$ **end**
> **procedure** *considernextcolumn*;
>   **begin** $j := j+1$; $x[j] := 0$ **end**
> **procedure** *reconsiderpriorcolumn*; $j := j-1$
> **procedure** *advancepointer*;
> $x[j] := x[j]+1$
> **Boolean procedure** *lastsquare*;
>   *lastsquare* $:= x[j] = 8$
> **Boolean procedure** *lastcoldone*;
>   *lastcoldone* $:= j > 8$
> **Boolean procedure** *regressoutoffirstcol*;
>   *regressoutoffirstcol* $:= j < 1$

At this stage, the program is expressed in terms of the instructions:

> *testsquare*
> *setqueen*
> *removequeen*

As a matter of fact, the instructions *setqueen* and *removequeen* may be regarded as vacuous, if we decide that the procedure *testsquare* is to determine the value of the variable *safe* solely on the grounds of the values $x_1 \ldots x_{j-1}$ which completely represent the positions of the $j-1$ queens so far on the board. But unfortunately the instruction *testsquare* is the one most frequently executed, and it is therefore the one instruction where considerations of efficiency are not only justified but essential for a good solution of the problem. Evidently a version of *testsquare* expressed only in terms of $x_1 \ldots x_{j-1}$ is inefficient at best. It should be obvious that *testsquare* is executed far more often than *setqueen* and *removequeen*. The latter procedures are executed whenever the column (j) is changed (say m times), the former whenever a move to the next square is undertaken (i.e. x_j is changed, say n times). However, *setqueen* and *removequeen* are the only procedures which affect the chessboard. Efficiency may therefore be gained by the method of *introducing auxiliary variables* $V(x_1 \ldots x_j)$ such that:

1.   Whether a square is safe can be computed more easily from $V(x)$ than from x directly (say in u units of computation instead of ku units of computation).

2. The computation of $V(x)$ from x (whenever x changes) is not too complicated (say of v units of computation).

The introduction of V is advantageous (apart from considerations of storage economy), if

$$n(k-1)u > mu \quad \text{or} \quad \frac{n}{m}(k-1) > \frac{v}{u},$$

i.e. if the gain is greater than the loss in computation units.

A most straightforward solution to obtain a simple version of *testsquare* is to introduce a Boolean matrix B such that $B[i, j] = $ **true** signifies that square (i, j) is not taken by another queen. But unfortunately, its recomputation whenever a new queen is removed (v) is prohibitive (why?) and will more than outweigh the gain.

The realization that the relevant condition for safety of a square is that the square must lie neither in a row nor in a diagonal already occupied by another queen, leads to a much more economic choice of V. We introduce Boolean arrays a, b, c with the meanings:

$a_k = $ **true** : no queen is positioned in row k
$b_k = $ **true** : no queen is positioned in the /-diagonal k
$c_k = $ **true** : no queen is positioned in the \-diagonal k

The choice of the index ranges of these arrays is made in view of the fact that squares with equal sum of their coordinates lie on the same /-diagonal, and those with equal difference lie on the same \-diagonal. With row and column indices from 1 to 8, we obtain:

Boolean array $a[1:8]$, $b[2:16]$, $c[-7:7]$

Upon every introduction of auxiliary data, care has to be taken of their *correct initialization*. Since our algorithm starts with an empty chessboard, this fact must be represented by initially assigning the value **true** to all components of the arrays $a, b,$ and c. We can now write:

```
procedure testsquare;
    safe := a[x[j]] ∧ b[j + x[j]] ∧ c[j−x[j]]
procedure setqueen;
    a[x[j]] := b[j+x[j]] := x[j−x[j]] := false
procedure removequeen;
    a[x[j]] := b[j+x[j]] := c[j−x[j]] := true
```

The correctness of the latter procedure is based on the fact that each queen currently on the board had been positioned on a safe square, and that all queens positioned after the one to be removed now had already been removed. Thus the square to be vacated becomes safe again.

A critical examination of the program obtained so far reveals that the variable $x[j]$ occurs very often, and in particular at those places of the program which are also executed most often. Moreover, examination of $x[j]$ occurs much more frequently than reassignment of values to j. As a consequence, the principle of introduction of auxiliary data can again be applied to increase efficiency: a new variable

integer i

is used to represent the value so far denoted by $x[j]$. Consequently $x[j] := i$ must always be executed before j is increased, and $i := x[j]$ after j is decreased. This final step of program development leads to the reformulation of some of the above procedures as follows:

```
procedure testsquare;
  safe := a[i] ∧ b[i+j] ∧ c[i−j]
procedure setqueen;
  a[i] := b[i+j] := c[i−j] := false
procedure removequeen;
  a[i] := b[i+j] := c[i−j] := true
procedure considerfirstcolumn;
  begin j := 1;  i := 0 end
procedure advancepointer;  i := i+1
procedure considernextcolumn;
  begin x[j] := i ;  j := j+1;  i := 0 end
Boolean procedure lastsquare;
  lastsquare := i = 8
```

The final program, using the procedures

```
testsquare
setqueen
regress
removequeen
```

and with the other procedures directly substituted, now has the form

```
j := 1;  i := 0;
repeat
  repeat i := i+1;  testsquare
  until safe ∨ (i = 8);
  if safe then
  begin setqueen x[j] := i;  j := j+1;  i := 0
  end else regress
until (j > 8) ∨ (j < 1);
if j > 8 then PRINT(x) else FAILURE
```

It is noteworthy that this program still displays the structure of the version designed in the first step. Naturally other, equally valid solutions can be suggested and be developed by the same method of stepwise program refinement. It is particularly essential to demonstrate this fact to students. One alternative solution was suggested to the author by E.W. Dijkstra. It is based on the view that the problem consists of a stepwise extension of the board by one column containing a safely positioned queen, starting with a null-board and terminating with 8 columns. The process of extending the board is formulated as a procedure, and the natural method to obtain a complete board is by *recursion* of this procedure. It can easily be composed of the same set of more primitive instructions which were used in the first solution.

```
procedure Trycolumn(j);
  begin integer i;  i := 0;
    repeat i := i+1; testsquare;
      if safe then
      begin setqueen; x[j] := i;
        if j < 8 then Trycolumn(j+1);
        if ¬ safe then removequeen
      end
    until safe ∨ (i = 8)
  end
```

The program using this procedure then is

> *Trycolumn*(1);
> **if** *safe* **then** PRINT (*x*) **else** FAILURE

(Note that due to the introduction of the variable *i* local to the recursive procedure, every column has its own pointer of inspection *i.* As a consequence, the procedures

> *testsquare*
> *setqueen*
> *removequeen*

must be declared locally within *Trycolumn* too, because they refer to the *i* designating the scanned square in the *current* column.)

5. The generalized 8-queens problem

In the practical world of computing, it is rather uncommon that a program, once it performs correctly and satisfactorily, remains unchanged forever. Usually its users discover sooner or later that their program does not deliver all the desired results, or worse, that the results requested were not the ones really needed. Then either an extension or a change of the program is called for, and it is in this case where the method of stepwise program design and systematic structuring is most valuable and advantageous. If the structure and the program components were well chosen, then often many of the constituent instructions can be adopted unchanged. Thereby the effort of redesign and reverification may be drastically reduced. As a matter of fact, the *adaptability* of a program to changes in its objectives (often called maintainability) and to changes in its environment (nowadays called portability) can be measured primarily in terms of the degree to which it is neatly structured.

It is the purpose of the subsequent section to demonstrate this advantage in view of a generalization of the original 8-queens problem and its solution through an extension of the program components introduced before.

The generalized problem is formulated as follows:

Find *all* possible configurations of 8 hostile queens on an 8 × 8 chessboard, such that no queen may be taken by any other queen.

The new problem essentially consists of two parts:

1. Finding a method to generate further solutions.
2. Determining whether all solutions were generated or not.

It is evidently necessary to generate and test candidates for solutions in some *systematic manner*. A common technique is to find an *ordering of candidates* and a condition to identify the last candidate. If an ordering is found, the solutions can be mapped onto the integers. A condition limiting the numeric values associated with the solutions then yields a criterion for termination of the algorithm, if the chosen method generates solutions strictly in increasing order.

It is easy to find orderings of solutions for the present problem. We choose for convenience the mapping

$$M(x) = \sum_{j=1}^{8} x_j 10^{j-1}$$

An upper bound for possible solutions is then

$$M(x_{max}) = 88888888$$

and the "convenience" lies in the circumstance that our earlier program generating one solution generates the minimum solution which can be regarded as the starting point from which to proceed to the next solution. This is due to the chosen method of testing squares strictly proceeding in increasing order of $M(x)$ starting with 00000000. The method for generating further solutions must now be chosen such that starting with the configuration of a given solution, scanning proceeds in the same order of increasing M, until either the next higher solution is found or the limit is reached.

6. The extended program

The technique of extending the two given programs finding a solution to the simple 8-queens problem is based on the idea of modification of the global structure only, and of using the same building blocks. The global structure must be changed such that upon finding a solution the algorithm will produce an appropriate indication — e.g. by printing the solution — and then proceed to find the next solution until it is found or the limit is reached. A simple condition for reaching the limit is the event when the first queen is moved beyond row 8, in which case regression out of the first column will take place. These deliberations lead to the following modified version of the nonrecursive program:

```
considerfirstcolumn;
repeat trycolumn;
  if safe then
  begin setqueen; considernextcolumn;
    if lastcoldone then
    begin PRINT(x); regress
    end
  end else regress
until regressoutoffirstcol
```

Indication of a solution being found by printing it now occurs directly at the level of detection, i.e. before leaving the repetition clause. Then the algorithm proceeds to find a next solution whereby a shortcut is used by directly regressing to the prior column; since a solution places one queen in each row, there is no point in further moving the last queen within the eighth column.

The recursive program is extended with even greater ease following the same considerations:

```
procedure Trycolumn(j);
begin integer i;
  〈declarations of procedures testsquare, advancequeen,
  setqueen, removequeen, lastsquare〉
  i := 0;
  repeat advancequeen; testsquare;
    if safe then
    begin setqueen; x[j] := i;
      if ¬ lastcoldone then Trycolumn(j+1) else PRINT(x);
      removequeen
    end
  until lastsquare
end
```

The main program starting the algorithm then consists (apart from initialization of *a, b,* and *c*) of the single statement *Trycolumn*(1).

In concluding, it should be noted that both programs represent the same algorithm. Both determine 92 solutions in the *same* order by testing squares 15720 times. This yields an average of 171 tests per solution; the maximum is 876 tests for finding a next solution (the first one), and the minimum is 8. (Both programs coded in the language Pascal were executed by a CDC 6400 computer in less than one second.)

7. Conclusions

The lessons which the described example was supposed to illustrate can be summarized by the following points.

1. Program construction consists of a sequence of *refinement steps*. In each step a given task is broken up into a number of subtasks. Each refinement in the description of a task may be accompanied by a refinement of the description of the data which constitute the means of communication between the subtasks. Refinement of the description of program and data structures should proceed in parallel.

2. The degree of *modularity* obtained in this way will determine the ease or difficulty with which a program can be adapted to changes or extensions of the purpose or changes in the environment (language, computer) in which it is executed.

3. During the process of stepwise refinement, a *notation* which is natural to the problem in hand should be used as long as possible. The direction in which the notation develops during the process of refinement is determined by the language in which the program must ultimately be specified, i.e. with which the notation ultimately becomes identical. This language should therefore allow us to express as naturally and clearly as possible the structures of program and data which emerge during the design process. At the same time, it must give guidance in the refinement process by exhibiting those basic features and structuring principles which are natural to the machine by which programs are supposed to be executed. It is remarkable that it would be difficult to find a language that would meet these important requirements to a lesser degree than the one language still used most widely in teaching programming: Fortran.

4. Each refinement implies a number of *design decisions* based upon a set of design criteria. Among these criteria are efficiency, storage economy, clarity, and regularity of structure. Students must be taught to be conscious of the involved decisions and to critically examine and to reject solutions, sometimes even if they are correct as far as the result is concerned; they must learn to weigh the various aspects of design alternatives in the light of these criteria. In particular, they must be taught to revoke earlier decisions, and to back up, if necessary even to the top. Relatively short sample problems will often suffice to illustrate this important point; it is not necessary to construct an operating system for this purpose.

5. The detailed elaborations on the development of even a short program form a long story, indicating that careful programming is not a trivial subject. If this paper has helped to dispel the widespread belief that programming is easy as long as the programming language is powerful enough and the available computer is fast enough, then it has achieved one of its purposes.

Acknowledgments. The author gratefully acknowledges the helpful and stimulating influence of many discussions with C.A.R. Hoare and E.W. Dijkstra.

References: Wirth

The following articles are listed for further reference on the subject of programming.

1.　Dijkstra, E.W.　A constructive approach to the problem of program correctness. *BIT 8* (1968), 174−186.

2.　Dijkstra, E.W.　Notes on structured programming.　EWD 249, Technical U. Eindhoven, The Netherlands, 1969.

3.　Naur, P.　Programming by action clusters.　*BIT 9* (1969), 250-258.

4.　Wirth, N.　Programming and programming languages.　Proc. Internat. Comput. Symp., Bonn, Germany, May 1970.

A Software Design and Evaluation System

One of the most difficult problems facing the software designer and implementer is that of evaluating the performance of a proposed design before it is actually implemented. Preimplementation evaluation is invaluable in assisting the designer to meet performance objectives of the system being designed. The problem of meeting these objectives is particularly severe for large multiprogramming, multiprocessing operating systems. These systems have become so complex that even the most experienced system designer is unable to evaluate a system's performance using intuition alone. Use of more formal methods is required. Existing techniques are handicapped by a severe time lag. To avoid costly reimplementation, feedback must get to the designers before the design is "cast in concrete." In this paper we describe a system which provides performance information at all stages in the design and implementation of a software system (which we will call the object system). Using this feedback, the designer can spot the problems which adversely affect performance early enough so that they can be corrected with only minor modifications to the design and implementation of the object system.

The key idea in our design and evaluation system is to use a single language to describe the object system at all stages of its design and implementation. This evolving source language description of the object system is used as direct input to evaluation procedures. The initial sketch of the object system's structure and data bases, which is the gross design specification, evolves into a final detailed implementation specification which can be compiled into executable object code. As soon as any part of the object system is specified, some evaluation information is available. As the design becomes

SOURCE: R.M. Graham, G.J. Clancy Jr. & D.B. DeVaney, *Communications of the ACM,* 1973.

more detailed, this information becomes more precise. Thus a fairly detailed and precise picture of the object system's performance is developed before it is completely implemented.

Problems in the evaluation of software

There are many problems associated with the preimplementation evaluation of a large software system. In this paper we address two of these problems: ensuring the validity of the evaluation and providing timely evaluation results. We believe that these are the most critical problems. To insure valid results, the system being evaluated must be the system which is being implemented. Since most evaluation techniques require use of a model, the model used must faithfully represent the system actually being implemented. If it does not, the evaluation results are apt to be misleading and changes based on them may well result in performance degradation rather than improvement. Even if the evaluation results are valid, they are of little use if they are not available until after the system has been implemented. In fact, the sooner the results are available, the more likely it is that costly redesign and reimplementation will be avoided.

A number of factors contribute to delaying the results. With the exception of simulation, current evaluation techniques make little or no use of a computer. Most analysis is done by hand. Thus, any detailed analysis takes a long time and results are usually too late. Since evaluation is not automatic it is almost always only of second priority, continually being postponed because of the pressure resulting from overoptimistic schedules and deadlines. No easily accessible central repository exists which contains all the knowledge about the object system — about both the software components and the hardware. Obtaining the information needed for evaluation may be difficult, resulting in a considerable delay in producing the desired results. Even though simulation usually uses the computer, a model of the object system has to be coded and debugged in some language which is different from that being used to specify the design and implementation. The process of interpreting the written documentation, designing the simulation model, coding it, and debugging it, is a major project of long duration. By the time this project has been completed, the object systems design will either have changed significantly or have already been implemented.

Establishing validity is an even more serious problem. Use of existing evaluation techniques usually requires more time and effort than it is practical for the designer to expend. Thus the evaluation and the attendant interpretation of the design specifications must be done by someone other than the designer. This interpretation is open to question, principally because of a lack of precision and uniformity in the design specification. Another factor which makes the validity of an evaluation, especially simulation, questionable is the difficulty of identifying the significant parameters when abstracting the object system to construct a model. If any of these parameters are omitted from the model, the results will probably be invalid. Since practically all evaluation techniques require some abstraction to a model which is separate from both the design specification and the implementation, changes in either may not get into the model. Minor software or hardware changes may have an effect which, when propagated throughout the system design, significantly affects performance. It is difficult to prevent whatever model is being used in evaluation from drifting away from the system actually being implemented when this model's description is separate from the implementation description.

A design and evaluation system

A system which integrates design specification, implementation, and evaluation can alleviate all of the problems mentioned in the previous section. Such a system, called DES, is currently under development. In the remainder of this paper we discuss the important features of this system, the kind of evaluation results which it produces, and the current status of the development. The two most significant features of DES are a single high level language, which is used for both design specification and implementation, and a single data base containing all known information about the object system. DES has the characteristics of a management information system combined with a simulator, analysis routines, and a compiler.

The use of high level languages for implementing software, while not yet commonplace, is not a new development. In particular, the Multics system was implemented in PL/I [3]. A special-purpose high level language has been used for describing implemented software systems in order to simulate them [9]. It has been recognized that the use of a special-purpose simulation language has certain advantages in the design, implementation, and evaluation of software [5, 10, 8]. The DES language described in more detail in the next section has many of the characteristics of a language like PL/I, plus some features found only in simulation languages. In addition, it contains features (not found in any current languages) which are specifically oriented toward the design and implementation of large, complex software systems.

DES maintains a single hierarchical data base containing all known information about the object system, both hardware and software. Every procedure and data component in the system must have an entry in this data base. These entries define the object system and constitute an official registry of the software components. Entries are also included for each hardware component and standard hardware configuration. The hierarchical structure permits the information to be organized by subsystem or project within the total object system. This structure also permits many levels of global definitions, each level having a wider scope. Thus each project may not automatically access another project's definitions. In fact, two projects may use the same names for their global definitions and no name conflict will result.

As soon as any part of the system design is known, it is expressed in the DES language and entered into the data base. Initially the information may consist of no more than a "registration" of each component. This consists of the component's name and type, the individual responsible for its definition, and the dates of its creation and last modification. As the design progresses, the designers gradually fill in additional information until the data base contains a complete description of the object system. The evaluation routines in DES give performance information consistent with the degree of detail and completeness of the component specifications. Whenever a component definition is modified or added to, DES automatically propagates this information throughout all components which are affected by the change, and the individuals responsible for these components are notified that there has been a change.

If a component is procedural, its definition will eventually include such items as its entry points, a description of each of its arguments, the names of other procedure and data components which it references, applicable restrictions and constraints, resource usage, and performance information. The definition of a data component will include information about the organization of the data, a description of its elements, access techniques used to reference it, a list of procedures which reference it, and size information such as the maximum and average number of entries in a table. The data base also includes information about the object system hardware, such as memory size, memory cycle time, instruction times, operational characteristics and timing for input-output devices, and the description of standard configurations. The placement of this data here rather than in the evaluation and simulation routines allows rapid reevaluation when hardware changes occur. It also makes it practical to experiment with different configurations.

The DES language

It has become common practice in software development to have a hierarchy of design documentation. Each level in the hierarchy is a reexpression, with some additional detail, of the previous level. Usually some degree of redesign is performed between levels. However, the higher level specification is seldom updated to reflect this redesign. Attempts to evaluate the system are stymied by the variation in level of detail of the component descriptions and the lack of consistent semantics used to express the design. Thus the final implementation may be far removed from the initial design specification.

DES eliminates these problems by providing a single language which is an extension of the implementation language, in this case PL/I, with additional statements which allow the designer to express the design at whatever level of detail he desires. This allows the total system design to be captured in a processable format at the initial design phase. Each iteration of a component's design, with changes and more detail, is automatically combined with all others to ensure that the total system is consistent at all times. Variations in the level of detail between components and within a single component can be noted for project control but do not prevent evaluation of parts or the whole at any time.

The new data types and other language extensions deal with the objects and concepts which are the basic building blocks of systems. The language deals with concepts such as general data structures, devices, files, access methods, and processes. The extensions dealing with physical resource usage include use of memory, the central processor, secondary storage, and input-output devices. The intent of these extensions is to make it possible for the designer to sketch his initial design in the extensions with little or no use of standard PL/I statements or declarations. As the design progresses, the designer fills in missing parameters in the statements of the extended language, inserts additional PL/I statements, and completes the data descriptions in the object system data base.

Since the intent of this paper is to discuss an evaluation concept, a detailed description of the language is not considered germane. Therefore, the language examples which follow are not necessarily syntactically accurate but are used simply to convey the concept. Three types of language elements are defined. The first is a data structure description which allows declaration of generalized data structures such as queues and tables. For example, the statement,

$dcls 1 d_free (queue,fifo);

declares a local data structure, d_free, which is a queue with fifo access characteristics. The description of the data items within an individual queue entry can be added when their detailed description is known. The statement,

$dclg fr_list;

directs DES to include in the source text a data declaration which is stored in a global library.

The second type of language element is used to specify conceptual operations, such as create, find and insert, on the generalized data structures. The statement,

$find fr_list;

indicates a search of the structure fr_list to locate an element. The statement,

$insert d_free;

specifies the insertion of an element into the structure d_free. The third type of language element is used to indicate the use of system resources such as input-output devices, memory, and central processor time. The statement,

$read(disk);

indicates a read operation on a disk device. The statement,

$process(1000);

indicates the use of the central processor for 1000 time units.

The following example shows how these language elements can be used to describe a basic system function:

```
get_element: proc;
        $dcls 1 d_free (queue,fifo);
        $dclg fr_list;
        $find d_free;
        $process (1000);
        $insert fr_list;
        end;
```

In this example an element on the queue d_free is located; an estimated amount of processing is performed; and an element is stored in the table fr_list.

Evaluation results produced by DES

DES produces information concerning both the dynamic and nondynamic aspects of the system. This information is generated for each procedure component and subsystem as well as for the entire object system. Component evaluation is concerned with performance and resource usage of the individual procedures, primarily nondynamic information such as total number of instructions in the procedure and upper and lower bounds on the execution time. Component evaluation also provides a model of the procedure which becomes input for subsystem and system evaluation. Subsystem evaluation builds a composite model of the subsystem which then may be subjected to processing similar to component evaluation. System evaluation, the final stage of evaluation, requires the use of simulation in order to determine the dynamic behavior of the system. The distinction between system and subsystem is of course somewhat arbitrary, and subsystems themselves may be subjected to the final stage of evaluation so that their dynamic behavior may be studied. Analysis of the dynamic aspects of the system, particularly simulation, appears in the next section. The remainder of this section focuses on component evaluation and nondynamic information concerning the object system as a whole.

The input to component evaluation is the DES source language description of a procedure component. The principal output includes:

- A model of the procedure.
- Information on external references.
- Resource usage.
- Interface and other constraint violations.

The model of the procedure is basically a directed graph representation of the control structure of the procedure. The nodes represent branch points and the branches represent execution. Each branch has two numbers associated with it: the amount of memory required to store the machine instructions corresponding to the branch and the total execution time for these instructions.

In addition to the memory requirement and execution time included in the model, component evaluation also gathers information on procedure and data references. DES can identify all global data and procedures which are referenced by a procedure. Information is also obtained on how data is referenced. This information is derivable from the find, copy, delete, and insert statements in the DES language. These statements allow the programmer to reference data elements and structures without requiring the access code itself. In effect, they indicate how the programmer intends to access the data, while the declarations for the data contain all of the information on the organization and other properties of the data.

In data acquisition, an additional benefit of this high level interface is that it is possible to defer the structuring of the data until a fairly accurate picture of how different procedures intend to access it is obtained. Moreover, the fact that a program declares "search on key" access to a queue currently defined to be ordered FIFO is instructive. Often structures are accessed by a variety of means, so it becomes important to know how often and by how many means. This enables the designer to reevaluate the efficiency of the currently defined ordering of the data. Another advantage of requiring that access be accomplished via the DES statements is that the access techniques can be designed and coded centrally. Further, compiler options can be provided to produce in-line data-specific code, in-line generalized code, or a call to a closed subroutine. This frees the programmer from the production of tedious routines, thereby letting him concentrate on more important design questions. It also permits automatic maintenance and evaluation of the system and provides feedback to the system design process on the use of data structures.

Device usage is also accounted for by component evaluation. This is accomplished via a device statement which can be replaced with the actual system function call when the latter becomes known. Since the data being sought is also identified, we can obtain information about the transience of particular data elements and structures in the system, feedback which aids in deciding if and when such data should be made resident rather than transient. Also, since timing and other performance information for the device are part of the object system data base rather than being explicitly in the input-output statements, greater flexibility results in being able to obtain timing for the system or subsystem across a variety of device types.

DES greatly reduces the time and effort required for system integration by guaranteeing interfaces which are syntactically, if not logically, correct before the system enters integration. A complete list of each procedure's parameters is kept in the object system data base. The parameters are identified as to position in the parameter list and data characteristics. During program evaluation, all call statements are identified, and their argument list is matched with the parameter list associated with the procedure identified by the entry name of the call statement. If an inconsistency between the two lists is found, this is noted on the program listing, where the correct argument list is also noted. In addition, the inconsistency is noted in the object system data base for inclusion in the project status report. When a new procedure is entered into the system, its parameter list is checked against the registry entry for the procedure, and any inconsistencies are noted.

Periodically, reports on the status of development are produced. The information in these reports varies in level of detail since different levels of information are of interest to different levels of management. A project status report may include the following.

- A list of all procedures called, to *n* levels, by each procedure in the system and all global data which are referenced.

- Estimates of the space and time requirements of all procedures in the system.

- Indicators of progress. This includes such information as the date of last update, the frequency of updates, the rate at which the DES extension statements like the process statement are being replaced by ordinary PL/I statements.

- A list of all recent changes to interfaces, and the procedures which are affected by them.

- A list of all inconsistencies and other constraint violations which have been noted.

By itself, the information is inconclusive about the state of system development. However, when a project manager combines this information with his own knowledge of the development effort within his organization, it can give him an accurate and complete picture of his project.

The simulation model

The model of a procedure component is a directed graph representing all significant paths within the procedure. With each branch in the graph is associated the amount of memory that the code representing that branch will occupy and the time it will take to execute this code. Each source statement is analyzed with regard to its space and time requirements, after which it is thrown away unless it qualifies as a node. A node is a statement which either initiates or terminates one or more paths in a procedure. Nodes are generated from all statements which are labeled and actually referenced, and from such PL/I statements as: go to, if, do, and return. In addition, call statements and function references are considered nodes for informational purposes.

The time that it takes for a program to execute is a function of such things as the hardware processor which executes it, the duration of any input-output which it initiates, the size of variable length data, and the probabilities of taking certain paths within the program. The processor is accounted for by making DES machine independent. Models of the processors in which we are interested are independently built and stored in the object system data base. During DES execution the appropriate object machine description is selected, and the component timing and space estimates become a function of that machine. Input/output timing is a function of record lengths and device characteristics. Here again, the machine models include configuration data with device properties enabling us to estimate seek and data transmission timing. At this point, however, it becomes necessary to distinguish between static and dynamic evaluation.

Static evaluation analyzes the behavior of a component to provide a statistical profile of the component in an idealized, interference-free environment, and produces a simplified model of the component for later use in dynamic evaluation. The statistical profile does not accurately represent a component's behavior within the total system, since external influences such as the number of active processes, I/O activity and arm contention, relative priorities, resource availability, and unrelated interrupts all have a potential influence on that behavior. The profile does, nevertheless, give us some valuable insight into the component. For example, we are able to determine such factors as minimum, maximum, and average execution times, resource requirements, and I/O activity. This profile can give us a feel for the best performance we can expect from a given component since outside influences can only degrade the static performance. It may well be that even the best static performance for some component is intolerable. This is significant.

Dynamic evaluation is simulation at the subsystem or system level rather than the component level, the environment in which component interaction exists. At this level cognizance must be taken of activity in the system being simulated. Time-dependent activity queues must be established for all significant events — events which affect either the state of the system or its resources. Component models must be sufficiently simplified so that simulation runs can be accomplished within a reasonable time frame, and yet not so oversimplified as to produce meaningless or questionable results. Driving data, in the form of job models, must be constructed in such a way that a representative mix of the expected usage of the system is achieved, or driving data must be weighted to test significant aspects or the functionalism of the system.

Because a valid model is central to the success of DES, the process of generating the model of a component is given considerable attention. This construction is an evolutionary, iterative, and in part, manual process. In any procedure of significance, the number of nodes in the graph can be tremendous. Such a large graph is difficult to evaluate, so every attempt is made to collapse the graph by eliminating nodes and branches. Following this, the component model is exercised by the designer to determine the procedure's sensitivity to various variables in an effort to further reduce the graph. This process is only partially automated, requiring manual inspection of the program and the selection of ranges of values for variables.

Several special cases of program structure, when detected, permit immediate collapsing. Do-loops with a constant iteration count, N, can be replaced by a single branch whose time estimate is N times the estimate for a single iteration. If the variation in the time estimates for all paths between two nodes is less than some tolerance factor, say half an order of magnitude, then all these paths can be replaced by a single branch whose time estimate is the average over those being replaced. Variables which specify lengths of varying length data can be replaced by the average length obtained from the data description in the object system data base.

A number of statistical techniques can also be applied to further collapse the graph. Exit probabilities are assigned to all the branches leaving each node. Various standard subgraphs can then be replaced by simpler ones [1]. Another method used, interactively with the designer, is to examine the sensitivity of the procedure's behavior to variations in the variables remaining after all automatic collapsing techniques have been applied. The results of all of these reduction techniques is a graph model of the procedures which contains only a small number of nodes and branches. The reduced models of all of the procedure components in the object system are then used as input to the simulator.

Implementation

A prototype version of DES has been implemented. The first phase of this prototype was implemented by a group at Honeywell Information Systems and was completed early in 1971. The final phase was completed early in 1972 [2]. The prototype was implemented using Multics [7] and the Multics PL/I compiler [4]. Use of Multics and its PL/I compiler substantially reduced the time and effort required to implement the prototype DES. The purpose of this prototype was to demonstrate the feasibility of the DES concept. Hence the focus was on system issues rather than sophisticated analysis. Thus the PL/I extensions, the model building, and the simulation are simple and straightforward.

The prototype DES maintains and uses an object system data base. This data base contains information on each component of the object system. In addition, it contains information needed to calculate statement execution times when building the component models and the device timing information needed during simulation. Maintenance routines exist for modifying this timing information and for producing various reports based on the contents of the data base. The Multics hierarchical file system is used extensively in maintaining the object system data base.

The Multics PL/I compiler is a key part of the static component analysis. A precompilation processor scans the DES source text for a procedure component and transforms all of the PL/I extensions into legal PL/I statements. Global data declarations are replaced by PL/I data declarations from the object system data base. All other language extensions are replaced with call statements which can be recognized by the post-compilation processor. The target of the call indicates the extension statement, and the arguments of the call are used to retain the remainder of the information in the replaced extension statement. The arguments of all external calls are validated against the argument description in the called procedure's entry in the object system data base.

After this preprocessing, the first four phases of the Multics PL/I compiler are invoked. The output from this processing is the source procedure in tree structure form. All declarative information is embedded in this tree. A post-compilation processor is then invoked. Its function is to construct the graph model of the procedure and compute the execution time and space requirements of the procedure. In addition, it reduces the resulting model as much as is possible. The final reduced model is saved for use in simulation.

When component analysis has been completed for all of the components of the object system, the individual component models can be used to simulate the object system. Each component graph model is translated into a PL/I program which consists mostly of calls to the simulation control program. Each of these translated models is compiled, and the entire set of compiled programs is executed with the simulation control program. The prototype simulation is relatively simple, with only minimal facilities for data collection and analysis and the specification of probability distributions.

Even though the language extensions, model building, and simulation are fairly simple in the prototype DES, it does contain enough of the essential features so that it can be used to design and implement nontrivial systems. In fact, the prototype DES can now be used to design and implement future versions of DES. Use of even a simple DES will be a significant help in gaining further insight into the problems of such an approach to system design and implementation.

Future development of DES

DES was designed to be an evolutionary system, and only the prototype version has been implemented. The major areas for further development are: the language, analysis and model building; simulation; and the coupling of analysis and simulation to the hardware description. The current extension of PL/I falls far short of being a satisfactory language for describing a software system design, especially in the area of asynchronous behavior. What is needed is a high level language which incorporates into its semantics the concepts of system structure and behavior which are central to the current work on abstract models of systems.

More powerful techniques for stochastic analysis need to be developed and incorporated into the model construction phase of DES. It is doubtful that the current techniques are capable of reducing the model of a large system like Multics to a tractable size. The entire area of interactive exploration and simplification of the model has yet to be investigated. This interaction between DES and the object system designers is a significant part of the design and implementation process, giving the designers a greatly improved insight into the system's behavior much sooner than possible today.

A special purpose simulator with built-in knowledge of software and hardware systems should be developed. Such a simulator would be much more efficient and useful in DES than any of the existing general purpose simulators. The coupling of the analysis and simulation routines to the hardware description can be greatly improved. The performance of the software is dependent on the hardware. DES obtains this information from the target system data base. However, the task of translating the hardware specifications into the form needed by DES is very time-consuming. Variations in hardware design could be evaluated rapidly if this transformation could be done automatically. For example, the timing figures for the general data structure statements depend on the code sequences used for accessing and manipulating the data. These code sequences are often very elaborate and lengthy. Automatic generation of these code sequences from a fairly simple description of the computer's order code and register structure is possible, and some work has been done on this problem [6].

We look upon DES as a small step in the direction of automating the production of large software and hardware systems. The state of the art in automation of hardware production is further advanced than it is in automated software production. The progress made in the past ten years in automating the production of compilers leads us to hope that significant progress can be made in automating the production of software systems. We must make evaluation an integral part of any automation we develop, so that the performance of the target system will be continuously monitored as it is developed, thus producing a system which has a realistic performance level, given the original objectives and constraints.

References: Graham, Clancy & DeVaney

1. Beizer, B. Analytical techniques for the statistical evaluation of program running time. Proc. 1970 FJCC, Vol. 37, AFIPS Press, Montvale, N.J., pp. 519-524.

2. Carlson, B. M.S. Thesis, Dep. of Elect. Eng., MIT, Cambridge, Mass. (to appear)

3. Corbató, F.J. PL/I as a tool for system programming. *Datamation* (May 1969).

4. Freiburghouse, R.A. The Multics PL/I compiler. Proc. AFIPS 1969 FJCC, Vol. 35, AFIPS Press, Montvale, N.J., pp.187-199.

5. Graham, R.M. The use of high level languages for systems programming. Proc. Invitational Workshop on Network of Computers, National Security Agency, Fort George G. Mead, Md., Oct. 1969, also, MAC TM 13, Proj. MAC, MIT, Cambridge, Mass., Sept. 1970.

6. Miller, P.L. Automatic code generation from an object machine description. MAC TM 18, Proj. MAC, MIT, Cambridge, Mass., Oct. 1970.

7. MIT, Project MAC. The multiplexed information and computing service: programmers manual. Proj. MAC, MIT, Cambridge, Mass., 1970.

8. Parnas, D.L. More on simulation languages and design methodology for computer systems. Proc. AFIPS 1969 SJCC, Vol. 34, AFIPS Press, Montvale, N.J., pp. 739-743.

9. Seaman, P.H., and Soucy, R.C. Simulation of operating systems. *IBM Syst. J. 8,* 4 (1969), 264-279.

10. Zurcher, F.W. and Randell, B. Iterative Multilevel modeling — a methodology for computer system design. Proc. IFIP Cong. 1968, North-Holland Pub. Co., Amsterdam, pp. 867-871. D138-142.

Design and Code Inspections to Reduce Errors in Program Development

Successful management of any process requires planning, measurement, and control. In programming development, these requirements translate into defining the programming process in terms of a series of operations, each operation having its own exit criteria. Next there must be some means of measuring completeness of the product at any point of its development by inspections or testing. And finally, the measured data must be used for controlling the process. This approach is not only conceptually interesting, but has been applied successfully in several programming projects embracing systems and applications programming, both large and small. It has not been found to "get in the way" of programming, but has instead enabled higher predictability than other means, and the use of inspections has improved productivity and product quality. The purpose of this paper is to explain the planning, measurement, and control functions as they are affected by inspections in programming terms.

An ingredient that gives maximum play to the planning, measurement, and control elements is consistent and vigorous *discipline*. Variable rules and conventions are the usual indicators of a lack of discipline. An iron-clad discipline on all rules, which can stifle programming work, is not required but instead there should be a clear understanding of the flexibility (or nonflexibility) of each of the rules applied to various aspects of the project. An example of flexibility may be waiving the rule that all main paths will be tested for the case where repeated testing of a given path will logically do no more than add expense. An example of necessary inflexibility would be that *all*

SOURCE: M.E. Fagan, *IBM Systems Journal,* 1976.

code must be inspected. A clear statement of the project rules and changes to these rules along with faithful adherence to the rules go a long way toward practicing the required project discipline.

A prerequisite of process management is a clearly defined series of operations in the process (Figure 1). The miniprocess within each operation must also be clearly described for closer management. A clear statement of the criteria that must be satisfied to exit each operation is mandatory. This statement and accurate data collection, with the data clearly tied to trackable units of known size and collected from specific points in the process, are some essential constituents of the information required for process management.

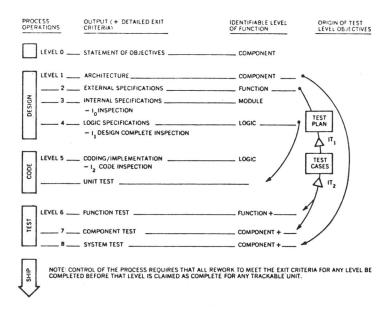

Figure 1. Programming process.

In order to move the form of process management from qualitative to more quantitative, process terms must be more specific, data collected must be appropriate, and the limits of accuracy of the data must be known. The effect is to provide more precise information in the correct process context for decision making by the process manager.

In this paper, we first describe the programming process and places at which inspections are important. Then we discuss factors that affect productivity and the operations involved with inspections. Finally, we compare inspections and walk-throughs on process control.

The process

A manageable process

A process may be described as a set of operations occurring in a definite sequence that operates on a given input and converts it to some desired output. A general statement of this kind is sufficient to convey the notion of the process. In a practical application, however, it is necessary to describe the input, output, internal processing, and processing times of a process in very specific terms if the process is to be executed and practical output is to be obtained.

In the programming development process, explicit requirement statements are necessary as input. The series of processing operations that act on this input must be placed in the correct sequence with one another, the output of each operation satisfying the input needs of the next operation. The output of the final operation is, of course, the explicitly required output in the form of a verified program. Thus, the objective of each processing operation is to receive a defined input and to produce a definite output that satisfies a specific set of exit criteria. (It goes without saying that each operation can be considered as a miniprocess itself.) A well-formed process can be thought of as a continuum of processing during which sequential sets of exit criteria are satisfied, the last set in the entire series requiring a well-defined end product. Such a process is not amorphous. It can be measured and controlled.

Exit criteria

Unambiguous, explicit, and universally accepted exit criteria would be perfect as process control checkpoints. It is frequently argued that universally agreed upon checkpoints are impossible in programming because all projects are different, etc. However, *all* projects do reach the point at which there is a project checkpoint. As it stands, any trackable unit of code achieving a clean compilation can be said to have satisfied a universal exit criterion or checkpoint in the process. Other checkpoints can also be selected, albeit on more arguable premises, but once the premises are agreed upon, the checkpoints become visible in most, if not all, projects. For example, there is a point at which the design of a program is considered complete. This point may be described as the level of detail to which a unit of design is reduced so that one design statement will materialize in an estimated three to 10 source code instructions (or, if desired, five to 20, for that matter). Whichever particular ratio is selected across a project, it provides a checkpoint for the process control of that project. In this way, suitable checkpoints may be selected throughout the development process and used in process management. (For more specific exit criteria see Reference 1.)

The cost of reworking errors in programs becomes higher the later they are reworked in the process, so every attempt should be made to find and fix errors as early in the process as possible. This cost has led to the use of the inspections described later and to the description of exit criteria which include assuring that all errors known at the end of the inspection of the new "clean-compilation" code, for example, have been correctly fixed. So, rework of all known errors up to a particular point must be complete before the associated checkpoint can be claimed to be met for any piece of code.

Where inspections are not used and errors are found during development or testing, the cost of rework as a fraction of overall development cost can be surprisingly high. For this reason, errors should be found and fixed as close to their place of origin as possible.

Production studies have validated the expected quality and productivity improvements and have provided estimates of standard productivity rates, percentage improvements due to inspections, and percentage improvements in error rates which are applicable in the context of large-scale operating system program production. (The data related to operating system development contained herein reflect results achieved by IBM in applying the subject processes and methods to representative samples. Since the results depend on many factors, they cannot be considered representative of every situation. They are furnished merely for the purpose of illustrating what has been achieved in sample testing.)

The purpose of the test plan inspection IT_1, shown in Figure 1, is to find voids in the functional variation coverage and other discrepancies in the test plan. IT_2, test case inspection of the test cases, which are based on the test plan, finds errors in the test cases. The total effects of IT_1 and IT_2 are to increase the integrity of testing and, hence, the quality of the completed product. And, because there are less errors in the test cases to be debugged during the testing phase, the overall project schedule is also improved.

A process of the kind depicted in Figure 1 installs all the intrinsic programming properties in the product as required in the statement of objectives (Level 0) by the time the coding operation (Level 5) has been completed — except for packaging and publications requirements. With these exceptions, all later work is of a verification nature. This verification of the product provides no contribution to the product during the essential development (Levels 1 to 5); it only adds error detection and elimination (frequently at one half of the development cost). I_0, I_1, and I_2 inspections were developed to measure and influence intrinsic quality (error content) in the early levels, where error rework can be most economically accomplished. Naturally, the beneficial effect on quality is also felt in later operations of the development process and at the end user's site.

An improvement in productivity is the most immediate effect of purging errors from the product by the I_0, I_1, and I_2 inspections. This purging allows rework of these errors very near their origin, early in the process. Rework done at these levels is 10 to 100 times less expensive than if it is done in the last half of the process. Since rework detracts from productive effort, it reduces productivity in proportion to the time taken to accomplish the rework. It follows, then, that finding errors by inspection and reworking them earlier in the process reduces the overall rework time and increases productivity even within the early operations and even more over the total process. Since less errors ship with the product, the time taken for the user to install programs is less, and his productivity is also increased.

The quality of documentation that describes the program is of as much importance as the program itself for poor quality can mislead the user, causing him to make errors quite as important as errors in the program. For this reason, the quality of program documentation is verified by publications inspections (PI_0, PI_1, and PI_2). Through a reduction of user-encountered errors, these inspections also have the effect of improving user productivity by reducing his rework time.

A study of coding productivity

A piece of the design of a large operating system component (all done in structured programming) was selected as a study sample (Figure 2). The sample was judged to be of moderate complexity. When the piece of design had been reduced to a level of detail sufficient to meet the Design Level 4 exit criteria [2] (a level of detail of design at which one design statement would ultimately appear as three to 10 code instructions), it was submitted to a design-complete inspection (100 percent), I_1. On conclusion of I_1, all error rework resulting from the inspection was completed, and the design was submitted for coding in PL/S. The coding was then done, and when the code was brought to the level of the first clean compilation [2], it was subjected to a code inspection (100 percent), I_2. The resultant rework was completed and the code was subjected to unit test. After unit test, a unit test inspection, I_3, was done to see that the unit test plan had been fully executed. Some rework was required and the necessary changes were made. This step completed the coding operation. The study sample was then passed on to later process operations consisting of building and testing.

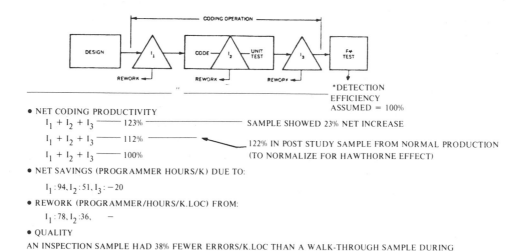

- NET CODING PRODUCTIVITY

  $I_1 + I_2 + I_3$ ———— 123% ———————————————— SAMPLE SHOWED 23% NET INCREASE

  $I_1 + I_2 + I_3$ ———— 112% ————————————————— 122% IN POST STUDY SAMPLE FROM NORMAL PRODUCTION

  $I_1 + I_2 + I_3$ ———— 100%   (TO NORMALIZE FOR HAWTHORNE EFFECT)

- NET SAVINGS (PROGRAMMER HOURS/K) DUE TO:

  $I_1 : 94, I_2 : 51, I_3 : -20$

- REWORK (PROGRAMMER/HOURS/K.LOC) FROM:

  $I_1 : 78, I_2 : 36,$ —

- QUALITY

AN INSPECTION SAMPLE HAD 38% FEWER ERRORS/K.LOC THAN A WALK-THROUGH SAMPLE DURING EQUIVALENT TESTING BETWEEN POST UNIT TEST AND SYSTEM TEST IN THIS STUDY.

Figure 2. A study of coding productivity.

Inspection sample

The inspection sample was considered of sufficient size and nature to be representative for study purposes. Three programmers designed it, and it was coded by 13 programmers. The inspection sample was in modular form, was structured, and was judged to be of moderate complexity on average.

Coding operation productivity

Because errors were identified and corrected in groups at I_1 and I_2, rather than found one-by-one during subsequent work and handled at the higher cost incumbent in later rework, the overall amount of error rework was minimized, even within the coding operation. Expressed differently, considering the inclusion of *all* I_1 time, I_2 time, and resulting error rework time (with the usual coding and unit test time in the total time to complete the operation), a *net* saving resulted when this figure was compared to the no-inspection case. This net saving translated into a 23 percent increase in the productivity of the coding operation alone. Productivity in later levels was also increased because there was less error rework in these levels due to the effect of inspections, but the increase was not measured directly.

An important aspect to consider in any production experiment involving human beings is the Hawthorne Effect [3]. If this effect is not adequately handled, it is never clear whether the effect observed is due to the human bias of the Hawthorne Effect or due to the newly implemented change in process. In this case a *control sample* was selected at random from many pieces of work *after the I_1 and I_2 inspections were accepted as commonplace*. (Previous experience without I_1 and I_2 approximated the net coding productivity rate of 100 percent datum in Figure 2.) The difference in coding productivity between the experimental sample (with I_1 and I_2 for the first time) and the control sample was 0.9 percent. This difference is not considered significant. Therefore, the measured increase in coding productivity of 23 percent is considered to validly accrue from the only change in the process: addition of I_1 and I_2 inspections.

Control sample

The control sample was also considered to be of representative size and was from the same operating system component as the study sample. It was designed by four programmers and was coded by seven programmers. And it was considered to be of moderate complexity on average.

Net savings

Within the coding operation only, the net savings (including inspection and re-work time) in programmer hours per 1000 Non-Commentary Source Statements (K.NCSS) [4] were I_1: 94, I_2: 51, and I_3: −20. As a consequence, I_3 is no longer in effect.

If personal fatigue and downtime of 15 percent are allowed in addition to the 145 programmer hours per K.NCSS, the saving approaches one programmer month per K.NCSS (assuming that our sample was truly representative of the rest of the work in the operating system component considered).

Error rework

The error rework in programmer hours per K.NCSS found in this study due to I_1 was 78, and 36 for I_2 (24 hours for design errors and 12 for code errors). Time for er-ror rework must be specifically scheduled. (For scheduling purposes it is best to develop rework hours per K.NCSS from history depending upon the particular project types and environments, but figures of 20 hours for I_1, and 16 hours for I_2 (*after the learning curve*) may be suitable to start with.)

Quality

The only comparative measure of quality obtained was a comparison of the in-spection study sample with a fully comparable piece of the operating system component that was produced similarly, except that walk-throughs were used in place of the I_1 and I_2 inspections. (Walk-throughs [5] were the practice before implementation of I_1 and I_2 inspections.) The process span in which the quality comparison was made was seven months of testing beyond unit test after which it was judged that both samples had been equally exercised. The results showed the inspection sample to contain 38 percent less errors than the walk-through sample.

Note that up to inspection I_2, no machine time has been used for debugging, and so machine time savings were not mentioned. Although substantial machine time is saved overall since there are less errors to test for in inspected code in later stages of the process, no actual measures were obtained.

Inspections in applications development

In the development of applications, inspections also make a significant impact. For example, an application program of eight modules was written in COBOL by Aetna Corporate Data Processing department, Aetna Life and Casualty, Hartford, Connecti-cut, in June 1975 [6]. Two programmers developed the program. The number of in-spection participants ranged between three and five. The only change introduced in the development process was the I_1 and I_2 inspections. The program size was 4,439 Non-Commentary Source Statements.

An automated estimating program, which is used to produce the normal program development time estimates for all the Corporate Data Processing department's projects, predicted that designing, coding, and unit testing this project would require 62 programmer days. In fact, the time actually taken was 46.5 programmer days including inspection meeting time. The resulting saving in programmer resources was 25 percent.

The inspections were obviously very thorough when judged by the inspection error detection efficiency of 82 percent and the later results during testing and usage as shown in Table 1.

Table 1
Error Detection Efficiency

Process Operations	Errors Found per K.NCSS	Percent of Total Errors Found
Design I_1 inspection Coding I_2 inspection	38*	82
Unit test Preparation for acceptance test	8	18
Acceptance test	0	
Actual usage (6 mo.)	0	
Total	46	100

*51% were logic errors, most of which were missing rather than due to incorrect design.

The results achieved in Non-Commentary Source Statements per Elapsed Hour are shown in Table 2. These inspection rates are four to six times faster than for systems programming. If these rates are generally applicable, they would have the effect of making the inspection of applications programs much less expensive.

Table 2
Inspection Rates in NCSS per Hour

Operations	I_1	I_2
Preparation	898	709
Inspection	652	539

Inspections

Inspections are a *formal, efficient,* and *economical* method of finding errors in design and code. All instructions are addressed at least once in the conduct of inspections. Key aspects of inspections are exposed in the following text through describing the I_1 and I_2 inspection conduct and process. I_0, IT_1, IT_2, PI_0, PI_1, and PI_2 inspections retain the same essential properties as the I_1 and I_2 inspections but differ in materials inspected, number of participants, and some other minor points.

The people involved

The inspection team is best served when its members play their particular roles, assuming the particular vantage point of those roles. These roles are described below:

1. *Moderator* — The *key person* in a successful inspection. He must be a competent programmer but need *not* be a technical expert on the program being inspected. To preserve objectivity and to increase the integrity of the inspection, it is usually advantageous to use a moderator from an unrelated project. The moderator must manage the inspection team and offer leadership. Hence, he must use personal sensitivity, tact, and drive in balanced measure. His use of the strengths of team members should produce a synergistic effect larger than their number; in other words, *he is the coach.* The duties of moderator also include scheduling suitable meeting places, reporting inspection results within one day, and follow-up on rework. *For best results the moderator should be specially trained.* (This training is brief but very advantageous.)

2. *Designer* — The programmer responsible for producing the program design.

3. *Coder/Implementor* — The programmer responsible for translating the design into code.

4. *Tester* — The programmer responsible for writing and/or executing test cases or otherwise testing the product of the designer and coder.

If the coder of a piece of code also designed it, he will function in the designer role for the inspection process; a coder from some related or similar program will perform the role of the coder. If the same person designs, codes, and tests the product code, the coder role should be filled as described above, and another coder — preferably with testing experience — should fill the role of tester.

Four people constitute a good-sized inspection team, although circumstances may dictate otherwise. The team size should not be artificially increased over four, but if the subject code is involved in a number of interfaces, the programmers of code related to these interfaces may profitably be involved in inspection. Table 3 indicates the inspection process and rate of progress.

Table 3
Inspection Process and Rate of Progress

Process Operations	Rate of Progress* (loc/hr) Design I_1	Code I_2	Objectives of the Operation
1. Overview	500	not necessary	Communication, education
2. Preparation	100	125	Education
3. Inspection	130	150	*Find errors*
4. Rework	20 hrs/K.NCSS	16 hrs/K.NCSS	Rework and resolve errors found by inspection
5. Follow-up	—	—	See that all errors, problems, and concerns have been resolved

*These notes apply to systems programming and are conservative. Comparable rates for applications programming are much higher. Initial schedules may be started with these numbers and as project history that is keyed to unique environments evolves, the historical data may be used for future scheduling algorithms.

Scheduling inspections and rework

The total time to complete the inspection process from overview through follow-up for I_1 and I_2 inspections with four people involved takes about 90 to 100 people-hours for systems programming. Again, these figures may be considered conservative but they will serve as a starting point. Comparable figures for applications programming tend to be much lower, implying lower cost per K.NCSS.

Because the error detection efficiency of most inspection teams tends to dwindle after two hours of inspection but then picks up after a period of different activity, it is advisable to schedule inspection sessions of no more than two hours at a time. Two two-hour sessions per day are acceptable.

The time to do inspections and resulting rework must be scheduled and managed with the same attention as other important project activities. (After all, as is noted later, for one case at least, it is possible to find approximately two thirds of the errors reported during an inspection.) If this is not done, the immediate work pressure has a tendency to push the inspections and/or rework into the background, postponing them or avoiding them altogether. The result of this short-term respite will obviously have a much more dramatic long-term negative effect since the finding and fixing of errors is delayed until later in the process (and after turnover to the user). Usually the result of postponing early error detection is a lengthening of the overall schedule and increased product cost.

Scheduling inspection time for modified code may be based on the algorithms in Table 3 *and on judgment.*

I_1 inspection process

Keeping the objective of each operation in the forefront of team activity is of paramount importance. Here is presented an outline of the I_1 inspection process operations.

1. *Overview* (whole team) − The designer first describes the overall area being addressed and then the specific area he has designed in detail− logic, paths, dependencies, etc. Documentation of design is distributed to all inspection participants on conclusion of the overview. (For an I_2 inspection, no overview is necessary, but the participants should remain the same. Preparation, inspection, and follow-up proceed as for I_1 but, of course, using code listings *and* design specifications as inspection materials. Also, at I_2 the moderator should flag for special scrutiny those areas that were reworked since I_1 errors were found *and other design changes* made.)

2. *Preparation* (individual) − Participants, using the design documentation, literally do their homework to try to understand the design, its intent and logic. (Sometimes flagrant errors are found during this operation, but in general, the number of errors found is not nearly as high as in the inspection operation.) To increase their error detection in the inspection, the inspection team should first study the ranked distributions of error types found by recent inspections. This study will prompt them to concentrate on the most fruitful areas. (See examples in Figures 3 and 4.) Checklists of clues on finding these errors should also be studied. (See partial examples of these lists in Figure 5 and 6

and complete examples for I_0 in Reference 1 and for I_1 and I_2 in Reference 7.)

VP	Individual Name	Missing	Wrong	Inspection file Extra	Errors	Error %
CD	CB Definition	16	2		18	3.5 ⎫ 10.4
CU	CB Usage	18	17	1	36	6.9 ⎭
FS	FPFS	1			1	.2
IC	Interconnect Calls	18	9		27	5.2
IR	Interconnect Reqts	4	5	2	11	2.1
LO	Logic	126	57	24	207	39.8 ←
L3	Higher Lvl Docu	1		1	2	.4
MA	Mod Attributes	1			1	.2
MD	More Detail	24	6	2	32	6.2
MN	Maintainability	8	5	3	16	3.1
OT	Other	15	10	10	35	6.7
PD	Pass Data Areas		1		1	.2
PE	Performance	1	2	3	6	1.2
PR	Prologue/Prose	44	38	7	89	17.1 ←
RM	Return Code/Msg	5	7	2	14	2.7
RU	Register Usage	1	2		3	.6
ST	Standards					
TB	Test & Branch	12	7	2	21	4.0
		295	168	57	520	100.0
		57%	32%	11%		

Figure 3. Summary of design inspections by error type.

VP	Individual Name	Missing	Wrong	Inspection file Extra	Errors	Error %
CC	Code Comments	5	17	1	23	6.6
CU	CB Usage	3	21	1	25	7.2
DE	Design Error	31	32	14	77	22.1 ←
F1			8		8	2.3
IR	Interconnect Calls	7	9	3	19	5.5
LO	Logic	33	49	10	92	26.4 ←
MN	Maintainability	5	7	2	14	4.0
OT	Other					
PE	Performance	3	2	5	10	2.9
PR	Prologue/Prose	25	24	3	52	14.9 ←
PU	PL/S or BAL Use	4	9	1	14	4.0
RU	Register Usage	4	2		6	1.7
SU	Storage Usage	1			1	.3
TB	Test & Branch	2	5		7	2.0
		123	185	40	348	100.0

Figure 4. Summary of code inspections by error type.

3. *Inspection* (whole team) — A "reader" chosen by the moderator (usually the coder) describes how he will implement the design. He is expected to paraphrase the design as expressed by the designer. Every piece of logic is covered at least once, and every branch is taken at least once. All higher-level documentation, high-level design specifications, logic specifications, etc., and macro and control block listings at I_2 must be available and present during the inspection.

I_1 Logic

Missing

1. Are all constants defined?
2. Are all unique values explicitly tested on input parameters?
3. Are values stored after they are calculated?
4. Are all defaults checked explicitly tested on input parameters?
5. If character strings are created are they complete, are all delimiters shown?
6. If a keyword has many unique values, are they all checked?
7. If a queue is being manipulated, can the execution be interrupted; if so, is queue protected by a locking structure; can queue be destroyed over an interrupt?
8. Are registers being restored on exits?
9. In queuing/dequeuing should any value be decremented/incremented?
10. Are all keywords tested in macro?
11. Are all keyword related parameters tested in service routine?
12. Are queues being held in isolation so that subsequent interrupting requestors are receiving spurious returns regarding the held queue?
13. Should any registers be saved on entry?
14. Are all increment counts properly initialized (0 or 1)?

Wrong

1. Are absolutes shown where there should be symbolics?
2. On comparison of two bytes, should all bits be compared?
3. On built data strings, should they be character or hex?
4. Are internal variables unique or confusing if concatenated?

Extra

1. Are all blocks shown in design necessary or are they extraneous?

Figure 5. Examples of what to examine when looking for errors at I_1.

INSPECTION SPECIFICATION

I_2 *Test Branch*

Is correct condition tested (If X = ON vs. If X = OFF)?
Is (Are) correct variable(s) used for test
(If X = ON vs. If Y = ON)?
Are null THENs/ELSEs included as appropriate?
Is each branch target correct?
Is the most frequently exercised test leg the THEN clause?

I_2 *Interconnection (or Linkage) Calls*

For each interconnection call to either a macro, SVC, or another module:
Are all required parameters passed set correctly?
If register parameters are used, is the correct register number specified?
If interconnection is a macro, does the in-line expansion contain all required code?
No register or storage conflicts between macro and calling module?
If the interconnection returns, do all returned parameters get processed correctly?

Figure 6. Examples of what to examine when looking for errors at I_2.

Now that the design is understood, *the objective is to find errors.* (Note that an error is defined as any condition that causes malfunction or that precludes the attainment of expected or previously specified results. Thus, deviations from specifications are clearly termed errors.) The finding of errors is actually done during the implementor/coder's discourse. Questions raised are pursued only to the point at which an error is recognized. It is noted by the moderator; its type is classified; severity (major or minor) is identified, and the inspection is continued. Often the solution of a problem is obvious. If so, it is noted, but no specific solution hunting is to take place during inspection. (The inspection is *not* intended to redesign, evaluate alternate design solutions, or to find solutions to errors; it is intended just to find errors!) A team is most effective if it operates with only one objective at a time.

Within one day of conclusion of the inspection, the moderator should produce a written report of the inspection and its findings to ensure that all issues raised in the inspection will be addressed in the rework and follow-up operations. Examples of these reports are given as Figures 7A, 7B, and 7C.

4. *Rework* — All errors or problems noted in the inspection report are resolved by the designer or coder/implementor.

5. *Follow-up* — It is imperative that every issue, concern, and error be entirely resolved at this level, or errors that result can be 10 to 100 times more expensive to fix if found later in the process (programmer time only, machine time not included). It is the responsibility of the moderator to see that all issues, problems, and concerns discovered in the inspection operation have been resolved by the designer in the case of I_1, or the coder/implementor for I_2 inspections. If more than five percent of the material has been reworked, the team should reconvene and carry out a 100 percent reinspection. Where less than five percent of the material has been reworked, the moderator at his discretion may verify the quality of the rework himself or reconvene the team to reinspect either the complete work or just the rework.

Commencing inspections

In Operation 3 above, it is one thing to direct people to find errors in design or code. It is quite another problem for them to find errors. Numerous experiences have shown that people have to be taught or prompted to find errors effectively. Therefore, it is prudent to condition them to seek the high-occurrence, high-cost error types (see example in Figures 3 and 4), and then describe the clues that usually betray the presence of each error type (see examples in Figures 5 and 6).

One approach to getting started may be to make a preliminary inspection of a design or code that is felt to be representative of the program to be inspected. Obtain a suitable quantity of errors, and analyze them by type and origin, cause, and salient indicative clues. With this information, an inspection specification may be constructed. This specification can be amended and improved in light of new experience and serve as an on-going directive to focus the attention and conduct of inspection teams. The objective of an inspection specification is to help maximize and make more consistent the error detection efficiency of inspections where

$$\begin{array}{c}\text{Error} \\ \text{detection} \\ \text{efficiency} \end{array} = \frac{\text{Errors found by an inspection}}{\text{Total errors in the product before inspection}} \times 100$$

Reporting inspection results

The reporting forms and form completion instructions shown in the Appendix may be used for I_1 and I_2 inspections. Although these forms were constructed for use in systems programming development, they may be used for applications programming development with minor modification to suit particular environments.

The moderator will make hand-written notes recording errors found during inspection meetings. He will categorize the errors and then transcribe counts of the errors, by type, to the module detail form. By maintaining cumulative totals of the counts by error type, and dividing by the number of projected executable source lines of code inspected to date, he will be able to establish installation averages within a short time.

Figures 7A, 7B, and 7C are an example of a set of code inspection reports. Figure 7A is a partial list of errors found in code inspection. Notice that errors are described in detail and are classified by error type, whether due to something being missing, wrong, or extra as the cause, and according to major or minor severity. Figure 7B is a module level summary of the errors contained in the entire error list represented by Figure 7A. The code inspection summary report in Figure 7C is a summary of inspection results obtained on all modules inspected in a particular inspection session or in a subcomponent or application.

1. PR/M/MIN   Line 3:   the statement of the prologue in the REMARKS section needs expansion.
2. DA/W/MAJ   Line 123:   ERR−RECORD−TYPE is out of sequence.
3. PU/W/MAJ   Line 147:   the wrong bytes of an 8-byte field (current−data) are moved into the 2-byte field (this year).
4. LO/W/MAJ   Line 169:   while counting the number of leading spaces in NAME, the wrong variable (I) is used to calculate "J."
5. LO/W/MAJ   Line 172:   NAME−CHECK is PERFORMED one time too few.
6. PU/E/MIN   Line 175:   In NAME−CHECK, the check for SPACE is redundant.
7. DE/W/MIN   Line 175:   the design should allow for the occurrence of a period in a last name.

Figure 7A. Error list.

CODE INSPECTION REPORT   DATE_____
MODULE DETAIL
MOD/MAC:_____CHECKER_____ SUBCOMPONENT/APPLICATION_____

SEE NOTE BELOW

PROBLEM TYPE:	MAJOR*			MINOR		
	M	W	E	M	W	E
LO: LOGIC		9			1	
TB: TEST AND BRANCH						
EL: EXTERNAL LINKAGES						
RU: REGISTER USAGE						
SU: STORAGE USAGE						
DA: DATA AREA USAGE		2				
PU: PROGRAM LANGUAGE		2				1
PE: PERFORMANCE						
MN: MAINTAINABILITY					1	
DE: DESIGN ERROR					1	
PR: PROLOGUE				1		
CC: CODE COMMENTS						
OT: OTHER						
TOTAL:		13			5	

REINSPECTION REQUIRED?____Y____

*A PROBLEM WHICH WOULD CAUSE THE PROGRAM TO MALFUNCTION. A BUG. M = MISSING.
W = WRONG. E = EXTRA
NOTE.   FOR MODIFIED MODULES, PROBLEMS IN THE CHANGED PORTION VERSUS PROBLEMS
        IN THE BASE SHOULD BE SHOWN IN THIS MANNER: 3(2). WHERE 3 IS THE NUMBER OF
        PROBLEMS IN THE CHANGED PORTION AND 2 IS THE NUMBER OF PROBLEMS IN THE BASE

Figure 7B. Example of module detail report.

CODE INSPECTION REPORT
SUMMARY   Date___11/20_____

To: Design Manager___KRAUSS_____Development Manager___GIOTTI_____
Subject: Inspection Report for___CHECKER_____Inspection Date_____11/19_____
            System/Application_____Release_____Build_____
            Component_____Subcomponent(s)_____

Mod/Mac Name	New or Mod	Full or Part Insp	Programmer	Tester	ELOC Added. Modified. Deleted									INSPECTION People-hours (X.X)				Sub-component
					Est. Pre			Est. Post			Rework			Prep	Insp Meetg	Re-work	Follow-up	
					A	M	D	A	M	D	A	M	D					
	n		McGINLEY	HALE	348			400			50			9.0	8.8	8.0	1.5	
				Totals														

Reinspection required?___YES_____Length of inspection (clock hours and tenths)___2.2_____
Reinspection by (date)____11/25/−_____Additional modules/macros?___NO_____
DCR #'s written____C-2_____
Problem summary: Major___13_____Minor___5_____Total___18_____
Errors in changed code: Major_____Minor_____Errors in base code: Major_____Minor_____
    LARSON   McGINLEY   HALE

| Initial Desr | Detailed Dr | Programmer | Team Leader | Other | Moderator's Signature |

Figure 7C. Example of code inspection summary report.

Inspections and languages

Inspections have been successfully applied to designs that are specified in English prose, flowcharts, HIPO (Hierarchy plus Input-Process-Output), and PIDGEON (an English prose-like meta language).

The first code inspections were conducted on PL/S and Assembler. Now, prompting checklists for inspection of Assembler, Cobol, Fortran, and PL/I code are available [7].

Personnel considerations

One of the most significant benefits of inspections is the detailed feedback of results on a relatively real-time basis. The programmer finds out what error types he is most prone to make and their quantity and how to find them. This feedback takes place within a few days of writing the program. Because he gets early indications from the first few units of his work inspected, he is able to show improvement, and usually does on later work even during the same project. In this way, feedback of results from inspections must be counted for the programmer's use and benefit: *they should not under any circumstances be used for programmer performance appraisal.*

Skeptics may argue that once inspection results are obtained, they will or even must count in performance appraisals, or at least cause strong bias in the appraisal process. The author can offer in response that inspections have been conducted over the past three years involving diverse projects and locations, hundreds of experienced programmers and tens of managers, and so far he has found no case in which inspection results have been used negatively against programmers. Evidently no manager has tried to "kill the goose that lays the golden eggs."

A preinspection opinion of some programmers is that they do not see the value of inspections because they have managed very well up to now, or because their projects are too small or somehow different. This opinion usually changes after a few inspections to a position of acceptance. The quality of acceptance is related to the success of the inspections they have experienced, the *conduct of the trained moderator,* and the *attitude demonstrated by management.* The acceptance of inspections by programmers and managers as a beneficial step in making programs is well-established amongst those who have tried them.

Process control using inspection and testing results

Obviously, the range of analysis possible using inspection results is enormous. Therefore, only a few aspects will be treated here, and they are elementary expositions.

Most error-prone modules

A listing of either I_1, I_2, or combined $I_1 + I_2$ data as in Figure 8 immediately highlights which modules contained the highest error density on inspection. If the error detection efficiency of each of the inspections was fairly constant, the ranking of error-prone modules holds. Thus if the error detection efficiency of inspection is 50 percent, and the inspection found 10 errors in a module, then it can be estimated that there are 10 errors remaining in the module. This information can prompt many actions to control the process. For instance, in Figure 8, it may be decided to reinspect module "Echo" or to redesign and recode it entirely. Or, less drastically, it may be decided to test it "harder" than other modules and look especially for errors of the type found in the inspections.

Module name	Number of errors	Lines of code	Error density, Errors/K.Loc	
Echo	4	128	31	
Zulu	10	323	31	
Foxtrot	3	71	28	
Alpha	7	264	27←	Average
Lima	2	106	19	Error
Delta	3	195	15	Rate
.	.	.	.	
.	.	.	.	
.	.	.	.	
	67			

Figure 8. Example of most error-prone modules based on I_1 and I_2.

Distribution of error types

If a ranked distribution of error types is obtained for a group of "error-prone modules" (Figure 9), which were produced from the same Process A, for example, it is a short step to comparing this distribution with a "Normal/Usual Percentage Distribution." Large disparities between the sample and "standard" will lead to questions on why Process A, say, yields nearly twice as many internal interconnection errors as the "standard" process. If this analysis is done promptly on the first five percent of production, it may be possible to remedy the problem (if it is a problem) on the remaining 95 percent of modules for a particular shipment. Provision can be made to test the first five percent of the modules to remove the unusually high incidence of internal interconnection problems.

	Number of errors	%	Normal/usual distribution, %
Logic	23	35	44
Interconnection/Linkage (Internal)	21	31 ?	18
Control Blocks	6	9	13
–	.	8	10
–	.	7	7
–	.	6	6
–	.	4	2
		100%	100%

Figure 9. Example of distribution of error types.

Inspecting error-prone code

Analysis of the testing results, commencing as soon as testing errors are evident, is a vital step in controlling the process since future testing can be guided by early results.

Where testing reveals excessively error-prone code, it may be more economical and saving of schedule to select the most error-prone code and inspect it before continuing testing. (The business case will likely differ from project to project and case to case, but in many instances inspection will be indicated.) The selection of the most error-prone code may be made with two considerations uppermost:

1. Which modules head a ranked list when the modules are rated by test errors per K.NCSS?

2. In the parts of the program in which test coverage is low, which modules or parts of modules are most suspect based on $(I_1 + I_2)$ errors per K.NCSS and programmer judgment?

From a condensed table of ranked "most error-prone" modules, a selection of modules to be inspected (or reinspected) may be made. Knowledge of the error types already found in these modules will better prepare an inspection team.

The reinspection itself should conform with the I_2 process, except that an overview may be necessary if the original overview was held too long ago or if new project members are involved.

Inspections and walk-throughs

Walk-throughs (or walk-thrus) are practiced in many different ways in different places, with varying regularity and thoroughness. This inconsistency causes the results of walk-throughs to vary widely and to be nonrepeatable. Inspections, however, having an established process and a formal procedure, tend to vary less and produce more repeatable results. Because of the variation in walk-throughs, a comparison between them and inspections is not simple. However, from Reference 8 and the walk-through procedures witnessed by the author and described to him by walk-through participants, as well as the inspection process described previously and in References 1 and 9, the comparison in Tables 4 and 5 is drawn.

Table 4
Inspection and Walk-through Processes and Objectives

Inspection		Walk-through	
Process Operations	*Objectives*	*Process Operations*	*Objectives*
1. Overview	Education (Group)	—	—
2. Preparation	Education (Individual)	1. Preparation	Education (Individual)
3. Inspection	Find errors! (Group)	2. Walk-through	Education (Group)
			Discuss design alternatives
4. Rework	Fix problems	—	Find errors
5. Follow-up	Ensure all fixes correctly installed	—	

Note the separation of objectives in the inspection process.

Table 5
Comparison of Key Properties of Inspections and Walk-throughs

Properties	*Inspection*	*Walk-through*
1. Formal moderator training	Yes	No
2. Definite participant roles	Yes	No
3. Who "drives" the inspection or walk-through	Moderator	Owner of material (Designer or coder)
4. Use "How to Find Errors" checklists	Yes	No
5. Use distribution of error types to look for	Yes	No
6. Follow-up to reduce bad fixes	Yes	No
7. Less future errors because of detailed error feedback to individual programmer	Yes	Incidental
8. Improve inspection efficiency from analysis of results	Yes	No
9. Analysis of data → process problems→ improvements	Yes	No

Effects on development process

Figure 10A describes the process in which a walk-through is applied. Clearly, the purging of errors from the product as it passes through the walk-through between Operations 1 and 2 is very beneficial to the product. In Figure 10B, the inspection process (and its feedback, feed-forward, and self-improvement) replaces the walk-through. The notes on the figure are self-explanatory.

Inspections are also an excellent means of measuring completeness of work against the exit criteria which must be satisfied to complete project checkpoints. (Each checkpoint should have a clearly defined set of exit criteria. Without exit criteria, a checkpoint is too negotiable to be useful for process control.)

Inspections and process management

The most marked effects of inspections on the development process is to change the old adage that, "design is not complete until testing is completed," to a position where a very great deal must be known about the design before even the coding is begun. Although great discretion is still required in code implementation, more predictability and improvements in schedule, cost, and quality accrue. The old adage still holds true if one regards inspection as much a means of verification as testing.

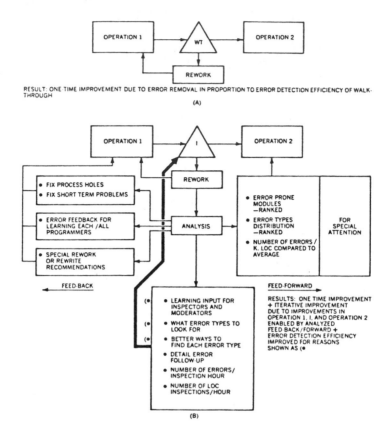

Figure 10A. Walk-through process.   **Figure 10B. Inspection process.**

Percent of errors found

Observations in one case in systems programming show that approximately two thirds of all errors reported during development are found by I_1 and I_2 inspections prior to machine testing. The error detection efficiencies of the I_1 and I_2 inspections separately are, of course, less than 66 percent. A similar observation of an application program development indicated an 82 percent find (Table 1). As more is learned and the error detection efficiency of inspection is increased, the burden of debugging on testing operations will be reduced, and testing will be more able to fulfill its prime objective of verifying quality.

Effect on cost and schedule

Comparing the "old" and "new" (with inspections) approaches to process management in Figure 11, we can see clearly that with the use of inspection results, error rework (which is a very significant variable in product cost) tends to be managed more during the first half of the schedule. This results in much lower cost than in the "old" approach, where the cost of error rework was 10 to 100 times higher and was accomplished in large part during the last half of the schedule.

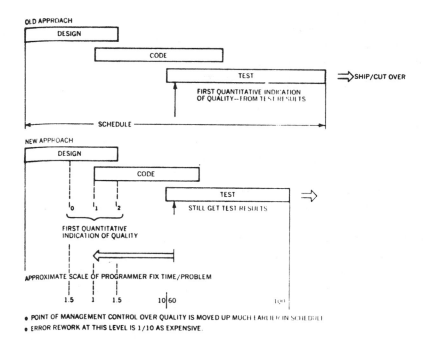

Figure 11. Effect of inspection on process management.

Process tracking

Inserting the I_1 and I_2 checkpoints in the development process enables assessment of project completeness and quality to be made early in the process (during the first half of the project instead of the latter half of the schedule, when recovery may be impossible without adjustments in schedule and cost). Since individually trackable modules of reasonably well-known size can be counted as they pass through each of these checkpoints, the percentage completion of the project against schedule can be continuously and easily tracked.

Effect on product knowledge

The overview, preparation, and inspection sequence of the operations of the inspection process give the inspection participants a high degree of product knowledge in a very short time. This important side benefit results in the participants being able to handle later development and testing with more certainty and less false starts. Naturally, this also contributes to productivity improvement.

An interesting sidelight is that because designers are asked at pre-I_1 inspection time for estimates of the number of lines of code (NCSS) that their designs will create, and they are present to count for themselves the actual lines of code at the I_2 inspection, the accuracy of design estimates has shown substantial improvement.

For this reason, an inspection is frequently a required event where responsibility for design or code is being transferred from one programmer to another. The complete inspection team is convened for such an inspection. (One-on-one reviews such as desk debugging are certainly worthwhile but do not approach the effectiveness of formal inspection.) Usually the side benefit of finding errors more than justifies the transfer inspection.

Inspecting modified code

Code that is changed in, or inserted in, an existing module either in replacement of deleted code or simply inserted in the module is considered modified code. By this definition, a very large part of programming effort is devoted to modifying code. (The addition of entirely new modules to a system count as new, not modified, code.)

Some observations of errors per K.NCSS of modified code show its error rate to be considerably higher than is found in new code (i.e., if 10.NCSS are replaced in a 100.NCSS module and errors against the 10.NCSS are counted, the error rate is described as number of errors per 10.NCSS, not number of errors per 100.NCSS). Obviously, if the number of errors in modified code are used to derive an error rate per K.NCSS for the whole module that was modified, this rate would be largely dependent upon the percentage of the module that is modified: this would provide a meaningless ratio. A useful measure is the number of errors per K.NCSS (modified) in which the higher error rates have been observed.

Since most modifications are small (e.g., 1 to 25 instructions), they are often erroneously regarded as trivially simple and are handled accordingly; the error rate goes up, and control is lost. In the author's experience, *all* modifications are well worth inspecting from an economic and a quality standpoint. A convenient method of handling changes is to group them to a module or set of modules and convene the inspection team to inspect as many changes as possible. But all changes must be inspected!

Inspections of modifications can range from inspecting the modified instructions and the surrounding instructions connecting it with its host module, to an inspection of the entire module. The choice of extent of inspection coverage is dependent upon the percentage of modification, pervasiveness of the modification, etc.

Bad fixes

A very serious problem is the inclusion in the product of bad fixes. Human tendency is to consider the "fix," or correction, to a problem to be error-free itself. Unfortunately, this is all too frequently untrue in the case of fixes to errors found by inspections and by testing. The inspection process clearly has an operation called Follow-Up to try and minimize the bad-fix problem, but the fix process of testing errors very rarely requires scrutiny of fix quality before the fix is inserted. Then, if the fix is bad, the whole elaborate process of going from source fix to link edit, to test the fix, to regression test must be repeated at needlessly high cost. The number of bad fixes can be economically reduced by some simple inspection after clean compilation of the fix.

Summary

We can summarize the discussion of design and code inspections and process control in developing programs as follows:

1. Describe the program development process in terms of operations, and define exit criteria which must be satisfied for completion of each operation.

2. Separate the objectives of the inspection process operations to keep the inspection team focused on one objective at a time:

Operation	Objective
Overview	Communications/education
Preparation	Education
Inspection	Find errors
Rework	Fix errors
Follow-up	Ensure all fixes are applied correctly

3. Classify errors by type, and rank frequency of occurrence of types. Identify *which types* to spend most time looking for in the inspection.

4. Describe *how* to look for presence of error types.

5. Analyze inspection results and use for constant process improvement (until process averages are reached and then use for process control).

Some applications of inspections include function level inspections I_0, design-complete inspections I_1, code inspections I_2, test plan inspections IT_1, test case inspections IT_2, interconnections inspections IF, inspection of fixes/changes, inspection of publications, etc., and post testing inspection. Inspections can be applied to the development of system control programs, applications programs, and microcode in hardware.

We can conclude from experience that inspections increase productivity and improve final program quality. Furthermore, improvements in process control and project management are enabled by inspections.

Acknowledgments

The author acknowledges, with thanks, the work of Mr. O.R. Kohli and Mr. R.A. Radice, who made considerable contributions in the development of inspection techniques applied to program design and code, and Mr. R.R. Larson, who adapted inspections to program testing.

Appendix: Reporting forms and form completion instructions

Instructions for Completing Design Inspection Module Detail Form

This form (Figure 12) should be completed for each module/macro that has valid problems against it. The problem-type information gathered in this report is important because a history of problem-type experience points out high-occurrence types. This knowledge can then be conveyed to inspectors so that they can concentrate on seeking the higher-occurrence types of problems.

1. MOD/MAC: The module or macro name.

2. SUBCOMPONENT: The associated subcomponent.

3. PROBLEM TYPE: Summarize the number of problems by type (logic, etc.), severity (major/minor), and by category (missing, wrong, or extra). For modified modules, detail the number of problems in the changed design versus the number in the base design. (Problem types were developed in a systems programming environment. Appropriate changes, if desired, could be made for application development.)

4. REINSPECTION REQUIRED?: Indicate whether the module/macro requires a reinspection.

DATE_____

DETAILED DESIGN INSPECTION REPORT

MODULE DETAIL

MOD/MAC_____ SUBCOMPONENT/APPLICATION_____

SEE NOTE BELOW

PROBLEM TYPE:	MAJOR*			MINOR		
	M	W	E	M	W	E
LO: LOGIC						
TB: TEST AND BRANCH						
DA: DATA AREA USAGE						
RM: RETURN CODES/MESSAGES						
RU: REGISTER USAGE						
MA: MODULE ATTRIBUTES						
EL: EXTERNAL LINKAGES						
MD: MORE DETAIL						
ST: STANDARDS						
PR: PROLOGUE OR PROSE						
HL: HIGHER LEVEL DESIGN DOC						
US: USER SPEC						
MN: MAINTAINABILITY						
PE: PERFORMANCE						
OT: OTHER						
TOTAL:						

REINSPECTION REQUIRED?_____

*A PROBLEM WHICH WOULD CAUSE THE PROGRAM TO MALFUNCTION: A BUG. M = MISSING.
W = WRONG. E = EXTRA.

NOTE: FOR MODIFIED MODULES, PROBLEMS IN THE CHANGED PORTION VERSUS PROBLEMS
IN THE BASE SHOULD BE SHOWN IN THIS MANNER: 3(2), WHERE 3 IS THE NUMBER OF PROBLEMS
IN THE CHANGED PORTION AND 2 IS THE NUMBER OF PROBLEMS IN THE BASE.

Figure 12. Design inspection module detail form.

All valid problems found in the inspection should be listed and attached to the report. A brief description of each problem, its error type, and the rework time to fix it should be given (see Figure 7A, which describes errors in similar detail to that required but is at a coding level).

Instructions for Completing Design Inspection Summary Form

Following are detailed instructions for completing the form in Figure 13.

1.   TO: The report is addressed to the respective design and development managers.

2.   SUBJECT: The unit being inspected is identified.

3.   MOD/MAC NAME: The name of each module and macro as it resides on the source library.

4.   NEW OR MOD: "N" if the module is new; "M" if the module is modified.

5.   FULL OR PART INSP: If the module/macro is "modified," indicate "F" if the module/macro was fully inspected or "P" if partially inspected.

6.   DETAILED DESIGNER: and PROGRAMMER: Identification of originators.

7.   PRE-INSP EST ELOC: The estimated executable source lines of code (added, modified, deleted). Estimate made prior to the inspection by the designer.

8.   POST-INSP EST ELOC: The estimated executable source lines of code. Estimate made after the inspection.

9. REWORK ELOC: The estimated executable source lines of code in rework as a result of the inspection.

10. OVERVIEW AND PREP: The number of people-hours (in tenths of hours) spent in preparing for the overview, in the overview meeting itself, and in preparing for the inspection meeting.

11. INSPECTION MEETING: The number of people-hours spent on the inspection meeting.

12. REWORK: The estimated number of people-hours spent to fix the problems found during the inspection.

13. FOLLOW-UP: The estimated number of people-hours spent by the moderator (and others if necessary) in verifying the correctness of changes made by the author as a result of the inspection.

14. SUBCOMPONENT: The subcomponent of which the module/macro is a part.

15. REINSPECTION REQUIRED?: Yes or no.

16. LENGTH OF INSPECTION: Clock hours spent in the inspection meeting.

17. REINSPECTION BY (DATE): Latest acceptable date for reinspection.

18. ADDITIONAL MODULES/MACROS?: For these subcomponents, are additional modules/macros yet to be inspected?

19. DCR #'S WRITTEN: The identification of Design Change Requests, DCR(S), written to cover problems in rework.

20. PROBLEM SUMMARY: Totals taken from Module Detail form(s).

21. INITIAL DESIGNER, DETAILED DESIGNER, etc: Identification of members of the inspection team.

Figure 13. Design inspection summary form.

Instructions for Completing Code Inspection Module Detail Form

This form (Figure 14) should be completed according to the instructions for completing the design inspection module detail form.

DATE_____

CODE INSPECTION REPORT

MODULE DETAIL

MOD/MAC:_____ SUBCOMPONENT/APPLICATION_____

SEE NOTE BELOW

PROBLEM TYPE:	MAJOR*			MINOR		
	M	W	E	M	W	E
LO: LOGIC						
TB: TEST AND BRANCH						
EL: EXTERNAL LINKAGES						
RU: REGISTER USAGE						
SU: STORAGE USAGE						
DA: DATA AREA USAGE						
PU: PROGRAM LANGUAGE						
PE: PERFORMANCE						
MN: MAINTAINABILITY						
DE: DESIGN ERROR						
PR: PROLOGUE						
CC: CODE COMMENTS						
OT: OTHER						
TOTAL:						

REINSPECTION REQUIRED?_____

*A PROBLEM WHICH WOULD CAUSE THE PROGRAM TO MALFUNCTION: A BUG. M = MISSING,
W = WRONG, E = EXTRA.
NOTE: FOR MODIFIED MODULES, PROBLEMS IN THE CHANGED PORTION VERSUS PROBLEMS
IN THE BASE SHOULD BE SHOWN IN THIS MANNER: 3(2), WHERE 3 IS THE NUMBER OF PROBLEMS
IN THE CHANGED PORTION AND 2 IS THE NUMBER OF PROBLEMS IN THE BASE.

Figure 14. Code inspection module detail form.

Instructions for Completing Code Inspection Summary Form

This form (Figure 15) should be completed according to the instructions for the design inspection summary form except for the following items.

1. PROGRAMMER AND TESTER: Identifications of original participants involved with code.

2. PRE-INSP ELOC: The noncommentary source lines of code (added, modified, deleted). Count made prior to the inspection by the programmer.

3. POST-INSP EST ELOC: The estimated noncommentary source lines of code. Estimate made after the inspection.

4. REWORK ELOC: The estimated noncommentary source lines of code in rework as a result of the inspection.

5. PREP: The number of people hours (in tenths of hours) spent in preparing for the inspection meeting.

CODE INSPECTION REPORT
SUMMARY   Date_____

To: Design Manager_____Development Manager_____
Subject: Inspection Report for_____Inspection Date_____
             System/Application_____Release_____Build_____
             Component_____Subcomponents(s)_____

Mod/Mac Name	New or Mod	Full or Part Insp.	Programmer	Tester	ELOC Added, Modified, Deleted									INSPECTION People-hours (X.X)				Sub-component
					Pre-insp.			Est. Post			Rework				Insp. Meetg	Re-work	Follow-up	
					A	M	D	A	M	D	A	M	D	Prep				
				Totals														

Reinspection required?_____Length of inspection (clock hours and tenths)_____
Reinspection by (date)_____Additional modules/macros?_____
DCR #'s written_____
Problem summary: Major_____Minor_____Total_____
        Errors in changed code: Major_____Minor_____Errors in base code: Major_____Minor_____

_____   _____   _____   _____   _____   _____
Initial Desr   Detailed Dr   Programmer   Team Leader   Other   Moderator's Signature

Figure 15. Code inspection summary form.

Cited References and Footnotes: Fagan

1. O.R. Kohli, *High-Level Design Inspection Specification,* Technical Report TR 21.601, IBM Corporation, Kingston, New York (July 21, 1975).

2. It should be noted that the exit criteria for I_1 (design complete where one design statement is estimated to represent 3 to 10 code instructions) and I_2 (first clean code compilations) are checkpoints in the development process through which every programming project must pass.

3. The Hawthorne Effect is a psychological phenomenon usually experienced in human-involved productivity studies. The effect is manifested by participants producing above normal because they know they are being studied.

4. NCSS (Non-Commentary Source Statements), also referred to as "Lines of Code," are the sum of executable code instructions and declaratives. Instructions that invoke macros are counted once only. Expanded macroinstructions are also counted only once. Comments are not included.

5. Basically in a walk-through, program design or code is reviewed by a group of people gathered together at a structured meeting in which errors/issues pertaining to the material and proposed by the participants may be discussed in an effort to find errors. The group may consist of various participants but always includes the originator of the material being reviewed who usually plans the meeting and is responsible for correcting the errors. How it differs from an inspection is pointed out in Tables 2 and 3.

6. *Marketing Newsletter,* Cross Application Systems Marketing, "Program inspections at Aetna," MS-76-006, S2, IBM Corporation, Data Processing Division, White Plains, New York (March 29, 1976).

7. J. Ascoly, M.J. Cafferty, S.J. Gruen, and O.R. Kohli. *Code Inspection Specification,* Technical Report TR21.630, IBM Corporation, Kingston, New York (1976).

8. N.S. Waldstein, *The Walk-Thru—A Method of Specification, Design and Review,* Technical Report TR 00.2536, IBM Corporation, Poughkeepsie, New York (June 4, 1974).

9. Independent study programs: *IBM Structured Programming Textbook,* SR20-7149-1, *IBM Structured Programming Workbook,* SR20-7150-0, IBM Corporation, Data Processing Division, White Plains, New York.

General References: Fagan

1. J.D. Aron, *The Program Development Process: Part 1: The Individual Programmer,* Structured Programs, 137-141, Addison-Wesley Publishing Co., Reading, Massachusetts (1974).

2. M.E. Fagan, *Design and Code Inspections and Process Control in the Development of Programs,* Technical Report TR 00.2763, IBM Corporation, Poughkeepsie, New York (June 10, 1976). This report is a revision of the author's *Design and Code Inspections and Process Control in the Development of Programs,* Technical Report TR 21.572, IBM Corporation, Kingston, New York (December 17, 1974).

3. O.R. Kohli and R.A. Radice, *Low-Level Design Inspection Specification,* Technical Report TR 21.629. IBM Corporation, Kingston, New York (1976).

4. R.R. Larson, *Test Plan and Test Case Inspection Specifications,* Technical Report TR 21.586, IBM Corporation, Kingston, New York (April 4, 1975).

Section 3
PROGRAMMING: LANGUAGES
AND CONSTRUCTS

The four papers on the subject of programming languages and constructs that I've chosen to include in this volume have similar themes, even though they span a ten-year period. That theme pertains to the merits and flaws of structured programming.

Knuth & Floyd: Notes on Avoiding "GO TO" Statements

Structured programming had become a major intellectual topic in 1971 in the more elite circles of computer scientists when Donald Knuth and Bob Floyd published "Notes on Avoiding 'GO TO' Statements." At the 25th National ACM Conference in 1971, structured programming was discussed and debated with more emotion than any other topic; at the triennial IFIP Conference held that year at Ljubljana, Yugoslavia, it was the subject of numerous papers and presentations. In addition, structured programming was being actively used commercially — by IBM in their now-famous New York Times project,* and in university programming projects at Stanford and Carnegie-Mellon, among other universities.

But it is obvious from the Knuth and Floyd paper that structured programming was being equated with GOTO-less programming — an issue of sufficient controversy to turn calm, rational adults into babbling fanatics. Knuth and Floyd, however, are quite the opposite of fanatics; in their paper, they go to some lengths to show just how foolish a literal-minded interpretation of GOTO-less programming can be. Their examples clearly show that a program can sometimes be more difficult to understand *without* GOTO statements than with them.

Most of the paper is devoted to a rather theoretical presentation of the techniques for converting an arbitrary unstructured program into an equivalent structured program. The authors point out, as have others, that the translation of an unstructured program into a structured program often requires blocks of duplicated code, or extra tests.

---

*Two papers describe the New York Times system. First is "Chief Programmer Team Management of Production Programming" by F.T. Baker, which originally appeared in *IBM Systems Journal,* Vol. 11, No. 1 (January 1972), pp. 56-73. The second is "System Quality Through Structured Programming," also by Baker, originally published in *AFIPS Proceedings of the 1972 Fall Joint Computer Conference,* Vol. 41 (Montvale, N.J.: AFIPS Press, 1972), pp. 339-44. Both articles are reprinted in *Classics in Software Engineering,* ed. E.N. Yourdon (New York: YOURDON Press, 1979), pp. 65-82, 129-38.

DeBalbine: Better Manpower Utilization Using Automatic Restructuring

The next paper, by Guy DeBalbine, carries this idea one step further. Although it is not at all apparent from the title, "Better Manpower Utilization Using Automatic Restructuring" discusses *mechanical* translation of unstructured programs into equivalent structured programs. The so-called structuring engine (presumably named after Babbage's historical "analytical engine") was developed by the consulting firm of Caine, Farber & Gordon to translate unstructured FORTRAN programs into a structured preprocessor language called S-FORTRAN. S-FORTRAN appears to be similar to languages like RATFOR* and other FORTRAN preprocessors that appeared in the mid-1970s.

The irony, of course, is that the structuring engine converts unstructured FORTRAN programs into a superset of FORTRAN; the S-FORTRAN preprocessor then translates *that* right back into FORTRAN, with GOTO statements reintroduced. Naturally, the programmer does all of his work at the S-FORTRAN level, so he doesn't see the blasphemous GOTOs reintroduced by the preprocessor.

The structuring engine addressed an issue that worried many of us in the early 1970s: Structured programming was a fine idea for *new* programs, but what about the enormous mountain of unstructured programs that had been developed over a period of twenty years? Why not translate mechanically? That it was theoretically possible to do so was something that everyone knew from the beginning — after all, the original Böhm and Jacopini[†] proof of structured programming was based on the concept of taking an arbitrary (unstructured) program and demonstrating that one could develop an equivalent structured program. And since structured programs seemed so much easier to understand and maintain, the potential market for a structuring engine seemed utterly enormous then.

And so DeBalbine's consulting firm developed its own structuring engine. In retrospect — in fact, even then, in 1975, when I first saw the paper in the *Proceedings* of the National Computer Conference — it seemed obvious to me that the structuring engine should have been used to restructure COBOL programs rather than FORTRAN. Why? Because FORTRAN programs are intrinsically ugly, whether structured or not.

Nevertheless, the package was built; DeBalbine's paper describes the technical approach, and some of the results. The developers found, for example, that the restructured code typically occupied approximately twenty percent more memory than the original code. They also found that if the structuring engine was unable to make a significant improvement in the organization of the code, it was a good indication that the original program needed to be redesigned from scratch.

While writing this introduction, I telephoned the firm of Caine, Farber & Gordon to discover if there were any recent developments with the structuring engine. Alas, it has fallen into disuse — nobody wanted it. There was a brief effort to convince a large client to underwrite the development of a structuring engine for COBOL, but that never came to pass. "Perhaps," Stephen Caine said to me, "we were just a few years ahead of our time." Perhaps so. Perhaps DeBalbine's paper will *truly* be seen as a classic in another five years.

---

*See B.W. Kernighan and P.J. Plauger, *Software Tools* (Reading, Mass.: Addison-Wesley, 1976).
[†]See C. Böhm and G. Jacopini, "Flow Diagrams, Turing Machines and Languages with Only Two Formation Rules," *Communications of the ACM*, Vol. 9, No. 5 (May 1966), pp. 366-71. Reprinted in *Classics in Software Engineering*, ed. E.N. Yourdon (New York: YOURDON Press, 1979), pp. 13-25.

Caine & Gordon: PDL — A Tool for Software Design

The third paper in this section is by Stephen Caine and Kent Gordon, of Caine, Farber & Gordon, and was published in the *Proceedings* of the 1975 National Computer Conference. Although it could also have been included in the collection of design papers, it is interesting to read this paper immediately after DeBalbine's discussion of the structuring engine.

Caine, Farber & Gordon's PDL is generally regarded as one of the first formal design languages. In many EDP organizations today, such a language is also called pseudocode or structured English. Indeed, as the authors point out, their language has the vocabulary of English and the syntax of a formal programming language.

Most of the paper is devoted to a description of the format and syntax of PDL; there is also a brief discussion of the authors' actual experience using PDL on software projects. They claim that PDL led to a fifty percent improvement in productivity over projects that used structured programming without a formal design language.

Hoare: The Emperor's Old Clothes

The final article in this section is a delightful paper by Tony Hoare, entitled "The Emperor's Old Clothes." It was presented as the 1980 Turing Award Lecture at the national ACM conference, and appeared in the *Communications of the ACM* in February, 1981. One might wonder why such a recent bit of writing is included with a collection of papers that are generally five or ten years old. The answer is simple: Hoare's paper is primarily a reminiscence of some twenty years of experience in the software field throughout the 1960s and 1970s.

Much of Hoare's work involved the design and development of programming languages, but he also describes a very interesting large, ambitious software development project that turned out to be a total disaster. As Hoare says, "I have learned more from my failures than can ever be revealed in the cold print of a scientific article, and now I would like you to learn from them, too." Anyone who has ever suffered through (and recovered from) a software development project that finally collapsed in failure would agree with this statement; anyone who has not yet had such an experience should read Hoare's paper several times over.

Hoare concludes with a passionate criticism of programming languages like Ada: ". . . I appeal to you, representatives of the programming profession in the United States, and citizens concerned with the welfare and safety of your own country and of mankind: Do not allow this language in its present state to be used in applications where reliability is critical. . . . The next rocket to go astray as a result of a programming language error may not be an exploratory space rocket on a harmless trip to Venus: It may be a nuclear warhead exploding over one of our own cities."

Strong words, indeed. But they are sincere words from an eminently wise man whose concern for our profession manifests itself in everything he states. I think you will find this one of the most appealing — and certainly the most thought-provoking — of all the articles in this book.

Additional References on Programming Languages and Constructs

The articles selected for this volume supplement the programming articles previously reprinted in *Classics in Software Engineering.* Because the bulk of *Classics* addresses the topic of programming, I will not cite each and every reference, but rather point the reader to the particularly relevant titles presented below:

1. E.W. Dijkstra, "Programming Considered as a Human Activity," *Proceedings of the 1965 IFIP Congress* (Amsterdam, The Netherlands: North-Holland Publishing Co., 1965), pp. 213-17. Reprinted in *Classics in Software Engineering,* ed. E.N. Yourdon (New York: YOURDON Press, 1979), pp. 3-9.

2. W.A. Wulf, "A Case Against the GOTO," *Proceedings of the 25th National ACM Conference* (New York: Association for Computing Machinery, 1972), pp. 791-97. Reprinted in *Classics in Software Engineering,* pp. 85-98.

3. M.E. Hopkins, "A Case for the GOTO," *Proceedings of the 25th National ACM Conference* (New York: Association for Computing Machinery, 1972), pp. 787-90. Reprinted in *Classics in Software Engineering,* pp. 101-09.

4. E.W. Dijkstra, "The Humble Programmer," *Communications of the ACM,* Vol. 15, No. 10 (October 1972), pp. 859-66. Reprinted in *Classics in Software Engineering,* pp. 113-25.

5. F.T. Baker, "System Quality Through Structured Programming," *AFIPS Proceedings of the 1972 Fall Joint Computer Conference,* Vol. 41 (Montvale, N.J.: AFIPS Press, 1972), pp. 339-44. Reprinted in *Classics in Software Engineering,* pp. 129-38.

6. D.L. Parnas, "On the Criteria to Be Used in Decomposing Systems into Modules," *Communications of the ACM,* Vol. 5, No. 12 (December 1972), pp. 1053-58. Reprinted in *Classics in Software Engineering,* pp. 141-50.

7. N. Wirth, "On the Composition of Well-Structured Programs," *ACM Computing Surveys,* Vol. 6, No. 4 (December 1974), pp. 247-59. Reprinted in *Classics in Software Engineering,* pp. 153-71.

8. B.W. Kernighan and P.J. Plauger, "Programming Style: Examples and Counterexamples," *ACM Computing Surveys,* Vol. 6, No. 4 (December 1974), pp. 303-19. Reprinted in *Classics in Software Engineering,* pp. 235-55.

Notes on Avoiding "GO TO" Statements

During the last decade there has been a growing sentiment that the use of "go to" statements is undesirable, or actually harmful. This attitude is apparently inspired by the idea that programs expressed solely in terms of conventional iterative constructions ("for," "while," etc.) are more readable and more easily proved correct. In this note we will make a few exploratory observations about the use and disuse of go to statements, based on two typical programming examples (from "symbol table searching" and "backtracking").

In the first place let us consider systematic ways for eliminating go to statements, without changing the sequence of computations specified by the program. There are two apparent ways to achieve this:

(a) *Recursive procedure method.* Suppose that each statement of a program is labeled. Replace each labeled statement

$$L : S$$

by   **procedure** L; **begin** S; L' **end**

where L' is the static successor of the statement S. A go to statement becomes simply a procedure call. The program ends by calling a null procedure. This construction shows that the mere elimination of go to statements does not automatically make a program better or easier to follow; "go to" is in some sense a special case of the procedure calling mechanism. (It is instructive in fact to consider this construction in reverse, realizing that it is sometimes more efficient to replace procedure calls by go to statements!)

SOURCE: D.E. Knuth & R.W. Floyd, *Information Processing Letters,* 1971.

153

(b) *Regular expression method.* For convenience, imagine a program expressed in flowchart form, as a directed graph. It is well known that all paths through this graph can be represented by "regular expressions" involving the operations of concatenation, alternation, and "star"; these latter correspond to familiar constructions in programming languages which do not depend on go to statements. Therefore it appears that "go to" statements can be eliminated, although it may be necessary to duplicate the code for other statements in several places.

Consider, for example, the following well-known programming situation

> **for** $i := 1$ **step** 1 **until** n **do**
>   **if** $A[i] = x$ **then go to** *found*;
> *not found*: $n := i$; $A[i] := x$; $B[i] := 0$;
> *found*: $B[i] := B[i] + 1$;

(Let us assume, for convenience, that $i = n + 1$ if the for loop is exhausted.) It is not obvious that the go to statement here is all that unsightly, but let us suppose that we are reactionary enough that we really want to abolish them from programming languages [4, 5]. One way to avoid the go to is to use a recursive procedure:

> **procedure** *find*;
>   **if** $i > n$ **then begin** $n := i$; $A[i] := x$; $B[i] := 0$ **end**
>   **else if** $A[i] \neq x$ **then begin** $i := i + 1$; *find* **end**;
> $i := 1$; *find*; $B[i] := B[i] + 1$;

An optimizing compiler could perhaps produce the same code for both programs, but again it is debatable which program is most readable and simple.

Other solutions change the structure of the program slightly:

(a)
> $i := 1$;
> **while** $i \leqslant n$ **and** $A[i] \neq x$ **do** $i := i + 1$;
> **if** $i > n$ **then begin** $n := i$; $A[i] := x$; $B[i] := 0$ **end**;
> $B[i] := B[i] + 1$;

(b)
> $i := 1$;
> **while** $A[i] \neq x$ **do**
> **begin** $i := i + 1$;
>   **if** $i > n$ **then begin** $n := i$; $A[i] := x$; $B[i] := 0$ **end**
> **end**;
> $B[i] := B[i] + 1$;

Solution (b) assumes that $n > 0$. Both solutions increase the amount of calculation that is specified: (a) tests "$i > n$" twice, while (b) tests "$A[i] \neq x$" after n has been increased.

The flowchart of the original program is:

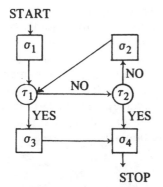

START

$\sigma_1 \equiv i := 1$

$\tau_1 \equiv i > n$?

$\tau_2 \equiv A[i] = x$?

$\sigma_2 \equiv i := i + 1$

$\sigma_3 \equiv n := i$; $A[i] := x$; $B[i] := 0$

$\sigma_4 \equiv B[i] := B[i] + 1$

STOP

By a suitable extension of BNF we can write a grammar for all flowcharts producible by a language without procedure calls or go to statements:

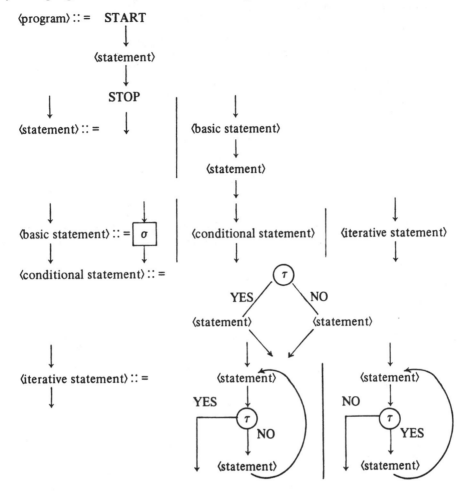

Here σ denotes a "statement" and τ denotes a "test."

We have not completely analyzed this grammar, although it appears to be unambiguous; there is probably an efficient parsing algorithm which will decide whether or not a given flowchart is derivable from the grammar, constructing a derivation when one exists. But we can easily prove that the above flowchart is *not* producible by this grammar. In fact, a stronger result is true:

> *Theorem.* No flowchart producible by the above grammar specifies precisely the computations of the above example flowchart (*).

This theorem contradicts our observations above about regular expressions being reducible to concatenation, alternation, and iteration; for our flowcharts provide each of these operations, yet they cannot reproduce the computations in (*). What went wrong? Perhaps it is that regular expressions are non-deterministic, while computations are inherently deterministic; but no, it is well known that regular expressions may be considered to be deterministic. The difference really lies in the nature of computational tests.

Thus, let us consider a special class R of regular expressions; R describes all computational sequences (paths in the flowchart) producible by flowcharts corresponding to a language without go to statements:

> the empty sequence is in R
>
> $\sigma \in R$, for all statements σ.
>
> $R_1 R_2 \in R$, for all R_1 and $R_2 \in R$.
>
> $(\tau_Y R_1 \mid \tau_N R_2)$, for all R_1 and $R_2 \in R$ and all tests τ.
>
> $(\tau_Y R_1)^* \tau_N \in R$, $(\tau_N R_1)^* \tau_Y \in R$, for all $R_1 \in R$ and all tests τ.

Here the subscripts Y and N denote the "YES" or "NO" branches in the flowchart.

To prove the theorem, consider the computational sequences producible by the flowchart (*); they may be described by the regular expression

$$\sigma_1(\tau_{1N}\tau_{2N}\sigma_2)^*(\tau_{1Y}\sigma_3 \mid \tau_{1N}\tau_{2Y})\sigma_4 . \qquad (**)$$

We will show that the corresponding regular event (the sequences defined by this regular expression) cannot be defined by any of the regular expressions in R. The following proof is due to J. Hopcroft.

Every regular expression $R \in R$ clearly has the property that τ_Y appears in some string of R if and only if τ_N appears in some string of R, for all tests τ. Since (**) contains strings with arbitrarily many occurrences of τ_{1N} separated by occurrences of τ_{2N}, it must contain a "star" construction including some regular $R \in R$ in which τ_{1N} or τ_{2N} appears. But R must also contain a string that includes τ_{1Y} or τ_{2Y}. Hence no regular expression in R can produce the regular event (**), and the theorem is proved.

Perhaps the reader feels that the above proof is too "slick," or that something has been concealed. In fact, this is quite true; we have penalized the class of flowcharts too severely! Compound tests such as "τ_1 and τ_2" have not been allowed sufficient latitude. Our flowchart grammar should be extended as follows: Replace

in the definitions of ⟨conditional statement⟩ and ⟨iterative statement⟩ by

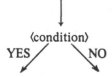

and add the new definition

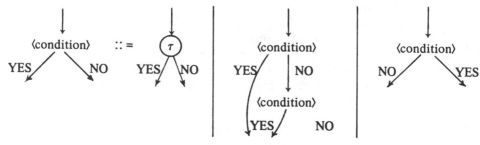

The grammar now becomes ambiguous in several cases, although the ambiguity can be removed at the expense of some complications which are irrelevant here. More important is the change to grammar R, where we are allowed to substitute

$$\tau'_Y \quad \text{for} \quad \tau_N, \qquad\qquad \tau'_N \quad \text{for} \quad \tau_Y$$

or

$$\tau'_N \tau''_N \quad \text{for} \quad \tau_N, \qquad (\tau'_Y | \tau'_N \tau''_Y) \quad \text{for} \quad \tau_Y$$

whenever τ, τ', τ'' are tests. Thus since $\sigma_1 (\tau_N \sigma_2)^* \tau_Y \sigma_4 \in R$, so is

$$\sigma_1 (\tau_{1N} \tau_{2N} \sigma_2)^* (\tau_{1Y} | \tau_{1N} \tau_{2Y}) \sigma_4 ,$$

and this is the same as (**) with σ_3 deleted. The theorem above is almost false! But we can still prove it by an exhaustive case analysis, considering all possible substitutions of compound tests and showing that none are permissible because of the presence of σ_3.

The theorem becomes almost false in another sense too, when compound conditions are considered, since the expression

$$\sigma_1 (\tau_{1N} \tau_{2N} \sigma_2)^* (\tau_{1Y} | \tau_{1N} \tau_{2Y})(\tau_{1Y} \sigma_3 | \tau_{1N}) \sigma_4$$

is in R and it differs from (**) only in that τ_{1Y} becomes $\tau_{1Y} \tau_{1Y}$ and $\tau_{1N} \tau_{2Y}$ becomes $\tau_{1N} \tau_{2Y} \tau_{1N}$. The sequences are essentially the same except that redundant tests are made. We could therefore consider equivalence operations on regular expressions, allowing commutativity of successive tests, and an idempotent law $\tau_Y \tau_Y = \tau_Y$. In that case our theorem would become false; but we can easily find another flowchart for which the theorem still applies: Simply put another statement box σ_5 between τ_1 and τ_2. Then no two tests are adjacent, and the original "slick" proof immediately shows that the regular event defined by

$$\sigma_1 (\tau_{1N} \sigma_5 \tau_{2N} \sigma_2)^* (\tau_{1Y} \sigma_3 | \tau_{1N} \sigma_5 \tau_{2Y}) \sigma_4$$

is not equivalent to any regular event definable with R. (When no two tests are adjacent, compound conditions cannot appear, nor do any of the equivalences apply, so none of the extensions affect the original proof of the theorem.)

Therefore, the "slick" proof is vindicated, and we have proved the existence of programs whose go to statements cannot be eliminated without introducing procedure calls. A somewhat stronger result has recently been obtained by Ashcroft and Manna [1].

Let us now consider a second example program, taken this time from a typical "backtracking" or exhaustive enumeration application. Most backtrack problems can be abstracted into the following form:

```
   start:  m[1]: = 0; k: = 0;
      up:  k: = k + 1; list(k); a[k]: = m[k];
     try:  if a[k] < m[k+1] then begin move(a[k]); go to up end;
    down:  k: = k − 1;
           if k = 0 then go to done;
           unmove(a[k]);
           a[k]: = a[k] + 1; go to try;
    done:
```

Here the procedures *list, move, unmove* may be regarded as manipulating a variable-width stack $s[0]$, $s[1]$, . . . of possible choices in this abstracted algorithm. Procedure *list(k)* determines all possible choices at the k-th level of backtracking, based on the previously made choices $a[1]$, . . ., $a[k−1]$. If there are c choices now possible, *list(k)* will set $m[k + 1] := m[k] + c$, and it will also set the stack entries $s[m[k] + 1], \ldots,$ $s[m[k] + c]$ to identify the choices. (Note that c can be zero. The choices might be, for example, where to place the k-th queen on a chessboard, given positions of $k-1$ other queens, if we are trying to solve the queens' problem.) Procedure *move* (t) makes the decision to choose alternative $s[t]$; this usually means that some internal tables need to be updated. Procedure *unmove* (t) reverses the decision made by *move* (t).

It is not necessary to understand the exact mechanism of this construction, although people familiar with backtracking should find the previous paragraph self-explanatory; the main point is that essentially all backtracking programs have the form of the above program, when appropriate sequences of code are substituted for *list* (k), *move* $(a[k])$, and *unmove* $(a[k])$, hence the program is worth considering from the standpoint of go to elimination.

First we can eliminate go to's by introducing a procedure:

```
procedure backtrack (k); value k; integer k;
  begin list (k); a[k] : = m[k];
    while a[k] < m[k + 1] do
      begin move (a [k]); backtrack (k + 1); unmove (a [k]);
        a[k] : = a[k] + 1
      end
    end backtrack;
  m[1] : = 0; backtrack (1);
```

This use of recursion is rather clean, so the above program is attractive except for the procedure-calling overhead (which is important since backtrack programs typically involve many millions of iterations). It is an interesting exercise to prove this program equivalent to our first version.

Now let's try to eliminate the go to statements without introducing a new procedure. The flowchart is:

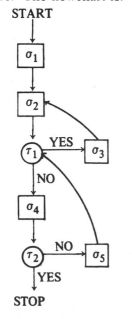

$\sigma_1 \equiv m[1] := 0; \ k := 0$

$\sigma_2 \equiv k := k + 1; \ list(k); a[k] := m[k]$

$\tau_1 \equiv a[k] < m[k + 1]$

$\sigma_3 \equiv move(a[k])$

$\sigma_4 \equiv k := k - 1$

$\tau_2 \equiv k = 0$

$\sigma_5 \equiv unmove(a[k]); a[k] := a[k] + 1$

Here we have the basic flowchart structure

instead of the previous situation when we had

It turns out that node-splitting works in this case but not the other; we can make two copies of node σ_2 in the above flowchart and we obtain

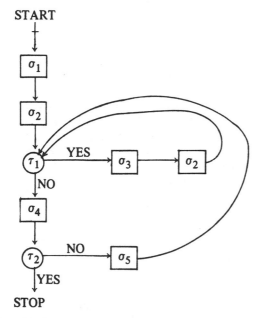

This diagram obviously satisfies the conditions of our flowchart grammar above, so we can avoid the go to statements.

What is the resulting program? Our flowchart grammar above allows more general iterative statements than present-day programming languages will admit. A general iterative construction might be written

      begin loop σ_1; **exit loop if** τ_1; σ_2 **end loop**;   (***)

but today's languages only consider the case that σ_1 is empty:

      while $\neg\,\tau_1$ **do** σ_2;

or if σ_2 is empty:

      do σ_1 **until** τ_1;

We can always rewrite (***) in the equivalent form

      σ_1; **while** $\neg\,\tau_1$ **do begin** σ_2; σ_1 *end*;

but this is quite unattractive when σ_1 is long, so a programmer will certainly prefer to use go to statements in that case. If we want to teach programmers to avoid go to statements, we must provide them with a sufficiently rich syntax of iterative statements to serve as a substitute.

Using (***) leads to the following program for backtracking without go to statements:

$m[1] := 0; k := 1; list(1); a[1] := 0;$

```
begin loop
   while a[k] < m[k + 1] do
      begin move(a[k]);
            k := k + 1; list(k); a[k] := m[k]
      end;
   k := k−1;
   exit loop if k = 0;
   unmove(a[k]); a[k] := a[k] + 1
end loop;
```

This code, although free of "go to statements," involves an uncomfortable element which may not make it very palatable: the "**while** $a[k] < m[k + 1]$" is a rather peculiar condition since k varies and the test involves different variables each time. This is quite different in effect from the appearance of the same clause in our recursive procedure *backtrack*(k). It is possible to think of the program in a fairly natural way nevertheless, for example (in tree language) as follows:

```
start at root of search tree;
begin loop
      while possible to go down and left in tree do so;
      move up one level in the tree;
exit loop if at the root;
      move to the right in the tree;
end loop;
```

this is a typical tree traversal algorithm.

The syntax in (***) is perhaps not the best way to improve iteration statements. An alternative proposal, based on some unpublished ideas of Wirth, has just been implemented as an extension to Stanford's ALGOL W compiler: The statement

   repeat ⟨block⟩

has the effect of

   L_1: ⟨block⟩; **go to** L_1; L_2:

and the statement

   exit

has the effect of

   go to L_2

where L_2 is the second implicit label corresponding to the smallest repeat block statically enclosing the *exit* statement. Thus, (***) becomes

   repeat begin σ_1; **if** τ_1 **then exit;** σ_2 **end;**

and we can even write our symbol table search routine without go to statements:

```
i := 1;
repeat begin
    while i ≤ n do if A[i] = x then exit else i := i + 1;
    n := i; A[i] := x; B[i] := 0; exit
end;
B[i] := B[i] + 1;
```

Here the "repeat loop" is never repeated, but the desired effect has been achieved. It appears doubtful that this repeat-exit mechanism will be able to eliminate go to statements in general, since it only allows a "one-level exit"; further study of these issues is indicated.

In this paper we have considered only transformations of the program which avoid go to statements, without introducing new variables or changing the sequence of computations and tests. Böhm and Jacopini [2] and Cooper [3] have observed that additional Boolean variables can be added in such a way that the program structure becomes very trivial and go to's are obviously unnecessary; but in fact, as Cooper has observed, these Boolean variables essentially simulate a program counter and they contribute nothing to the clarity of the program. Ashcroft and Manna [1] have recently found a more meaningful way to introduce variables into programs so that go to's can be omitted without changing the program's "topology."

References: Knuth & Floyd

1. E. Ashcroft and Z. Manna, "The Translation of GO TO Programs into WHILE Programs," Computer Science Department Report CS 188 (Stanford University, January 1971).

2. C. Böhm and G. Jacopini, "Flow Diagrams, Turing Machines and Languages with Only Two Formation Rules," *Comm. ACM,* 9 (1966), pp. 366-371.

3. D.C. Cooper, "Böhm and Jacopini's Reduction of Flow Charts," *Comm. ACM,* 10 (1967), pp. 463, 473.

4. E.W. Dijkstra, "GO TO Statement Considered Harmful," *Comm. ACM,* 11 (1968), pp. 147-148.

5. D.V. Schorre, "Improved Organization for Procedural Languages," System Development Corp. Techn. Memo 3086/022/00 (August 6, 1966).

Better Manpower Utilization Using Automatic Restructuring

Introduction

Our intent is to introduce the concept of automatic restructuring as a powerful method for improving the quality of software developed before the advent of structured programming. The quality improvements we are concerned with are neither execution time efficiency nor core size requirements but, rather, higher readability and clear structured code. These, in turn, should improve the reliability and reduce the maintenance costs by making human verification more efficient.

The fact that arbitrary flow diagrams can be mapped into equivalent structured flow diagrams by introducing new Boolean variables has been established by Böhm and Jacopini [2] (see Reference 1 for an example of a program that cannot be restructured without additional Boolean variables). The first steps toward systematizing this mapping are taken in Reference 9.

In practice, however, we have found that adding Boolean variables (whose names are meaningless since they would have to be program generated) makes the code often harder to read. Thus Dijkstra's comment [4] that "the exercise to translate an arbitrary flow diagram more or less mechanically into a jumpless one is not to be recommended" because "the resulting flow diagram cannot be expected to be more transparent than the original one."

On the other hand, if we allow certain constrained forms of the GO TO statement, many of the difficulties vanish and readability can be enhanced. One form of the constrained GO TO, which we call UNDO, is used to exit from nested structures when necessary, the jump always being a forward jump to the end of a DO group. This is similar to the LEAVE statement in BLISS [10].

SOURCE: G. DeBalbine, *AFIPS Proceedings of the 1975 National Computer Conference*, 1975.

Figure 1 shows an example derived from Reference 1. With the UNDO construct, a natural straightforward representation can be obtained.

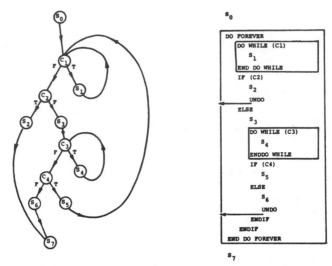

Figure 1. Example of UNDO usage.

Based on the hypothesis that the restructuring process could be applied systematically to existing unstructured programs and enhance their clarity, we have designed and implemented a software tool known as the "structuring engine." We shall now describe in more detail some of our motivations and the experimental results that we have obtained while using the "structuring engine."

Improving the human ⟷ software interface

Most production software in existence today was developed using no precise design methodology. The programming languages generally used (FORTRAN, COBOL) were invented over a decade ago and have hardly evolved due to the severe binds imposed by upward compatibility. Maintaining and extending the huge software inventory is a difficult and inefficient task which is becoming even more so year by year. The software documentation is poor, the logic is often obscure, and the authors are most likely to be gone or assigned to other projects. Operational programs still break down with bugs that have managed to escape the most careful scrutiny. Modifications and extensions are dreaded and postponed since they are likely to cause perturbations whose far ranging effects cannot be easily and reliably assessed.

We do not claim to have a panacea that can cure all of these problems instantly. However, the experience gained while developing large scale software using structured programming has shown some of the important factors that influence software reliability and maintenance costs. In our experience, the quality of the human ⟷ software interface is one such factor since it influences the efficiency of all manhours invested at the program level, both during development and maintenance.

To benefit from a better human ⟷ software interface applicable to future software development, as well as to current software, we suggest extending commonly available programming languages, imposing some constraints to ensure proper language usage, emphasizing the need for visual improvement of programs, and providing transitional tools to assist in the conversion of existing software to meet the new interface specifications.

Language extensions

The only precise, and by definition up-to-date, source of internal documentation for most software in existence today lies in the programs themselves. Understanding what programs accomplish implies an understanding in the formalism and at the level of detail imposed by the programming language used as a vehicle for implementation. Thus, any shortcomings of the implementation language have a direct impact on the effort needed to understand what the programs do and to modify and extend them successfully.

The two most widespread programming languages, FORTRAN and COBOL, do not contain adequate mechanisms to support structured coding. The limited facilities they provide can be exploited very cleverly to look somewhat like structured code. However, a substantial effort is needed to maintain proper indentation and the legibility is never as good as that obtainable with a structured language.

The obvious step is to build preprocessors to provide the necessary syntactic extensions and perform some of the manual chores such as automatic indentation. Several dozen preprocessors have already been built to translate various brands of structured FORTRAN into pure FORTRAN [7]. Our effort along these lines has led to the design and implementation of the S-FORTRAN language and translator. S-FORTRAN embodies a small but powerful set of structured constructs. S-FORTRAN was designed to serve both as a target language for restructured programs and as an implementation language for new programs. It is not only simple but easy to remember unambiguously. The S-FORTRAN language is succinctly described in the Appendix.

We do not wish at this point to discuss at length the individual merits of each S-FORTRAN feature and whether LOOP is a better term than DO FOREVER or should DO UNTIL test first rather than execute first. These decisions are mostly conventions. Let us simply express the hope that a consensus will soon develop so that a ''de facto'' standard will prevail. Structured FORTRAN programs will then be unambiguously understood by all.

Language usage

Providing extended languages to permit structured coding is not sufficient to guarantee software clarity. Programmers can still misuse structured languages to follow their traditional thought processes, the result being obscure programs under the guise of structured code.

Rather than resort to building enforcement tools, it is our belief that the simplicity and intellectual appeal of a well formed program will generate the necessary motivation among programmers to adopt a new standard of quality.

Visual improvement

Structured coding techniques require that programs be systematically indented to stress the relationships between code segments. This hierarchical arrangement allows a quick grasp of the global as well as the local structure of the code. Understanding the code no longer requires keeping track of many scattered items such as labels and transfers. Rather, it means perceiving visual patterns that can be precisely mapped into our analytical understanding of the solution. Each part and subpart corresponds to a block of code, carefully delimited to facilitate its verification. Systematic indentation makes it easy to collect the conditions controlling the execution of each indentation level down to the code segment being examined.

The power of visual perception can be readily tapped by developing patterns whenever feasible. Symmetry, lack of symmetry, block indentation, regularity, recurring patterns, aligned similar items, . . . are characteristics that can be detected at a glance by the eye. Interestingly enough, these are characteristics whose global nature is usually hard to detect and utilize automatically with software tools.

How to benefit from the new interface

Formulating a better human ↔ software interface is clearly valuable for software that has not yet been written. The important point is that such an improvement can also be applied to a large part of the software inventory in existence today. It is our belief that this should lead to a significant reduction in the maintenance effort by better utilizing the available manpower.

Until very recently, the main route for modernizing existing unstructured software was to start over with a clean top-down design and structured implementation. Needless to say, such complete manual reprogramming should not be undertaken without a very careful evaluation of the potential gain versus the effort involved. We have found that the major obstacles to manual reprogramming are the need for top talent during the redesign phase, the manpower expenditure, the elapsed time before a new system is up and running and the penalty for having to go through a full testing and debugging period again.

As an alternative, we have developed a method which is much easier to apply in practice. It consists in keeping the global design as is, in particular the data structures, and in automatically transforming every program into an equivalent structured program, visually improved to make its reading easier and its understanding more thorough. This method is supported by a software tool known as the "structuring engine." We have applied this tool to a variety of FORTRAN programs. We shall now describe the characteristics of the tool and some of the experimental results that we have obtained so far.

The "structuring engine"

Capabilities

The "structuring engine," as it now exists, is a large task running on an IBM/370 under VS. It consists of over 30,000 lines of structured PL/I code. It will restructure programs written in FORTRAN including any language extensions acceptable by IBM, Univac, CDC and Honeywell compilers.

Each program or subprogram is restructured independently. The complete flow graph of each program or subprogram is analyzed to determine the best strategy for obtaining a well structured program. Machine dependencies are taken into account when building the flow graph because the interpretation of some statements depends on the particular compiler that the program was intended for. For instance, values outside the range of a computed GO TO can be handled in three distinct ways depending upon the particular compiler implementation. Such variations are taken into account by the "structuring engine" which generates the necessary statements to guarantee consistency in the restructured output.

In general, the restructured programs will bear little resemblance to the original unstructured ones, particularly if the logic was complex and somewhat twisted to start with. In the output, the logic flows from top to bottom, from the single entry to the single exit.

Figure 2 is an example of a simple program before and after restructuring. Similarly, Figure 3 shows what happens in the case of a heavily folded program.

```
CFG. INC.          PROGRAM                              18:03:30     01 DEC 74          PAGE   1
                                                    FORTRAN PROGRAM INPUT
----------------------------------------------------------------------------------------------
          LINE
         NUMBER                                     INPUT FORTRAN STATEMENT

           1        C******************** M S I N C    12 ***********************************
           2              SUBROUTINE FORIT (FNT,N,M,A,B)
           3              IMPLICIT REAL*8 (A-H,O-Z)
           4        C
           5              DIMENSION FNT(1),A(M),B(M)
           6        C
           7        C     ... SET CONSTANTS
           8              COEF=1.0/(N+0.5)
           9              CONST=3.141593*COEF
          10              S1=DSIN(CONST)
          11              C1=DCOS(CONST)
          12              C=1.0
          13              S=0.0
          14              FNTZ=FNT(1)
          15              J=1
          16              M1=M+1
          17              N2=N+N+1
          18        C
          19        C     ... COMPUTE FOURIER COEFFICIENTS RECURSIVELY
          20           70 U2=0.0
          21              U1=0.0
          22              I=N2
          23           75 U0=FNT(I)+2.0*C*U1-U2
          24              U2=U1
          25              U1=U0
          26              I=I-1
          27              IF (I-1) 80,80,75
          28           80 A(J)=COEF*(FNTZ+C*U1-U2)
          29              B(J)=COEF*S*U1
          30              IF (J-M1) 90,100,100
          31           90 Q=C1*C-S1*S
          32              S=C1*S+S1*C
          33              C=Q
          34              J=J+1
          35              GO TO 70
          36          100 A(1)=A(1)*0.5
          37              RETURN
          38              END
```

```
CFG. INC.          PROGRAM  FORIT                    18:03:30     01 DEC 74          PAGE  13
                                               STRUCTURED SFORTRAN PROGRAM
----------------------------------------------------------------------------------------------
CORRESPONDING   LINE
FORTRAN LINE    NUMBER                         OUTPUT SFORTRAN STATEMENT

                   1     C     ************************* FORIT    ENTRY *************************
----------------------------------------------------------------------------------------------
                   2     C******************** M S I N C    12 ***********************************
       2           3           SUBROUTINE FORIT (FNT,N,M,A,B)
       3           4                 IMPLICIT REAL*8 (A-H,O-Z)
                   5     C
       5           6                 DIMENSION FNT(1),A(M),B(M)
----------------------------------------------------------------------------------------------
                   7     C     ************************** LOGIC START **************************

                   8     C
                   9     C                                               ... SET CONSTANTS
       8          10                 COEF=1.0/(N+0.5)
       9          11                 CONST=3.141593*COEF
      10          12                 S1=DSIN(CONST)
      11          13                 C1=DCOS(CONST)
      12          14                 C=1.0
      13          15                 S=0.0
      14          16                 FNTZ=FNT(1)
      15          17                 J=1
      16          18                 M1=M+1
      17          19                 N2=N+N+1
                  20                 EXECUTE (AFR PROCEDURE001)

                                     ------------------------------------------------------------
                                     I                                                          I
      30          21                 IDO WHILE ((J-M1) .LT. 0)                                  I
      31          22                 I    Q=C1*C-S1*S                                           I
      32          23                 I    S=C1*S+S1*C                                           I
      33          24                 I    C=Q                                                   I
      34          25                 I    J=J+1                                                 I
                  26                 I    EXECUTE (AFR PROCEDURE001)                            I
                  27                 IEND DO WHILE                                              I
                                     I-----------------------------------------------------------

      36          28                 A(1)=A(1)*0.5
      37          29                 RETURN
                         <--------
----------------------------------------------------------------------------------------------

                  30     C     ****************** AFR PROCEDURE001 PROCEDURE ********************
----------------------------------------------------------------------------------------------
                  31           PROCEDURE (AFR PROCEDURE001)
                  32     C
                  33     C                         ... COMPUTE FOURIER COEFFICIENTS RECURSIVELY
      20          34                 U2=0.0
      21          35                 U1=0.0
      22          36                 I=N2
                                     ------------------------------------------------------------
                                     I                                                          I
      27          37                 IDO UNTIL ((I-1) .LE. 0)                                   I
      23          38                 I    U0=FNT(I)+2.0*C*U1-U2                                 I
      24          39                 I    U2=U1                                                 I
      25          40                 I    U1=U0                                                 I
      26          41                 I    I=I-1                                                 I
                  42                 IEND DO UNTIL                                              I
                                     I-----------------------------------------------------------

      28          43                 A(J)=COEF*(FNTZ+C*U1-U2)
      29          44                 B(J)=COEF*S*U1
                  45           END PROCEDURE

                  46     C     *********************** FORMAT STATEMENTS ***********************
----------------------------------------------------------------------------------------------
                  47     C     ************************ END PROGRAM UNIT ***********************

                  48           END
----------------------------------------------------------------------------------------------

                                          PROCEDURE CROSS_REFERENCE TABLE
----------------------------------------------------------------------------------------------
PROCEDURE                            LOCATION   REFERENCES

AFR PROCEDURE001                        31          20     26
```

Figure 2. Sample program FORIT before and after restructuring.

The restructured programs are equivalent to those from which they are derived in the sense that they behave identically at run time. That is, they carry out the same sequence of operations on the data structures, great care being taken that the ordering of operations not be modified. For instance, a three way arithmetic IF cannot be simply converted into two nested S-FORTRAN IF statements because the arithmetic expression would then be evaluated twice.

```
CFG, INC.        PROGRAM                         03:56:54     31 JAN 75        PAGE   1
                                       FORTRAN PROGRAM INPUT
   LINE
  NUMBER                               INPUT FORTRAN STATEMENT

      C....... REF: LSTAT         ALIAS  URDB
      C******* ELEMENT NAME:ORDB                            ***************************
            INTEGER FUNCTION LSTAT(LINE,FLAG)
            IMPLICIT INTEGER (A-Y)
            DATA NIV/5/
            COMMON/ARRAY/C,LINOWN,CL:ARD(80),PICTUR(1320),BUFFER(15,200)
            COMMON/DEBUG/DEBUG
            COMMON /EFNARR/LENGTH,NREF,REFMAX,MAXLIN,EFNLIS(1567),CREF(3000)
            COMMON/RANGE/K1,K2
            LOGICAL FLAG
            L=LINE
            TARGET=LINE
            SWITCH=1
         65 KOUNT=1
         70 L=MOD(L   -1,LENGTH)+1
            LINOLD=FLD(0,18,EFNLIS(L))
            IF (LINOLD.EQ.TARGET)GO TO(115,180,140,150),SWITCH
            IF (LINOLD.EQ.0)GU TJ 255
            IF (KOUNT.EQ.LENGTH)GU TO 255
            IF (KOUNT.EQ.1)LINC=MJD(L-1,LENGTH-1)+1
            L=L+LINC
            KOUNT=KOUNT+1
            GO TO 70
        115 LINEW=FLD(18,18,EFNLIS(L))
            LTEMP=K1*LINEW+K2
      C   FLAG IS TRUE IF LINE IS A STATEMENT EFN
      C           FALSE IF LINE IS A REFERENCE TO AN EFN
            IF (FLAG.OR.NREF.LT.0)GO TO 260
      C   BUILD CROSS REF LIST
            IF (NREF.EQ.REFMAX)GO TO 235
            IF (LINOWN.GE.MAXLIN)GO TO 195
      C   OLD EFN FOR CURRENT LINE IS LINOWN
            IF (SWITCH.LT.4)SWITCH=SWITCH+1
            TARGET=LINOWN
            L=LINOWN
            GO TO 65
        180 CURLIN=FLD(18,18,EFNLIS(L))
            CURNEW=K1*CURLIN+K2
            GO TO 200
        195 CURNEW=K1*(LINOWN-MAXLIN)+K2
        200 NREF=NREF+1
            FLD(0,18,CREF(NREF)) =LTEMP
            FLD(18,18,CREF(NREF))=CURNEW
            IF(DEBUG.GT.NIV)PRINT 220,NIV,LTEMP,CURNEW,NREF,CREF(NREF)
        220 FORMAT(' NIV',I3,': ORDB LTEMP=',I5,' CURNEW=',I5,
           1' CREF(',I4,')=',O12)
            GO TO 260
        235 PRINT 240
        240 FORMAT(1X,10(1H*),28H CROSS REFERENCE TABLE FULL ,90(1H*))
            NREF=-NREF
            GO TO 260
        140 CURNEW=CURLIN+K2
            GO TO 200
        150 CURLIN=FLD(18,18,EFNLIS(L))
            GO TO 140
        255 LTEMP=0
        260 LSTAT=LTEMP
            IF(DEBUG.GT.NIV)PRINT 270,NIV,LINE,FLAG,LTEMP
        270 FORMAT(' NIV',I3,': ORDB LINE=',I5,' FLAG=',L1,' LSTAT=',I5)
            RETURN
            END
```

Figure 3. Sample program ORDB unstructured (Part I).

In that case, incorrect results might be obtained if the arithmetic expression contains calls to abnormal functions, i.e., functions which do not always produce the same results from a given set of inputs.

One of the basic processes used in restructuring is known as node splitting. If a node of the subgraph can be reached from two different paths that must be separated, the node is split into two identical nodes so that each path can have its own copy of the node.

If the node splitting operations were carried out indiscriminately, the resulting S-FORTRAN programs would often become so large as to be virtually useless. Not only would clarity be lost but the object program would be likely not to fit in the target machine. To circumvent that difficulty, the "structuring engine" tries recognizing proper subgraphs that can be turned into procedures instead of being duplicated in line.

```
CFG, INC.        PROGRAM LSTAT                    03:56:54   31 JAN 75      PAGE  3
                                     STRUCTURED SFORTRAN PROGRAM

INPUT   OUTPUT   NEST
LINE    LINE     LEVEL                            OUTPUT SFORTRAN STATEMENT

          1       C   ****************** LSTAT    ENTRY ******************
          2       C....... REF: LSTAT        ALIAS  ORDB
          3       C....... ELEMENT NAME:ORDB                    ******************
 3        4           INTEGER FUNCTION LSTAT(LINE,FLAG)
 4        5           IMPLICIT INTEGER (A-Y)
 5        6           DATA NIV/5/
 6        7           COMMON /ARRAY/L,LINNUM,LLCARD(80),PICTUR(1320),BUFFER(15,230)
 7        8           COMMON /DEBUG/DEBUG
 8        9           COMMON /EFNARR/LENGTH,NREF,REFMAX,MAXLIN,EFNLIS(1567),CREF(
          10        1         3000)
 9        11          COMMON /RANGE/K1,K2
10        12          LOGICAL FLAG

          13      C   ****************** LOGIC START ******************

11        14          L=LINE
12        15          TARGET=LINE
13        16          SWITCH=1
14        17          KOUNT=1

                  18  18  DO FOREVER
15        19       1      L=MOD(L -1,LENGTH)+1
16        20       1      LINULD=FLD(0,16,EFNLIS(L))
17        21       1      IF (LINULD.NE.TARGET)
18        22       2         IF (LINULD.EQ.0)
56        23       3            LTEMP=0
          24       3         UNDO 18

19        25       2      ELSEIF (KOUNT.EQ.LENGTH)
56        26       3         LTEMP=0
          27       3         UNDO 18

          28       2      END IF
          29       2      EXECUTE (AFR PROCEDURE002)
          30       1      ELSE

                             DO CASE SWITCH
17        31       2

                                CASE 1
32        3                       LINE=FLD(16,16,EFNLIS(L))
24        33       4              LTEMP=K1*LINE+K2
25        34       4              FLAG IS TRUE IF LINE IS A STATEMENT EFN
          35       4   C          FALSE IF LINE IS A REFERENCE TO AN EFN
          36       4   C          IF (FLAG.OR.NREF.LT.0)
28        37       4              UNDO 18
          38       5

                                                 BUILD CROSS REF LIST
          39       4   C
30        40       4              ELSEIF (NREF.EQ.REFMAX)
48        41       4                 PRINT 9002U
50        42       5                 NREF=-NREF
          43       5              UNDO 18

31        44       4              ELSEIF (LINOWN.GE.MAXLIN)
40        45       4                 CURNEW=K1*(LINOWN-MAXLIN)+K2
          46       5                 EXECUTE (AFR PROCEDURE001)
          47       5              UNDO 18

          48       4              END IF
          49       4   C                    OLD EFN FOR CURRENT LINE IS LINOWN
33        50       4              IF (SWITCH.LT.4)
33        51       5                 SWITCH=SWITCH+1
          52       5              END IF
34        53       4              TARGET=LINOWN
35        54       4              L=LINOWN
14        55       4              KOUNT=1

                                CASE 2
37        56       3              CURLIN=FLD(16,16,EFNLIS(L))
38        57       4              CURNEW=K1*CURLIN+K2
          58       4              EXECUTE (AFR PROCEDURE001)
          59       4              UNDO 18
          60       4

                                CASE 3
52        61       3              CURNEW=CURLIN+K2
62        4              EXECUTE (AFR PROCEDURE001)
63        4              UNDO 18
64        4

                                CASE 4
54        65       3              CURLIN=FLD(16,16,EFNLIS(L))
52        66       4              CURNEW=CURLIN+K2
67        4              EXECUTE (AFR PROCEDURE001)
68        4              UNDO 18
69        4

                                CASE OTHER
18        70       3              IF (LINULD.EQ.0)
56        71       4                 LTEMP=0
72        5              UNDO 18
73        5

19        74       4              ELSEIF (KOUNT.EQ.LENGTH)
56        75       5                 LTEMP=0
76        5              UNDO 18

          77       4              END IF
78        4              EXECUTE (AFR PROCEDURE002)
79        2              END DO CASE

          80       1      END IF
81          END DO FOREVER

57        82          LSTAT=LTEMP
58        83          IF (DEBUG.GT.NIV)
59        84       1      PRINT 9003U, NIV,LINE,FLAG,LTEMP
          85          END IF
60        86          RETURN
```

Figure 3. Sample program ORDB restructured (Parts II and III).

A procedure is simply a section of code with one entry and one exit. This concept corresponds to the PERFORMed group in COBOL, but with additional constraints to guarantee a clean invocation and a clean return. Once a procedure has been extracted and given a name, it can be referenced from many locations within the restructured program, including from other procedures. The example in Figure 2 contains one procedure, the one in Figure 3 contains two. The decision whether to expand code in line or create procedures can be externally controlled using a threshold which indicates how complex a subgraph must be before it becomes a procedure. Procedures are not separate subprograms. Rather, they are segments of code that can be executed from various locations within a particular program or subprogram. The EXECUTE command hides the ASSIGNed GO TO linkage that a FORTRAN programmer would have to set up otherwise.

To visually improve the resulting code, every statement is laid out according to its logical indentation level. This stresses its relationship with other statements in the same program unit. A box is built around each complete DO group to enhance the scope of the DO statements. Statements such as UNDO, CYCLE, and RETURN are followed by an arrow that attracts the attention of the reader and shows him immediately what implications these statements have on the logic flow. Consecutive comment cards are right adjusted by block in order to make them as unobtrusive as possible.

Of course, if the modules to be restructured contain logic errors, the same errors will be found in the structured output. In general, the "structuring engine" is incapable of detecting errors except for some obvious language violations. The input programs are supposed to have compiled correctly so that the errors we are really trying to eliminate are errors in the logic that cannot be identified without an intimate understanding of the problem. Only a programmer aware of the problem being solved can discover and correct these errors.

Emphasis in building the "structuring engine" has been on reliability rather than efficiency. This has been achieved through a combination of structured design techniques, self identifiable data structures and dynamic assertion verification at run time, i.e., the constant verification that the assumptions underlying the design are never violated during production runs.

Figure 3. Continued.

Experimental results

We are currently applying the "structuring engine" to a wide variety of unstructured FORTRAN code. Although our analysis is far from complete, we would like to comment on some of the experimental results that we have obtained so far.

Clarity of the restructured programs

A reliable assessment of clarity improvements is obviously quite difficult to obtain until we get some figures on maintenance costs. The familiarity of the end user with structured code is a factor as noted in Reference 6. The cleverness of the "structuring engine" in making the right choices is obviously another important factor since there are not one but many solutions to the restructuring problem. So far, we have found that:

- the majority of the programs (about 90 percent) will come out extremely clear, at least in our opinion and in that of end users that have worked with restructured programs.

- the rest (about 10 percent) will either remain complex or become lengthy or both. In this group, we find a number of programs that could be handled more cleverly by the "structuring engine" and, therefore, move into the above category. We are obviously building the necessary improvements into the "structuring engine." Still, there are some programs that will probably never look very good. They are ill-designed. The problem that they are supposed to solve should be reexamined and a complete redesign and reprogramming of these programs may be necessary.

Execution characteristics of the restructured programs

Let us now try to answer some of the most common questions regarding this automatic restructuring process. What price do we pay for the improved clarity of the restructured programs? In particular, how do the restructured programs execute compared to the original ones?

To answer these questions, we must first examine the various components in the processing chain as shown in Figure 4. The "structuring engine" transforms unstructured FORTRAN into structured S-FORTRAN. The resulting S-FORTRAN programs are then translated back into FORTRAN using the S-FORTRAN to FORTRAN translator. At that point, we have pure FORTRAN source code again which can be compiled, loaded and executed. Thus, the characteristics that we are reporting on involve not only the "structuring engine" but also the translator and a compiler.

The core size of the object modules produced from the restructured programs has been found to always be larger than that of the original modules, typically by about 20 percent.

We know from Reference 9 that arbitrary programs cannot be restructured without increasing their running time or their core size. In the present case, we have chosen to accept a limited increase in memory size. The creation of internal procedures is our method for preventing a program from growing beyond an acceptable point.

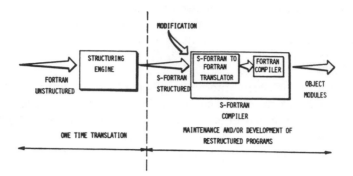

Figure 4. The restructuring chain.

Figure 5 shows a typical distribution of core size expansion ratios (1 would mean no increase) as a function of the size of the object module for the unstructured program when compiled with IBM's FORTRAN G compiler. The circled data point corresponds to a program that the "structuring engine" could not structure without producing three times as many S-FORTRAN cards as there were FORTRAN cards. This "abnormal" expansion factor was caused by a deeply nested section of code that could not be turned into procedure because it would then have contained an UNDO outside its scope. Such an UNDO outside the scope of a procedure is not permitted in S-FORTRAN. Consequently, the same section of code was duplicated 18 times throughout the program.

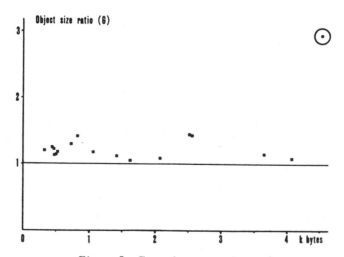

Figure 5. Core size expansion ratios.

Data on the execution speed of the restructured programs has been harder to get because most of the programs we have restructured so far were components of much larger systems which we could not run ourselves. Preliminary results show that we should expect slight variations in the running time with a trend toward a reduction rather than an increase. This may seem paradoxical at first but can be explained as follows.

There are two major factors that influence the running time in opposite ways:

(i) the size of the basic block: the restructuring process cannot decrease the average size of the basic block and in general will increase it. Thus, an optimizing compiler should generate better code within each basic block of the restructured programs.

(ii) the control flow statements produced by the translator to support branching, looping and procedure referencing: These require, in general, more instructions than are needed to implement the original control logic.

The first factor tends to make restructured programs run faster whereas the latter tends to slow them down. This means that with a translator generating very good code we should be able to have programs run faster restructured than unstructured. In fact, we have now built more sophistication into the translator than had been originally planned in order to make full use of the capabilities of optimizing compilers. For instance, with IBM's FORTRAN H (OPT=2) compiler, changes in the translation of IF statements have reduced in one instance the core size by 12 percent and the running time by 8 percent when compared with earlier versions of the translator.

Conclusions

Automatic restructuring as implemented by the "structuring engine" is proposed as a method to modernize existing programs. It should prove much more practical than manual reprogramming, particularly with regards to manpower requirements, conversion time and the reliability of the conversion process itself.

Manpower requirements are reduced since no major human effort is invested redoing what already exists. On the contrary, programmer time is devoted to perusing restructured programs, implementing improvements wherever deficiencies show up, and correcting errors. In particular, any program which still appears to be overly complex after restructuring compared to what it is supposed to accomplish, becomes a good candidate for an in-depth investigation of the reasons underlying its apparent complexity. Poor algorithms may be pinned down fast and replaced accordingly. The overall result is that the programmer understands the structured code more rapidly and can, therefore, allocate more time to difficult areas. Consequently, his error detection rate increases, thus justifying our claim to improved software reliability.

Conversion time is negligible compared to that required for manual reprogramming. In particular, the project's clock is not set back since the restructuring process does not introduce any new errors.

Of course, there may still be cases where complete redesign and reprogramming appear to be absolutely necessary. Under those circumstances, the "structuring engine" can still play an important role. Indeed, no matter how unstructured and clumsy the original software may be, it represents an approximate solution to the problem, correct in most if not all of the cases. As such, it acts as a repository for a wealth of details that were added throughout the life cycle of the software to handle unusual and certainly unforeseen cases. Starting from this rich data, the "structuring engine" becomes a very valuable tool since it produces an up-to-date structured picture of the solution currently implemented. This picture may then be used to base a thorough evaluation of the status of the project, including any needs for manual redesign and reprogramming.

Appendix

The main characteristics of S-FORTRAN are:

(a)   S-FORTRAN is a superset of FORTRAN (including the FORTRAN language extensions provided by various manufacturers).

(b)   Any construct with a scope has both an opening and a closing delimiter. If the opening statement is XXX, the ending statement is of the form END XXX (e.g., IF . . . END IF, DO WHILE . . . END DO WHILE).

(c)   The IF includes any number of ELSEIF clauses and an optional ELSE clause. ELSEIF's are often convenient to prevent very deep indentation levels (and the so-called "wall to wall" ENDIF's).

(d)   *Repetitive DO groups* include a DO FOR analogous to the FORTRAN DO loop, a DO WHILE, a DO UNTIL (which is in fact a DO AT LEAST ONCE UNTIL), and a DO FOREVER (any infinite loop).

(e)   *Non repetitive DO groups* include a DO for bracketing statements, a powerful DO CASE, a DO CASE SIGN OF which is the equivalent of a three way arithmetic IF, and a DO LABEL to handle abnormal returns from subroutines and functions and end and error exits from I/O statements.

(f)   UNDO is a mechanism to exit from a DO group prematurely. We have found this multilevel exit mechanism to be superior to introducing switch variables which tend to clutter the program and make its logic harder to follow. UNDO is applicable to any DO group, repetitive or not. It can be followed by a label if another DO group besides the innermost one is to be exited from.

(g)   CYCLE is similar to UNDO but implies skipping any statement until the closing delimiter of a DO group is found. The test controlling the repeated execution of the DO group is then performed to determine whether to exit or repeat. CYCLE is only applicable to repetitive-DO groups.

(h)   Internal parameterless procedures can be defined using PROCEDURE . . . END PROCEDURE. Their execution can only be triggered by an EXECUTE (proc-name) statement. Premature termination of a procedure can be accomplished by an EXIT statement. Procedures share the same data space as the program in which they are contained.

References: DeBalbine

1. Ashcroft, E.A., and Z. Manna, "The Translation of 'GOTO' Programs to 'WHILE' Programs," *Proc. IFIP Congress 71,* Ljubljana, Aug. 1971.

2. Böhm, C., and G. Jacopini, "Flow Diagrams, Turing Machines and Languages with Only Two Formation Rules," *Comm. ACM,* May 1966, pp. 366-371.

3. Caine, S.H., *Reference Guide to the XXX Language,* CFG 708-001, Feb. 1971.

4. Dijkstra, E.W., "GO TO Statements Considered Harmful," *Comm. ACM,* March 1968, pp. 147-148.

5. Donaldson, J.R., "Structured Programming," *Datamation,* Dec. 1973, pp. 52-54.

6. Holmes, C.E., and L.W. Miller, "Chief Programmer Experience," *GUIDE 37,* Nov. 1973.

7. Miller, E.F., *Extensions to FORTRAN and Structured Programming — An Experiment,* General Research Corp., RM-1608, Feb. 1972.

8. Mills, H.D., "On the Development of Large Reliable Programs," *IEEE Symp. Computer Software Reliability,* 1973, pp. 155-159.

9. Peterson, W.W., T. Kasami and N. Tokura, "On the Capabilities of WHILE, RE-PEAT, and EXIT Statements," *Comm. ACM,* Aug. 1973, pp. 503-512.

10. Wulf, W.A., "A case against the GO TO," *SIGPLAN Notices,* Nov. 1972, pp. 63-69.

PDL — A Tool
for Software
Design

Introduction

During the past several years, industry has seen an explosion in the cost of software production coupled with a decline in the quality and reliability of the results. A realization that structured programming, top-down design, and other changes in techniques can help has alerted the field to the importance of applying advanced design and programming methods to software production [1, 2].

For the past four years, Caine, Farber & Gordon, Inc. has used such advanced techniques as structured programming, top-down design and system implementation, centralized program production libraries, and egoless programming teams for all of its programming [3−8]. With these techniques we have achieved a level of productivity comparable to that recently reported by others employing similar techniques.

However, within the last year, we greatly refined these techniques, applying them to design as well as to programming. This has resulted in increased productivity, greatly decreased debugging effort, and clearly superior products. On recent complex projects we have achieved production rates, over the full development cycle, of 60-65 lines of finished code per man-day and computer utilization of less than 0.25 CPU hours per thousand lines of finished code. For comparison, these production rates are approximately half again better than our best efforts using just structured programming techniques and 4-6 times better than average industrial experience using classical techniques. Computer usage was four times smaller than our experience with just structured programming techniques and more than 10 times smaller than classical industrial averages.

As an example, consider the two CFG projects shown in Table 1. Project "A" is a major component of a seismic data

SOURCE: S.H. Caine & E.K. Gordon, *AFIPS Proceedings of the 1975 National Computer Conference*, 1975.

processing system for oil exploration. It was produced using "classical" structured programming techniques and production rates compare favorably to other projects [3] which used similar techniques. Project "B" is a system for the automatic restructuring of Fortran programs [9]. It was developed using the latest CFG methods. Production rates were 50 percent better than for project "A" and the amount of computer time used in development was approximately one quarter of that used for the first project. In each case, a "line" of code was taken to be one 80-column source card with common data definitions counted only once. Both projects were developed using an IBM 370/158.

Table 1
Production Comparisons

	PROJECT "A"	PROJECT "B"
DEVELOPMENT METHOD	CLASSICAL STRUCTURED	LATEST CFG
PROGRAMMING LANGUAGE	PL/I DIALECT	PL/I
SIZE OF PROGRAM (LINES)	32,000	27,000
SIZE OF TEAM	3−6	3−5
ELAPSED TIME (MONTHS)	9	6
LINES PER MAN-DAY	40	65
CPU HOURS PER 1000 LINES (IBM 370/158)	0.90	0.16

In order to achieve the results that we are currently experiencing, we have developed a comprehensive software production methodology which places its greatest emphasis on design. Before *any* code is written, a complete design is produced which contains:

- all external and internal interface definitions
- definitions of all error situations
- identification of all procedures
- identification of all procedure calls
- definition of all global data
- definition of all control blocks
- specification of the processing algorithms of all procedures

The design is produced and presented top-down and is oriented toward understandability by people. While in no sense is our design process automated, it is supported by a series of tools − both computerized and procedural.

This paper is not intended to present our complete design and implementation methodology. Rather, it discusses one of the design tools − the "Program Design Language" (PDL) and its computerized processor. Both of these have been in extensive use since the autumn of 1973.

The purpose of PDL

PDL is designed for the production of structured designs in a top-down manner. It is a "pidgin" language in that it uses the vocabulary of one language (i.e., English) and the overall syntax of another (i.e., a structured programming language). In a sense, it can be thought of as "structured English."

While the use of pidgin languages is also advocated by others, we have taken the additional steps of imposing a degree of formalism on the language and supplying a processor for it. Input to the processor consists of control information plus design for procedures (called "segments" in PDL). The output is a working design document which can, if desired, be photo-reduced and included in a project development workbook.

The output of the processor completely replaces flowcharts since PDL designs are easier to produce, easier to change, and easier to read than are designs presented in flowchart form.

Designing for people in PDL

Like a flowchart, and unlike a program, PDL can be written with whatever level of detail is appropriate to the problem at hand. A designer can start with a few pages giving the general structure of his system and finish, if necessary, with even more precision than would exist in the corresponding program.

In our experience, the purpose of a design is to communicate the designer's idea to other people — not to a computer. Figure 1 shows a sample design "segment" for a simple exchange sort.

```
SORT (TABLE, SIZE OF TABLE)

    IF SIZE OF TABLE > 1
        DO UNTIL NO ITEMS WERE INTERCHANGED
            DO FOR EACH PAIR OF ITEMS IN TABLE (1-2, 2-3,
                3-4, ETC.)
                IF FIRST ITEM OF PAIR > SECOND ITEM OF PAIR
                INTERCHANGE THE TWO ITEMS
                ENDIF
            ENDDO
        ENDDO
    ENDIF
```

Figure 1. PDL design of a simple sorting algorithm.

Note that we are *not* attempting to illustrate efficient sorting methods. Rather, having decided to use this particular sorting method, we wish to present the algorithm in a way that it can be easily comprehended. Given that the "DO UNTIL" construct represents a loop whose completion test occurs at the *end* of the loop, the operation of the algorithm is apparent. It is clearly better, from the viewpoint of understandability, than either the flowchart of Figure 2 or the translation of the algorithm into PL/I as shown in Figure 3.

A virtue of PDL is that a rough outline of an entire problem solution can be quickly constructed. This level of design can be easily understood by people other than the designer. Thus, criticisms, suggestions, and modifications can be quickly incorporated into the design, possibly resulting in complete rewrites of major sections. When the design has stabilized at this level, more detail can be added in successive passes through the design with decisions at each point affecting smaller and smaller areas.

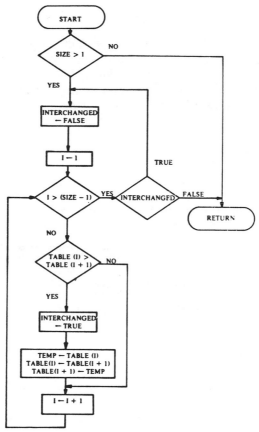

Figure 2. Flowchart for sorting algorithm of Figure 1.

```
SORT:
  PROCEDURE(TABLE);
  DECLARE TABLE(*) FIXED BIN;
  DECLARE INTERCHANGED BIT(1);
  DECLARE TEMP FIXED BIN;
  IF DIM(TABLE,1) > 1 THEN
    DO;
      INTERCHANGED = '1'B;
      DO WHILE (INTERCHANGED);
        INTERCHANGED = '0'B;
        DO I = LBOUND(TABLE,1) TO
        HBOUND(TABLE,1)−1;
          IF TABLE(I) >TABLE(I+1) THEN
            DO;
              INTERCHANGED = '1'B;
              TEMP = TABLE(I);
              TABLE(I) = TABLE(I+1);
              TABLE(I+1) = TEMP;
            END;
          END;
        END;
      END;
END SORT;
```

Figure 3. PL/I procedure for sorting algorithm.

The form of a design in PDL

A design produced in PDL consists of a number of "flow segments," each corresponding roughly to a procedure in the final implementation. A sample of a high-level flow segment from a large design is shown in Figure 4. If a statement in a segment references another flow segment, the page number of the referenced segment is shown to the left of the referencing statement. A sample low-level segment is shown in Figure 5.

```
CFG, INC.   AIL CEVELCPMENT WORKBCCK (14.90)                                06 JUL 74   PAGE  39
            EXPRESSICN AND REFERENCE PRCCESSING


      PRCCESS EXPRESSICN

 REF
 PAGE  ***********************************************************************************************
      *                                                                                              *
      *  1    PUSh "SCE" (START CF EXPRESSICN) CNTC CPERATCR STACK                                    *
  40  *  2    PROCESS OPERAND                                                                         *
      *  3    DC WHILE NEXT TOKEN IS AN CPERATCR                                                      *
      *  4       DO WHILE OPERATCR IS NOT SAME AS CPERATCR CN TCF CF OPERATOR STACK AND ITS PRECEDENCE IS LESS  /*
      *             THAN OR ECUAL TC PRECECENCE CF CPERATCR CN THE TOP OF THE OPERATOR STACK          *
  42  *  5          BUILD TOP NCCE                                                                    *
      *  6          PCP OPERATOR STACK                                                                *
      *  7       ENDDD                                                                                *
      *  8       IF NEW OPERATOR IS SAME AS TCP OPERATCR CN CPERATCR STACK                            *
      *  9          INCREMENT OPERAND CCLNT IN TCF CF CPERATCR STACK BY CNE                           *
      * 10       ELSE                                                                                 *
      * 11          PUSH NEW OPERATOR ANC OPERAND COUNT CF 2 CNTC OPERATCR STACK                      *
      * 12       ENDIF                                                                                *
  40  * 13       PROCESS OPERAND                                                                      *
      * 14    ENDDU                                                                                   *
      * 15    DO WHILE TCP OF OPERATOR STACK IS NCT "SCE"                                             *
  42  * 16       BUILD TOP NODE                                                                       *
      * 17       POP OPERATOR STACK                                                                   *
      * 18    ENDDD                                                                                   *
      * 19    POP OPERATOR STACK                                                                      *
      * 20    (TCP OF OPERANC STACK CCNTAINS TCP NCCE IN EXPRESSION)                                  *
      *                                                                                              *
      ***********************************************************************************************
```

Figure 4. Sample of a high-level PDL flow segment.

```
CFG, INC.   LOCOMOTOR DATA REDUCTION                                        15 UCT 74   PAGE  21
            DATA COMPRESSION


      AVERAGE OVER PUINTS (RADIUS)

 REF
 PAGE  ***********************************************************************************************
      *                                                                                              *
      *  1    IF DEBUGGING                                                                            *
  29  *  2       START LINE (CURRENT CYCLE)                                                           *
  28  *  3       PRINT POINTS IN BUFFER (CURRENT BUFFER)                                              *
      *  4    ENDIF                                                                                   *
      *  5    POINTS <- 0                                                                             *
      *  6    SX <- 0                                                                                 *
      *  7    SY <- 0                                                                                 *
      *  8    BUFFER <- PREVIOUS OF PREVIOUS BUFFER                                                   *
      *  9    DO FOR 5 BUFFERS                                                                        *
  22  * 10       MOVE GOOD POINTS TO WORK BUFFER (BUFFER,RADIUS)                                      *
      * 11       IF DEBUGGING                                                                         *
  28  * 12          PRINT POINTS IN BUFFER (WORK BUFFER)                                              *
      * 13       ENDIF                                                                                *
      * 14       IF POINT COUNT OF WORK BUFFER > 0                                                    *
      * 15          DO FOR POINTS IN WORK BUFFER                                                      *
      * 16             ADD X TO SX                                                                    *
      * 17             ADD Y TO SY                                                                    *
      * 18          ENDO                                                                              *
      * 19          ADD POINT CUUNT OF WORK BUFFER TO PCINTS                                          *
      * 20       ENDIF                                                                                *
      * 21       BUFFER <- NEXT BUFFER                                                                *
      * 22    ENDO                                                                                    *
      * 23    IF POINTS > 0                                                                           *
      * 24       AX <- SX/POINTS                                                                      *
      * 25       AY <- SY/POINTS                                                                      *
      * 26    ELSE (NO DATA FUR POINT)                                                                *
      * 27       AX <- NEGATIVE                                                                       *
      * 28       AY <- 0                                                                              *
      * 29    ENDIF                                                                                   *
      *                                                                                              *
      ***********************************************************************************************
```

Figure 5. Sample low-level PDL flow segment.

The statements which compose a flow segment are entered in free form. The PDL processor automatically underlines keywords, indents statements to correspond to structure nesting levels, and provides automatic continuation from line to line.

Design information may also be entered in "text segments." These contain purely textual information such as commentary, data formats, assumptions, and constraints.

The document output by the PDL processor is in a form ready for photo-reduction and publication. It contains:

- a cover page giving the design title, data, and processor identification

- a table of contents (Figure 6)

- the body of the design, consisting of flow segments and text segments

- a "reference tree" showing how segment references are nested (Figure 7)

- a cross-reference listing showing the page and line number at which each segment is referenced (Figure 8)

```
LFG, INC.    AIL CEVELOPMENT WORKBCCK (14.90)
             TABLE CF CCNTENTS

TABLE UF CONTENTS
-----------------

    INTRODUCTION . . . . . . . . . . . . . . . . . . . . . . . .   2
      PURPOSE OF SECTICN. . . . . . . . . . . . . . . . . . . .    3

    DICTIONARY ALGURITHMS. . . . . . . . . . . . . . . . . . . .   4
      FIND CICTICNARY ENTRY . . . . . . . . . . . . . . . . . .    5
      SEARCH CNE BLOCK. . . . . . . . . . . . . . . . . . . . .    6
      SEE IF MATCH. . . . . . . . . . . . . . . . . . . . . . .    7

    TOKEN SCANNING . . . . . . . . . . . . . . . . . . . . . . .   8
      BACK UP SCANNER . . . . . . . . . . . . . . . . . . . . .    9
      SCAN CNE TCKEN. . . . . . . . . . . . . . . . . . . . . .   10
      SKIP BLANKS . . . . . . . . . . . . . . . . . . . . . . .   11
      SKIP COMMENT. . . . . . . . . . . . . . . . . . . . . . .   12
      SCAN IDENTIFIER . . . . . . . . . . . . . . . . . . . . .   13
      SCAN SPECIAL CHARACTER. . . . . . . . . . . . . . . . . .   14
      GET NEXT CHARACTER. . . . . . . . . . . . . . . . . . . .   15

    SOURCE INPUT . . . . . . . . . . . . . . . . . . . . . . . .  16
      READ NEXT SOURCE CARD . . . . . . . . . . . . . . . . . .   17
      LIST SCURCE CARC. . . . . . . . . . . . . . . . . . . . .   18

    MAIN PROCESSING LCCP . . . . . . . . . . . . . . . . . . . .  19
      MAIN LCOP . . . . . . . . . . . . . . . . . . . . . . . .   20
      PROCESS CNE STATEMENT . . . . . . . . . . . . . . . . . .   21
      SETUP STATEMENT . . . . . . . . . . . . . . . . . . . . .   22
      VERIFY STATEMENT PLACEMENT. . . . . . . . . . . . . . . .   23
      PROCESS IF STATEMENT. . . . . . . . . . . . . . . . . . .   24
      PROCESS PROCEDURE STATEMENT . . . . . . . . . . . . . . .   25
      PROCESS DO STATEMENT. . . . . . . . . . . . . . . . . . .   26
      PROCESS ENC STATEMENT . . . . . . . . . . . . . . . . . .   27
      PROCESS END OF STATEMENT. . . . . . . . . . . . . . . . .   28

    DECLARATICN PROCESSING . . . . . . . . . . . . . . . . . . .  29
      PROCESS DECLARATION LIST. . . . . . . . . . . . . . . . .   30
      SCAN DECLARATICN LIST . . . . . . . . . . . . . . . . . .   31
      SCAN DECLARATICN ITEM . . . . . . . . . . . . . . . . . .   32
      SCAN ATTRIBUTES . . . . . . . . . . . . . . . . . . . . .   33
      INSTALL DECLARATION ITEMS . . . . . . . . . . . . . . . .   34
      INSTALL BASIC ENTRY . . . . . . . . . . . . . . . . . . .   35
      INSTALL STRUCTURE ENTRIES . . . . . . . . . . . . . . . .   36
      INSTALL CECLARATICN ATTRIBUTES. . . . . . . . . . . . . .   37

    EXPRESSICN AND REFERENCE PROCESSING. . . . . . . . . . . . .  38
      PROCESS EXPRESSION. . . . . . . . . . . . . . . . . . . .   39
      PROCESS OPERAND . . . . . . . . . . . . . . . . . . . . .   40
      BUILD UNARY NODE. . . . . . . . . . . . . . . . . . . . .   41
      BUILD TOP NODE. . . . . . . . . . . . . . . . . . . . . .   42
      PROCESS REFERENCE . . . . . . . . . . . . . . . . . . . .   43
      PROCESS BASIC REFERENCE . . . . . . . . . . . . . . . . .   44
      FORM POSSIBLE <SR> NODE . . . . . . . . . . . . . . . . .   45
      PROCESS SINGLE REFERENCE. . . . . . . . . . . . . . . . .   46
```

Figure 6. Sample table of contents from a PDL design.

```
CFG, INC.    LOCOMOTOR DATA REDUCTION              CFG, INC.    AIL DEVELOPMENT WORKBOOK (20.90)
             SEGMENT REFERENCE TREES                            INDEX TO GROUPS AND SEGMENTS

STOW                                                3    GP    MAIN PHASE FLOW
----
                                                    8    SG    MAKE SUCCESSOR EDGE
                                                                   7:08    7:11    7:19
LN   DEF   SEGMENT
--   ---   -------                                  31   SG    MARK LOOP ENTRY BLOCKS
                                                                   30:02
 1    4    STOW
 2   11      SET DEFAULTS                           39   SG    MARK LOOP MEMBERSHIP
 3   35      FIND STARTING SECTOR                                  37:13
 4    6      WRITE ON TAPE
 5   38        CONVERT TO TANK ID                   32   SG    MARK ONE LOOP ENTRY BLOCK
 6   19        BUILD PROCESSED DATA ARRAY                          31:13
 7   24          INITIALIZE INPUT BUFFERS
 8   31            GET POINTS                        4    SG    OPTIMIZE
 9   34              GET BATCH
10   36                READ DISK                     54   SG    PERFORM BACKWARD MOVEMENT
11   32                MOVE AND COUNT POINTS                       37:17
12   26              MOVE TO BUFFER
13   20          PROCESS A POINT                     45   SG    PERFORM LOCAL CSE ELIMINATION
14   21            AVERAGE OVER POINTS                             44:01
15   29              START LINE
16   28              PRINT POINTS IN BUFFER          36   SG    PERFORM TRANSFORMATIONS
17   22              MOVE GOOD POINTS TO WORK BUFFER                4:06
18   28              PRINT POINTS IN BUFFER
19   25          ADVANCE INPUT BUFFERS               47   SG    PROCESS ASSIGNMENT FOR CSE
20   31            GET POINTS                                      45:07    51:10    52:16
21   34              GET BATCH
22   36                READ DISK                     48   SG    PROCESS CALL FOR CSE
23   32                MOVE AND COUNT POINTS                       45:09    51:12    52:18
24   26              MOVE TO BUFFER
25   17        BUILD COMPRESSED DATA ARRAY           46   SG    PROCESS COMPUTATIONAL TRIPLE FOR CSE
26   10        DISPLAY COMPRESSED POINTS                          45:05
27    5      EXECUTE A COMMAND
28    6        WRITE ON TAPE                         17   SG    PROCESS FETCH INFORMATION
29   38          CONVERT TO TANK ID                               16:05  16:08  16:10  16:12  16:13  16:15  16:18
30   19          BUILD PROCESSED DATA ARRAY
31   24            INITIALIZE INPUT BUFFERS          18   SG    PROCESS STORE INFORMATION
32   31              GET POINTS                                   16:06
33   34                GET BATCH
34   36                  READ DISK                   56   SG    REDUCE STRENGTH
35   32                  MOVE AND COUNT POINTS                     37:18
36   26                MOVE TO BUFFER
37   20            PROCESS A POINT                   65   SG    REDUCE STRENGTH OF ONE TRIPLE
38   21              AVERAGE OVER POINTS                           56:07
39   29                START LINE
40   28                PRINT POINTS IN BUFFER        27   SG    RESOLVE TENTATIVE BACK DOMINATORS
41   22                MOVE GOOD POINTS TO WORK BUFFER               25:09
42   28                PRINT POINTS IN BUFFER
43   25            ADVANCE INPUT BUFFERS             55   GP    STRENGTH REDUCTION PART OF TRANSFORMATIONS SUBPHASE
44   31              GET POINTS
45   34                GET BATCH                     22   SG    TRACE CALLS
46   36                  READ DISK                                 4:03
47   32                  MOVE AND COUNT POINTS
48   26                MOVE TO BUFFER               23   SG    TRACE ONE NODE
```

Figure 7. Sample of a segment reference tree.   Figure 8. Part of an index to a design.

Design constructs

What goes into a design segment is generally at the discretion of the designer. In choosing the form of presentation, he is guided by a compendium of style which has been developed through extensive experience. However, the language and the processor have been defined to encourage and support design constructs which relate directly to the constructs of structured coding. The two primary constructs are the IF and the DO.

The IF construct

The IF construct provides the means for indicating conditional execution. It corresponds to the classical IF . . . THEN . . . ELSE construct of Algol-60 [10] and PL/I, augmented by the ELSEIF of languages such as Algol-68 [11]. The latter is used to prevent excessive indentation levels when cascaded tests are used.

The general form of the construct is shown in Figure 9. Any number (including zero) ELSEIF's are allowed and at most one ELSE is allowed.

```
IF condition
   one or more statements
ELSEIF condition
   one or more statements

   .

   .

   .

ELSEIF condition
   one or more statements
ELSE
   one or more statements
ENDIF
```

Figure 9. General form of IF construct.

The DO construct

This construct is used to indicate repeated execution and for case selection. The reasons for the dual use of this construct are historic in nature and closely map several of the in-house implementation languages we frequently use. It may be effectively argued that a separate construct for case selection would be better.

The iterative DO is indicated by:

```
DO iteration criteria
   one or more statements
ENDDO
```

The "iteration criteria" can be chosen to suit the problem. As always, bias toward human understandability is preferred. Statements such as:

```
DO WHILE THERE ARE INPUT RECORDS
DO UNTIL "END" STATEMENT HAS BEEN
PROCESSED
DO FOR EACH ITEM IN THE LIST EXCEPT
THE LAST ONE
```

occur frequently in actual designs.

Our experience, and that of others [7], has shown that a provision for premature exit from a loop and premature repetition of a loop are frequently useful. To accomplish this, we take the statement

```
UNDO
```

to mean that control is to pass to the point following the ENDDO of the loop. Likewise,

```
CYCLE
```

is taken to mean that control is to pass to the loop termination test.

Since we may wish that an UNDO or CYCLE apply to an outer loop in a nest of loops, any DO may be labelled and the label may be placed after the UNDO or CYCLE.

Case selection is indicated by

```
DO CASE selection criteria
```

Again, we advocate the use of understandable selection criteria such as

DO CASE OF TRANSACTION TYPE
DO CASE OPERATOR TYPE
DO CASE OF CONTROL CARD VERB

Generally, we use labels in the body of the DO to indicate where control passes for each case. This is illustrated in Figure 10.

```
        DO CASE OF TRANSACTION TYPE
ADD:
        CREATE INITIAL RECORD
DELETE:
        IF DELETION IS AUTHORIZED
          CREATE DELETION RECORD
        ELSE
          ISSUE ERROR MESSAGE
        ENDIF
CHANGE:
        INCREMENT CHANGE COUNT
        CREATE DELETION RECORD
"OTHER":
        ISSUE ERROR MESSAGE
        ENDDO
```

Figure 10. Example of DO CASE construct.

Future directions

The results we have achieved with PDL have exceeded our original expectations. However, it is clear that further development is both possible and desirable. The areas which we are currently exploring include:

- *handling of data:* The current PDL presents a procedural design — a design of control flow and processing actions. It would be very desirable to have a similar mechanism for the design of data structures and data flow. A method for integrating the data and procedural designs and performing mutual cross-referencing would be very powerful, indeed.

- *interactive versions:* the current PDL processor is batch oriented. The ability to compose and, more importantly, to modify a design on-line in a manner specifically planned for interactive use would be of great assistance. This would be particularly advantageous during the early stages of a project when design changes are often frequent and extensive.

- *total design system:* an integrated computer system for software design, such as the DES system of Professor R.M. Graham [12], is a natural outgrowth of our work with PDL. Such a system would act as an information management system maintaining a data base of designs. Designs could be entered and modified; questions about a design and the inter-relations of its parts could be asked and answered; reports on design status and completeness could be prepared. Provision for simulation of a design for performance estimation and a mechanism for transition from design to code are also important.

Conclusions

In the autumn of 1973, we integrated the use of PDL and its processor into our software design and implementation methodology. Since then, it has been used on a number of projects of varying sizes. The results have been comparable to those discussed earlier.

PDL is not a "panacea" and it is certainly possible to produce bad designs using it. However, we have found that our designers and programmers quickly learn to use PDL effectively. Its emphasis on designing for people provides a high degree of confidence in the correctness of the design. In our experience, it is almost impossible to "wave your hands" in PDL. If a designer doesn't really yet see how to solve a particular problem, he can't just gloss over it without the resulting design gap being readily apparent to the reader of a design. This, plus the basic readability of a PDL design, means that clients, management, and team members can both understand the proposed solution and gauge its degree of completeness.

We have also found that PDL works equally well for large and small projects. Because it is so easy to use, persons starting to work on even a "quick and dirty" utility will first sketch out a solution in PDL. In the past, such programs were usually written with little or no design preceding the actual coding.

References: Caine & Gordon

1. Boehm, B.W., "Software and Its Impact: A Quantitative Assessment," *Datamation*, May 1973, pp. 48-59.

2. Goldberg, J., (editor), *Proceedings of a Symposium on the High Cost of Software*, Stanford Research Institute, 1973.

3. Baker, F.T., "Chief Programmer Team Management of Production Programming," *IBM Sys. J.*, Vol. 11, No. 1, 1972, pp. 56-73.

4. Böhm, C., and G. Jacopini, "Flow Diagrams, Turing Machines and Languages With Only Two Formation Rules," *Comm. ACM*, May 1966, pp. 366-371.

5. Dijkstra, E., "GO TO Statements Considered Harmful," *Comm. ACM*, March 1968, pp. 147-148.

6. Mills, Harlan D., "On the Development of Large Reliable Programs," *IEEE Symp. Computer Software Reliability*, 1973, pp. 155-159.

7. Peterson, W.W., T. Kasami and N. Tokura, "On the Capabilities of WHILE, REPEAT and EXIT Statements," *Comm. ACM*, August 1973, pp. 503-512.

8. Stevens, W.P., G.J. Myers and L.L. Constantine, "Structured Design," *IBM Sys. J.*, Vol. 13, No. 2, 1974, pp. 115-139.

9. De Balbine, G., *Better Manpower Utilization Using Automatic Restructuring*, Caine, Farber & Gordon, Inc., 1974 (in publication). [Ed. note: Reprinted in this volume, paper 9.]

10. Naur, P., et al., "Report on the Algorithmic Language ALGOL 60," *Comm. ACM*, May 1960, pp. 299-314.

11. Van Wijngaarden, A., et al., "Report on the Algorithmic Language ALGOL 68," *Numerische Mathematik*, 14, 1969, pp. 79-218.

12. Graham, R.M., G.J. Clancy and D.B. Devaney, "A Software Design and Evaluation System," *Comm. ACM*, February 1973, pp. 110-116. [Ed. note: Reprinted in this volume, paper 6.]

The Emperor's Old Clothes

My first and most pleasant duty in this lecture is to express my profound gratitude to the Association for Computing Machinery for the great honor which they have bestowed on me and for this opportunity to address you on a topic of my choice. What a difficult choice it is! My scientific achievements, so amply recognized by this award, have already been amply described in the scientific literature. Instead of repeating the abstruse technicalities of my trade, I would like to talk informally about myself, my personal experiences, my hopes and fears, my modest successes, and my rather less modest failures. I have learned more from my failures than can ever be revealed in the cold print of a scientific article and now I would like you to learn from them, too. Besides, failures are much more fun to hear about afterwards; they are not so funny at the time.

I start my story in August 1960, when I became a programmer with a small computer manufacturer, a division of Elliott Brothers (London) Ltd., where in the next eight years I was to receive my primary education in computer science. My first task was to implement for the new Elliott 803 computer, a library subroutine for a new fast method of internal sorting just invented by Shell. I greatly enjoyed the challenge of maximizing efficiency in the simple decimal-addressed machine code of those days. My boss and tutor, Pat Shackleton, was very pleased with my completed program. I then said timidly that I thought I had invented a sorting method that would usually run faster than SHELLSORT, without taking much extra store. He bet me sixpence that I had not. Although my method was very difficult to explain, he finally agreed that I had won my bet.

I wrote several other tightly coded library subroutines but after six months I was given a much more important task —

SOURCE: C.A.R. Hoare, *Communications of the ACM*, 1981.

that of designing a new advanced high level programming language for the company's next computer, the Elliott 503, which was to have the same instruction code as the existing 803 but run sixty times faster. In spite of my education in classical languages, this was a task for which I was even less qualified than those who undertake it today. By great good fortune there came into my hands a copy of the Report on the International Algorithmic Language ALGOL 60. Of course, this language was obviously too complicated for our customers. How could they ever understand all those **begins** and **ends** when even our salesmen couldn't?

Around Easter 1961, a course on ALGOL 60 was offered in Brighton, England, with Peter Naur, Edsger W. Dijkstra, and Peter Landin as tutors. I attended this course with my colleague in the language project, Jill Pym, our divisional Technical Manager, Roger Cook, and our Sales Manager, Paul King. It was there that I first learned about recursive procedures and saw how to program the sorting method which I had earlier found such difficulty in explaining. It was there that I wrote the procedure, immodestly named QUICKSORT, on which my career as a computer scientist is founded. Due credit must be paid to the genius of the designers of ALGOL 60 who included recursion in their language and enabled me to describe my invention so elegantly to the world. I have regarded it as the highest goal of programming language design to enable good ideas to be elegantly expressed.

After the ALGOL course in Brighton, Roger Cook was driving me and my colleagues back to London when he suddenly asked, "Instead of designing a new language, why don't we just implement ALGOL 60?" We all instantly agreed — in retrospect, a very lucky decision for me. But we knew we did not have the skill or experience at that time to implement the whole language, so I was commissioned to design a modest subset. In that design I adopted certain basic principles which I believe to be as valid today as they were then.

(1) The first principle was *security:* The principle that every syntactically incorrect program should be rejected by the compiler and that every syntactically correct program should give a result or an error message that was predictable and comprehensible in terms of the source language program itself. Thus no core dumps should ever be necessary. It was logically impossible for any source language program to cause the computer to run wild, either at compile time or at run time. A consequence of this principle is that every occurrence of every subscript of every subscripted variable was on every occasion checked at run time against both the upper and the lower declared bounds of the array. Many years later we asked our customers whether they wished us to provide an option to switch off these checks in the interests of efficiency on production runs. Unanimously, they urged us not to — they already knew how frequently subscript errors occur on production runs where failure to detect them could be disastrous. I note with fear and horror that even in 1980, language designers and users have not learned this lesson. In any respectable branch of engineering, failure to observe such elementary precautions would have long been against the law.

(2) The second principle in the design of the implementation was *brevity of the object code produced by the compiler and compactness of run time working data.* There was a clear reason for this: The size of main

storage on any computer is limited and its extension involves delay and expense. A program exceeding the limit, even by one word, is impossible to run, especially since many of our customers did not intend to purchase backing stores.

This principle of compactness of object code is even more valid today, when processors are trivially cheap in comparison with the amounts of main store they can address, and backing stores are comparatively even more expensive and slower by many orders of magnitude. If as a result of care taken in implementation the available hardware remains more powerful than may seem necessary for a particular application, the applications programmer can nearly always take advantage of the extra capacity to increase the quality of his program, its simplicity, its ruggedness, and its reliability.

(3)   The third principle of our design was that *the entry and exit conventions for procedures and functions should be as compact and efficient as for tightly coded machine-code subroutines.* I reasoned that procedures are one of the most powerful features of a high level language, in that they both simplify the programming task and shorten the object code. Thus there must be no impediment to their frequent use.

(4)   The fourth principle was that *the compiler should use only a single pass.* The compiler was structured as a collection of mutually recursive procedures, each capable of analyzing and translating a major syntactic unit of the language — a statement, an expression, a declaration, and so on. It was designed and documented in ALGOL 60, and then coded into decimal machine code using an explicit stack for recursion. Without the ALGOL 60 concept of recursion, at that time highly controversial, we could not have written this compiler at all.

I can still recommend single-pass top-down recursive descent both as an implementation method and as a design principle for a programming language. First, we certainly want programs to be read by *people* and people prefer to read things once in a single pass. Second, for the user of a time-sharing or personal computer system, the interval between typing in a program (or amendment) and starting to run that program is wholly unproductive. It can be minimized by the high speed of a single pass compiler. Finally, to structure a compiler according to the syntax of its input language makes a great contribution to ensuring its correctness. Unless we have absolute confidence in this, we can never have confidence in the results of any of our programs.

To observe these four principles, I selected a rather small subset of ALGOL 60. As the design and implementation progressed, I gradually discovered methods of relaxing the restrictions without compromising any of the principles. So in the end we were able to implement nearly the full power of the whole language, including even recursion, although several features were removed and others were restricted.

In the middle of 1963, primarily as a result of the work of Jill Pym and Jeff Hillmore, the first version of our compiler was delivered. After a few months we began to wonder whether anyone was using the language or taking any notice of our occasional reissue, incorporating improved operating methods. Only when a customer had a complaint did he contact us and many of them had no complaints. Our customers have now moved on to more modern computers and more fashionable languages but many have told me of their fond memories of the Elliott ALGOL System and the fondness is not due just to nostalgia, but to the efficiency, reliability, and convenience of that early simple ALGOL System.

As a result of this work on ALGOL, in August 1962, I was invited to serve on the new Working Group 2.1 of IFIP, charged with responsibility for maintenance and development of ALGOL. The group's first main task was to design a subset of the language which would remove some of its less successful features. Even in those days and even with such a simple language, we recognized that a subset could be an improvement on the original. I greatly welcomed the chance of meeting and hearing the wisdom of many of the original language designers. I was astonished and dismayed at the heat and even rancor of their discussions. Apparently the original design of AL-GOL 60 had not proceeded in that spirit of dispassionate search for truth which the quality of the language had led me to suppose.

In order to provide relief from the tedious and argumentative task of designing a subset, the working group allocated one afternoon to discussing the features that should be incorporated in the next design of the language. Each member was invited to suggest the improvement he considered most important. On October 11, 1963, my suggestion was to pass on a request of our customers to relax the ALGOL 60 rule of compulsory declaration of variable names and adopt some reasonable default convention such as that of FORTRAN. I was astonished by the polite but firm rejection of this seemingly innocent suggestion: It was pointed out that the redundancy of ALGOL 60 was the best protection against programming and coding errors which could be extremely expensive to detect in a running program and even more expensive not to. The story of the Mariner space rocket to Venus, lost because of the lack of compulsory declarations in FORTRAN, was not to be published until later. I was eventually persuaded of the need to design programming notations so as to maximize the number of errors which cannot be made, or if made, can be reliably detected at compile time. Perhaps this would make the text of programs longer. Never mind! Wouldn't you be delighted if your Fairy Godmother offered to wave her wand over your program to remove all its errors and only made the condition that you should write out and key in your whole program three times! The way to shorten programs is to use procedures, not to omit vital declarative information.

Among the other proposals for the development of a new ALGOL was that the **switch** declaration of ALGOL 60 should be replaced by a more general feature, namely an array of label-valued variables and that a program should be able to change the values of these variables by assignment. I was very much opposed to this idea, similar to the assigned GO TO of FORTRAN, because I had found a surprising number of tricky problems in the implementation of even the simple labels and switches of ALGOL 60. I could see even more problems in the new feature including that of jumping back into a block after it had been exited. I was also beginning to suspect that programs that used a lot of labels were more difficult to understand and get correct and that programs that assigned new values to label variables would be even more difficult still.

It occurred to me that the appropriate notation to replace the ALGOL 60 switch should be based on that of the conditional expression of ALGOL 60, which selects between two alternative actions according to the value of a Boolean expression. So I suggested the notation for a "case expression" which selects between any number of alternatives according to the value of an integer expression. That was my second language design proposal. I am still most proud of it, because it raises essentially no problems either for the implementor, the programmer, or the reader of a program.

Now, after more than fifteen years, there is the prospect of international standardization of a language incorporating this notation — a remarkably *short* interval compared with other branches of engineering.

Back again to my work at Elliott's. After the unexpected success of our ALGOL Compiler, our thoughts turned to a more ambitious project: To provide a range of operating system software for larger configurations of the 503 computer, with card readers, line printers, magnetic tapes, and even a core backing store which was twice as cheap and twice as large as main store, but fifteen times slower. This was to be known as the Elliott 503 Mark II software system.

It comprised:

(1)   An assembler for a symbolic assembly language in which all the rest of the software was to be written.

(2)   A scheme for automatic administration of code and data overlays, either from magnetic tape or from core backing store. This was to be used by the rest of the software.

(3)   A scheme for automatic buffering of all input and output on any available peripheral device — again, to be used by all the other software.

(4)   A filing system on magnetic tape with facilities for editing and job control.

(5)   A completely new implementation of ALGOL 60, which removed all the nonstandard restrictions which we had imposed on our first implementation.

(6)   A compiler for FORTRAN as it was then.

I wrote documents which described the relevant concepts and facilities and we sent them to existing and prospective customers. Work started with a team of fifteen programmers and the deadline for delivery was set some eighteen months ahead in March 1965. After initiating the design of the Mark II software, I was suddenly promoted to the dizzying rank of Assistant Chief Engineer, responsible for advanced development and design of the company's products, both hardware and software.

Although I was still managerially responsible for the 503 Mark II software, I gave it less attention than the company's new products and almost failed to notice when the deadline for its delivery passed without event. The programmers revised their implementation schedules and a new delivery date was set some three months ahead in June 1965. Needless to say, that day also passed without event. By this time, our customers were getting angry and my managers instructed me to take personal charge of the project. I asked the senior programmers once again to draw up revised schedules, which again showed that the software could be delivered within another three months. I desperately wanted to believe it but I just could not. I disregarded the schedules and began to dig more deeply into the project.

It turned out that we had failed to make any overall plans for the allocation of our most limited resource — main storage. Each programmer expected this to be done automatically, either by the symbolic assembler or by the automatic overlay scheme. Even worse, we had failed to simply count the space used by our own software which was already filling the main store of the computer, leaving no space for our customers to run *their* programs. Hardware address length limitations prohibited adding more main storage.

Clearly, the original specifications of the software could not be met and had to be drastically curtailed. Experienced programmers and even managers were called back from other projects. We decided to concentrate first on delivery of the new compiler for ALGOL 60, which careful calculation showed would take another four months. I impressed upon all the programmers involved that this was no longer just a prediction; it was a promise; if they found they were not meeting their promise, it was their personal responsibility to find ways and means of making good.

The programmers responded magnificently to the challenge. They worked nights and days to ensure completion of all those items of software which were needed by the ALGOL compiler. To our delight, they met the scheduled delivery date; it was the first major item of working software produced by the company over a period of two years.

Our delight was short-lived; the compiler could not be delivered. Its speed of compilation was only two characters per second which compared unfavorably with the existing version of the compiler operating at about a thousand characters per second. We soon identified the cause of the problem: It was thrashing between the main store and the extension core backing store which was fifteen times slower. It was easy to make some simple improvements, and within a week we had doubled the speed of compilation — to four characters per second. In the next two weeks of investigation and reprogramming, the speed was doubled again — to eight characters per second. We could see ways in which within a month this could be still further improved; but the amount of reprogramming required was increasing and its effectiveness was decreasing; there was an awful long way to go. The alternative of increasing the size of the main store so frequently adopted in later failures of this kind was prohibited by hardware addressing limitations.

There was no escape: The entire Elliott 503 Mark II software project had to be abandoned, and with it, over thirty man-years of programming effort, equivalent to nearly one man's active working life, and I was responsible, both as designer and as manager, for wasting it.

A meeting of all our 503 customers was called and Roger Cook, who was then manager of the computing division, explained to them that not a single word of the long-promised software would ever be delivered to them. He adopted a very quiet tone of delivery, which ensured that none of the customers could interrupt, murmur in the background, or even shuffle in their seats. I admired but could not share his calm. Over lunch our customers were kind to try to comfort me. They had realized long ago that software to the original specification could never have been delivered, and even if it had been, they would not have known how to use its sophisticated features, and anyway many such large projects get cancelled before delivery. In retrospect, I believe our customers were fortunate that hardware limitations had protected them from the arbitrary excesses of our software designs. In the present day, users of microprocessors benefit from a similar protection — but not for much longer.

At that time I was reading the early documents describing the concepts and features of the newly announced OS 360, and of a new time-sharing project called Multics. These were far more comprehensive, elaborate, and sophisticated than anything I had imagined, even in the first version of the 503 Mark II software. Clearly IBM and MIT must be possessed of some secret of successful software design and implementation whose nature I could not even begin to guess at. It was only later that they realized they could not either.

So I still could not see how I had brought such a great misfortune upon my company. At the time I was convinced that my managers were planning to dismiss me.

But no, they were intending a far more severe punishment. "O.K. Tony," they said. "You got us into this mess and now you're going to get us out." "But I don't know how," I protested, but their reply was simple. "Well then, you'll have to find out." They even expressed confidence that I could do so. I did not share their confidence. I was tempted to resign. It was the luckiest of all my lucky escapes that I did not.

Of course, the company did everything they could to help me. They took away my responsibility for hardware design and reduced the size of my programming teams. Each of my managers explained carefully his own theory of what had gone wrong and all the theories were different. At last, there breezed into my office the most senior manager of all, a general manager of our parent company, Andrew St. Johnston. I was surprised that he had even heard of me. "You know what went wrong?" he shouted — he always shouted — "You let your programmers do things which you yourself do not understand." I stared in astonishment. He was obviously out of touch with present day realities. How could one person ever understand the whole of a modern software product like the Elliott 503 Mark II software system?

I realized later that he was absolutely right; he had diagnosed the true cause of the problem and he had planted the seed of its later solution.

I still had a team of some forty programmers and we needed to retain the good will of customers for our new machine and even regain the confidence of the customers for our old one. But what should we actually plan to do when we knew only one thing — that all our previous plans had failed? I therefore called an all-day meeting of our senior programmers on October 22, 1965, to thrash out the question between us. I still have the notes of that meeting. We first listed the recent major grievances of our customers: Cancellation of products, failure to meet deadlines, excessive size of software, ". . . not justified by the usefulness of the facilities provided," excessively slow programs, failure to take account of customer feedback; "Earlier attention paid to quite minor requests of our customers might have paid as great dividends of goodwill as the success of our most ambitious plans."

We then listed our own grievances: Lack of machine time for program testing, unpredictability of machine time, lack of suitable peripheral equipment, unreliability of the hardware even when available, dispersion of programming staff, lack of equipment for keypunching of programs, lack of firm hardware delivery dates, lack of technical writing effort for documentation, lack of software knowledge outside of the programming group, interference from higher managers who imposed decisions, ". . . without a full realization of the more intricate implications of the matter," and overoptimism in the face of pressure from customers and the Sales Department.

But we did not seek to excuse our failure by these grievances. For example, we admitted that it was the duty of programmers to educate their managers and other departments of the company by ". . . presenting the necessary information in a simple palatable form." The hope ". . . that deficiencies in original program specifications could be made up by the skill of a technical writing department . . . was misguided; the design of a program and the design of its specification must be undertaken in parallel by the same person, and they must interact with each other. A lack of clarity in specification is one of the surest signs of a deficiency in the program it describes, and the two faults must be removed simultaneously before the project is embarked upon." I wish I had followed this advice in 1963; I wish we all would follow it today.

My notes of the proceedings of that day in October 1965 include a complete section devoted to failings within the software group; this section rivals the most abject self-abasement of a revisionist official in the Chinese cultural revolution. Our main failure was overambition. "The goals which we have attempted have obviously proved to be far beyond our grasp." There was also failure in prediction, in estimation of program size and speed, of effort required, in planning the coordination and interaction of programs, in providing an early warning that things were going wrong. There were faults in our control of program changes, documentation, liaison with other departments, with our management, and with our customers. We failed in giving clear and stable definitions of the responsibilities of individual programmers and project leaders — Oh, need I go on? What was amazing was that a large team of highly intelligent programmers could labor so hard and so long on such an unpromising project. You know, you shouldn't trust us intelligent programmers. We can think up such good arguments for convincing ourselves and each other of the utterly absurd. Especially don't believe us when we promise to repeat an earlier success, only bigger and better next time.

The last section of our inquiry into the failure dealt with the criteria of quality of software. "In the recent struggle to deliver any software at all, the first casualty has been consideration of the quality of the software delivered. The quality of software is measured by a number of totally incompatible criteria, which must be carefully balanced in the design and implementation of every program." We then made a list of no less than seventeen criteria which has been published in a guest editorial in Volume 2 of the journal, *Software Practice and Experience.*

How did we recover from the catastrophe? First, we classified our 503 customers into groups, according to the nature and size of the hardware configurations which they had bought — for example, those with magnetic tapes were all in one group. We assigned to each group of customers a small team of programmers and told the team leader to visit the customers to find out what they wanted; to select the easiest request to fulfill, and to make plans (but no promises) to implement it. In no case would we consider a request for a feature that would take more than three months to implement and deliver. The project leader would then have to convince *me* that the customers' request was reasonable, that the design of the new feature was appropriate, and that the plans and schedules for implementation were realistic. Above all, I did not allow anything to be done which I did not myself understand. It worked! The software requested began to be delivered on the promised dates. With an increase in our confidence and that of our customers, we were able to undertake fulfilling slightly more ambitious requests. Within a year we had recovered from the disaster. Within two years, we even had some moderately satisfied customers.

Thus we muddled through by common sense and compromise to something approaching success. But I was not satisfied. I did not see why the design and implementation of an operating system should be so much more difficult than that of a compiler. This is the reason why I have devoted my later research to problems of parallel programming and language constructs which would assist in clear structuring of operating systems — constructs such as monitors and communicating processes.

While I was working at Elliott's, I became very interested in techniques for formal definition of programming languages. At that time, Peter Landin and Christopher Strachey proposed to define a programming language in a simple functional notation, that specified the effect of each command on a mathematically defined abstract machine. I was not happy with this proposal because I felt that such a definition must incorporate a number of fairly arbitrary representation decisions and would not be much simpler in principle than an implementation of the language for a real machine. As an alternative, I proposed that a programming language definition should be formalized as a set of axioms, describing the desired properties of programs written in the language. I felt that carefully formulated axioms would leave an implementation the necessary freedom to implement the language efficiently on different machines and enable the programmer to prove the correctness of his programs. But I did not see how to actually do it. I thought that it would need lengthy research to develop and apply the necessary techniques and that a university would be a better place to conduct such research than industry. So I applied for a chair in Computer Science at the Queen's University of Belfast where I was to spend nine happy and productive years. In October 1968, as I unpacked my papers in my new home in Belfast, I came across an obscure preprint of an article by Bob Floyd entitled, "Assigning Meanings to Programs." What a stroke of luck! At last I could see a way to achieve my hopes for my research. Thus I wrote my first paper on the axiomatic approach to computer programming, published in the *Communications of the ACM* in October 1969.

Just recently, I have discovered that an early advocate of the assertional method of program proving was none other than Alan Turing himself. On June 24, 1950 at a conference in Cambridge, he gave a short talk entitled, "Checking a Large Routine" which explains the idea with great clarity. "How can one check a large routine in the sense of making sure that it's right? In order that the man who checks may not have too difficult a task, the programmer should make a number of definite *assertions* which can be checked individually, and from which the correctness of the whole program easily follows."

Consider the analogy of checking an addition. If the sum is given [just as a column of figures with the answer below] one must check the whole at one sitting. But if the totals for the various columns are given, [with the carries added in separately], the checker's work is much easier, being split up into the checking of the various assertions [that each column is correctly added] and the small addition [of the carries to the total]. This principle can be applied to the checking of a large routine but we will illustrate the method by means of a small routine viz. one to obtain *n* factorial without the use of a multiplier. Unfortunately there is no coding system sufficiently generally known to justify giving this routine in full, but a flow diagram will be sufficient for illustration. That brings me back to the main theme of my talk, the design of programming languages.

During the period, August 1962 to October 1966, I attended every meeting of the IFIP ALGOL working group. After completing our labors on the IFIP ALGOL subset, we started on the design of ALGOL X, the intended successor to ALGOL 60. More suggestions for new features were made, and in May 1965, Niklaus Wirth was commissioned to collate them into a single language design. I was delighted by his draft design which avoided all the known defects of ALGOL 60 and included several new features, all of which could be simply and efficiently implemented, and safely and conveniently used.

The description of the language was not yet complete. I worked hard on making suggestions for its improvement and so did many other members of our group. By the time of the next meeting in St. Pierre de Chartreuse, France in October 1965, we had a draft of an excellent and realistic language design which was published in June 1966 as "A Contribution to the Development of ALGOL," in the *Communications of the ACM*. It was implemented on the IBM 360 and given the title ALGOL W by its many happy users. It was not only a worthy successor of ALGOL 60, it was even a worthy predecessor of PASCAL.

At the same meeting, the ALGOL committee had placed before it, a short, incomplete and rather incomprehensible document, describing a different, more ambitious and, to me, a far less attractive language. I was astonished when the working group, consisting of all the best known international experts of programming languages, resolved to lay aside the commissioned draft on which we had all been working and swallow a line with such an unattractive bait.

This happened just one week after our inquest on the 503 Mark II software project. I gave desperate warnings against the obscurity, the complexity, and overambition of the new design, but my warnings went unheeded. I conclude that there are two ways of constructing a software design: One way is to make it so simple that there are *obviously* no deficiencies and the other way is to make it so complicated that there are no *obvious* deficiencies.

The first method is far more difficult. It demands the same skill, devotion, insight, and even inspiration as the discovery of the simple physical laws which underlie the complex phenomena of nature. It also requires a willingness to accept objectives which are limited by physical, logical, and technological constraints, and to accept a compromise when conflicting objectives cannot be met. No committee will ever do this until it is too late.

So it was with the ALGOL committee. Clearly the draft which it preferred was not yet perfect. So a new and final draft of the new ALGOL language design was promised in three months' time; it was to be submitted to the scrutiny of a subgroup of four members including myself. Three months came and went, without a word of the new draft. After six months, the subgroup met in the Netherlands. We had before us a longer and thicker document, full of errors corrected at the last minute, describing yet another, but to me, equally unattractive language. Niklaus Wirth and I spent some time trying to get removed some of the deficiencies in the design and in the description, but in vain. The completed final draft of the language was promised for the next meeting of the full ALGOL committee in three months' time.

Three months came and went — not a word of the new draft appeared. After six months, in October 1966, the ALGOL working group met in Warsaw. It had before it an even longer and thicker document, full of errors corrected at the last minute, describing equally obscurely yet another different, and to me, equally unattractive language. The experts in the group could not see the defects of the design and they firmly resolved to adopt the draft, believing it would be completed in three months. In vain, I told them it would not. In vain, I urged them to remove some of the technical mistakes of the language, the predominance of references, the default type conversions. Far from wishing to simplify the language, the working group actually asked the authors to include even more complex features like overloading of operators and concurrency.

When any new language design project is nearing completion, there is always a mad rush to get new features added before standardization. The rush is mad indeed, because it leads into a trap from which there is no escape. A feature which is omitted can always be added later, when its design and its implications are well understood. A feature which is included before it is fully understood can never be removed later.

At last, in December 1968, in a mood of black depression, I attended the meeting in Munich at which our long-gestated monster was to come to birth and receive the name ALGOL 68. By this time, a number of other members of the group had become disillusioned, but too late: The committee was now packed with supporters of the language, which was sent up for promulgation by the higher committees of IFIP. The best we could do was to send with it a minority report, stating our considered view that, " . . . as a tool for the *reliable creation* of sophisticated programs, the language was a failure." This report was later suppressed by IFIP, an act which reminds me of lines of

Hilaire Belloc,

> But scientists, who ought to know
> Assure us that it must be so.
> Oh, let us never, never doubt
> What nobody is sure about.

I did not attend any further meetings of that working group. I am pleased to report that the group soon came to realize that there was something wrong with their language and with its description; they labored hard for six more years to produce a revised description of the language. It is a great improvement but I'm afraid that, in my view, it does not remove the basic technical flaws in the design, nor does it begin to address the problem of its overwhelming complexity.

Programmers are always surrounded by complexity; we cannot avoid it. Our applications are complex because we are ambitious to use our computers in ever more sophisticated ways. Programming is complex because of the large number of conflicting objectives for each of our programming projects. If our basic tool, the language in which we design and code our programs, is also complicated, the language itself becomes part of the problem rather than part of its solution.

Now let me tell you about yet another overambitious language project. Between 1965 and 1970 I was a member and even chairman of the Technical Committee No. 10 of the European Computer Manufacturers Association. We were charged first with a watching brief and then with the standardization of a language to end all languages, designed to meet the needs of all computer applications, both commercial and scientific, by the greatest computer manufacturer of all time. I had studied with interest and amazement, even a touch of amusement, the four initial documents describing a language called NPL, which appeared between March 1 and November 30, 1964. Each was more ambitious and absurd than the last in its wishful speculations. Then the language began to be implemented and a new series of documents began to appear at six-monthly intervals, each describing the final frozen version of the language, under its final frozen name PL/I.

But to me, each revision of the document simply showed how far the initial F-level implementation had progressed. Those parts of the language that were not yet implemented were still described in free-flowing flowery prose giving promise of unalloyed delight. In the parts that *had* been implemented, the flowers had withered; they were choked by an undergrowth of explanatory footnotes, placing arbitrary and unpleasant restrictions on the use of each feature and loading upon a programmer the responsibility for controlling the complex and unexpected side-effects and interaction effects with all the other features of the language.

At last, March 11, 1968, the language description was nobly presented to the waiting world as a worthy candidate for standardization. But it was not. It had already undergone some seven thousand corrections and modifications at the hand of its original designers. Another twelve editions were needed before it was finally published as a standard in 1976. I fear that this was not because everybody concerned was satisfied with its design, but because they were thoroughly bored and disillusioned.

For as long as I was involved in this project, I urged that the language be simplified, if necessary by subsetting, so that the professional programmer would be able to understand it and be able to take responsibility for the correctness and cost-effectiveness of his programs. I urged that the dangerous features such as defaults and ON- conditions be removed. I knew that it would be impossible to write a wholly reliable compiler for a language of this complexity and impossible to write a wholly reliable program when the correctness of each part of the program depends on checking that every other part of the program has avoided all the traps and pitfalls of the language.

At first I hoped that such a technically unsound project would collapse but I soon realized it was doomed to success. Almost anything in software can be implemented, sold, and even used given enough determination. There is nothing a mere scientist can say that will stand against the flood of a hundred million dollars. But there is one quality that cannot be purchased in this way — and that is reliability. The price of reliability is the pursuit of the utmost simplicity. It is a price which the very rich find most hard to pay.

All this happened a long time ago. Can it be regarded as relevant in a conference dedicated to a preview of the Computer Age that lies ahead? It is my gravest fear that it can. The mistakes which have been made in the last twenty years are being repeated today on an even grander scale. I refer to a language design project which has generated documents entitled *strawman, woodenman, tinman, ironman, steelman, green* and finally now ADA. This project has been initiated and sponsored by one of the world's most powerful organizations, the United States Department of Defense. Thus it is ensured of an influence and attention quite independent of its technical merits and its faults and deficiencies threaten us with far greater dangers. For none of the evidence we have so far can inspire confidence that this language has avoided any of the problems that have afflicted other complex language projects of the past.

I have been giving the best of my advice to this project since 1975. At first I was extremely hopeful. The original objectives of the language included reliability, readability of programs, formality of language definition, and even simplicity. Gradually these objectives have been sacrificed in favor of power, supposedly achieved by a plethora of features and notational conventions, many of them unnecessary and some of them, like exception handling, even dangerous. We relive the history of the design of the motor car. Gadgets and glitter prevail over fundamental concerns of safety and economy.

It is not too late! I believe that by careful pruning of the ADA language, it is still possible to select a very powerful subset that would be reliable and efficient in implementation and safe and economic in use. The sponsors of the language have declared unequivocally, however, that there shall be no subsets. This is the strangest paradox of the whole strange project. If you want a language with no subsets, you must make it *small*.

You include only those features which you know to be needed for *every* single application of the language and which you know to be appropriate for *every* single hardware configuration on which the language is implemented. Then extensions can be specially designed where necessary for particular hardware devices and for particular applications. That is the great strength of PASCAL, that there are so few unnecessary features and almost no need for subsets. That is why the language is strong enough to support specialized extensions — Concurrent PASCAL for real time work, PASCAL PLUS for discrete event simulation, UCSD PASCAL for microprocessor work stations. If only we could learn the right lessons from the successes of the past, we would not need to learn from our failures.

And so, the best of my advice to the originators and designers of ADA has been ignored. In this last resort, I appeal to you, representatives of the programming profession in the United States, and citizens concerned with the welfare and safety of your own country and of mankind: Do not allow this language in its present state to be used in applications where reliability is critical, i.e., nuclear power stations, cruise missiles, early warning systems, anti-ballistic missile defense systems. The next rocket to go astray as a result of a programming language error may not be an exploratory space rocket on a harmless trip to Venus: It may be a nuclear warhead exploding over one of our own cities. An unreliable programming language generating unreliable programs constitutes a far greater risk to our environment and to our society than unsafe cars, toxic pesticides, or accidents at nuclear power stations. Be vigilant to reduce that risk, not to increase it.

Let me not end on this somber note. To have our best advice ignored is the common fate of all who take on the role of consultant, ever since Cassandra pointed out the dangers of bringing a wooden horse within the walls of Troy. That reminds me of a story I used to hear in my childhood. As far as I recall, its title was:

The Emperor's Old Clothes

Many years ago, there was an Emperor who was so excessively fond of clothes that he spent all his money on dress. He did not trouble himself with soldiers, attend banquets, or give judgement in court. Of any other king or emperor one might say, "He is sitting in council," but it was always said of him, "The emperor is sitting in his wardrobe." And so he was. On one unfortunate occasion, he had been tricked into going forth naked to his chagrin and the glee of his subjects. He resolved never to leave his throne, and to avoid nakedness, he ordered that each of his many new suits of clothes should be simply draped on top of the old.

Time passed away merrily in the large town that was his capital. Ministers and courtiers, weavers and tailors, visitors and subjects, seamstresses and embroiderers, went in and out of the throne room about their various tasks, and they all exclaimed, "How magnificent is the attire of our Emperor."

One day the Emperor's oldest and most faithful Minister heard tell of a most distinguished tailor who taught at an ancient institute of higher stitchcraft, and who had developed a new art of abstract embroidery using stitches so refined that no one could tell whether they were actually there at all. "These must indeed be splendid stitches," thought the Minister. "If we can but engage this tailor to advise us, we will bring the adornment of our Emperor to such heights of ostentation that all the world will acknowledge him as the greatest Emperor there has ever been."

So the honest old Minister engaged the master tailor at vast expense. The tailor was brought to the throne room where he made obeisance to the heap of fine clothes which now completely covered the throne. All the courtiers waited eagerly for his advice. Imagine their astonishment when his advice was not to add sophistication and more intricate embroidery to that which already existed, but rather to remove layers of the finery, and strive for simplicity and elegance in place of extravagant elaboration. "This tailor is not the expert that he claims," they muttered. "His wits have been addled by long contemplation in his ivory tower and he no longer understands the sartorial needs of a modern Emperor." The tailor argued loud and long for the good sense of his advice but could not make himself heard. Finally, he accepted his fee and returned to his ivory tower.

Never to this very day has the full truth of this story been told: That one fine morning, when the Emperor felt hot and bored, he extricated himself carefully from under his mountain of clothes and is now living happily as a swineherd in another story. The tailor is canonized as the patron saint of all consultants, because in spite of the enormous fees that he extracted, he was never able to convince his clients of his dawning realization that their clothes have no Emperor.

Section 4
PROGRAMMING: MATHEMATICAL
PROOFS OF PROGRAM CORRECTNESS

The fourth section of the book contains three papers that discuss programming, and especially structured programming, from a mathematical point of view. Many readers will want to skim through the papers, since they require a level of mathematics far beyond what one normally encounters in day-to-day work in the data processing field. However, it is precisely because of this that the papers are interesting to read — that is, the papers by Cooper, Hoare, and Mills give one an idea of the level of mathematical expertise one ought to acquire in order to pursue computer programming with the degree of rigor and precision that is usually associated with structured programming.

Cooper: Böhm and Jacopini's Reduction of Flow Charts

The selection written by David Cooper consists simply of a brief Letter to the Editor of *Communications of the ACM,* and comments on the classic Böhm and Jacopini proof of structured programming.* The letter is interesting because it expresses Cooper's view that Böhm and Jacopini did not go far enough — that, in fact, one could prove that an arbitrary program could be reduced to a form even simpler than that suggested by Böhm and Jacopini.

Hoare: Proof of a Program: FIND

Tony Hoare's paper is much more substantial than Cooper's letter, and is equally challenging to read. It provides a formal mathematical proof of a subroutine, FIND, that is used in sorting algorithms. The subroutine itself is not likely to be terribly interesting to anyone except those who are concerned with classical sorting algorithms, but it is presented in an eminently understandable fashion.

The primary reason for reading Hoare's paper is to get an appreciation for the amount of effort — and the level of expertise — required to provide a formal proof of correctness of a relatively small piece of code. The discussion requires some eight pages of text and eighteen lemmas to prove the correctness of fifteen program state-

---

*See C. Böhm and G. Jacopini, "Flow Diagrams, Turing Machines and Languages with Only Two Formation Rules," *Communications of the ACM,* Vol. 9, No. 5 (May 1966), pp. 366-71. Reprinted in *Classics in Software Engineering,* ed. E.N. Yourdon (New York: YOURDON Press, 1979), pp. 13-25.

ments. Even if the average computer programmer were capable of such effort (which is certainly not true in the United States at the current time!), how could we justify such an investment of time and effort for a typical programming project?

Most programmers, managers, and users would argue, of course, that such an enormous investment of time and effort would be impractical. On the other hand, if the computer program is being used to control a nuclear missile, or a nuclear reactor, perhaps it is worth the effort. The thought is indeed humbling: It suggests that if we really do want computers to assume responsibility for such critical life-and-death applications, then we should be prepared to develop the software with a level of expertise far beyond what we are really capable of accomplishing today. It is significant, I think, to note that Hoare's paper was published more than ten years ago — and there has still not been any noticeable trend toward formal proofs of program correctness in real-world applications.

Mills: Mathematical Foundations for Structured Programming

The last paper in this section is a massive one. Written by Harlan Mills, at IBM, the paper's original publication date was February 1972, which means that most of it was probably written in 1971 — the period during which the Federal Systems Division of IBM was getting its first substantial experience with structured programming, top-down design, and chief programmer teams on the New York Times project.*

Even if you've decided to skip this entire section of papers to avoid the mathematics, you should read the first five or six pages of Mills's paper. It presents structured programming almost as if it were a religious gospel — suggesting, for example, that ". . . a radical change is possible now . . . that in structured programming the techniques and tools are at hand to permit an entirely new level of precision in programming." His whole introduction to the subject matter of structured programming is convincing and eloquent, even if one has already *been* convinced! One has the distinct impression that much of this was necessary in order for Mills to convince his colleagues throughout IBM to adopt this alien new programming approach.

After the first few pages, Mills launches into a very long, very formal presentation of the mathematics of structured programming. However, it appears to be written for non-mathematicians and it should be possible for any serious programmer to read and understand it. The best part of this presentation, in my opinion, is the first two paragraphs of the section entitled "The Correctness of Structured Programs." In it, Mills reminds us, "There is no such thing as an absolute proof of logical correctness. There are only degrees of rigor, such as 'technical english,' 'mathematical journal proof,' 'formal logic,' etc., which are each informal descriptions of mechanisms for creating agreement and belief in a process of reasoning."

I think this makes an important point. Even if a programmer cannot (or will not) develop a formal proof of correctness along the lines of Hoare's proof of the FIND program, he should not abdicate *all* responsibility for developing some kind of convincing

---

*The New York Times system is described in F.T. Baker's "Chief Programmer Team Management of Production Programming," which originally appeared in *IBM Systems Journal,* Vol. 11, No. 1 (1972), pp. 56-73; and in "System Quality Through Structured Programming," also by Baker, which was originally published in *AFIPS Proceedings of the 1972 Fall Joint Computer Conference,* Vol. 41 (Montvale, N.J.: AFIPS Press, 1972), pp. 339-44. Both papers are reprinted in *Classics in Software Engineering,* ed. E.N. Yourdon (New York: YOURDON Press, 1979), pp. 65-82, 129-38.

demonstration that his program does what it ought to do. And of course, it is immensely easier to develop some kind of convincing argument, whether it takes the form of an informal walkthrough or a formal mathematical proof, if the program is organized according to the principles of structured programming.

Additional References on Mathematical Proofs of Program Correctness

The articles selected for this volume supplement those previously reprinted in *Classics in Software Engineering.* For a more complete view of programming techniques, see the following:

1. C. Böhm and G. Jacopini, "Flow Diagrams, Turing Machines and Languages with Only Two Formation Rules," *Communications of the ACM,* Vol. 9, No. 5 (May 1966), pp. 366-71. Reprinted in *Classics in Software Engineering,* ed. E.N. Yourdon (New York: YOURDON Press, 1979), pp. 13-25.

2. E. Ashcroft and Z. Manna, "The Translation of 'go to' Programs to 'while' Programs," *Proceedings of the 1971 IFIP Congress,* Vol. 1 (Amsterdam, The Netherlands: North-Holland Publishing Co., 1971), pp. 250-55. Reprinted in *Classics in Software Engineering,* pp. 51-61.

Böhm and Jacopini's Reduction of Flow Charts

Editor:

In the first part of the paper by Böhm and Jacopini, "Flow Diagrams, Turing Machines and Languages with Only Two Formation Rules" [*Comm. ACM* 9, 5 (May 1966)], it is proved that any program may be mechanically transformed into an equivalent program whose flowchart is "decomposable into II Φ Δ." This last phrase means that all loops are properly nested; this concept is equivalent to the block form I have defined in "Some Transformations and Standard Forms of Graphs, with Applications to Computer Programs," to be published shortly (in *Machine Intelligence 2*, D. Michie, ed., Oliver and Boyd, Edinburgh). However, even by making the same assumptions as Böhm and Jacopini, a stronger reduction than theirs is possible.

In order to prove their result, Böhm and Jacopini introduce new Boolean variables into the program (or equivalently a single Boolean stack, but a bound for the maximum depth required for this stack may easily be given). As they point out, it is not usually necessary to add a new concept such as "Boolean variable" because in most applications we would expect to find some existing concept which would serve the same purpose. However, for simpler exposition we assume new variables have been added. New predicates to test these variables are also needed, together with assignments to set them true or false.

If we allow these additions to a program, then it is clear that any two nodes (*P* and *Q*) of the directed graph which is the program's flowchart may be coalesced into one new node *N*. The node *N* has as input all the arcs leading into *P* and also all those leading into *Q*, and similarly for the outputs. Loops *PP* or *QQ* do not affect this argument. A new Boolean variable,

SOURCE: D.C. Cooper, *Communications of the ACM*, 1967.

B_N, is introduced and instructions added to set it true on all arcs originally leading into P, and false on those originally leading into Q. By testing this variable the correct output arc of N may be chosen. By repeating this process, all the nodes of a program may be collapsed into a single node; the resulting program will have a trivial flowchart consisting of node A with loops AA and arcs to A from the input and from A to the output. In Böhm and Jacopini's terminology we have reduced the program to one whose flowchart is decomposable into Π, Φ, and Δ, with at most one Φ.

The result may be illustrated using ALGOL as follows: Let L_0 and L_n be labels on the start and exit, respectively, of a program P, and let $L_1, \ldots, L_{n-1}$ be all the other labels. For $0 \leq i \leq n-1$ and $0 \leq j \leq n$, let $P_{i,j}$ be the condition for control to pass from L_i to L_j without passing any other label, and let $S_{i,j}$ be the sequence of assignment statements obeyed on this path. Define new Boolean variables $B_0, B_1, \ldots, B_n$. Then P is equivalent to the program:

$START$: $B_0 \leftarrow$ **true**; $B_1 \leftarrow$ **false**; $\ldots$; $B_n \rightarrow$ **false**;

L: **if** B_n **then go to** $EXIT$;

    if $B_0 \wedge P_{0,0}$ **then begin** $B_0 :=$ **false**; $S_{0,0}$;

    $B_0 :=$ **true end else**

    $\ldots$

    $\ldots$

    if $B_i \wedge P_{i,j}$ **then begin** $B_i :=$ **false**; $S_{i,j}$;

    $B_j :=$ **true end else**

    $\ldots$

    $\ldots$

    if $B_{n-1} \wedge P_{n-1,n}$ **then begin** $B_{n-1} :=$ **false**; $S_{n-1,n}$;

    $B_n :=$ **true end**;

    go to L;

$EXIT$:

This program has a trivial flowchart of the form indicated above.

Böhm and Jacopini are interested in reducing as far as possible the number of concepts used and it is then reasonable to code up previous flow of control into variables, as this can usually be done within the existing framework. If, however, one's motivation is to simplify the program's structure so that we may better answer questions such as whether the program loops indefinitely, then this coding of the control into variables is no help at all. It remains true though that the block form is a very natural standard form to use, and it is certainly possible to transform many programs into equivalent programs in block form without resorting to the coding of control features as values of variables. Some preliminary conjectures along this line are reported in my paper referred to above.

Proof of a Program: FIND

1. Introduction

In a number of papers [1, 2, 3] the desirability of proving the correctness of programs has been suggested and this has been illustrated by proofs of simple example programs. In this paper the construction of the proof of a useful, efficient, and nontrivial program, using a method based on invariants, is shown. It is suggested that if a proof is constructed as part of the coding process for an algorithm, it is hardly more laborious than the traditional practice of program testing.

2. The program "Find"

The purpose of the program Find [4] is to find that element of an array $A[1:N]$ whose value is fth in order of magnitude; and to rearrange the array in such a way that this element is placed in $A[f]$; and furthermore, all elements with subscripts lower than f have lesser values, and all elements with subscripts greater than f have greater values. Thus on completion of the program, the following relationship will hold:

$$A[1], A[2], \ldots, A[f-1] \leqslant A[f] \leqslant A[f+1], \ldots, A[N]$$

This relation is abbreviated as Found.

One method of achieving the desired effect would be to sort the whole array. If the array is small, this would be a good method; but if the array is large, the time taken to sort it will also be large. The Find program is designed to take advantage of the weaker requirements to save much of the time which would be involved in a full sort.

The usefulness of the Find program arises from its application to the problem of finding the median or other quantiles

SOURCE: C.A.R. Hoare, *Communications of the ACM*, 1971.

of a set of observations stored in a computer array. For example, if N is odd and f is set to $(N + 1)/2$, the effect of the Find program will be to place an observation with value equal to the median in $A[f]$. Similarly the first quartile may be found by setting f to $(N + 1)/4$, and so on.

Table I

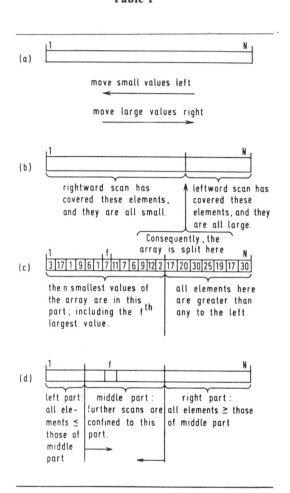

The method used is based on the principle that the desired effect of Find is to move lower valued elements of the array to one end — the "left-hand" end — and higher valued elements of the array to the other end — the "right-hand" end. (See Table I(a)). This suggests that the array be scanned, starting at the left-hand end and moving rightward. Any element encountered which is small will remain where it is, but any element which is large should be moved up to the right-hand end of the array, in exchange for a small one. In order to find such a small element, a separate scan is made, starting at the right-hand end and moving leftward. In this scan, any large element encountered remains where it is; the first small element encountered is moved down to the left-hand end in exchange for the large element already encountered in the rightward scan. Then both scans can be resumed until the next exchange is necessary. The process is repeated until the scans meet somewhere in the middle of the array. It is then known that all elements to the left of this meeting point will be small, and all elements to the right will be large. When this condition holds, we will say that the array is *split at* the given point into two parts (see Table I(b)).

The reasoning of the previous paragraph assumes that there is some means of distinguishing small elements from large ones. Since we are interested only in their comparative values, it is sufficient to select the value of some arbitrary element before either of the scans starts; any element with lower value than the selected element is counted as small, and any element with higher value is counted as large. The fact that the discriminating value is arbitrary means that the place where the two scans will meet is also arbitrary; but it does not affect the fact that the array will be split at the meeting point, wherever that may be.

Now consider the question on which side of the split the fth element in order of value is to be found. If the split is to the right of $A[f]$, then the desired element must of necessity be to the left of the split, and all elements to the right of the split will be greater than it. In this case, all elements to the right of the split can be ignored in any future processing, since they are already in their proper place, namely to the right of $A[f]$ (see Table I(c)). Similarly, if the split is to the left of $A[f]$, the element to be found must be to the right of the split, and all elements to the left of the split must be equal or less than it; furthermore, these elements can be ignored in future processing.

In either case, the program proceeds by repeating the rightward and leftward scans, but this time one of the scans will start at the split rather than at the beginning of the array. When the two scans meet again, it will be known that there is a second split in the array, this time perhaps on the other side of $A[f]$. Thus again, we may proceed with the rightward and leftward scans, but we start the rightward scan at the split on the left of $A[f]$ and the leftward scan at the split on the right, thus confining attention only to that part of the array that lies between the two splits; this will be known as the *middle part* of the array (see Table I(d)).

When the third scan is complete, the middle part of the array will be split again into two parts. We take the new middle part as that part which contains $A[f]$ and repeat the double scan on this new middle part. The process is repeated until the middle part consists of only one element, namely $A[f]$. This element will now be equal to or greater than all elements to the left and equal to or less than all elements to the right; and thus the desired result of Find will be accomplished.

This has been an informal description of the method used by the program Find. Diagrams have been used to convey an understanding of how and why the method works, and they serve as an intuitive proof of its correctness. However, the method is described only in general terms, leaving many details undecided; and accordingly, the intuitive proof is far from watertight. In the next section, the details of the method will be filled in during the process of coding it in a formal programming language; and simultaneously, the details of the proof will be formalized in traditional logical notation. The end product of this activity will be a program suitable for computer execution, together with a proof of its correctness. The reader who checks the validity of the proof will thereby convince himself that the program requires no testing.

3. Coding and proof construction

The coding and proof construction may be split into several stages, each stage dealing with greater detail than the previous one. Furthermore, each stage may be systematically analyzed as a series of steps.

3.1. Stage 1: Problem definition

The first stage in coding and proof construction is to obtain a rigorous formulation of what is to be accomplished, and what may be assumed to begin with. In this case we may assume

(a) The subscript bounds of A are 1 and N.

(b) $1 \leqslant f \leqslant N$.

The required result is:

$$\forall p, q(1 \leqslant p \leqslant f \leqslant q \leqslant N \supset A[p] \leqslant A[f] \leqslant A[q]) \qquad \text{[Found]}$$

3.2. Stage 2: The general method

(1) The first step in each stage is to decide what variables will be required to hold intermediate results of the program. In the case of Find, it will be necessary to know at all times the extent of the middle part, which is currently being scanned. This indicates the introduction of variables m and n to point to the first element $A[m]$ and the last element $A[n]$ of the middle part.

(2) The second step is to attempt to describe more formally the purpose of each variable, which was informally described in the previous step. This purpose may be expressed as a formula of logic which is intended to remain true throughout the execution of the program, even when the value of the variable concerned is changed by assignment.* Such a formula is known as an *invariant*. As mentioned above, m is intended to point to the leftmost element of the middle part of the array; and the middle part at all times contains $A[f]$; consequently m is never greater than f. Furthermore, there is always a split just to the left of the middle part, that is between $m - 1$ and m. Thus the following formula should be true for m throughout execution of the program:

$$m \leq f \;\&\; \forall p, q(1 \leq p < m \leq q \leq N \supset A[p] \leq A[q]) \qquad \text{[m-invariant]}$$

Similarly, n is intended to point to the rightmost element of the middle part; it must never be less than f, and there will always be a split just to the right of it:

$$f \leq n \;\&\; \forall p, q(1 \leq p \leq n < q \leq N \supset A[p] \leq A[q]) \qquad \text{[n-invariant]}$$

(3) The next step is to determine the initial values for these variables. Since the middle part of the array is intended to be the part that still requires processing, and since to begin with the whole array requires processing, the obvious choice of initial values of m and n are 1 and N, respectively, indicating the first and last elements of the whole array. The code required is:

$$m := 1; \quad n := N$$

(4) It is necessary next to check that these values satisfy the relevant invariants. This may be done by substituting the initial value for the co⁓ ⁓ondin⁓ ⁓ariable in each invariant, and ensuring that the result follows from facts al⁓⁓⁓ know⁓

$$1 \leq f \leq N \supset 1 \leq f \;\&$$
$$\forall p, q(1 \leq p < 1 \leq q \leq N \supset A[p] \leq A[q]) \qquad \text{[Lemma 1]}$$

$$1 \leq f \leq N \supset f \leq N \;\&$$
$$\forall p, q(1 \leq p \leq N < q \leq N \supset A[p] \leq A[q]) \qquad \text{[Lemma 2]}$$

The quantified clause of each lemma is trivially true since the antecedents of the implications are always false.

(5) After setting the initial values, the method of the program is repeatedly to reduce the size of the middle part, until it contains only one element. This may be accomplished by an iteration of the form:

while $m < n$ **do** "reduce middle part"

---

*Except possibly in certain "critical regions."

(6) It remains to prove that this loop accomplishes the objectives of the program as a whole. If we write the body of the iteration properly (i.e. in such a way as to preserve the truth of all invariants) then all invariants will still be true on termination. Furthermore, termination will occur only when $m < n$ goes false. Thus it is necessary only to show that the combination of the truth of the invariants and the falsity of the while clause expression $m < n$ implies the truth of Found.

$$m \leqslant f \,\&\, \forall p, q (1 \leqslant p < m \leqslant q \leqslant N \supset A[p] \leqslant A[q])$$
$$\&\, f \leqslant n \,\&\, \forall p, q (1 \leqslant p \leqslant n < q \leqslant N \supset A[p] \leqslant A[q])$$
$$\&\, \neg\, m < n$$
$$\supset \forall p, q (1 \leqslant p \leqslant f \leqslant q \leqslant N \supset A[p] \leqslant A[f] \leqslant A[q]) \qquad \text{[Lemma 3]}$$

The antecedents imply that $m = n = f$. If $1 \leqslant p \leqslant f \leqslant q \leqslant N$, then either $p = f$, in which case $A[p] \leqslant A[f]$ is obvious, or $p < f$, in which case substituting f for both m and q in the first quantified antecedent gives $A[p] \leqslant A[f]$. A similar argument shows that $A[f] \leqslant A[q]$.

At this point, the general structure of the program is as follows:

$m := 1; n := N;$

while $m < n$ **do** "reduce middle part"

Furthermore, this code has been proved to be correct, provided that the body of the contained iteration is correct.

3.3. Stage 3: Reduce the middle part

(1) The process for reducing the middle part involves a scan from the left and from the right. This requires two pointers, i and j, pointing to elements $A[i]$ and $A[j]$ respectively. In addition, a variable r is required to hold the arbitrary value which has been selected to act as a discriminator between "small" and "large" values.

(2) The i pointer is intended to pass over only those array elements with values smaller than r. Thus all array elements strictly to the left of the currently scanned element $A[i]$ will be known always to be equal to or less than r:

$$m \leqslant i \,\&\, \forall p (1 \leqslant p < i \supset A[p] \leqslant r) \qquad \text{[i-invariant]}$$

Similarly the j pointer passes over only large values, and all elements strictly to the right of the currently scanned element $A[j]$ are known always to be equal to or greater than r:

$$j \leqslant n \,\&\, \forall q (j < q \leqslant N \supset r \leqslant A[q]) \qquad \text{[j-invariant]}$$

Since the value of r does not change, there is no need for an r-invariant.

(3) The i pointer starts at the left of the middle part, i.e. at m; and the j pointer starts at the right of the middle part, i.e. at n. The initial value of r is taken from an arbitrary element of the middle part of the array. Since $A[f]$ is always in the middle part, its value is as good as any.

(4) The fact that the initial values satisfy the i- and j-invariants follows directly from the truth of the corresponding m- and n-invariants; this is stated formally in the following lemmas:

$$f \leqslant N \,\&\, m \leqslant f \,\&\,$$
$$\forall p, q (1 \leqslant p < m \leqslant q \leqslant N \supset A[p] \leqslant A[q])$$
$$\supset m \leqslant m \,\&\, \forall p (1 \leqslant p < m \supset A[p] \leqslant A[f]) \qquad \text{[Lemma 4]}$$

$$1 \leq f \& f \leq n \&$$
$$\forall p, q(1 \leq p \leq n < q \leq N \supset A[p] \leq A[q])$$
$$\supset n \leq n \& \forall q(n < q \leq N \supset A[f] \leq A[q]) \qquad \text{[Lemma 5]}$$

The first of these is proved by setting q to f and the second by setting p to f.

(5) After setting the initial values, the method is to repeatedly add one to i and subtract one from j, until they cross over. This may be achieved by an iteration of the form:

while $i \leq j$ **do** "increase i and decrease j"

On exit from this loop, $j < i$ and all invariants are intended to be preserved.

If j and i cross over above f, the proposed method assigns j as the new value of n; if they cross over below f, i is assigned as the new value of m.

if $f \leq j$ **then** $n := j$

else if $i \leq f$ **then** $m := i$

else go to L

The destination of the jump will be determined later.

(6) The validity of these assignments is proved by showing that the new value of n or m satisfies the corresponding invariant whenever the assignment takes place. In these proofs it can be assumed that the i- and j-invariants hold; and furthermore, since the assignment immediately follows the iteration of (5), it is known that $j < i$. Thus the appropriate lemma is:

$$j < i \& \forall p(1 \leq p < i \supset A[p] \leq r)$$
$$\& \forall q(j < q \leq N \supset r \leq A[q])$$
$$\supset \text{if } f \leq j \text{ then } f \leq j \&$$
$$\forall p, q(1 \leq p \leq j < q \leq N) \supset A[p] \leq A[q))$$
$$\text{else if } i \leq f \text{ then } i \leq f \&$$
$$\forall p, q(1 \leq p < i \leq q \leq N \supset A[p] \leq A[q]) \qquad \text{[Lemma 6]}$$

The proof of this is based on the fact that if $1 \leq p \leq j < q \leq N$, then $p < i$ (since $j < i$), and both $A[p] \leq r$ and $r \leq A[q]$. Hence $A[p] \leq A[q]$. Similarly, if $1 \leq p < i \leq q \leq N$, then $j < q$, and the same result follows.

It remains to determine the destination of the jump **go to** L. This jump is obeyed only if $j < f < i$, and it happens that in this case it can be proved that the condition Found has already been achieved. It is therefore legitimate to jump straight to the end of the program. The lemma which justifies this is:

$$1 \leq f \leq N \& j < f < i \& \forall p(1 \leq p < i \supset A[p] \leq r)$$
$$\& \forall q(j < q \leq N \supset r \leq A[q])$$
$$\supset \forall p, q(1 \leq p \leq f \leq q \leq N \supset A[p] \leq A[f] \leq A[q]) \qquad \text{[Lemma 7]}$$

This may be readily proved: if f is put for q in the antecedent, we obtain $r \leq A[f]$. Similarly, putting f for p in the antecedent we obtain $A[f] \leq r$. Hence $A[f] = r$. If $1 \leq p \leq f \leq q \leq N$, then $1 \leq p < i$ (since $f < i$) and $j < q \leq N$ (since $j < f$) and hence the i-invariant states that $A[p] \leq r$ and the j-invariant states that $r \leq A[q]$. But r has already been proved equal to $A[f]$.

This concludes the outline of the program required to reduce the middle part:

$r := A[f]; i := m; j := n;$

while $i \leqslant j$ **do** "increase i and decrease j ";

if $f \leqslant j$ **then** $n := j$

else if $i \leqslant f$ **then** $m := i$

else go to L

This program has been proved to be correct, in that it preserves the truth of both the m- and n-invariants, provided that the body of the contained loop preserves these invariants as well as the i- and j-invariants.

3.4. Stage 4: Increase i and decrease j

At this stage there is no need to introduce further variables and no further invariants are required. The construction of the code is not therefore split into the steps as before.

The first action of this part of the program is to use the i-pointer to scan rightward, passing over all elements with value less than r. This is accomplished by the loop:*

while $A[i] < r$ **do** $i := i + 1$

The fact that this loop preserves the truth of the invariant is expressed in the obvious lemma:

$$A[i] \leqslant r \,\&\, m \leqslant i \,\&\, \forall p(1 \leqslant p < i \supset A[p] \leqslant r)$$
$$\supset m \leqslant i + 1 \,\&\, \forall p(1 \leqslant p < i + 1 \supset A[p] \leqslant r) \qquad \text{[Lemma 8]}^\dagger$$

The next action is to use the j-pointer to scan leftward, passing over all elements greater than r. This is accomplished by the loop:

while $r < A[j]$ **do** $j := j - 1$

which is validated by the truth of:

$$r \leqslant A[j] \,\&\, j \leqslant n \,\&\, \forall q(j < q \leqslant N \supset r \leqslant A[q])$$
$$\supset j - 1 \leqslant n \,\&\, \forall q(j - 1 < q \leqslant N \supset r \leqslant A[q]) \qquad \text{[Lemma 9]}$$

On termination of the first loop, it is known that $r \leqslant A[i]$, and on termination of the second loop $A[j] \leqslant r$. If i and j have not crossed over, an exchange of the elements they point to takes place. After the exchange, it is obvious that

$$A[i] \leqslant r \leqslant A[j],$$

---

*The reason for the strict inequality is connected with termination. See Section 4.

†This lemma is not strictly true for some implementations of computer arithmetic. Suppose that N is the largest number representable in the integer range, that $m = i = N$, and that modulo arithmetic is used. Then $i + 1$ will be the smallest number representable, and will certainly be less than m. The easiest way to evade this problem is to impose on the user of the algorithm the insignificant restriction that $N < $ maxint, where maxint is the largest representable integer.

and hence Lemmas 8 and 9 justify a further increase in i and decrease in j:

> **if** $i \leq j$ **then**
> **begin** "exchange $A[i]$ and $A[j]$";
> $\quad i := i + 1; \quad j := j - 1$
> **end**

Thus the process of increasing i and decreasing j preserves the truth of all the invariants, provided that the exchange of $A[i]$ and $A[j]$ does so, and the program takes the form:

> **while** $A[i] < r$ **do** $i := i + 1$;
> **while** $r < A[j]$ **do** $j := j - 1$;
> **if** $i \leq j$ **then**
> $\quad$ **begin** "exchange $A[i]$ and $A[j]$";
> $\quad\quad i := i + 1; \quad j := j - 1$
> $\quad$ **end**

3.5. Stage 5: Exchange $A[i]$ and $A[j]$

The code for performing the exchange is:

$$w := A[i]; \quad A[i] := A[j]; \quad A[j] := w$$

Although this code uses a new variable w, there is no need to establish an invariant for it, since its value plays a purely temporary role.

The proof that the exchange preserves the invariants is not trivial, and depends critically on the fact that $i \leq j$. Let A' stand for the value of the array as a whole after the exchange has taken place. Then obviously:

$$A'[i] = A[j] \tag{1}$$

$$A'[j] = A[i] \tag{2}$$

$$\forall s(s \neq i \,\&\, s \neq j \supset A'[s] = A[s]) \tag{3}$$

The preservation of the i-invariant is stated in the lemma:

$$m \leq i \leq j \,\&\, \forall p(1 \leq p < i \supset A[p] \leq r)$$
$$\supset m \leq i \,\&\, \forall p(1 \leq p < i \supset A'[p] \leq r) \tag{Lemma 10}$$

This is proved by observing that if $p < i \leq j$ then $p \neq i$ and $\mathrm{p} \neq j$ and by (3), $A'[p] = A[p]$.

Similarly the preservation of the j-invariant is guaranteed by the lemma:

$$i \leq j \leq n \,\&\, \forall q(j < q \leq N \supset r \leq A[q])$$
$$\supset j \leq n \,\&\, \forall q(j \leq q \leq N \supset r \leq A'[q]) \tag{Lemma 11}$$

The proof likewise proceeds by observing that $i \leq j < q$ implies that $q \neq i$ and $q \neq j$, and therefore by (3), $A'[q] = A[q]$.

The preservation of the m-invariant is guaranteed by the truth of the following lemma:

$$m \leq i \leq j \,\&\, \forall p, q(1 \leq p < m \leq q \leq N \supset A[p] \leq A[q])$$
$$\supset \forall p, q(1 \leq p < m \leq q \leq N \supset A'[p] \leq A'[q]) \tag{Lemma 12}$$

Outline proof:

Assume $1 \leq p < m \leq q \leq N$; hence $p \neq i$ and $p \neq j$ (since $p < m \leq i \leq j$). Therefore by (3),

$$A'[p] = A[p]. \tag{4}$$

Substituting i and then j for q in the antecedent, we obtain $A[p] \leq A[i]$ and $A[p] \leq A[j]$. Consequently $A'[p] \leq A'[j]$ and $A'[p] \leq A'[i]$ (from (4), (1), and (2)). Furthermore, for all $q \neq i$ and $q \neq j$, $A'[p] = A[p] \leq A[q] = A'[q]$ (by (4) and (3)). Hence $A'[p] \leq A'[q]$ for all $q(m \leq q \leq N)$.

The preservation of the n-invariant is guaranteed by a similar lemma:

$$i \leq j \leq n \,\&\, \forall p, q(1 \leq p \leq n < q \leq N \supset A[p] \leq A[q])$$
$$\supset \forall p, q(1 \leq p \leq n < q \leq N \supset A'[p] \leq A'[q]) \qquad \text{[Lemma 13]}$$

The proof is very similar to that of Lemma 12, and is left as an exercise.

3.6. The whole program

The gradual evolution of the program code and proof through several stages has been carried out in the previous sections. In presenting the code of the program as a whole, the essential invariants and other assertions have been preserved as comments. Thus a well-annotated version of the program appears in Table II.

Table II

```
begin
  comment  This program operates on an array A[1:N], and a value of
    f(1 ≤ f ≤ N). Its effect is to rearrange the elements of A in such a way that:
      ∀p, q(1 ≤ p≤ f≤ q ≤ N ⊃ A[p] ≤ A[f] ≤ A[q]);
  integer m, n; comment
      m ≤ f & ∀p, q(1 ≤ p < m≤ q ≤ N ⊃ A[p] ≤ A[q]),
      f ≤ n & ∀p, q(1 ≤ p ≤ n< q ≤N ⊃ A[p] ≤A[q]);
    m := 1; n := N;
  while m < n do
  begin integer r, i, j, w;
    comment
          m ≤ i & ∀p(1≤p<i ⊃ A[p]≤r),
          j ≤ n & ∀q(j < q ≤ N ⊃ r ≤ A[q]);
      r := A[f]; i := m; j := n;
    while i ≤ j do
    begin while A[i] < r do i := i + 1;
      while r < A[j] do j := j − 1
      comment  A[j] ≤ r ≤ A[i];
      if i ≤ j then
      begin w := A[i];  A[i] := A[j];  A[j] := w;
          comment  A[i] ≤ r ≤ A[j];
          i := i + 1; j := j − 1;
      end
    end increase i and decrease j;
    if f ≤ j then n := j
  else if i ≤ f then m  := i
    else go to L
  end reduce middle part;
  L:
end Find
```

4. Termination

The proof given so far has concentrated on proving the correctness of the program supposing that it terminates; and no attention has been given to the problem of proving termination. It is easier in this case to prove termination of the inner loops first.

The proof of the termination of:

while $A[i] < r$ **do** $i := i + 1$

depends on the recognition that at all times there will be an element in the middle part to the right of $A[i]$ whose value is equal to or greater than r. This element will act as a "stopper" to prevent the value of i from increasing beyond the value n. More formally, it is necessary to establish an additional invariant for i, which is true before and during the loop; i.e. throughout execution of "reduce middle part." This invariant is:

$$\exists p(i \leqslant p \leqslant n \, \& \, r \leqslant A[p]) \tag{5}$$

Obviously if this is true, the value of i is necessarily bounded by n; it cannot increase indefinitely, and the loop must therefore terminate.

The fact that (5) is an invariant for the duration of the particular loop is established by the following lemmas:

$$m \leqslant f \leqslant n \supset \exists p(m \leqslant p \leqslant n \, \& \, A[f] \leqslant A[p]) \qquad \text{[Lemma 14]}$$

Proof: take f for p.

$$A[i] < r \, \& \, \exists p(i \leqslant p \leqslant n \, \& \, r \leqslant A[p])$$
$$\supset \exists p(i + 1 \leqslant p \leqslant n \, \& \, r \leqslant A[p]) \qquad \text{[Lemma 15]}$$

Proof: consider the p whose existence is asserted by the antecedent. Since $r \leqslant A[p] \, \& \, A[i] < r$, $p \neq i$. Hence $i + 1 \leqslant p$.

$$r \leqslant A[i] \, \& \, i + 1 \leqslant j - 1 \, \& \, j \leqslant n$$
$$\supset \exists p(i + 1 \leqslant p \leqslant n \, \& \, r \leqslant A'[p]) \qquad \text{[Lemma 16]}$$

Proof: Take j for p. Then $A'[p] = A'[j] = A[i] \geqslant r$.

Lemma 14 shows that the invariant is true after the initialization of "reduce middle part." Lemma 15 shows that the invariant is preserved by **while** $A[i] < r$ **do** $i := i + 1$, and Lemma 16 shows that the invariant is preserved by the final compound statement of "reduce middle part," providing that $i \leqslant j$ after the execution of this statement. Since the body of the loop is not reentered unless this condition is satisfied, the invariant is unconditionally true at the beginning of the second and subsequent repetitions of "reduce middle part."

The termination of the loop

while $r < A[j]$ **do** $j := j - 1$

is established in a very similar manner. The additional invariant is

$$\exists q(m \leqslant q \leqslant j \, \& \, A[q] \leqslant r) \tag{6}$$

and the lemmas required are Lemma 14 and

$$r < A[j] \& \exists q(m \leqslant q \leqslant j \& A[q] \leqslant r)$$
$$\supset \exists q(m \leqslant q \leqslant j - 1 \& A[q] \leqslant r) \qquad \text{[Lemma 17]}$$

$$A[j] \leqslant r \& i + 1 \leqslant j - 1 \& m \leqslant i$$
$$\supset \exists q(m \leqslant q \leqslant j - 1 \& A'[q] \leqslant r) \qquad \text{[Lemma 18]}$$

The proofs of these lemmas are very similar to those for Lemmas 15 and 16.

This proof of termination is more than usually complex; if the program were rewritten to include an extra test ($i \leqslant n$ or $m \leqslant j$) in each loop, termination would have been obvious. However, the innermost loops would have been rather less efficient.

The proof of termination of the middle loop is rather simpler. The loop for increasing i and decreasing j must terminate; since if the conditional statement it contains is not obeyed then j is already less than i and termination is immediate; whereas if $j \geqslant i$ then i is necessarily incremented and j decremented, and they must cross over after a finite number of such operations.

Proof of the termination of the outermost loop depends on the fact that on termination of the middle loop both $m < i$ and $j < n$. Therefore whichever one of the assignments $m := i$ or $n := j$ is executed, the distance between n and m is strictly decreased. If neither assignment is made, **go to** L is executed, and terminates the loop immediately.

The proof that at the end of the middle loop both $m < i$ and $j < n$ depends on the fact that on the first execution of the loop body the conditional **if** $i \leqslant j$ **then** . . . is actually executed. This is because at this stage $A[f]$ is still equal to r, and therefore the rightward scan of i cannot pass over $A[f]$. Similarly the leftward scan of j cannot pass over $A[f]$. Thus on termination of both innermost loops $i \leqslant f \leqslant j$. Thus the condition $i \leqslant j$ is satisfied, and i is necessarily incremented, and j is necessarily decremented. Recall that this reasoning applies only to the first time round this loop — but once is enough to ensure $m < i$ and $j < n$ since i is a nondecreasing quantity and j is a nonincreasing quantity.

5. Reservation

In the proof of Find, one very important aspect of correctness has not been treated, namely, that the program merely rearranges the elements of the array A, without changing any of their values. If this requirement were not stated, there would be no reason why the program Find should not be written trivially:

for $i := 1$ **step** 1 **until** N **do**

$A[i] := i$

since this fully satisfies all the other criteria for correctness.

The easiest way of stating this additional requirement is to forbid the programmer to change the array A in any other way than by exchanging two of its elements. This requirement is clearly met by the Find program and not by its trivial alternative.

If it is desired to formulate the requirement in terms of conditions and invariants, it is necessary to introduce the concept of a permutation; and to prove that for arbitrary A_0,

A is a permutation of A_0, $\qquad$ [Perm]

is an invariant of the program. Informally this may be proved in three steps:

(a) "exchange $A[i]$ and $A[j]$," is the only part of the program which changes A,

(b) exchanging is a permutation,

(c) the composition of two permutations is also a permutation.

The main disadvantages of the formal approach are illustrated by this example. It is far from obvious that the invariance of Perm expresses exactly what we want to prove about the program; when the definition of Perm is fully and formally expressed, this is even less obvious; and finally, if the proof is formulated in the manner of the proofs of the other lemmas of this paper, it is very tedious.

Another problem which remains untreated is that of proving that all subscripts of A are within the bounds 1 to N.

6. Conclusion

This paper has illustrated a methodology for systematic construction of program proofs together with the programs they prove. It uses a "top-down" method of analysis to split the process into a number of stages, each stage embodying more detail than the previous one; the proof of the correctness of the program at each stage leads to and depends upon an accurate formulation of the characteristics of the program to be developed at the next stage.

Within each stage, there are a number of steps: the decision on the nature of the data required; the formulation of the invariants for the data; the construction of the code; the formulation and proof of the lemmas. In this paper, the stages and steps have been shown as a continuous progress, and it has not been necessary to go back and change decisions made earlier. In practice, reconsideration of earlier decisions is frequently necessary, and this imposes on the programmer the need to reestablish the consistency of invariants, program, lemmas, and proofs. The motivation for taking this extra trouble during the design and coding of a program is that it is hoped to reduce or eliminate trouble at phases which traditionally come later − program testing, documentation, and maintenance.

Similar systematic methods of program construction are described in [5] and [6]; this present paper, however, places greater emphasis on the formalization of the characteristics of the program as an aid to the avoidance of logical and coding errors. In the future, it may be possible to enlist the aid of a computer in formulating the lemmas, and perhaps even in checking the proofs [7, 8].

Acknowledgments. The author is grateful to the referee and to the retiring editor for his meticulous comments and general encouragement in the preparation of this paper.

References: Hoare

1. Naur, P. Proof of algorithms by general snapshots. *BIT 6* (1966), 310-316.

2. Dijkstra, E.W. A constructive approach to the problem of program correctness. *BIT 8* (1968), 174-186.

3. Hoare, C.A.R. An axiomatic approach to computer programming. *Comm. ACM 12,* 10 (Oct. 1969), 576-580, 583.

4. Hoare, C.A.R. Algorithm 65, Find. *Comm. ACM 4,* 7 (July 1961), 321.

5. Naur, P. Programming by action clusters. *BIT 9* (1969), 250-258.

6. Dijkstra, E.W. Structured programming [EWD249] T.H.E. (privately circulated).

7. Floyd, R.W. Assigning meanings to programs. Proc. Amer. Math. Soc. Symposium in Applied Mathematics, Vol. 19, 19-31.

8. King, J.C. A program verifier. Ph.D. Th., Carnegie-Mellon U., Pittsburgh, Pa., Sept. 1969.

Mathematical Foundations for Structured Programming

Foreword

The first name in structured programming is Edsger W. Dijkstra (Holland), who has originated a set of ideas and a series of examples for clear thinking in the construction of programs. These ideas are powerful tools in mentally connecting the static text of a program with the dynamic process it invokes in execution. This new correspondence between program and process permits a new level of precision in programming. Indeed, it is contended here that the precision now possible in programming will change its industrial characteristics from a frustrating, trial and error activity to a systematic, quality controlled activity.

However, in order to introduce and enforce such precision programming as an industrial activity, the ideas of structured programming must be formulated as technical standards, not simply as good ideas to be used when convenient, but as basic principles which are always valid. A good example of a technical standard occurs in logic circuit design. There, it is known, from basic theorems in boolean algebra, that any logic circuit, no matter how complex its requirement, can be constructed using only AND, OR, and NOT gates.

Our interest is similar, to provide a mathematical assurance, for management purposes, that a technical standard is sound and practical. This mathematical assurance is due, in large part, to Corrado Böhm and Giuseppe Jacopini (Italy), who showed how to prove that relatively simple (structured) program control logics were capable of expressing any program requirements.

Initial practical experience with structured programming indicates there is more than a technical side to the matter.

SOURCE: H.D. Mills, *IBM Corp. Report No. FSC 72-6012*, 1972.

There is a psychological effect, as well, when programmers learn of their new power to write programs correctly. This new power motivates, in turn, a new level of concentration, which helps avoid errors of carelessness. This new psychology of precision has a mathematical counterpart in the theory of program correctness, which we formulate in a new way.

The mathematical approach we take in formulating structured programming and the correctness problem emphasizes these combinatorial aspects, in order to demonstrate for programmers that correct programming involves only combinatorial selection, and not problems requiring perfect precision, on a continuous scale. Because of this, we are confident that programmers will soon work at a level of productivity and precision which will appear incredible compared to early experience with the programming problem.

Complexity and precision in programming

The digital computer has introduced a need for highly complex, precisely formulated, logical systems on a scale never before attempted. Systems may be large and highly complex, but if human beings, or even analog devices, are components in them, then various error tolerances are possible, which such components can adjust and compensate for. However, a digital computer, in hardware and software, not only makes the idea of perfect precision possible — it requires perfect precision for satisfactory operation. This complete intolerance to the slightest logical error gives programming a new character, little known previously, in its requirements for precision on a large scale.

The combination of this new requirement for precision, and the commercial demand for computer programming on a broad scale, has created many false values and distorted relationships in the past decade. They arise from intense pressure to achieve complex and precision results in a practical way without adequate technical foundations. As a result, a great deal of programming uses people and computers highly inefficiently, as the only means presently known to accomplish a practical end.

It is universally accepted today that programming is an error-prone activity. Any major programming system is presumed to have errors in it. Only the very naive would believe otherwise. The process of debugging programs and systems is a mysterious art. Indeed, more programmer time goes into debugging than into program designing and coding in most large systems. But there is practically no systematic literature on this large undertaking.

Yet, even though errors in program logic have always been a source of frustration, even for the most careful and meticulous, this may not be necessarily so in the future. Programming is very young as a human activity — some twenty years old. It has practically no technical foundations yet. Imagine engineering when it was twenty years old. Whether that was in 1620 or 1770, it was not in very good technical shape at that stage either! As technical foundations are developed for programming, its character will undergo radical changes.

We contend here that such a radical change is possible now — that in structured programming the techniques and tools are at hand to permit an entirely new level of precision in programming.

This new level of precision will be characterized by programs of large size (from tens of thousands to millions of instructions) which have mean time between detected errors of a year or so. But to accomplish that level of precision a new attitude toward programming expectations will be required in programmers, as well.

The psychology of precision

A child can learn to play the game of tic tac toe perfectly — but a man can never learn to saw a board exactly in half. Playing tic tac toe is a combinatorial problem, selecting, at every alternative, one of a finite number of possibilities. Sawing a board exactly in half is a physical problem, for which no discrete level of accuracy is sufficient.

The child who has learned to play tic tac toe need never make a mistake, except through a loss of concentration. In any game he believes important (say played for a candy bar) he is capable of perfect play.

Computer programming is a combinatorial activity, like tic tac toe not like sawing a board in half. It does not require perfect resolution in measurement and control — it only requires correct choices out of finite sets of possibilities at every step. The difference between tic tac toe and computer programming is complexity. The purpose of structured programming is to control complexity through theory and discipline. And with complexity under better control, it now appears that men can write substantial computer programs correctly. In fact, just as a child moves from groping and frustration to confidence and competence in tic tac toe, so men can now find solid ground for program development.

A child, in learning to play tic tac toe, soon develops a little theory, dealing with "center squares," "corner squares," "side squares," and the self discipline to block possible defeats before building threats of his own. In programming, theory and discipline are critical, as well, at a man's level of intellectual activity. Structured programming is such a theory, which provides a systematic way of coping with complexity in program design and development. It makes possible a discipline for program design and construction on a level of precision not previously possible.

But for the child, knowing how to play tic tac toe perfectly is not enough. He must know that he knows. This knowing that he knows is a vital ingredient in his self discipline — knowing that he is capable of analyzing the board, and doesn't need to guess and hope.

It is the same with the programmer. If a programmer knows that what is in his mind is correct, then getting it onto paper precisely is more important, as is checking details of data definitions, and whatever, in his coding process. On the other hand, if a programmer thinks what is in his mind is probably all right, but is subconsciously counting on debugging and integration runs to iron out logic and interface errors, then the entire process of getting it onto paper and into the computer suffers in small ways to later torment him.

It takes some learning on the part of experienced programmers to discover that structured programs can be written with unprecedented logical and interface precision. As with the child, it is not enough to be able to program with precision. The programmer must know his capability for precision programming in order to supply the concentration to match his capability.

The problem of complexity

Five hundred years ago men did not know that the air we breathe, and move through so freely, has weight. Air is hard to put on a scale, or even identify as any specific quantity for weighing at all. But now we know that air has weight — at sea level, the weight of a column of water 34 feet high.

It is easy to imagine, in hindsight, the frustrations of a well pump manufacturer, whose "research department" is operating on the theory that "nature abhors a vacuum." Water can be raised up a well pipe 15, 20, then 25 feet, by using a plunger and tightening its seals better and better. All this merely seems to confirm the "current theory" about the operation of such pumps. But at 35 feet, total frustration ensues. No matter how tight the seals, the water cannot be raised.

In computer programming today, we do not yet know that "complexity has weight." Since it is not easily measured or described, like storage requirements or throughput, we often ignore the complexity of a planned program or subprogram. But when this complexity exceeds certain unknown limits, frustration ensues. Computer programs capsize under their own logical weight, or become so crippled that maintenance is precarious and modification is impossible. Problems of storage and throughput can always be fixed, one way or another. But problems of complexity can seldom be adequately recognized, let alone fixed.

The syndrome of creating unsolvable problems of complexity because of anticipated problems of storage and throughput is well known. It is the work of amateurs. It arises in a misguided arrogance that "what happened to them won't happen to me!" But it keeps happening, over and over.

The idea of structured programming

Closely related to many original ideas of E. Dijkstra [10], and using key results of C. Böhm and G. Jacopini [5], P. Naur [32], and R. Floyd [13], structured programming is based on new mathematical foundations for programming (in contrast to the use of programming to implement mathematical processes, or to study foundations of mathematics). It identifies the programming process with a step by step expansion of mathematical functions into structures of logical connectives and subfunctions, carried out until the derived subfunctions can be directly realized in the programming language being used. The documentation of a program is identified with proof of the correctness of these expansions. Aspects of this approach are illustrated as well in the work of Ashcroft and Manna [3], Hoare [17], and Wirth [39]. A major application to a programming system of considerable size is described by Baker [4].

Four mathematical results are central to this approach. One result, a "Structure Theorem," due in original form to Böhm and Jacopini, guarantees that any flowchartable program logic can be represented by expansions of as few as three types of structures, e.g., (1) f THEN g, (2) IF p THEN f ELSE g, (3) WHILE p DO f, where f, g, are flowcharts with one input and one output, p is a test, THEN, IF, ELSE, WHILE, DO, are logical connectives. This is in sharp contrast to the usual programming practice of flowcharting arbitrary control logic with unrestricted control branching operations.

In block structured programming languages, such as Algol or PL/I, such structured programs can be GOTO-free, and be read sequentially without mentally jumping from point to point. In a deeper sense, the GOTO-free property is superficial. Structured programs should be characterized not simply by the absence of GOTO's, but by the presence of structure. Structured programs can be further organized into trees of program "segments," such that each segment is at most some prescribed size, e.g., a page (some 50 lines) in length, and with entry only at the top and exit at the bottom of the segment. Segments refer to other segments at the next level in such trees, each by a single name, to represent a generalized data processing operation at that point, with no side effects in control. In this way, the size and complexity of any programming system can be handled by a tree structure of segments, where each segment — whether high level or low level in the system hierarchy — is of precisely limited size and complexity.

The Structure Theorem has a constructive proof, which provides insight, itself, into program design and construction techniques. Although a flowchart may be of any size, the Structure Theorem guarantees that its control logic can be represented in a finite basis, with a corresponding reduction in the complexity characteristic of arbitrary flowcharts. The Structure Theorem also provides a canonical form for documenting and validating programs, to help define operational procedures in programming.

The second mathematical result is a "Top Down Corollary," which guarantees that structured programs can be written or read "top down," i.e., in such a way that the correctness of each segment of a program depends only on segments already written or read and on the functional specifications of any additional segments referred to by name. The application of this Corollary requires a radical change in the way most programmers think today, although advocates of "functional programming" have proposed such ideas independently, e.g., Randell and Zurcher [40], Landin [22], Strachey [37], Burge [6], and Scott [35]. It is a nearly universal practice, at the present time, to write large programs "bottom up" — coding and unit testing program modules, then subsystems, and finally systems integration and testing. In top down programming, the integration code is written first, at the system, then subsystem levels, and the functional modules are written last. As discussed by Mills [29], top down programming can eliminate the necessity for the simultaneous interface assumptions that frequently result in system errors during integration.

The third mathematical result is a "Correctness Theorem," which shows how the problem of the correctness of structured programs can be reduced to function theoretic questions to which standard mathematical practices apply. These questions necessarily go into the context of intentions and operations available for writing programs. Ordinarily, they will require specific mathematical frameworks and procedures for their resolution. Indeed, for complex programs, the mathematical questions may be more comprehensive and detailed than is practical to resolve at some acceptable level of mathematical rigor. But, in any case, the questions can be formulated on a systematic basis, and technical judgements can then be applied to determine the level of validation which is feasible and desirable for a given program.

In this connection, we note that mathematics consists of a set of logical practices, with no inherent claim to absolute rigor or truth, e.g., see Wilder [38, p. 196]. Mathematics is of human invention, and subject to human fallibilities, in spite of the aura of supernatural verities often found in a schoolboy world. But even so, the reduction of the problem of program meanings to such mathematical practices permits the classification and treatment of ideas in terms of processes which have been subjected to considerable analysis and criticism by mankind.

The fourth mathematical result is an "Expansion Theorem" which defines the freedom available in expanding any functional specification into a structure at the next level. Perhaps the most surprising aspect of this result is how little freedom a programmer has in correctly expanding programs top down. For example, it will be clear in defining the structure "IF p THEN f ELSE g," that the choice of p automatically defines f and g — that the only freedom in such a structure is in its predicate. Even more surprising, is the result that in the expansion "WHILE p DO f," no freedom exists at all in the selection of p — the looping predicate will be seen to be totally determined by the functional specification itself.

Our motivation in this final result is to exhibit programming as an analysis, rather than a synthesis, activity, that is, to identify the top down programming process as a sequence of decompositions and partitions of functional specifications and sub-specifications, each of which produces simpler subspecifications to handle, until finally the level of programming language instructions or statements is reached. This is in contrast to programming as a synthesis of instructions or statements that "accomplish" the functional specifications. It is in this distinction that programming emerges as a readily perceived combinatorial activity.

The correctness of structured programs

With structured programming, programmers are capable of high precision programming, but, as in tic tac toe, it is important for their concentration to know their own capability for this high precision. The Correctness Theorem provides concepts and procedures for realizing this precision in programming. Correctness proofs are demonstrations of human devising for human consumption. There is no such thing as an absolute proof of logical correctness. There are only degrees of rigor, such as "technical english," "mathematical journal proof," "formal logic," etc., which are each informal descriptions of mechanisms for creating agreement and belief in a process of reasoning.

It is clear that a whole spectrum of rigor will be useful in correctness proofs. A casual program, used in an experimental investigation, may warrant no more than a few lines of explanation. A heavily used program — say a text editor or a compiler — may warrant a much more formal proof. London has furnished several realistic examples of proof at a mathematics level [23, 24, 25], including the proof of an optimizing LISP compiler. Jones [20] has given an example of a proof in more formal terms. King [21] and Good [14] have developed more automatic machinery. Dijkstra [9] has illustrated less formal ideas which may be even more convincing in some programs. The persuasion of a proof depends not only on its formality, but on its brevity. Unfortunately, formality and brevity do not often cooperate, and the programmer has a difficult balancing problem in selecting the best compromise between formality and brevity.

Our approach is functional (or denotational, as used by Ashcroft [2]), rather than computational — instead of proving assertions about computational steps in a program (as introduced by Naur [31], Floyd [12], et al.), we formulate assertions about functions whose values are computed by programs and subprograms. In this approach, the set theoretic definition of a function as a set of ordered pairs is of critical convenience. For example, an IFTHENELSE subprogram corresponds to a partition of a corresponding function into two subsets of ordered pairs, which, as subfunctions, correspond to the THEN clause and ELSE clause of the original subprogram.

As noted, structured programs admit decompositions into subprograms of very simple types, such as THEN, IFTHENELSE, and DOWHILE subprograms. Our main interest is to show that each type leads to a characteristic logical assertion about the correctness of a subprogram. These assertions are eventually embodied in function theoretic questions, dealing with composition and partition of functions, e.g., for some sets f, g, h (not necessarily distinct), it is to be proved that

$$f = g * h \qquad \text{or} \qquad f = g \cup h.$$

These relations assert equalities between sets of ordered pairs. There are many acceptable ways in current mathematical practice to prove such assertions, such as an induction over some common structural feature of the sets involved. But such ways are outside our current interest in formulating the assertions themselves.

We recognize, with Floyd [12], that the question of program correctness is simply the question of program meaning, i.e., knowing what a program does. Any program, including pure gibberish, exhibits some behavior, and it is correct with respect to that behavior, independent of what other capabilities may be envisioned for it. In this context, it is crucial to distinguish between correctness and capability. A program under construction top down can be correct at every stage, but not capable of its eventual requirements until completed. An error in a program is an unexpected action. A function theoretic description of the behavior of a program can thus be regarded as a pure description or a normative prescription, but the correctness problem comes down to the agreement between a functional description and a program behavior.

Functions

We adopt the common mathematical notion that a *function* is a set of ordered pairs, cf. Halmos [15], say

$$f = \{(x_1, y_1), (x_2, y_2), \ldots\}$$

such that if $(x,y) \in f$, $(u,v) \in f$, $x = u$, then $y = v$. The relation $(x,y) \in f$ is often written as

$$y = f(x),$$

and x is called the *argument,* y is called the *value* of function f. The sets of first, second members of the ordered pairs of a function are called the *domain, range* of the function, respectively. In the example above,

$$\text{domain (f)} = \{x_1, x_2, \ldots\}$$

$$\text{range (f)} = \{y_1, y_2, \ldots\}$$

Note these definitions for domain, range include *only* arguments, values of the function, and no other elements.

Since a function is a set, it makes sense to use the terms "empty function," "subfunction," "function partition," etc., with the word, suffix or prefix "set" replaced by "function," whenever the conditions further required by a function can be guaranteed to hold. Instances which violate these conditions include the case of the power set — the set of subsets of a function is not itself a function, but is a set of functions — and the union of functions — the uniqueness of a value for a given argument — may be lost in forming the union of two functions. However, the union of disjoint functions or intersection of two functions is again a function, as is the difference (set) of two functions.

Functions and rules

In the description of a function f as a set of ordered pairs, it is often convenient to give a *rule* for calculating the second member from the first, as in

$$f = \{(x,y) \mid y = x^2 + 3x + 2\},$$

or

$$(x, x^2 + 3x + 2) \in f,$$

or even

$$f(x) = x^2 + 3x + 2,$$

where domain (f) is given in some broader context. A rule used in defining a function in this way is not unique. For example, if

$$x^2 + 3x + 2 = (x + 1) (x + 2),$$

then the new function and rule

$$g = \{(u,v) \mid v = (u+1) (u+2)\}$$

or

$$g(u) = (u+1) (u+2)$$

defines the same set as before, i.e., f=g (as sets).

If a function is finite, then its enumeration can serve in a rule. The rule is to find any given argument as a first member of an ordered pair, if possible, and to extract the second member, if found, as the value for that argument. Otherwise, if enumeration is impossible or impracticable, a rule must be expressed as an algorithm, possibly very complex, but with unambiguous outcome for every argument.

In programming, there is a direct correspondence to the relationship between functions and rules — it is between functional specifications and programs. The problem of program correctness then becomes the problem of showing that a given function is defined by a given rule. Perhaps the simplest form of the program correctness problem is defined by function rules of enumeration, or "table lookup." If a table lookup program has been proved to be correct previously, then any finite functional specification, entered as a table, can be verified to be correct by verifying the table entries therein.

Since functions are merely sets of ordered pairs, we regard the usual idea of a "partial function" to be a relationship between two sets, one of which is the domain of some function under consideration. In our case, we use the term *partial rule* to mean a rule of computation not always defined over some given set.

Function composition and completion

Beyond operations directly inherited from sets, *function composition* is based on the fact that functions are sets of ordered pairs. A composition of two functions is a new function which represents the successive use of the values of one function as the arguments of the other. That is, we define the new function composition, using an infix notation, i.e.,

$$f * g = \{(x,y) \mid \exists z \ (z=g(x) \ \wedge \ y = f(z))\}.$$

If range (g) and domain (f) are disjoint, then f * g is the empty function; otherwise, f * g is just the set of ordered pairs which is defined through the application of g then f to arguments of g to get values of f.

Conversely, we say an ordered pair of functions, (f,g), is a *decomposition* of a function, h, if h = f * g. Clearly, for any function h, there may be many decompositions.

It is clear that function composition is associative — i.e., that

$$(f * g) * h = f * (g * h)$$

for all functions f, g, h; hence, the parentheses can be omitted without ambiguity, as in

$$f * g * h$$

Then, the composition of a function with itself can also be denoted simply by an exponent notation, i.e.,

$$f^2 = f * f$$
$$f^3 = f * f^2 = f^2 * f = f * f * f$$
$$f^4 = f * f^3 = f * f * f * f.$$

It will be occasionally convenient to permit a zero exponent, and interpret f^0 as an identity function (see below).

Given a function, we consider its repeated composition with itself, reusing values as new arguments, until, if ever, such values are not members of the domain of the function. The number of compositions then possible depends on the original argument, of course. Thus, we define a *function completion,* say for function f, to be

$$*f* = \{(x,y) \mid \exists\, k\, ((x,y) \in f^k) \land y \notin \text{domain } (f)\}.$$

Special functions

We identify, for future convenience, several general classes of functions, namely:

    a. Identity Functions: $I = \{f \mid (x,y) \in f \supset y = x\}$

    b. Constant Functions: $C(a) = \{f \mid (x,y) \in f \supset y = a\}$

    c. Permutation Functions: $P = \{f \mid \text{domain } (f) = \text{range } (f)\}$

    d. Inverse Function Pairs: $R = \{(f,g) \mid f * g = g * f \in I\}$

             (If $(f,g) \in R$, we say $g = f^{-1}$ or $f = g^{-1}$.)

Programs

We abstract the commonly known idea of a (computer) *program* as a finite set of functions, called *instructions,* each with a finite domain contained in a common set, called the *data space,* and a finite range contained in the cartesian product of the data space and the program, called the *state space.* Members of the data space, state space are called data values, state values, respectively.

A program *execution* is a sequence of state values, say

$$s_i = (d_i, f_i),\ i = 0, 1, \ldots$$

such that

$$s_{i+1} = f_i(d_i),\ i = 0, 1, \ldots$$

which terminates, if ever, when $f_i(d_i)$ fails to exist — i.e., when $d_i \notin \text{domain } (f_i)$. The state value s_0 is called the *initial value* of the execution. If the execution is finite, say

$$s = s_0, s_1, \ldots, s_n = t$$

then t is called the *final value* of the execution.

Since the state space of a program is finite, it is decidable, for every initial value, s, whether that execution terminates, and, if so, what the final value, t, is. Therefore, a program automatically defines a function of ordered pairs (s,t) defined by terminating executions, called the *program function.* If a program is given by a set P, we denote its program function by [P]. In retrospect, a program is a specific (non-unique) rule for calculating the values of its program function.

A *subprogram* is a subset of a program, which inherits its state space. A *subprogram execution* is a contiguous subsequence of a program execution which terminates, if ever, when an instruction not in the subprogram appears in the state value. To each subprogram corresponds a *subprogram function,* as well.

Control graphs

The instructions (functions) of a program determine a directed *control graph* whose nodes are instructions and whose directed lines are the next possible instructions. A node of such a graph may have several *input lines* and several *output lines* which denote the direction of control flow, as shown:

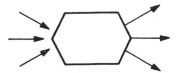

An instruction (node) has a natural decomposition between control and data effects which can be displayed by its partition (of its set of ordered pairs) into subsets, each of whose values contain identical (next) instruction components. The instruction node displayed above then has the form:

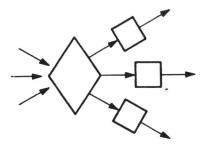

where the diamond (control node) represents an identity function for values in the data space and a square (*process node*) represents a constant function for values in the program (next instruction). Since the program (set) is finite, this partition can be refined so that control nodes each contain exactly two output lines, called *predicate nodes*.

From these considerations we are led to directed graphs with predicate and process nodes of the form shown.

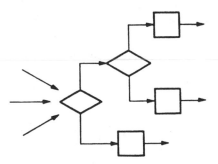

It will be convenient to introduce a symmetry into such directed graphs, by augmenting the original program with "noop" instructions (*collecting nodes*) which collect and transfer control from exactly two input lines each, which we diagram as shown:

Control graphs are also called program schemas [19].

Programs in flowchart form

We can represent a program in *flowchart* form. A flowchart is defined by a control graph, and by operations and tests to be carried out on data in a sequence determined by that control graph. As noted, we consider control graphs with only three types of nodes:

Process   Predicate   Collecting

The upper and lower lines out of a predicate node are labeled "True" and "False," respectively, just to be definite, unless otherwise noted.

In a flowchart, each process node is associated with a function, or data transformation, and each predicate node is associated with a predicate function, or a binary valued data test. Each line of a flowchart is associated with a set of possible data states. A set of data states may be the set of all possible machine states, for a program in a machine language, or may be the set of all variables allocated at a point in a program in a programming language. The function associated with a process node maps a set of data states associated with its input line into a set of data states associated with its output line. A function f from X to Y is identified in a flowchart as:

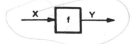

This mapping is a subfunction, say g, of f, namely:

$$g = \{ (x,y) \mid x \in X \ \wedge \ (x,y) \in f \ \wedge \ y \in Y \}.$$

If $x \notin X$, no such input is possible; if $y \notin Y$, no such output is possible; if $x \in X$ but $(x,y) \notin f$ or $y \notin Y$, the operation is not completed.

The predicate function associated with a predicate node maps the set of data states associated with its input line into the set {True, False} but does not transform data otherwise, that is, the flowchart figure

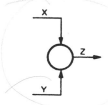

is associated with the identity mappings of data from input to output. But in order to satisfactorily complete the test, the condition

$$x \in X \land (((x, \text{True}) \in p \land x \in Y) \lor (x, \text{False}) \in p \land x \in Z))$$

must be satisfied.

The collecting node is also associated with an identity mapping, from the flowchart figure:

Also, to complete the transfer of control, the condition

$$(x \in X \land x \in Z) \lor (y \in Y \land y \in Z)$$

must be satisfied. In early practice and in current programming theory, the sets associated with control lines are often taken to be identical — a "state vector" set. However, with data scoping and dynamic storage allocation, as found in contemporary practice, the data space is variable, rather than constant, over a program or flowchart.

Program execution

The execution of a program is easily visualized in a flowchart, using the control graph to identify the sequence of operations and tests on data required. For example, consider the program f in flowchart form:

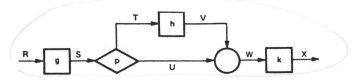

Where possible, *initial data* $r \in R$ is converted by f into *intermediate data* $s \in S$, then $t \in T$ and $v \in V$, or $u \in U$, then $w \in W$, and ultimately into *final data* $x \in X$, by functions g, h, and k, under the control of predicate p. I.e., the program function [f] of program f has values, when they exist, given by:

$$x = k(h(g(r))) \quad \text{if} \quad p(g(r)) = \text{True}$$
$$x = k(g(r)) \quad \text{if} \quad p(g(r)) = \text{False}.$$

More precisely, we mean:

$$[f] = \{ (r,x) \mid r \in R \; \wedge \; (\exists s, v \; ((r,s) \in g \; \wedge \; (s, \text{True}) \in p \; \wedge$$
$$(s,v) \in h \; \wedge \; (v,x) \in k)) \; \vee \; (\exists s((r,s) \in g \; \wedge$$
$$(s, \text{False}) \in p \; \wedge \; (s,x) \in k) \; \wedge \; x \in x \}.$$

Proper programs

We define a *proper program* to be a program in which:

a. There is precisely one input line and one output line

b. For every node, there exists a path from the input line through that node to the output line.

Note we admit the possibility of programs with no nodes, a single input/output line. We call such a program λ. Clearly, the program function [λ] is an identity function; i.e., [λ] ∈ I. In illustration, the following are not proper programs.

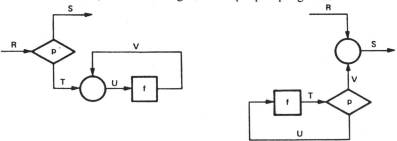

This definition of proper programs is primarily motivated by the interchangeability of proper programs and process nodes in larger programs.

Henceforth, we take the "proper program" and "program" to be synonymous. If necessary, we will use the term "improper program" to refer to a program which is not a proper program.

Program equivalence

We will say two proper programs are *equivalent* when they define the same program function, whether or not they have identical control graphs, require the same number of operations, etc. For example, the two programs

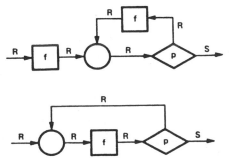

and

have the same program function, as do the two programs:

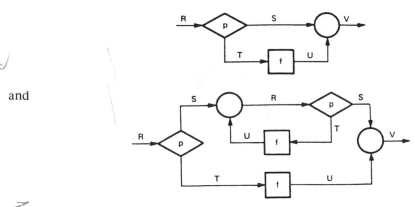

and

That is, two programs are equivalent if they define the same program function, even though the programs may represent different rules for computing the values of the program function. In particular, given program f and its program function [f], the new program g

domain ([f]) → [f] → range ([f])

is equivalent to f. In this case g is a table lookup version of f.

Program expansions

If a program contains a process node, as

R → f → S

it may happen that a rule for computing the values of f is defined as another program. We call such a program an *expansion* of the function f, such as shown next.

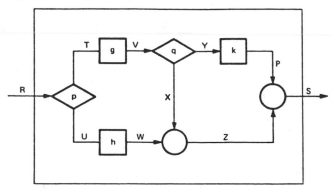

In this case, it is asserted that the program function of the latter program is f. That is, any expansion of a function is simply a rule for computing its values, possibly using other functions and predicates to do so.

Programs with loops may or may not terminate. This property of termination partitions an input set R into R_t and $R-R_t$, where R_t is the subset of inputs for which the evaluations terminate. If $R_t \neq R$, then the program defines a partial rule, rather than a rule. Note, in fact, that a program may terminate by reaching an output line (*normal termination*) or by reaching a node with a data value not in the domain of the corresponding function (*abnormal operation termination*) or by reaching a line with a data value not in the data space (*abnormal storage termination*).

Control graph labels

The set of all control graphs of proper programs can be enumerated and labeled. The beginning of such an enumeration is given in Figure 1.

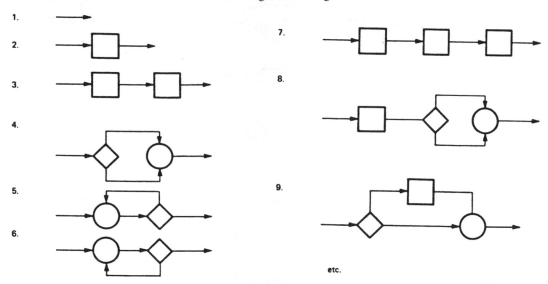

Figure 1. Control graphs.

In fact, a few such control graphs are given special mnemonic labels in various programming languages. For example, the following labels are common:

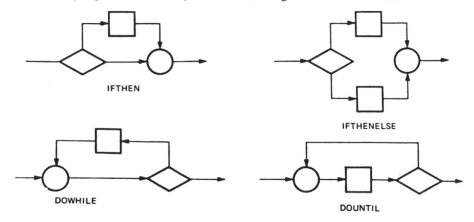

(IFTHEN is 9, in the enumeration started above, IFTHENELSE might be 37, 42, etc.)

However, there is nothing special about these graphs except for their simplicity. Any control graph possibly more complicated than these might be so labeled if it were useful. In particular, we label the sequence of two process nodes

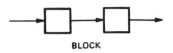

BLOCK

for future reference.

Program formulas

A program can be given as a *formula,* by associating an ordering with the set of process nodes, predicate nodes and control lines of its control graph, and by listing the label of its control graph, followed by labels for the functions, predicates and state sets of the program. For notational convenience, we will use parentheses and commas to denote the list structure of a program formula, e.g.,

(A, p, q, f, g, h, R, S, T, U)

means a program given by a control graph labeled A, with predicates p, q, functions f, g, h, and state sets R, S, T, U, associated with the nodes and lines of A. For example

(BLOCK, f, g, R, S, T)

defines a program

$$R \rightarrow \boxed{f} \xrightarrow{S} \boxed{g} \xrightarrow{T}$$

whose action on an input r ∈ R is to produce output t ∈ T if it exists, such that

t = g(f(r)),

more precisely,

[(BLOCK,f,g,R,S,T)] = { (r,t) |∃ s (r ∈ R

∧ s ∈ S ∧ t ∈ T ∧ (r,s) ∈ f ∧ (s,t) ∈ g) }.

The list

IFTHENELSE, p, f, g, R, S, T, U, V, W)

defines a program

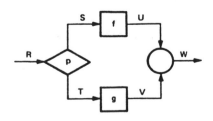

which maps any $r \in R$ into some $w \in W$, if it exists, such that

$$w = \begin{cases} f(r) \text{ if } p(r) = \text{True} \\ g(r) \text{ if } p(r) = \text{False} \end{cases}$$

More precisely,

$$[(\text{IFTHENELSE}, p,f,g,R,S,T,U,V,W)]$$
$$= \{ (r,w) \mid r \in R \ \wedge w \in W \ \wedge \ (((r, \text{True}) \in p \ \wedge$$
$$r \in S \ \wedge \ (r,w) \in f \ \wedge \ w \in U) \ \vee$$
$$((r, \text{False}) \in p \ \wedge r \in T \ \wedge \ (r,w) \in g \ \wedge \ w \in V)) \}.$$

In much of what follows, the list of data sets is not central to the ideas under development. In this case, they will be suppressed. However, such data sets are always implicit to program descriptions and discussions.

Since function composition is associative, i.e.,

$$(f * g) * h = f * (g * h),$$

so is BLOCK formation, i.e.,

$$[(\text{BLOCK}, [(\text{BLOCK},f,g)], h)] = [(\text{BLOCK},f, [(\text{BLOCK},g,h))]]$$

and no ambiguity results by extending the meaning of BLOCK to several nodes, e.g.,

$$(\text{BLOCK3},f,g,h) = (\text{BLOCK},(\text{BLOCK},f,g),h),$$

etc. In particular, we permit zero or one nodes in a BLOCK, as in

(BLOCK0) = λ   (BLOCK1, f) .

Then, for example, we have the identity

$$f = [(\text{BLOCK1},f,\text{domain}(f), \text{range}(f))].$$

It may happen that a function listed in a program formula is, itself, a program function given by another formula, such as

$$(\text{IFTHEN},p, [(\text{BLOCK},g,h)]).$$

We extend the idea of program formula to permit the replacement of a program function by its program formula, such as

$$(\text{IFTHEN},p,(\text{BLOCK},g,h)).$$

It is clear that, while these are different programs, they have identical program functions, just by the definition of program functions.

Program descriptions

Flowcharts and formulas are simply two alternative ways of describing (possibly partial) rules, with some internal structure, in terms of other rules (or partial rules). Still another way of description is in programming language text such as

```
IF p THEN
    f
ELSE
    g
ENDIF
```

and

```
WHILE p DO
    f
ENDDO
```

and

```
BLOCK
    f
    g
ENDBLOCK
```

etc. We find all three types of description useful in various circumstances in programming. Typically, flowcharts are useful in general discussions because of their graphics, formulas are useful in stating and proving theoretical properties of such rules, the text is useful in the actual construction of large complex programs. For example, the same program is given in the formula

(IFTHENELSE,p ,(DOWHILE,q,f), (BLOCK,g,h)),

the flowchart,

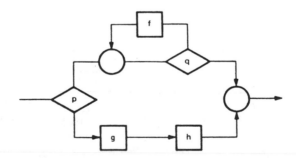

or in program text,

```
IF p THEN
        WHILE q DO
            f
        END DO
ELSE
        BLOCK
            g
            h
        END BLOCK
END IF
```

Structured programs

As flowcharts increase in size, we can often identify patterns which give more coherence and understandability to a whole flowchart. For example, the control graph next

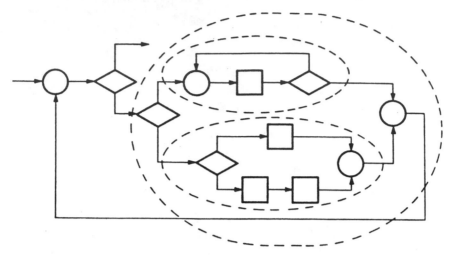

has three definite nested substructures, which are control graphs for proper programs, which make the whole more easily considered. But the following control graph

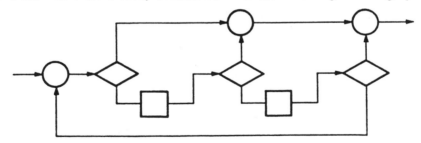

admits no such structuring. By simply continuing this last pattern indefinitely, it is easy to see that indecomposable control graphs exist of any size.

Having noted that programs of arbitrary size may be indecomposable, we next add the possibility of operations and tests on data outside the original data sets of a program. The additional operations and tests correspond to "flag" setting and testing. But we can couch these operations in the concept of a push down stack to show their economy. In addition to the functions and predicates original to a given program, we introduce three new functions and one predicate.

More specifically, we define process nodes with functions named TRUE, FALSE, POP, and a predicate node with function named TOP, which add truth values True, False, remove, and test such truth values in an input data set, respectively. That is, for any data set Y, and $y \in Y$ and $z \in \{True, False\}$,

$$
\begin{aligned}
\text{TRUE}(y) &= (y, True) \\
\text{FALSE}(y) &= (y, False) \\
\text{POP}(y,z) &= y \\
\text{TOP}(y,z) &= z
\end{aligned}
$$

These new functions and predicate allow us to construct explicit control logic in the form of flags. For example, a program whose control structure is in the indecomposable pattern above is shown next.

This program is equivalent to the new program, where the output line X and return line Y are tagged and the tag later tested.

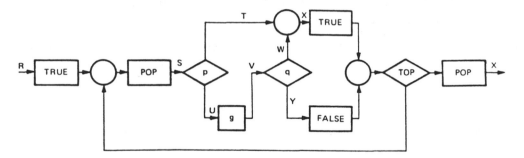

Only the original data sets have been shown; the remaining ones can be inferred from the definitions above. Close inspection will reveal that the net effect of TRUE, FALSE, POP, and TOP is to present just the correct original data set to each of the original functions and predicates of the program. It may not be obvious that this equivalent program is of any value in this case. It seems rather more complex — except that there is now a substructure, a proper program, which contains all the original functions and predicates, and furthermore, has no loop in it. This particular application previews a fundamental construction in the proof of the main Structure Theorem below. As a result, this new program can now be decomposed into two sections, of the forms

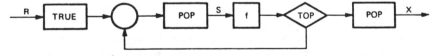

where process node f is given by

Before proving this Theorem, we introduce a simple Lemma which counts the control lines of a proper program in terms of its function and predicate nodes.

The number of control lines in a proper program

Lemma

If the number of function, predicate, and collecting nodes is ϕ, π, γ, respectively, and the number of control lines, i.e., (edges) is e, in a proper program, then

$$\pi = \gamma$$

and

$$e = 1 + \phi + 3\pi.$$

Proof

In order to prove this Lemma, count the "heads and tails" of the control lines, adjacent to all the nodes, and at the input and output of the program, to get:

Control Line	Input	Function Node	Predicate Node	Collecting Node	Output	Total
Heads		ϕ	π	2γ	1	$\phi + \pi + 2\gamma + 1$
Tails	1	ϕ	2π	γ		$\phi + 2\pi + \gamma + 1$

Since the total number of heads must equal the total number of tails, and each equal e,

$$\phi + \pi + 2\gamma + 1 = e = \phi + 2\pi + \gamma + 1$$

and the equations of the Lemma follow.

Structure theorem

Any proper program is equivalent to a program whose formula contains at most the graph labels BLOCK, IFTHENELSE, and DOUNTIL, and additional functions TRUE, FALSE, POP and predicate function TOP.

Proof*

We prove the Theorem by induction on the number of lines of a proper program. The induction step is constructive, and identifies, for any proper program of more than one node, an equivalent proper program which is a formula in at most graph labels BLOCK, IFTHENELSE, and DOUNTIL and new proper programs, each with fewer lines than the initial program.

In order to carry out the induction, we first define a structuring process, S, on any proper program, f, whose result we denote by S(f), as follows. For convenience, we abbreviate the graph labels BLOCK, IFTHENELSE, DOUNTIL to BLK, IF, DO, respectively, in the remainder of the proof.

---

*Thanks go to J. Misra for suggestions and assistance in developing the following Proof. Thanks are also due to S. Cole for discussions about the Theorem and methods for its Proof.

Since f is a proper program, it has exactly one input and one output. We identify several cases that are possible.

Case 1 — No Nodes

If f has no nodes, we define

$S(f) = \lambda$.

Case 2 — One or More Nodes

If f has at least one node, we examine the unique node reached by the input line. There are three possible cases:

Case 2a — Predicate Node. If the first node is a predicate node, then f is of the form

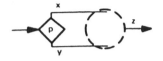

Since f is a proper program, the line z can be reached from both x and y,* and we construct two *constituent* programs which consist of all nodes accessible in f from x and y, respectively, calling them g and h, respectively.

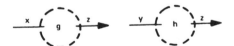

The constituents may contain identical nodes from f, so that g and h represent duplications of parts of f. If a collecting node in g or h is reached by only one input line (the other line in f being in the other constituent), we suppress that collecting node, i.e.,

becomes ⟶

Note g and h are each proper programs; otherwise f is not a proper program. Note also g and/or h may be λ, a program with no nodes.

Since each g and h contain at least one less predicate node than does f, at least one collecting node is suppressed in each constituent. Next, we consider the new proper program, (IF,p,g,h),

---

*Our definition of proper programs is necessary for this assertion. The proof of Böhm and Jacopini [5] breaks down at this point.

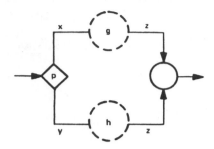

with the original predicate p and the constituents g and h of f (and a new collecting node, not from g or h). In this case, we define

$$S(f) = (\text{IF},p,g,h).$$

Also, in this case, we observe that

$$e(g) \leq \phi(f)+3(\pi(f)-1)+1 = e(f) -3$$
$$e(h) \leq \phi(f)+3(\pi(f)-1)+1 = e(f) -3$$

since g and h at least do not contain predicate node f. (We use $e(f)$, $\phi(f)$, and $\pi(f)$ to denote the number of lines, function nodes, and predicate nodes, respectively, in f, etc.)

Finally, it is clear by construction that $S(f)$ is equivalent to f.

Case 2b — Function Node. If the first node is a function node, then f is of the form

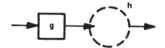

and h is a proper program, possibly λ. In this case, we define

$$S(f) = (\text{BLK},g,h).$$

Also, in this case, it is easy to count the number of lines in h, given that there are $e(f)$ lines in f. The number is

$$e(h) = (\phi(f)-1)+3\pi(f)+1 = e(f)-1.$$

Finally, it is clear by construction that $S(f)$ is equivalent to f.

Case 2c — Collecting Node. If the first node is a collecting node, then f must be of the form

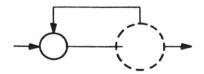

and we examine the next unique node reached from this collecting node. It is clear that such a next node exists, because a predicate node, at least, must be reached in the remaining improper program in order to have two output lines. There are three sub-cases to be examined.

2.c.(1) Predicate Node — If the next node is a predicate node, then f is of the form

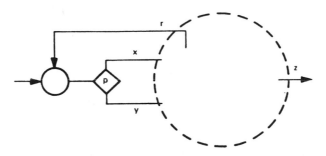

As before, we construct two programs which consist of all nodes which can be reached from x and y, which terminate in z or r. We suppress collecting nodes with only one input, as before. These programs will not be proper programs if both r and z can be reached from x or y. However, since f is a proper program, we know that each constructed program must reach at least z or r, and that each z and r must be reached by at least one constructed program. These constructed programs have the form

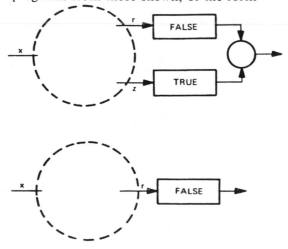

where the solid output line is necessary, and the dotted output line may or may not exist. We use TRUE, FALSE function nodes (to set flags) and possibly collecting nodes to construct new proper programs from these shown, of the form

or

and

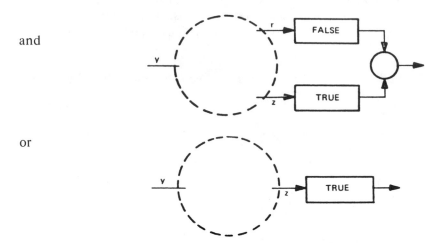

or

depending on whether or not the dotted output lines r and z exist.

We label these proper programs g and h (such that g has at least the r output line and h has at least the z output line). Now, we consider the new program

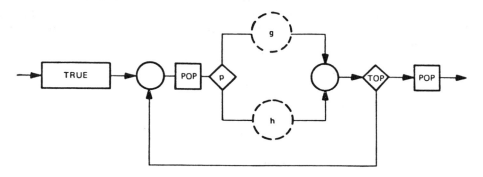

with g and h as constituent programs. In this case, we define

$$S(f) = (\text{BLK},\text{TRUE},(\text{BLK},(\text{DO},\text{TOP},(\text{BLK},\text{POP},(\text{IF},p,g,h))),\text{POP})).$$

We observe that g and h does not have the predicate node p and each has at most two more function nodes. Hence,

$$e(g) \leq \phi(f)+2+3(\pi(f)-1)+1 = e(f)-1$$
$$e(h) \leq \phi(f)+2+3(\pi(f)-1)+1 = e(f)-1$$

Finally, it can be verified that $S(f)$ is equivalent to f.

2.c.(2) Function Node — If the next node is a function node, then f is of the form

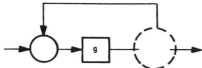

and we consider the new program

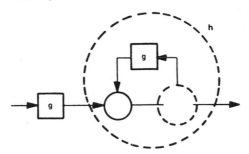

with new program labeled h. In this case, we define

$$S(f) = (\text{BLK},g,h).$$

Also, in this case, we observe directly that

$$e(h) = e(f)$$

but that also, the number of lines, say i(f), required to reach the first predicate of f is reduced by one, i.e., that

$$i(h) = i(f)-1$$

Finally, it is clear that S(f) is equivalent to f.

2.c.(3) Collecting Node — If the next node is a collecting node, then f is of the form

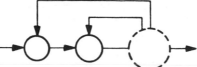

and we consider the new program

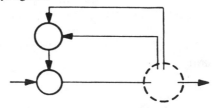

called g. In this case we define

$$S(f) = g$$

Also, in this case, we observe directly that

$$e(g) = e(f)$$
$$i(g) = i(f)-1$$

It is clear that $S(f)$ is equivalent to f.

Summary

This completes the analysis of cases for the input region of f, and the definition of the structuring process S. In summary, in each case, we have defined a new program, $S(f)$, equivalent to f, such that $S(f)$ is a formula in, at most, graph labels BLOCK, IFTHENELSE, DOUNTIL, functions, predicates, and constituent proper programs. In several cases, the number of edges of the constituents of f are seen to be less than the number of edges in f. In two cases, this number of edges was not decreased, but the number of edges from input to the first predicate node was decreased. It is clear that the number of edges from input to the first predicate node is bounded by the number of edges of a program. When we apply this information to that generated in the case analyses above, we get Table 1.

Table 1
Case Analysis — Structuring Process

Case	e values		i values
2a	$e(g) \leq e(f)-3$	,	$i(f) \leq e(f)-3$
	$e(h) \leq e(f)-3$	,	$i(h) = e(f)-3$
2b	$e(h) = e(f)-1$	,	$i(h) \leq e(f)-1$
2c(1)	$e(g) \leq e(f)-1$	,	$i(g) \leq e(f)-1$
	$e(h) \leq e(f)-1$	,	$i(g) \leq e(f)-1$
2c(2)	$e(h) = e(f)$	,	$i(h) = i(g)-1$
2c(3)	$e(g) = e(f)$	,	$i(g) = i(f)-1$

We are now ready to summarize our proof, as follows:

First, it is clear that the Theorem is true for proper programs with one line, for such a program is simply λ.

Next, suppose the Theorem is true for proper programs of n lines or less for n > 1. Let f be a proper program with n + 1 lines. We apply S to f. If cases 2a, 2b, or 2c(1) apply, we have a new equivalent program, whose constituent programs are proper and have at most n lines; and each such constituent, by our induction hypothesis, satisfies the Theorem. Moreover, the new equivalent program has a formula in, at most, graph labels BLOCK, IFTHENELSE, DOUNTIL, predicates and its constituents. Therefore, the new program satisfies the Theorem. If none of cases 2a, 2b, or 2c(1) apply, then $i(f) \leq n$, and case 2c(2) or 2c(3) must apply. In each such case, there remains only one constituent, say g, and

$$e(g) = e(f), i(g) = i(f)-1$$

Therefore, after, at most, n such applications, case 2c(1) must apply, and the final equivalent program satisfies the Theorem.

This completes the Proof of the Structure Theorem.

Top down corollary

Any proper program is equivalent to a program of one of the forms

(BLOCK,g,h)
(IFTHENELSE,p,g,h)
(DOUNTIL,p,g)

where p is a predicate of the original program or TOP, and g,h are each proper programs, functions of the original program, TRUE, FALSE, or POP.

S-Structured programs

The Structure Theorem motivates the definition of a structured program as follows:

Let S be any finite set of labels associated with control graphs of proper programs. Then any program whose formula contains only graph labels from S is said to be an S-structured program.

When the prefix "S" is not critical, or understood, it will be suppressed.

Program representations

The result of the Structure Theorem is similar to representation theorems in other branches of mathematics, in which it is shown that all elements of a set, or "space," can be represented by combinations of a subset of "basic elements" of the space. For example, three nonplanar vectors span a three-dimensional Euclidean space, the set $\{\sin nx, \cos nx \mid n=0,1, \ldots \}$ span a set of real functions in the interval $[0, 2\pi]$ — i.e., a "function space." The foregoing examples refer to linear combination for representation.

In the Structure Theorem, it is shown that three simple types of programs, defined by BLOCK, IF-THEN-ELSE, and DO-UNTIL control graphs, span the set of all proper programs, using substitution of proper programs for process nodes as the only rule of combination. Such a representation theorem permits the resolution of questions of the adequacy of a programming language simply and effectively. For example, all one needs to show a new set of basis programs will span the set of all proper programs is that one can represent BLOCK, IF-THEN-ELSE, and DO-UNTIL programs in this new set.

One simple illustration of a new basis is to represent DOUNTIL in terms of BLOCK and DOWHILE, as follows

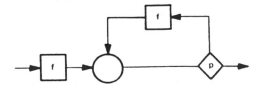

or

(DOUNTIL,p,f) = (BLOCK,f, (DOWHILE,p,f)).

Hence, BLOCK, IFTHENELSE, and DOWHILE provide a sufficient control structure to represent all proper programs as well as BLOCK, IFTHENELSE, and DOUNTIL.

Program trees

The formula of a structured program can be displayed in a program tree in a natural way, with the graph labels, functions and predicates assigned to nodes of the tree. For example, the formula

(IFTHENELSE,p,g,h)

defines the program tree

and the formula

(DOWHILE,p,(IFTHENELSE,q,g,(BLOCK,h,k)))

defines the program tree

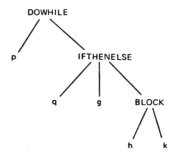

Conversely, given any program tree of graph labels, functions and predicates, the original program can be recovered. In particular, any subtree defined by a node plus all its successors in the tree defines a subprogram of the original program.

The program tree provides a convenient way of visualizing program structure in the form of subprograms. By labeling subprograms, and referring to their program functions at higher levels in the program, an original program of any size can be organized as a set of subprograms, each of a prescribed maximum size.

It is clear that the subprograms so defined are each proper programs. That is, they each map an input data set into an output data set, with no control side effects.

Program correctness

We have already noted that program correctness is a question of predictability. More precisely, given a program, f, and a function, g, we are interested in whether g is the same as the program function [f]. If we know both g and [f], we can resolve the question by comparison. Carrying out such a comparison of two sets is a general mathematics problem whose solution will depend on how the sets are defined. In few cases they will be enumerated. In that case their elements can be ordered and matched, a pair at a time. In most cases such sets will be defined by conditions or rules in some broader (less formal) context than set theory per se. There may be natural numbers involved, in which case inductive definitions and comparisons may be possible. In any case, the techniques for comparison are beyond our present interest, and must be formulated in whatever terms are available.

In the case of structured programs, the program tree permits the decomposition of the correctness problem into a series of nested problems, each of a simple type which can be prescribed in advance.

Correctness theorem

If the formula of a program contains at most graph labels BLOCK, IFTHEN, IFTHENELSE, DOWHILE, and DOUNTIL, and satisfies a loop qualification, then it can be proved correct by a tour of its program tree, in which, at each node, the relevant one of five cases must be proved (data sets suppressed — see below for data set versions):

If f = (BLOCK,g,h), prove

$$[f] = \{(r,t) \mid \exists\, s((r,s) \in [g] \;\wedge\; (s,t) \in [h])\}$$

If f = (IFTHEN,p,g), prove

$$[f] = \{(r,s) \mid ((r, \text{True}) \in p \;\wedge\; (r,s) \in [g] \;\vee$$
$$((r, \text{False}) \in p \;\wedge\; (r,s) \in p \;\wedge\, r = s)\}$$

If f = (IFTHENELSE,p,g,h), prove

$$[f] = \{(r,s) \mid ((r, \text{True}) \;\wedge\, p \;\wedge\; (r,s) \;\wedge\, [g]) \;\vee$$
$$((r, \text{False}) \in p \;\wedge\; (r,s) \in [h])\}$$

If f = (DOWHILE,p,g), prove

$$[f] = [(\text{IFTHEN},p,(\text{BLOCK},[g], [f]))]$$

If f = (DOUNTIL,p,g), prove

$$[f] = [(\text{BLOCK},[g], (\text{IFTHEN},p,[f]))]$$

Proof

By hypothesis each node in the program tree is one of the five types listed. Beginning at the root of the tree, the program function [f] of program f is determined by possibly a predicate, and program functions [g], [h] of constituent subprograms g, h, and so on, until functions are reached at the endpoints of the tree. If the program function at each node is known with respect to program functions of its successor nodes, then by finite induction, the program function at the root of the tree is known with respect to the functions in the program.

It remains to validate the detailed assertions case by case.

Case f = (BLOCK,g,h)

In flowchart form,

Now

by the definition of program functions [g], [h]. Then, program function [f] can be formulated directly as

$$[f] = \{(r,t) \mid r \in R \; \exists \; s((r,s) \in [g] \; s \in S \; (s,t) \in [h]) \; t \in T\}.$$

This agrees with the statement of the Theorem with the data sets suppressed.

Case f = (IFTHEN,p,g)

In flowchart form,

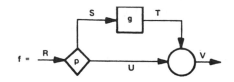

Now

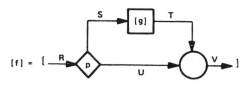

Then

$$[f] = \{(r,v) \mid r \in R \; \wedge$$
$$(((r, True) \in p \; \wedge \; r \in S \; \wedge \; (r,v) \in [g] \; \wedge \; v \in T)$$
$$\vee((r,False) \in p \; \wedge \; r = v \; \wedge \; v \in U)) \; \wedge \; v \in V\}.$$

This agrees with the statement of the Theorem with the data sets suppressed.

Case f = (IFTHENELSE,p,g,h)

In flowchart form,

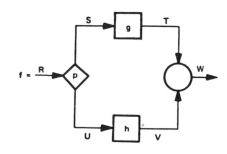

Now

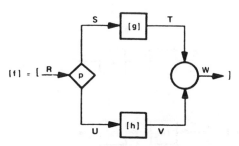

Then

$$[f] = \{(r,w) \mid r \in R \; \bigwedge$$

$$(((r, \text{True}) \in p \; \bigwedge \; r \in S \; \bigwedge \; (r,w) \in [g] \; \bigwedge \; w \in T)$$

$$\bigwedge \; ((r, \text{False}) \in p \; \bigwedge \; r \in U \; \bigwedge \; (r,w) \in [h] \; \bigwedge \; w \in V)) \; \bigwedge \; w \in W\}.$$

This agrees with the statement of the Theorem with the data sets suppressed.

Case $f = (\text{DOWHILE},p,g)$

In flowchart form,

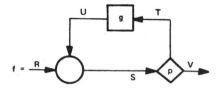

Now

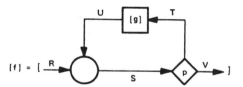

and, indeed,

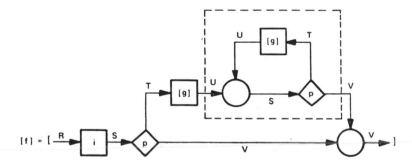

by construction and inspection, where i is an identity function. We note that if $R = U$ then the DOWHILE subprogram in the dotted section has program function $[f]$ i.e.,

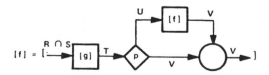

This agrees with the statement of the Theorem with the data sets suppressed. We call the condition $R = U$ the *loop qualification* on f; i.e., both input lines to the collecting node have identical data spaces.

Case f = (DOUNTIL,p,g)

In flowchart form,

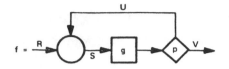

Now,

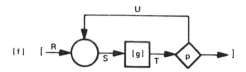

and, indeed,

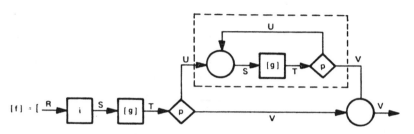

by construction and inspection. If R = U, (the loop qualification), then the DOUNTIL subprogram in the dotted section has program function [f], i.e.,

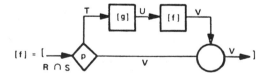

This agrees with the statement of the Theorem with the data sets suppressed.
    With this case, the proof of the Theorem is completed.

Correctness notes

    At first glance, the verification conditions for DOWHILE and DOUNTIL seem to involve a recursive relation in program function [f]. But this is not the case; the verification conditions involve [f] as an input, not as an unknown to be solved for.

It is also noteworthy that the top down approach to correctness avoids the problem of incomplete rules (or in other formulations, incomplete functions, for which we have no counterparts), and termination. In a program equation such as

> f = WHILE p DO g ,

the functions p and [g] are usually taken to be the "independent variables" and the function [f] to be the "dependent variable," a "bottom up" viewpoint. Of course, even through p and [g] may be given by complete rules, the new rule "WHILE p DO g" may turn out to be partial because of nontermination. However, in the top down viewpoint, the function [f] is the "independent variable," and the program equation defines "dependent variables" p and [g] implicitly, (and meaningfully). Now, since [f] is a function, p and [g] must be defined such that the rule "WHILE p DO g" terminates for any input in the domain of [f].

The loop qualification required in the Correctness Theorem is a serious restriction with respect to the allocation and freeing of storage space. If the body of a DO loop allocates or frees space, then the loop qualification is not satisfied, and the reduction of a loop verification to the form of the Theorem is not valid.

Top down program expansions

Thus far, we have considered programs first, and then their meanings as program functions. In top down programming, we want to reverse that order of conception. That is, given a function (a program specification) we want to find some program (a rule) which has that program function. This reversal of conception allows us to avoid questions of "partial rules," "partial correctness," and the general termination problem, because they never arise. In the usual way of looking at program equations, such as

> f = (DOWHILE,p,g)

the graph label DOWHILE, predicate p, and function or subprogram g, are usually taken to be the "independent variables" and program f taken to be the "dependent variable." In this case, even though p and g are given by rules defined everywhere on their domains, the new program (DOWHILE,p,g) may not terminate and thus be called a partial rule. One may prove properties relating p and g to f in case of termination to get partial correctness, but one must also establish termination separately to get total correctness.

We observe that if we take f to be the independent variable in the foregoing equation, then these partial rule and partial correctness problems disappear. If f denotes a complete rule, then p and g must denote complete rules, in order to satisfy the equation as dependent variables. That is the essence of top down programming, regarding the constituent subprograms and predicates of an expansion as dependent variables which satisfy a prescribed equation which is inherited top down.

When this approach is taken, perhaps the most surprising result is the amount of freedom available to a programmer in writing a correct program. In the bottom up approach, programming appears to be an activity with almost unlimited freedom to improvise or solve problems in various ways. But in developing a program top down, it is clear that this freedom is highly restricted. At first glance it may seem there is less freedom in programming top down than in bottom up, but a second thought shows that is not the case. They must lead to equivalent results and, in fact, what really is exhibited in the bottom up approach is a false freedom that is subsequently paid for in a painful error elimination process, following an original "gush of originality."

In order to exhibit the degree of freedom available in programming, we formulate the Expansion Theorem below in both a verbal and a set theoretic version. The Structure Theorem exhibits characteristics of a completed program, while the Expansion Theorem shows how programs can look at every intermediate stage of their construction. At every such intermediate stage, a program developed in a top down discipline can be guaranteed to be correct, insofar as it is developed, without the necessity of altering parts of the program already done, in order to accommodate the remaining parts of the program yet to be developed. It is a familiar experience in large program development to get "90% done" and to remain at that 90% level for a lengthy period. That phenomena occurs not because the last 10% is difficult to write, but because in order to write the last 10%, critical sections of the first 90% need to be altered. The Expansion Theorem and top down programming can guarantee that the first 90% can remain intact while the last 10% is finished on schedule.

Expansion theorem (verbal version)

In a program function expansion of the form (data sets suppressed — see below for more detail):

(1) $f = [(\text{BLOCK},g,h)]$
Any pair (g,h) whose composition is f may be chosen.

(2) $f = [(\text{IFTHENELSE},p,g,h)]$
Any predicate p with the same domain as f may be chosen, then g and h are fully determined, as the members of the partition of f defined by p.

(3) $f = [(\text{DOWHILE},p,g)]$
The program function f must be the identity in the intersection of its domain and range, any function g may be chosen whose completion is the varying part of f, and p is fully determined by f and g.

In short, the invention of an IFTHENELSE program is equivalent to a partition of a prescribed program function, while the invention of a DOWHILE program is equivalent to the determination of a function whose completion is a prescribed program function. That is, the only freedom in an IFTHENELSE program is its predicate, and the only freedom in a DOWHILE program is its iterative process — all other freedoms, in the THEN or ELSE clauses, in the WHILE predicate, are illusions. THEN and ELSE clauses are frequently used for elaborating functional specifications not fully stated; but these are not freedoms of choice, but interpretations of intentions at more detailed levels. The point is that if functional specifications are sufficiently well defined to decide whether a program satisfies them, then there is no freedom beyond the choice of the predicate in an IFTHENELSE program. In the case of the DOWHILE, the question is more subtle, and relates to the character of the termination questions in programming top down, in contrast to bottom up. The WHILE predicate is completely determined on the domain and range of the function (specification). The DOWHILE program must terminate on reaching any element of the range, and must continue otherwise; because, if not, it cannot possibly satisfy the prestated (top down inherited) function specification.

In order to formulate a more concise, set theoretic version of the Expansion Theorem, we introduce a reinterpretation of the logical constant "True." Ordinarily, a predicate is taken to be a function, p, such that

$$\text{range}(p) = \{\text{True, False}\}.$$

We reinterpret the constant True by the statement for an associated function

$$\bar{p} = \{(x,y) \mid (x,\text{True}) \in p\} ;$$

i.e., if p(x) is true, then for any element y, $(x,y) \in \bar{p}$.

We also introduce the idea of a refinement of a function, corresponding to the ordinary idea of the refinement of a partition. (A refinement of a partition is simply a new partition, each of whose members is a subset of some member of the original partition.) We form a partition of the domain of a function, called a partition of *level sets*, or the *contour* of the function, by grouping arguments which have identical values into subsets of the domain. Then we say one function is a refinement of another if its contour is a refinement of the others.

Finally, we define the *fixed points* of a function f, denoted as the fixed(f) subset

$$\text{fixed}(f) = \{(x,y) \mid (x,y) \in f \land x = y\}.$$

Expansion theorem (set theoretic version)

In a program expansion of the form (data sets suppressed — see below for more detail):

(1) f = [(BLOCK,g,h)]

    (a) choose function g as any refinement of program function f

    (b) then h is uniquely determined by the relation f = g * h

(2) f = [(IFTHENELSE,p,g,h)]

    (a) choose predicate p such that domain(p) = domain(f)

    (b) then g and h are uniquely determined by the relations
        g = $\bar{p}$ ∩ f
        h = f − g

(3) f = [(DOWHILE,p,g)]

    (a) verify that domain(fixed(f)) = domain(f) ∩ range (f)

    (b) choose function g such that * g * = f − fixed(f).

    (c) then p is uniquely determined such that
        p(x) = True if x ∈ domain(g)−range(f)
        p(x) = False if x ∈ range(f)

Proof

Case f = [(BLOCK,g,h)]

In flowchart form

$$f = [\xrightarrow{\text{R}} \boxed{g} \xrightarrow{\text{S}} \boxed{h} \xrightarrow{\text{T}}]$$

Consider the following construction of g, h, R, S, T:

Set R = domain(f).

Set T = range(f).

Choose any refinement of f, say g; then for any x ∈ R, y ∈ R,

$$g(x) = g(y) \supset f(x) = f(y)$$

Set S = range(g)

Set h = {(s,t) | (r,s) ∈ g ∧ (r,t) ∈ f}

Now, it is easy to verify by this construction that

$$[(\text{BLOCK } g,h,)] = [(x,y) | (x,y) ∈ f]$$

as was to be shown. The function h is uniquely determined in the construction by f and g.

Case f = [(IFTHENELSE,p,g,h)]

In flowchart form

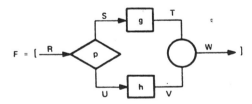

Consider the following construction of p, g, h, R, S, T, U, V, W:

Set R = domain(f)

Choose any predicate p such that domain(p) = domain(f) = R

Set S = { s | (s,True) ∈ p}

Set g = {(s,t) | s ∈ S ∧ (s,t) ∈ f}

Set T = range(g)

Set U = {u | (u,False) ∈ p}

Set h = {(u,v) | u ∈ U ∧ (u,v) ∈ f}

Set V = range(h)

Set W = T ∪ V

Now, it is easy to verify by this construction that

$$[(\text{IFTHENELSE},p,g,h)] = \{(x,y) \mid (x,y) \in f\}$$

as was to be shown. Note that g is a subset of f defined by p, i.e., $\bar{p} \cap f$, and h is the complement of g in f, i.e., $f - g$.

Case f = [(DOWHILE,p,g)]

In flowchart form

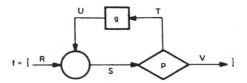

Consider $(s,v) \in f$, i.e., $v \in \text{range}(f)$. We note that necessarily $p(v) = $ False. Otherwise the control path to g is taken, and the program cannot terminate with value v, which contradicts the correctness of the expansion.

Next, consider $(r,v) \in f$ such that $r \in \text{domain}(f) \cap \text{range}(f)$; then $p(v) = $ False by the foregoing remark, and the function g is bypassed, so that necessarily $v = r$, or $r \in \text{domain}(\text{fixed}(f))$. Conversely, if $r \in \text{domain}(\text{fixed}(f))$, then $r \in \text{range}(f)$ and $p(r) = $ False, hence $r \in \text{domain}(f) \cap \text{range}(f)$. That is, $\text{domain}(\text{fixed}(f)) = \text{domain}(f) \cap \text{range}(f)$ as needed to be shown.

Next, choose function g such that $* g * = f - \text{fixed}(f)$. At least one such choice is possible, namely for $g = f - \text{fixed}(f)$, since the domain and range of $f - \text{fixed}(f)$ is disjoint.

Finally, we have already seen that necessarily $p(x) = $ False when $x \in \text{range}(f)$. But clearly, we must have $p(x) = $ True when $x \in \text{domain}(g)$, in order that the correct control path be taken to finally reach an output $v \in \text{range}(f)$; in addition, since $* g * \supset f$, then necessarily $\text{domain}(g) \supset \text{domain}(*g*) \supset \text{domain}(f)$, so that $x \in \text{domain}(g)$ implies $x \in \text{domain}(f)$. Thus, in summary,

$p(x) = $ True if $x \in \text{domain}(g) - \text{range}(f)$

$p(x) = $ False if $x \in \text{range}(f)$

as was to be shown.

The data sets required are as follows:

Set R = domain(f)

Set V = range(f)

Set T = domain(g)

Set U = range(g)

Set S = R ∪ U

This discussion is concluded with a combinatorial characterization of g, the iterative process of a DOWHILE program:

For function f, consider any superfunction h, such that range(h) = range(f). For each level set, or contour, of h, define any arbitrary set of rooted trees on its elements. If x of domain(h) is a root of such a tree, then we set

$$y(x) = h(x).$$

If x ∈ domain(h) is not a root of such a tree, let y denote the parent of x in that tree, and define

$$g(x) = y.$$

It is easily verified that any function g so defined, and no other, will satisfy the relation * g * = f.

With this, it is clear that in all three cases, the entire freedom of choice is a combinatorial one. In a BLOCK program, it is the choice of a function; in an IFTHENELSE program, the choice is a partition of a function; in a DOWHILE program, the choice is a tree structure within the level sets of a function.

Indeterminate programs

In certain applications, particularly those of artificial intelligence [33], it is convenient to generalize the idea of a program to a construct which permits ambiguity in execution, rather than uniqueness. For example, an algorithm may specify a selection of a member of some set for processing, without naming a specific member. In this event, intermediate and/or final results may be indeterminate. Such "indeterminate algorithms" are often useful in describing the essentials of a process, without getting unduly involved with its specifics. Indeterminate algorithms are also useful for treating a man-machine computing system, in which the actions of men — say at terminals — are indeterminate. Then, an entire system can be defined to be governed by an indeterminate algorithm.

Our development of programs, which we call "determinate programs," where necessary, can be generalized to include "indeterminate programs" by a very simple extension — namely, by extending the idea of function, throughout, to the idea of relation. A *relation* is defined to be a set of ordered pairs, without the additional qualification required of a function to provide unique values for given arguments. As with functions, relations inherit set properties. In fact, not only the intersection and difference of two relations are new relations (as in the case of functions), but the union of two relations is also a relation (not generally so for functions). Domains and ranges of relations are defined as for functions.

Next, we define an *indeterminate program* to be a finite set of relations, called *indeterminate instructions*, whose domains are each included in a data space, and whose ranges are each included in the cartesian product of the data space and the indeterminate program, again called the state space. An *indeterminate program execution* is, again, a sequence of state values

$$s = (d_i, r_i), i = 0, 1, \ldots$$

such that

$$(d_i, s_{i+1}) \in r_i, i = 0, 1, \ldots$$

which terminates, if ever, when $d_i \notin$ domain (r_i). Precisely as before, all executions which terminate define a set of ordered pairs, now a relation, instead of a function, which we call the *indeterminate program relation;* i.e., in retrospect, an indeterminate program is a (nonunique) rule for calculating the members of its relation, using other relations in so doing.

At this point, we leave it to the reader to observe that every construction and theorem goes through for indeterminate programs and their relations, just as for determinate programs and their functions.

References: Mills

1. Allen, C.D., "The Application of Formal Logic to Programs and Programming," *IBM Systems Journal,* Vol. 10, No. 1 (1971), pp. 2-38.

2. Ashcroft, E.A., "Program Correctness Methods and Language Definition," *Proceedings of the ACM Conference on Proving Assertions About Programs,* New Mexico State University (January 1972).

3. Ashcroft, E.A., and Z. Manna, "The Translation of 'GO TO' Programs to 'WHILE' Programs," Stanford Artificial Intelligence Project, Memo AIM-138, Computer Sciences Department Report No. STAN-CS-71-188 (January 1971).

4. Baker, F.T., "Chief Programmer Team Management of Production Programming," *IBM Systems Journal,* Vol. 11, No. 1 (1972), pp. 56-73.

5. Böhm, C., and G. Jacopini, "Flow Diagrams, Turing Machines and Languages With Only Two Formation Rules," *Communications of the ACM,* Vol. 9, No. 5 (1966), pp. 366-371.

6. Burge, W.H., "Some Examples of Programming Using a Functional Notation," Second Symposium of Special Interest Group Association for Computing Machinery on Symbolic and Algebraic Manipulation, Los Angeles (March 1971).

7. Burstall, R.M., "An Algebraic Description of Programs with Assertions, Verification and Simulation," *Proceedings of the ACM Conference on Proving Assertions About Programs,* New Mexico State University (January 1972).

8. Church, A., *Introduction to Mathematical Logic,* Vol. 1, Princeton, N.J.: Princeton University Press (1956).

9. Dijkstra, E.W., "A Constructive Approach to the Problem of Program Correctness," *BIT,* Vol. 8, No. 3 (1968), pp. 174-186.

10. Dijkstra, E.W., *Notes on Structured Programming,* Technische Hogeschool Eindhoven, Report No. EWD-248, 70-WSK-0349, Eindhoven, The Netherlands (1970).

11. Dijkstra, E.W., "Structured Programming," *Software Engineering Techniques,* Eds.: J.N. Buxton and B. Randell, NATO Science Committee (1969), pp. 88-93.

12. Floyd, R.W., "Assigning Meanings to Programs," *Proceedings of the Symposium in Applied Mathematics,* Vol. 19, Ed.: J.T. Schwartz, American Mathematical Society, Providence, R.I. (1967), pp. 19-32.

13. Floyd, R.W., "Nondeterministic Algorithms," *Journal of the ACM,* Vol. 14, No. 4 (October 1967), pp. 636-644.

14. Good, D.I., "Toward a Man-machine System for Proving Program Correctness," Ph.D. Thesis, University of Wisconsin (1970).

15. Halmos, P.R., *Naive Set Theory,* Eds.: J.L. Kelley and P.R. Halmos, Princeton, N.J.: D. Van Nostrand Co., Inc. (1960).

16. Hoare, C.A.R., "An Axiomatic Approach to Computer Programming," *Communications of the ACM,* Vol. 12, No. 10 (October 1969), pp. 576-580, 583.

17. Hoare, C.A.R., "Proof of a Program: FIND," *Communications of the ACM,* Vol. 14, No. 1 (January 1971), pp. 39-45. [Ed. note: Reprinted in this volume, paper 13.]

18. Horning, J.J., and B. Randell, "Structuring Complex Processes," IBM T.J. Watson Research Center, Report RC 2459 (May 1969).

19. Ianov, I., "The Logical Schemas of Algorithms," *Problems of Cybernetics,* Vol. 1, English translation (Pergamon Press) (1960).

20. Jones, C.B., "Formal Development of Correct Algorithms: An Example Based on Earley's Recognizer," *Proceedings of the ACM Conference on Proving Assertions About Programs,* New Mexico State University (January 1972).

21. King, J.C., "A Program Verifier," Ph.D. Thesis, Carnegie-Mellon University (1969).

22. Landin, P.J., "A Correspondence Between ALGOL 60 and Church's Lambda-Notation," *Communications of the ACM,* Vol. 8, No. 3 (March 1965).

23. London, R.L., "Certification of Algorithm 245 Treesort 3: Proof of Algorithms — A New Kind of Certification," *Communications of the ACM,* Vol. 13 (1970), pp. 371-373.

24. London, R.L., "Correctness of a Compiler for a LISP Subset," *Proceedings of the ACM Conference on Proving Assertions About Programs,* New Mexico State University (January 1972).

25. London, R.L., "Proving Programs Correct: Some Techniques and Examples," *BIT,* Vol. 10, No. 2 (1970), pp. 168-182.

26. McCarthy, J., "Towards a Mathematical Science of Computation," *Proceedings of the IFIP Congress,* Amsterdam: North-Holland (1962).

27. Mendelson, E., *Introduction to Mathematical Logic,* Princeton, N.J.: D. Van Nostrand Co., Inc. (1964).

28. Mills, H.D., "Syntax-Directed Documentation for PL360," *Communications of the ACM,* Vol. 13, No. 4 (April 1970), pp. 216-222.

29. Mills, H.D., "Top Down Programming in Large Systems," *Debugging Techniques in Large Systems,* Courant Computer Science Symposium, Vol. 1, Ed.: R. Rustin, New York University (1971), pp. 41-55.

30. Nahikian, H.M., *Topics in Modern Mathematics,* Ed.: C.B. Allendoerfer, London: The Macmillan Co., Collier-Macmillan Ltd. (1966).

31. Naur, P., "Programming by Action Clusters," *BIT,* Vol. 9, No. 3 (1969), pp. 250-258.

32. Naur, P., "Proof of Algorithms by General Snapshots," *BIT,* Vol. 6, No. 4 (1966), pp. 310-316.

33. Nilsson, N.J., *Problem-Solving Methods in Artificial Intelligence,* New York: McGraw-Hill, Inc. (1971).

34. Scott, D., "The Lattice of Flow Diagrams," *Programming Research Group,* Oxford University (1970).

35. Scott, D., "An Outline of a Mathematical Theory of Computation," *Programming Research Group,* Oxford University (1970).

36. Snowdon, R.A., *PEARL: An Interactive System for the Preparation and Validation of Structured Programs,* Tech. Report No. 28, Ed.: Dr. B. Shaw, University of Newcastle Upon Tyne, Computing Laboratory (1971).

37. Strachey, C., "Towards a Formal Semantics," *Formal Language Description Languages,* Ed.: T.B. Steel, Amsterdam: North-Holland (1966), pp. 198-220.

38. Wilder, R.L., *Evolution of Mathematical Concepts — An Elementary Study,* New York: John Wiley & Sons, Inc. (1968).

39. Wirth, N., "Program Development by Stepwise Refinement," *Communications of the ACM,* Vol. 14, No. 4 (April 1971), pp. 221-227. [Ed. note: Reprinted in this volume, paper 5.]

40. Zurcher, F., and B. Randell, "Iterative Multi-Level Modelling — A Methodology for Computer System Design," *Proceedings of the IFIP Congress* (1968), pp. D138-D142.

Section 5
PROJECT MANAGEMENT:
CONTROL AND COST ESTIMATION

The previous papers in this book have dealt with techniques: systems analysis, design, programming, and the arcane area of mathematical correctness proofs. This next group addresses the *management* of the systems development process.

To paraphrase a comment from my colleague and friend Tom DeMarco, "You can't manage what you can't measure, and what you don't measure is out of control." This theme is evident throughout all four of the papers in this section: The emphasis is on management, but all of the papers stress that the only effective way to manage a software development project is to measure and monitor what takes place during the project.

Boehm: Software and Its Impact: A Quantitative Assessment

The first paper in the group is by Barry Boehm. Published in *Datamation* in 1973, this article was probably the first to establish Boehm as *the* American authority on statistics and measurement in the business of developing computer systems. Indeed, it's hard to provide a preview of Boehm's paper without focussing on his informative statistics, most of which are still valid, or can be easily extrapolated from, nearly ten years later. For example, Boehm provides convincing figures to indicate that software represented approximately seventy-five percent of the total cost of an EDP system. It was a startling proportion in 1973, but in the 1980s people are gradually becoming aware that software represents almost ninety percent of the cost of a system. Similarly, Boehm points out that in the early 1970s software represented roughly one percent of the U.S. Gross National Product. It's fascinating to draw a comparison between our current situation with computer software and the situation with telephone technology in the 1920s. The telephone industry extrapolated from the trend that they could see then, and predicted that by the 1970s or 1980s almost every man, woman, and child in the United States would have to be a telephone operator — which is exactly what has happened with touch-tone telephones. Could the same phenomenon apply to computer software?

Barry Boehm also suggested in his paper that the three major methods of solving the software crisis are

- increasing productivity of individual programmers

- improving management of software projects
- starting software development much earlier in the life cycle of systems development projects

Were these ideas new in 1973? I must say that they probably were not. However, when these more-or-less obvious suggestions were supported by dozens, and possibly hundreds, of pieces of hard statistical evidence, suddenly a lot of bits of advice and folklore in the data processing business began to take on some of the authority of an engineering discipline, if not a science.

I have treasured Boehm's article since I first read it; I've reread it a dozen times since, and I'm sure I'll read it another dozen times over the next ten years. I'll let you discover on your own his amazing, and amusing, facts and statistics, and let you decide for yourself whether his suggestions and remedies are the right ones. As you read, keep in mind that most of the impact of Boehm's article comes from the fact that he and his colleagues actually *had* measurements of real software projects, and were thus able to draw conclusions that few EDP managers are able to draw.

Belady & Lehman: A Model of Large Program Development

Belady and Lehman expound on the management-by-measurement theme in their paper "A Model of Large Program Development," published in the *IBM Systems Journal* in the fall of 1976. They gathered measurements and data about only one system — but what a system! The OS/360 operating system was the subject of their study, which covered some twenty releases of OS from 1964 to 1976.

I found two things fascinating about Belady and Lehman's approach. First of all, they considered OS largely as a black box; rather than looking closely at its internal construction, they appear to have concentrated on its visible, *external* characteristics: such things as the number of reported errors and the time between releases of OS. Second, by observing OS/360 in this fashion, they were able to treat it almost as a living organism, writing, "The system and the metasystem — the project organization that is developing it — constitute an organism that is constrained by conservation laws."

The "conservation laws" suggested by Belady and Lehman are the following three:

- *the law of continuing change:* A system undergoes continuing change until it is judged more cost-effective to freeze the system and recreate it.

- *law of increasing entropy:* The entropy (unstructuredness) of a system increases with time, unless specific work is executed to maintain or reduce it.

- *law of statistically smooth growth:* Growth trend measures of global system attributes may appear to be stochastic locally, but statistics show them to be cyclically self-regulating, with well-defined long-range trends.

I'll let you read the paper to discover just what the cycles and trends are. You'll find it enlightening, I think; but you may be tempted to discount the paper as applying only to IBM's unique, mammoth operating system. However, it is becoming increasingly obvious to all of us that there are *many* EDP projects underway, or in the planning stage, that rival OS in size and complexity. Belady and Lehman's approach, particularly their emphasis on studying the hardware/software system *and* the people who build it, should be applicable to large systems of any sort.

Donelson: Project Planning and Control

The next paper in the section, by William Donelson, was published in *Datamation* in 1976. It continues the theme of measuring the activities and the available resources in an EDP project; it also repeats Boehm's point that a database of past project experience should be used to help predict the behavior of future projects.

Indeed, Donelson provides a number of statistics from projects in his own organization — but, unfortunately, the environment (a batch processing IBM 360/40) is hardly similar to anyone's environment today. Although Donelson's statistics might not be applicable to *your* organization, his paper shows how one person and one organization went about gathering sufficient statistics to better manage themselves; as such, it has probably served as an inspiration to many project managers over the years.

Putnam & Fitzsimmons: Estimating Software Costs

The last paper in this section is by Larry Putnam and Ann Fitzsimmons, and was published in three parts in *Datamation* in the fall of 1979. It provides an interesting contrast to the article Donelson published some three years earlier: Instead of a few statistics gleaned from a small sample of projects, it provides very sophisticated formulas for project estimating derived from literally hundreds of observed projects.

In addition to providing formulas for estimating the size, cost, and schedule of a software project, Putnam and Fitzsimmons provide tremendous guidance in determining the *accuracy* of the estimates. They quote Aristotle: "It is the mark of an instructed mind to rest satisfied with the degree of precision which the nature of the subject admits and not to seek exactness when only an approximation of the truth is possible." All EDP project managers know that there is a degree of uncertainty in their estimates; this paper seems to be the first widely circulated one to provide practical guidance in determining that uncertainty.

The final part of the Putnam and Fitzsimmons paper addresses another crucial management issue: the trade-off between time and people, and the strategies for bringing people into a project at an optimum time. All veteran project managers know that doubling the number of programmers on a project will *not* cause the schedule to be cut in half. But what is the proper manpower loading for a typical project? What is the effect of adding more people — and *when* should they be added? These are all questions that are nicely addressed by Putnam and Fitzsimmons. Their techniques should become standard tools of the trade for professional project managers.

Additional References on Project Management

The articles selected for this volume supplement those previously reprinted in *Classics in Software Engineering.* For more on project management, see the following:

1. J.D. Aron, "The 'Super-Programmer Project,'" *Software Engineering, Concepts and Techniques,* eds. J.M. Buxton, P. Naur, and B. Randell (New York: Van Nostrand Reinhold, 1976), pp. 188-90. Reprinted in *Classics in Software Engineering,* ed. E.N. Yourdon (New York: YOURDON Press, 1979), pp. 37-39.

2. F.T. Baker, "Chief Programmer Team Management of Production Programming," *IBM Systems Journal,* Vol. 11, No. 1 (January 1972), pp. 56-73. Reprinted in *Classics in Software Engineering,* pp. 65-82.

3. F.T. Baker and H.D. Mills, "Chief Programmer Teams," *Datamation,* Vol. 19, No. 12 (December 1973), pp. 58-61. Reprinted in *Classics in Software Engineering,* pp. 195-204.

4. B.W. Boehm, "Software Engineering," *IEEE Transactions on Computers,* Vol. C-25, No. 12 (December 1976), 1226-41. Reprinted in *Classics in Software Engineering,* pp. 325-61.

Software and Its Impact: A Quantitative Assessment

"You software guys are too much like the weavers in the story about the Emperor and his new clothes. When I go out to check on a software development the answers I get sound like, 'We're fantastically busy weaving this magic cloth. Just wait a while and it'll look terrific.' But there's nothing I can see or touch, no numbers I can relate to, no way to pick up signals that things aren't really all that great. And there are too many people I know who have come out at the end wearing a bunch of expensive rags or nothing at all."

— An Air Force decisionmaker

Recently, the Air Force Systems Command* completed a study, "Information Processing/Data Automation Implications of Air Force Command and Control Requirements in the 1980s," or CCIP-85 for short. The study projected future Air Force command and control information processing requirements and likely future information processing capabilities into the 1980s, and developed an Air Force R&D plan to correct the mismatches found between likely capabilities and needs.

Although many of the CCIP-85 conclusions are specific to the Air Force, there are a number of points which hold at least as well elsewhere. This article summarizes those transferable facts and conclusions.

SOURCE: B.W. Boehm, *Datamation*, 1973.

*The views in this article do not necessarily reflect those of the United States Air Force.

Basically, the study showed that for almost all applications, software (as opposed to computer hardware, displays, architecture, etc.) was "the tall pole in the tent" — the major source of difficult future problems and operational performance penalties. However, we found it difficult to convince people outside the software business of this. This was primarily because of the scarcity of solid quantitative data to demonstrate the impact of software on operational performance or to provide perspective on R&D priorities.

The study did find and develop some data which helped illuminate the problems and convince people that the problems were significant. Surprisingly, though, we found that these data are almost unknown even to software practitioners. (You can test this assertion via the Software Quiz, p. 269.) The main purpose of this article is to make these scanty but important data and their implications better known, and to convince people to collect more of it.

Before reading further, though, please try the Software Quiz. It's intended to help you better appreciate the software issues which the article goes on to discuss.

Software is big business

One convincing impact of software is directly on the pocketbook. For the Air Force, the estimated dollars for FY 1972 are in Fig. 1; an annual expenditure on software of between $1 billion and $1.5 billion, about three times the annual expenditure on computer hardware and about 4 to 5% of the total Air Force budget. Similar figures hold elsewhere. The recent World Wide Military Command and Control System (WWMCCS) computer procurement was estimated to involve expenditures of $50 to $100 million for hardware and $722 million for software [1]. A recent estimate for NASA was an annual expenditure of $100 million for hardware, and $200 million for software — about 6% of the annual NASA budget.

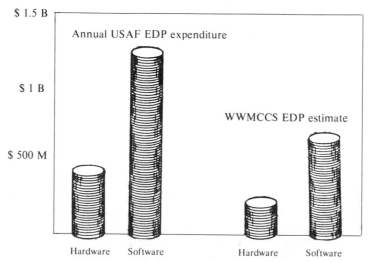

Figure 1. USAF software is big business.

For some individual projects, here are some overall software costs:

IBM OS/360	$ 200,000,000 [2]
SAGE	250,000,000 [3]
Manned Space Program, 1960-70	1,000,000,000 [3]

A Software Quiz

Very little in the way of quantitative data has been collected about software. But there is some which deserves to be better known than it is. Because, otherwise, we have nothing but our intuition to guide us in making critical decisions about software, and often our intuition can be quite fallible. The four questions below give you a chance to test how infallible your software intuition is. **Answers to the quiz appear on the following two pages.**

1A. Where Does the Software Effort Go?

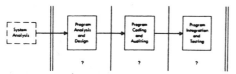

If you're involved in planning, staffing, scheduling or integrating a large software effort, you should have a good idea of how much of the effort will be spent on analysis and design (after the functional specification for the system has been completed), on coding and auditing (including desk checking and software module unit testing), and on checkout and test. See how well you do in estimating the effort on a percentage basis for the three phases. The results for such different large systems as SAGE, OS/360, and the Gemini space shots have been strikingly similar.

2A. How Do Hardware Constraints Affect Software Productivity?

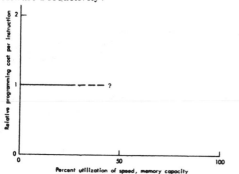

Another useful factor to know in planning software development is the extent to which hardware constraints affect software productivity. As you approach complete utilization of hardware speed and memory capacity, what happens to your software costs? Do they stay relatively constant or do they begin to bulge upward somewhat? The data here represent 34 software projects at North American Rockwell's Autonetics Division with some corroborative data points determined at Mitre.

3A. Where Are Software Errors Made?

	Batch (all errors)	Real-time (final validation phase only)
Computation and assingment	?	?
Sequencing and control	?	?
Input - output	?	?
Declarations	?	?
Punctuation	?	Not available
Correction to errors	Not available	?
Total	100 %	100 %

If you're setting test plan schedules and priorities, designing diagnostic aids for compilers and operating systems, or contemplating new language features (e.g., GOTO-free) to eliminate sources of software errors, it would be very useful to know how such errors are distributed over the various software functions. See how well you do in estimating the distribution of errors for typical batch programs and for the final validation of a critical real-time program.

4A. How Do Compilers Spend Their Time?

(Knuth study: 440 Lockheed programs; 250,000 statements)

Number of operands	%
1 (A = B)	?
2 (A = B ⊕ C)	?
3 (A = B ⊕ C ⊕ D)	?
>3	?

Recently, Donald Knuth and others at Stanford performed a study on the distribution of complexity of FORTRAN statements. Try to estimate what percentage of their sample of 250,000 FORTRAN statements were of the simple form A=B, how many had two operands on the right-hand side, etc. If you're a compiler designer, this should be very important, because it would tell you how to optimize your compiler — whether it should do simple things well or whether it should do complex things well. Here the results refer to aerospace application programs at Lockheed; however, a sample of Stanford student programs showed roughly similar results.

Answers to Software Quiz

1B. Where Does the Software Effort Go?

	Analysis and Design	Coding and Auditing	Checkout and Test
SAGE	39%	14%	47%
NTDS	30	20	50
GEMINI	36	17	47
SATURN V	32	24	44
OS/360	33	17	50
TRW Survey	46	20	34

How close did you come to that large 45−50% for checkout? Whatever you estimated, it was probably better than the planning done on one recent multimillion dollar, multiyear (nondefense) software project by a major software contractor which allowed two weeks for acceptance testing and six weeks for operational testing, preceded by a two-man-month test plan effort. Fortunately, this project was scrapped in midstream before the testing inadequacies could show up. But similar schedules have been established for other projects, generally leading to expensive slippages in phasing over to new systems and prematurely delivered, bug-ridden software.

Another major mismatch appears when you compare the relative amount of effort that goes into the three phases with the relative magnitude of R&D expenditures on techniques to improve effectiveness in each of the phases. Relatively little R&D support has been going toward improving software analysis, design, and validation capabilities.

The difference in the later TRW data probably reflects another insight: that more thorough analysis and design more than pays for itself in reduced testing costs.

(Refs.: Boehm, B.W., "Some Information Processing Implications of Air Force Space Missions: 1970-1980," *Astronautics and Aeronautics*, January 1971. Wolverton, R., *The Cost of Developing Large-Scale Software*, TRW Paper, March 1972.)

2B. How Do Hardware Constraints Affect Software Productivity?

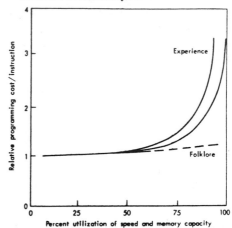

Hopefully, your estimate was closer to the "experience" curve than the "folklore" one. Yet, particularly in hardware procurements, people make decisions as if the folklore curve were true. Typically, after a software job is sized, hardware is procured with only about 15% extra capacity over that determined by the sizing, presenting the software developers with an 85% saturated machine just to begin with. How uneconomic this is will be explained by Fig. 7 in the text.

Those data also make an attractive case for virtual memory systems as ways to reduce software costs by eliminating memory constraints. However, the strength of this case is reduced to the extent that virtual memory system inefficiencies tighten speed constraints.

(Ref.: Williman, A.O., and C. O'Donnell, "Through the Central 'Multiprocessor' Avionics Enters the Computer Era," *Astronautics and Aeronautics*, July 1970.

3B. Where Are Software Errors Made?

	7 batch programs (all errors)		Benchmark space booster control (all errors)	On-board space booster control (final validation phase only)
	PL/I	2 COBOL 2 JOVIAL 3 FORTRAN		
Computation and assignment	9%	25%	28%	20%
Sequencing and control	20	17	27	51
Input-output	8	8	7	6
Declarations	32	35	38	16
Punctuation	31	15	n.a.	n.a.
Corrections to errors	n.a.	n.a.	n.a.	7
Total (%)	100%	100%	100%	100%
Errors (No.)	214	140	313	87

Several points seem fairly clear from the data. One is that GOTO-free programming is not a panacea for software errors, as it will eliminate only some fraction of sequence and control errors. However, as Column 4 shows, the sequence and control errors are the most important ones to eliminate, as they currently tend to persist until the later, more difficult stages of validation on critical real-time programs. Another point is that language features can make a difference, as seen by comparing error sources and totals in PL/I with the other languages (FORTRAN, COBOL, and JOVIAL), although in this case an additional factor of less programmer familiarity with PL/I also influences the results.

(Refs.: Rubey, R.J., et al., *Comparative Evaluation of PL/I*, United States Air Force Report, ESD-TR-68-150, April 1968. Rubey, R.J., *Study of Software Quantitative Aspects*, United States Air Force Report, CS-7150-R0840, October 1971.)

4B. How Do Compilers Spend Their Time?

NUMBER OF OPERANDS IN FORTRAN STATEMENTS
(Knuth study: 440 Lockheed Programs, 250,000 statements)

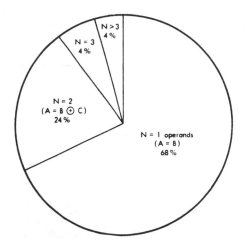

It's evident from the data that most FORTRAN statements used in practice are quite simple in form. For example, 68% of these 250,000 statements were of the simple form A=B. When Knuth saw this and similar distributions on the dimensionality of arrays (58% unindexed, 30.5% with one index), the length of DO loops (39% with just one statement), and the nesting of DO loops (53.5% of depth 1, 23% of depth 2), here was his reaction:

"The author once found . . . great significance in the fact that a certain complicated method was able to translate the statement
$$C(I*N+J):=((A+X)*Y) +2.768((L-M)*(-K))/Z$$
into only 19 machine instructions compared with the 21 instructions obtained by a previously published method. . . . The fact that arithmetic expressions usually have an average length of only two operands, in practice, would have been a great shock to the author at that time."

Thus, evidence indicates that batch compilers generally do very simple things and one should really be optimizing batch compilers to do simple things. This could be similarly the case with compilers and interpreters for on-line systems; however, nobody has collected the data for those.

(Ref.: Knuth, D.E., "An Empirical Study of FORTRAN Programs," *Software Practice and Experience*, Vol. 1, 1971, p. 105.)

Overall software costs in the U.S. are probably over $10 billion per year, over 1% of the gross national product.

If the software-hardware cost ratio appears lopsided now, consider what will happen in the years ahead, as hardware gets cheaper and software (people) costs go up and up. Figure 2 shows the estimate for software expenditures in the Air Force going to over 90% of total adp system costs by 1985: this trend is probably characteristic of other organizations, also.

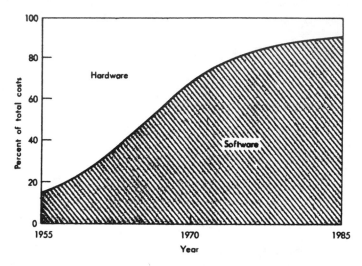

Figure 2. Hardware/software cost trends.

One would expect that current information-processing research and development projects would be strongly oriented toward where the future problems are. However, according to recent Congressional testimony by Dr. Ruth Davis of the National Bureau of Standards (NBS) on federally-funded computing R&D projects:

". . . 21% of the projects were concerned with hardware design, 40% were concerned with the needs of special interest communities such as natural sciences, engineering, social and behavioral sciences, humanities, and real-time systems, 14% were in the long-range payoff areas of metatheory, while only 9% were oriented to the highly agonizing software problems identified by most customers as their major concern."*

One result of the CCIP-85 study has been to begin to reorient Air Force information processing R&D much more toward software. Similar R&D trends are evident at DOD's Advanced Research Projects Agency (ARPA), National Science Foundation, and the National Bureau of Standards. But much remains to be done.

---

*"Government Bureau Takes on Role of Public Protector Against Computer Misuse," *ACM Communications,* November 1972, p. 1018.

Indirect costs even bigger

Big as the direct costs of software are, the indirect costs are even bigger, because software generally is on the critical path in overall system development. That is, any slippages in the software schedule translate directly into slippages in the overall delivery schedule of the system.

Let's see what this meant in a recent software development for a large defense system. It was planned to have an operational lifetime of seven years and a total cost of about $1.4 billion — or about $200 million a year worth of capability. However, a six-month software delay caused a six-month delay in making the system available to the user, who thus lost about $100 million worth of needed capability — about 50 times the direct cost of $2 million for the additional software effort. Moreover, in order to keep the software from causing further delays, several important functions were not provided in the initial delivery to the user.

Again, similar situations develop in domestic applications. IBM's OS/360 software was over a year late [2]. The U.S. air traffic control system currently operates much more expensively and less effectively because of slippages of years in software (and also hardware, in this case) development, which have escalated direct software costs to over $100 million [4]. Often, organizations compensate for software development slippages by switching to a new system before the software is adequately tested, leading to such social costs as undelivered welfare checks to families with dependent children, bad credit reports, and even people losing their lives because of errors in medical software.

Getting software off the critical path

Once software starts slipping along the critical path, there are several more or less unattractive options. One option is to add more people in hopes that a human wave of programmers will quickly subdue the problem. However, Brooks' excellent article [5] effectively shows that software is virtually incompressible with respect to elapsed time, and that such measures more often make things worse rather than better. Some other unhappy options are to skimp on testing, integration, or documentation. These usually cost much more in the long run. Another is just to scrap the new system and make do with the old one. Generally, the most attractive option is to reduce the system to an austere but expandable initial capability.

For the future, however, several opportunities exist for reducing software delays and getting software off the critical path. These fall into three main categories:

1. Increasing each individual's software productivity.

2. Improving project organization and management.

3. Initiating software development earlier in the system development cycle.

Increasing software productivity: definitions

Figure 3 shows a simplistic view of likely future trends in software productivity. It is probably realistic in maintaining at least a factor-of-10 spread between the 10th and 90th percentiles of software productivity, but it begs a few important questions.

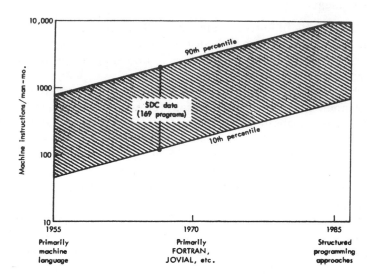

Figure 3. Technology forecast: software productivity.

One is, "What is software?" Even the courts and the Internal Revenue Service have not been able to define its metes and bounds precisely. The figures above include computer program documentation, but exclude operating procedures and broad system analysis. Clearly, a different definition would affect software productivity figures significantly.

Another important question is, "What constitutes software production?" As early as the mid-1950s there were general-purpose trajectory analysis systems with which an analyst could put together a modular, 10,000-word applications program in about 10 minutes. Was this "software production"? With time, more and more such general-purpose packages as ICES (MIT's Integrated Civil Engineering System), Programming-by-Questionnaire, RPG, MARK IV, and SCERT have made the creation of significant software capabilities so easy that they tend to be eliminated from the category of "software productivity," which continues to refer to those portions of the software directly resulting from handwritten strings of assembly or FORTRAN-level language statements. Figure 4 is an attempt to characterize this trend in terms of a "50% automation date": the year in which most of the incoming problems in an area could be "programmed" in less than an hour by a user knowledgeable in his field, with one day of specialized training.

Thus, if we want to speak objectively about software productivity, we are faced with the dilemma of:

1. Either redefining it in terms of source instructions rather than object instructions — thereby further debasing the unit of production (which isn't completely objective even using object instructions as a base) — or

2. Continuing to narrow the range of definition of "software productivity" to the more and more difficult programs which can't be put together more or less automatically.

The eventual result of ARPA's major "automatic programming" effort will be to narrow this latter range even further [6].

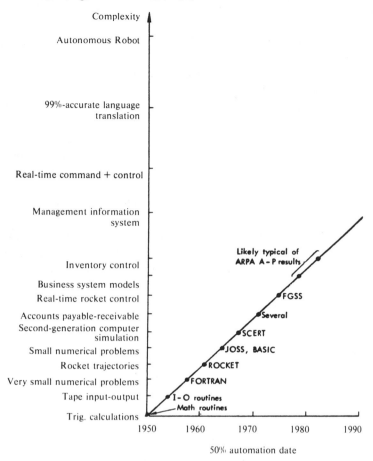

Figure 4. Growth of automatic programming.

Increasing software productivity: factors

However, the fact remains that software needs to be constructed, that various factors significantly influence the speed and effectiveness of producing it, and that we have at least some measure of control over these factors. Thus, the more we know about those factors, the more our decisions will lead to improved rather than degraded software productivity. What are the important factors?

One is computer system response time. Studies by Sackman and others [7] comparing batch versus on-line programming have shown median improvements of 20% in programming efficiency using on-line systems.

However, in these same studies, *variations between individuals* accounted for differences in productivity of factors up to 26:1. Clearly, selecting the right people provides more leverage than anything else in improving software productivity. But this isn't so easy. Reinstedt [8] and others have shown that none of the selection tests developed so far have an operationally-dependable correlation with programmer performance. Weinberg, in his excellent book [9], illustrates the complexity of the issue by citing two programmer attributes for each letter of the alphabet (from age and agility through zygosity and zodiacal sign), each of which might be a plausible determinant of programmer performance. Still, the potential payoffs are so large that further work in the areas of personnel selection, training, and evaluation should be closely followed. For example, the Berger Test of Programming Proficiency has proved fairly reliable in assessing the programming capability of experienced programmers.

Other factors such as *programming languages* have made significant differences in software productivity. Rubey's PL/I study showed differences of up to 2:1 in development time for the same program written in two different languages. In a related effort, Kosy obtained a 3.5:1 productivity improvement over one of the Rubey examples by using ECSS, a special-purpose language for simulating computer systems.

Weinberg has also shown [9, 10] that the choice of *software development criteria* exerts a significant influence on software productivity. In one set of experiments, programmers were given the same program specification, but were told either (Group P) to finish the job as promptly as possible or (Group E) to produce as efficient a program as possible. The results were that Group E finished the job with an average of over twice as many runs to completion, but with programs running an average of six times faster.

Another important factor is the software *learning curve*. The table below shows the estimated and actual programming effort involved in producing three successive FORTRAN compilers by the same group [11].

Compiler	Man-Months	
Effort No.	Estimated	Actual
1	36	72
2	24	36
3	12	14

Clearly, software estimation accuracy has a learning curve, also.

But other factors in the programming environment make at least as large a contribution on any given project. The most exhaustive quantitative analysis done so far on the factors influencing software development was an SDC study done for the Air Force Electronic Systems Division in 1965 [12], which collected data on nearly 100 factors over 169 software projects and performed extensive statistical analysis on the results. The best fit to the data involved 13 factors, including stability of program design, percent mathematical instructions, number of subprograms, concurrent hardware development, and number of man-trips — but even that estimate had a standard deviation (62 man-months) larger than the mean (40 man-months).

Increasing software productivity: prescriptions

Does all this complexity mean that the prospect of increasing software productivity is hopeless? Not at all. In fact, some of the data provide good clues toward avenues of improvement. For example, if you accurately answered question 1 on the Software Quiz, you can see that only 15% of a typical software effort goes into coding. Clearly, then, there is more potential payoff in improving the efficiency of your analysis and validation efforts than in speeding up your coding.

Significant opportunities exist for doing this. The main one comes when each of us as individual programmers becomes aware of where his time is really going, and begins to design, develop and use thoughtful test plans for the software he produces, beginning in the earliest analysis phases. Suppose that by doing so, we could save an average of one man-day per man-month of testing effort. This would save about 2.5% of our total expenditure on software. Gilchrist and Weber [13] estimate about 360,000 software practitioners in the U.S.; even at a somewhat conservative total cost quotation of $30,000 per man-year, this is about $10.8 billion annually spent on software, yielding a testing savings above of about $270 million per year.

Another opportunity lies in the area of programming languages. Except for a few experiments such as Floyd's "Verifying Compiler," programming languages have been designed for people to express programs with a minimum of redundancy, which tends to expedite the coding process, but makes the testing phase more difficult. Appropriate additional redundancy in a program language, requiring a programmer to specify such items as allowable limits on variables, inadmissible states and relations between variables [14], would allow a compiler or operating system to provide much more help in diagnosing programming errors and reducing the time-consuming validation phase. For example, of the 93 errors detected during execution in Rubey's PL/I study, 52 could have been caught during compilation with a validation-oriented programming language containing features such as those above.

Another avenue to reducing the validation effort lies in providing tools and techniques which get validation done more efficiently during the analysis phase. This is the approach taken in *structured programming*. This term has been used to describe a variety of on-line programming tool boxes, programming systems, and innovative structurings of the software production effort. An example of the first is the Flexible Guidance Software System, currently being developed for the Air Force Space and Missile Systems Organization. The second is exemplified by the Technische Hogeschool Eindhoven (THE) [15] and automated engineering design (AED) systems, while innovative structuring may be seen in experiments such as the IBM chief programmer team (CPT) effort [16]. Although they are somewhat different, each concept represents an attempt to bring to software production a "top-down" approach and to minimize logical errors and inconsistencies through structural simplification of the development process. In the case of the THE system, this is reinforced by requiring system coding free of discontinuous program control ("GO-TO free"). In the chief programmer approach, it is accomplished by choosing a single individual to do the majority of actual design and programming and tailoring a support staff around his function and talents.

As yet, none of the systems or concepts described has been rigorously tested. Initial indications are, however, that the structured approach can shorten the software development process significantly, at least for some classes of programs and programmers. In one case, the use of AED reduced the man-effort of a small system from an envisioned six man-months to three man-weeks. A major experiment using the CPT concept (on an 83,000-instruction system for the *New York Times*) cut expected project costs by 50% and reduced development time to 25% of the initial estimate.

The validation statistics on this project were particularly impressive. After only a week's worth of system integration, the software went through five weeks of acceptance testing by *Times* personnel. Only 21 errors were found, all of which were fixed in one day. Since then during over a year's worth of operational experience, only 25 additional errors have been found in the 83,000-instruction package [17].

At this point, it's still not clear to what extent this remarkable performance was a function of using remarkably skilled programming talent, and to what extent the performance gains could be matched by making a typical programming team into a Chief Programmer Team. Yet the potential gains were so large that further research, experimentation and training in structured programming concepts was one of the top priority recommendations of the CCIP-85 study.

Improving software management

Even though an individual's software productivity is important, the CCIP-85 study found that the problems of software productivity on medium or large projects are largely problems of management: of thorough organization, good contingency planning, thoughtful establishment of measurable project milestones, continuous monitoring on whether the milestones are properly passed, and prompt investigation and corrective action in case they are not. In the software management area, one of the major difficulties is the transfer of experience from one project to the next. For example, many of the lessons learned as far back as SAGE are often ignored in today's software developments, although they were published over 10 years ago in Hosier's excellent 1961 article on the value of milestones, test plans, precise interface specifications, integrated measurement capabilities, formatted debugging aids, early prototypes, concurrent system development and performance analysis, etc. [18].

Beyond this, it is difficult to say anything concise about software management that doesn't sound like motherhood. ●Therefore, this article will simply cite some good references in which the subject is explored in some detail [19, 20, 21].

Getting an earlier start: the software-first machine

Even if software productivity never gets tremendously efficient, many of the most serious software agonies would be alleviated if we could get software off the critical path within an overall system development. In looking at the current typical history of a large software project (Fig. 5) you can see that the year (or often more) spent on hardware procurement pushes software farther out onto the critical path, since often the software effort has to wait at least until the hardware source selection is completed.

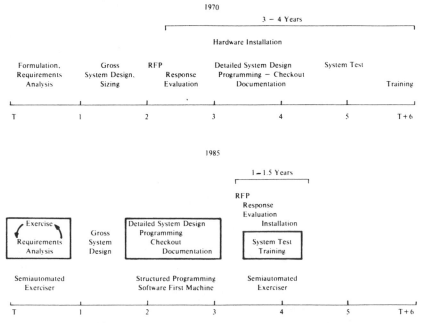

Figure 5. The software development cycle.

One of the concepts developed in the CCIP-85 study for getting software more off the critical path was that of a "software-first machine." This is a highly generalized computer, capable of simulating the behavior of a wide range of hardware configurations. Figure 6 provides a rough plan of such a software-first machine. It would have the capability of configuring and exercising through its microprogrammed control, a range of computers, and could also simultaneously provide some additional hardware aids to developing and testing software.

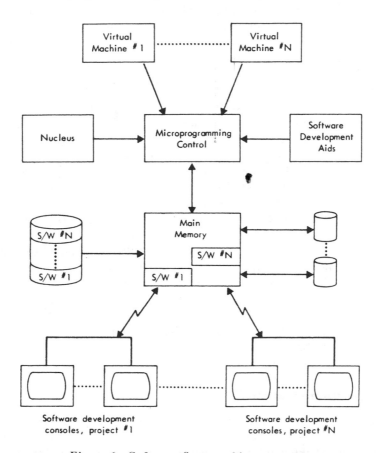

Figure 6. Software-first machine concept.

Suppose a large organization such as the Air Force owned such a machine. The following events could then take place: a contractor who is trying to develop software for an airborne computer could start with a need for a machine which is basically the IBM 4PI, but with a faster memory and different interrupt structure. This software contractor could develop, exercise, store, and recall his software based on the microprogrammed model of the machine. When it turned out that this architecture was hampering the software developers, they could do some hardware/software tradeoffs rather easily by changing the microprogrammed machine representation; and when they were finished or essentially finished with the software development, they would have detailed design specifications for the hardware that could be produced through competitive procurement in industry. Similarly, another contractor could be developing software for interface message processors for communications systems, based on variants of the

Honeywell DDP 516; another could be improving a real-time data processing capability based on an upgrade of a CDC 3800 computer on another virtual machine.

The software-first machine could be of considerable value in shortening the time from conception to implementation of an integrated hardware/software system. In the usual procurement process (Fig. 5), the hardware is chosen first, and software development must await delivery of the hardware. With the software-first machine, software development can avoid this wait, as hardware procurement can be done during the system test phase: the necessary hardware fabrication will start from a detailed design and, with future fabrication technology, should not introduce delays. This saving translates also into increased system operating life, as the hardware installed in the field is based on more up-to-date technology.

However, the software-first machine concept has some potential drawbacks. For example, it might produce a "centrifugal tendency" in hardware development. Allowing designers to tailor hardware to software might result in the proliferation of a variety of similar although critically different computers, each used for a special purpose.

A final question concerning the software-first machine remains moot: Can it be built, at any rate, at a "reasonable" cost? Architectures such as the CDC STAR, ILLIAC IV, and Goodyear STARAN IV would be virtually impossible to accommodate in a single machine. Thus, it is more likely that various subsets of the software-first machine characteristics will be developed for various ranges of applications.

One such variant is under way already. One Air Force organization, wishing to upgrade without a simultaneous hardware and software discontinuity, acquired some Meta 4 microprogrammed machines which will originally be installed to emulate the existing second-generation hardware. Once the new hardware is in operation, they will proceed to upgrade the system software using a different microprogrammed base. In this way they can upgrade the system with a considerably reduced risk of system downtime.

Another existing approach is that of the microprogrammed Burroughs B1700, which provides a number of the above characteristics plus capabilities to support "direct" execution of higher-level-language programs.

Other hardware-software tradeoffs

In addition, there are numerous other ways in which cheaper hardware can be traded off to save on more expensive software development costs. A most significant one stems from the striking difference between "folklore" and "experience" in the hardware-software curves shown in Fig. 2B of the Software Quiz. This tradeoff opportunity involves buying enough hardware capacity to keep away from the steep rise in software costs occurring at about the 85% saturation point of cpu and memory capacity.

Thus, suppose that one has sized a data-processing task and determined that a computer of one-unit capacity (with respect to central processing unit speed and size) is required. Figure 7 shows how the total data-processing system cost varies with the amount of excess cpu capacity procured for various estimates of the ratio of ideal software-to-hardware costs for the system. ("Ideal software" costs are those that would be incurred without any consideration of straining hardware capacity.) The calculations are based on the previous curve of programming costs and two models of hardware cost: the linear model assumes that cost increases linearly with increases in cpu capacity; the "Grosch's Law" model assumes that cost increases as the square root of cpu capacity. Sharpe's data [22] indicates that most applications fall somewhere between these models.

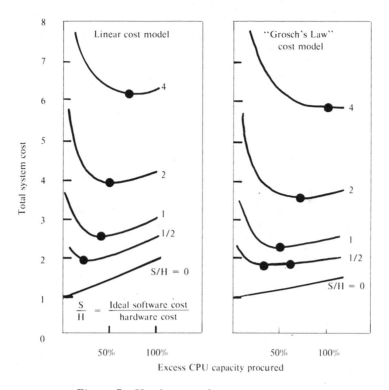

Figure 7. Hardware-software systems costs.

It should be remembered that the curves are based on imprecise observations; they clearly cannot be used in "cookbook" fashion by system designers. But even their general trends make the following points quite evident:

1. Overall system cost is generally minimized by procuring computer hardware with at least 50% to 100% more capacity than is absolutely necessary.

2. The more the ratio of software-to-hardware cost increases (as it will markedly during the seventies), the more excess computing capacity one should procure to minimize the total cost.

3. It is far more risky to err by procuring a computer that is too small than one that is too large. This is especially important, since one's initial sizing of the data-processing job often tends to underestimate its magnitude.

Of course, buying extra hardware does not eliminate the need for good software engineering thereafter. Careful configuration control must be maintained to realize properly the benefits of having extra hardware capability, as there are always strong Parkinsonian tendencies to absorb excess capacity with marginally useful tasks.

Software responsiveness

Another difficulty with software is its frequent unresponsiveness to the actual needs of the organization it was developed for. For example, the hospital information system field has several current examples of "wallflower" systems which were developed without adequately consulting and analyzing the information requirements of doctors, nurses, and hospital administrators. After trying to live with these systems for a while, several hospital administrators have reluctantly but firmly phased them out with such comments as, "We know that computers are supposed to be the way to go for the future, but this system just doesn't provide us any help," or, "Usage of the system began at a very low level — and dropped off from there."

The main difficulties stem from a lack of easily transferable procedures to aid in the software requirements analysis process. This process bears an all-too-striking resemblance to the class of folk tales in which a genie comes up to a man and tells him he has three wishes and can ask for anything in the world. Typically, he spends his first two wishes asking for something like a golden castle and a princess, and then when he discovers the operations, maintenance, and compatibility implications of his new acquisitions, he is happy to spend the third wish getting back to where he started.

Similarly, the computer is a sort of genie which says, "I'll give you any processed information you want. All you need to do is ask — by writing the software to process it." Often, though, we go the man in the folk tale one better by canvassing a number of users (or nonusers) and putting their combined wish lists into a software requirements analysis. But our technology base for assessing the operations, maintenance, and compatibility implications of the resulting software system is just as inadequate. Thus, large airline reservations software developments (Univac/United, Burroughs/TWA) have reached the point that the customer preferred to wish them out of existence rather than continue them — but only after the investment of tens of millions of dollars. In other cases, where no alternative was available, software rewrites of up to 67% (and in one very large system, 95%) have taken place — *after* the "final" software package had been delivered — in order to meet the user's operational needs.

Considering the major needs for better requirements analysis techniques, the relative lack of available techniques, and the added fact (from Fig. 1B of the Software Quiz) that about 35% of the total software effort goes into analysis and design, it is not surprising that the top-priority R&D recommendation made by the CCIP-85 study was for better techniques for performing and validating information system requirements analyses, and for generating and verifying the resulting information system designs.

The recent *Datamation* articles on automated system design [23, 24] indicated some promising initial developments in this area such as Teichroew's ISDOS project, FOREM, and IBM'S TAG (Time-Automated Grid) system. Other significant aids are being developed in the area of special languages and packages such as SCERT, CASE, CSS, SAM, and ECSS to accelerate the process of design verification by simulating information-processing systems. Also, ARPA's major research effort in automatic programming is focused strongly on automating the analysis and design processes [6].

Software reliability and certification

Another major area in which the CCIP-85 study identified a serious mismatch between future needs and likely software capabilities was in the area of software certification: of providing guarantees that the software will do what it is supposed to do. (Other significant problem or opportunity areas identified by CCIP-85 included, in order, data security, airborne computing power, multisource data fusion, data communications, source data automation, image processing, performance analysis, parallel processing, and software transferability.)

This is a significant concern right now, but it becomes even more pressing when one extrapolates current trends toward more complex software tasks and toward more and more automated aids to decision making. Just consider the trends implicit in the results of the recent AFIPS/Time survey [25] which indicated that currently *30% of the labor force must deal with computers in their daily work, but only 15% of the labor force is required to have any understanding of computers.* Extrapolating this trend into the 1980s, as is done in Fig. 8, indicates that perhaps 40% of the labor force will be trusting implicitly in the results produced by computer software.

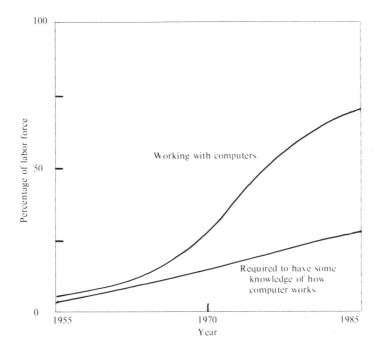

Figure 8. Growth of trust in computers and software.

Software reliability: problem symptoms

Will software be deserving of such trust? Not on its past record. For example, some of the most thoroughly tested software in the world is that of the Apollo manned spaceflight efforts. Yet on Apollo 8, an unforeseen sequence of astronaut actions destroyed the contents of a word in the computer's erasable memory — fortunately, not a critical error in this case. And on Apollo 11, the data flow from the rendezvous radar was not diverted during the critical lunar landing sequence, causing a computer overload that required astronaut Armstrong to divert his attention from the process of landing the spacecraft — fortunately again, without serious consequences. And during the 10-day flight of Apollo 14, there were 18 discrepancies found in the software — again fortunately, without serious consequences.

Other space missions haven't been so fortunate. Recently a software error aboard a French meteorological satellite caused it to "emergency destruct" 72 out of 141 high-altitude weather balloons, instead of interrogating them. An early U.S. Mariner interplanetary mission was lost due to a software error. And the Soviet Union has had missions fail because of software errors.

Down on earth, software reliability isn't any better. Each new release of OS/360 contains roughly 1,000 new software errors. On one large real-time system containing about 2,700,000 instructions and undergoing continuous modifications, an average of one software error per day is discovered. Errors in medical software have caused people to lose their lives. And software errors cause a constant stream of social dislocations due to false arrests, incorrect bank balances or credit records, lost travel reservations, or long-delayed payments to needy families or small businesses. Also, lack of certification capabilities makes it virtually impossible to provide strong guarantees on the security or privacy of sensitive or personal information.

Software reliability: technical problems

As the examples above should indicate, software certification is not easy. Ideally, it means checking all possible logical paths through a program; there may be a great many of these. For example, Fig. 9 shows a rather simple program flowchart. Before looking at the accompanying text, try to estimate how many different possible paths through the flowchart exist.

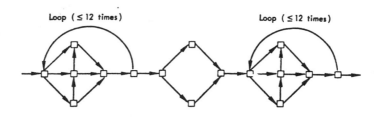

Figure 9.

Even through this simple flowchart, the number of different paths is about ten to the twentieth. If one had a computer that could check out one path per nanosecond (10^{-9} sec), and had started to check out the program at the beginning of the Christian era (1 A.D.), the job would be about half done at the present time.

So how does one certify a complex computer program that has incredibly more possible paths than this simple example? Fortunately, almost all of the probability mass in most programs goes into a relatively small number of paths that can be checked out.

But the unchecked paths still have some probability of occurring. And, furthermore, each time the software is modified, some portion of the testing must be repeated.

Figure 10 shows that, even for small software modifications, one should not expect error-free performance thereafter. The data indicate that small modifications have a better chance of working successfully than do large ones. However, even after a small modification the chance of a successful first run is, at best, about 50%. In fact, there seems to be a sort of complacency factor operating that makes a successful first run less probable on modifications involving a single statement than on those involving approximately five statements — at least for this sample.

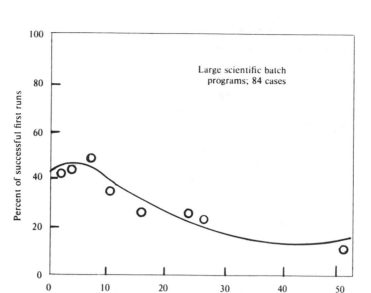

Large scientific batch
programs; 84 cases

Figure 10. Reliability of software modifications.

At this point, it's not clear how representative this sample is of other situations. One roughly comparable data point is in Fig. 3B of the Software Quiz, in which only 7% of the errors detected were those made in trying to correct previous errors. The difference in error rates is best explained by both the criticality of the application and the fact that the modifications were being made in a software validation rather than a software maintenance environment.

In another analysis of software error data performed for CCIP-85 by McGonagle [26], 19% of the errors resulted from "unexpected side effects to changes." Other sources of errors detected over three years of the development cycle of a 24,000-instruction command and control program are shown in Table 1. These data are of particular interest because they provide insights into the *causes* of software errors as well as their variation with type of program.

Table 1
Distribution of Software Error Causes

	Hardware Diagnostics (%)	Executive (%)	User Programs (%)	Total (%)
Unexpected side effects to changes	5	25	10	19
Logical flaws in the design				
Original design	5	10	2	8
Changes	5	15	8	12
Inconsistencies between design and implementation	5	30	1ᴏ	22
Clerical errors	40	20	50	-
Inconsistencies in hardware	40	—	20	11
	100	100	100	100
Total errors detected, 3-year sample	36	108	18	162
Number of instructions	4K	10K	10K	24K

Certification technology

Against the formidable software certification requirements indicated above, the achievements of current technology leave a great deal to be desired. One organization paid $750,000 to test an 8,000-instruction program, and even then couldn't be guaranteed that the software was perfect, because testing can only determine the *presence* of errors, not their *absence*. The largest program that has been mathematically proved correct was a 433-statement ALGOL program to perform error-bounded arithmetic; the proof required 46 pages of mathematical reasoning.

However, there are several encouraging trends. One is the impressive reduction of errors achieved in the structured programming activities discussed earlier in this article. Another is the potential contribution of appropriately redundant programming languages, also discussed earlier. A third trend is the likely development of significant automated aids to the program-proving process, currently an extremely tedious manual process. Another is the evolutionary development and dissemination of better software test procedures and techniques and the trend toward capitalizing on economies of scale in validating similar software items, as in the DOD COBOL Compiler Validation System. But even with these trends, it will take a great deal of time, effort, and research support to achieve commonly usable solutions to such issues as the time and cost of analytic proof procedures, the level of expertise required to use them, the difficulty of providing a valid program specification to serve as a certification standard, and the extent to which one can get software efficiency and validability in the same package.

Where's the software engineering data base?

One of the major problems the CCIP-85 study found was the dearth of hard data available on software efforts which would allow us to analyze the nature of software problems, to convince people unfamiliar with software that the problems were significant, or to get clues on how best to improve the situation. Not having such a data base forces us to rely on intuition when making crucial decisions on software, and I expect, for many readers, your success on the Software Quiz was sufficiently poor to convince you that software phenomena often tend to be counterintuitive. Given the magnitude of the risks of basing major software decisions on fallible intuition, and the opportunities for ensuring more responsive software by providing designers with usage data, it is surprising how little effort has gone into endeavors to collect and analyze such data. Only after a decade of R&D on heuristic compilers, optimizing compilers, self-compiling compilers and the like, has there been an R&D effort to develop a *usage-measuring* compiler. Similar usage-measuring tools could be developed for keeping track of error rates and other software phenomena.

One of the reasons progress has been slow is that it's just plain difficult to collect good software data — as we found on three contract efforts to do so for the CCIP-85 study. These difficulties included:

1. Deciding which of the thousands of possibilities to measure.

2. Establishing standard definitions for "error," "test phase," etc.

3. Establishing what had been the development performance criteria.

4. Assessing subjective inputs such as "degree of difficulty," "programmer expertise," etc.

5. Assessing the accuracy of *post facto* data.

6. Reconciling sets of data collected in differently defined categories.

Clearly, more work on these factors is necessary to insure that future software data collection efforts produce at least roughly comparable results. However, because the data collection problem is difficult doesn't mean we should avoid it. Until we establish a firm data base, the phrase "software engineering" will be largely a contradiction in terms. And the software components of what is now called "computer science" will remain far from Lord Kelvin's standard:

> "When you can measure what you are speaking about, and express it in numbers, you know something about it; but when you cannot measure it, when you cannot express it in numbers, your knowledge is of a meager and unsatisfactory kind: it may be the beginning of knowledge, but you have scarcely, in your thoughts, advanced to the stage of *science*."

But, in closing, I'd like to suggest that people should collect data on their software efforts because it's really in their direct best interest. Currently, the general unavailability of such software data means that whoever first provides system designers with quantitative software characteristics will find that the resulting system design tends to be oriented around his characteristics.

For example, part of the initial design sizing of the ARPA Network was based on two statistical samples of user response, on Rand's JOSS system and on MIT'S Project MAC. This was not because these were thought to be particularly representative of future network users; rather, they were simply the only relevant data the ARPA working group could find.

Another example involves the small CCIP-85 study contracts to gather quantitative software data. Since their completion, several local software designers and managers have expressed a marked interest in the data. Simply having a set of well-defined distributions of program and data module sizes is useful for designers of compilers and operating systems, and chronological distributions of software errors are useful for software management perspective. Knuth's FORTRAN data, excerpted in Fig. 4B of the Software Quiz, have also attracted considerable designer interest.

Thus, if you're among the first to measure and disseminate your own software usage characteristics, you're more likely to get next-generation software that's more responsive to your needs. Also, in the process, there's a good chance that you'll pick up some additional clues which begin to help you produce software better and faster right away.

Acknowledgments. Hundreds of people provided useful inputs to CCIP-85 and this extension of it; I regret my inability to properly individualize and acknowledge their valuable contributions. Among those providing exceptionally valuable stimulation and information were Generals L. Paschall, K. Chapman, and R. Lukeman; Colonels G. Fernandez and R. Hansen; Lieutenant Colonel A. Haile, and Captain B. Engelbach of the United States Air Force; R. Rubey of Logicon; R. Wolverton and W. Hetrick of TRW; J. Aron of IBM; A. Williams of NAR/Autonetics; D. McGonagle of Anderson, Inc.; R. Hatter of Lulejian Associates; W. Ware of Rand; and B. Sine. Most valuable of all have been the never-ending discussions with John Farquhar and particularly Don Kosy of Rand.

References: Boehm

1. *Datamation,* March 1, 1971, p. 41.

2. T. Alexander, "Computers Can't Solve Everything," *Fortune,* May 1969.

3. B.W. Boehm, "System Design," in *Planning Community Information Utilities,* eds. H. Sackman and B.W. Boehm, AFIPS Press, 1972.

4. P. Hirsch, "What's Wrong With the Air Traffic Control System?" *Datamation,* August 1972, pp. 48-53.

5. F. Brooks, "Why Is the Software Late?" *Data Management,* August 1971.

6. Robert M. Balzer, *Automatic Programming,* Institute Technical Memorandum, University of Southern California, Information Sciences Institute, September 1972.

7. H. Sackman, *Man-Computer Problem Solving,* Auerbach Publishers, Inc., 1970.

8. R.N. Reinstedt, "Results of a Programmer Performance Prediction Study," *IEEE Trans. Engineering Management,* December 1967, pp. 183-87.

9. G. Weinberg, *The Psychology of Computer Programming,* Van Nostrand Reinhold, 1971.

10. G.M. Weinberg, "The Psychology of Improved Programming Performance," *Datamation,* November 1972.

11. R.M. McClure, "Projection vs. Performance in Software Production," in *Software Engineering,* eds. P. Naur and B. Randell, NATO Science Committee, January 1969.

12. E.A. Nelson, *Management Handbook for the Estimation of Computer Programming Costs,* SDC, TM-3224, Oct. 31, 1966.

13. B. Gilchrist and K.E. Weber, "Employment of Trained Computer Personnel — A Quantitative Survey," *Proceedings, 1972 SJCC,* pp. 641-48.

14. D.W. Kosy, *Approaches to Improved Program Validation Through Programming Language Design,* The Rand Corporation, P-4865, July 1972.

15. E.W. Dijkstra, "The Structure of the 'THE'-Multiprogramming System," *ACM Communications,* May 1968. [Ed. note: Reprinted in this volume, paper 4.]

16. F.T. Baker, "Chief Programmer Team," *IBM Systems Journal,* Vol. 11, No. 1, 1972, pp. 56-73.

17. F.T. Baker, "System Quality Through Structured Programming," *Proceedings, 1972 FJCC,* pp. 339-44.

18. W.A. Hosier, "Pitfalls and Safeguards in Real-Time Digital Systems with Emphasis on Programming," *IEEE Transactions on Engineering Management,* Vol. EM-8, June 1961, pp. 99-115.

19. P. Naur and B. Randell, eds., *Software Engineering,* NATO Science Committee, January 1969.

20. J.N. Buxton and B. Randell, eds., *Software Engineering Techniques,* NATO Science Committee, April 1970.

21. G. Weinwurm, ed., *On the Management of Computer Programming,* Auerbach, 1970.

22. W.F. Sharpe, *The Economics of Computers,* Columbia University Press, 1969.

23. D. Teichroew and H. Sayari, "Automation of System Building," *Datamation,* August 15, 1971, pp. 25-30.

24. R.V. Head, "Automated System Analysis," *Datamation,* August 15, 1971, pp. 23-24.

25. *A National Survey of the Public's Attitudes Toward Computers,* AFIPS and Time, Inc., November 1971.

26. J.D. McGonagle, *A Study of a Software Development Project,* James P. Anderson and Co., September 21, 1971.

27. D.I. Good and R.L. London, "Computer Interval Arithmetic: Definition and Proof of Correct Implementation," *ACM Journal,* October 1970, pp. 603-12.

A Model of Large Program Development

As a need for a discipline of software engineering has been recognized, the design, implementation, and maintenance of computer software have come into the forefront. The formulation of concepts of programming methodology, exemplified by Dijkstra's structured programming [1], strikes at the root of the problem. The realization is that a program, much as a mathematical theorem, should and can be provable. Recognition that a program can be proved correct as it is developed and maintained [2], and before its results are used, may ultimately change the nature of the programming task and the face of the programming world. Clearly these developments are of fundamental importance. They appear to point to long-term solutions to problems that will be encountered in creating the great amount of program text that the world appears to require. But even though progress in mastering the science of program creation, maintenance, and expansion has also been made, there is still a long way to go.

The system approach

Such progress as is currently being made stems primarily from the personal involvement of researchers and developers in the programming process at a detailed level. Often they tackle a single problem area: algorithm development, language, structure, correctness proving, code generation, documentation, or testing. Others view the process as a whole, yet they are primarily concerned with the individual steps that, together, take one from concept to computation. Still this type of study is essential if real insight is to be gained and progress made.

SOURCE: L.A. Belady & M.M. Lehman, *IBM Systems Journal,* 1976.

The scientific method has made progress in revealing the nature of the physical world by pursuing courses other than studying individual phenomena in exquisite detail. Similarly, a system, a process, or a phenomenon may be viewed from the outside, by acts of observing; clarifying; and by measuring and modeling identifiable attributes, patterns, and trends. From such activities one obtains increasing knowledge and understanding, based on the behavior of both the system and its subsystems, the process and its subprocesses.

Starting with the initial release of OS/360 as a base, we have studied the interaction between management and the evolution of OS/360 by using certain independent variables of the improvement and enhancement (i.e., maintenance) process. We cannot say at this time that we have used all the key independent variables. There is undoubtedly much more to be learned about the variables and the data that characterize the programming process. Our method of study has been that of regression − outside in − which we have termed "structured analysis." Starting with the available data, we have attempted to deduce the nature of consecutive releases of OS/360. We give examples of the data that support this systematic study of the programming process. Again, however, we wish to emphasize that this study is but the beginning of a new approach to analyzing man-made systems.

The programming process

The authors have studied the programming process [3] as it pertains to the development of OS/360, and now give a preliminary analysis of some project statistics of this programming system, which had already survived a number of versions or releases when the study began. The data for each release included measures of the size of the system; the number of modules added, deleted or changed; the release date; information on manpower and machine time used and costs involved in each release. In general there were large, apparently stochastic, variations in the individual data items from release to release.

All in all, the data indicated a general upward trend in the size, complexity, and cost of the system and the maintenance process, as indicated by components, modules, statements, instructions, and modules handled in Figure 1. The various parameters were averaged to expose trends. When the averaged data were plotted as shown in Figure 2, the previously erratic data had become strikingly smooth.

Some time later, additional data were plotted as shown in Figure 3 and confirmed suspicions of nonlinear − possibly exponential − growth and complexity. Extrapolation suggested further growth trends that were significantly at odds with the then current project plans. The data were also highly erratic with major, but apparently serially correlated, fluctuations shown in Figure 4 by the broken lines from release to release. Nevertheless, almost any form of averaging led to the display of very clear trends as shown by the dashed line in Figure 4. Thus it was natural to apply uni- and multivariate regression and autocorrelation techniques to fit appropriate regression and time-series models to represent the process for purposes of planning, forecasting, and improving it in part or as a whole. As the study progressed, evidence accumulated that one might consider a software maintenance and enhancement project as a self-regulating organism, subject to apparently random shocks, but − overall − obeying its own specific conservation laws and internal dynamics.

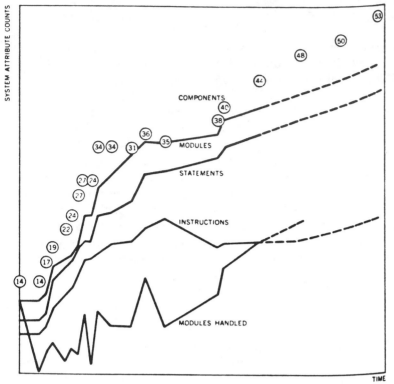

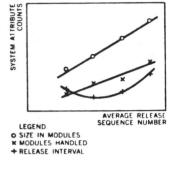

Figure 1. Growth trends of system attribute counts with time.

Figure 2. Average growth trends of system attributes.

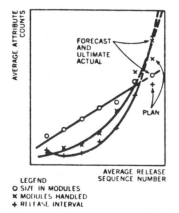

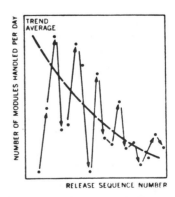

Figure 3. Average growth trends of system attributes compared with planned growth.

Figure 4. Serial and average growth trends of a particular attribute.

Thus these first observations encouraged the search for models that represented laws that governed the dynamic behavior of the metasystem of organization, people, and program material involved in the creation and maintenance process, in the evolution of programming systems.

Laws of program evolution

It is perhaps necessary to explain here why we allege continuous creation, maintenance, and enhancement of programming systems. It is the actual experience of all who have been involved in the utilization of computing equipment and the running of large multiple-function programs, that such systems demand continuous repair and improvement. Thus we may postulate the First Law of Program Evolution Dynamics [4].

I. *Law of continuing change.* A system that is used undergoes continuing change until it is judged more cost effective to freeze and recreate it.

Software does not face the physical decay problems that hardware faces. But the power and logical flexibility of computing systems, the extending technology of computer applications, the ever-evolving hardware, and the pressures for the exploitation of new business opportunities all make demands. Manufacturers, therefore, encourage the continuous adaptation of programs to keep in step with increasing skill, insight, ambition, and opportunity. In addition to such external pressures for change, there is the constant need to repair system faults, whether they are errors that stem from faulty implementation or defects that relate to weaknesses in design or behavior. Thus a programming system undergoes continuous maintenance and development, driven by mutually stimulating changes in system capability and environmental usage. In fact, the evolution pattern of a large program is similar to that of any other complex system in that it stems from the closed loop cyclic adaptation of environment to system changes and vice versa.

As a system is changed, its structure inevitably degenerates. The resulting system complexity and reduction of manageability are expressed by the Second Law of Program Evolution Dynamics.

II. *Law of increasing entropy.* The entropy of a system (its unstructuredness) increases with time, unless specific work is executed to maintain or reduce it.

This law too expresses vast experience, in part by data to be presented later in this paper. This, in turn, leads to the formulation of the Third Law of Program Evolution Dynamics.

III. *Law of statistically smooth growth.* Growth trend measures of global system attributes may appear to be stochastic locally in time and space, but, statistically, they are cyclically self-regulating, with well-defined long-range trends.

The system and the metasystem — the project organization that is developing it — constitute an organism that is constrained by conservation laws. These laws may be locally violated, but they direct, constrain, control, and thereby regulate and smooth the long-term growth and development patterns and rates. Observation, measurement, and interpretation of the latter can thus be used to plan, control, and forecast better the product of an existing process and to improve the process so as to obtain desired or desirable characteristics.

The "laws" that we are expounding upon have gradually evolved as we have pursued our study of the programming task. When we began our studies, observations led to the concept that we termed "programming systems growth dynamics" [5]. We have now renamed this subdiscipline "programming evolution dynamics."

The remainder of this paper describes some of the statistical and formal models of the programming process that we have been able to develop by pursuing the consequences of the laws of programming evolution dynamics. It is our conviction that the extension of these studies can lead to an increasing understanding of the nature and dynamics of the programming process. Hence, studies such as these may yield significant advances in the ability to engineer software, i.e., to plan and control program creation and maintenance.

The process observed — a statistical model

The basic assumptions of programming evolution dynamics spring from viewing the program being implemented, enhanced, and maintained and its metasystem — the organization that generated and undertook the development of OS/360 — as interacting systems. The evolutionary process and life cycle of a program are at least partially governed by the structural and functional attributes of both the program and the human organization. Their size, complexity, and numerous internal interactions suggest the use of statistical techniques for interpreting observed behavior.

Detailed studies of available data in conjunction with the almost universal experience of the programming community indicate that a large programming project has many of the properties of a multiple loop, self-stabilizing feedback system. The overall trend has been summarized in the previously discussed three laws that underlie the dynamics of evolution of large programs. The present section presents some of the accumulated numerical evidence derived from experience with OS/360 — one model of one system from one environment.

Available data

The project data presented here originate from OS/360, which is now some twelve years old. This system has been made available to an increasing number of users in a series of over twenty user-oriented releases. These releases have extended the capability of the operating system by correcting faults, improving performance, supporting new hardware, and by adding newly conceived functions.

These and other intermediate releases were assigned names or numbers as identifiers. Each release may, however, also be identified as a program that — with its documentation — forms an identifiable and stable text in an otherwise continuously changing environment. Assigning *Release Sequence Numbers* (*RSN*s) to versions receiving the same degree of exposure, yields a sequence of integers that forms a pseudo time measure in the sense of Cox and Lewis [6] that may be used to describe the time-dependent behavior of program evolution.

Of the releases considered, the first represents the culmination of the basic design and build (i.e., system integration) process. The iterative process that yields the specification, architecture, design, and the first implementation of a large program system differs significantly from subsequent maintenance and enhancement activity. In particular, there is at this stage no feedback of fault reporting or performance assessment by independent users. Hence data relating to that first release are not included in this analysis. The build process itself may, however, be studied by using data obtained periodically during the development activity.

Data from a second release were also unused because they were shown to represent a component development somewhat off the main stream. In the final analysis, the model and the plots to be presented are based on twenty-one sets of observations. This relatively small number of data points implies that extreme care must be exercised in interpreting the results of the statistical analysis. Subsequent data from the OS/360 augmented by data from other environments have generally confirmed our observations and conclusions.

Observables of system evolution

The release sequence number (RSN) is taken as the first of the system evolution parameters. The second is the age of the system D_R at release with $RSN = R$. Equivalently, D_R is the inter-release interval I_R; in other words, the interval in days between releases with $RSN = R-1$ and R, respectively. A third available parameter M_R measures the size of the system in modules. We present the results of our analysis in terms of modules, though other size measures — such as numbers of components or instructions in the system — could also have been used. The suitability of the module stems from the fact that in OS/360 the concept of module — though imprecisely defined — represents at one and the same time a functional and implementation entity and, for execution, a unit of system generation and storage allocation.

A fourth parameter MH_R records the number of system modules that have received attention, i.e., those that have been handled during the release interval and, more specifically, during the integration process. We have used this as an initial estimator of the amount of activity undertaken in each release. The measure is imprecise, but represents the best available information over the entire sequence. From MH_R and I_R, in turn, we determine an estimate of the handle rate HR_R for the activity that produced the release with $RSN = R$.

From the very first beginnings of this study of the programming process [5], it has been clear that the changing complexity of a system, as it is modified, plays a vital role in the aging process. Unfortunately there is no clear or unique understanding of what complexity is and how it can be defined and measured. The choice of complexity definition cannot, in fact, be disassociated from the use to which it is to be put. But complexity of the system, of the organization, and of each particular series of changes is fundamental to the maintenance and to the resultant aging process. Hence some measures of complexity must be established.

For the purposes of the present analysis, *complexity* C_R has been defined as the fraction of the released system modules that were handled during the course of the release with $RSN = R$. This definition is clearly inadequate. It does not separately measure the various independent complexity factors involved. It does not discriminate between system organization and the nature of the work undertaken. Nor does it measure the amount of activity involved. But at least it is a measure for which real data exist. Moreover the data give interpretable results. Hence $C_R = MH_R / M_R$ will suffice until better measures become available.

The present model

We have just identified five observable and measurable parameters of the programming process. Our hypothesis implies that these parameters do not vary independently, at least when viewed over a relatively long period of time. In fact, we have been able to determine, for example, four bivariate relationships among them. The complexity parameter, however, is derived from two of the others. Hence, on the basis of present data, we are entitled to fit only three independent functions. The fourth relationship, then, must be derived from the other three and tested for fit. As in all data fitting, the forms selected must also pass a test of conceptual reasonableness.

We stress that, in general, any statistical goodness of fit test is insufficient to establish any relationship as an element of the total model — as an expression of causal relationships — unless it can be convincingly interpreted in the light of one's insight into the process. Ultimately, it is only through the interplay and iteration of observation, modeling, and interpretation that real progress can be made in understanding and mastering the large-scale programming process.

Nature of the relationships

The statistically derived relationships to be presented here comprise a model of the programming process with respect to this system's life cycle. The relationships represent a simple, but recognizably incomplete, model of what is happening. In practice the statistical model has been used to improve the planning for this particular system. With the insight gained from the model's development, further statistical and analytic models have been and will continue to be developed that may explain the process and eventually lead to the insight that permits improvement of process planning, control, and cost-effectiveness.

In the first instance, we must identify the global nature of the process as expressed in the relationships to be, or that have been, developed. The previously stated Third Law suggests that smooth long-term trends can be seen in the measures even if short-term behavior tends to be erratic. This is supported by the fact that we have been able to construct statistically significant relationships consisting of three parts: the first expresses the long-term, deterministic trend; the second describes short-term cyclic effects; and the third part expresses any system-relative stochastic influences on the process.

The stochastic influences arise, in part, from a certain arbitrariness in the selection of the new function and, therefore, new code to be included in any given release. It is influenced to a significant degree by user and management pressure, the availability of new hardware devices, and by business considerations that are not directly related to the internal dynamics of the process. Equally, the release target date, and hence the age of the system at the release point, are strongly influenced by factors external to the programming process.

The cyclic trends that we have observed in the data, and that have long been accepted on a heuristic basis by managers and observers of programming practice, may well contain the clue to current limitations of the process. In part, at least, inter-release effects arise from the interaction of repair and enhancement activity, particularly when they share common resources and are undertaken in parallel. It is probably the interplay between the levels and rates of the various activities and, in particular, their divisions at any given time between repair, functional improvements, and new capability additions that charts the fate of a programming system. Long-term trends, however, are perhaps of greatest significance in understanding the process and in foreseeing and influencing the future. It is this effect that we shall mainly stress in our analysis.

Figure 5 shows the size of OS/360 in modules plotted with respect to release sequence numbers. Relative to the nonuniform time measure, growth in size is more or less linear. Indicated by arrows around the linear trend line is a visible ripple. This cyclic effect can be understood if the total organization is viewed as a self-stabilizing feedback system. That is, the design-programming-distribution-usage system has a feedback-driven and controlled transfer function and input-output relationship.

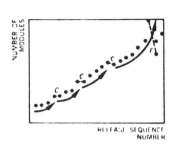

Figure 5. History of growth in number of modules. C: consolidation effect; F: fission effect.

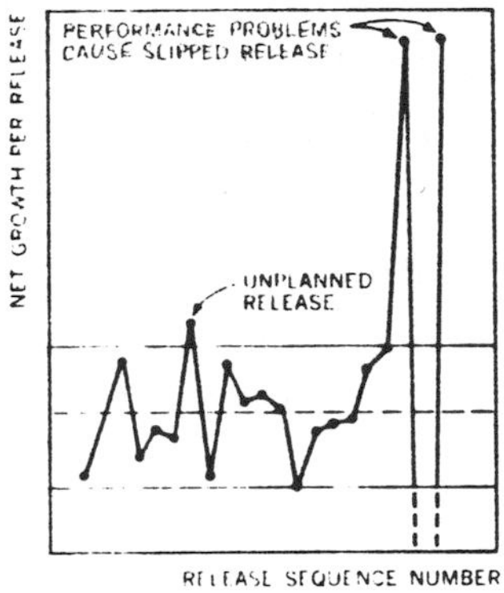

Figure 6. Cyclic nature of net growth of operating system releases.

Some feedback results, for example, from constant pressure to supplement system capability and power. As the growth rate and work pressures build up, thereby increasing the size and complexity of the operating system, reduced quality of design, coding and testing, lagging documentation, and other factors emerge to counter the increasing growth rate. Sooner or later, as indicated by the segments marked C, these lead, at best, to a need for a system consolidation, a release that contains little or no functional enhancement and in which correction, restructuring, and rewriting activities predominate. As a result the system size does not grow significantly during such a release and may even shrink. At the worst a fission effect F may occur, as at $RSN = 20$ to 21 where excessive prior growth has apparently led to a break up of the system.

Figure 6 presents the net growth of OS/360 in each release. Analysis confirms the cyclicity of the growth process as indicated in the figure. A second observation may, however, be of even greater significance in estimating the limits of growth. With three exceptions, the net growth points may be seen to lie in a band bounded at about the 400-module level, a level that does not appear to have changed significantly in size during the lifetime of the system. Moreover, in the three instances where this growth level of OS/360 was exceeded, the record shows that, in the first case, the release was of such quality that it had to be followed by an unplanned clean-up release. The latter two cases had equally unplanned consequences, significant schedule slippages, relatively disappointing performance, and — in the case of release 20 — the previously unplanned division of the operating system into at least two independent systems. Moreover, note that releases with net growth near or in excess of the indicated bound tend to be followed by one or more releases with a much reduced net growth.

If we may generalize our conclusion, it is that as a large system grows through the addition of new and modified code, the system requires the regular establishment of a unique base reference to both code and documentation, such as is attained when the system is to be released for significant usage outside the development and maintenance group.

Also, in the present state of the art, complete and unambiguous specifications of changes or additions to be made are not normally achieved or even achievable. Nor is it possible to continuously prove the specifications to be consistent, and their subsequent implementation to be correct with respect to the new program behavior desired (or even with respect to previous program behavior). Hence the code and the system are tested. But tests can reveal only deviations from desired or expected behavior [7], they do not demonstrate absolutely correct behavior or the absence of faults. Furthermore, the extent to which testing reveals deviations or faults is limited by both the resources that can be consumed to conduct them and by the view that test designers and interpreters have of the total program, the changes, and the intended behavior of both.

Thus, a further intrinsic consequence of system release is that the program is suddenly exposed to an environment in which both the expected behavior and the actual usage may — and usually do — differ from that to which the system was exposed in the development, maintenance, and test environments. Inevitably, therefore, release of the code results in the discovery of new faults. We conclude that sufficiently early release to users of stabilized code and documentation prevents a build-up of undiscovered faults. On the other hand, too many code changes that are undertaken without exposure to a wider usage pattern than can be generated in any test shop causes an accumulation of interrelated faults and system weaknesses, such as poor performance, that are far more complex to unravel. The data on which Figure 6 is based suggest that there existed a nonlinear effect with a critical growth mass in the operating system we are discussing of some four hundred modules.

This critical growth mass had been essentially invariant in almost a decade of OS/360 project and system life, despite methodological and technological improvements: increasing use of high-level languages and programming support tools; and increasing experience of designers, implementers, and management. Thus the characteristic is likely to be an attribute of the entire organization that relates to this system. That is, we appear to have identified a combined system and metasystem invariance. In view of the posited multiloop feedback nature of the process, one can expect to change and improve this characteristic growth rate only when one begins to understand the structure of the process and its relationship to the organization and to the system.

Without speculating further about the nature of the process, we may represent its invariance as observed in the present data by the following relationship:

$$\Delta M_R = K_{11} + S'_1 + Z'_1 \tag{1}$$

or by

$$M_R = K_{10} + K_{11} R + S_1 + Z_1 \tag{2}$$

Here ΔM_R represents the net growth of the system between $(RSN) = (R - 1)$ and $(RSN) = R$. A least-squares fit to the available data yields values of 760 and 200 for K_{10} and K_{11}, respectively. The S and Z terms represent the cyclic and stochastic components whose nature and magnitude can be determined using statistical techniques, such as those described in Reference 8. The small number of available data points, however, restricts the possible significance. We note that Equations 1 and 2 reflect directly the First and Third Laws proposed in the introduction of this paper.

In the absence of a more satisfactory measure, we represent the complexity of the activity required during the interval preceding release R by the fraction C_R (of modules of the total system) handled. Figure 7 shows this measure plotted against RSN.

One possible (and least square-wise significant) fit is by a quadratic in R. Other functional forms (particularly an exponential fit) are also significant. Both the quadratic and exponential representations appeal to our need for models and limitations on the program development process, but more data will have to be obtained to determine the one that more closely reflects a particular process.

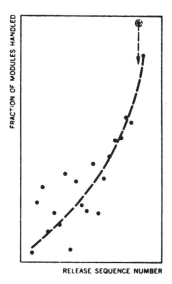

Figure 7. Complexity growth during the interval prior to each release.

On the basis of the principle of parsimony [8], we select the following quadratic form for the current model:

$$C_R = K_{20} + K_{21} R + K_{22} R^2 + S_2 + Z_2 \tag{3}$$

For the present data, K_{20}, K_{21}, and K_{22} are respectively 0.14, 0, and 0.0012.

We note immediately that the monotonic growth trend implied by Equation 3 supports the Second of our three Laws. The Third Law is once again supported by the identification of a significant trend.

Notice that the residuals for this quadratic fit, and equally those for an exponential fit, are generally rather large for $R = 2$ through, say, $R = 14$. This variation is, of course, absorbed by the cyclic and stochastic terms, but in fact the residuals correlate very strongly with the handle rate HR_R. This correlation is not statistically conclusive, since both measures are in the present instance derived from related parameters. Nevertheless, it suggests a more complete representation of the following form:

$$C_R = K'_{20} + K'_{21} R + K'_{22} R^2 + K'_{23} HR_R + S'_2 + Z'_2 \tag{4}$$

where a least squares fit to the present data yields the values 0.037, 0, 0.0013, and 0.008 respectively, for coefficients K'_{20}, K'_{21}, K'_{22}, and K'_{23}.

An interpretation of this model suggests that more rapid work leads to greater pressures on the team, and hence to more errors — which, in turn, require greater repair activity. The data indicate that this is mainly incurred in the same release rather than discovered and undertaken thereafter. Furthermore, since it appears to lead to an increase in the fraction of the system handled, it suggests that the maintenance teams tend to remove the symptoms of a fault rather than to locate and repair its cause. This deduction has been confirmed independently by a number of observers of — and participants in — the process, a fact that strengthens one's confidence in Equation 4 as a more complete representation of one aspect of the process.

Work rate

The work associated with each release is measured in this instance by modules handled MH_R. This measure is, in each case, associated with a particular release and also with the release interval that separates the release from its predecessor. However, many releases overlap — particularly those releases that include major functional growth — and a new release may be integrated successively against two or even more predecessor releases.

Data on the degree of overlap between the various releases were not available to us. Therefore, we first examine the cumulative sum of modules handled (CMH) as compared with the age of the system, in an attempt to neutralize the overlap effect in determining the handle rate. Figure 8 shows these data fitted, as a first approximation, by a straight line. Such a fit suggests that the major changes that have occurred during the lifetime of the operating system in methodology, tooling, and staffing levels have had no significant impact on handle rate. This has stayed essentially constant over the period at some eleven modules per day.

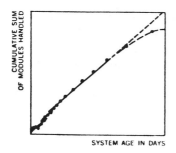

Figure 8. Handle rate of modules over system lifetime.

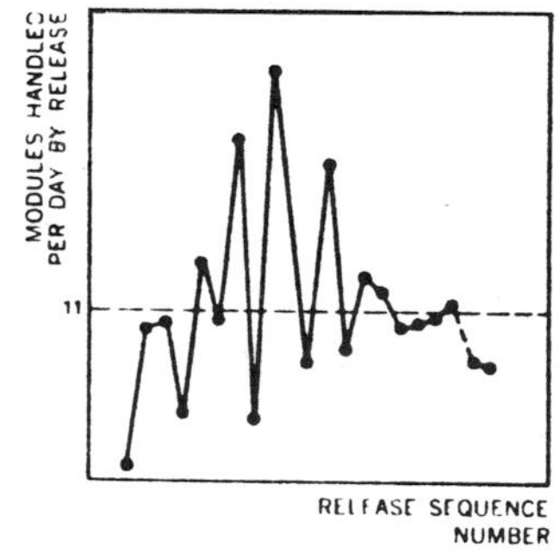

Figure 9. Handle rate as a function of release number.

The data at the extremes of Figure 8 suggest that in the early life of the system, and in the most recent two releases, the handle rate may have been a little lower. This can no longer be confirmed for the older data. As far as present trends are concerned, however, since the handle fraction is approaching unity, we expect the scope of the cumulative handle plot versus system age to drop off from its previously constant value. It appears that even though the straight line fit is adopted as an initial model, an *S*-curve provides a more faithful representation over the life to date of the operating system.

We may now usefully examine the handle rate HR_R as determined by the ratio of the handle-to-release interval for each release, as shown in Figure 9. Because of the effect of release overlap, the range of rates achieved is exaggerated, but it is indeed centered around an average of about eleven modules per day. Also note that where the release rate has exceeded this average, the figure for the next release is lower. We conclude from the data for Figures 8 and 9 that the handle rate is stationary with cyclic and stochastic components that are confirmed by analysis to be significant and to have a three-release cycle.

Thus we adopt as our third relationship an expression of the following form:

$$HR_R = K'_{31} + S'_3 + Z'_3 \tag{5}$$

or

$$CMH_D = K_{30} + K_{31} D + S_3 + Z_3 \tag{6}$$

Size as a function of age

CMH_D counts the total number of modules handled between the first release of the system and day D, that is, when its age from release 1 is D days. HR_R represents the module handle rate in the Rth release interval. The S and Z terms once again represent the cyclic and stochastic components. For the present system, K_{30} and K_{31} are 1100 and 11 respectively. The statistically significant determination of a long-range trend with cyclic and stochastic components once again confirms the proposed Third Law.

We must now consider the data of Figure 5 which we have presented as a function of real time in Figure 10, where system size in modules is plotted as a function of system age in days. As indicated earlier in this paper, the relationship developed to represent this trend must be compatible with those already expressed in Equations 1 through 6. Of the alternative forms that can be significantly fitted, we have selected the following expression:

$$M_D = K_{40} + K_{41} \log (1 + D/K_{42}) + S_4 + Z_4 \tag{7}$$

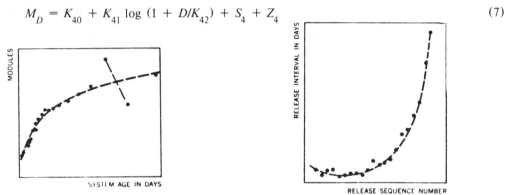

Figure 10. System size as an indication of declining growth rate.   **Figure 11. Increasing release interval.**

Here, a least squares fit yields K_{40}, K_{41}, and K_{42} as 89, 1350, and 51 respectively. The value of the intercept is not significant because the representation is not meaningful where D approaches zero. In reality, of course, system age was not zero at the time of $R = 1$, which is the assumed origin of our time scale. Nor, in view of the assumption that the build and maintenance processes are intrinsically different, may we expect to express the actual system age at first release in the same terms, even if this were known.

We note that the logarithmic representation is not asymptotic. Nevertheless, it suggests unlimited growth potential, though at a decreasing rate. This corresponds to our intuitive understanding that, as a system ages, it is always possible to change another instruction or add another module. However, the time required to do this tends to increase, unless the system is restructured and cleaned up.

One further observation of interest follows from the logarithmic representation selected. This representation is compatible with the constant incremental growth implied by Equation 1, provided that the release interval is growing polynomially, or, in the limit, exponentially. But this is precisely the behavior of interval growth, as shown in Figure 11. As it so happened, the earliest and very successful forecasting undertaken by us was based on this very observation and on the resultant exponential fits to the data.

Summary

Equations 1 through 7 provide a model of the maintenance process for the operating system, OS/360, based on five parametric concepts, but with only four available measures. The model would be complete with the determination of the statistical parameters of the cyclic and stochastic terms. The small number of data points, however, precludes the determination of significant values.

Recognizing the essential interdependence of the various parameters, one can also gain in descriptive power by determining compatible multivariate relationships such as are shown in Equation 4. These relationships could, of course, involve additional or lower-level breakdowns of existing parameters.

The number of basic relationships presented has been deliberately restricted to the number that is necessary and sufficient with respect to the existing degrees of freedom. Equations 1 through 4 have been selected because they bring out apparent invariants of the process. The recognition of invariances is fundamental to the application of the scientific method. As such, invariant detection in an analysis of the programming process not only strengthens our basic assumption of regularity in the process development, but it also provides hope that the analysis can be further developed and eventually permit improvement of the process.

Although the present model represents the observed behavior, it does, however, not explain it. Moreover, the representations break down at the extrema of observation. We have commented on this in the case of Equation 7 when D approaches zero from above. Similarly, Equations 3 through 6 are seen to be invalid representations as the fraction handled approaches its intrinsic limit of one. In fact, the expected non-linear trend is visible in Figure 8. Good reasons have been given, however, for expecting a constant handle rate to be valid over the major portion of the interval considered. Thus it is not surprising that forecasting and planning techniques based on these representations have been useful in providing accurate data to improve planning in this particular environment.

It now appears that further development of statistical process models should be directed toward an examination of the behavior of other systems from both the same and from other program development organizations, so as to determine the range of applicability of the observed phenomena. First confirmation has come from data on a second though smaller operating system that originated in the same organization. With minor differences, this operating system shows the same characteristics and trends, though with markedly different parameters. Preliminary data from a totally different organizational environment have also been examined [9]. As indicated in Figures 12 through 14, the smaller operating system confirms the basic observations of constant growth trends, cyclicity, overall smoothness, and declining work rates. The confirmation that this implies is of particular interest because the source is a programming organization outside IBM that created structured programs in ALGOL for IBM use only. Thus the organizational environment is quite different, but the phenomena are visibly present.

Clearly, these data — especially the invariants — should be studied further, for example by examining actual work rates within a release interval. With further study, one hopes to discover the reasons for the phenomena and ultimately to remove the limitations that they imply.

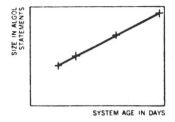

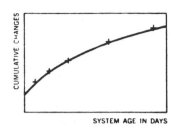

Figure 12. Constant growth rate exhibited by a second operating system.

Figure 13. Number of changes as a function of release number of a second operating system.

Figure 14. Declining work rate exhibited by a second operating system.

In parallel with the study of invariants, one should also proceed with the development of abstract models that represent and formalize our perception and understanding of the large-program development process itself or of aspects of the process. We describe examples of our earliest approaches to this problem in the following section.

Formal modeling of the program development process

Since our goal is to understand and to learn to control the programming process, one view of the process is to see it as the interaction between two entities. On the one hand, the large program in all its representations and with its documentation we call the "object." On the other hand, the human organization that implements the process in its manipulation of the object is termed the "team." The function of the team is to execute changes in the object.

In conjunction with user-provided data, the object enables a computing machine to perform useful work. During its lifetime, all kinds of changes to the object are necessary. The (hardware) machine or some of its components may be changed or replaced. New devices may be added. Computing requirements may be redefined to serve new uses. New ways of using the system may be devised. In general, the behavior of the system deviates from that anticipated or desired because of *faults* in the system. We term faults related to changes in the environment *defects,* whereas an *error* relates to the difference between actual and anticipated behavior. When faults manifest themselves, the team is required to undertake corrective action, to perform changes on the object.

Observations related to those discussed in the previous section suggest that system evolution is to some considerable extent influenced by fault repair activity. Our earliest formal models, therefore, have been designed to examine fault distribution in the system. These models were based on the following assumptions:

- Changes, that is, object handlings, are, in general, imperfect. When changes are performed, errors are injected by the team with probability greater than zero. This by itself would imply a continuous need for change, even if the environment were fixed.

- There is a delay between the injection of an error and its first detection and recording, and another delay exists between recording the error and its final elimination.

- Some errors are ordered in that one of them must be repaired before the other can be detected. That is, there is a layering of errors in the object that is representable by a directed graph.

- The team creates and uses documents, which are kinds of representations of the object, to study faults and possible courses of action. The documentation may be viewed as an integral part of the object.

- Team members, while involved with changes, communicate with each other in the language of these documents.

- Team members have to be educated in the documentation; moreover, the team has the additional task of updating the documentation to reflect changes performed on the remainder of the object.

- Deficiencies in documentation influence the effectiveness of the process and, therefore, cause deficiencies in the object.

From these assumptions, we have developed two classes of models. The first emphasizes the internal distribution and propagation of errors in the object. The role of the team is simply to eliminate observed faults.

The second class of models gives the team a more active role. Management is free to make decisions as to those particular tasks, error repair, documentation, or other activities to which the team should turn. The object responds to these actions by manifesting different error generation rates.

Model of fault penetration

The model of fault penetration that we now discuss is a measure of complexity due to aging. Consider an elementary change activity in the time interval $(i, i + 1)$. This is depicted in Figure 15, where the width of each arrow band may be interpreted to be proportional to the number of faults it represents.

At time i, a number of faults is assumed to exist. As a result of team activities, the following occurrences are likely:

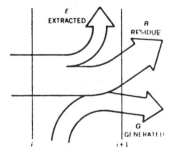

- A fraction E of the total faults is removed (extracted).

- New faults G are injected (generated) due to imperfection in the activity.

Thus at time $i + 1$ a new composition of faults appears that consists of residual R and generated errors.

Figure 15. Primitive model of fault penetration.

Preserving the distinction between residual and newly generated errors is fundamental to an understanding of the evolutionary process. A system cannot be effectively maintained if that distinction is not understood. And complete understanding demands a knowledge of the history as well as of the state of the object at all times.

The primitive change activity of Figure 15 spans the network of Figure 16, where i is a discrete measure of age (or release number) and j is a variable used to introduce the tree structure. For each node, the residual design faults R and the generated faults

G may be expressed as follows:

$$R_{i-1,j} = R_{i,2j-1} + E_{i,2j-1} \tag{8}$$

or

$$G_{i-1,j} = R_{i,2j} + E_{i,2j} \tag{9}$$

and $G_{i,2j-1}$ and $G_{i,2j}$ are to be defined for each node by the following additional assumptions:

- $G_{i,j} > 0$ (imperfection hypothesis)

- We define $C_i = 2^{i-1}$ *fault classes* for every i. Each class has a unique label that consists of a two-valued $\{R,G\}$ character string of length i, with the first element always R, meaning residual design faults. For example, $R\ R\ G\ R\ G\ G\ R$ represents a node or fault class at $i = 7$. More specifically, faults in this class are the

residue (. . . R) of
    faults generated (. . . GR)
        while extracting faults generated (. . . GGR)
            while extracting the residue (. . . $RGGR$) of
            faults generated (. . $GRGGR$)
                while extracting the residue (. $RGRGGR$) of
                faults in the original design ($RRGRGGR$)

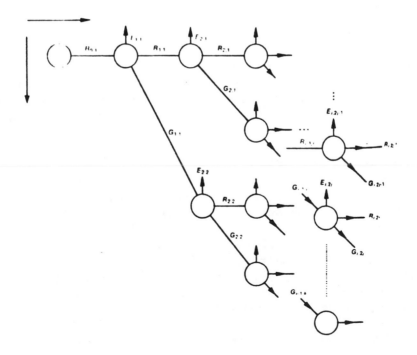

Figure 16.   Network showing faults extracted and faults generated.

The model as described represents an increasingly large and complex network of fault trajectories or histories, even though the total number of faults present may have been stable or even declining as a consequence of nonzero Es. Faults are identified in terms of unexpected or undesired system behavior in execution. Thus we have excluded from consideration here simple faults that manifest themselves locally in a single element of the system. That is, we may omit from consideration those faults that may be detected or removed by operating with or on any one element alone, and consider those situations where rectification of a fault requires coordinated changes in two or more system elements and in their interfaces. Interactions among interelement and intergeneration effects represent the conceptual complexity of the fault pattern. And it is the increasingly complex fault structure that underlies increasing object complexity. Thus periodic restructuring of the object is necessary to reduce complexity because increasing object complexity is itself a fault that impinges on the maintainability of the system.

The connection between the relational complexity of errors and the structural complexity of the system implies that relational complexity may be a measure of communication requirements for the team and the underlying cause of fault extraction and generation over the entire lifetime of the object.

We now give a quantitative interpretation of the fault penetration model, which is a simplified view of structural aging. To analyze the above fault generation model so as to obtain even a simplified view of the resultant structural aging, additional assumptions must be made about the fault extraction and generation variables E and G.

The simplest hypothesis is that, for each node,

$$E = G \tag{10}$$

that is, as many faults are extracted as are generated. Under this assumption the system appears to be in a steady state.

Let us consider the number of fault classes C_i as a measure of *complexity* of the system. Analysis has shown that complexity increases even in steady state, that is, when the number of faults in the system remains constant.

A degree of freedom can be eliminated by establishing a relation between fault extraction and the fault content of a given class. A reasonable assumption could be that $E_{i,2j-1}$ is in fixed proportion to $R_{i-1,j}$, and no new errors are generated. Thus we have the following fault elimination-to-fault residue ratio:

$$\frac{E_{i,2j-1}}{R_{i-1,j}} = (1-p) \tag{11}$$

and fault decay follows a geometric distribution with parameter p, which is constant such that $0 < p < 1$. After i intervals, and having started with a given collection of faults S, the remaining number of faults in the original collection is $S(1-p)^i$, whereas $S(1-(1-p)^i)$ faults must have been extracted. Since $G_i \equiv 0$ for all nodes, the system approaches an error-free state asymptotically (approximately exponentially). Thus in all cases considered the geometric distribution reflects the reasonable assumption that the smaller the fault content the fewer the faults there are to be discovered and extracted. This, however, still implies a monotonically increasing C_i until, if ever, a fault-free state is reached.

More elaborate relations between E and G may be required, so as to represent currently observed situations. It is important to note that E and G at each node are not independent, but are coupled via the team and the process.

Qualitative interpretation of fault penetration

As already indicated, even with decreasing fault content $(E > G)$, the complexity measure C increases monotonically. This results from and reflects the increasing stratification of the system because of the increasing heterogeneity of faults.

The resultant structural deterioration experienced as an increasing difficulty in executing change alerts the team to the need to counteract the aging process. On the basis of our previous assumptions, the latter may be considered proportional to $2^{G(i)}$, where $G(i)$ is a monotonically increasing function of i that reflects higher-order variations not considered here, as well as the complex relationship between fault and system structure.

To cope with the situation, the state of the system has to be precisely defined. Documentation must be accurate, complete and accessible. In addition, the administrative organization or responsibility of team members must be well defined. Finally, team members must be aware of the state of the system by learning. Fulfillment of these needs can effectively reduce the effect of growing complexity, and can be represented symbolically as follows:

$$C_i(\text{modified}) = \frac{2^{G(i)}}{2^{DAL(i)}} = 2^{G(i)-DAL(i)} \tag{12}$$

where DAL means "Documentation, Accessibility, and Learning," which are constructive factors. Equation 12 is a qualitative one, and one that is closely related to our earlier fault penetration model. Real-life situations are much more complex. Communication complexity required to overcome system stratification may, for example, be further increased by geographic scattering of the team activity. Nevertheless, the model enables one to address some very real questions about the program maintenance process. For example, since the model mirrors a domain that is discrete (indexed with i), the model suggests that perhaps increasing the number of intervals i (i.e., decreasing the inter-release time) should permit faster extraction of faults. This would occur if such an increase were to imply an increase in the frequency of restructuring and of providing adequate team knowledge of the state of the system. That is, $G(i)$ and $DAL(i)$ must be kept in step. Whether more frequent intervals would indeed be beneficial is by no means clear. As a consequence of one of our early assumptions, namely, that faults are layered and manifest themselves in a partially ordered fashion, one has to go through the process of gradually repairing the system, with the inevitable result of generating complexity. In addition, short intervals provide less opportunity to exercise the system in actual use for fault manifestation, thus reducing the number of faults that can be extracted. The size of the optimum interval is, therefore, undecided. A more detailed model is required if this is to be formally explored with the objective of helping solve a problem that arises in real system development.

Management decision model

We now discuss our management decision model, which reflects our earlier formulation [4, 10, 11], and which is based on the following assumptions.

Budget B, the available budget, bounds the total activity. During the change process, every unit of fault extraction (termed "progressive" P) activity, measured by $G(i)$ in the model given by Equation 12, is associated with a certain amount of documentation, administration, communication, and learning activity (termed "antiregressive" A) as measured by $DAL(i)$ in Equation 12.

Neglect of A activity results in the accumulation of additional work demand to cope with increasing complexity C. This cumulative demand can be removed only by a (temporary) increase in the intensity of *A*, which, as a result of the limited budget *B*, causes a (temporary) decrease in progressive activity *P*.

Management is assumed to have full control of the allocation of its resources and the division of effort between *P*- and *A*-type activities. Management cannot, however, directly control the growth in complexity that accumulates, except by utter concentration on complexity control through restructuring. This is an activity that is strictly antiregressive and, as such, is psychologically difficult to inspire, since it yields no direct, short-term, benefits.

To examine these concepts further, we now present an alternative formulation of the model. In a somewhat simplified fashion, we assume that resources are fixed (by budget) and that they are equally applicable to either *P* or *A* activity. *B* and activities *P*, *A*, and *C* can be measured in cost per unit of time, which express the budget rate and its expenditure rate on progressive, antiregressive, and complex control activities, respectively. In addition, we use the following relationships:

$k = A/P$ represents the inherent *A* activity required for each unit of *P* activity, so that complexity does not grow.

m = management factor, which is the fraction of progress kP that is actually dedicated by management to *A* activity.

At any time, the total expenditure on all activities must be equal to the budget, hence the formula for the budget is given as follows

$$B = P + A + C \tag{13}$$

The formula for antiregressive activities is

$$A = mkP \tag{14}$$

and

$$C_A = \int_0^t (1-m)\,kP\,dt \tag{15}$$

where

$$C_A(t_0) = 0$$

The expression C_A or complexity reflects the cumulative decay caused by the neglect of *A* activity.

Since the values k and m are left free to vary with time, the model can be used for the investigation of the consequences of various possible management strategies in controlling the maintenance process. Further freedom can be introduced by inserting variable-length delays among the three major expenditure components. A large problem space thus results that can be explored by interactive modeling for increased insight. In this environment, real-life observed phenomena can be approached in the model by stepwise changes in model parameters.

Management simulation

A graphic modeling facility has been used by the authors. This system was essentially an analog computer that was implemented on a digital machine such that the analog components (delays, adders, integrators, etc.) could be connected into a network on a cathode ray tube by the use of a lightpen. Upon request, the computer accepted the network and numerical parameters as inputs for a stored program. The system then computed the response, as described in References 12 and 13.

During the numerous experimental sessions with this facility, many real-life phenomena were successfully reproduced. One example was the cyclic pattern of object growth for the statistical model discussed earlier. The network consisted of a nested two-loop feedback system; preset threshold values for k simulated the management decisions.

More precisely, in our simulation, after a period of persistent neglect of A-activities ($m < 1$), management becomes alarmed by the rapid reduction of P due to increasing C. Consequently, an increase in A is scheduled ($m > 1$) until the situation noticeably improves. At this point, management again becomes optimistic and relaxes k to a lower level. In the long run, however, C grows monotonically. A sample output of a run is presented in Figure 17.

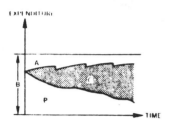

Figure 17. Example output of a budgeting simulation.

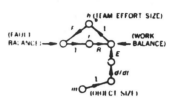

Figure 18. Model of growth in the presence of error generation that is proportional to effort.

The authors are convinced that this type of interactive modeling is perhaps the most fertile, and certainly the fastest, way of developing a feel for the interactions involved, and gradually developing a more complex model that has the power of predicting real-life behavior.

In contrast to previous models, management decision modeling yields an optimistic prognosis, since it includes parameters that reflect management discretion. Thus it permits the counteraction to remove the consequences of growing complexity, action that occurs in real-life situations. On the other hand, of course, the model does not reflect the internal structure of the object. In our earlier models, internal structure was modeled by combining the management model with an extension of the fault penetration model.

Model of limited growth

Suppose that management is free to allocate resources to grow the object, as well as to extract faults as in the previous model. Of course, both activity classes are essentially imperfect in that, while performing them, errors are injected into the object.

As the simplest case, we would like to show how the size m of the object, measured, for example, by the number of modules it contains, develops in the presence of error generation that is proportional to growth activity. In signal-flow-graph form, the linear relations can be represented by Figure 18. Here E and R convert growth rate and error repair to work demand (measured in man-hours). F is the error generation rate (the number of errors per man hour) and r is the number of errors.

The corresponding equations are:

$$h = Rr + E \, dm/dt \tag{16}$$

$$r = Fh \tag{17}$$

Assuming a constant work force h, the solution is given as follows:

$$m = m_0 + \frac{1 - RF}{E} ht \tag{18}$$

where growth is a linear function of time. The greater the work force and the smaller the error generation, the more rapid is the growth, which is, in principle, unlimited. The reason is that, on the basis of our previous assumptions, the effort not used for repair is available to grow the object at a rate that is independent of its size.

Observations on our previous models, however, have suggested that larger and older objects are more complex and receive more errors as they evolve — through growth and through fault removal. Retaining the linear character of the relationships, the flowgraph given in Figure 19 represents the modified assumption, namely, that increasing size causes more errors to be generated, with a gain D per unit size. The somewhat modified equations appear as follows:

$$h = Rr + E \, dm/dt \tag{19}$$

and

$$r = Fh + Dm \tag{20}$$

where Equation 19 represents a negative feedback to control size. The solution now becomes the following:

$$m = m_{er} \left(1 - \frac{1}{m_{er}} e^{\frac{RD_t}{E}} \right) \tag{21}$$

$$m_{er} = \frac{h(1 - FR)}{RD} \tag{22}$$

Equations 19 through 22 indicate that under the assumptions of this section growth is limited to m_{er}. This critical size can only be reached asymptotically. The reader may be wise to compare this result with the real-life observations previously reported.

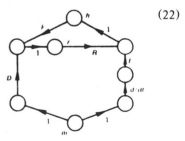

Figure 19. Model of limited growth in which increasing size generates increasing errors.

The critical size can be increased by increasing the size of the work force. However, this means that a subsequent reduction of the work force can create a new critical size that is smaller than the one already reached. Thus a situation of monotonically increasing error content is created.

This model has been studied under differing assumptions. The main conclusion remains, however, that object size is limited with even the slightest negative feedback of size.

This section has presented several models each throwing different, though related, light on the program maintenance or enhancement process. Our aim has not been to present completed models. Rather, we have wished to illustrate how the modeling may be approached, and how interpretation of the models may be used to study and to improve the programming process.

Concluding remarks

Currently, the process of large-scale program development and maintenance appears to be unpredictable; its costs are high and its output is a fragile product. Clearly, one should try to reach beyond understanding and attempt to change the process for the better.

As a first step toward ultimate improvement, we are studying the process as it is, and as it is evolving, much as the physicist studies nature. Our immediate goal is an organized quantized record of observations that formalizes the perception of what is happening and what is being done. With such global studies, one may hope to identify specific points or sources of trouble and perhaps identify areas of the process that are major causes of concern. When that which is happening is understood in the context of the process as a whole, one may attempt to understand why it is happening. Only then will one attempt to change the process without risking local optimization that is very likely to reduce significantly the degree of global optimization. At the present time, for example, it is not clear to what extent improvements should be sought by attention to the human organization, management, or by emphasis on the product side of the process, in order to achieve the most significant gain in and from the process.

We do speculate that communication is a major problem. If this can be confirmed then, for example, a design methodology that expresses the understanding and intention of the designer unambiguously and completely might eliminate many difficulties. One may also hope to avoid problems in the performance area as a consequence of overspecification. Thus one might equally consider that a reduction in product complexity, by better partitioning, for example, could lessen the need for communication and, at the same time, improve performance potential. To do this effectively, however, we must be able to identify those parts of the product that are most interlaced in their logical structure.

Our data so far have been largely limited to that of a few rather large operating systems that were produced within the same large administrative organization. Even these data are meager. Since the initial design phase, no one anticipated the long series of changes that was to follow the initial development. We now know much better and are able to specify the kinds of data that are necessary for future analysis of the development, implementation, and maintenance processes.

We are also enlarging our scope beyond the environments studied so far. It is already clear that qualitative observations similar to ours have been made at other places where large-scale programming has been undertaken. This suggests an urgent need for the definition and standardization of process measures to facilitate meaningful comparison between dissimilar systems, processes, and organizations.

Clearly, we still must test the generality of the hypotheses presented in this paper. It will, for example, be of major interest to determine the degree of generality and the range of validity of the various invariants discovered so far, after filtering new data to remove noise due to environmental factors. This should improve the usability of program evolution dynamics concepts and techniques as planning tools, an improvement much needed by managers who are, in general, not very successful in assessing, predicting, and controlling schedules and resources in the software process.

It is important for an emerging discipline, such as program evolution dynamics, to summarize its most essential concepts into unambiguously defined and measurable quantities at an early stage in its development. This makes it possible to use appropriate techniques and tools from established disciplines. Mathematics, for example, facilitates comparisons between derived results and real life, and may even help the development and communication of new ideas.

One of the most frequently used — but as yet undefined — concepts encountered in our studies is that of complexity. Particular definitions that have been established in the somewhat narrow context of computational magnitude do not appear to be useful or applicable for the study of structure and interaction. After some preliminary studies, we have concluded that a measure of complexity, applicable to the large scale programming environment, could be developed by using established concepts that are related to information, uncertainty, and entropy. Further investigation in this direction forms an ongoing activity in the authors' groups.

Given a measure of complexity expressed in terms of simple structural properties — such as the number of interactions between product or organizational elements — normalized measures for programming effort, productivity, system reliability, and security can be derived and comparisons between different products or methodologies made meaningful. Without such a measure, many of the essential parts of the developing discipline remain unconnected and phenomena are easily misunderstood. An early result in the study, for example, suggests the consideration of complexity of software and its documentation in a unified fashion. In this case, the total project workload can be better quantified, and plans and schedules made more accurate, provided that the manpower need is strongly related to complexity.

Many of the directions pursued in our exploration of evolution dynamics appear to relate to the global properties of complex systems rather than to properties that result specifically from the software environment.

Thus we assume that the results of our studies may be generalizable to other complex technological projects, and to the study of sociological, economic, and biological systems or organisms. In the immediate future, however, we shall concentrate our studies on the evolution of large programs, since in this area change is observable over a relatively short period of time, and experimentation is possible without the serious penalties that could be incurred in other fields. Thus program evolution dynamics may be interpreted as a suitable prototype or test bed for the study of more general system evolution dynamics.

Acknowledgment

The authors appreciate the contributions of their many colleagues in IBM and in the Imperial College, and in particular their discussions with Heinz Beilner and Lip Lim. The CSMP modeling was a contribution made by Steve Morse.

References: Belady & Lehman

1. E.W. Dijkstra, "Notes on structured programming," pp. 1-82. O.J. Dahl, E.W. Dijkstra, and C.A.R. Hoare, *Structured Programming*, Academic Press, New York, New York (1972).

2. E.W. Dijkstra, "A constructive approach to the problem of program correctness," *BIT* 8, 174-186 (1968).

3. M.M. Lehman, *The Programming Process*, IBM Research Report RC 2722 (December 5, 1969), IBM Thomas J. Watson Research Center, Yorktown Heights, New York 10598.

4. M.M. Lehman, *Programs, Cities and Students — Limits to Growth?* Inaugural Lecture, Imperial College of Science and Technology (University of London), London, England (May 14, 1974).

5. L.A. Belady and M.M. Lehman, *Programming Systems Dynamics, or the Meta-Dynamics of Systems in Maintenance and Growth*, IBM Research Report RC 3546 (September 1971), IBM Thomas J. Watson Research Center, Yorktown Heights, New York 10598.

6. D.R. Cox and P.A.W. Lewis, *The Statistical Analysis of Series of Events*, John Wiley & Sons, New York, New York (1966).

7. E.W. Dijkstra, "The humble programmer," *Communications of the ACM* 15, pp. 859-866 (October 1972).

8. G.E.P. Box and G.M. Jenkins, *Time Series Analysis*, Holden-Day, Inc., 500 Sansome St., San Francisco, California 94111.

9. D.H. Hooton, *A Case Study in Evolution Dynamics*, M.Sc. Thesis, Department of Computing and Control, Imperial College of Science and Technology (University of London), London, England (September 1975).

10. L.A. Belady and M.M. Lehman, "An introduction to growth dynamics," *Statistical Computer Performance Evaluation*, Academic Press, New York, New York (1972).

11. L.A. Belady and M.M. Lehman, *A Systems Viewpoint of Programming Projects*, Imperial College Research Report 72/31, Imperial College of Science and Technology (University of London), London, England (1972).

12. H.B. Baskin and S.P. Morse, "A multilevel modeling structure for interactive graphic design," *IBM Systems Journal* 7, pp. 3-4, 218-228 (1968).

13. *1130 Continuous System Modeling Program*, Order No. H20-0209-1, IBM Data Processing Division, White Plains, New York 10504.

Project Planning
and Control

Management information system projects generally have two distinguishing characteristics: 1) they are late, and 2) there is usually a significant cost overrun. There may be other related problems such as improper definition, inadequate scope, poor design, poor programming, inadequate testing, cryptic documentation, and incomplete implementation. Attention to the two main characteristics should also shed some light on these.

There are, of course, many successful implementations of systems which have proven well worth their cost. The difference between the successful and unsuccessful systems may well lie in the manner in which the projects were managed. With better MIS project management tools, virtually all dp system implementations can be successful and cost effective.

Return on investment

If we look at a dp system as a purchased product (which it really is), what do we expect for our money? We might be tempted to say: profound problem definition, creative design, well-engineered execution, etc. But these items are conceptual attributes, not products. Just like any other purchase of goods and services, we are looking for a tangible product and effective service which performs as advertised and has a set of instructions telling us how to use it. We are buying a "bill of material" combination of product and service which may be defined as follows:

1. *A number of modules or programs* which permit data entry, detectable error identification and reentry, file maintenance, analysis, and reporting. These modules should work correctly.

SOURCE: W.S. Donelson, *Datamation*, 1976.

2. *Implementation and operating tools,* including module linking "job control" decks, data base creation or conversion utilities, data backup and retention utilities, and job control decks for periodic operation.

3. *Instructions for use,* including a user manual with illustrated samples and step-by-step procedures for data preparation, error correction, and report utilization; and an operating manual for installation, data entry, and periodic operation.

4. *Technical documentation* for the systems analyst and programmer (and interested user) to aid in understanding the system.

5. *Training or educational service* to enable users, systems, programming and operations personnel to make optimum use of the system.

Summing up, when we buy a system we are buying programs, JCL, and documentation, and we expect some training services to enable us to implement and use them.

If we are purchasing a "package" from an outside vendor, we have in mind performance and economy requirements, and the price we can afford. Our task is matching the capability of various alternatives to our requirements at a given cost. We generally compromise in one or more areas, or we end up making modifications to meet our requirements.

If we are developing a package in-house (hopefully, because the capability cannot be purchased), the big difference is that we must state objectives and define requirements which must be converted into specifications. We then employ people with the technological capability to develop and deliver the product, hopefully in accordance with specification, at the proper due date, and at an agreed-upon price.

The goals are the same, for purchasing or developing systems, but there is an advantage in purchasing — the buyer gets to examine all the parts and then make his decision. In developing an in-house system, the parts won't be there to examine unless some careful planning and carrying out is done. There's no magic to this; in fact, in-house development can be reduced to a six part recipe: producing a user manual, planning a framework for project control, estimating, scheduling, project control, and analysis of variance from estimates.

The user manual, it turns out, is very important to do first rather than last.

Part one: the user manual

The critical issues are stating objectives, defining and establishing specifications, and these are not trivial tasks! In virtually every area of enterprise, these items are conceived mentally and manifested on paper (text and drawings). For project oriented (as opposed to mass produced product) businesses, in only a few instances is it financially feasible to provide a tangible working prototype or model prior to development of the real thing. The finished product must be constructed from "paper" ideas and, all too often, both the quantity and quality of this "paper" is insufficient to determine the adequacy of design and to predict the success or failure of the outcome. In fact, too many systems definitions and specifications exist only orally and are not reduced to paper until after programming or implementation has started, if ever.

Would you buy a million dollar computer without reading its specifications and principles of operation manuals? The obvious answer is "no." Then why buy a dp system without demanding the same privileges? You don't have to.

To the user, the "system" is synonymous with the outputs (reports, crt screens, audio response, graphics, etc.) and inputs. The user should determine his reporting requirements and provide specifications with the aid of (not through delegation to) a systems analyst, using concrete objectives as a guideline. The systems analyst must then determine the data base requirement to support this reporting capability, and the user should participate aggressively in this data base definition activity. Finally, both the systems analyst and the user must determine the inputs, sources and timing of data needed to support the data base, and the reporting capability. The user must then be willing to bear the burden and expense of providing the input to gain the benefit of the output.

In many cases, the provider of the input resides in another department or division, and interdepartmental or interdivisional cooperation will be required to carry out the plan successfully. Keeping in mind that each functional area has its own objectives, incentives, and motivations which may conflict with those of other functional areas, this element of cooperation is a crucial matter.

As a result of having defined the outputs, data base and inputs (which are the "first cut" at requirements definition and specifications), we should be in a good position to construct a user manual with the following sections:

1. *Annotated sample reports* which are mocked up by writing proposed report formats on data entry sheets, keypunching, and listing the data with conventional dp utilities to produce realistic report facsimiles. (The keypunch approach is recommended over typing because changes are easier to make.) The annotation should cover the name, purpose, source, content, sequence, distribution, frequency and disposition of the report.

2. *Preliminary data base layouts* showing master file and detail record layouts and data base structure (list, hierarchy, network, sequential, etc.).

3. *Preliminary input layouts,* and procedures for entry including source of data, applicable edit rules and balancing procedures, error correction and reentry procedures with illustrated samples.

4. *Proposed coding structure tables* which identify and define the meaning of codes to be used by the user (customer type code, credit limit code, inventory ordering rule code, etc.). Even if the codes have not been defined at this point, there should be pages indicating that codes will be developed to represent data elements so that the users can clearly identify what will be required of them.

5. *A preliminary system flowchart* of input, processing and reporting modules and flows. This chart should depict interfaces to existing and planned systems and should be supported by a narrative explaining interface plans and anticipated problems, production schedule changes, etc.

6. *A system narrative* stating the requirements, scope, objectives, description, benefits, capability and limitations of the system (10 to 15 pages).

For a typical commercial system (receivables, materials requirements planning, general ledger), this manual will be about 100 pages and can be constructed fairly quickly if it is made a prerequisite to systems development (and this is a top management consideration). It may take 90 to 120 man-days to complete the user manual at a cost of $5,000−$15,000, but keep in mind that the whole project may cost $75,000−$150,000 or more and at the point this preliminary user manual is completed, no program specifications have been written, no programming has commenced, no computer test time has been consumed, no implementation has proceeded, and therefore, no costly mistakes have been made.

The manual must show on paper what the system will do, how it will work, who must support it and in what capacity, who will specifically benefit from it and how the total organization will benefit from it. Every participant in the system will have the opportunity to see what they are buying, to determine if the merchandise is good, and to propose (or insist upon) design modifications to better meet their requirements before they get locked into an inflexible system.

Part two: a framework

By identifying the object of planning, more than half the project planning battle is won. If a system is a set of programs, JCL, documentation (user reference material and procedures) and training, a project is nothing other than the framework in which the system is commissioned, defined, constructed and implemented. This framework is conceived and animated by people. Thus, the planning of a project is the planning of the framework within which the project will gain its identity, planning which addresses the following issues:

1. *Problem Definition.* Who wants the system (the user), why do they want the system (suspected problem), what do they want the system to do (scope), and how will the system benefit them (objectives).

2. *Project Organization.* Who will authorize the project (management), who will manage the project (project manager or steering committee), and who will participate in the project (project team consisting of users, MIS personnel and dp personnel).

3. *Problem Analysis.* What is the real problem and what is the cause? Can the problem be eliminated or mitigated, or do we have to construct a system to handle it? (A lot of "make work" systems could stop here because there is no real problem).

4. *System Definition.* The environment, inputs, data base, flows, rules and procedures which will solve the problem. This should manifest itself in the form of a user manual as defined earlier.

5. *System Review and Approval.* The formal process of reviewing the requirements and specifications against proposed capability to ensure a good match. The focal point is the user manual and the project turning point is here. The project can proceed with review and approval by all functional area managers affected by the system and final authorization by top management; it can go back to any prior step for rework; or it can, as scrap, be terminated. If a positive decision is not made within a reasonable time, usually the project will continue into detail

design and programming stages without approval and authorization until a cost, time, design, or some other obstacle is encountered. This may be the reason for a high project failure rate — the system never gets completed for lack of cooperation, or never gets implemented because of lack of consent by required contributors.

6. *Detail Design.* Program specifications relating to processing of inputs, maintenance of files and production of reports.

7. *Programming and Testing.* The conversion of the ideas on paper into the bill of deliverable products. Along with this should go a high degree of project management, project control, and revision of documentation.

8. *Training and Implementation.* The delivery of the product and performance of related services.

9. *Post-Implementation Review.* The *formal* process measuring how well the capabilities of the project and service matched the requirements, and the subsequent fine tuning of the system to accomplish a good match.

Project planning has only these two essential ingredients: a framework for conduct, and a user manual for manifestation. Without these, it is not possible to estimate, schedule and control the project and to analyze the deviation from the plan. Items 4 and 5 provide the proper background for project estimation, scheduling and control. Items 6, 7 and 8 are the proving ground for the estimation, scheduling and control and Item 9 provides the opportunity for analysis of variance from plan.

Part three: estimating

The preliminary user manual provides the focal point for project estimation. The quantifiable components for estimating are the numbers of each functional type of module or program which will be required to construct the system, and by this time we should have an accurate forecast of the number of each type due to the preliminary system flowchart in the manual. A typical commercial system has at least 12 categories of functional components:

1. *Data definition books.* File, record and transaction layouts which are stored in a library and *copied* into programs as required.

2. *One-time utilities.* Programs to create files, generate test data, simulate processing, and test called subroutines.

3. *Conversion utilities.* Programs to convert or reformat data files and transactions from existing systems to the new system format.

4. *General purpose utilities.* Modules to perform repeated functions which are used by different control modules (date conversions, table lookups, calculations, etc.).

5. *Data base interface utility.* Here I am advocating the use of a "bridge" between application programs and *most* data base management systems to provide a higher degree of data independence, to assure physical integrity of the data base (by auditing adds, deletes and updates), and to

provide file content and utilization statistics. This bridge relates functional entry points (open, close, read, write, explode, implode, etc.) for application modules to technique-oriented entry points and commands supplied by data base management packages (MRAN, CDIR, ADD-M, DELVD, GET UNIQUE, etc.).

6. *Edit modules.* Programs which assure the logical integrity of data entered into the system and which provide error listings or alerts. (One module per transaction type or family of transactions is assumed.)

7. *Update modules.* Programs which update the data base. (This function may be performed within the same module as the editing function, but it is, nevertheless, a separate function which produces audit trails or activity reports.)

8. *Processing modules.* Programs which do extensive calculations, analyses, and manipulations of data, resulting in possible additional file maintenance.

9. *Major data base extracts.* Programs which select data from the data base for subsequent (or simultaneous) analysis and reporting.

10. *Minor data base extracts.* Same as Item 9, but less complex.

11. *Major Reports.* Programs which report the results of major extracts and processing and which are complex in nature (multiple levels of control breaks and totals, sophisticated row and column formatting, and possibly further access to the data base).

12. *Minor Reports.* Same as Item 11, but simple in structure.

(Note that the project manager who tightly controls the data definition books and data base interface utility will produce a well constructed system in terms of architecture and adaptability to change. Also, if the file maintenance function is strictly confined to file maintenance modules, there will be less latitude for the occurrence of difficult to locate system bugs.)

For typical commercial application systems, each class or type of module has a mean number of statements per module (and standard deviation), and also has a measurable programming rate in terms of mean and standard deviation of numbers of statements per hour. Computer test requirements are also a quantifiable by module type. Comprehensive study by the author has revealed the statistics in Table 1, based upon new applications development using COBOL in a batch processing IBM 360/40 environment. (For system modifications, as opposed to new systems development, other languages, on-line processing, or other hardware, different statistics will have to be compiled. These statistics will no doubt vary somewhat by installation due to differences in methods, standards, and personnel experience levels, and each installation should adjust these statistics to account for these differences. As explained later, the analysis of variance technique will be instrumental in providing the basis for refinement of these statistics.)

System analysis and design hours are approximately 110% of programming hours for an entire project, assuming that this function has responsibility for project management, analysis, design, user manual preparation, program specification writing, program quality control, test results analysis, user training, system implementation (as opposed to program implementation and operations support, which is typically done by lead programmers), and post implementation review. COBOL programs may be keyed and verified at the rate of 125 statements per hour, assuming an average of 32 characters per statement (if more characters per statement are coded, the number of statements per module should decrease, and the total keystrokes per module class should remain fairly constant).

Table 1
Programming and Testing Estimates for New Applications
Developed in COBOL in a Batch Processing IBM 360/40 Environment

Module Class	STATEMENTS* PER MODULE		PROGRAMMING RATE (Statements per hour)		COMPUTER TEST HOURS PER MODULE
	Mean	Standard Deviation	Mean	Standard Deviation	
1. Data definition	62	52	16	N/A	.7
2. One-time utility	177	92	30	N/A	.7
3. Conversion utility	449	179	24	N/A	3.2
4. General utility	260	120	5	4.5	8.9
5. Data base interface "bridge"	450	150	10	1.8	8.1
6. Edits	1715	415	16	4.2	19.0
7. Updates	1278	528	20	7.8	11.3
8. Processing	1186	~108	8	1.4	27.0
9. Major extracts	530	29	15	3.9	6.1
10. Minor extracts	186	76	7	3.0	4.6
11. Major reports	907	436	8	2.5	19.7
12. Minor reports	260	95	9	5.1	5.0
(N/A = Not Available)					

*does not include COPIED data definition statements.

By determining the number of modules in each class, it becomes feasible to forecast systems analysis and design hours, programming hours, keypunch hours and computer test hours. Knowing the cost per hour of these resources (approximations are $20/hour for systems analysis and design, $15/hour for programming, $9/hour for keypunch and $50/hour for computer time — although computer chargeout rates can vary substantially), it is possible to estimate project costs as follows:

$$\text{Total Cost} = \sum_{i=1}^{12} M_i \left[\left[\frac{(S_i + \alpha_i\ \sigma s_i)}{(P_i + \beta_i\ \sigma p_i)} \frac{(1.1\ R_s + R_p)}{} \right] + \left[\frac{S_i + \alpha_i\ \sigma s_i)\ R_k}{125} \right] + T_i\ R_c \right]$$

Where i = module class or type
M = number of modules per class (from planner's estimate)
S = mean number of statements per module per class (from Table 1)
σS = standard deviation of S (from Table 1)
α = selected multiple of σs (from planner's estimate)
P = programming statements per hour (from Table 1)
σP = standard deviation of P (from Table 1)
β = selected multiple of σp (from planner's estimate)
T = mean number of computer test hours per module per class (from Table 1)
Rs = hourly charge for systems analysis and design
Rp = hourly charge for programming
Rk = hourly charge for keypunch
Rc = hourly charge for computer test time

This cost algorithm and set of statistics address the costs of project development through implementation and post implementation review which accrue within the MIS/DP department.*

The specific costs associated with user participation during development have been purposely omitted from the cost estimation algorithm for various reasons (the author believes this type of cost must be estimated on an incremental cost basis or on an opportunity cost basis). However, the total hours of user involvement are believed to be about 50 to 100% of total systems analysis and design hours, and can run even higher in some cases. Also, clerical effort required for one-time data conversion can be very substantial, but is rather easily estimated.

Part four: scheduling

Once a project estimate is established in terms of man-hours and dollars, we are in a position to establish a master project schedule. Analysis of prior projects has revealed the distribution of resource consumption over project duration (again, these statistics may require some refinement by the reader in order to be applicable to their specific environment) shown in Table 2.

Table 2
Estimated Resource Consumption Over the Life of a Project
(Again Using Batch COBOL on an IBM 360/40)

Resource	Systems Analysis	Detail Design	Programming and Test	Training and Implementation	Post Implementation Review
Systems analysts	24%	26%	30%	13%	7%
Programmers	0%	16%	55%	24%	5%
Keypunch	0%	0%	90%	10%	0%
Computer	0%	0%	68%	30%	2%

If each project phase is treated as a separate entity and the rule is made that subsequent phases cannot be initiated until the current phase is completed, then we can establish a master schedule for each phase. The estimated hours for each resource are multiplied by the percent of resource consumed in each phase, yielding resource hours per phase. A safe assumption is that a project participant can contribute a maximum of 123 productive hours per calendar month (2087 hours/year−80 hours holiday−80 hours sick leave−80 hours vacation ÷ 12 months/year × 0.8 productivity factor). If the project personnel are 100% allocated to the project, we can compute minimum elapsed months for each phase of systems analyst and programmer utilization as follows:

Required hours by resource by phase ÷ (# personnel allocated × 123).

---

*Note that this estimation technique is very much akin to building construction cost estimating, a primary tool of which is cost per square foot.

We may also wish to establish a constraint on computer test time utilization in any one month based upon a reasonable limit per programmer (say, 20 hours/month) or based upon a total availability of x hours/month. This can be converted into minimum elapsed months per phase as follows:

Computer hours required in each phase ÷ (# programmers allocated to phase × 20)

or,

Computer hours required in each phase ÷ x.

In most cases, we can assume infinite capacity for keypunching because of the number of outside service bureaus available and the relatively minor cost of this resource (1−3% of project total).

We then take the largest elapsed months figure (systems analyst, programmer or computer) in each phase as one would establish a critical path with PERT analysis. The sum of the largest figures from each phase represents the minimum total project duration. Design review time (two to four weeks or longer) should be allowed between analysis and detail design, and several months should be allowed between implementation and post-implementation review to establish a system performance record (keep in mind, the system is operational at the end of implementation, but the project should continue until fine tuning of the system is completed).

In the elapsed time between implementation and post-implementation review, problems should be noted; however, attempts to correct minor problems should be discouraged and only major disruptive system, programming, and operational problems should be fixed immediately. In this manner, the level of program and system bugs builds up to a meaningful work load which is most efficiently handled at one time, the time being when 95% of all problems have been detected. This is usually three to four months after implementation, provided that the system operates on a minimum weekly basis. (Systems whose cycles are monthly or longer rarely achieve bug-free status.) This technique of allowing minor bugs to accumulate minimizes the disruption caused by frequent changes, some of which cause additional problems.

From the project master schedule, it is possible to establish a detail schedule for each activity and each participant. In doing this, timing, sequence, and resource availability problems will appear which did not appear at the master or macro-schedule level, and the planner can make schedule adjustments to handle them. When the final detail schedule is summed back up to a macro level, the overall duration of the project may change ± 15% or more from the first iteration of the master schedule.

This top-to-bottom and bottom-back-to-top approach preserves the principle that the whole is equal to the sum of its parts, and we end up with detail schedules for each activity and each participant. This detail will be useful for project control.

Part five: project control

Project control implies and requires a controllable situation and a means of accountability to measure progress against the plan. If every person records hours worked against one project control number, the project is automatically out of control because there is no "individual" accountability. Therefore, a participant code or name must be assigned to every participant and a subproject code or name to every activity, so that actual progress against plan can be recorded at the micro level. In this manner, overall progress of the project can be measured, problem areas can be identified or predicted, and action can be taken in advance to prevent an out-of-control activity from resulting in disruption. To measure progress, however, to-date actual progress versus plan is not sufficient. If the plan calls for 100 hours to complete an activity, and 60 hours have been consumed to-date, we cannot assume that the activity is 60% complete. An independent estimate of percentage of completion of each activity by each participant is needed. With the "percent complete" known at the activity level, dividing actual hours to date (times 100) by percent complete yields a *projected actual.* If the summation of projected actuals adversely affects the project estimate and schedule for the current phase to an unrecoverable degree, alternative plans should be established and cleared with management. A revised schedule and budget generally results, being strangely characteristic of building construction and product development projects.

The estimation of percent completion at the detail activity level is a tenuous task, as the person who is doing the detail work has a subconscious desire to report good news to the project administrator in order to appear to be where he is expected to be. Typically, dp personnel report 25% completion when they start an activity, 50% completion when they are really 25% complete, 75% completion when they are really 50% complete, and 95% completion for the remaining duration until they are really 100% complete. A well thought out antilogarithmic function combined with independent estimates of hours to complete lagging activities will smooth this reporting problem. For individual performers who consistently operate within expectations, detail progress review may not be necessary. These people know their capabilities and limitations, and will advise the project manager of anticipated problems. (They also are the type who will take work home and do it when necessary to prevent project disruption and avoid personal embarrassment, so one may never know they had a problem.) For inconsistent performers, a regularly scheduled progress review meeting should be held.

The percentage completion reporting method is not free of major pitfalls, however. In fact, the method is a highly subjective exercise. In the early stages of a project, it is difficult to distinguish between 5% completion and 10% completion, yet the resultant projection can vary 100% based on which number is chosen. Thus, for perhaps the first half of a project, this method is at best unreliable and may cause project control alarms to sound needlessly.

Project milestone reporting is perhaps a more suitable alternative. Using this method, each task or subproject is divided into scheduled elementary steps (for example: flowcharting, coding, first compile, first unit test, first volume test, final test, etc.), and the completion of each step is reported on a master project schedule. If the master schedule is established using a PERT or critical path technique, it is possible to measure the overall impact on the master schedule caused by schedule variances of individual tasks. This places much more emphasis on getting tasks done on time and focuses attention on critical areas which are running behind schedule.

The ideal method of project control would be based on a marriage of the two techniques. If cumulative percent time distributions were established over all phases of each typical subproject, milestone reporting of each would automatically yield an associated percentage of completion, thereby giving a project manager both current status and an estimate to completion. There is much room for creativity and applied research in the discipline of project control.

Part six: analysis of variance

The purpose for analysis of variance from plan is to identify specific factors which caused project cost and schedule under- and overruns (mostly the latter), and to help us do a better job of estimating, scheduling and control of the next project. To illustrate the concept, let's take a specific example. The hours and cost estimation technique shows that programming cost is a function of four factors:

Number of programs × Statements per program ÷
Statement coding rate per hour × Hourly cost of programmers

The programming estimation technique employs two standards: statements per program and statement coding rate per hour. The numbers embodied in these standards may be questioned. However, these standards are a starting point, and positive decision rules can improve them to the point where they work for a particular environment, staff, language, and computer.

Let us make the following representations:

$$P \ = \ \text{number of planned programs}$$
$$\Delta P \ = \ \text{actual number of programs} - P$$
$$S \ = \ \text{standard statements per program}$$
$$\Delta S \ = \ \text{actual statements per program} - S$$
$$H \ = \ \text{standard hours per coded statement (reciprocal of statements per hour)}$$
$$\Delta H \ = \ \text{actual hours per statement} - H$$
$$R \ = \ \text{planned hourly cost}$$
$$\Delta R \ = \ \text{actual hourly cost} - R$$

Our initial cost plan is $P \times S \times H \times R$. The actual cost will be $(P + \Delta P) \times (S + \Delta S) \times (H + \Delta H) \times (R + \Delta R)$ which expands into 16 compound factors. We are interested in five of the compound factors, and we allocate the other 11 using standard cost accounting methods. The five factors of interest are:

A. The original plan: $\quad P \times S \times H \times R$
B. Change due to ΔP: $\quad \Delta P \times S \times H \times R$
C. Change due to ΔS: $\quad P \times \Delta S \times H \times R$
D. Change due to ΔH: $\quad P \times S \times \Delta H \times R$
E. Change due to ΔR: $\quad P \times S \times H \times \Delta R$

We are now prepared to explain actual results which deviate from plan in a meaningful and analytical manner. If the number of programs changed, we should have known early in design phase, and, although our original master plan should never be changed, we can have a working plan which gets revised by upper management consent. If the hourly cost rates changed, we should have known about that in advance and called this to the attention of upper management. The only remaining elements to explain are C and D. If there was a significant variance either way (say, more than $\pm$ 10%) due to ΔS, an analysis should be made of the programs in question to explain the variance in terms of the manner in which the programs were written. If the programs are acceptable, and the relationship $-0.1 < (\text{Item C} \div \text{Item A}) < 0.1$ does not hold, a change in the "S" standard may be appropriate for future use. If the programs are not acceptable, project control administration or programming standards may have been inadequate. If there was more than $\pm$ 10% variance in the plan due to ΔH, a performance review should be held on an exception basis with those doing the work to explain the variance. If these people's performance is judged to be acceptable, and the relationship $-0.1 < (\text{Item D} \div \text{Item A}) < 0.1$ does not hold, a change in the "H" standard may be advisable. If the performance was judged to be substandard, project control administration may have been inadequate or personnel recruitment and development practices may be poor.

The analysis of variance and subsequent review provide an explanation for variance from plan and suggest areas for improvement in future projects.

Voilà

There is no substitute for managerial capability, good judgment and a conservative approach in planning, estimating, scheduling and controlling a project, but these quantitative methods can significantly reduce errors in estimating and scheduling MIS projects, and can lead to improved planning and control.

Estimating
Software Costs

PART I

Few managers are able to predict the time and resources needed to develop large-scale software systems. Progress is often measured by the rate of expenditure of resources rather than by some count of accomplishments. Unrealistic estimates often result in last minute efforts to get code written quickly, resulting in cost overruns and poor quality software.

Software development can be brought under control. It requires an understanding of how application software behaves, what factors management can control and what factors are limited by the process itself.

The basis of effective management is the fact that the software development process exhibits a characteristic behavior, which can be exploited, so that the expensive results of unrealistic approaches can be avoided.

Traditionally, managers make two incorrect assumptions about software development: that people and time are interchangeable and that productivity levels are relatively constant for all software projects within the same organization.

The first assumption is that development effort is simply the product of people and time and that the time can be specified arbitrarily by management. Thus, the manning level is the development effort (in man-years) divided by the predetermined development time (see Fig. A1).

For example, suppose that the organization has to work under constraints. If the manpower available were limited to 25 people, the time would be determined as 100 man-years divided by 25 people, or four years. However, if the system had to be finished in two years, the relation would become: Manpower equals 100 man-years/2 years, which equals 50 people.

SOURCE: L.H. Putnam & A. Fitzsimmons, *Datamation,* 1979.

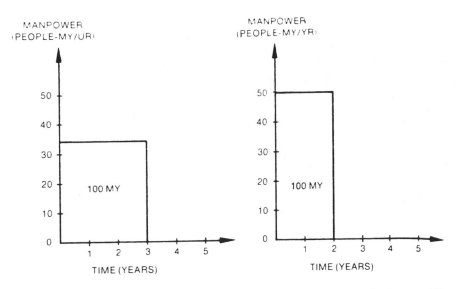

Figure A1. The assumption that 50 people for two years is equivalent to 33 people for three years turned out not to be valid for large-scale software development.

Managers arrive at the second assumption by taking some overall productivity figures from previous projects that they think are similar. However, they do not examine closely the precise characteristics of that similarity. An estimate of total source statements derived from the specifications is divided by the productivity figures to give a man-year estimate. For example, assume that we have to build a system of 100,000 source statements ($SS = 100,000$) and our productivity is 1,000 source statements per man-year, by analogy with a previous project. The development effort thus equals 100,000 SS/1,000, which equals 100 man-years.

Unfortunately, our experience shows that these relationships are too simple, except in the case of very small programs, such as those of less than 7,500 source statements, or that employ a few people for a few months.

For larger programs we now know that people and time are not interchangeable. Fred Brooks, manager of the IBM 360 operating system project, has described this phenomenon so graphically that a variant of it has become known as Brooks' law: "Adding people to a late project only makes it later." The reason is clear. As the number of people on a project increases arithmetically, the number of human interactions increases geometrically. More and more time must be spent on human communication and less and less on productive work. The only way to avoid this inevitability is to reduce the number of people who must interact by stretching out the time.

We also now know that productivity is not constant. Rather, it is a complex function of the effort, time and technology tools being applied to the development task. You can't improve productivity without changing these factors. It is not unusual for a group of programmers to achieve a productivity of, say, 5,000 source statements per man-year on a small, relatively simple business application while doing only 1,000 source statements per man-year on a large real-time system.

With this kind of variation in productivity, it is little wonder that estimates based on the constant productivity assumption are not reliable.

Software life cycle

Over the last five years we have studied the manpower vs. time pattern of several hundred medium- to large-scale software development projects of different classes. These projects all exhibited the same life cycle pattern — a rise in manpower, a peaking and a tailing off (see Fig. A2). Use of the manpower curve and the corresponding equation allows us to determine the number of people needed at any time t. The time of peak effort is denoted by t_d; this time is very close to the development time for the system, which is also the time when the system reaches full operational capability. The falling part of the curve corresponds to the operations and maintenance phase of the system life cycle. During this phase the principal work is modification, minor enhancements and remedial repair (fixing bugs).

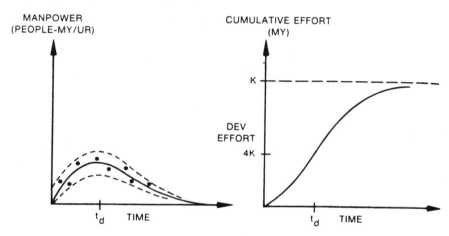

Figure A2. The curves defined by this equation, originally applied by Lord Rayleigh to describe other scientific phenomena, have been found to fit reasonably well the manpower pattern of software development, at least within the "noise" of the data points (lefthand curve).

The data points shown on the manpower diagram indicate that there is scatter or noise in the data underlying the process. Empirical evidence suggests that the noise component may be up to $\pm$ 25 percent of the expected manpower value during the rising part of the curve. This part of the curve corresponds to the development effort.

The form of the equation is:

$$\dot{Y} = K/t_d^2 \bullet t \bullet e^{-t^2/2t_d^2}$$

where: $\dot{Y}$ is the manpower at any time t.

K is the area under the curve and corresponds to the total life cycle effort in man-years.

t_d is the development time (time of peak manpower).

Large software systems and some small ones seem to follow this general pattern, called the Rayleigh curve. Other small systems, however, seem to have a more rectangular manpower pattern (see Fig. A1), probably because the manpower applied is determined by management or by contractual agreements. Many small projects are established as level-of-effort contracts, leading to rectangular manloading.

Rectangular manloading patterns are seldom found in large projects, apparently because managers have so little intuitive feel for the resources needed to do the job that they hesitate to specify the loading pattern. Rather, they tend to react to the needs of the system. This reactive approach results in time lags and on occasion in underapplication of effort, but the overall effect is a reasonable approximation to Rayleigh manloading.

As we have seen, the manpower equation allows us to determine our manloading — if we know the total effort (K) and the development time (t_d). We can find K and t_d once we know the expected size of the system, but first we must obtain the best estimate of the system size, and do it before development begins.

Before we begin to size the system, we should decide what we really want from a sizing technique. Obviously we need an estimate of the expected number of source statements. We use source statements rather than machine language instructions because they are what people write and what people can most easily relate to. People have some intuition for the size in source statements, whereas to get machine language estimates requires an uncertain conversion which introduces additional possibilities for error.

Less obvious is the need for an estimate of the uncertainty (or range) of the source statement number. The uncertainty estimate allows us to project the risk associated with our source statement estimate — something every manager should have. It also permits us to generate risk estimates for cost, schedule, and manpower — information we never had before.

At least three different estimates should be made before development of the system begins. They should be made once during the systems definition phase and at least twice during the functional design and specifications phase.

More than one estimate should be made because better and better data are available as we go from early systems definition into the functional design phase. A look at the system life cycle (Fig. A3) helps us decide when these estimates can be made.

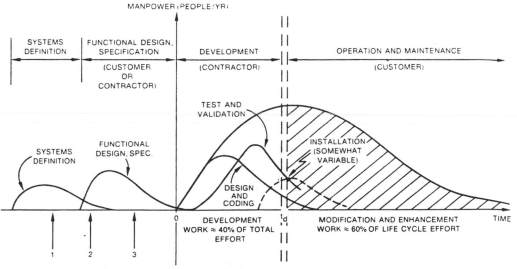

THE SOFTWARE LIFE CYCLE

Figure A3. Formal development begins at time 0, but before that, as information about the system is developed in the systems definition and functional design and specifications phases, it becomes possible to estimate the size of the system with increasing precision at points 1, 2, and 3.

Feasibility sizing

During the early systems definition phase we need broad estimates of the ultimate system size, development time and cost so that we can establish basic economic feasibility. At this point we have no hard data about the system we are considering because it is too early — no design has been done. Therefore, all we really can do is make an intelligent guess as to the range of size of the system, based on what we've done in the past and what little we do know about it. If we let a equal the lowest possible number of source statements and let b equal the highest possible number of source statements, we can determine the expected size and its standard deviation (or uncertainty) by using the laws of statistics and probability.

Let us assume that we are two weeks into the systems definition of a large-scale inventory control system called SAVE. Based on past experience and what we know about this system at this point, we might broadly estimate it to be between 50,000 and 140,000 source statements. Using our statistical equations, we know that the expected number of source statements is:

$$SS = (a + b)/2 = 190,000/2 = 95,000$$

The standard deviation is:

$$\sigma SS = 1b - a1/6 = 90,000/6 = 15,000$$

The expected size is:

$$95,000 \pm 15,000$$

By "expected" statisticians mean that there are 68 chances out of 100 that the true size lies within one standard deviation of the mean, i.e., between 80,000 and 110,000 source statements. There are 99 chances out of 100 that the true size falls within three standard deviations of the mean, i.e., between 50,000 and 140,000 source statements and less than one chance that it lies outside these limits.

While this method results in what seems to be a disconcertingly large range, it is important to understand that it is as good as we can do at this time, considering that we have almost no solid information about the system we want to build. Managers who insist on getting better estimates (meaning smaller ranges or even absolute numbers) must learn instead to work with averages of the quantities and a measure of the variability of the quantities, i.e., the standard deviation.

This is an important philosophical point because it means that only a certain level of accuracy and precision is possible at this stage and all efforts to do better are futile. As Aristotle wrote, "It is the mark of an instructed mind to rest satisfied with the degree of precision which the nature of the subject admits and not to seek exactness when only an approximation of the truth is possible."

As we continue into the life cycle and learn more about the final system, the statistics improve and uncertainty is reduced. Thus, as we approach the start of detailed design, we can reduce our risk to ranges that are considered to be within the limits of engineering accuracy in other branches of the engineering art. We achieve this result by breaking the system into pieces and estimating the pieces separately. Then we combine the pieces by means of our equations, letting the statistics of aggregation reduce our uncertainty.

Toward the beginning of functional design, we should know what the major subsystems will be. At this point, the members of the project team who have worked on the systems definition should estimate the size of each of the major subsystems as follows:

Let *a* be the smallest possible size (in source statements).
Let *m* be the most likely size.
Let *b* be the largest possible size.

The averages of these estimates for SAVE — in effect, a Delphi polling of experts — resulted in the first three columns of Table A1.

Table A1. A polling of the project team for SAVE at the early functional design phase provided the smallest, most likely, and largest estimates (average of team) of the number of source statements in each subsystem. From each range the expected value and its standard deviation was calculated.

Function	Smallest	Most Likely	Largest	Expected	Std Dev
File Handlers	25000.	40000.	70000.	42500.	7500.
Utilities	5000.	15000.	26000.	15167.	3500.
System Procs	12000.	36000.	50000.	34333.	6333.
Total				92000.	10422.

Parenthetically, we might note that we went through this procedure with several groups of systems engineers and they are quite comfortable with it. Most analysts or engineers are reluctant to give a single estimate of size. When they are forced to do so, they will bias it on the high side. They prefer to give a range of sizes, because they can make this range as large or as small as they need to, depending on what they know about the system at the time. Psychologically, giving a range is not a threatening commitment.

The estimates for the three subsystems in SAVE resulted in a broad range of possible sizes. Note that the distribution is skewed on the high side in each case. This bias is typical of the beta distribution, the characteristics of which are used in PERT estimating. The PERT technique has been used successfully in other fields for more than 15 years and we adopted it here in order to find the overall system size range and distribution.

1. *Expected value.* An estimate of the expected value of a beta distribution is:

$$E_i = (a + 4m + b)/6$$

   This formula simply biases the result so that the expected value falls on the side about which we are more uncertain. The expected value for each subsystem is listed in the fourth column. Then the overall expected value is just the sum of the individual expected values.

2. *Standard deviation.* An estimate of the standard deviation of any distribution (including the beta) may be found by dividing the range within which 99% of the values are likely to occur by six:

$$\sigma i = | b - a | /6$$

The standard deviation of each subsystem is shown in the fifth column. The overall standard deviation is the square root of the sum of the squares of the individual standard deviations. This value turns out to be much smaller than one would guess by just looking at the individual ranges. The reason is that some actual values will be lower than expected and others will be higher. Such variations cancel each other to some extent.

At this phase the results for SAVE were:

Expected value: $SS = 92,000$
Standard deviation: $\sigma = 10,422$
68% range: 81,578 to 102,422
99% range: 60,735 to 123,264

The chances are fifty-fifty that the actual value will turn out to be either greater than or less than 92,000 source statements. In each case the chance that the ultimate size will be in the range shown is qualified by the proviso that the input estimates do not change. Note that we have reduced the uncertainty significantly — from 15,000 to 10,422 — simply by knowing enough about the system to divide it into three major subsystems.

Functional design phase

When the functional design is a little more than half complete, a final investment decision must be made, as well as a manning plan, a life-cycle cost and a milestone schedule. At this time the preliminary specification and system design is nearly completed or at least reasonably well defined. System analysts and engineers should now be able to break the system down into its major functions and have a fairly good idea of the size range of each one.

Now we simply repeat the statistical process we have described, using the larger number of different functions. In effect, breaking the system down into more functions enables us to reduce the uncertainty in our estimate and to obtain a better estimate of the expected size.

The results with the greater number of functions now available are shown in Table A2. At the time of this analysis the project team had been working on the system about 12 weeks, and the key results were:

Expected value: $SS = 98,475$
Standard deviation: $\sigma = 7,081$
68% range: 91,394 to 105,556
99% range: 77,231 to 119,718

Several properties of the successive sets of data may be noted. The expected value of the size has remained within one standard deviation of the previous estimates. The size of the standard deviation has steadily declined — from 15,000 to 10,422, and on the third iteration to 7,081. In addition, what may be called our uncertainty ratio (standard deviation divided by source statements, or $\sigma SS/SS$) has dropped from 16% to 7%.

Table A2. Midway through the functional design phase of SAVE, the project team had enough information to break out 11 functions. At this level of detail the uncertainty (standard deviation) was reduced to less than half that of the first set of estimates. Moreover, at about ± 7 percent the uncertainty is no worse than that of many other engineering values.

Pert Sizing					
Title: Save (Functional Design Phase)				**Date: 15-Feb-79**	
Function	**Smallest**	**Most Likely**	**Largest**	**Expected**	**Std Dev**
Maintained	8675.	13375.	18625.	13467.	1658.
Search	5577.	8988.	13125.	9109.	1258.
Route	3160.	3892.	8800.	4588.	940.
Status	850.	1425.	2925.	1579.	346.
Browse	1875.	4052.	8250.	4389.	1063.
Print	1437.	2455.	6125.	2897.	781.
User Aids	6875.	10625.	16250.	10938.	1563.
Incoming Msg	5830.	8962.	17750.	9905.	1987.
Sys Mon	9375.	14625.	28000.	15979.	3104.
Sys Mgt	6300.	13700.	36250.	16225.	4992.
Comm Proc	5875.	8975.	14625.	9400.	1458.
Total				98475.	7081.

Moreover, the results of applying this sizing technique to SAVE — from early systems definition through functional design phase — were similar to our experiences with groups of analysts on other projects.

PART II

There is a fundamental relationship in software development between the number of source statements in the system and the effort, development time, and the state of technology being applied to the project. This relationship was discovered by Larry Putnam partly from theory and partly from an empirical fit of a substantial body of productivity data. The equation that describes this relationship is:

$$S_5 = C_k \, K^{1/3} \, t_d , \quad \text{where}$$

S_5 is the number of end product source lines of code delivered

K is the life cycle effort in man-years,

t_d is the development time, and

C_k is a state of technology constant.

Figure B1 shows a parametric graph of this equation. We have substituted development effort (DE) for life cycle effort (K) in this graph since this is usually the information that managers need. This relationship is approximately DE = $0.4K$ for large systems.

In Fig. B1 the darker line labeled constraint represents the minimum time in which a system can be developed. The area below this line represents the region in which it is not feasible to attempt development of a software system. For example, in this graph we can see that it is not feasible to develop a system of 200,000 lines of code in less than 2½ years. There are other constraint conditions, depending on the type of system. This particular constraint applies to a new standalone system that must be designed and coded from scratch.

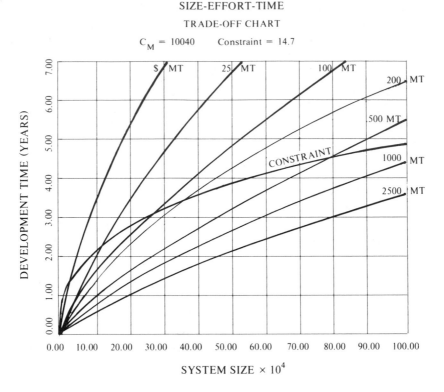

Figure B1

While this graph shows the functional relationship between size, time, and effort for all systems, the absolute values will differ for most organizations and even for different projects within a single organization. The C_k value in the equation determines what these absolute values will be (and actually represents the state of technology an organization is applying to a system). This value will be determined by the use of modern programming practices, the language used, the development environment (on-line, interactive development versus batch), and the availability of the development machine, among other factors. While C_k is difficult to determine from its individual components because identification of these components and their relative importance is not well understood, nevertheless this value can be calibrated easily for an organization by looking at past projects. The constant should remain quite consistent for similar projects within an organization. The C_k value used in Fig. B1 (10040) represents an average state of the art development environment using on-line, interactive development.

A feasible region for development

In PART I, we described a real world estimating problem for a system called SAVE. In this example, analysts were 12 weeks into the functional design of the system and had estimated the size to be 98,475, plus or minus 7,081 source statements. We will now use this estimate and the graph shown in Fig. B1 to establish a feasible region for our development effort and development time for this system. Table B1 presents three scenarios for five different points of the size distribution curve.

Table B1

	SS	t_d = 2 yrs		FASTEST TIME	
		DEV. EFF. (MY) (COST × $1,000)	t_d	DEV. EFF. (MY) (COST × $1,000)	
-3σ	77000	11.28 ($564.00)	1.63	25.80 ($1,290.00)	
-1σ	91394	18.86 ($943.00)	1.75	32.16 ($1,610.00)	
Exp	98475	23.59 ($1,180.00)	1.81	35.40 ($1,770.00)	
$+1\sigma$	105556	29.05 ($1,450.00)	1.86	38.71 ($1,840.00)	
$+3\sigma$	120000	42.69 ($2,135.00)	1.97	45.65 ($2,280.00)	

From this table, we can see that the minimum time for development of the system at the expected size (98,475 source statements) is approximately 1.8 years, with a corresponding development effort of about 35 man-years. However, if we take two years to do the job, we can reduce our effort to 25 man-years. We call this the trade-off law in software development. Basically, this law states that if we can relax our schedule, taking more time, we can save a considerable amount of money. Conversely, if we compress the schedule, the cost will go up dramatically.

To many managers this trade-off law may not make sense. However, as we noted above, there is a logical reason for it. As the number of people who must interact and work together on a project rises arithmetically, the number of interactions will go up geometrically. This results in more and more time being spent on human communication and less and less being spent on productive work. One way to handle this problem is to limit the number of people working on a project at any one time, and the only way to do this in software development is to stretch out the time schedule.

From Table B1 we can also see what the minimum time schedule (and maximum development effort) would be for a broad range of sizes. Using the probability laws, we know there is less than a 1% probability that the size will be less than 77,000 source statements (as long as our initial input estimates do not change). At this size, the minimum time would be 1.63 years with a development effort of 25.8 man-years. Similarly, at the 99% level for size, the minimum time is two years with a required effort of 45.7 man-years.

We now have estimates of the expected time and effort as well as a 99% range on these parameters. How do we determine the costs?

Most of the costs associated with software development are people costs. Any extra costs, such as computer costs, supplies, etc., can be factored into the average labor rate if we assume this rate to be a fully burdened number, including overhead. Every financial department has a very good idea of what this will be for its particular organization; in fact, this is the only really good (stable) number we have in software development. In many industrial environments, this will be around $50,000 to $60,000 per man-year; government labor rates typically run about 10% to 30% less because of different methods of accounting for overhead. For SAVE, we assumed an average labor rate of $50,000 per man-year.

Multiplying this value by the estimates of man-years, we get an expected total cost of $1.77 million, with the range going from $1.3 million to $2.3 million. While this may seem like a disconcertingly large range, it is the best we can do at this time, given the uncertainties in our estimates of size. Moreover, it is very important to know that this uncertainty range exists and how big it is. Better to be approximately right than exactly wrong!

Simulation and risk analysis

While Table B1 gives a fairly broad range of solutions that answer many "what if" questions, they are based on the assumption that we know the input information exactly. Of course, we don't. Each input into the software equation (e.g., "the expected size of the final system is 98,475 source statements") involves its own degree — often a high degree — of uncertainty. This is where the element of risk enters the problem, and it is in the evaluation of this risk that the software manager has been able to get little help from currently available tools and techniques.

Let us look, then, at what the software manager really needs to know before he makes an investment decision.

Suppose a company is considering bidding on a large software project. The "best estimate" of the company's development cost is $1.75 million. However, there is also a 1-in-4 chance that the cost will be as high as $2.5 million, and a 1-in-4 chance that the cost will be as low as $1 million. Suppose this were a small software house and if the actual cost came in at $2.5 million it would put the company out of business. Management would be taking a 1-in-4 chance of going bankrupt if only the "best estimate" (expected value) were used. If a risk analysis had been performed, management might have chosen a safer approach.

How, then, does one determine this risk? Since almost every factor entering into our estimate of cost and schedule is subject to some degree of uncertainty, the manager needs to portray the effects of the uncertainty associated with each of these factors. Our objective is to get a realistic picture of the relative risk and the probable odds of coming out greater or less than the expected solution.

This is generally not feasible to do analytically but is nicely handled by Monte Carlo simulation. To carry out the analysis for SAVE, we performed the following steps.

1. Estimate the range of values for each of the key input factors — size of the system, difficulty of the system (handled by the constraint condition described earlier), average software development labor rate, and the probability distribution of the occurrence of each value.

2. Select at random from the distribution of values for each factor a single value. Combine each of these values for all factors and compute the time, effort, and cost for this combination of factors. For example, one combination might be a system size of 110,000 source statements, a gradient constraint of 18, and an average labor rate of $58,000/man-year. (More factors can be entered, depending on the particular problem being analyzed.)

3. Run this problem on the computer several thousand times to define the outcome probability distribution. In other words, we want to find out not only that the expected (average) minimum development time is 1.8 years; we also want to know the probability of being able to complete the system by a contract deadline of two years.

The results of the simulation yield a much better estimate than just a single number answer. Note that the expected development effort is the same as the single point deterministic value. The expected development time is also the same. This is as it should be. The simulation produces the right expected (average) values. The real value of the simulation is an estimate of the variability of the outcome values — a feature heretofore not used in software cost estimating, but one that has been badly needed in view of the poor accuracy we have experienced.

The results of the SAVE simulation for development time, development effort, and development cost can be shown in the form of probability plots to generate the projections of risk as shown in Fig. B2. We can see from these plots that there is more than a 99% probability that the cost will not exceed $2.25 million. There is only a 1% probability (one chance in 100) that the cost will be as low as $1.25 million — given the uncertainties in our input information. As we learn more and more about the final system and development environment, we can reduce the uncertainties in our inputs, thereby reducing the risks in the final estimates.

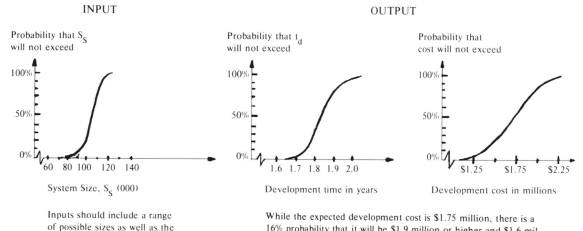

INPUT

OUTPUT

Probability that S_s will not exceed

System Size, S_s (000)

Inputs should include a range of possible sizes as well as the probability of occurrence of any value within that range.

Probability that t_d will not exceed

Development time in years

Probability that cost will not exceed

Development cost in millions

While the expected development cost is $1.75 million, there is a 16% probability that it will be $1.9 million or higher and $1.6 million or lower. In other words, management can be 68% certain that the cost will be between $1.6 and $1.9 million.

Figure B2

The result for the development time is extremely important from a conceptual point of view. The small variability is both a curse and a blessing. It says we can determine the development time very accurately, but at the same time it tells us we have little latitude in adjusting the development time to meet contractual requirements.

For example, the standard deviation is 0.063 years or 3.28 weeks; this means that our 99% range on time is 6(3.28) ∼ 20 weeks.

This means that there is less than a 1% chance that development can be done in less than 1.6 years or a little over 19 months (1.8 years − .19 years = 1.6 years). Therefore, if the time schedule has been arbitrarily set by management or the customer at, say, 1.5 years, there is less than 1 chance in 100 of meeting this schedule. Similarly, we can be 99% certain that the minimum time schedule will not exceed two years.

This does not mean that if requirements change or delivery of a computer is late, the software will still come in at plus or minus 10 weeks of the expected time. These are external factors that will change t_d (development time) and must be specifically accounted for.

This is the curse. The system is very sensitive to external perturbation. Requirements changes and external disturbances (say, a 90-day delay in test bed computer delivery) will generally cause development time increments greater than two or three standard deviations.

However, management can use the knowledge of this great time sensitivity effectively in planning and contracting so that risk is always acceptable. The critical point is that time is not a free good. Development time cannot be specified by management; it is determined by the system. Software systems are inherently narrow band processes with sharp cutoff characteristics, and decisions need to be made with the minimum development time known beforehand. Until this fact is recognized and used, software projects will continue to "slip" and "overrun."

Linear programming technique

The solutions just presented are based primarily on characteristics of the software system itself. However, most managers must also deal with everyday concerns, such as cost ceilings, contract deadlines, hiring practices, and capabilities.

Linear programming is a technique that produces the best possible solution to a problem bounded by an array of constraints. Typically, it is used on very large problems, such as optimizing the output of an oil refinery which is subject to such constraints as market demands and varying feedstock mixes. In the case of the software application, the mathematics is trivial, but all the power of the linear programming concept is brought to bear. More important, the manager has, for the first time, an opportunity to apply his own management constraints to the problem of developing large scale software systems.

The linear programming algorithm allows us to enter as many of these management constraints as we need into the problem. Then we can solve the problem to either minimize or maximize some objective function (such as cost). In our case, we have two objective functions — cost and time — and usually a manager wants to minimize one or the other. For SAVE, we will solve the linear program twice, first minimizing time and then cost.

Table B2 shows the constraints entered by the manager and the two solutions provided by the linear program.

Table B2

Inputs (Management constraints)		
• Maximum number of people available at peak manloading (hiring constraint)	28 people	
• Minimum number of people you want to have at peak manloading ("old faithfuls")	15 people	
• Maximum cost	$2 million	
• Maximum time (contract deadline)	2 years	
Outputs (Two solutions)		
	Minimum time	Minimum cost
t_d	1.83 years	2.0 years
Dev Effort (MY)	33.6 MY	24.4 MY
Cost	$1.68 M	$1.22 M

Our feasible development region is now identified in between these two solutions. In being able to invoke this powerful technique, we produce two constrained optimal solutions, the best that can be done within the constraints, and all other feasible effort-time choices. The simplicity of this statement should not cause us to overlook its importance. We have progressed from an inability to guarantee even one feasible solution to the ability to get all feasible choices and to select the best possible one from among those identified.

Let's examine the range of feasible, time-effort-cost combinations for SAVE identified in Table B3. This will let us identify excellent opportunities to save money on the project.

Table B3

Dev time (Years)	Man-years	Cost	
1.83	33.6	$1.68M	Min. time solution
1.87	30.3	$1.52M	
1.91	27.8	$1.39M	
1.95	25.5	$1.28M	
2.00	24.4	$1.22M	Min. cost solution

Note that we can save almost $500,000 by taking the maximum time and minimum cost solution. However, in doing this we increase our risk exposure. If we plan the job at $t_d = 1.8$ years and 35 man-years ($1.77 million), the probability that it will not take us more than two years to do is very high. But if we elect to take advantage of the trade-off law by planning the job at two years with 24 man-years ($1.2 million), we have reduced the probability that it will not take us more than the contract delivery time to 50%.

These odds are too low for most situations. However, a 90% probability may be very acceptable. This occurs at a planned development time of $t_d = 1.92$ years with 28 man-years of effort or $1.4 million. So it is possible to keep risk reasonable ($<10\%$ chance of exceeding delivery time) and save $300,000 compared with the minimum time solution.

The managerial questions — "Can I do it? How much? How long? How many people? What's the risk? What's the trade-off?" — can be answered with numbers.

With the application techniques described we have been able to quantitatively come to grips with the software cost estimating problem and produce reasonable engineering answers. We need only know the state of technology we are going to apply to development (C_k), estimates of the number of lines of code, and the software equation which we solve along with a constraint relationship to get the management parameters (K, t_d) of the Rayleigh/Norden equation. Simulation provides suitable statistics for risk estimation. The linear programming alternative provides constrained optimal solutions and the range of all feasible solutions.

The economics of the software development process is startling. The indications are clear that apparently innocent management choices can be made that affect cost by multiples of 5 to 10. With that kind of variation on multimillion dollar projects, managers need to know the choices, sensitivities, and influences they can bring to bear, over the whole life cycle, and in numbers.

PART III

Most large-scale software takes one to three years to develop and has an operational life of six to 10 years. This is a life cycle. We have studied the behavior of this life cycle, just as other businesses study the life cycle of a new product. We have developed a model of the software life cycle that can be used by management to forecast and manage the schedules and manloading requirements of software projects. Understanding the life cycle can help prevent managers from misapplications or inefficient management of the available manpower.

Large-scale software development can be thought of as a series of interrelated tasks. At the beginning of the project there may be only one or two major tasks, for example, defining the major system modules and the interactions among them. Each of these major tasks is broken into more and more subtasks. There must eventually come a time when the number of subtasks remaining reaches a peak, levels off, and finally begins to decline.

At the beginning of development, when only a few major tasks have been defined, only a few key people can actually do productive work on the project. These key people must become intimately familiar with the overall function and design of the system. They are responsible for breaking the problem down into manageable pieces — a task that becomes virtually impossible as more and more people are applied to it. However, as the problem becomes better defined, additional people can be applied successfully.

If people are applied as useful work becomes available for them we begin to see a manloading pattern like the one shown in Fig. C1.

MANLOADING PATTERN

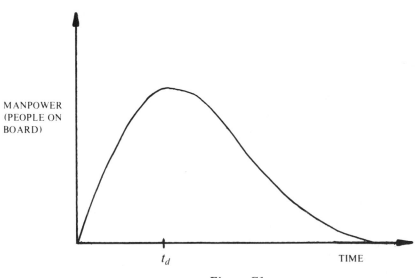

Figure C1

We have looked at data from hundreds of past software systems and noticed that almost all large software development efforts show a pattern of manloading very similar to Fig. C1. Moreover, for all large systems, the peak of the curve occurs at approximately the same time the system reaches full operational capability. (We will call this the development time for the system, and denote it as t_d.)

There is a logical reason for this. Just before the system reaches full operational capability, the total development task has been subdivided into many subtasks — testing and final integration, installation, writing documentation, fixing remaining bugs, etc. It is possible to have many types of personnel — programmers, analysts, quality assurance personnel, clerical, administrative and training support — all usefully employed. This was not true earlier in the development phase.

At the time the system is accepted and becomes fully operational we move into the operations and maintenance phase of the software life cycle. This corresponds to the falling part of the curve. The principal work during this phase is modification, minor enhancements, and remedial repair (fixing bugs).

The form of the curve and the accompanying equation allow us to project what the manpower requirements and cashflow for system development will be at any given time. The equation representing this curve is:

$$\dot{Y} = K/t_d{}^2 \bullet t \bullet e^{-t^2/2t_d{}^2} \text{, where}$$

K is the life cycle effort in man-years,
t_d is the development time for the system, and
t is the independent variable representing any point in the life cycle — current elapsed time.

Obviously, K and t_d can take on a range of values. A change in K or a change in t_d (or both) will result in a change in the shape and magnitude of the curve. Let's look at what this means to a manager faced with the real problem of applying manpower in the most effective way.

We will assume that $K = 100$ man-years for a given system. Figure C2 shows what happens to the distribution of this effort simply by varying the time to reach peak manpower. If the development of the system is set at two years, then the system would require a relatively gradual application of manpower, peaking at 30 people 24 months into the project. However, notice what happens when we reduce the development time to one year (assuming this were feasible) — this would require hiring and assimilating 61 people in 12 months. While this may be possible in some larger corporations, many organizations would find the practical problems associated with hiring — and productively applying — this many people in this short time nearly impossible.

This is a good example of what project management must contend with when the development time for a system is arbitrarily set by senior management.

There is another factor in software development that makes it unreasonable to try to compress development time. The tasks in a software project must interact with each other; for example, the initiation of one task may depend on the successful completion of a preceding task. Thus the software schedule can be compressed only so much; attempts to reduce it more will result in wasted effort, at best, and may even result in negative effort — work that will have to be redone.

Determining the best manloading

PART II of this article described a software estimating problem for a system called SAVE. We showed that there exists a fundamental relationship between the size of the system, the effort (K), the development time (t_d) and the state of technology an organization applies to the project. Using this fundamental relationship, we determined that the minimum feasible schedule for development of SAVE was 1.81 years with a corresponding development effort of 35.1 man-years and a life cycle effort (K) of 89.2

man-years. Because there was a time constraint on the system, management elected to develop the system in the minimum time (1.81 years).

ALTERNATE MANLOADING PATTERNS

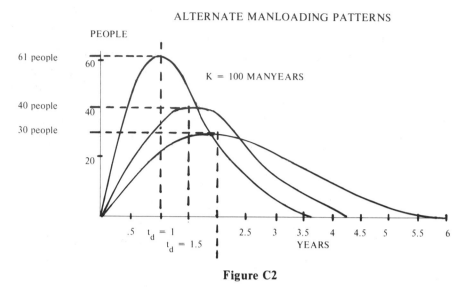

Figure C2

Using our manpower equation, we can determine the best manloading for this system over the 1.81 years, and even project ahead throughout the life cycle. We substitute our management parameters into the Rayleigh equation,

$$\dot{Y} = 89 \ / \ (1.81)^2 \bullet t \bullet e^{-t^2/2(1.81)^2}$$

Figure C3 shows a plot of the expected manloading for SAVE.

The range of values to either side of the curve in Fig. C3 represents the uncertainty in our estimate of how many people can be expected to be working on the project at any time. For example, our best estimate is that there will be 22 people working on the project one year into development, but there is a 16% chance that the number will be 19 or lower, and 25 or higher — simply as a result of the uncertainties in our estimates of K and t_d.

Every experienced software manager knows that behind most precise calculations in business are data that are not so precise. The software development field is certainly not excluded from this situation; in fact, the data in software development are notoriously imprecise. In this example, we had estimated that the life cycle effort was 89 man-years with a statistical uncertainty of ± nine man-years. Similarly, the minimum development was 1.81 years ± .063 years.

By solving the manloading equation several thousand times at each time interval, and varying our inputs (K and t_d) according to this statistical uncertainty, we can get a more realistic picture of the odds of having more or less people on board than the expected number at any time.

Now that we have a good estimate of the manpower requirements each month we can determine what our cashflow requirements will be throughout the project. All we need is the average burdened labor rate (including overhead) for software development. For this organization, we knew from past experience that this figure was $50,000/MY. Multiplying this figure by the manpower each month, we obtain the instantaneous and cumulative costs requirements shown in Table C1.

PROJECTED MANLOADING CURVE

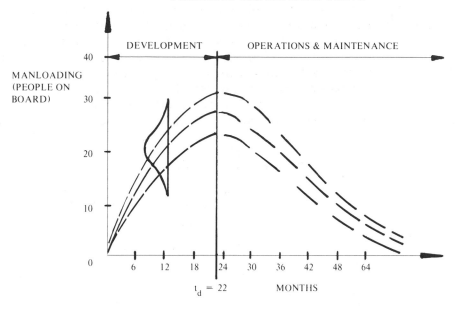

Figure C3

Table C1
Cashflow Projections

| MONTH | PEOPLE | | COST/MTH (× $1000) | | CUM COST (× $1000) | |
	MEAN	STD DEV	MEAN	STD DEV	MEAN	STD DEV
Jan 79	1.	0.	5.	1.	5.	1.
Feb 79	3.	0.	14.	2.	18.	3.
Mar 79	5.	1.	23.	4.	41.	7.
Apr 79	8.	1.	33.	6.	73.	12.
May 79	10.	2.	41.	8.	115.	19.
Jun 79	12.	2.	50.	8.	165.	27.
Jul 79	14.	2.	59.	11.	223.	37.
Aug 79	16.	2.	69.	13.	292.	49.
Sep 79	18.	3.	78.	15.	369.	62.
Oct 79	19.	3.	84.	15.	454.	76.
Nov 79	21.	3.	94.	18.	547.	91.
Dec 79	22.	3.	101.	19.	648.	108.
Jan 80	23.	3.	104.	19.	753.	126.
Feb 80	25.	3.	109.	19.	863.	144.
Mar 80	26.	4.	120.	21.	980.	164.
Apr 80	27.	4.	123.	22.	1104.	184.
May 80	27.	4.	126.	22.	1231.	206.
Jun 80	28.	4.	128.	23.	1359.	227.
Jul 80	29.	4.	136.	24.	1493.	249.
Aug 80	29.	4.	136.	24.	1630.	272.
Sep 80	29.	4.	136.	23.	1767.	295.
Oct 80	29.	4.	139.	22.	1905.	318.

An interesting pattern in the occurrence of major milestones during development can be seen. Data from several hundred systems representing all types of development environments have shown that the relative occurrence of these milestones to the total development time is extremely stable in most organizations and environments. This pattern has been noted even in organizations where the milestones have been arbitrarily (and often unrealistically) set by management; e.g., "Critical Design Review will occur three months after project start." In almost all these situations, the actual milestone accomplishment has slipped to the demands of the system itself.

Table C2 shows the time from project start that these major milestones should occur.

Table C2
Times of Major Milestones

EVENT	t/t_d	TIME FROM START (MONTHS) FOR 'SAVE'
Critical design review	.43	9
Systems integration test	.67	15
Prototype test	.80	17
Start installation	.93	20
Full operational capability	1.0	22

This analysis should be used not only as a planning tool, but can be very helpful in measuring actual accomplishment once the project has begun. Past data have shown that if a single milestone slips, there is little hope of catching up later on.

For instance, in the Table C2 plan, if we successfully accomplish the Critical Design Review at 11 months, rather than at nine months, we should rework our proposed schedule rather than trying to speed up development. One of the best methods of preventing severe slippages and minimizing the impact of any slippage is to recognize them early, bite the bullet right then, and immediately review project plans.

In the past, application software development has been unnecessarily characterized by cost overruns, manpower shortages, and schedule slippages. How much will it cost? How long will it take? What are the chances of the system not being operational on time? How many people will be required? Without reliable answers to these questions, a manager cannot expect to effectively manage the software development process.

A proven model of the software development process has been developed and used in this series of articles to provide numerical answers to the manager's questions. Some of the most powerful problem-solving techniques known today — the PERT algorithm, linear programming and simulation — have been simply applied to provide accurate size, cost, time, people, and milestone estimates for computer software systems development. Limiting constraints and viable alternatives are identified, permitting real design-to-cost and design-to-schedule options. Probability risk profiles can be calculated to provide the decision-maker with the hard numbers required to make sound decisions about software projects. Like ships upon the sea, software people need some numbers to guide them in the right direction at the right time to arrive on schedule at cost.

Section 6
METRICS

This section is concerned with the measurement of software, a field that has come to be known as *software metrics,* and contains six papers, published between 1967 and 1979. While the management papers reprinted in the previous section tended to take a macroscopic view of software, the papers in this section take a somewhat microscopic view: Their concern is with the atomic-level operation of computer programs — on a statement-by-statement basis.

Interestingly, many (although not all) of the papers in this section were motivated by intense interest in the so-called programmer productivity techniques that exploded upon the data processing profession in the early 1970s. Everyone had the impression that the concepts of structured programming were going to have an enormous impact upon the productivity and quality of computer programming — but exactly how much of an impact? And for that matter, exactly what did we mean by "productivity" and "quality"? The papers that follow shed some light on questions such as these.

Martin & Estrin: Models of Computations and Systems . . .

Written by David Martin and Gerald Estrin in 1967, our first paper is entitled "Models of Computations and Systems — Evaluation of Vertex Probabilities in Graph Models of Computations." When you read through it, you'll get a good idea of the kind of "metrics" that people were interested in in the late 1960s: measures of the *CPU speed* of computer programs! These days, it is rare for anyone to care how fast a computer program executes — if it isn't fast enough, one simply invests another $1.98 for a faster processor and/or more memory. I've included the paper for a single reason that is not at all apparent on first reading: The graphic models used in the paper provided the inspiration for "data flow diagrams" of the form introduced by Larry Constantine.* It's very doubtful that Martin and Estrin ever intended to provide the basis for new ideas in systems design and systems analysis — but, intentionally or not, they do indeed deserve a substantial amount of credit for their notions on graphics!

Sackman et al.: Exploratory Experimental Studies . . .

"Exploratory Experimental Studies Comparing Online and Offline Programming Performance" was written by Harold Sackman, Bill Erikson, and Ed Grant, and was published in the January 1968 issue of *Communications of the ACM.* It was written so

---

*See E. Yourdon and L.L. Constantine, *Structured Design: Fundamentals of a Discipline of Computer Program and Systems Design,* 2nd ed. (New York: YOURDON Press, 1978), pp. 38-41.

long ago that one might wonder how it could have any significance to our current life. But the paper presents statistics that are relevant as well as informative — and the fact that no other paper remotely like it has been published in the past dozen years suggests to me that it may well be read and consulted for many years to come.

There is a certain irony here, as there is with the earlier paper of Martin and Estrin, in that Sackman, Erikson, and Grant did not choose to address the field of software engineering or software metrics *per se*. It's true that they did share some concerns that we see in many current articles — as witnessed by the comment in the first paragraph of their paper: "As . . . computer hardware costs go down . . . the human costs of programming continue to rise and one day will probably greatly exceed hardware costs."

While this was indeed a rather prophetic statement, it must be read with an understanding of the authors' primary perspective: Because software development was already becoming a major issue, perhaps it would be appropriate to determine whether an on-line, software development environment was more cost-effective or less cost-effective than a batch environment. For computer professionals entering the field in the early 1980s, this seems inconsequential. Batch? What is batch? Of course all computer programmers have terminals at their desks — or at least some reasonable form of remote job-entry that ensures that they will see results of their compilations and test runs within a matter of minutes. It is educational — and perhaps humbling — to read that it wasn't always so.

But the major impact of the Sackman, Erikson, and Grant paper had nothing to do with the issue of on-line versus off-line; rather, it had to do with the fact that a dozen experienced people and nine trainees had all been put to work on the *same* computer problem, and that their performance had been closely monitored. This is something that had never been done before (according to the paper) and that has not, to my knowledge, been done since. Consider the typical EDP environment: Every programmer strives to convince his boss that his job is unique, and that it cannot be compared with anyone else's programming assignment. But in the Sackman, Erikson, and Grant study (and in similar informal experiments conducted by EDP teachers around the world), it was an entirely different situation: A group of people all had the same project, under the same conditions.

Were it not for this, the results might not have attracted anyone's attention. The fact that Sackman, Erikson, and Grant reported results from people who worked on the *same* programming problem has led to an enormous amount of credibility in their fundamental finding: *Within a group of experienced EDP professionals, there is likely to be an order of magnitude difference between the best and the worst.* Indeed, there are some areas in which the authors showed that the best performers were twenty-eight times better than the worst performers.

Most interesting about the Sackman, Erikson, and Grant study is their statement that, for experienced programmers, actual performance bore little statistical correlation to scores on a basic programming knowledge test. For those who spend a considerable amount of time reading programmers' resumes, this might not be a surprise — but it certainly does emphasize the authors' point that

> When a programmer is good,
> He is very, very, good,
> But when he is bad,
> He is horrid.

Halstead: Toward a Theoretical Basis . . .

In contrast to Sackman et al., most technical papers these days don't concentrate so much on the people who write computer programs — rather, they concentrate on the characteristics of the finished program. A good example of the latter approach is presented in "Toward a Theoretical Basis for Estimating Programming Effort," by Maurice Halstead. The paper provides a brief glimpse at the kind of ideas that Halstead eventually published in his book *The Elements of Software Physics,* and its basic premise is that one can *measure* the complexity of a computer program without knowing anything about the person who wrote it.

For decades, programmers have tended to associate program complexity with program length — longer programs are more complicated than shorter programs (except in APL). With any serious thought, though, anyone in the EDP field would agree that this is a crude measure at best — if nothing else, we must admit that some hundred-statement programs are more complex than other hundred-statement programs. But what is it that contributes to the complexity? Halstead argues that the complexity of a program is a direct function of the number of *operators* and *operands* in the program, and he provides a precise mathematical formula to express the relationship. More interesting, he provides some experimental evidence to demonstrate that his theoretical formula can give a good estimate of the length of time that will be required to develop the program. Other experimental studies (not reported in this paper) have also shown a strong correlation between the theoretical complexity of a program, as predicted by Halstead's formula, and the number of errors that were reported in the program after it was put into operation.

Intriguing though this paper may be, I must report that it has not yet had any significant impact in the EDP industry: The vast majority of EDP organizations still use the simpler formula relating complexity to program length — as illustrated in the typical programming standard, "Thou shalt not write a module more than fifty statements long." Perhaps Halstead's ideas are still a few years ahead of their time.

Walston & Felix: A Method of Programming Measurement and Estimation

"A Method of Programming Measurement and Estimation" appeared in the January 1977 issue of *IBM Systems Journal.* When it was first published, it was widely seen as a major endorsement of the "programmer productivity" techniques, for it contained impressive evidence indicating that, for example, structured programming had had a significant positive impact on productivity. But the paper is really much more than that: It is concerned with identifying *all* of the factors in a typical development project that might affect productivity — positively or adversely — so that a project manager might be better able to estimate the productivity of his own project. As was the case with many of the other authors whose work is reprinted in this book, Walston and Felix approached this job by collecting information from a sample of several existing projects — in their case, some sixty projects. The projects cover an enormous range — from one person-year of effort to a thousand person-years — and an enormous variety of applications, involving twenty-eight different high-level languages and sixty-six different types of computers.

The particular statistics that Walston and Felix present are indeed informative — it was interesting, for example, to see that design and code inspections apparently increased productivity by almost fifty percent. But the most valuable part of the paper is the identification of sixty-six project "variables" (for example, the decision to use, or not use, structured programming). Twenty-nine of the variables were found to have a significant impact on productivity.

Jones: Measuring Programming Quality and Productivity

With all of this emphasis on productivity, it is useful to read Capers Jones's article, which appears next in this section of the book. Jones makes two fundamental points: the units of measure with which we discuss productivity must be carefully chosen, and productivity should be discussed not only in terms of the *quantity* of the delivered product, but also its *quality.*

It has long been known that "lines of code" is a crude way to measure programming productivity — although that is the most common measure, and the one used in the Walston and Felix study discussed above. Jones presents a good summary of the well-known reasons why counting lines of code might give a misleading (or even false) measure of productivity; he also points out that emphasizing lines of code tends to discourage "re-usable" code.

After an initial discussion about measuring productivity, Jones makes what appears to be a rather abrupt switch to a discussion about programming quality — which he defines simply as the "absence of defects." Eventually, the connection between the two ideas becomes evident: Much of the job of programming is spent removing defects. Hence, better measurement of the defect-removal process, and better techniques for avoiding defects, can ultimately lead to higher productivity.

Woodward et al.: A Measure of Control Flow Complexity . . .

The final paper in this section is entitled "A Measure of Control Flow Complexity in Program Text," and was published in the *IEEE Transactions on Software Engineering* in January 1979. Unfortunately, as this journal is not as widely read as some others in the industry, the paper may not have had the readership it deserved. However, it summarizes simply and elegantly some ideas previously published in a more esoteric form by Tom McCabe and by Glen Myers.*

The basic premise is similar to Halstead's: There are characteristics of a program that contribute to its complexity, and these characteristics can be measured in a straightforward way. For Woodward, Hennell, and Hedley, the interesting characteristic is a "knot" — a situation in which a line of control flow, as represented on a flowchart, crosses another line of control flow. Knots are easy to identify, easy to count, and thus serve as an easily determined measure of program complexity.

As with Halstead's work, the disappointing aspect of this paper is that its ideas have not been adopted more widely. However, I think it deserves to be read and read again, and I expect that its influence may be more apparent in the years to come than it is today.

---

*See T.J. McCabe, "A Complexity Measure," *IEEE Transactions on Software Engineering,* Vol. SE-2 (December 1976), pp. 308-20; and G.J. Myers, "An Extension to the Cyclomatic Measure of Program Complexity," *Sigplan Notices,* Vol. 12 (October 1977), pp. 61-64.

Models of Computations and Systems — Evaluation of Vertex Probabilities in Graph Models of Computations

A priori estimates of expected computation time for given problems on given processing systems may be generated by modeling the computation with a transitive directed graph [1].

A computational algorithm is first represented by a directed graph containing cycles, with vertices representing macro-operations and arcs representing sequence, branching control conditions and data transfer. Cycles may then be removed in a systematic transformation resulting in a transitive directed graph [2−5]. The model of the computation can be assigned to a model of a computer system and a successive relaxation procedure used to obtain a suboptimal assignment and sequencing of tasks on machines. In this process a measure of expected path length, which takes into account branching probabilities, serves as a criterion.

A fundamental aspect of the above process involves the computation of vertex probabilities which are then used in computing the estimates of expected path length through a graph.

In this paper the nature of transitive directed graphs representing computations is discussed, a systematic enumerative procedure for calculating vertex probabilities is described, and then a more practicable algorithm useful in a priori assignment and sequencing experiments is established.

A computer program for calculating vertex probabilities is presented and results summarized for several graphs abstracted from complex problems.

SOURCE: D. Martin & G. Estrin, *Journal of the ACM*, 1967.

Graph model of computation

Consider a graph (such as Figure 8) consisting of two sets (W, U), viz., a set of vertices and a set of directed arcs which connect the vertices together; let us establish a correspondence between mathematical formulas and the graph.

A computational statement representing a formula specifies the generation of a set of data by means of a defined transformation upon the elements of another set of data. Let the input set be s_i and let s_0 be the set into which s_i is mapped through the transformation, f. Then we can write

$$s_0 = f(s_i),\qquad(1)$$

and we usually state that s_0 is a function of s_i. The formula (1) is represented graphically in Figure 1. If w_i represents an initial input operation, then the source of s_i is unambiguous. If w_i represents an interior operation in the graph, the input set for w_f may have been generated by w_i or its predecessors and transported to accessible storage until required. Under any conditions, the presence of the arc from w_i to w_f unambiguously establishes that the operation (computations) represented by w_f cannot be executed until w_i has generated s_i.

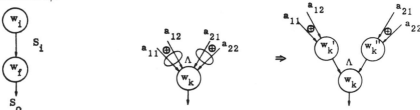

Figure 1. The operation represented by w_i generates s_i; the operation (function) represented by w_f "transforms" s_i into s_0.

Figure 2.

Vertex input logic

Since the computational tasks (vertices) represent functions whose arguments are either conveyed along the arcs incident into a given vertex or were previously stored in an accessible location, it is possible to specify when a given vertex may "begin" by writing a Boolean expression whose truth value indicates that all precedence conditions have been satisfied. There are three types of "vertex-input" logic described in what follows.

Conjunctive Input. Let a given vertex require *all* of several sets of data, each set coming from a different source (vertex). Let the availability of these sets of data be represented by Boolean variables, $a_1, a_2, \ldots, a_n$. Then the event "all data available" is represented by the truth value of the conjunction $a_1 \wedge a_2 \wedge, \ldots, \wedge a_n$.

Mutually Exclusive Inputs. Let a given vertex require only one set of input data, but let this set of data be generated from one of several mutually exclusive origins (vertices). Let the event "all data available" be represented by the Boolean variable, a_1, and its alternate forms by $a_{11}, a_{12}, \ldots, a_{1m}$. Then the condition for vertex initiation is

$$a_1 = a_{11} \oplus a_{12} \oplus \ldots \oplus a_{1m},\qquad(2)$$

under the condition that all the a_{ij} are mutually exclusive events.

Compound Input. If the initiation of a vertex requires *several* sets of data, each of which has several mutually exclusive origins, we are interested in the truth value of the expression $(a_{11} \oplus \ldots \oplus a_{1m}) \wedge \ldots \wedge (a_{n1} \oplus \ldots \oplus a_{nm_n})$.

For purposes of calculation it is convenient to decompose vertices with compound input logic into several vertices with simple, i.e., only $\land$ or $\oplus$, input logic. This is easily done by introduction of an appropriate number of pseudo-vertices as shown in Figure 2.

Whenever a computation is described in terms of INCLUSIVE OR input conditions we require a transformation such that only $\land$, $\oplus$ input conditions exist and thereby avoid complex definition of data distributions in the model.

Vertex output logic

The existence of mutually exclusive alternate origins of sets of data is due to the presence of *branching* or *decision* vertices in the graph. An arc incident out from a branching vertex may be traversed with a probability less than unity and may be selected conditional upon data being generated. In the usual language of computer programming such an operation is called a conditional transfer.

A branching vertex is defined as a vertex with EXCLUSIVE OR output logic as follows: If B is a Boolean variable representing the event that there is an output from a vertex and b_1, b_2, . . ., b_n are the Boolean variables representing *mutually exclusive events* at the output of the branching vertex, we can write

$$B \equiv b_1 \oplus b_2 \oplus . . . \oplus b_n, \tag{3}$$

where the two sides of the expression are logically equivalent [6].

Program flow may also occur from a given vertex along several different arcs simultaneously, i.e., there may be a bundle of arcs, each with the same origin vertex and different terminal vertices, that are incident out from a vertex (or pseudo-vertex) jointly. Then, if for any event represented by b_i as above, we define Boolean variables b_{i1}, b_{i2}, . . ., b_{im} such that there is a logical equivalence between any pair of b_{ij}, we can unambiguously denote the simultaneity of output arcs on the graph. We choose to use the symbol, $*$, to mark the logical equivalence of events on output arcs and obtain

$$b_i \equiv b_{i1} * b_{i2} * . . . * b_{im} \tag{4}$$

as a representation of simultaneous vertex output events. The $*$ output condition is sometimes referred to as an AND output condition in this paper.

If the sets $\{b_{j1}, b_{j2}, . . ., b_{jm_j}\}$, $j = 1, 2, . . ., n$, represent all of the possible output events that can occur upon completion of a vertex, then the occurrence of a compound output event will be represented by the expression

$$(b_{11} * . . . * b_{1m_1}) \oplus . . . \oplus (b_{n_1} * . . . * b_{nm_n}). \tag{5}$$

As in the case of compound input logic, pseudo-vertices are introduced to decompose compound output logic into simple output logic. This is illustrated in Figure 3 for the condition where w_k initiates w_a, w_b, w_c, w_d under the conditions $(w_a * w_b) \oplus (w_c * w_d)$.

Let us consider the probabilities associated with branching arcs. If w_i and w_j are origin and terminal vertices of an arc, u_{ij}, let the probability of reaching w_j via u_{ij} be q_{ij}. In general, q_{ij} is a conditional probability of traversing u_{ij} given that w_i has been reached. We now require that program flow be "conserved," i.e., if $u_{k1}, u_{k2}, . . ., u_{kn}$ are the mutually exclusive arcs incident out from a branching vertex w_k with simple EXCLUSIVE OR output logic, then

$$\sum_{i=1}^{n} q_{ki} = 1. \tag{6}$$

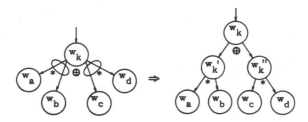

Figure 3.

It is instructive to compare our graphical network with two types of networks used in other contexts. The first is the PERT [7] network, in which all vertices have AND input and output logic. Hence all vertices are reached with probability one. Another special network is the graph representation of the sequential machine, where vertices correspond to the internal states of the machine and arcs represent the transitions between states. All vertices in the latter cases have EXCLUSIVE OR input and output logic and the arc traversal probabilities are the state-to-state transition probabilities. The probabilistic properties of such a network can be represented as a simple Markov chain. Our network is a more general form of these two cases and the computational probabilities are more difficult to determine.

Vertices

A computational vertex on a directed graph represents an unambiguously defined computational statement. The execution of the statement may imply the execution of several other more elementary operations or "microstatements." A certain amount of "fine structure" may not explicitly appear in the graph dependent upon the relative complexity of functions represented by single vertices. In fact the fine structure implied by any particular vertex might itself be represented by a graph whose characteristics are identical to those discussed above. Hence if the assumption is now made that vertex properties (such as time required for the operation) are known, then treatment of the problem of representing collections of vertices by a single vertex [2] will indicate the effect of the implied fine structure.

Vertex probabilities

In the following two procedures are considered for determining the probability, p_k, of ever reaching a given vertex, w_k, on the graph. It is assumed that the directed graphs are acyclic, that all vertices possess simple input and output logic and that all branching decisions are independent. A properly connected graph is defined as one in which $0 < p_k \leqslant 1$ and p_k is just the probability of w_k being linked to a subset of the set of origin vertices which have no logical predecessors.

Vertex probability computational procedure I

A partially ordered set of computations represented on a directed graph can be regarded as a collection of mutually exclusive subgraphs whose vertices possess no exclusive-OR input or output logic within any subgraph. These subgraphs we call AND-type subgraphs. Each branching vertex can be regarded as a multiway switch in which one and only one position (emergent arc) is selected each time the vertex is executed. Each switch position is chosen according to the set of arc traversal probabilities assigned to the arcs incident out from a given branching vertex.

If any given graph could be partitioned into a number of mutually exclusive subsets (AND-type subgraphs) whose union was equivalent to the set represented by the graph, then the following procedure would determine the probability of ever reaching a vertex w_i.

1. For each AND-type subgraph establish the arc traversal probabilities of all arcs contained in it.

2. Compute the probability of traversing each AND-type subgraph as the product of the arc traversal probabilities found in step 1.

3. Consider each vertex in turn and find the set of AND-type subgraphs containing that vertex. The probability of ever reaching that vertex is the sum of the probabilities computed for the subgraphs in step 2.

We are left with the need for a systematic procedure to find all the distinct AND-type subgraphs into which a computational network can be partitioned. It is helpful to introduce two structural indices associated with the vertices, called the precedence and ante numbers.

A connection matrix $[Z]$ describes graph linkages with a nonzero Z_{ji} entry whenever there is an arc u_{ij} from vertex w_i to vertex w_j. From $[Z]$ is obtained [2, 3, 5] a square Boolean precedence matrix, $[D]$, which has dimensions equal to the number of vertices, contains nonzero entries in its kth row to mark the predecessor (not necessarily immediate) vertices of vertex w_k and contains nonzero entries in its kth column to mark the successor (not necessarily immediate) vertices of vertex w_k. We define

$$d_k \overset{\Delta}{=} \sum_{1=1}^{N_w} d_{ki} \tag{7}$$

as the precedence number of w_k and

$$f_k \overset{\Delta}{=} \sum_{1=1}^{N_w} d_{ik} \tag{8}$$

as the ante number of w_k, where d_{ij} is an element of $[D]$ and N_w is the number of vertices in the graph. The precedence and ante numbers of a given vertex have certain properties that are simply related to the partial orderings between vertices, viz., if w_i precedes w_j then $d_i < d_j$ and $f_i > f_j$, but not conversely.

Now let S be the set of branching vertices in the graph and execute the following procedure.

1. Find the set of branching vertices S.

2. Let the set of (branching) arcs incident out from each $w_i \in S$ be U_i^+, and let I_i be the index set of the arcs in U_i^+, i.e., $u_j \in U_i^+ \longleftrightarrow j \in I_i$. Note that u_j just represents an indexing of the branching arcs emerging from a vertex w_i. We imply that we retain a mapping between the u_j and the previously described u_{ij}. Now form a distinct combination of indices $C(k)$ (the kth such distinct combination, say) by selecting one index from each of the index sets I_i, $w_i \in S$, and form the union set of arcs

$$V_k \overset{\Delta}{=} \bigcup_{j \in C(k)} u_j ,$$

(9)

where V_k will be used to form an AND-type subgraph as follows.

3. Find the set of arcs

$$E_k \overset{\Delta}{=} \bigcup_{w_i \in S} U_i^+ - V_k ,$$

(10)

i.e., the set of branching arcs which are *excluded* from the AND-type subgraph being formed.

4. We must now "purge" the graph, i.e., remove those vertices and arcs whose presence in the graph is precluded by the removal of arcs in E_k from the graph. To accomplish this with an iterative procedure we define $R_k(-)$ as the set of arcs and vertices removed from the graph during formation of the subgraph. Initially, $R_k(-) = E_k$. Define W_n as the set of vertices with precedence number n. Now, in order of increasing precedence number, examine all the vertices in the (original) graph as indicated in the steps that follow.

5. Examine the vertices in the sets W_0, W_1, W_2, etc., *in that order,* and determine their input logic. Let w_i be the vertex under examination. Determine the input logic of w_i:

    a. w_i *has* AND *input logic.* Find the set of arcs incident into w_i, viz., U_i^-. If any of the arcs in U_i^- are also in $R_k(-)$, add $w_i \cup U_i^- \cup U_i^+$ to $R_k(-)$, i.e., w_i and the arcs both incident into and out from w_i. If $U_i^- = \phi$, i.e., $w_i \in W_0$, no additions are made to $R_k(-)$.

    b. w_i *has* EXCLUSIVE OR *input logic.* If *all* the arcs in U_i^- are in $R_k(-)$, then add $w_i \cup U_i^+$ to $R_k(-)$. If not all the arcs in U_i^- are in $R_k(-)$, i.e., $U_i^- \not\subset R_k(-)$, then there should be one and only one arc in U_i^- not in $R_k(-)$. If there are more, then the input logic at w_i is not EXCLUSIVE OR, and the graph has improper logical structure. If there is properly only one arc U_i^- not in $R_k(-)$, $R_k(-)$ is unchanged.

6. When the complete set W has been exhausted, the vertices and arcs that have not been removed from the original graph, i.e., the set $(W, U) - R_k(-)$, constitute the AND-type subgraph that results from a choice of branching arcs whose indices are in the set $C(k)$.

All the other AND-type subgraphs into which (W, U) can be partitioned are found by repeating the above procedure using all other distinct combinations $C(k)$ defined in step 2 above. It is worth noting here that the procedure given above for finding the AND-type subgraphs into which a given acyclic directed graph can be partitioned depends not only upon the structure of the original graph but more importantly upon the input and output logic possessed by the vertices. Hence even though we select structurally distinct sets V_i and V_j, $V_i \neq V_j$, the AND-type subgraph completion procedure above may yield the same AND-type subgraph by the discarding of subgraphs reached with probability zero but containing index selected branching arcs. This point is illustrated by Figure 4, in which selection of $V \overset{\Delta}{=} \{u_{12}, u_{34}\}$ and $V' \overset{\Delta}{=} \{u_{12}, u_{35}\}$ yields only one AND-type subgraph $G = G' = \{w_1, w_2, w_6, u_{12}, u_{26}\}$. Furthermore, it must be noted that the above procedure is essentially enumerative and therefore the size of the problem must be considered. An upper bound for the number N of AND-type subgraphs obtainable from a graph containing n branching vertices with m_i arcs incident out from the ith branching vertex $i = 1, 2, \ldots, n$ is

$$\overline{N} = \prod_{i=1}^{n} m_i .$$

(11)

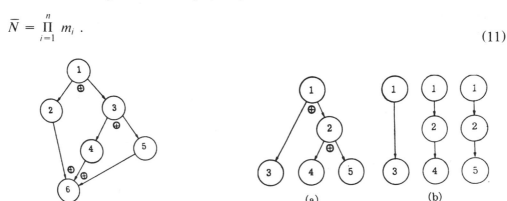

Figure 4. A graph illustrating the non-uniqueness of AND-type subgraph selection.

Figure 5. An example graph: a, original graph; b, partition.

The small example illustrated in Figure 5 indicates that N is generally much less than the upper bound. However, the complexity with which it might be possible to deal using the above enumerative procedure seems so small that we now leave aside this procedure and consider a nonenumerative procedure based on a more restrictive assumption about the original graph.

Vertex probability computational procedure II

A nonenumerative procedure becomes possible if a certain amount of semantics is introduced into the process of generating a precedence matrix which picks out select predecessors and successors only if they also satisfy logical conditions and maintain proper connectivity. The following discussion attempts to clarify these remarks.

Consider a vertex w_k in the interior of a graph. w_k is reached from a subset of the origin vertices via a subgraph consisting of w_k, its logical predecessors and associated connecting arcs. We choose to distinguish at this point between *structural* predecessors denoted D_k^- (defined by nonzero entries in the kth *row* of the matrix $[D]$) and the set of *logical* predecessors, denoted E_k^-, which are a subset of D_k^- that are reached with a nonzero probability given that w_k has been reached. In a similar vein, topological and logical *successor* sets D_k^+ and E_k^+ are defined. To clarify further it must be recognized that the subgraph consisting of the set of vertices $D_k^- \cup w_k$ and the associated connecting arcs can be partitioned into a number of distinct AND-type subgraphs. The condition for elements of the E_k^- sets is then equivalent to stating that a logical predecessor of w_k must be included in at least one of the distinct AND-type subgraphs into which $D_k^- \cup w_k$ and the associated connecting arcs is partitioned. A similar condition holds between E_k^+ and $D_k^+ \cup w_k$. It follows that

$$E_k^- \subseteq D_k^-, \qquad E_k^+ \subseteq D_k^+.$$

(12)

For illustration, consider the directed graph in Figure 6 where we have

$$D_5^- = \{1, 2, 3\}, \qquad E_5^- = \{1, 2, 3\}, \tag{13}$$

and Figure 7 where we have

$$D_6^- = \{1, 2, 3, 4, 5\}, \qquad E_6^- = \{1, 3, 5\}. \tag{14}$$

One very important difference between $D_k^{\pm}$ and $E_k^{\pm}$ lies in their determination. The sets $D_k^{\pm}$ can be obtained directly from the precedence matrix $[D]$. $E_k^{\pm}$ may require the enumeration of the AND-type subgraphs into which $D_k^{\pm} \cup w_k$ and the associated connecting arcs are partitioned.

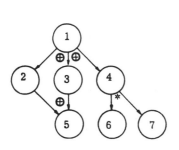

Figure 6. A graph in which $D_k^{\pm} = E_k^{\pm}$.   **Figure 7. A graph in which $D_k^{\pm} \neq E_k^{\pm}$.**

In the remainder of this study, we concern ourselves with directed graphs for which $E_k^{\pm} = D_k^{\pm}$, $w_k \in W$, a condition which holds for all the complex graphs encountered in our experiments [3] and which may hold always if the logic implied by the original computational formulas is retained in defining a graph and no artificial graph linkages are arbitrarily inserted.

With the above discussion in mind we proceed to describe a practicable algorithm for computing vertex probability.

Consider a subgraph G_k^- incident into a vertex w_k and including w_k. The probability, p_k, of ever reaching w_k depends upon the traversal probabilities of arcs incident out from branching vertices in G_k^-. We find the latter formulation useful whenever w_k has conjunctive input logic. In the case that w_k has disjunctive input logic we note that the probability of the union of a number of mutually exclusive events is equal to the sum of their individual probabilities of occurrence.

If we make use of the above observations and the assumptions that branching decisions are mutually independent and $D_k^{\pm} = E_k^{\pm}$, the algorithm for computing the probability of ever reaching a vertex w_k follows.

1.   Examine in order of subscript the vertex sets w_i, $i = 0, 1, 2, \ldots$, where i is the precedence number. Let w_k be a vertex under consideration.

2.   Find Z_k^-, the set of immediate predecessors of w_k. Four cases can occur:

       a. $Z_k^- = \phi$, i.e., w_k is an initial vertex and $p_k = 1$.

b. Z_k^- consists of a single vertex, e.g., $Z_k^- = \{w_a\}$. Then $p_k = p_a q_{ak}$.

c. Z_k^- consists of more than one vertex and w_k has exclusive-OR input logic. Then

$$p_k = \sum_{w_i \in Z_k^-} p_i q_{ik}.$$ (15)

d. Z_k^- consists of more than one vertex and w_k has AND input logic. We deal with a subset of D_k^-, S_k^-, which contains only the branching vertices preceding w_k. Then

$$p_k = 1 - \sum_{w_i \in S_k^-} p_i \sum_{w_j \in Z_i^+ - Z_i^+ \cap D_k^-} q_{ij}.$$ (16)

Computational experiments

Figures 8−12 depict graphs representing computations arising in X-ray crystallography (Figure 8), Numerical Weather Prediction (Figures 9, 10) and the Assignment and Sequencing Computation (Figures 11, 12).

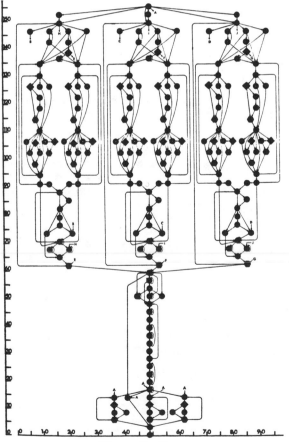

Figure 8. X-ray.

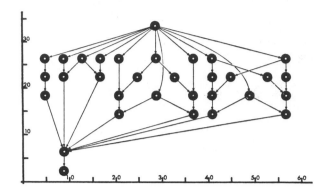

Figure 9. NWP32.

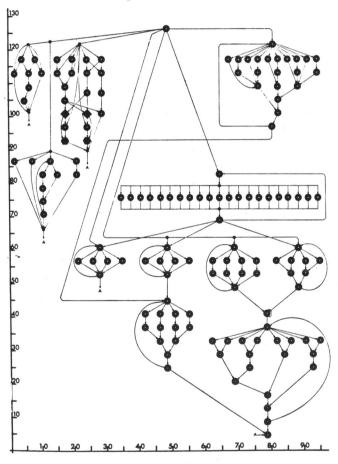

Figure 10. NWP147.

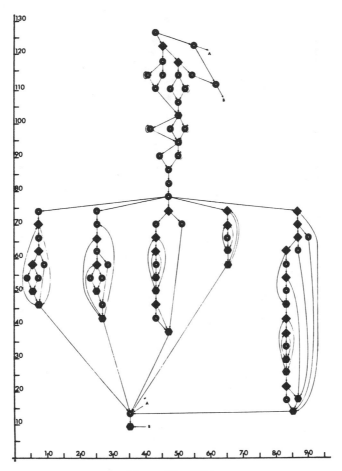

Figure 11. 82V

Cyclic to acyclic transformations [3] remove all feedback arcs leaving the nonfeedback topology unchanged but primarily affecting the estimated operation times. Instead of explicitly labeling the input and output control conditions, the vertex shapes are varied as follows:

1. Circle: AND INPUT, AND OUTPUT
2. Diamond: AND INPUT, OR OUTPUT
3. Hexagon: OR INPUT, AND OUTPUT

The OR input-OR output condition did not explicitly appear in the graphs studied. The coordinates are merely a convenience for locating vertices. Table 1 is a summary of graph statistics for the computations modeled as vehicles for assignment and sequencing experiments which used the vertex probability calculations.

The results of these computations then serve as inputs to programs which are used in assignment and sequencing of operations on computers and estimating the resulting expected computation time [3]. Figures 13–15 illustrate the preparation of graph description (LINK 1) and the assignment and sequencing perturbation process (LINK 2). The vertex probability computation occurs in the former.

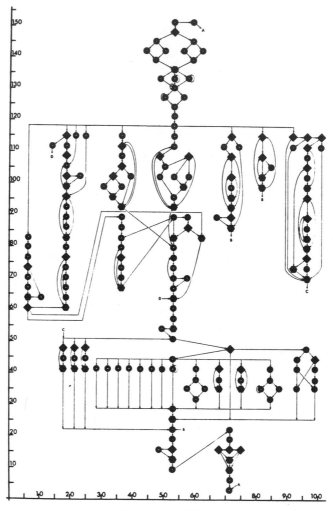

Figure 12. L2

Dependent branching decisions

Thus far, the vertex computational probability algorithm has been derived on the assumption that all the branching decisions executed in the computational network were mutually independent. We now modify our algorithm to include the case where the branching decisions are not mutually independent.

First of all, it would be instructive to give a couple of instances where nonindependence of branching decisions arises. Consider the following ALGOL statements:

$L1$: **if** $a_1 \leqslant x \; \wedge \; x \leqslant a_2$ **then go to** $L2$ **else go to** $L3$;
$L2$: **if** $a_3 \leqslant y \; \wedge \; y \leqslant a_4$ **then go to** $L4$;
$L3$: ...

$\qquad \vdots$

$L4$: ...

Table 1
Graph Statistics

GRAPH STATISTICS	GRAPH									
Statistic	NWP32		82V		NWP147		L2		XRAY	
No. of Vertices	32		82		147		193		223	
No. of Vertex Clusters	32		74		147		176		202	
No. of Arcs	47		129		246		294		413	
No. of Feedback Arcs (cycles)	0		14		12		24		45	
No. of Vertices with										
OR input logic	0		16		2		33		24	
OR output logic	0		21		2		40		24	
AND input logic	32		66		145		160		199	
AND output logic	32		61		145		153		199	
*	WFB	NFB	WFB	NFB	WFB	NFB	WFB	NFB	WFB	NFB
Avg. no. arcs input to any vertex	1.47	1.47	1.57	1.40	1.67	1.59	1.52	1.40	1.85	1.65
Max. no. of arcs input to any vertex	7	7	6	6	21	21	12	12	5	4
Avg. no. of arcs output from:										
any vertex	1.47	1.47	1.57	1.40	1.67	1.59	1.52	1.40	1.85	1.65
vertex w/AND output logic	---	1.47	---	1.18	---	1.59	---	1.22	---	1.61
vertex w/OR output logic	---	---	---	2.05	---	2.00	---	2.07	---	2.00
Max. no. of arcs output from any vertex	11	11	5	5	25	25	12	12	11	11

*WFB: includes feedback arcs; NFB: does not include feedback arcs.

These statements may be represented on a directed graph, with decision vertices represented by diamond-shaped boxes, as shown in Figure 16. Now if x and y are independent of each other, i.e., their values are not linked computationally or otherwise, then the arc traversal probability $q_{L2,L4}$ is determined independently of $q_{L1,L2}$. On the other hand, if x and y are computationally related, there is a conditional probabilistic relation between $q_{L2,L4}$ and $q_{L1,L2}$, determined by the relation between x and y, i.e., by the probability distributions of x and y over the intervals $[a_1,a_2]$ and $[a_3,a_4]$, respectively. In particular, let $y = Tx$, where T is a computation that maps x into y, and let $f(x)$ be the probability density function of x on the interval $[a_1,a_2]$. Then, knowing the relation $y = Tx$, we can determine the region, i.e., the union set of disjoint intervals, into which the interval $[a_1,a_2]$ maps. Although it is an abuse of notation, let this union set be denoted by $[a_1',a_2']$. We can then determine the probability density function of $y = Tx$ over $[a_1',a_2']$, and hence also the density function of y on the intersection set $[a_1',a_2']$ $[a_3,a_4]$. From this information, we can finally determine the conditional probability for $(y \in [a_3,a_4] \mid x \in [a_1,a_2])$, i.e., the probability that $y \in [a_3,a_4]$ given $x \in [a_1,a_2]$. Now if the branching decisions made in vertices $L1$ and $L2$ were statistically independent, the probability of executing vertex $L4$ would be

$$p_{L4} = p_{L1}q_{L1,L2}q_{L2,L4} \qquad \text{(independence). (17)}$$

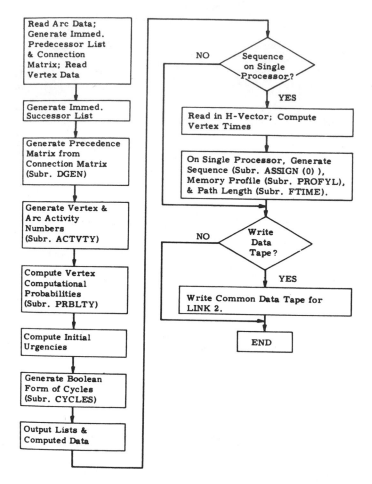

Figure 13. Flowchart of LINK 1 of the a priori assignment and sequencing program.

However, if these branching decisions were *not* statistically independent (as we have postulated), then

$$p_{L4} = p_{L2}q_{L1,L2}(q_{L2,L4} \mid q_{L1,L2}) \qquad \text{(dependence)}, \quad (18)$$

where $(q_{L2,L4} \mid q_{L1,L2})$ is the conditional probability of traversing arc $(L2, L4)$ given that arc $(L1, L2)$ has been traversed. The conditional probability $(q_{L2,L4} \mid q_{L1,L2})$ can be determined from the conditional probability for $(y \in [a_3,a_4] \mid x \in [a_1,a_2])$.

Let us give one more instance where the simplifying assumption of statistical independence is incorrect.

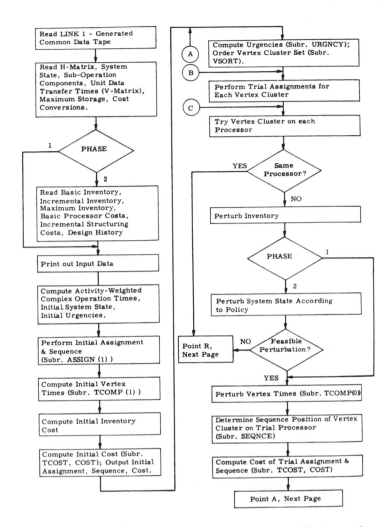

Figure 14. Flowchart of LINK 2 of the a priori assignment and sequencing program.

Consider the graph in Figure 17. The branching decisions in vertices 1 and 2 are made in parallel. Let $p_1 = p_2 = 1$, and let us compute p_3. Now the branching decisions classify the same datum, x, into the two classes c_1 and c_2, and we wish to determine the probability that $x \in c_1$ and $x \in c_2$. This probability clearly depends upon whether c_1 and c_2 do not intersect ($c_1 \cap c_2 = \phi$), partially intersect ($c_1 \cap c_2 \neq \phi$) or totally intersect (either $c_1 \cap c_2 = c_1$ or $c_1 \cap c_2 = c_2$). If $c_1 \cap c_2 = \phi$, it is clear that $p_3 = 0$ (this case would not be properly representable by the graph in Figure 17, since w_3 would be redundant). On the other hand, if $c_1 \cap c_2 \neq \phi$, then $(q_{23} | q_{13}) \neq q_{23}$. The conditional probability $(q_{23} | q_{13})$ is determined from a knowledge of the probability density functions of x on c_1 and c_2, and the relation between c_1 and c_2. Specifically,

$$(q_{23} | q_{13}) = \begin{cases} 0, & c_1 \cap c_2 = \phi, \\ (q_{23} | q_{13}), & c_1 \cap c_2 \neq \phi, \\ 1, & c_1 \cap c_2 = c_1 (c_1 c_2), \\ q_{23} / q_{13}, & c_1 \cap c_2 = c_2 (c_2 c_1), \end{cases} \qquad (19)$$

and hence, since $p_3 = q_{13}(q_{23}|q_{13})$,

$$p_3 = \begin{cases} 0, & c_1 \cap c_2 = \phi, \\ q_{13}(q_{23}|q_{13}), & c_1 \cap c_2 \neq \phi, \\ q_{13}, & c_1 \cap c_2 = c_1, \\ q_{23}, & c_1 \cap c_2 = c_2. \end{cases} \tag{20}$$

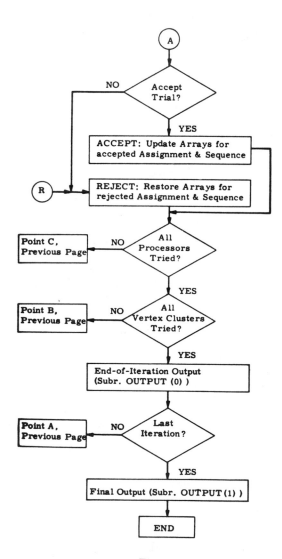

Figure 15.

In cases where there are more than two branching decisions that are dependent upon one another, expressions similar to the ones above can be written, except that the number of different cases might become large. Generally speaking, if we are concerned with n dependent branching decisions, then expressions of the form

$$q_1(q_2|q_1)(q_3|q_2q_1) \ldots (q_n|q_{n-1} \ldots q_1) \tag{21}$$

will arise where the q_i are arc traversal probabilities.

Let us now address ourselves to the problem of incorporating these cases into the vertex computational probability algorithm. Let us begin by assuming that we have chosen a particular vertex w_k, found the sets D_k^- and S_k^- and chosen the ith mutually exclusive AND-type subgraph. The probability that w_k will be connected to the origin vertices by means of the ith AND-type subgraph can be regarded as the probability of the joint occurrence of a number of mutually dependent binary-valued events, i.e., *dependent* Bernoulli trials. If $\{u_1, u_2, \ldots u_{m_i}\}$ is the set of arcs in the ith AND-type subgraph and $\{q_1, q_2, \ldots, q_{m_i}\}$ is the set of corresponding arc traversal probabilities, then the probability that all the arcs will be traversed is

$$p_{ki} = q_1(q_2 \mid q_1) \ldots (q_{m_i} \mid q_{m_{i-1}} \ldots q_1). \tag{22}$$

Now those conditional arc traversal probabilities that correspond to arcs incident out from nonbranching vertices represent events that occur with certainty, and hence they are really not conditional upon the outcome of any of the branching decisions. Thus, as before, these unity probabilities need not be included in the formula for p_{ki}. Hence,

$$p_{ki} = q_1(q_2 \mid q_1) \ldots q_{m_i}' \mid q_{m_{i-1}}' \ldots q_1), \tag{23}$$

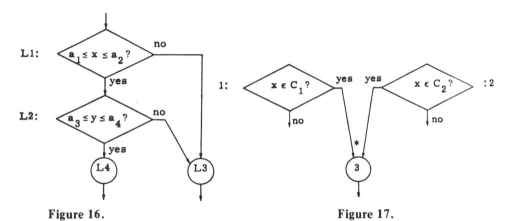

Figure 16.   Figure 17.

where $\{u_1, u_2, \ldots, u_{m_i}\}$ represents the set of arcs incident out from branching vertices in the ith AND-type subgraph. Having computed all the p_{ki}, we may obtain p_k through

$$p_k = \sum_i p_{ki}. \tag{24}$$

The foregoing algorithm is an extension of the enumerative vertex computational probability algorithm previously derived, and it presumes that sufficient information is available for the evaluation of all the required conditional arc traversal probabilities.

Unfortunately, due to the conditional relations between the various arc traversal probabilities, our extended algorithm cannot be recast into a more compact form as was done when the branching decisions were mutually independent. Hence, the extended algorithm remains essentially enumerative.

Conclusion

This paper has formulated procedures for determining the probability of reaching vertices in a transitive directed graph representation of computations and has discussed a number of problems arising in such modeling.

The algorithms are essential to methods for a priori estimation of computation time on models of computer systems and have proven themselves effective in a number of experimental studies.

Further work is needed to handle branching dependency, to automatically generate estimates of arc traversal probabilities from initial formulas or programs and to test for improperly connected graphs.

Other papers will deal with cyclic to acyclic transformations, path length calculations and experiments in automatic assignment and sequencing.

References: Martin & Estrin

1. Berge, C. *The Theory of Graphs and Its Applications.* John Wiley & Sons, New York, 1962.

2. Estrin, G., and Turn, R. Automatic assignment of computations in a variable structure computer system. *IEEE Trans. EC-12* (Dec. 1963), 755-773.

3. Martin, D. The automatic assignment and sequencing of computations on parallel processor systems. Ph.D. thesis, U. of California, Los Angeles, Jan. 1966.

4. Elmaghraby, S.E. An algebra for the analysis of generalized activity networks. *Manage. Sci. 10* (April 1964), 494-514.

5. Russell, E.C. Automatic assignment of computational tasks in a variable structure computer. M.S. thesis in Engineering, U. of California, Los Angeles, 1963.

6. Carnap, R. *Introduction to Symbolic Logic and Its Applications.* Dover Publications, New York, 1958, pp. 19-23.

7. Kelley, J.E., Jr. Parametric programming and the primal-dual algorithm. *Oper. Res. 7* (May-June 1959), 327-334.

Exploratory Experimental Studies Comparing Online and Offline Programming Performance

Introduction

Computer programming is a multibillion dollar industry. Major resources are being expended on the development of new programming languages, new software techniques, and improved means for man-computer communications. As computer power grows and computer hardware costs go down because of the advancing computer technology, the human costs of computer programming continue to rise and one day will probably greatly exceed hardware costs.

Amid all these portents of the dominating role that computer programming will play in the emerging computer scene, one would expect that computer programming would be the object of intensive applied scientific study. This is not the case. There is, in fact, an applied scientific *lag* in the study of computer programmers and computer programming — a widening and critical lag that threatens the industry and the profession with the great waste that inevitably accompanies the absence of systematic and established methods and findings and their substitution by anecdotal opinion, vested interests, and provincialism.

The problem of the applied scientific lag in computer programming is strikingly highlighted in the field of online versus offline programming. The spectacular increase in the number of time-shared computing systems over the last few years has raised a critical issue for many, if not most, managers of computing facilities. Should they or should they not convert from a batch-processing operation, or from some other form of noninteractive information processing, to time-shared operations? Spirited controversy has been generated at professional meetings, in the literature, and at grass roots, but virtually no exper-

SOURCE: H. Sackman, W.J. Erikson & E.E. Grant, *Communications of the ACM,* 1968.

imental comparisons have been made to test and evaluate these competing alternatives objectively under controlled conditions. Except for related studies by Gold 1967 [4], and by Schatzoff, Tsao, and Wiig 1967 [11], the two experimental studies reported in this paper are, to our knowledge, the first on this central issue to have appeared. They illustrate the problems and pitfalls in doing applied experimental work in computer programming. They spell out some of the key dimensions of the scientific lag in computer programming, and they provide some useful guidelines for future work.

Time-sharing systems, because of requirements for expanded hardware and more extensive software, are generally more expensive than closed-shop systems using the same central computer. Time-sharing advocates think that such systems more than pay for themselves in convenience to the user, in more rapid program development, and in manpower savings. It appears that most programmers who have worked with both time-sharing and closed-shop systems are enthusiastic about the online way of life.

Time sharing, however, has its critics. Their arguments are often directed at the efficiency of time sharing; that is, at how much of the computational power of the machine is actually used for productive data processing as opposed to how much is devoted to relatively nonproductive functions (program swapping, idle time, etc.). These critics (see Patrick 1963 [8], Emerson 1965 [2], and Macdonald 1965 [7]) claim that the efficiency of time-sharing systems is questionable when compared to modern closed-shop methods, or with economical small computers. Since online systems are presumably more expensive than offline systems, there is little justification for their use except in those situations where online access is mandatory for system operations (for example, in realtime command and control systems). Time-sharing advocates respond to these charges by saying that, even if time sharing is more costly with regard to hardware and operating efficiency, the savings in programmer man-hours and in the time required to produce working programs more than offset such increased costs. The critics, however, do not concede this point either. Many believe that programmers grow lazy and adopt careless and inefficient work habits under time sharing. In fact, they claim that instead of improving, programmer performance is likely to deteriorate.

The two exploratory studies summarized here are found in Grant and Sackman 1966 [5] and in Erikson 1966 [3]. The original studies should be consulted for technical details that are beyond the scope of this paper. They were performed by the System Development Corporation for the Advanced Research Projects Agency of the Department of Defense. The first study is concerned with online versus offline debugging performance for a group of twelve experienced programmers (average of seven years' experience). The second investigation involved nine programmer trainees in a comparison of interactive versus noninteractive program debugging. The highlights of each study are discussed in turn, and the composite results are interpreted in the concluding section. For easier reference, the first experiment is described as the "Experienced Programmer" study, and the second as the "Programmer Trainee" study.

The two experiments were conducted using the SDC Time-Sharing System (TSS) under the normal online condition and simulated offline or noninteractive conditions. TSS is a general purpose system (see Schwartz, Coffman, and Weissman 1964 [14], and Schwartz and Weissman 1967 [15]) similar in many respects to the Project MAC system (see Scherr 1966 [12]) at the Massachusetts Institute of Technology. Schwartz 1965 [13] has characterized this class of time-sharing system as providing four important properties to the user: "instantaneous" response, independent operation for each user, essentially simultaneous operation for several users, and general purpose capability.

TSS utilizes an IBM AN/FSQ-32 computer. The following is a general description of its operation. User programs are stored on magnetic tape or in disk file memory. When a user wishes to operate his program, he goes to one of several teletype consoles; these consoles are direct input/output devices to the Q-32. He instructs the computer, through the teletype, to load and activate his program. The system then loads the program either from the disk file or from magnetic tape into active storage (drum memory). All currently operating programs are stored on drum memory and are transferred, one at a time, in turn, into core memory for processing. Under TSS scheduling control, each program is processed for a short amount of time (usually a fraction of a second) and is then replaced in active storage to await its next turn. A program is transferred to core only if it requires processing; otherwise it is passed up for that turn. Thus, a user may spend as much time as he needs thinking about what to do next without wasting the computational time of the machine. Although a time-sharing system processes programs sequentially and discontinuously, it gives users the illusion of simultaneity and continuity because of its high speed.

1. Experienced programmer study

1.1 Experimental design

The design used in this experiment is illustrated in Figure 1.

	Online		*Offline*	
GROUP I	Algebra	(6)	Maze	(6)
GROUP II	Maze	(6)	Algebra	(6)
Totals		(12)		(12)

Figure 1. Experimental design for the experienced programmer study.

The 2 × 2 Latin-square design with repeated measures for this experiment should be interpreted as follows. Two experimental groups were employed with six subjects in each; the two experimental treatments were online and offline program debugging; and the Algebra and Maze problems were the two types of programs that were coded and debugged. Repeated measures were employed in that each subject, serving as his own control, solved one problem task under online conditions and the other under offline conditions. Note in Figure 1 that each of the two program problems appears once, and only once, in each row and column to meet the requirements of the 2 × 2 Latin-square. Subjects were assigned to the two groups at random, and problem order and online/offline order were counterbalanced.

The statistical treatment for this design involves an analysis of variance to test for the significance of mean differences between the online and offline conditions and between the Algebra and Maze problems. There are two analyses of variance, corresponding to the two criterion measures — one for programmer man-hours spent in debugging and the other for central processor time. A leading advantage of the Latin-square design for this experiment is that each analysis of variance incorporates a total of 24 measurements. This configuration permits maximum pooled sample size and high statistical efficiency in the analysis of the results — especially desirable features in view of the small subject samples that were used.

1.2 Method

A number of problems were encountered in the design and conduct of this experiment. Many are illustrative of problems in experimenting with operational computer systems, and many stemmed from lack of experimental precedent in this area. Key problems are described below.

1.2.1 *Online and Offline Conditions.* Defining the online condition posed no problems. Programmers debugging online were simply instructed to use TSS in the normal fashion. All the standard features of the system were available to them for debugging. Defining the offline condition proved more difficult. It was desired to provide a controlled and uniform turnaround time for the offline condition. It was further desired that this turnaround time be short enough so that subjects could be released to their regular jobs and the experiment completed in a reasonable amount of time; on the other hand, the turnaround time had to be long enough to constitute a significant delay. The compromise reached was two hours — considerably shorter than most offline systems and yet long enough so that most of the programmer-subjects complained about the delay.

It was decided to simulate an offline system using TSS and the Q-32 by requiring the programmer to submit a work request to a member of the experimental staff to have his program operated. The work request contained specific instructions from the programmer on the procedures to be followed in running the program — essentially the same approach used in closed-shop computer facilities. Strictly speaking, then, this experiment was a comparison between online and *simulated* offline operations.

Each programmer was required to code his own program using his own logic and to rely on the specificity of the problem requirements for comparable programs. Program coding procedures were independent of debugging conditions; i.e., regardless of the condition imposed for checkout — online or offline — all programmers coded offline. Programmers primarily wrote their programs in JTS (JOVIAL Time-Sharing — a procedure-oriented language for time sharing).

1.2.2 *Experimental Problems.* Two program problem statements were designed for the experiment. One problem required the subjects to write a program to interpret teletype-inserted, algebraic equations. Each equation involved a single dependent variable. The program was required to compute the value of the dependent variable, given teletype-inserted values for the independent variables, and to check for specific kinds of errors in teletype input. All programmers were referred to a published source (Samelson and Bauer 1960 [10]) for a suggested workable logic to solve the problem. Programs written to solve this problem were referred to as Algebra programs.

The other problem called for writing a program to find the one and only path through a 20 × 20 cell maze. The programs were required to print out the designators of the cells constituting the path. Each cell was represented as an entry in a 400-item table, and each entry contained information on the directions in which movement was possible from the cell. These programs were referred to as Maze programs.

1.2.3 *Performance Measures.* Debugging time was considered to begin when the programmer had coded and compiled a program with no serious format errors detected by the compiler. Debugging was considered finished when the subject's program was able to process, without errors, a standard set of test inputs. Two basic criterion measures were collected for comparing online and offline debugging — programmer man-hours and central processor (CPU) time.

Man-hours for debugging were actual hours spent on the problem by the programmer (including turnaround time). Hours were carefully recorded by close personal observation of each programmer by the experimental staff in conjunction with a daily time log kept by the subjects. Discrepancies between observed time and reported time were resolved by tactful interviewing. TSS keeps its own accounting records on user activity; these records provided accurate measures of the central processor time used by each subject. The recorded CPU time included program execute time, some system overhead time, and times for dumping the contents of program or system registers.

A variety of additional measures was obtained in the course of the experiment to provide control data, and to obtain additional indices of programmer performance. Control measures included: TSS experience, general programming experience (excluding TSS experience), type of programming language used (JTS or machine language), and the number of computer runs submitted by each subject in the offline condition. Additional programmer performance measures included: man-hours spent on each program until a successful pass was made through the compiler (called coding time), program size in machine instructions, program running time for a successful pass through the test data, and scores on the Basic Programming Knowledge Test (BPKT) — a paper-and-pencil test developed by Berger, et al., 1966 [1] at the University of Southern California.

1.3 Results

1.3.1 *Criterion Performance.* Table I shows the means and standard deviations for the two criterion variables, debug man-hours and CPU time. These raw score values show a consistent and substantial superiority for online debug man-hours, from 50 percent to 300 percent faster than the offline condition. CPU time shows a reverse trend; the offline condition consistently required about 30 percent less CPU time than the online mode. The standard deviations are comparatively large in all cases, reflecting extensive individual differences. Are these results statistically significant with such small samples?

Table I
Experienced Programmer Performance

| | DEBUG MAN-HOURS | | | |
| | Algebra | | Maze | |
	Online	Offline	Online	Offline
Mean	34.5	50.2	4.0	12.3
SD	30.5	58.9	4.3	8.7

| | CPU TIME (sec) | | | |
| | Algebra | | Maze | |
	Online	Offline	Online	Offline
Mean	1266	907	229	191
SD	473	1067	175	136

Table II shows three types of analysis of variance applied to the Latin-square experimental design. The first is a straightforward analysis of raw scores. The second is an analysis of square root transformed scores to obtain more normal distributions. The third is also an analysis of variance on the square root scores but with the covariance associated with programmer coding skill parceled out statistically; that is, individuals were effectively equated on coding skill so that online/offline differences could be tested more directly.

Table II
Comparative Results of Three Analyses of Variance

Performance measures	Significance levels		
	Raw Scores	Square root	Square root with covariance
1. DEBUG MAN-HOURS			
Online vs. Offline	None	.10	.025
Algebra vs. Maze	.025	.001	.10
2. CPU TIME			
Online vs. Offline	None	None	None
Algebra vs. Maze	None	.001	.05

These applications resulted in six analyses of variance (three for each criterion measure) as shown in Table II. The columns in Table II represent the three kinds of analysis of variance; the rows show the two criterion measures. For each analysis of variance, tests for mean differences compared online versus offline performance and Algebra versus Maze differences. The entries in the cells show the level of statistical significance found for these two main effects for each of the six analyses of variance.

The results in Table II reveal key findings for this experiment. The first row shows results for online versus offline performance as measured by debug man-hours. The raw score analysis of variance shows no significant differences. The analysis on square root transformed scores shows a 10 percent level of significance in favor of online performance. The last analysis of variance, with covariance, on square root scores, shows statistically significant differences in favor of the online condition at the .025 level. This progressive trend toward more clearcut mean differences for shorter debug man-hours with online performance reflects the increasing statistical control over individual differences in the three types of analyses. In contrast to debug man-hours, no significant trend is indicated for online versus offline conditions for CPU time. If real differences do exist along the lines indicated in Table I for more CPU time in the online mode, these differences were not strong enough to show statistical significance with these small samples and with the large individual differences between programmers, even with the square root and covariance transformations.

The results for Algebra versus Maze differences were not surprising. The Algebra task was obviously a longer and harder problem than the Maze task, as indicated by all the performance measures. The fairly consistent significant differences between Algebra and Maze scores shown in Table II reflect the differential effects of the three tests of analysis of variance, and, in particular, point up the greater sensitivity of the square root transformations over the original raw scores in demonstrating significant problem differences.

1.3.2 *Individual Differences.* The observed ranges of individual differences are listed in Table III for the ten performance variables measured in this study. The ratio between highest and lowest values is also shown.

Table III
Range of Individual Differences in Programming Performance

Performance measure	Poorest score	Best score	Ratio
1. Debug hours Algebra	170	6	28:1
2. Debug hours Maze	26	1	26:1
3. CPU time Algebra (sec)	3075	370	8:1
4. CPU time Maze (sec)	541	50	11:1
5. Code hours Algebra	111	7	16:1
6. Code hours Maze	50	2	25:1
7. Program size Algebra	6137	1050	6:1
8. Program size Maze	3287	651	5:1
9. Run time Algebra (sec)	7.9	1.6	5:1
10. Run time Maze (sec)	8.0	.6	13:1

Table III points up the very large individual differences, typically by an order of magnitude, for most performance variables. To paraphrase a nursery rhyme:

> When a programmer is good,
> He is very, very good,
> But when he is bad,
> He is horrid.

The "horrid" portion of the performance frequency distribution is the long tail at the high end, the positively skewed part which shows that one poor performer can consume as much time or cost as 5, 10, or 20 good ones. Validated techniques to detect and weed out these poor performers could result in vast savings in time, effort, and cost.

To obtain further information on these striking individual differences, an exploratory factor analysis was conducted on the intercorrelations of 15 performance and control variables in the experimental data. Coupled with visual inspection of the empirical correlation matrix, the main results were:

a. A substantial performance factor designated as "programming speed," associated with faster coding and debugging, less CPU time, and the use of a higher order language.

b. A well-defined "program economy" factor marked by shorter and faster running programs, associated to some extent with greater programming experience and with the use of machine language rather than higher order language.

This concludes the description of the method and results of the first study. The second study on programmer trainees follows.

2. Programmer trainee study

2.1 Experimental design

A 2 × 2 Latin-square design was also used in this experiment. With this design, as shown in Figure 2, the Sort Routine problem was solved by Group I (consisting of four subjects) in the noninteractive mode and by Group II (consisting of the other five subjects) in the interactive mode. Similarly, the second problem, a Cube Puzzle, was worked by Group I in the interactive mode and by Group II in the noninteractive mode.

Analysis of variance was used to test the significance of the differences between the mean values of the two test conditions (interactive and noninteractive) and the two problems. The first (test conditions) was the central experimental inquiry, and the other was of interest from the point of view of control.

	Interactive	*Noninteractive*
GROUP I (4)	Cube Puzzle	Sort Routine
GROUP II (5)	Sort Routine	Cube Puzzle
Total	9 Subjects	

Figure 2. Experimental design for the programmer trainee study

2.2 Method

Nine programmer trainees were randomly divided into two groups of four and five each. One group coded and debugged the first problem interactively while the other group did the same problem in a noninteractive mode. The two groups switched computer system type for the second problem. All subjects used TINT (Kennedy 1965 [6]) for both problems. (TINT is a dialect of JOVIAL that is used interpretively with TSS.)

2.2.1 *Interactive and Noninteractive Conditions.* "Interactive," for this experiment, meant the use of TSS and the TINT language with all of its associated aids. No restrictions in the use of this language were placed upon the subjects.

The noninteractive condition was the same as the interactive except that the subjects were required to quit after every attempted execution. The subjects ran their own programs under close supervision to assure that they were not inadvertently running their jobs in an interactive manner. If a member of the noninteractive group immediately saw his error and if there were no other members of the noninteractive group waiting for a teletype, then, after he quit, he was allowed to log in again without any waiting period. Waiting time for an available console in the noninteractive mode fluctuated greatly but typically involved minutes rather than hours.

2.2.2 *Experimental Problems.* The two experimental tasks were relatively simple problems that were normally given to students by the training staff. The first involved writing a numerical sort routine, and the second required finding the arrangement of four specially marked cubes that met a given condition. The second problem was more difficult than the first, but neither required more than five days of elapsed time for a solution by any subject. The subjects worked at each problem until they were able to produce a correct solution with a run of their program.

2.2.3 *Performance Measures.* CPU time, automatically recorded for each trainee, and programmer man-hours spent debugging the problem, recorded by individual work logs, were the two major measures of performance. Debugging was assumed to begin when a subject logged in for the first time, that is, after he had finished coding his program at his desk and was ready for initial runs to check and test his program.

2.3 Results

2.3.1 *Criterion Performance.* A summary of the results of this experiment is shown in Table IV. Analysis of variance showed the difference between the raw score mean values of debug hours for the interactive and the noninteractive conditions to be significant at the .13 level. The difference between the two experimental conditions for mean values of CPU seconds was significant at the .08 level. In both cases, better performance (faster solutions) was obtained under the interactive mode. In the previous experiment, the use of square root transformed scores and the use of coding hours as a covariate allowed better statistical control over the differences between individual subjects. No such result was found in this experiment.

Table IV
Programmer Trainee Performance

| | DEBUG MAN-HOURS | | | |
| | Sort Routine | | Cube Puzzle | |
	Interactive	Noninteractive	Interactive	Noninteractive
Mean	0.71	4.7	9.2	13.6
SD	0.66	3.5	4.2	7.0
	CPU TIME (sec)			
	Sort Routine		Cube Puzzle	
	Interactive	Noninteractive	Interactive	Noninteractive
Mean	11.1	109.1	290.2	875.3
SD	9.9	65.6	213.0	392.6

If each of the subjects could be directly compared to himself as he worked with each of the systems, the problem of matching subjects or subject groups and the need for extensive statistical analysis could be eliminated. Unfortunately, it is not meaningful to have the same subject code and debug the same problem twice; and it is extremely difficult to develop different problems that are at the same level of difficulty. One possible solution to this problem would be to use some measure of problem difficulty as a normalizing factor. It should be recognized that the use of any normalizing factor can introduce problems in analysis and interpretation. It was decided to use one of the more popular of such measures, namely, the number of instructions in the program. CPU time per instruction and debug man-hours per instruction were compared on the two problems for each subject for the interactive and noninteractive conditions. The results showed that the interactive subjects had significantly lower values on both compute seconds per instruction (.01 level) and debug hours per instruction (.06 level).

2.3.2 *Individual Differences.* One of the key findings of the previous study was that there were large individual differences between programmers. Because of differences in sampling and scale factors, coefficients of variation were computed to compare individual differences in both studies. (The coefficient of variation is expressed as a percentage; it is equal to the standard deviation divided by the mean, multiplied by 100.) The overall results showed that coefficients of variation for debug man-hours and CPU time in this experiment were only 16 percent smaller than coefficients of variation in the experienced programmer study (median values of 66 percent and 82 percent, respectively). These observed differences may be attributable, in part, to the greater difficulty level of the problems in the experienced programmer study, and to the much greater range of programming experience between subjects which tended to magnify individual programmer differences.

In an attempt to determine if there are measures of skill that can be used as a preliminary screening tool to equalize groups, data were gathered on the subject's grades in the SDC programmer training class, and as mentioned earlier, they were also given the Basic Programming Knowledge Test (BPKT). Correlations between all experimental measures, adjusted scores, grades, and the BPKT results were determined. Except for some spurious part-whole correlations, the results showed no consistent correlation between performance measures and the various grades and test scores. The most interesting result of this exploratory analysis, however, was that class grades and BPKT scores showed substantial intercorrelations. This is especially notable when only the first of the two BPKT scores is considered. These correlations ranged between .64 and .83 for Part I of the BPKT; two out of these four correlations are at the 5 percent level and one exceeds the 1 percent level of significance even for these small samples. This implies that the BPKT is measuring the same kinds of skills that are measured in trainee class performance. It should also be noted that neither class grades nor BPKT scores would have provided useful predictions of trainee performance in the test situation that was used in this experiment. This observation may be interpreted three basic ways: first, that the BPKT and class grades are valid and that the problems do not represent general programming tasks; second, that the problems are valid, but that the BPKT and class grades are not indicative of working programmer performance; or third, that interrelations between the BPKT and class grades do in fact exist with respect to programming performance, but that the intercorrelations are only low to moderate, which cannot be detected by the very small samples used in these experiments. The results of these studies are ambiguous with respect to these three hypotheses; further investigation is required to determine whether one or any combination of them will hold.

3. Interpretation

Before drawing any conclusions from the results, consider the scope of the two studies. Each dealt with a small number of subjects — performance measures were marked by large error variance and wide-ranging individual differences, which made statistical inference difficult and risky. The subject skill range was considerable, from programmer trainees in one study to highly experienced research and development programmers in the other. The programming languages included one machine language and two subsets of JOVIAL, a higher order language. In both experiments TSS served as the online or interactive condition whereas the offline or noninteractive mode had to be simulated on TSS according to specified rules. Only one facility was used for both experiments — TSS. The problems ranged from the conceptually simple tasks administered to the programmer trainees to the much more difficult problems given to the experienced programmers. The representativeness of these problems for programming tasks is unknown. The point of this thumbnail sketch of the two studies is simply to emphasize their tentative, exploratory nature — at best they cover a highly circumscribed set of online and offline programming behaviors.

The interpretation of the results is discussed under three broad areas, corresponding to three leading objectives of these two studies: comparison of online and offline programming performance, analysis of individual differences in programming proficiency, and implications of the methodology and findings for future research.

3.1 Online vs. offline programming performance

On the basis of the concrete results of these experiments, the online conditions resulted in substantially and, by and large, significantly better performance for debug man-hours than the offline conditions. The crucial questions are: to what extent may these results be generalized to other computing facilities; to other programmers; to varying levels of turnaround time; and to other types of programming problems? Provisional answers to these four questions highlight problem areas requiring further research.

The online/offline comparisons were made in a time-shared computing facility in which the online condition was the natural operational mode, whereas offline conditions had to be simulated. It might be argued that in analogous experiments, conducted with a batch-processing facility, with real offline conditions and simulated online conditions, the results might be reversed. One way to neutralize this methodological bias is to conduct an experiment in a hybrid facility that uses both time-sharing and batch-processing procedures on the same computer so that neither has to be simulated. Another approach is to compare facilities matched on type of computer, programming languages, compilers, and other tools for coding and debugging, but different in online and offline operations. It might also be argued that the use of new and different programming languages, methods, and tools might lead to entirely different results.

The generalization of these results to other programmers essentially boils down to the representativeness of the experimental samples with regard to an objective and well-defined criterion population. A universally accepted classification scheme for programmers does not exist, nor are there accepted norms with regard to biographical, educational and job experience data.

In certain respects, the differences between online and offline performance hinge on the length and variability of turnaround time. The critical experimental question is not whether one mode is superior to the other mode, since, all other things equal, offline facilities with long turnaround times consume more elapsed programming time than either online facilities or offline facilities with short turnaround times. The critical comparison is with online versus offline operations that have short response times. The data from the experienced programmer study suggest the possibility that, as offline turnaround time approaches zero, the performance differential between the two modes with regard to debug man-hours tends to disappear. The programmer trainee study, however, tends to refute this hypothesis since the mean performance advantage of the interactive mode was considerably larger than waiting time for computer availability. Other experimental studies need to be conducted to determine whether online systems offer a man-hour performance advantage above and beyond the elimination of turnaround time in converting from offline to online operations.

The last of the four considerations crucial to any generalization of the experimental findings — type of programming problem — presents a baffling obstacle. How does an investigator select a "typical" programming problem or set of problems? No suitable classification of computing systems exists, let alone a classification of types of programs. Scientific versus business, online versus offline, automated versus semiautomated, realtime versus nonrealtime — these and many other tags for computer systems and computer programs are much too gross to provide systematic classification. In the absence of a systematic classification of computer programs with respect to underlying skills, programming techniques and applications, all that can be done is to extend the selection of experimental problems to cover a broader spectrum of programming activity.

In the preceding discussion we have been primarily concerned with consistent findings on debug man-hours for both experiments. The opposite findings in both studies with regard to CPU time require some comment. The results of the programmer trainee study seem to indicate that online programming permits the programmer to solve his problem in a direct, uninterrupted manner, which results not only in less human time but also less CPU time. The programmer does not have to "warm up" and remember his problem in all its details if he has access to the computer whenever he needs it. In contrast, the apparent reduction of CPU time in the experienced programmer study under the offline condition suggests an opposing hypothesis; that is, perhaps there is a deliberate tradeoff, on the part of the programmer, to use more machine time in an exploratory trial-and-error manner in order to reduce his own time and effort in solving his problem. The results of these two studies are ambiguous with respect to these opposing hypotheses. One or both of them may be true to different degrees under different conditions. Then again, perhaps these explanations are too crude to account for complex problem-solving in programming tasks. More definitive research is needed.

3.2 Individual differences

These studies revealed large individual differences between high and low performers, often by an order of magnitude. It is apparent from the spread of the data that very substantial savings can be effected by successfully detecting low performers. Techniques measuring individual programming skills should be vigorously pursued, tested and evaluated, and developed on a broad front for the growing variety of programming jobs.

These two studies suggest that such paper-and-pencil tests may work best in predicting the performance of programmer trainees and relatively inexperienced programmers. The observed pattern was one of substantive correlations of BPKT test scores with programmer trainee class grades but of no detectable correlation with experienced programmer performance. These tentative findings on our small samples are consistent with internal validation data for the BPKT. The test discriminates best between low experience levels and fails to discriminate significantly among highest experience levels. This situation suggests that general programming skill may dominate early training and initial on-the-job experience, but that such skill is progressively transformed and displaced by more specialized skills with increasing experience.

If programmers show such large performance differences, even larger and more striking differences may be expected in general user performance levels with the advent of information utilities (such as large networks of time-shared computing facilities with a broad range of information services available to the general public). The computer science community has not recognized (let alone faced up to) the problem of anticipating and dealing with very large individual differences in performing tasks involving man-computer communications for the general public.

In an attempt to explain the results of both studies in regard to individual differences and to offer a framework for future analyses of individual differences in programmer skills, a differentiation hypothesis is offered, as follows: when programmers are first exposed to and indoctrinated in the use of computers, and during their early experience with computers, a general factor of programmer proficiency is held to account for a large proportion of observed individual differences. However, with the advent of diversified and extended experience, the general programming skill factor differentiates into separate and relatively independent factors related to specialized experience.

From a broader and longer range perspective, the trend in computer science and technology is toward more diversified computers, programming languages, and computer applications. This general trend toward increasing variety is likely to require an equivalent diversification of human skills to program such systems. A pluralistic hypothesis, such as the suggested differentiation hypothesis, seems more appropriate to anticipate and deal with this type of technological evolution, not only for programmers, but for the general user of computing facilities.

3.3 Future research

These studies began with a rather straightforward objective — the comparison of online and offline programmer debugging performance under controlled conditions. But in order to deal with the online/offline comparison, it became necessary to consider many other factors related to man-machine performance. For example, it was necessary to look into the characteristics and correlates of individual differences. We had to recognize that there was no objective way to assess the representativeness of the various experimental problems for data processing in general. The results were constrained to a single computing facility normally using online operations. The debugging criterion measures showed relationships with other performance, experience, and control variables that demanded at least preliminary explanations. Programming languages had to be accounted for in the interpretation of the results. The original conception of a direct statistical comparison between online and offline performance had to give way to multivariate statistical analysis in order to interpret the results in a more meaningful context.

In short, our efforts to measure online/offline programming differences in an objective manner were severely constrained by the lack of substantive scientific information on computer programming performance — constrained by the applied scientific lag in computer programming, which brings us back to the opening theme. This lag is not localized to computer programming; it stems from a more fundamental experimental lag in the general study of man-computer communications. The case for this assertion involves a critical analysis of the status and direction of computer science which is beyond the scope of this article; this analysis is presented elsewhere (Sackman 1967 [9]). In view of these various considerations, it is recommended that future experimental comparisons of online and offline programming performance be conducted within the broad framework of programmer performance and not as a simple dichotomy existing in a separate data-processing world of its own. It is far more difficult and laborious to construct a scientific scaffold for the man-machine components and characteristics of programmer performance than it is to try to concentrate exclusively on a rigorous comparison of online and offline programming.

Eight broad areas for further research are indicated:

a. Development of empirical, normative data on computing system performance with respect to type of application, man-machine environment, and types of computer programs in relation to leading tasks in object systems.

b. Comparative experimental studies of computer facility performance, such as online, offline, and hybrid installations, systematically permuted against broad classes of program languages (machine-oriented, procedure-oriented, and problem-oriented languages), and representative classes of programming tasks.

c. Development of cost-effectiveness models for computing facilities, incorporating man and machine elements, with greater emphasis on empirically validated measures of effectiveness and less emphasis on abstract models than has been the case in the past.

d. Programmer job and task analysis based on representative sampling of programmer activities, leading toward the development of empirically validated and updated job classification procedures.

e. Systematic collection, analysis, and evaluation of the empirical characteristics, correlates, and variation associated with individual performance differences for programmers, including analysis of team effectiveness and team differences.

f. Development of a variety of paper-and-pencil tests, such as the Basic Programming Knowledge Test, for assessment of general and specific programmer skills in relation to representative, normative populations.

g. Detailed case histories on the genesis and course of programmer problem-solving, the frequency and nature of human and machine errors in the problem-solving process, the role of machine feedback and reinforcement in programmer behavior, and the delineation of critical programmer decision points in the life cycle of the design, development and installation of computer programs.

h. And finally, integration of the above findings into the broader arena of man-computer communication for the general user.

More powerful applied research on programmer performance, including experimental comparisons of online and offline programming, will require the development in depth of basic concepts and procedures for the field as a whole — a development that can only be achieved by a concerted effort to bridge the scientific gap between knowledge and application.

References: Sackman, Erikson & Grant

1. Berger, Raymond M., et al. Computer personnel selection and criterion development: III. The basic programming knowledge test. U. of S. California, Los Angeles, June 1966.

2. Emerson, Marvin. The "small" computer versus time-shared systems. *Comput. Autom.,* Sept. 1965.

3. Erikson, Warren J. A pilot study of interactive versus noninteractive debugging. TM-3296, System Development Corp., Santa Monica, Calif., Dec. 13, 1966.

4. Gold, M.M. Methodological for evaluating time-shared computer usage. Doctoral dissertation, Alfred P. Sloan School of Management, M.I.T., 1967.

5. Grant, E.E., and Sackman, H. An exploratory investigation of programmer performance under online and offline conditions. SP-2581, System Development Corp., Santa Monica, Calif., Sept. 2, 1966.

6. Kennedy, Phyllis R. TINT users guide. TM-1933/00/03, System Development Corp., Santa Monica, Calif., July 1965.

7. Macdonald, Neil. A time shared computer system — the disadvantages. *Comput. Autom.,* Sept. 1965.

8. Patrick, R.L. So you want to go online? *Datamation 9,* 10 (Oct. 1963), 25-27.

9. Sackman, H. *Computers, System Science, and Evolving Society,* John Wiley & Sons, New York (in press) 1967.

10. Samelson, K., and Bauer, F. Sequential formula translation. *Comm. ACM 3* (Feb. 1960), 76-83.

11. Schatzoff, M., Tsao, R., and Wiig, R. An experimental comparison of time sharing and batch processing. *Comm. ACM 10* (May 1967), 261-265.

12. Scherr, A.L. Time sharing measurement. *Datamation 12,* 4 (April 1966), 22-26.

13. Schwartz, J.I. Observations on time shared systems. Proc. ACM 20th Nat. Conf., 1965, pp. 525-542.

14. ———, Coffman, E.G., and Weissman, C. A general purpose time sharing system. Proc. AFIPS 1964 Spring Joint Comp. Conf., Vol. 25, pp. 397-411.

15. ———, and Weissman, C. The SDC time sharing system revisited. Proc. ACM 22nd Nat. Conf., 1967, pp. 263-271.

Toward a Theoretical Basis for Estimating Programming Effort

The measurement of programmer productivity is certainly one of the most complex areas in Computer Science. Since Ida Rose [1] of the National Bureau of Standards noted, more than 20 years ago, that coding time approximated four instructions per manhour, the field has been aware that longer programs usually (but not always) take longer to program than short ones. As recently as his 1973 Turing lecture, Dijkstra [2] noted that there was as yet no proof on the question of whether the time to implement a program increases linearly or as the square of program length.

The present note will borrow from the field of software physics [3−7] to obtain a theoretical relationship between a computer program and the mental effort required to implement it, and then test this relationship against one set of experimental data as reported by another author [8].

Given the four countable (hence measurable) parameters:

n_1 = Unique Operators Used,

n_2 = Unique Operands Used,

N_1 = Total Operators Used,

N_2 = Total Operands Used,

in any algorithm in any language, and letting:

$$n = n_1 + n_2$$

and

$$N = N_1 + N_2,$$

SOURCE: M.H. Halstead, *Proceedings of the ACM Conference*, 1975.

it has been shown [4, 5] and independently confirmed [12] that the relationship:

$$\hat{N} = n_1 \log_2 n_1 + n_2 \log_2 n_2 \tag{1}$$

yields a good estimate of the program length, N.

Further it has been shown experimentally [6] that the volume, V, and the level, L, when measured by:

$$V = N \log_2 n \tag{2}$$

and

$$\hat{L} = \frac{n_1^*}{n_1} \frac{n_2}{N_2} \tag{3}$$

where

$$n_1^* = 1 + M \tag{4}$$

and

$M =$ Number of modules,

have a product $L \times V = V^*$ \hfill (5)

which depends only upon the algorithm, and is reasonably invariant as the algorithm is translated from one programming language to another.

It can also be suggested that, to a first approximation, the total number of mental discriminations required to implement a preconceived algorithm in any language with which the programmer is fluent might be obtained in the following way.

Assume that each of the N items in a program is selected from its vocabulary, n, by means of a binary search. The number of comparisons required for each binary search will be, on the average, $\log_2 n$. Consequently, the total number of comparisons required to generate a program of length N will be $N\log_2 n$, which is nothing more than the program volume, V, of eq. (2). Now recall that the level, as the term is intuitively used, and in the sense of eq. (3) also, is intended to represent the inverse of program difficulty. If these two assumptions are valid, then the total number of effective mental discriminations, E, required to generate a given program can be calculated from:

$$\hat{E} = \frac{V}{L} \tag{6a}$$

Noting that $V^* = V \times L$, it follows that eq. (6a) can also be expressed as:

$$\hat{E} = \frac{V^2}{V^*} \tag{6b}$$

In order to convert eq. (6) from units of effective mental discriminations to units of time, we may either proceed experimentally, or adopt previous results from Psychology. According to a most pertinent paper, "On the Fine Structure of Psychological Time" [9], if we let S represent the number of "moments" per second for the human brain, then:

$$5 \leqslant S \leqslant 20 \tag{7}$$

Eq. (6) then becomes:

$$\hat{T} = \frac{V}{SL} \tag{8a}$$

or
$$\hat{T} = \frac{V^2}{SV^*}$$
(8b)

provided, of course, that we are dealing with a programmer who is enforcing the equivalent of the hardware instruction: "Inhibit all Interrupts." If he is not concentrating on the programming task, then eq. (8) should yield only a lower bound. Since computer programmers might be expected to fall near the high end of Stroud's range, and since an unpublished technical report on machine language rates [10] yielded the value experimentally, we will take $S = 18$ per second in the following analysis. (In an unreported, but seemingly valid test, Dijkstra apparently sustained a rate of 51/second for a three minute period, but then, even Stroud would not have expected a Dijkstra in his population.)

Experimental procedure

In an exhaustive report, Zislis [8] details the following procedure.

Non-procedural specifications were written for the twelve algorithms numbered 14, 16, 17, 19, 20, 21, 23, 24, 25, 29, 31 and 33 published in the *Communications of the ACM* [11]. He then programmed each of these algorithms in a language selected at random from the set: FORTRAN, PL/I and APL, recording the times spent in coding, coding declarations, desk checking, and correcting errors revealed by desk checking. Times were recorded to the nearest minute, and summed for each program. (The experiment was then repeated with a second, a third, and the original language, but because of uncertainty in eliminating the effect of learning from those data, they will not be treated here.) After all programming had been completed, Zislis measured the parameters n_1, n_2, N_1, and N_2. His data, taken from Appendix D, iteration 1, and Appendix F, n and N counts, are reproduced in Table 1.

Table 1
Data from Zislis Algorithm Implementation Experiment

Algorithm (CACM Nr.)	Implementation Time (Minutes)	n_1	n_2	N_1	N_2
14	33	15	17	64	51
16	135	20	35	223	303
17	33	15	15	78	81
19	7	10	6	25	19
20	12	14	19	59	38
21	43	23	25	106	97
23	21	17	13	50	50
24	16	15	14	81	82
25	62	26	34	179	163
29	25	7	11	72	67
31	20	17	25	53	54
33	4	6	8	9	15

For purposes of calculation, eq. (8) may be expanded, algebraically, to:

$$\hat{T} = \frac{n_1}{n_1^* S} \times \frac{n_1}{n_2} \times N_2 (N_1 + N_2) \log_2 (n_1 + n_2) \tag{9}$$

where, for $\hat{T}$ in minutes, $S = 18 \times 60 = 1080/\text{Min}$.

Now n_1^*, the only parameter not recorded by Zislis, is defined as the number of operators required to express a procedure call upon a given algorithm. Since in most cases this may consist merely of a single grouping or assignment operator, plus the name of the procedure itself, its value is usually 2. However, a procedure call may need to specify another procedure among its operands, and since any procedure or function name is an operator, this has the effect of increasing n_1^*. Examining the twelve algorithms in the sample, we find that ten of them are indeed single procedures, for which $n_1^* = 2$. Algorithm 16, on the other hand, consists of the three procedures CROUT, INNERPRODUCT, and SOLVE, hence for it $n_1^* = 1 + 3 = 4$. Similarly, algorithm 25 specifies both the procedure ZEROS and FUNCTION, for an $n_1^* = 1 + 2 = 3$.

Table 2 contains the result of applying eq. (9) to the data of Table 1, and in addition it also contains a count of the number of executable statements in each of the original Algol implementations. The latter can be taken as a measure of "Program Length" in its historical sense, hence the algorithms have been ordered according to that parameter. The steps performed in the calculation of coefficients of correlation between "Length" and observed programming times, and between observed and theoretically calculated programming times are shown at the bottom of the table.

Table 2
Analysis of Zislis Experiment

Algorithm (CACM Nr.)	Number of Statements	T (obs) (Minutes)		T (Eq. 9) (Minutes)
33	1	4		0.5
19	5	7		2.6
20	6	12		6.3
23	7	21		14.9
24	8	16		32.2
17	9	33		29.3
21	12	43		46.8
29	14	25		11.4
31	15	20		9.8
14	22	33		12.0
16	35	135		121.9
25	57	62		77.7
Σx	191	411		365.4
$\bar{x}$	15.92	34.25		30.45
Σx^2	5779	28027		25261
$n\bar{x}^2$	3041	14077		11126
$\sqrt{\Sigma x^2 - n\bar{x}^2}$	52.33	118.11		120.40
$\Sigma x_{obs} x_i$		10834	26054	
$n\bar{x}_{obs} \bar{x}_i$		6543	12515	
$\Sigma x_{obs} x_i - n\bar{x}_{obs} \bar{x}_i$		4291	13539	
		.694	.952	

$$r = \frac{\Sigma x_{obs} x_i - n\bar{x}_{obs} \bar{x}_i}{\sqrt{\Sigma x_{obs}^2 - n\bar{x}_i^2} \sqrt{\Sigma x_i^2 - n\bar{x}_i^2}}$$

The analysis in Table 2 clearly indicates two things. First, while the coefficient of correlation, r, between the times required to program these algorithms and a classical measure of their lengths is both positive and acceptably high, 0.694, the correlation between the observed times and those calculated with eq. (9) is considerably higher, 0.952.

Second, in the case of $\hat{T}$, the units are also in minutes.

Clearly, just as one robin does not make a spring, one experiment can not validate a theory. As had long been recognized in the natural sciences, however, additional experiments at one installation can never guarantee their reproducibility. All that can be said is that the results presented here appear to be of sufficient potential interest to warrant additional experimentation by others.

References: Halstead

[1] Rose, Ida, "Programming Productivity" (With the proper reference lost in antiquity, this information passed from one computer center manager to another during the 1950s).

[2] Dijkstra, Edsger W., "The Humble Programmer," *Comm. ACM,* Vol. 15, No. 10 (Oct. 1972), pp. 859-866.

[3] Halstead, M.H., "Natural Laws Controlling Algorithmic Structure?" *ACM SIGPLAN Notices,* Vol. 7, No. 2 (Feb. 1972).

[4] Halstead, M.H., and Rudolf Bayer, "Algorithm Dynamics," *Proc. ACM Annual Conference,* 1973.

[5] Bulut, Necdet, M.H. Halstead, and Rudolf Bayer, "The Experimental Verification of a Structural Property of Fortran Programs," *Proc. ACM Annual Conference,* 1974.

[6] Bulut, Necdet, "An Invariant Property of Algorithms," Ph.D. Thesis, Purdue, August 1973.

[7] Halstead, M.H., "Software Physics Comparison of a Sample Program in DSL ALPHA and COBOL," *IBM Research Report,* R.J. 1460, October 1974.

[8] Zislis, Paul, "An Experiment in Algorithm Implementation," *CSD Tech. Rpt. No. 96,* Purdue, June 1973.

[9] Stroud, John M., "The Fine Structure of Psychological Time," *Annals of the New York Academy of Sciences,* 1966, pp. 623-631.

[10] Halstead, M.H., "A Theoretical Relationship Between Mental Work and Machine Language Programming," *CSD Tech. Rpt. No. 67,* Purdue, May 1972.

[11] Beam, A., "Algorithm 14, Complex Exponential Integral," *Comm. ACM,* Vol. 3, No. 7 (July 1960), p. 406 and following.

[12] Bohrer, Robert, "Halstead's Criterion and Statistical Algorithms," *Proc. 8th Computer Science/Statistics Interface Symposium,* Los Angeles, February 1975.

A Method of Programming Measurement and Estimation

New materials technologies and architectures are significantly affecting computing system hardware. While the cost per bit of storage and the execution cost per instruction have both been decreasing, the same trend has not been true for software. Since software development has continued to be a people-oriented activity, a higher percentage of the cost to acquire a computing system is accruing to software development [1].

New management and programming techniques have been developed to improve programming efficiency. Among the improved programming technologies are the following:

- *Chief programmer team,* a programming organization built around a chief programmer, a backup chief programmer, and a librarian that effectively produces code in a disciplined and open environment [2].

- *Hierarchy plus Input-Process-Output* (HIPO), a graphic design and documentation method that is used to describe program functions from the topmost level to great detail [3].

- *Development support library,* a tool that provides current information about project programs, data, and status [4].

- *Structured programming,* a programming method based on the mathematical Structure Theorem [5] that enables programmers to understand and enhance programs that have been written by others [6], as well as one's own programs.

SOURCE: C.E. Walston & C.P. Felix, *IBM Systems Journal,* 1977.

- *Design and code inspections,* a review of program design, code, and documentation to detect errors prior to program execution [7].

- *Top-down development,* an ordering of program development and testing that begins at the topmost functional level and proceeds decrementally to the lowest functional level.

This paper discusses research into programming measurements, with emphasis on one phase of that research: a search for a method of estimating programming productivity. The method we present is aimed at measuring the rate of production of lines of code by projects, as influenced by a number of project conditions and requirements. We do not, however, measure the performance of individual programming project members. As we continue our research, we are continuing to learn more about the attributes of the programming process, about programming itself, and about better ways of analyzing the data.

Before starting the programming measurements research reported here we analyzed the literature on programming measurements and productivity that includes the work of Aron [8], Weinwurm and Zagorski [9], and Nelson [10]. We also wanted to isolate the effects of improved programming technologies from the effects of monetary inflation, variations in computing cost, and ambiguities in the definition of computing quantities (such as that of the size of the delivered program product).

The software measurements project began in 1972 when we decided to assess the effects of structured programming on the software development process. To do that, a rigorous program was established to measure the then current software methodologies so that changes that result from the introduction of new methodologies could be measured. The initial phase of the measurements program was to identify variables to be measured, to design a questionnaire (called the Programming Project Summary questionnaire), and to develop a system for processing the data to be collected. The first report entered the system on January 23, 1973, and data have continued to be received and entered into the system from that time on. Since the establishment of the Programming Project Summary, two new reporting formats have been designed: the Software Development Report and the Software Service Report.

Objectives

We understood at the outset that the established objectives might change as the project matured and as data were accumulated. Current objectives of the project discussed in this paper are the following:

- Provide data for the evaluation of improved programming technologies.
- Provide support for proposals and contract performance.
- Gather and preserve historical records of the software development work performed.
- Provide programming data to management.
- Foster a common programming terminology.

Key to a software measurement program are the analysis of measurements and feedback of results to the suppliers of the raw data and to management. This paper discusses the data reporting and analysis in the software measurements program of the IBM Federal Systems Division. Described first are the measurements data base, the services that are available to users of the data, and descriptive statistics from the data base. The next section covers the analysis of programming productivity and describes a productivity estimation technique. Following this, the results of other analyses that have been performed with respect to factors such as documentation, staffing, and computer costs are presented. The last section briefly describes analysis efforts that are being contemplated for future research. In the measurements project discussed here, a sufficiently large quantity of data is being collected so that a programming project measurement system is used to provide the necessary flexibility and capability of storage control and analysis. The Programming Project Measurement System is briefly described in the Appendix.

Measurements data base

Data contained in questionnaires submitted by line projects at prescribed reporting periods are stored in a computer data base where they are accessible for answering queries, preparing reports, or for analytical studies.

The basic measurements data base is structured so that it contains all the reports received, as described in Table 1. Each Programming Project Summary milestone report is given a unique number when received and is assigned a separate record in the file. Project milestones are the following: start of work; preliminary design review; midway through software development; acceptance test completion; and every three months during the maintenance or service phase. Each initial and final Software Development and Software Service Report is also filed as a separate record.

Table 1
Software Project Measurements Reports

Report Name	Nature of the Report
Programming Project Summary	Detailed report on the software development environment, the product (including errors), resources, and schedule.
Software Development Report	Detailed report on the software development environment, the product (including changes and errors), resources and schedule.
Monthly Software Development Report	One report on product, resource, and schedule status. Changes in software development environment are noted.
Software Service Report	Report on project size and on the software service environment.
Quarterly Software Service Report	Detailed data on product being serviced, resource status, and changes in software service environment.

The monthly Software Development Reports plus any changes to the initial submission constitute separate records, as do the quarterly Software Service Reports and any changes to the initial Software Service Report. Each record is structured into fields, or variables, that correspond to the question response fields in the questionnaires.

Sixty completed software development projects are now in the data base. These completed projects, which represent a wide variety of programming technology, are summarized in Table 2. Their delivered source lines of code range from 4000 to 467000, and their effort ranges from 12 to 11758 man-months. These programs include real-time process control, interactive, report generators, data-base control, and message switching programs. Some of the programs have severe timing or storage constraints and other programs have both types of constraints. Twenty-eight different high-level languages and 66 different computers are represented in the listing in Table 2.

Table 2

Characterization of Programs in the Programming Project Data Base

A. Small less-complex systems
- Batch storage and retrieval
- Batch inventory
- Batch information management
- Batch languages preprocessor and information management
- Batch reporting
- Batch financial information
- Batch scientific processing simulation
- Batch utility
- Batch operating system exerciser

B. Medium less-complex systems
- Special-purpose data management [2]
- Batch storage and retrieval [2]
- Process control simulation
- Batch reporting
- Batch data-base utility [2]
- On-line scientific processing simulation
- Batch on-line scientific information management
- On-line business information management
- On-line storage and retrieval
- Batch hardware test support
- Batch scientific algorithm feasibility [3]
- Interactive scientific processing [2]
- System test support
- Batch planning [3]
- Batch military information management
- Special-purpose operating system

C. Medium complex systems
- Real-time, special-purpose system exerciser
- Special-purpose operating system [2]
- Batch information modification
- Batch information conversion
- Data management
- Sensor-based mission control
- On-line scheduling
- Sensor-based mission simulation
- Interactive scientific processing
- Process control [3]
- On-line graphics
- System performance monitoring and measurement [3]
- Terminal data management
- Interactive information conversion
- Operating system extensions

D. Large complex systems
- Sensor-based mission monitoring and control
- Interactive information acquisition
- Process control
- Sensor-based system exerciser [3]
- Sensor-based mission processing and communication [2]

Services

With the previously described data base and with the capabilities provided by the Programming Project Measurement System, a wide variety of services can be provided to line project personnel. Queries can be answered, analyses performed, and programming project productivity estimation provided for new or on-going projects. Examples of services are discussed throughout the remainder of this paper.

Queries that can be answered by direct retrieval of data from the data base are of two general types. First is a request for data about a specific project. In this case, the Programming Project Measurement System generates a report that lists the answers to the questions submitted by personnel of the specified project. The second type of query is a more general request for information, an example of which is, "What has been the utilization of improved programming technologies by projects in the data base and what was the effect on project productivity?" The answer is provided in the form of a listing of productivity data sorted by project. The following breakdown indicates the types of reported and derived data that can be provided in response to a general inquiry:

Programming project data:

- Number of lines of delivered source code ordered by project. (Source lines are 80-character source records provided as input to a language processor. Job control languages, data definitions, link edit language, and comment lines are included. Reused code is not included.)
- Pages of documentation (including program source listings) delivered.
- Source languages used to develop code.

Resource data:

- Total effort (in man-months, including management, administration, analysis, operational support, documentation, design, coding, and testing) required to produce the lines of source code by project.
- Duration of project in months.

Use of improved programming technologies (expressed as a percentage of code developed using each technique):

- Structured programming.
- Top-down development.
- Chief programmer team.
- Design and code inspections.

Derived data:

- Productivity achieved, ordered by project. *Programming productivity* is defined as the ratio of the delivered source lines of code to the total effort (in man-months) required to produce the lines of code, and is computed from product and resource data.
- Average number of people required to work on the project, computed by dividing the total effort in man-months by the duration of the project in calendar months.

More complex and extensive search and analysis questions can also be answered. These are supported by a question analysis subsystem of the Programming Project Measurement System, which incorporates a statistical package for the manipulation and statistical analysis of many types of data. The more complex requests can be grouped into two types, descriptive and analytical. A descriptive request requires searching the data base for specific variables or derived variables and computing characteristics about their distributions such as the mean, mode, and standard deviation, in order to prepare the report. Table 3 illustrates one such report for the completed projects in the data base.

Table 3
Programming Project Descriptive Data Report for Completed Projects

	Median 50%	Quartiles 25–75%
Productivity		
Source lines per man-month of total effort	274	150–440
Product		
Source lines (thousands)	20	10–59
Percentage of code lines not to be delivered	5	0–11
Documentation per thousand lines of source code (pages)	69	27–167
Resource		
Computer cost (as a percentage of project cost)	18	10–34
Total effort (man-months)	67	37–186
Average manning	6	3.8–14.5
Effort distribution of preliminary design review (percent)	18	11–25
Distribution of effort (percent)		
Management and administration	18	12–20
Analysis	18	6–27
Programming and design	60	50–70
Other	4	0–6
Duration (months)	11	8–19
Development error detection		
Errors per thousand source lines	3.1	0.8–8.0
Incorrect function	76	50–86
Omitted function (percent)	8	0.22
Misinterpreted function (percent)	17	7–25
Errors per programming man month	0.9	0.3–2.4

Because of the variability in the measurement data, the statistics in Table 3 are presented in terms of medians and quartiles. The median for the size of the delivered software product is 20 thousand lines and fifty percent of the projects reported that the sizes of their delivered source code ranged from 10 thousand to 59 thousand lines. The effort for software development reported was distributed into the major categories as shown. The error detection section of the table shows the distribution of errors reported during the development phase.

Table 4 provides descriptive statistical data for completed service projects. Most service activity is not purely maintenance, but includes development efforts as well. The ratio of developed source lines of code to maintained lines of code was 4 percent at the median.

Table 4
Data for Completed Service Projects

	Median 50%	Quartiles 25 – 75%
Product		
Lines of maintained source code (thousands)	103	56 – 474
Ratio of developed to maintained code	0.04	0 – 0.19
Resources		
Average manning per project	6	4 – 11
Maintained source lines per man (thousands)	15	5 – 24
Distribution of effort		
Management and administration (percent)	15	10 – 20
Analysis (percent)	10	4 – 30
Programming (percent)	72	40 – 80
Other (percent)	3	0 – 7
Duration (months)	18	11 – 31
Errors detected		
Errors per thousand lines of maintained code	1.4	0.2 – 2.9
Incorrect function (percent)	73	
Omitted function (percent)	11	
Misinterpreted function (percent)	13	

Table 5 presents data on on-going programming and service projects. Since only a small percentage of these projects have been completed at this time, the statistics represent a mixture of actual measurements and estimates at various stages of completion.

Table 5
Descriptive Data from On-Going Projects

Programming	Median 50%	Quartiles 25 – 75%
Source lines (thousands)	12.5	5.4 – 30
Percentage of code lines not to be delivered	2.6	0 – 11
Effort (man-months)	72	30 – 205
Distribution of effort:		
System analysis (percent)	15	10 – 20
System design (percent)	20	15 – 25
Code and unit test (percent)	30	20 – 35
Integration and test (percent)	20	15 – 30
Other (percent)	5	0 – 10
Duration (months)	12	9 – 18

Service	Median 50%	Quartiles 25 – 75%
Maintained source lines (thousands)	148	55 – 340
Ratio of developed to maintained code	0.05	0 – 0.09
Effort (man-months)	88	27 – 185
Average manning (persons)	5	3 – 19
Duration (months)	10.5	6.5 – 12

Productivity analysis

We have identified five major parameters that can help programming project personnel make estimates. These parameters, productivity, schedule, cost, quality, and size, are listed in order of increasing difficulty and complexity of analysis. Some of the difficulties arise from a lack of detailed data in the data base, as in the case of schedule data. Complexity of the quantitative data can create other difficulties. One significant difficulty is in identifying and measuring independent variables that can be used to estimate the desired variable, as is the case in estimating the size of the product to be delivered.

Productivity, which can be defined in terms of the quantitative measures that are in the data base, is a vital factor in all software estimating processes and, therefore, is of immediate value to project personnel. For this reason, the analysis performed to date has focused on productivity estimation. Productivity has often been defined as the ratio of output to input. *Programming productivity* is defined here as the ratio of the delivered source lines of code (DSL) to the total effort in man-months (MM) required to produce that delivered product.

The basic relationship between delivered lines of code and effort is shown in Figure 1. Each plotted point represents the data reported by a completed project in the data base. A number on the chart indicates a position where a number of data points are grouped sufficiently close together that they cannot be individually identified on the plot. The data have been plotted in the log-log domain so that they become approximately linear. The linear coefficients become power relationships when transformed back to the original domain of the data. The least squares fit to the data as plotted in Figure 1, yields the result:

$$E = 5.2L^{0.91}$$

where

E = total effort in man months

and

L = thousands of lines of delivered source code.

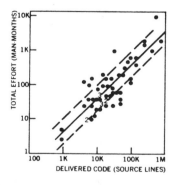

Figure 1. Relationship between delivered lines of code and effort.

Productivity index

This relationship is nearly a first-power (or linear) relationship between effort and product size. The dashed lines indicate the standard error of the estimate on either side of the least squares fit. To identify the sources of scatter or variation of Figure 1, those variables that are related to productivity have been investigated. Preliminary findings have led to the development of a productivity estimator that provides an on-line capability to support proposed as well as on-going projects. A set of sixty-eight variables was selected from the data base, and those variables were analyzed to determine which were significantly related to productivity. Twenty-nine of the variables showed a significantly high correlation with productivity and have therefore been retained for use in estimating. Table 6 lists these variables and the responses associated with them. To illustrate the meaning of Table 6, consider the first entry, which is derived from a multiple-choice question that asks the information supplier to circle his response to the following statement: Customer interface is (less than, equal to, greater than) normal complexity.

Table 6

Variables That Correlate Significantly with Programming Productivity

Question or Variable	Response Group Mean Productivity (DSL/MM)			Productivity Change (DSL/MM)
Customer interface complexity	Normal 500	Normal 295	> Normal 124	376
User participation in the definition of requirements	None 491	Some 267	Much 205	286
Customer originated program design changes	Few 297		Many 196	101
Customer experience with the application area of the project	None 318	Some 340	Much 206	112
Overall personnel experience and qualifications	Low 132	Average 257	High 410	278
Percentage of programmers doing development who participated in design of functional specifications	< 25% 153	25 — 50% 242	> 50% 391	238
Previous experience with operational computer	Minimal 146	Average 270	Extensive 312	166
Previous experience with programming languages	Minimal 122	Average 225	Extensive 385	263
Previous experience with application of similar or greater size and complexity	Minimal 146	Average 221	Extensive 410	264
Ratio of average staff size to duration (people/month)	< 0.5 305	0.5 — 0.9 310	> 0.9 173	132
Hardware under concurrent development	No 297		Yes 177	120
Development computer access, open under special request	0% 226	1 — 25% 274	> 25% 357	131
Development computer access, closed	0 — 10% 303	11 — 85% 251	> 85% 170	133
Classified security environment for computer and 25% of programs and data	No 289		Yes 156	133

Table 6
Continued

Question or Variable	Response Group Mean Productivity (DSL/MM)			Productivity Change (DSL/MM)
Structured programming	0−33% 169	34−66% −	66% 301	132
Design and code inspections	0−33% 220	34−66% 300	> 66% 339	119
Top-down development	0−33% 196	34−66% 237	> 66% 321	125
Chief programmer team usage	0−33% 219	34−66% −	> 66% 408	189
Overall complexity of code developed	< Average 314		> Average 185	129
Complexity of application processing	< Average 349	Average 345	> Average 168	181
Complexity of program flow	< Average 289	Average 299	> Average 209	80
Overall constraints on program design	Minimal 293	Average 286	Severe 166	107
Program design constraints on main storage	Minimal 391	Average 277	Severe 193	198
Program design constraints on timing	Minimal 303	Average 317	Severe 171	132
Code for real-time or interactive operation, or executing under severe timing constraint	< 10% 279	10−40% 337	> 40% 203	76
Percentage of code for delivery	0−90% 159	91−99% 327	100% 265	106
Code classified as non-mathematical application and I/O formatting programs	0−33% 188	34−66% 311	67−100% 267	79
Number of classes of items in the data base per 1000 lines of code	0−15 334	16−80 243	> 80 193	141
Number of pages of delivered documentation per 1000 lines of delivered code	0−32 320	33−88 252	> 88 195	125

When the mean productivity was computed for all the completed reports in the data base that indicated less than normal customer interface complexity, the result obtained was 500 delivered source lines of code per man-month of effort (DSL/MM). By a similar computation, the mean productivity for all projects that reported normal complexity was 295 DSL/MM, and the mean productivity for those reporting greater than normal complexity experience was 124 DSL/MM. The change in productivity between less-than-normal and greater-than-normal customer interface is 376 DSL/MM, as noted in the final column in Table 6. Three variables in the table (overall personnel experience, code complexity, and design constraints) were formed by combining the answers to several questions in the questionnaire. It should be noted that this analysis was performed on each variable independently and does not take into account either the possibility that these variables may be correlated, or that there may be interrelated effects associated with them.

The twenty-nine variables were then combined into an index, based on the effect of each variable on productivity, as indicated by the above analysis, to form a productivity index. The productivity index is computed as follows:

$$I = \sum_{i=1}^{29} W_i X_i \, ,$$

where

$I =$ productivity index for a project

$W_i =$ question weight, calculated as one-half $\log_{10}$ of the ratio of total productivity change indicated for a given question i

$X_i =$ question response $(+1, 0,$ or $-1)$, depending on whether the response indicates increased, nominal, or decreased productivity

An index was computed for fifty-one projects, and a plot of actual productivity for each project versus the computed productivity index and the least squares fit to this relationship is shown in Figure 2. The standard error of the estimate (standard deviation of the residuals) is shown as dashed lines.

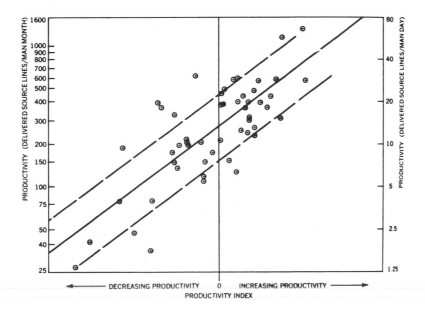

Figure 2. Relationship between productivity and productivity index for twenty-nine variables.

Rapid estimates

To support project estimates, a shortened version of the data collection form is used that contains excerpted questions associated with the twenty-nine variables used in the index. A program, running in the Time Sharing Option of OS/VS (TSO) was developed to compute and list the index estimates. This terminal-based program allows rapid response to project requests for information. The estimate of expected productivity is returned to the requester in the form of a report that contains a comparison between the project estimate and the one derived from the data base. Also included is a list of the reported attributes or variables that had a significant influence on the estimate. Where possible, detailed discussions are held on special factors associated with a project that may not be properly handled in the present algorithm.

Figure 3 is a plot similar to the one shown in Figure 2, which is presented for a hypothetical project. The productivity index is computed for the project from responses to the proposal questionnaire and yields the expected productivity to be attained, as determined by the measurements data base. In the case shown in Figure 3, the estimated productivity is seen to be two hundred delivered source lines of code per man-month (DSL/MM), with one standard error range of 115 to 340 DSL/MM. The project team's independently developed productivity estimate for the same conditions was 150 DSL/MM. Thus, in this case, the project estimate is a more conservative estimate than that given by the productivity index.

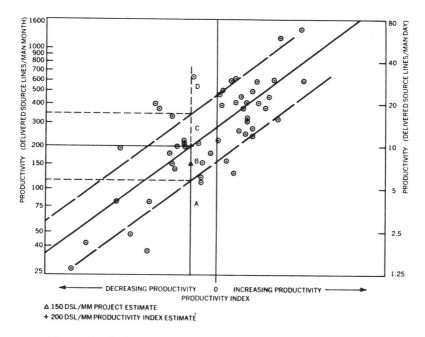

Figure 3. Estimated productivity for a hypothetical project.

Other estimates

Consider additional conclusions that can be drawn from Figure 3. If we assume a normal distribution for the observations, when they are plotted as a log of the productivity versus a log of the productivity index in Figure 3, the probability P_A that the project would have a productivity estimate in region A (i.e., less than 2.06 or the $\log_{10}$ of 115 DSL/MM) is about 0.17. The probability that the productivity estimate would be in region B (i.e., between 2.06 and 2.30, the log of 115 and 200 DSL/MM) is about 0.33. Similarly, P_C is 0.33 and P_D is 0.17. This is the probability distribution of productivity estimates, not the cumulative probability that a project will (or will not) achieve or exceed the productivity that was estimated.

Investigation is continuing into other variables from the data base that may also be related to productivity. Figure 4 shows several distributions that appear to have a significant relationship to productivity, although in two of these cases they are based on a limited number of observations. Table 7 expresses the net effect of the data plotted in Figure 4 in tabular form. Figure 4(A) shows productivity (in source lines of code per man-month) plotted against the ratio of developed source code to the sum of any original (or reused) code plus the developed code. The plot in Figure 4(A) suggests that productivity is highest when there is no original or reused code, that is, when all the code is developed from the inception of the project. As the percentage of reused code grows, the expected productivity decreases.

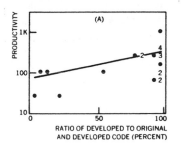
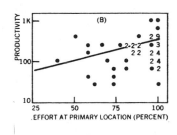
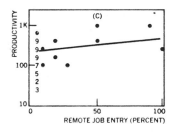

Figure 4. Additional productivity relationships.

Table 7
Additional Productivity Related Variables

Variable	Response Change (low to high percent)	Productivity Change* (percent)
Ratio of developed to original plus developed code	0 to 100	705
Effort at primary development location	50 to 100	215
Remote job entry computer access	0 to 100	205

*Based on least squares fit to data in Figure 4

Figure 4(B), although it contains a large amount of scatter, suggests that when the development effort is spread across more than one location, i.e., as the percentage of effort at the primary location becomes less than 100 percent, the productivity decreases. Another question currently of interest is the impact of remote job entry on productivity. Most of the completed projects in the data base were developed without the use of terminals, as Figure 4(C) shows. On the basis of a least squares fit, however, those projects that use remote job entry do appear to have an increase in productivity.

Other results of programming analysis

Although the primary effort has been directed toward productivity analysis, other analyses have been performed on the data base. Results of these efforts to the present time are presented here. The data can be used to check productivity estimates, and to check current project parameters against past experience, as reflected by the data base. Such results provide a multidimensional approach to crosschecking a number of the factors that enter into estimates of effort: productivity, duration, documentation, and computer costs. These results also indicate the nature of the analyses that can be performed against the data base.

Documentation is a critical product of every software project, and documentation costs are an important component of the estimation process. A useful parameter for measuring documentation is number of pages. Figure 5 is a plot of delivered documentation in number of pages versus delivered source lines of code. Documentation is defined here as program functional specifications and descriptions, users' guides, test specifications and results, flow charts, and program source listings that are delivered as part of the documentation. As a first approximation, the least squares fit indicates that a linear or first-order relationship exists; that is, the number of pages of delivered documentation varies directly as the number of lines of source code.

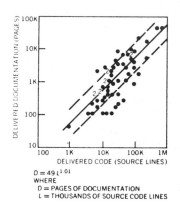

$$D = 49 L^{1.01}$$
WHERE
D = PAGES OF DOCUMENTATION
L = THOUSANDS OF SOURCE CODE LINES

Figure 5. Relationship between documentation and delivered code.

After programming project estimates have been completed, those estimates can be checked against the data base by using the plots in Figures 5-10. If, for example, the size of the delivered software product is estimated as ten thousand lines of source code (as shown in Figure 5), it can be seen from past experience that the expected number of pages of documentation to be delivered is five hundred. The range for one standard error for this given value is one hundred eighty to thirteen hundred pages. This provides an independent calibration point that the manager can use to compare his estimate against the experience of past projects. A significant difference between the two does not necessarily imply an error on the part of the manager, but it does suggest that the assumptions and estimates might be re-examined.

Project duration

The question of how much time to allow for the development of software is always difficult to assess. The relationship between duration (expressed in months) and delivered source lines of code is shown in Figure 6. Project duration as a function of total effort in man-months is shown in Figure 7. Initial analysis indicates that a cubic relationship fits the data in both of these figures. This implies that the duration of effort increases by the cube root of the number of source lines of code delivered or by the cube root of the total effort applied to the development of the code. For example, for a project that is developing a software product of 10 thousand lines of source code, the expected duration of the effort is $4.0 \times 10.0^{0.38}$ or 9.6 months. Figure 7 does not imply that simply reducing total effort automatically permits a reduction in project duration. Such a reduction would more likely make it impossible to produce and test the required volume of code.

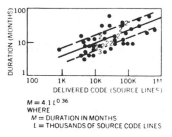

M = 4.1 L^{0.36}
WHERE
M = DURATION IN MONTHS
L = THOUSANDS OF SOURCE CODE LINES

Figure 6. Relationship between project duration and delivered code.

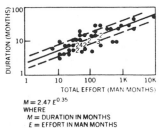

M = 2.47 E^{0.35}
WHERE
M = DURATION IN MONTHS
E = EFFORT IN MAN MONTHS

Figure 7. Relationship between project duration and total effort.

Staff size

The staff size utilized to develop a given software product is influenced by a number of factors, including the time allowed for development, the amount of code to be developed, and the staffing rates that can be achieved. After a project has been estimated, one convenient measure used to describe the size of the project is the average number of people required. Figure 8 shows a relationship that can be used as another check on the estimating process. It shows the relationship between the staff size — expressed in terms of the average number of people (defined as total man-months of effort divided by the duration) — and the total effort applied.

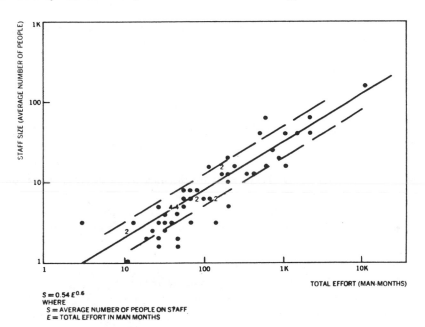

S = 0.54 E^{0.6}
WHERE
S = AVERAGE NUMBER OF PEOPLE ON STAFF
E = TOTAL EFFORT IN MAN MONTHS

Figure 8. Relationship between average staff size and total effort.

Computer cost

Estimating computer costs is very difficult, but at the same time it can also be a very significant fraction of the total cost. Although only eighteen of the completed projects in the data base had computer costs reported, some interesting relationships are indicated when computer costs are compared with the amount of delivered code and the total effort, as is shown in Figures 9 and 10. In Figure 9, two observations (circled) are evidently out of bounds when plotted against delivered code. These same two observations, however, fit well with the total effort, as shown by the plot in Figure 10. Based on this limited evidence, it appears that computer costs are closely related to effort, and they appear to have nearly a first-power (or linear) relationship. Note that in Figure 9, the two out-of-bounds points are not included in determining the least square fit.

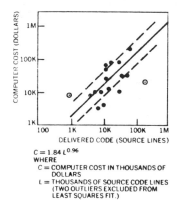

$C = 1.84\,L^{0.96}$
WHERE
C = COMPUTER COST IN THOUSANDS OF DOLLARS
L = THOUSANDS OF SOURCE CODE LINES
(TWO OUTLIERS EXCLUDED FROM LEAST SQUARES FIT.)

Figure 9. Relationship between computer cost and delivered code.

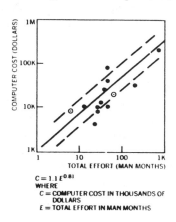

$C = 1.1\,E^{0.81}$
WHERE
C = COMPUTER COST IN THOUSANDS OF DOLLARS
E = TOTAL EFFORT IN MAN MONTHS

Figure 10. Relationship between computer cost and total effort.

Concluding remarks

Regression method

The present approach to productivity estimation, although useful, is far from being optimized. Based on the results of the variable analysis described in this paper, and supplemented by the results of the continued investigation of additional variables related to productivity, an experimental regression model has been developed. Preliminary results indicate that the model reduces the scatter. Further work is being done to determine the potential of regression as an estimating tool, as well as to extend the analyses of the areas of computer usage, documentation volume, duration, and staffing.

Appendix

The effective utilization of programming measurements data requires the ability to store, retrieve, process, and report data. Specialized capabilities to do various types of statistical analyses are also required. These capabilities are provided by a Programming Project Measurement System. This system is composed of two subsystems, the question processing subsystem and the question analysis subsystem. The basic functions provided by the question processing subsystem are the maintenance of the data base (which contains the information submitted in response to the questionnaire), the retrieval and listing of data from the data base in various report formats, and the extraction of data for transfer to the question analysis subsystem for statistical analysis. Figure 11 shows the overall flow of information in the Programming Project Measurement System. The question analysis subsystem uses the Statistical Package for the Social Sciences (a product of SPSS, Inc.), which is an integrated system of computer programs for the analysis of data, and provides the user with a large set of procedures for data selection, transformation, and file manipulation, and offers a large number of commonly used statistical routines.

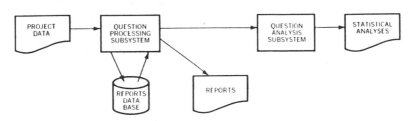

Figure 11. Programming Project Measurement System.

Statistical routines include descriptive statistics, frequency distributions, cross tabulations, correlation, partial correlation, multiple regression, and factor analysis. The package has its own internal data management facilities that can be used to modify analysis files of data and can be used in conjunction with any of the statistical procedures. These facilities enable the user to generate variable transformations, recode variables, sample, select or weight specified cases, and add to or alter the data or the analysis files.

Project data enter the Programming Project Measurement System by way of questionnaires that are answered by project personnel. At the inception of the measurement program discussed in this paper, one questionnaire was used for both development and service (maintenance) contracts. On service contracts, questionnaires were to be submitted quarterly. For development projects, four questionnaires were to be prepared by the project at major milestones during the life of the project. Identical questionnaires were to be submitted, but not every item required an answer at each submission. The four reporting milestones were the following:

- Start of work.
- Preliminary design review or equivalent.
- Top-down programming — completion of integration of one-half of the program units, or
  Bottom-up programming — completion of unit test of three quarters of the program units.
- Acceptance test completion.

Problems arose when project personnel tried to use the same questionnaire form for both development and service contracts; differences between those two types of activities made it difficult to fit all the necessary questions into one questionnaire format. A further problem was the reporting frequency of development contracts. The four milestones might often be six months to two years apart, and many changes could occur in project organization, in project specifications, and in the definitions of products to be delivered, so that it was difficult to correlate questionnaire responses from milestone to milestone.

For these reasons changes were made in the questionnaires and frequency of reporting. Separate questionnaires were created for development projects (Software Development Reports) and for service efforts (Software Service Reports). Development reports, which cover detailed qualitative items as well as quantitative data, are submitted at the start of work and again at acceptance test completion. Between these two submittals, a Monthly Software Development Report is submitted. This is a one-page summary of the status of a product, cost, and effort that is submitted each month. The Software Service Report is an overview of a product that is being serviced and is submitted at the start and end of service. The Quarterly Software Service Report is a summary of the product, cost, and effort status, plus a detailed reporting of errors and their impact. Reporting is done by programming projects that are developing or servicing products in the form of lines of code and that employ two or more programmers with an expenditure of twelve or more man-months of effort.

References: Walston & Felix

Cited References

1. B.W. Boehm, "Software and its impact: a quantitative assessment," *Datamation* **19,** No. 5, 48-59 (May 1973).

2. F.T. Baker, "Chief programmer team management of production programming," *IBM Systems Journal* **11,** No. 1, 56-73 (1972).

3. *HIPO — A Design Aid and Documentation Technique*, Order No. GC20-1851, IBM Corp., Data Processing Division, White Plains, New York 10504.

4. F.M. Luppino and R.L. Smith, *Programming Support Library Functional Requirements*, U.S. Air Force, Headquarters, Rome Air Development Center, Griffis Air Force Base, New York (July 1974). See also Rome Air Development Center, Structured Programming Series, Vol. V.

5. E.W. Dijkstra, "Notes on structured programming," pp. 1-82. O.J. Dahl, E.W. Dijkstra, and C.A.R. Hoare, *Structured Programming*, Academic Press, New York, New York (1972).

6. F.T. Baker, "System quality through structured programming," *AFIPS Conference Proceedings* **41,** Part I, 339-343 (1972).

7. M.E. Fagan, "Design and code inspections to reduce errors in program development," *IBM Systems Journal* **15,** No. 3, 182-211 (1976).

8. J.D. Aron, "Information systems in perspective," *Computing Surveys* **1,** No. 4 (December 1969).

9. G.F. Weinwurm and H.J. Zagorski, *Research into the Management of Computer Programming: A Transition Analysis of Cost Estimation Techniques,* SDC Report TM-2712, System Development Corp., Santa Monica, California (1965).

10. E.A. Nelson, *Research into the Management of Computer Programming: Some Characteristics of Programming Cost Data from Government and Industry,* System Development Corp., Santa Monica, California (November 1965).

General References

1. *Improved Programming Technologies — An Overview,* IBM Systems Reference Library, Order No. GC20-1850, IBM Corp., Data Processing Division, White Plains, New York 10504.

2. P. Van Leer, "Top-down development using a program design language," *IBM Systems Journal* **15,** No. 2, 155-170 (1976).

3. G.J. Myers, "Characteristics of composite design," *Datamation* **19,** No. 9, 100-102 (September 1973).

4. W.P. Stevens, G.J. Myers, and L.L. Constantine, "Structured design," *IBM Systems Journal* **13,** No. 2, 115-139 (1974).

5. E.W. Dijkstra, "Notes on structured programming," T.H.E. Report WSK-03, Second Edition, Technical University Eindhoven, The Netherlands (April 1970).

6. E.W. Dijkstra, "GOTO statement considered harmful," *Communications of the ACM* **11,** No. 3, 147-148 (March 1968).

7. H.D. Mills, *Mathematical Foundations for Structured Programming,* FSC 72-6012, IBM Corp., Gaithersburg, Maryland 20760 (February 1972). [Ed. note: Reprinted in this volume, paper 14.]

8. H.D. Mills, *Structured Programming,* FSC 70-1070, IBM Corp., Gaithersburg, Maryland 20760 (October 1970).

9. J.G. Rogers, "Structured programming for virtual storage systems," *IBM Systems Journal* **14,** No. 4, 385-406 (1975).

10. G.J. Myers, *Software Reliability: Principles and Practices,* Wiley-Interscience, New York, to be published.

11. G.J. Myers, *Reliable Software Through Composite Design,* New York: Petrocelli/Charter (1975). Also see W.P. Stevens, G.J. Myers, and L.L. Constantine, "Structured Design," *IBM Systems Journal* **13,** No. 2, 115-139 (1974).

12. D.L. Parnas, "On the criteria to be used in decomposing systems into modules," *Communications of the ACM* **15,** No. 12, 1053-1058 (1972).

13. N. Wirth, *Systematic Programming: An Introduction,* Prentice-Hall, Inc., Englewood Cliffs, New Jersey (1973).

14. J.F. Stay, "HIPO and integrated program design," *IBM Systems Journal* **15,** No. 2, 143-154 (1976).

15. M.F. Fagan, "Design and code inspections to reduce errors in program development," *IBM Systems Journal* **15,** No. 3, 182-211 (1976). [Ed. note: Reprinted in this volume, paper 7.]

16. G.J. Myers, "Composite design facilities of six programming languages," *IBM Systems Journal* **15,** No. 3, 212-224 (1976).

Measuring Programming Quality and Productivity

Although it is not always appreciated, the great advances in chemistry, physics, and other scientific disciplines in the 19th and 20th centuries were preceded by advances in the measurement of physical attributes and the development of accurate measuring instruments in the 17th and 18th centuries. Indeed, it can almost be said that scientific progress of any kind is totally dependent on the ability to measure quantities precisely. Therefore, the work of men like Gabriel Daniel Fahrenheit, who made the first mercury thermometer in 1714; of John Harrison, who made the first practical chronometer in 1728, and many other measurement specialists, are the fundamental underpinnings of modern scientific achievements.

It is because of the vital significance of measurement to progress that so many common words and units of measure today are taken from the names of those who explored better ways of measuring new phenomena: Ampere, Celsius, Coulomb, Curie, Henry, Hertz, Joule, Ohm, and Watt were all researchers whose names have been applied to common units of measure, and there are others such as Faraday, Galvani, and Volta who have indirectly lent their names to measurement.

In the field of computer programming, the lack of precise and unambiguous units of measure for quality and productivity has been a source of considerable concern to programming managers throughout the industry. In 1972, there was established in the San Jose Programming Center of the IBM Corporation a study group to explore the interrelated topics of program quality, programmer productivity, and the units of measure that could clearly display trends in both areas.

One of the projects carried out by that group was a detailed analysis of common units of measure used to assess pro-

SOURCE: T.C. Jones, *IBM Systems Journal,* 1978.

ductivity and quality throughout the open literature of the entire industry. Some of the findings were surprising, and it soon became evident that a number of widespread units of measure were misleading and even paradoxical. For example, the unit *cost per defect* was discovered to yield the lowest values for the most defective programs, thus making obsolete technologies appear more favorable in some instances than modern ones. The unit *lines of code written per programmer-month* was found to consistently penalize high-level languages, and tended to favor programs written in Assembler language. These findings are of some importance to the industry, because they make it difficult to compare productivity and quality from program to program. In extreme cases, they can slow down the acceptance of new methods because the methods may — when measured — give the incorrect impression of being less effective than former techniques, even though the older approaches actually were more expensive. This paper attempts to describe the common units of measure, and point out the nature of the paradoxes that occasionally occur. When the paradoxes and measurement variables are clearly understood, it becomes possible to make reasonable assessments of programming quality and productivity, and to apply units of measure that behave in a predictable manner.

Counting lines of code

A fundamental problem of all measurement techniques involving computer programs is that of knowing exactly what is meant by the phrase "lines of code." This topic is discussed in References 1 and 2. The conclusions there and the one here are generally the same; namely, that programs consist of more than executable lines of code. Programs also contain commentary lines, data declarations, Job Control Language (JCL) in some cases, and macroinstructions. Some counting methods consider every statement to be a line, whereas other methods consider only a subset, such as executable lines and data declarations, in the counts of the program. Between the extremes of counting everything and counting only executable lines there may be more than a two-to-one variability for the same program.

This problem is not really too serious provided it is recognized. Counting methods become troublesome when productivity rates are being discussed without knowing the line-counting rules in effect. The convention used at one programming center calls for counting executable lines and data declarations, but not counting comments or JCL. Macroinstructions are counted once when expanded, and calls that invoke macroinstructions are counted once. There is no inference that this method is either better or worse than the other possibilities. The key is to state the counting rules when reporting on quality and productivity. Otherwise, there is no way of knowing what the results mean.

A more subtle problem occurs when counting lines of code for programs written in high-level languages. In PL/I, for example, a line might be everything that occurs between semicolons, or everything that is written on a single line of a coding pad. Here, too, it is important to state the conventions in effect for the data to be meaningful.

To avoid such variations associated with counting lines of source code, an alternative is to count bytes or object instructions. Although this method has much to recommend it and is often used successfully, it is not always easy to estimate the final, compiled size of programs written in high-level languages. Since compilers differ in efficiency, and since individual programming styles can interact with the compilers in astonishingly diverse ways [3], it is incorrect to assume that X number of source code lines in a given high-level language compile into Y number of object code lines.

As an example of the difficulty of doing source-to-object code expansions consistently, a number of cost-estimating reference manuals recommend different ratios for expanding high-level source lines into object lines for a particular language. The lowest expansion is 1.6 object lines for each source line, and the greatest expansion is 6 object lines per source line. It is a simple matter to count object lines in completed programs, but it is not easy to estimate expansion factors before a program has been written, without knowing the programmers' styles and the compilers to be used.

Still another possibility is to accept the uncertainties of line counting and accumulate multiple counts of source lines, object lines, and bytes. Identify the compilers used. Then publish the line-counting conventions in effect for the programs being reported.

With any method, there are even more variables associated with counting lines of code than those so far discussed. For example, some programs are written in mixed languages. Other programs require scaffold code or throwaway code for testing and integrating the main program, yet that code does not become part of the final, delivered product. One might question the counting of such code. How should one count the changing of an existing program? Should only the new lines be counted, or should the base lines in the existing program also be counted?

In counting as in accounting, experience and practice require that whatever the counting method, it should be (1) documented and clearly understood by all who work on the program; and (2) the significant programming reality is the final version — its quality and cost — that is delivered to the users. The size of this final version, counted by whatever method is agreed upon, is the key to uniformly assessing productivity and defect rates.

Once delivered, of course, programs become candidates for changes and modifications, as defects are noted and the original requirements change. Here, too, the basic concept applies that what is important is the version of the program actually delivered after modifications.

As in building a house, in which the scaffolding is part of the cost, programs seem to be characterized by the same kind of thinking. For initial creation, the important aspect is the cost of the delivered program. Intermediate versions are significant only because they are part of the cost of producing the final program. After installation, the costs of program changes and extensions are important both as they occur, and because they are part of cumulative costs of the program. In other words, the size of the change and the cost of the change are important, as well as the size of the total program after the change and the cumulative cost of the program after the change. These concepts are discussed in detail later in this paper. Because of the uncertainties in counting lines of code, object lines, or bytes, one might come to believe that the entire issue is irrelevant. Programs, after all, are written to provide functions, and the number of lines of code it takes to supply a function is of much less importance than the cost of the function itself. In fact, it is not important that the function be supplied via a program. If microcode or an electronic circuit can supply the same function for a lower cost than programming, it might be preferable to measure *cost per function* rather than cost per line of code.

Although such an evaluative approach may become increasingly important, this paper does not explore these issues for several reasons. There is a great deal still to be learned about quality and productivity normalized against lines of code. We have not explored the limits of knowledge, and comparisons between different kinds of programs — with lines of code counted the same way for both — almost daily yield new insights and discoveries. It is premature to abandon this method, just when results are becoming encouraging. Also, to explore such things as cost per function, it is necessary to be able to define and count functions. At present, the methodology for doing this seems too uncertain, although some progress is visible.

Measuring program quality

The term *quality* is used here to mean an absence of defects that would cause a program to behave unpredictably or stop successful execution. There are two fundamental ways of minimizing programming defects that significantly determine quality measurements. One is to prevent defects from occurring. The other is to remove defects that have occurred. Therefore, quality measurements are related to restricting the quantity of defects that come into existence, and their efficient removal by various kinds of reviews and tests used in programming.

A theory of defect removal

The pivotal concepts in the defect removal portion of quality measurement are those of *defect removal efficiency* and *cumulative defect removal efficiency*. Defect removal efficiency is the reduction of the defects that are present at the beginning of a defect removal operation by a certain percentage. Cumulative defect removal efficiency is the percentage of defects that have been removed by a series of removal operations, based on the number of defects that are present at the beginning of the series, or added while the series is in progress. The concept of cumulative defect removal efficiency is illustrated by Figure 1.

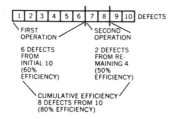

Figure 1. Cumulative defect removal efficiency.

The nature of cumulative defect removal efficiency is shown by the results of the second defect removal operation, and in combining the results of the first and second operations. Note that although the second removal operation has found two defects out of the total of ten in the hypothetical program, its efficiency is actually fifty percent (not twenty percent) because only four defects remain in the program at the time the operation is carried out.

Since the sum of the effects of the two operations is eight defects out of ten removed, the cumulative efficiency is eighty percent. Even though the first operation had a sixty percent efficiency and the second operation had an efficiency of fifty percent, the cumulative efficiency clearly is not one hundred ten percent.

Bad fixes are another aspect of defect removal that require quantification when the efficiency of a given defect removal operation is being measured with accuracy. *Bad fix injection* is the introduction of a new defect, one not previously in the program, while repairing a defect in that program. It is useful to keep independent records of bad fixes so that separate statistics can be maintained for both detection efficiency and repair effectiveness.

Estimating program defects

Given defect removal efficiency and cumulative defect removal efficiency, programming defect removal operations become more open to analysis and calibration. Indeed, it is largely through direct measurements of defect removal efficiency that improved forms of removal operations, such as design and code inspections [4] have come into existence.

Since defect removal efficiency statistics imply a knowledge of all, or almost all, defects found during the life of a program, the question arises of how such a theory of defect removal efficiency can be turned into a practical tool for everyday programming. We believe that this can be done as follows. As a program moves through the development cycle, records are kept of the quantities of defects found in all removal operations. Later, when the program has reached its intended users, records are also kept of the defects found in actual utilization of the program in its production environment. After several years, we sum all the defect records and find both the total quantity of discovered defects and the defect removal efficiencies of the series of reviews, inspections, and tests that were used to bring the program into existence.

We have been seeking trends based on experience that might prove to be useful in making predictions. Therefore, the procedure just given is not usually much help to the first few programs to be analyzed because too much time elapses before a sufficient quantity of data have been collected to carry out the analysis. Indeed, a program may already have been replaced or discarded before the data are sufficient. However, as more programs are measured and the results are analyzed, trends and problem areas become visible, and gradually significant improvements in cumulative defect removal efficiency become possible. Thus, real-time results may not always be possible, but long-term improvement in knowledge of removal efficiency eventually repays the effort. This is not unlike experience in other fields, such as medicine, in which the development of a cure for a disease is generally preceded by careful epidemiological studies on the causes of the disease, its outbreaks, the vectors that transmit it, and all other observations that relate to the disease.

Another problem in accumulating statistics of defect removal efficiency concerns major program changes between defect removal operations. A change in user requirements or a design change might take place between two defect removal operations. The result might be that the program that enters the second operation is quite different from the program that exited after the first operation. Our experience suggests two methods of dealing with this problem, a simpler method that tends to introduce distortions into the records (which may be tolerable), and a sophisticated method that preserves the accuracy of the data, but with added expense.

By the simpler method, cumulative defect removal is expressed by the following formula:

$$\text{Cumulative defect removal efficiency} = \frac{\text{defects found before release}}{\text{defects found before and after release}}$$

By this formula, if 100 defects are found in a program during its entire life — in both development and in production — and 90 of the defects are found before release, then the cumulative defect removal efficiency is considered to be 90 percent. We often find this coarse measure to be useful.

Detailed method

The more sophisticated and detailed method requires the flagging of changes in the programming work products, including lines of code themselves. Although our goal is to arrive at the same formula as has just been described, the more detailed approach of flagging calls for analyzing the defect data and adjusting the quantities, depending on whether the problems were true defects or were caused by changing requirements. An adjunct of this method is that of analyzing the sources of programming defects. Given in Reference 2 are the following six causes of programming defects:

- Functional problems and the misunderstanding of user requests.
- Problems of logic and internal program design.
- Coding problems.
- Documentation problems.
- Incorrect repairs or bad fixes.
- Miscellaneous causes (a small category).

If a flagging system were utilized, and if records were kept against each work product during each defect removal operation, the resulting information could be displayed in a table that shows the contribution of each defect source to the overall total of defects, and the contribution of each defect removal operation toward the elimination of defects in each source. For simplicity, Table 1 gives an example display that is characteristic of the data we have collected, although this specific example is a hypothetical one. (All data are given in units of percent.)

Table 1
Sources of Defects and Defect Removal Efficiency by Source

A. Percentages of defects by source

Functional design and misunderstandings	15
Logic design and misunderstandings	20
Coding problems	30
Documentation and others (not shown)	35

B. Percentage of defect removal efficiency by source

Activity	Efficiency percentage against defects in			Percentage of incorrect repairs to defects
	function	logic	coding	
Functional specification review	50	—	—	+1
Logic specification review	40	50	—	+2
Module logic inspection	60	70	—	+2
Module code inspection	65	75	70	+3
Unit test	10	10	25	+4
Function test	20	25	55	+5
Component test	15	20	65	+5
Subsystem test	15	15	55	+7
System test	10	10	40	+10
Cumulative efficiency	98	98	99	
Net cumulative efficiency		98		

Suppose that a program's defect causes fall into only two categories, A and B. Suppose also the program is known to have 100 total defects, of which 40 are caused by category-A problems and 60 are caused by category-B problems. Then it is clear that category A causes 40 percent of the program's initial problems, and category B causes 60 percent of the problems. Now suppose that the program is to be tested by a single defect removal operation that is known to have an efficiency of 50 percent against category-A defects and 70 percent against category-B defects. After the completion of the defect removal operation, the 40 category-A defects would have been reduced by 50 percent, so 20 undetected category-A defects are presumed to remain in the program for discovery by subsequent defect removal operations. The 60 category-B defects would have been reduced by 70 percent. Thus, 42 category-B defects would have been removed and 18 such defects would remain for subsequent removal. Since a total of 62 defects out of 100 have been removed, the cumulative detection efficiency against both sources is 62 percent in this example.

Of course, in operational situations it is necessary to adjust such elementary calculations as these to include bad fixes, to handle more than a single defect removal operation, and to recognize defects against more than two sources. In our experience, the necessary recordkeeping has been rather complicated, but the long-term value of the data and the insights that are gained have proved to be quite beneficial.

There is a great amount of record-keeping complexity associated with the more detailed flagging method of defect removal efficiency analysis. Therefore, the simpler method may prove to be useful initially, even considering the vagaries that this method introduces. These may be tolerable for crude calculations and rough analyses.

Simpler method

To make the simpler method truly simple, however, it is necessary to normalize the data. Because programs vary widely in size and in other attributes that can cause defect quantities to fluctuate, it is not convenient to measure the raw quantities of defects alone. It is more practical to express defect levels in terms of some general unit, such as *defects per thousand lines of source code.* (Let the term "lines" be defined by local convention.) This method of normalization is useful for both quality and productivity measures, as is explained later in this paper.

In working with the simpler form of defect removal efficiency analysis, it is necessary to make the following two simplifying assumptions:

- All defects, regardless of source or of origin (whether design problems, coding problems, or some other) are lumped together and counted as the single variable, *defects.*

- The defect removal efficiencies of all reviews, inspections, tests, and other defect removal operations are lumped together and counted as the single variable, *cumulative defect removal efficiency.*

With these two simplifying assumptions and with the data for defect quantities in normalized form as defects per thousand lines of code, the results are both easy to work with and surprisingly powerful. Even though some imprecision is unavoidable, the value of this approach is that it breaks down the topic of quality into the two pivotal concepts of defect prevention and defect removal. The method also allows program data to be displayed as a matrix or table of data.

Maintenance potential

The most basic display is that of total defects per thousand lines of code as one axis, and the cumulative defect removal efficiency as the other axis. Elements of the resulting matrix might be called the *maintenance potential* of a program. The maintenance potential of a program is the quantity of defects not found during defect removal operations. Undiscovered defects are sources of potential maintenance activity, if such defects occur during the actual use of a program. Table 2 is an example of such a matrix that is typical of values for selected ranges of the two variables.

Table 2 shows that if the total quantity of defects in a particular program ranges between 30 and 35 per thousand lines of code, and the cumulative defect removal efficiency of all reviews, inspections, and tests ranges between 90 and 95 percent, then the maintenance potential or quantity of undiscovered defects that might cause maintenance changes ranges between 1.5 and 3.5 potential maintenance problems per thousand lines of code. For example, the best case in this situation is 30 defects per thousand lines of code, 95 percent cumulative defect removal efficiency, for a potential maintenance load of 1.5 problems per thousand lines. This is shown in the lower right corner of Table 2.

Table 2
Maintenance Potential* or Undiscovered Defects as a Function
of Cumulative Defect Removal Efficiency and Initial Total Defects
Per Thousand Lines of Code

Total defects per thousand lines of code	Cumulative defect removal efficiency percentage					
	90	*91*	*92*	*93*	*94*	*95*
35	3.5	3.15	2.8	2.45	2.1	1.75
34	3.4	3.06	2.72	2.38	2.04	1.7
33	3.3	2.97	2.64	2.31	1.98	1.65
32	3.2	2.88	2.56	2.24	1.92	1.6
31	3.1	2.79	2.48	2.17	1.86	1.55
30	3.0	2.7	2.4	2.1	1.8	1.5

*Maintenance potential = total defects − defect removal efficiency

As has been mentioned, a whole family of interesting and useful data displays can be constructed from the basic concepts already presented, when augmented by other kinds of programming data. For example, suppose there is uncertainty regarding how many lines of code must be written for a new program. All that is known is that the quantity probably falls somewhere between 15 and 20,000 lines. In such a case, it is possible to link a series of graphs together to display all key variables. For example, the best case for the program just cited in connection with Table 2 consists of the smallest quantity of lines, the lowest number of defects, and the highest defect removal efficiency. That means 15,000 lines multiplied by 30 defects per thousand lines, for a lifetime potential of 450 defects. If the cumulative defect removal efficiency is 95 percent for the program in question one would calculate a potential of 1.5 defects per thousand lines, or 23 defects in all.

The worst case for the program is 20 thousand lines multiplied by 35 defects per thousand lines, for a lifetime potential of 700 defects. If the cumulative defect removal efficiency is 90 percent in this case, then the program is estimated to contain 3.5 defects per thousand lines, or 70 defects in all.

Probability rectangle

The general form for displaying the linkage of ranges of variables together is what I call a *probability rectangle* because it bounds the probable ranges within which the program is to be developed. A series of such rectangles, each based on at least one variable from a previous rectangle in the series, is what I call *linked probability rectangles*.

Table 3
Maintenance Potential as a Function
of Hypothetical Program Size Range

Range in undetected defects per thousand lines	Program size range (thousands of lines)	
	15	20
3.5	52.5	70
1.5	18	30

Such rectangles take the form of a matrix, with the base of the rectangle indicating the range of one variable, and the height indicating the range of another variable. The elements of the matrix indicate the interaction of the two variables. The size of a matrix (or number of elements) depends on the ranges of the variables and the granularity — degree of coarseness — with which the data are displayed.

Table 3 illustrates a probability rectangle for the number of maintenance changes that might be expected in the hypothetical program. Here the size range is 15,000 to 20,000 lines and defects range from 30 to 35 per thousand lines. The cumulative defect removal efficiency ranges from 90 to 95 percent. Table 3 is the simplest form of the probability rectangle and shows only the extreme ends of the ranges, with no intervening values. In reality, more information is usually displayed. We have used this simple form to clarify the principle.

Note in this probability rectangle that although none of the intermediate variables used in its construction varies enormously, the difference between the best and worst case is quite large. Indeed, the best case is 18 potential problems (or defects remaining to be fixed) and the worst case is 70 defects, or 3.88 times the potential problems of the best case. When the variables that affect a program's defect rate are separated and analyzed independently, and then recombined, it becomes evident that small changes yield large results.

It is often said that quality cannot be tested into a program. The combined impact of improving the defect removal efficiency by even a few percentage points, if coupled with reducing the quantity of defects by another few percentage points, yields a large reduction of defects in the delivered program.

Before discussing productivity measurements, it is well to observe that the term quality has been used here to mean an absence of defects. Of course, there are many other attributes associated with quality than defect rate. However, when discussing the problem of quality, defect rates and defect removal efficiency are certainly reasonable starting points. Although there are programs with low defect rates that may not properly be called high-quality programs, there is usually a correlation between overall satisfaction with a program and its defect levels. On the other hand, few if any programs that have high defect levels engender much satisfaction or merit the admittedly subjective feeling that high quality has been achieved.

The improved programming technologies that have been introduced since 1968 may be exemplified by three groups. (1) Top-down design and structured code are defect prevention techniques, and act by reducing the quantity of defects that have to be found and repaired. (2) Design reviews and inspections are defect removal techniques and act by increasing the efficiency with which defects are removed. (3) On-line debugging methods are direct aids and act by facilitating the work of programming. Since the main thrust of modern programming includes defect prevention and removal, the measurement of these attributes is vital to demonstrating the efficiency of the improved programming methodologies [5].

Measuring programming productivity

Two measures of programming productivity are the speed and the cost of the programming. The common meaning of *productivity* is completing an activity as expeditiously as possible. The term also has the economic connotation of goods and services produced per unit of labor or expense. The common meaning is used when discussing how fast programming tasks are carried out, and the economic meaning is used when discussing program costs.

Units of measure

The units of measure of programming speed I have called *work units* because they relate to the speed at which programmers work. Thus work units might be characterized as natural, human-oriented measures. Examples of work units common to programmers are the following:

- Lines of code written per programmer-month.
- Pages of documentation written per writer-month.
- CPU hours and connect hours per programmer-month.
- Test cases written and executed per programmer-month.

At the present time, the most common unit of measure for productivity in the industry is lines of code written per programmer-month. Variants of that measure include such possibilities as lines of code per programmer-year or per programmer-day. The concept of lines per unit time has limitations that are discussed later in this paper.

The units of measure of programming cost I have called *cost units*. These units concern the program itself, rather than the human activities that go into creating the program. Examples of programming cost units include the following:

- Programmer-months of effort per thousand lines of code.
- CPU hours and connect hours per thousand lines of code.
- Dollars expended per thousand lines of code.
- Cost per page for documentation.
- Cost per defect for maintenance.

Here too there are variations, such as hours per line instead of months per thousand lines. Also bytes may replace lines in a definition. The general concept is the same, however, to normalize by the product rather than by the work of creating the product.

Lines of code per programmer-month

Both work units and cost units are needed in evaluating programming productivity. A basic difference between the two units is that each is the reciprocal of the other. A misunderstanding of this difference has sometimes led to one of the problems with lines of code per programmer-month. In such a case, for example, the work unit has mistakenly been pressed into service as a cost unit, where it has sometimes served unsuccessfully. As a general unit of measure, lines of code per programmer-month has a number of weaknesses to which industry-wide variations in reported programming productivity may be attributed.

Noted here are five problem areas that involve lines of code per programmer-month:

- Sensitivity to line-counting variations.
- Ineffectiveness for noncoding tasks.
- Tendency to penalize high-level language programs in favor of programs written in Assembler language.
- Arithmetic awkwardness in accounting for subtasks.
- Attention focusing on the act of coding, which is a misdirection, since the coding of a program is but a small part of the total effort required.

Line counting

Line counting variations have been discussed earlier in this paper and in Reference 1. We merely add that they can lead to perhaps a two-to-one variation in apparent productivity, depending on the line counting method used.

Noncoding tasks

The problem of ineffectiveness in measuring noncoding tasks is summarized here from a fuller discussion in Reference 6. The complete job of developing a computer program requires more than coding activities and these activities must also be measured. Therefore, when lines of code per programmer-month is used on noncoding tasks, the results are apt to be questionable. Results may even approach being nonsensical, as illustrated by this scenario. With modern defect prevention and defect removal techniques in programming, it sometimes happens that no defects are discovered during testing because the program has no defects at the time the test is carried out. If testing is done by an independent group rather than by the programmers themselves this tends to introduce slack time into development. By normal program development practice, the programmer usually cannot be fully reassigned until testing is over, in case defects should be discovered. Since it is nonproductive, slack time does not contribute to lines of code per programmer-month. It is therefore inaccurate to say for example, that one's productivity is one thousand lines of code per month during testing when there is no coding, and much of the time is spent waiting for bugs that may never occur. It is reasonable to say that slack time has added one month to a project but it is not reasonable to say that slack has proceeded at a rate of one thousand lines of code per month.

High-level languages

The problem of penalizing high-level language programs has only recently been explored, and it has been found to be quite important. Many portions of a programming development project are language-independent, and take the same amount of time regardless of the programming language selected. Such things as understanding user requirements, writing specifications, writing test cases and writing user documentation are not affected in any way by the programming language selected. We know that high-level languages require fewer source statements to program a given function than does Assembler language. But language-independent activities proceed at the same rate as in Assembler language programs, yet fewer lines of code are written in high-level language than in Assembler language. The result is an apparent productivity lowering for the whole development cycle with high-level languages, even though development costs have actually been reduced. This is one of the paradoxes of programming measurement.

Table 4 illustrates an apparent loss of productivity when a program is written in a high-level language instead of Assembler language. Note that the true cost for the high-level language version of the same program was actually lower. The paradox lies in the unit of measure itself. Lines of code per programmer-month often displays this paradox, if activities other than pure coding are included in the measurements.

Table 4
The Paradox of Lines of Code Per Programmer-Month

Activity	Assembler program	High-level program
Design	4 weeks	4 weeks
Coding	4 weeks	2 weeks
Testing	4 weeks	2 weeks
Documentation	2 weeks	2 weeks
Management/support	2 weeks	2 weeks
Total effort	16 weeks (4 months)	12 weeks (3 months)
Lines of source code	2000	500
Lines of source code per programmer-month	500	167

Table 4 illustrates that although the high-level language version of the program has actually required four weeks less time than the Assembler language version (both versions assumed to offer identical functions), the high-level language apparent productivity expressed in terms of lines of code per programmer-month is only about one-third as great as that of Assembler language.

Although the Assembler language version in the example in Table 4 has 2000 lines and the high-level language version has 500 lines, this does not imply a general statement that one high-level language statement is equivalent to four Assembler language statements. As was mentioned earlier in this paper, there is no reason to believe that any expansion factor for any high-level language can yield uniformly acceptable results. This is one of the reasons why it is important to define line-counting rules when discussing productivity rates. It is also one of the reasons why it is generally advisable to establish separate productivity targets for programs in each source language, and to use extreme caution in comparing productivity rates (for source lines, object lines, or bytes) from language to language.

Subtasks

Another problem with lines of code per programmer-month is the cumbersome arithmetic it entails, when one tries to measure all parts of a programming development cycle. The point is illustrated by the following example. Suppose a program consisting of 1000 lines of source code has been developed. The development cycle consists of four separate activities, each of which has taken one month to complete and has yielded a total development expenditure of four programmer-months. The sum of four consecutive activities, each of which proceeded at a rate of 1000 lines of code per month, is not 4000 lines of code per month, but 250 lines of code per programmer-month. Although simple in this example, the concept is cumbersome if data for a number of programs are being analyzed, and each program is divided into a large number of subactivities.

Coding

The fifth problem with lines of code per programmer-month is that it contributes to a mental set toward the coding, a task that is not always a major activity.

The productivity measure of lines of code per programmer-month originated in the early days of programming, when writing a program was usually a one-person effort. This main activity may well have consisted of actual coding. Today, programs are often developed by teams of specialists, of which the coder is only one part. Further, in modular programming where programs are constructed from reusable modules, rather than being hand-coded, there may be no new coding to be measured.

Modern programming methods are moving rapidly in the direction of developing reusable modules that can be catalogued in a library, and then obtained from the library to create new programs with little or no additional coding. The trend of attention is now away from work units and toward cost units, as is discussed in this paper.

Other work units

As has been previously mentioned, there are work units other than lines of code per programmer-month. The most common way of estimating and measuring machine time during programming projects is that of CPU hours and/or connect hours per programmer-month. This unit, however, shares the vagaries of other work units, and tends to fluctuate widely from person to person and program to program. Experience leads to the conclusion that it is wise to discard the work unit form of machine time measurement. A preferable measure is CPU hours per thousand lines, a topic that is discussed later in the paper.

Another work unit of questionable reliability is that of pages written per writer-month for documentation and publications. To be useful, it is obviously necessary to define the page, and even then the results tend to be erratic and of marginal utility. Here also the cost unit form, which might be expressed as documentation cost per thousand lines of code, seems more reliable as a way of gaining understanding about this important area.

Programming cost units

Of the several programming cost units mentioned — cost per byte, cost per line, cost per thousand lines, and others — from my experience, cost per thousand lines of code serves best. Here, lines of code means source lines of executable instructions and data declarations, but not commentary lines. Source lines are natural units for most managers and programmers, and selecting a thousand lines or bytes helps to visualize a realistic development cycle. Of course, for programs smaller than a thousand lines some other unit, such as a hundred lines, might be preferable.

The advantage of cost units as opposed to work units is that all development and maintenance expenses, including manpower, machine time, and dollars can be expressed in terms of this basic unit, and can be used to derive complete project costs by summing the subactivity costs. The summing of cost units is simpler than summing work units, and is one of the reasons why cost units are more useful and versatile than work units.

Table 5 illustrates the differences between a work unit (lines of code per programmer-month) and a cost unit (programmer-months of effort per thousand lines). The example is taken from the 2000 line Assembler language program shown in Table 4. In this example, the work unit data under lines of code per programmer-month do not add up directly. The net productivity at the end must be calculated by dividing 2000 lines of source code by the four months of effort. The data under programmer-months per thousand lines of source code can be added directly, and lead to a cost/value analysis that is discussed later in this paper.

Table 5
Comparison of Work Units and Cost Units

Activity	Raw time expended	Lines of code per programmer month	Programmer-months per thousand lines of source code
Design	4 weeks	2000	0.5
Coding	4 weeks	2000	0.5
Testing	4 weeks	2000	0.5
Documentation	2 weeks	4000	0.25
Management/support	2 weeks	4000	0.25
Totals	16 weeks (4 months)	500	2.0
Lines of source code	2000		

Example

Tables 6 and 7 give a hypothetical example comparison of work versus cost units wherein the data are typical of those found in the literature. Assume that a company is debating the merits of various improved programming technologies, and wishes to know whether they are cost justified. Suppose also that an experimental program is developed for comparison, using improved programming methods. Expenditure of personnel time is to be compared to the experience of several past programming projects.

Table 6
Work Unit Comparison of Past Experience
and Improved Programming Technologies

Activity	Past experience	Improved programming technologies
User analysis and requirements statement	3 programmer-weeks	3 programmer-weeks
Design	20 pages per week	20 pages per week
Coding	60 lines per day	110 lines per day
Testing/debugging	10 tests per day	20 tests per day
Documentation	5 pages per day	6 pages per day
Maintenance	4 hours per change	6 hours per change

On the basis of the information in Table 6, it is difficult to compare the two programs definitively because each method has advantages and disadvantages. Compared on the basis of programmer-months per thousand lines, as shown in Table 7, the cost advantage of the improved programming technologies stands out clearly.

Table 7
Cost Unit* Comparison of Past Experience
and Improved Programming Technologies

Activity	Past experience	Improved programming technologies
User analysis and requirements statement	0.24	0.24
Design	0.72	1.08
Coding	1.5	0.66
Testing/debugging	1.5	0.72
Documentation	0.48	0.36
Maintenance	1.56	0.72
Total	6.00	3.78

*Programmer-months per thousand lines of source code.

Productivity analysis using probability rectangles

By using a cost unit, a series of useful productivity analyses can be made. To visualize these analyses, the probability rectangle approach, discussed earlier in this paper, is used again. In the particular probability rectangles used here, the cost units are dollars spent per thousand lines. Other measures, however, such as CPU hours per thousand lines or programmer-months per thousand lines, are equally possible and useful.

Programs have two attributes that lend themselves to a display of their cost of productivity ranges. They have size, which can be displayed in units such as thousands of lines of code. They also have costs and expenditures that can be expressed in such terms as dollars, programmer-months, or CPU hours.

The fundamental units of size and cost make possible the plotting of those parameters and the comparison of programs. Such data plots also highlight major uncertainties and the ranges of those uncertainties that confront a programming manager and cost estimator. Typical of the factors that such a person must estimate are the number of lines of code to be produced and the unit cost per line or per thousand lines.

In the following example, a company plans to develop a new program, the size of which is estimated to fall between three and five thousand lines of code. Previous unit costs for programs at the company have ranged between $20,000 and $25,000 per thousand lines (a typical cost range). In Figure 2, these estimates are plotted as a probability rectangle.

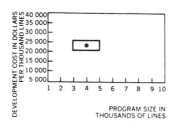

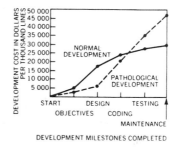

Figure 2. Probability rectangle for development cost and program size.

Figure 3. Normal and pathological program development.

The best case for the program being estimated is 3000 lines of code produced at a unit cost of $20,000 per thousand, yielding a total expenditure of $60,000, i.e., the lower left corner of the rectangle. The worst case is 5000 lines of code produced at a unit cost of $25,000 per thousand yielding a total expenditure of $125,000, i.e., the upper right corner of the rectangle. The center point of the rectangle is the mean of both variables. This point indicates that an expected size of 4000 lines has been produced at a unit cost of $22,500 per thousand, thus yielding a total expenditure of $90,000.

While the programming project is under way, both the size of a program and the unit cost of a program tend to fluctuate independently. Therefore, it is helpful to be able to separate these variables, so they can be analyzed independently. Such information aids in business decisions about whether the project is worthwhile and should be continued. Such an analysis also provides feedback about potentially dangerous situations before they become pathological and cannot be corrected. The probability rectangle approach provides management with the expected boundary conditions of program size and program costs, and facilitates making decisions about whether to continue a project in the event that worst-case situations occur.

A probability rectangle analysis also aids in heading off what we term *pathological* programming situations. Generally, a pathological program is one where unit costs and/or size far exceeded worst-case expectations. Figure 3 illustrates the contrasts between a normal development and maintenance expenditure pattern and a pathological one. The curves plotted here are not a probability rectangle, but ones that have been derived from the concept of normalizing data to display various costs on a per-thousand-lines basis. This graph is one of the family of several possible data displays that use cost units and normalization.

In normal development, early expenditures are usually high because of the tooling up and necessary learning that accompany requirements, specifications, functional definition, and design. This spending pattern typically levels off during coding, testing, and maintenance. On the other hand, pathological development is often characterized by hasty requirements analysis, incomplete design, and the premature start of coding. The discovery of overlooked functional needs frequently triggers the rewriting and recompiling of much of the code. Such programs may be termed *rear loaded,* as illustrated in Figure 3 by low initial expenditures and by steeply increasing costs late in the project. One of the values of data normalization and cost units is that such patterns can be seen as they are developing, and corrective action can be taken.

Measuring productivity in a complex environment

We now explore more realistic program development situations that involve complex programs in which development and maintenance are intermixed at the same time. One of the few items of wisdom in programming about which almost everyone seems to agree is that there is no such thing as a final program; changes always occur.

The concepts of normalization and programming cost units are useful in describing complex and realistic changing situations, as well as hypothetical cases. To do so, however, it is necessary to measure or evaluate the following costs:

- Costs of changing a program as circumstances change.
- Cumulative costs of program ownership.

Assume a programming system that has been developed and put into production status. Its initial size was 50,000 lines of code, developed at a unit cost of $40,000 per thousand lines. Thereafter, major changes were made to the system that added or deleted lines of code. Table 8 summarizes events in the life cycle of this hypothetical programming system.

Table 8
Life Cycle of a Hypothetical Programming System

Event	Size in thousands of lines	Cost in dollars per thousand lines of code	Cumulative cost in dollars
Creation	50	40,000	2,000,000
Addition	10	50,000	500,000
Deletion	−5	40,000	200,000
Addition	5	60,000	300,000
Subtotal	60	50,000	3,000,000

The basic programming system entered production status with a unit cost of $40,000 per thousand lines, or $2,000,000 in total costs. Later there were two additions and one deletion. Although the additions and deletions were presumably made at different times for different reasons, and had varying unit costs, the cumulative cost of ownership always increases. Furthermore, after the additions and deletions, the unit cost for the whole system had risen from $40,000 per thousand lines at its initial completion to $50,000 per thousand lines after the third change. Although it is possible for the unit cost to decrease (such as when many lines are added for a very low cost) the general trend is usually upward with time, and the cumulative cost of ownership is always upward.

The main goals of productivity improvement are to lower the unit cost for development and the cumulative cost of ownership during the entire life of the program. It is important to be clear about these goals because technologies and strategies that tend to minimize unit costs and ownership costs are not always the same as those that lead to the most rapid coding or hand crafting of programs. For example, if a program were to be developed and there were a choice between writing the program from scratch or modifying an existing program, the following things might occur. Assume the new program to be 5000 lines of code in size and could be produced at a work-unit rate of 500 lines of code per month, or 10 programmer-months in all.

To offer the same set of functions via modification might require 2400 lines of new code added to a base of 2600 lines of code borrowed from an existing program. Because of the difficulty of understanding or learning the base, productivity on writing the 2400 lines might drop to only 300 lines of code per month, or 8 months in all. Yet regardless of the apparent productivity rates, the costs are lower via modification. That is, if the delivered versions of the equivalent programs are contrasted in cost units, then the new program would require 2 programmer-months per thousand lines of code, and the modified version would require only 1.6 programmer-months per thousand lines.

This example illustrates the observation that on the average, productivity rates on new programs decline as size increases — with small programs of less than 2000 lines of code often taking in the vicinity of 1 programmer month per thousand lines, and large systems of over 512,000 lines often taking 10 programmer-months per thousand lines or more. When the cost of maintaining or changing a program is measured, however, a reverse trend is noted. That is, the smaller the change, the larger the unit cost is likely to be. This is because it is necessary to understand the base program even to add or modify a single line, and the overhead of the learning curve exerts an enormous leverage on small changes. Additionally, it is often necessary to test the entire program and perhaps recompile much of it, even though only a single line has been modified. This subject is discussed in somewhat more detail in Reference 2.

The cost saving that is often associated with reusing code that has already been written, rather than hand crafting it, is one of the main economic incentives leading to an increasing interest in modular programming and reusable module structures. It is in analyzing the potential cost saving that cost units as a means of comparison are showing their value.

If a program is being created from a library of precoded functions, the unit of lines of code per programmer-month has no meaning, since the work of the programmer has changed. Still, there are costs associated with assembling the products. Measuring with cost units leads to speculation about new ways of doing business, and about productivity gains similar to those in engineering and manufacture through the use of interchangeable parts.

Reusable code may significantly change one's perception of productivity. If, for example, one is developing a program function that is expected to be catalogued for reuse in many future programs, it might be well to invest in exhaustive testing, so as to approach zero program defects.

Problems of cost units

Although my experience indicates that cost units are more useful than work units in measuring programs at the present time, there are problems with cost units. Discussed here are limitations of two cost units, cost per defect for maintenance repairs and cost per page for publications and documentation.

In the context of programming, both units are in fact peripheral to the main concept of what a program is. With respect to programming, cost units aim at the product itself — lines of code or bytes. Thus cost per defect is a supplemental unit; the real indicator and true cost unit is defect removal cost per thousand lines or, alternatively, defect removal cost per line.

Similarly for documentation and publications, cost per page is a reasonable unit in a localized sense. However, it is preferable to measure documentation costs per thousand lines or documentation cost per line, so that these costs can be added to the other subactivity costs.

Cost per defect

Of the two units of measure, cost per defect is likely to cause the greater misunderstanding. Cost per defect is a key unit because, as mentioned in Reference 2, about half the money ever spent on programming has been used for defect removal and repair. As it is commonly measured and used, cost per defect is one of the paradoxical units of measure, and tends to penalize high-quality programs because it often assumes its lowest values for the most defective programs. High-quality programs tend to be relatively free of simple defects, which are cheap to repair, and only have a residue of rather elusive problems. Also, cost per defect is a compound unit of measure, and one should understand both parts of the compound. All defect removal operations, such as testing, have two distinct expense elements. One element is preparation, which includes writing test cases, reading specifications, and many other activities. Preparation costs accrue whether a program has any defects in it or not, and these costs increase more or less as a function of program size. The other expense element is repair, which includes fixing bugs that are found and retesting after repairing the defects. Suppose, for example, that two similar programs are being tested, and we are interested in comparing their defect removal costs in some normalized form. Assume that both programs consist of one thousand lines of Assembler code, but one program has been written using improved programming methods, such as topdown design and structured code, for defect prevention. The other program, however, has been using older methodologies. Assume also that in testing only one problem is found in the modern program, whereas the old style program has ten problems reported. Preparation costs for the test are identical for both programs and run ten hours each. Defect repair costs for the modern program are only six hours, but total thirty hours for the old-style program. By adding the preparation and repair hours and dividing by the number of defects in each case the cost per defect is sixteen hours for the single modern program defect and four hours for the old-style program. The paradox lies in the observation that the greater the number of defects found in the program, the cheaper they are to repair. It might be thought that by separating the preparation costs from the repair costs the paradox would be resolved. This, however, is not the case. The low-defect program shows six hours per defect for repair alone, whereas the high-defect program requires only three hours per defect in repair costs.

Cost per page

The overall conclusion is that cost per defect is not a reliable unit of measure, since it penalizes high-quality programs. A better method is to look at defect removal and repair costs per thousand lines. With this unit, the true expenses of high-defect levels are revealed, i.e., sixteen hours of test cost per thousand lines of code for high quality programs, and forty hours of test cost per thousand lines of code for old-style programs.

The situation with cost per page of documentation is not quite as traumatic as it is with cost per defect, since page costs do not tend to favor high-defect work products. The problem with cost per page is that it tends to achieve its lowest values for pages with the greatest amount of white space. If white space is held constant, cost per page tends to be lower for documents with the greatest number of pages (although this latter point is not a definite rule).

The problems with cost per page can be shown by the following example. Suppose that two identical programs are being documented, and both are one thousand lines of code in size. In one case, the writer merely converts a specification into a publication, and produces a fifty-page document at a cost of $3000. This yields a cost per page of $60. In the second case, the writer works hard to condense the materials, and produces a thirty-page document at a cost of $2400, or $80 per page. Even though the cost per page favors the large document, the smaller publication is the less expensive of the two. If documentation costs per thousand lines of code is the unit of measure, this fact is clearly revealed. The small book costs $2400 per thousand lines of code, whereas the larger costs $3000 per thousand lines of code. With documentation as with programming, care must be used in selecting units of measure for the results to be truly meaningful.

Ratios and percentages

Of all the ways to discuss productivity data, ratios and percentages tend to be the least reliable and the most likely to cause serious misunderstandings. Ratios show, for example, percentages of time, expenses, or CPU hours devoted to different aspects of development. It is extremely common — perhaps more common than any other method — to see reports that indicate such things as "design took twenty percent of the time and fifteen percent of the programmer-months while coding took thirty percent of the time and forty percent of the programmer-months."

The fundamental problem with ratios and percentages is that they assume that various development activities are connected in such a way that if you know one of the activities, you can derive the others. For example, there is an assumption (implicit in the use of ratios) that if you can estimate coding costs accurately, then you can derive testing costs by assuming that testing is some percentage of the coding cost. These basic assumptions are incorrect, and there are no known fundamental ratios between the various activities of programming. Consider the two activities of coding and testing. Coding expenses are a function of the completeness of the design, the skills of the coders, and the tools and methods used. Testing expenses are a function of preparation costs and defect repair costs. It is possible — in fact quite common — for two programs A and B to have virtually identical coding expenses, but very different testing expenses. The assumption that a ratio of coding costs to testing costs developed for program A will work for program B is a common misconception, and one of the key sources of estimating error.

The alternative to ratios and percentages is straightforward. Calculate the costs of each development activity on its own merits and then sum all the subactivity costs to arrive at the total programming cost. This way, even if one activity is grossly incorrect, the problem does not propagate itself throughout other activities, which might be the case if ratios had been used.

Without multiplying examples, it may easily be seen that ratios are extremely simplistic, and supply little or no useful information. Indeed, the only thing that ratios do well is preserve secret or proprietary information about how much time or money were actually spent.

Summary and conclusions

To a large extent, the units used to measure program quality and productivity tend to lead the mind along certain channels of thought. An analysis of the commonly used units of measure in programming has revealed deficiencies in some units that lead to incorrect and even to paradoxical conclusions.

This analysis has shown directions in which further progress can be made in understanding both programming itself and ways of measuring it. We have shown that by subdividing the general topic of quality into the subcategories of defect prevention and defect removal for separate analysis, great insights into programming productivity may result.

In the general area of productivity it has been shown that it is useful to distinguish between work units (which try to assess how fast programs are developed) and cost units (which try to assess how much will be spent). My experience so far indicates that this distinction is important, because techniques that reduce costs are sometimes quite different from techniques that increase speed.

Even though great progress is being made in programming and in measuring programming, it cannot yet be said that programming has fully reached the level of an exact science. In spite of this, however, the results are increasingly encouraging.

References: Jones

Cited References

1. J.R. Johnson, "A working measure of productivity," *Datamation* **23**, No. 2, 106-112 (February 1977).

2. T.C. Jones, *Program Quality and Programmer Productivity,* TR02.764, IBM Corporation, General Products Division, 5600 Cottle Road, San Jose, California 95193.

3. S.L. de Freitas and P.J. Lavelle, "A method for the time analysis of programs," *IBM Systems Journal* **17**, No. 1 (January 1978).

4. M.E. Fagan, "Design and code inspections to reduce errors in program development," *IBM Systems Journal* **15**, No. 3, 182-211 (1976).

5. C.E. Walston and C.P. Felix, "A method of programming measurement and estimation," *IBM Systems Journal* **16**, No. 1, 54-73 (1977).

6. T.C. Jones, "Productivity measurements," *Proceedings of GUIDE 44,* San Francisco, California (May 1977).

General References

1. B.W. Boehm, "Software and its impact: a quantitative assessment," *Datamation* **19,** No. 5, 48-59 (May 1973).

2. T. Gilb, *Software Metrics,* Winthrop Computer Systems Series, Winthrop Publishing Co., Englewood, NJ (1976).

3. M.H. Halstead, *Elements of Software Science,* Elsevier North-Holland Incorporated, New York, NY (1977).

A Measure of Control
Flow Complexity
in Program Text

I. Introduction

Increasing importance is being attached to the idea of measuring software characteristics [2]. It is only by such a process of measurement that it will be possible to determine whether new programming techniques are having the desired effect in reducing the problems of reliable software production. Unfortunately many of the qualities of interest such as clarity, ease of testing and maintenance, etc., are highly subjective and so experiments have been performed to correlate objective grading of programs with measured structural characteristics of source programs [1]. Although it may be possible to mimic professional judgment of programs by objective metrics in this fashion it seems likely that such a process will be very dependent on the language used and in-house programming standards.

Other related aspects are to measure objectively the complexity and unstructuredness of programs and then investigate the relationship between such metrics and error histories of programs. Intuitively one might expect that the more complex a program is, in some sense, the greater will be the expected incidence of errors in that program. It will also be of great interest to compare the use, or lack of use, of the principles of structured programming with error rates.

First, however, one needs suitable measures of complexity and unstructuredness and it is with this purpose that this paper is concerned. There exists a number of complexity metrics as outlined in the next section. However, it has been noted by Thayer [14] that "evaluation of metrics is part of the study process, and it will take several iterations on a number of differing software systems to identify the more universally applicable

SOURCE: M.R. Woodward, M.A. Hennell & D. Hedley, *IEEE Transactions on Software Engineering,* 1979.

metrics." In Section III we put forward a simple language independent concept which can be used as a measure of complexity. Then in Section IV we develop the idea for use as a measure of unstructuredness. Finally in Section V we relate our experience with these and other metrics.

II. Some complexity and unstructuredness metrics

In his letter entitled "Goto Statement Considered Harmful," Dijkstra [5] observed that the "quality of programmers is a decreasing function of the density of goto statements." This suggests then a very simple measure, namely the number of gotos in a program. Whilst this may be useful as a measure of unstructuredness for some languages (e.g., the Algol type languages) it is not for others (e.g., Fortran). It has been recognized for example that gotos are an essential ingredient for writing structured Fortran [12].

Gilb in his book *Software Metrics* [8] states that logical complexity is a measure of the degree of decision making within a system and that the number of if statements is a rough measure of this complexity. Indeed he reports the experience of Farr and Zagorski [6] who have found this metric to be a significant factor in predicting software costs. More generally it seems reasonable to count not only the ifs, but all the branch creating statements (decision points) in a program.

An interesting link exists between this last measure and the intellectually very appealing cyclomatic complexity measure $V(G)$ of McCabe [10]. A program is first represented as a directed graph and then:

$$V(G) = \text{number of edges} - \text{number of nodes} + 2.$$

McCabe has shown that this number equals the number of predicates (i.e., decision points) in the program plus one.

III. "Knots" as a measure of complexity

Let us temporarily restrict attention to Fortran programs. At some stage most Fortran programmers will probably have laid out their program text in front of them and then proceeded to draw arrowed lines on one side of the text indicating where a jump occurs from one line of text to another line of text, as for example in Fig. 1. (This routine is in fact Routine A of [4].) Such a time honored procedure sometimes aids the programmer in following the flow of control through the program. The more intertwined these arrowed lines become, the less useful is such a procedure in providing the programmer with a mental map of the program. It was this consideration which led us to define a "knot" as occurring when one is forced to draw two such directional lines crossing each other at some point. This can be stated more mathematically and without ambiguity as follows.

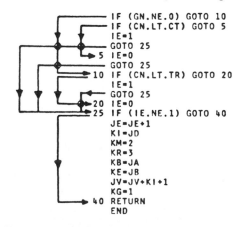

Figure 1. Example with 4 knots. This is in fact Routine A of [4].

If a jump from line a to line b is represented by the ordered pair of integers (a,b), then jump (p,q) gives rise to a "knot" or crossing point with respect to jump (a,b) if either

1) $\min(a,b) < \min(p,q) < \max(a,b)$
     and $\max(p,q) > \max(a,b)$

or

2) $\min(a,b) < \max(p,q) < \max(a,b)$
     and $\min(p,q) < \min(a,b)$

Then by counting the number of "knots" in a program a measure of complexity can be obtained.

It is to be noted that the above definition is in terms of line numbers and although we have only discussed the notion of a "knot" for Fortran programs it can be extended to other languages. The characteristic of Fortran which makes knots so natural and simple to obtain is that it is a language with one statement per line. For languages permitting many statements per line the number of knots becomes ill defined. For example in the following code:

label 1: . . . ; label 2: . . . ;
if a = b then goto label 1 else goto label 2 fi;

applying the definition with jumps in terms of the line numbers alone is not sufficient to expose the crossing of control flow.

There are two approaches which resolve this difficulty. The first is to number the lexemes (or even individual characters) sequentially from the start of the program code. Having characterized the jumps in terms of this numbering we can now apply the knots definition.

The second approach is to reformat the program in such a way as to remove the difficulties [9]. The example above would become:

label 1: . . . ;
label 2: . . . ;
    if a = b
    then
        goto label 1
    else
        goto label 2
    fi;

The advantages are twofold. Firstly the ability to draw in the knots by hand is retained. Secondly the readability of the program is vastly improved. It is well-known that in any language with powerful control structures, the layout of the program is an important consideration. Thus, since the programs will have the required layout anyway, the line number characterization has considerable appeal.

Although the definition of knots is dependent on knowledge of program control flow jumps in terms of line numbers, it is possible to obtain upper and lower bounds on the number of knots in a program from a directed graph representation, provided we also know the ordering of the nodes to make the transition from a two-dimensional graph to a one-dimensional program. The inability to extract the precise number of knots is to be expected, because information concerning the physical source test is discarded in constructing a directed graph of a program.

In order to obtain the lower bound we just apply the definition as it stands, where now the ordered pairs of integers (a,b) and (p,q) represent the edges of the directed graph. The strict inequalities in the definition ensure that no knots arise which involve transfer of control to the next node, i.e., edges (a,a+1) as for example in the transfer of control via natural succession, and the number obtained in this fashion is a definite lower bound.

Since the nodes in a directed graph usually represent basic blocks [7] which may involve several source lines with a unique entry point at the head of the block (first line), no branching within the block, and a unique exit point at the tail of the block (last line), there exist situations in which there is insufficient information to resolve the existence or nonexistence of a knot. For example the number of knots in a construction such as in Fig. 2 depends on whether node B corresponds to several lines (1 knot) or just one line (0 knots). By including all such doubtful cases in our count we can obtain an upper bound to the number of knots.

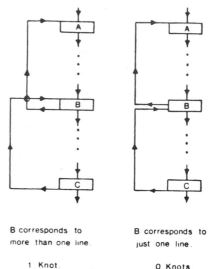

B corresponds to more than one line.

1 Knot.

B corresponds to just one line.

0 Knots.

Figure 2. Example showing the difficulty in determining the number of knots in a program from its directed graph representation.

We notice that we can obtain these lower and upper bounds from the incidence matrix corresponding to the directed graph. If we have an edge (i,j) with $i > j$ or $i < j$ then by setting $p = \min(i,j)$ and $q = \max(i,j)$ the lower bound can be obtained by counting the number of entries to nodes strictly between p and q to nodes strictly outside the range p to q, and also the number of exits from nodes strictly between p and q to nodes strictly outside the range p to q. This corresponds to counting the number of nonzero entries in the shaded region of the incidence matrix, as in Fig. 3, for each edge (i,j).

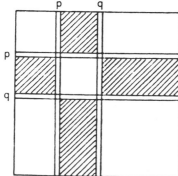

Figure 3. To obtain a lower bound on the number of knots, count the number of nonzero entries in the shaded region of the incidence matrix for each edge (i,j) where p = min(i,j) and q = max(i,j).

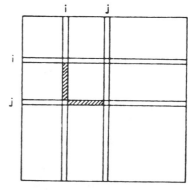

Figure 4. For each edge (i,j) with i < j, include the number of nonzero entries in this additional shaded region of the incidence matrix to obtain an upper bound on the number of knots.

The upper bound can be obtained by adding into the count the number of nonzero elements in the additional shaded regions of Fig. 4 if i < j and of Fig. 5 if i > j. Since each knot arises as a crossing of two jumps, a count performed in this fashion for each nonzero element of the incidence matrix will include every knot twice.

It is to be noted that calculating a lower bound and an upper bound in this way provides a complexity interval in a manner resembling Myers' extension of McCabe's cyclomatic complexity [11].

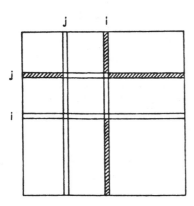

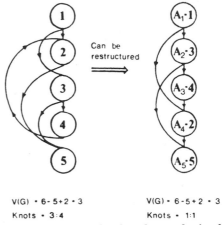

Can be restructured

$V(G) \cdot 6 - 5 + 2 \cdot 3$

Knots $\cdot$ 3:4

$V(G) \cdot 6 - 5 + 2 \cdot 3$

Knots $\cdot$ 1:1

Figure 5. For each edge (i, j) with i > j, include the number of nonzero entries in this additional shaded region of the incidence matrix to obtain an upper bound on the number of knots.

Figure 6. An example of reduced complexity by restructuring. In the original version the knot count lower bound arises from the crossings of edge (1,3) with edge (4,2), edge (1,3) with edge (2,5), and edge (3,5) with edge (4,2). The upper bound also includes the crossing of edge (2,5) with edge (4,2). In the restructured version the single knot arises from the crossing of edge (A_1, A_4) with edge (A_2, A_5).

One of the advantages the knot count has over the cyclomatic complexity $V(G)$ is that the number of knots in a program is dependent on the ordering of the statements in the program. Since a directed graph, like a flow chart, is two dimensional, linearization of it must take place in the actual construction of a program. There will be many ways of ordering the nodes of a directed graph to produce equivalent programs and some will be more complex than others [3]. This will not be reflected in $V(G)$ since McCabe's measure is independent of the ordering. Consider an example of reordering (Fig. 6) given by Ramamoorthy and Ho [13], consisting of 5 nodes and 6 edges so that:

$$V(G) = 6 - 5 + 2 = 3.$$

In the first version the knots interval is 3:4 but the second restructured (less complex) version has a knots interval of 1:1.

Other program transformations aimed at code improvement also have the desired property of reducing the knot count. For example the three Fortran routines considered by Brown and Nelson [4], when rewritten so that they no longer contain "phantom" paths, i.e., paths which cannot be exercised for any input data, all have reduced knot counts. The number of knots in their Routine A drops from 4 to 0, in their Routine B from 6 to 4, and in their Routine C from 9 to 3. This last case is included here in Figs. 7 and 8. It demonstrates once again an advantage of considering knots rather than the cyclomatic complexity, since $V(G) = 3$ for both the original (Fig. 7) and the undoubtedly less complex version (Fig. 8) which has no "phantom" paths.

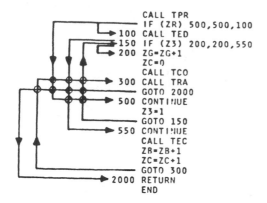

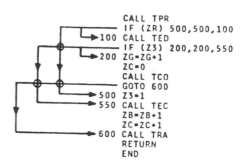

Figure 7. Original version of Routine C from [4], having 9 knots. It has two branch creating statements and so V(G) = 2+1 = 3.

Figure 8. Rewritten version of Routine C from [4] having no "phantom" paths and 3 knots. It still has two branch creating statements and so V(G) = 2+1 = 3.

One might also consider the problem of counting the knots when the directional lines are allowed on both sides of the source text such as a programmer might attempt on a program listing. However, problems then arise on how the jumps should be partitioned when both sides are permitted in this manner and the additional information does not appear worth the necessary expenditure of effort [15].

IV. "Knots" and structured programming

Since the number of knots is determined from the program text, the complexity of the usual constructs in structured programming will depend upon the language used and the way the constructs are implemented. Consider for example the implementation in Fortran of the simple choice clause:

_if_ bool <u>then</u> . . . A . . . <u>else</u> . . . B . . .

The most natural way of writing this in Fortran is given in Fig. 9 and has 1 knot. Another way of implementing this construct which does not involve negation of the Boolean expression, but results in more complicated control flow, is given in Fig. 10 and has 2 knots.

The use of the Fortran arithmetic IF or computed GOTO to provide a 3-way choice results in 3 knots (Fig. 11) and in general an n-way case simulated using the computed GOTO will have a knot count of:

$$\sum_{r=1}^{n-1} r = (n-1).n/2.$$

The <u>while</u> and <u>repeat until</u> looping constructs can be implemented with zero knots.

The contribution to the program complexity arising from the use of structured programming can be removed to provide a measure which reflects the lack of structure in a program. The usual reduction of the directed graph can be performed replacing the admitted primitives of structured programming by single nodes. If this process is continued until no further reduction of the graph is possible and the knots interval of the remaining graph G' is determined, this will provide a measure of program "unstructuredness.'' A structured program will be reducible to a single node with zero knots. This leads to a definition of the remaining knots as the essential knots of the program and it can be stated that a structured program will have zero essential knots. This is analogous to McCabe's calculation of the cyclomatic complexity of the reduced graph $V(G')$ which equals his essential complexity $EV(G)$ provided each proper subgraph with unique entry and unique exit is one of the structured programming primitives. Note that $EV(G) = V(G') = 1$ for a structured program.

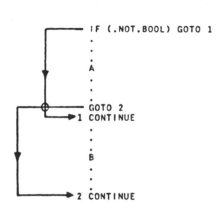

Figure 9. One way of implementing an if then else construct in Fortran having 1 knot.

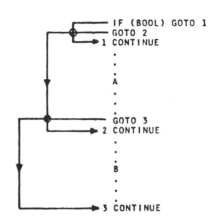

Figure 10. An alternative way of implementing an if then else construct in Fortran having 2 knots.

Figure 11. An example of a 3-way case construct in Fortran having 3 knots.

Figure 12. Table of metrics for a sample of 26 Fortran subroutines from a numerical algorithms library.

Routine	Lines	Gotos	Ifs	V(G)	Knots	EV(G)	Essential Knots
A	3	0	0	1	0	1	0:0
B	7	1	1	3	0	1	0:0
C	8	0	1	2	0	1	0:0
D	16	1	1	3	0	1	0:0
E	17	2	3	7	0	1	0:0
F	21	2	5	5	3	5	2:3
G	21	1	1	7	0	1	0:0
H	24	2	3	8	0	1	0:0
I	39	0	0	6	0	1	0:0
J	43	7	9	17	0	1	0:0
K	47	4	10	10	11	7	6:7
L	50	11	11	14	9	7	5:6
M	51	4	4	13	1	1	0:0
N	55	9	7	13	2	4	0:2
O	58	6	8	19	3	8	1:3
P	59	5	15	17	12	14	10:11
Q	68	7	2	7	2	3	2:2
R	69	4	18	19	27	8	15:16
S	74	7	7	22	1	1	0:0
T	77	12	12	18	7	9	3:6
U	93	13	13	22	5	6	2:4
V	95	11	19	27	83	25	79:83
W	112	15	14	24	15	5	3:4
X	210	52	42	62	30	14	4:6
Y	249	23	32	62	42	22	30:31
Z	310	59	54	85	33	15	13:17

V. Experience

We have an automatic tool for obtaining the number of knots in Fortran programs using a list of jumps in terms of line numbers. In a survey of some 330 Fortran subroutines from a numerical algorithms library it was found that one third of the routines had zero knots, another third had less than 10 knots, and only 50 routines had more than 20 knots.

We also have a tool for determining the knots interval for the directed graph using the incidence matrix representation. It also performs the previously described reduction process and enables us to determine the cyclomatic complexity and the essential knots. In Fig. 12 we give a list of various metrics mentioned in this paper for a sample of 26 Fortran subroutines from a numerical algorithms library. From this small random sample it would appear that $V(G)$ increases almost linearly with the size of a program. In fact the correlation coefficient between $V(G)$ and the number of lines was 0.98 and was the highest correlation encountered between any pair of columns in Fig. 12. It could be argued that this is a desirable feature of a complexity metric especially since size in source statements has been shown in a study by TRW [14] to be the metric that correlated best with the occurrence of actual software errors. We note that only one routine (Routine Q) with more than 50 lines has $V(G)$ less than 10, the upper limit on cyclomatic complexity for a single module suggested by McCabe.

However we feel that the knot count provides a much clearer indication of program readability. From Fig. 12 it is possible to see that the cyclomatic complexity $V(G)$ is usually greater than the number of knots. Routines R and V are significant exceptions to this. The high knot counts for these routines confirm not only the visual impression of high complexity but also the difficulty actually encountered in translating them to other languages (viz., Algol 60 and Algol 68). In the correlation analysis it was found that the correlation coefficient between $V(G)$ and the number of knots was 0.60. The lowest correlation was between the essential knots and the number of gotos with a coefficient of 0.21.

To highlight the differences between $V(G)$ and the knot count consider a program of n nested loops as represented by the directed graph of Fig. 13. Since this has $(3n+2)$ edges and $(2n+3)$ nodes the cyclomatic complexity is given by:

$$V(G) = (3n+2) - (2n+3) + 2 = n+1.$$

However it has zero knots. If now any extra exits are inserted from the center of the nested loops at node $n+2$, we start to obtain a nonzero knot count. Indeed if we consider n exits from the center of the nest, as represented by Fig. 14, we find that $V(G)$ increases linearly as a function of n but the number of knots increases as a function of n^2.

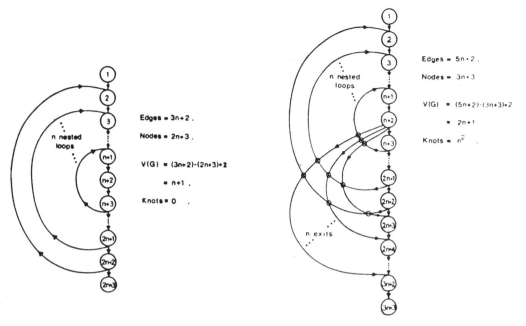

Figure 13. An example with V(G) increasing linearly as a function of n, but having zero knots.

Figure 14. An example with V(G) increasing linearly as a function of n, but with the number of knots increasing as a function of n^2.

It is this feature of knots in penalizing those areas of code for which the control flow is highly interwoven which we have found useful. Furthermore, if the knots remain, even after reduction of structured programming constructs to single nodes, then this would appear to indicate a code segment in need of reevaluation.

Acknowledgment

The authors would like to acknowledge the NAG (Numerical Algorithms Group) organization for permission to analyze their library.

References: Woodward, Hennell & Hedley

1. S.J. Amster, E.J. Davis, B.N. Dickman, and J.P. Kuoni, "An experiment in automatic quality evaluation of software," in *Proc. Symp. Computer Software Eng.,* MRI Symposia Series, vol. XXIV, J. Fox, Ed., Polytechnic Institute of New York, Apr. 1976, pp. 171-197.

2. B.W. Boehm, J.R. Brown, and M. Lipow, "Quantitative evaluation of software quality," in *Proc. 2nd Int. Conf. Software Eng.,* San Francisco, Oct. 1976, pp. 592-605.

3. T.B. Boffey, "The linearisation of flow charts," *BIT,* vol. 15, pp. 341-350, 1975.

4. J.R. Brown and E.C. Nelson, "Functional programming," Final Tech. Rep. on contract F30602-76-C-0315 by TRW Defense and Space Systems Group for Rome Air Development Center, July 15, 1977.

5. E.W. Dijkstra, "Goto statement considered harmful," *Commun. Ass. Comput. Mach.,* vol. 11, pp. 147-148, 1968.

6. L. Farr and H.J. Zagorski, "Quantitative analysis of programming cost factors: A progress report," in "Economics of automatic data processing" in *1965 ICC Symp. Proc.,* Rome, A.B. Frielink, Ed. Amsterdam, The Netherlands: North-Holland, 1965.

7. L.D. Fosdick, "BRNANL—A FORTRAN program to identify basic blocks in FORTRAN programs," Tech. Rep. CU-CS-040-74, Dep. Comput. Sci., Univ. Colorado, Boulder, Mar. 1974.

8. T. Gilb, *Software Metrics.* Cambridge, MA: Winthrop, 1977.

9. M.A. Hennell and D. Hedley, "An experimental testbed for numerical software: II Algol 68," *Comput. J.,* to be published.

10. T.J. McCabe, "A complexity measure," *IEEE Trans. Software Eng.,* vol. SE-2, pp. 308-320, Dec. 1976.

11. G.J. Myers, "An extension to the cyclomatic measure of program complexity," *Sigplan Notices,* vol. 12, pp. 61-64, Oct. 1977.

12. P.M. Neely, "The new programming discipline," *Software — Practice and Experience,* vol. 6, pp. 7-27, 1976.

13. C.V. Ramamoorthy and S.F. Ho, "Testing large software with automated software evaluation systems," in *Proc. 1975 Int. Conf. Reliable Software,* Los Angeles, Apr. 1975, pp. 382-394.

14. T.A. Thayer, "Understanding software through empirical reliability analysis," in *1975 Spring Joint Comput. Conf., AFIPS Conf. Proc.,* vol. 44. Montvale, NJ: AFIPS Press, May 1975, pp. 335-341.

15. M.R. Woodward, M.A. Hennell, and D. Hedley, "The analysis of control flow structure in computer programs," in *Proc. Liverpool Univ. Conf. Combinatorial Programming* (CP77), T.B. Boffey, Ed., Sept. 1977, pp. 190-201.

Section 7
HUMAN CONCEPTUAL LIMITS

Miller: The Magical Number Seven . . .

The concluding paper in this collection is the most classic of all: "The Magical Number Seven, Plus or Minus Two: Some Limits on Our Capacity for Processing Information." Written by George Miller, and published in *The Psychological Review* in 1956, its basic message has appeared in dozens — if not hundreds — of papers and books in the data processing field in the past fifteen years. Yet Miller's paper doesn't deal with the area of data processing at all; it simply discusses the limited "channel capacity" of the human mind.

His examples are intriguing: Most humans can only discriminate between six musical tones; can distinguish roughly five levels of loudness of sound; and can only differentiate about four levels of saltiness in a taste test. All of these have to do with the ability of people to distinguish between different values of a single variable; this ability — which Miller calls *absolute judgment* — seems to be severely limited by the number of "bits" of information being presented to the human observer.

Miller then goes on to define *immediate memory:* Unlike absolute judgment, which is the ability to make an *instant* response to a stimulus, immediate memory is the ability to withhold a response until several stimuli in succession have been given. Once again, it is found that there is a limit — the same magical number seven. However, numerous experiments have demonstrated that while a person's absolute judgment is limited by the amount of information — expressed in bits of information — the immediate memory is limited by the number of "chunks" of information. By appropriately recoding information into larger, richer chunks, we are able to maintain a larger amount of information in our immediate memory.

Miller's demonstration of this is terribly familiar to anyone with a computer programming background. He points out that the average person can only remember a string of approximately seven binary digits; however, we can compress the binary digits into, say, octal digits and maintain an immediate memory of seven (plus or minus two) octal digits — or twenty-four bits of information.

All of this would be fascinating reading even if it had nothing to do with data processing. But of course, it *does* have a lot to do with the ideas presented in several of the other papers in this book. The whole notion of levels of abstraction espoused by Dijkstra, Hoare, Wirth, Mills, and others is what Miller would call recoding — the ability of the human mind to group several discrete pieces of information into a meaningful abstraction. Without Miller's paper, one might be inclined to think that levels of abstraction, or stepwise refinement, or top-down design were just nice ideas. After reading the paper, it is obvious that such ideas are absolutely essential if we are to develop complex software properly — for our ability to develop complex software is absolutely limited by the ability of the human mind to comprehend it. And the ability of the human mind, as Miller shows us, is indeed limited.

The Magical Number Seven, Plus or Minus Two: Some Limits on Our Capacity for Processing Information

My problem is that I have been persecuted by an integer. For seven years this number has followed me around, has intruded in my most private data, and has assaulted me from the pages of our most public journals. This number assumes a variety of disguises, being sometimes a little larger and sometimes a little smaller than usual, but never changing so much as to be unrecognizable. The persistence with which this number plagues me is far more than a random accident. There is, to quote a famous senator, a design behind it, some pattern governing its appearances. Either there really is something unusual about the number or else I am suffering from delusions of persecution.

I shall begin my case history by telling you about some experiments that tested how accurately people can assign numbers to the magnitudes of various aspects of a stimulus. In the traditional language of psychology these would be called experiments in absolute judgment. Historical accident, however, has decreed that they should have another name. We now call them experiments on the capacity of people to transmit information. Since these experiments would not have been done without the appearance of information theory on the psychological scene, and since the results are analyzed in terms of the concepts of information theory, I shall have to preface my discussion with a few remarks about this theory.

SOURCE: G.A. Miller, *The Psychological Review,* 1956.

Information measurement

The "amount of information" is exactly the same concept that we have talked about for years under the name of "variance." The equations are different, but if we hold tight to the idea that anything that increases the variance also increases the amount of information we cannot go far astray.

The advantages of this new way of talking about variance are simple enough. Variance is always stated in terms of the unit of measurement — inches, pounds, volts, etc. — whereas the amount of information is a dimensionless quantity. Since the information in a discrete statistical distribution does not depend upon the unit of measurement, we can extend the concept to situations where we have no metric and we would not ordinarily think of using the variance. And it also enables us to compare results obtained in quite different experimental situations where it would be meaningless to compare variances based on different metrics. So there are some good reasons for adopting the newer concept.

The similarity of variance and amount of information might be explained this way: When we have a large variance, we are very ignorant about what is going to happen. If we are very ignorant, then when we make the observation it gives us a lot of information. On the other hand, if the variance is very small, we know in advance how our observation must come out, so we get little information from making the observation.

If you will now imagine a communication system, you will realize that there is a great deal of variability about what goes into the system and also a great deal of variability about what comes out. The input and the output can therefore be described in terms of their variance (or their information). If it is a good communication system, however, there must be some systematic relation between what goes in and what comes out. That is to say, the output will depend upon the input, or will be correlated with the input. If we measure this correlation, then we can say how much of the output variance is attributable to the input and how much is due to random fluctuations or "noise" introduced by the system during transmission. So we see that the measure of transmitted information is simply a measure of input-output correlation.

There are two simple rules to follow. Whenever I refer to "amount of information," you will understand "variance." And whenever I refer to "amount of transmitted information," you will understand "covariance" or "correlation."

The situation can be described graphically by two partially overlapping circles. Then the left circle can be taken to represent the variance of the input, the right circle the variance of the output, and the overlap the covariance of input and output. I shall speak of the left circle as the amount of input information, the right circle as the amount of output information, and the overlap as the amount of transmitted information.

In the experiments on absolute judgment, the observer is considered to be a communication channel. Then the left circle would represent the amount of information in the stimuli, the right circle the amount of information in his responses, and the overlap the stimulus-response correlation as measured by the amount of transmitted information. The experimental problem is to increase the amount of input information and to measure the amount of transmitted information. If the observer's absolute judgments are quite accurate, then nearly all of the input information will be transmitted and will be recoverable from his responses. If he makes errors, the transmitted information may be considerably less than the input. We expect that, as we increase the amount of input information, the observer will begin to make more and more errors; we can test the limits of accuracy of his absolute judgments. If the human observer is a reasonable kind of communication system, then when we increase the amount of input information the transmitted information will increase at first and will eventually level off at some asymptotic value. This asymptotic value we take to be the *channel capacity* of the observer: it represents the greatest amount of information that he can give us about the stimulus on the basis of an absolute judgment. The channel capacity is the upper limit on the extent to which the observer can match his responses to the stimuli we give him.

Now just a brief word about the *bit* and we can begin to look at some data. One bit of information is the amount of information that we need to make a decision between two equally likely alternatives. If we must decide whether a man is less than six feet tall or more than six feet tall and if we know that the chances are 50−50, then we need one bit of information. Notice that this unit of information does not refer in any way to the unit of length that we use − feet, inches, centimeters, etc. However you measure the man's height, we still need just one bit of information.

Two bits of information enable us to decide among four equally likely alternatives. Three bits of information enable us to decide among eight equally likely alternatives. Four bits of information decide among 16 alternatives, five among 32, and so on. That is to say, if there are 32 equally likely alternatives, we must make five successive binary decisions, worth one bit each, before we know which alternative is correct. So the general rule is simple: every time the number of alternatives is increased by a factor of two, one bit of information is added.

There are two ways we might increase the amount of input information. We could increase the rate at which we give information to the observer, so that the amount of information per unit time would increase. Or we could ignore the time variable completely and increase the amount of input information by increasing the number of alternative stimuli. In the absolute judgment experiment we are interested in the second alternative. We give the observer as much time as he wants to make his response; we simply increase the number of alternative stimuli among which he must discriminate and look to see where confusions begin to occur. Confusions will appear near the point that we are calling his "channel capacity."

Absolute judgments of unidimensional stimuli

Now let us consider what happens when we make absolute judgments of tones. Pollack [17] asked listeners to identify tones by assigning numerals to them. The tones were different with respect to frequency, and covered the range from 100 to 8000 cps in equal logarithmic steps. A tone was sounded and the listener responded by giving a numeral. After the listener had made his response, he was told the correct identification of the tone.

When only two or three tones were used, the listeners never confused them. With four different tones confusions were quite rare, but with five or more tones confusions were frequent. With fourteen different tones the listeners made many mistakes.

These data are plotted in Fig. 1. Along the bottom is the amount of input information in bits per stimulus. As the number of alternative tones was increased from 2 to 14, the input information increased from 1 to 3.8 bits. On the ordinate is plotted the amount of transmitted information. The amount of transmitted information behaves in much the way we would expect a communication channel to behave; the transmitted information increases linearly up to about 2 bits and then bends off toward an asymptote at about 2.5 bits. This value, 2.5 bits, therefore, is what we are calling the channel capacity of the listener for absolute judgments of pitch.

Figure 1. Data from Pollack [17, 18] on the amount of information that is transmitted by listeners who make absolute judgments of auditory pitch. As the amount of input information is increased by increasing from 2 to 14 the number of different pitches to be judged, the amount of transmitted information approaches as its upper limit a channel capacity of about 2.5 bits per judgment.

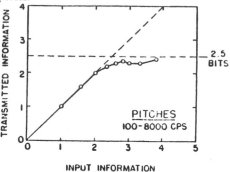

So now we have the number 2.5 bits. What does it mean? First, note that 2.5 bits corresponds to about six equally likely alternatives. The result means that we cannot pick more than six different pitches that the listener will never confuse. Or, stated slightly differently, no matter how many alternative tones we ask him to judge, the best we can expect him to do is to assign them to about six different classes without error. Or, again, if we know that there were N alternative stimuli, then his judgment enables us to narrow down the particular stimulus to one out of $N/6$.

Most people are surprised that the number is as small as six. Of course, there is evidence that a musically sophisticated person with absolute pitch can identify accurately any one of 50 or 60 different pitches. Fortunately, I do not have time to discuss these remarkable exceptions. I say it is fortunate because I do not know how to explain their superior performance. So I shall stick to the more pedestrian fact that most of us can identify about one out of only five or six pitches before we begin to get confused.

It is interesting to consider that psychologists have been using seven-point rating scales for a long time, on the intuitive basis that trying to rate into finer categories does not really add much to the usefulness of the ratings. Pollack's results indicate that, at least for pitches, this intuition is fairly sound.

Next you can ask how reproducible this result is. Does it depend on the spacing of the tones or the various conditions of judgment? Pollack varied these conditions in a number of ways. The range of frequencies can be changed by a factor of about 20 without changing the amount of information transmitted more than a small percentage. Different groupings of the pitches decreased the transmission, but the loss was small. For example, if you can discriminate five high-pitched tones in one series and five low-pitched tones in another series, it is reasonable to expect that you could combine all ten into a single series and still tell them all apart without error. When you try it, however, it does not work. The channel capacity for pitch seems to be about six and that is the best you can do.

While we are on tones, let us look next at Garner's [7] work on loudness. Garner's data for loudness are summarized in Fig. 2. Garner went to some trouble to get the best possible spacing of his tones over the intensity range from 15 to 110 db. He used 4, 5, 6, 7, 10, and 20 different stimulus intensities. The results shown in Fig. 2 take into account the differences among subjects and the sequential influence of the immediately preceding judgment. Again we find that there seems to be a limit. The channel capacity for absolute judgments of loudness is 2.3 bits, or about five perfectly discriminable alternatives.

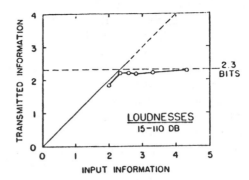

Figure 2. Data from Garner [7] on the channel capacity for absolute judgments of auditory loudness.

Since these two studies were done in different laboratories with slightly different techniques and methods of analysis, we are not in a good position to argue whether five loudnesses is significantly different from six pitches. Probably the difference is in the right direction, and absolute judgments of pitch are slightly more accurate than absolute judgments of loudness. The important point, however, is that the two answers are of the same order of magnitude.

The experiment has also been done for taste intensities. In Fig. 3 are the results obtained by Beebe-Center, Rogers, and O'Connell [1] for absolute judgments of the concentration of salt solutions. The concentrations ranged from 0.3 to 34.7 gm. NaCl per 100 cc. tap water in equal subjective steps. They used 3, 5, 9, and 17 different concentrations. The channel capacity is 1.9 bits, which is about four distinct concentrations. Thus taste intensities seem a little less distinctive than auditory stimuli, but again the order of magnitude is not far off.

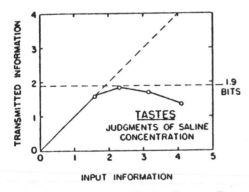

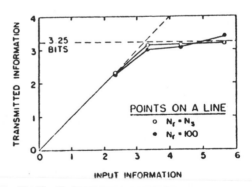

Figure 3. Data from Beebe-Center, Rogers, and O'Connell [1] on the channel capacity for absolute judgments of saltiness.

Figure 4. Data from Hake and Garner [8] on the channel capacity for absolute judgments of the position of a pointer in a linear interval.

On the other hand, the channel capacity for judgments of visual position seems to be significantly larger. Hake and Garner [8] asked observers to interpolate visually between two scale markers. Their results are shown in Fig. 4. They did the experiment in two ways. In one version they let the observer use any number between zero and 100 to describe the position, although they presented stimuli at only 5, 10, 20, or 50 different positions. The results with this unlimited response technique are shown by the filled circles on the graph. In the other version the observers were limited in their responses to reporting just those stimulus values that were possible. That is to say, in the second version the number of different responses that the observer could make was exactly the same as the number of different stimuli that the experimenter might present. The results with this limited response technique are shown by the open circles on the graph. The two functions are so similar that it seems fair to conclude that the number of responses available to the observer had nothing to do with the channel capacity of 3.25 bits.

The Hake-Garner experiment has been repeated by Coonan and Klemmer. Although they have not yet published their results, they have given me permission to say that they obtained channel capacities ranging from 3.2 bits for very short exposures of the pointer position to 3.9 bits for longer exposures. These values are slightly higher than Hake and Garner's, so we must conclude that there are between 10 and 15 distinct positions along a linear interval. This is the largest channel capacity that has been measured for any unidimensional variable.

At the present time these four experiments on absolute judgments of simple, unidimensional stimuli are all that have appeared in the psychological journals. However, a great deal of work on other stimulus variables has not yet appeared in the journals. For example, Eriksen and Hake [6] have found that the channel capacity for judging the sizes of squares is 2.2 bits, or about five categories, under a wide range of experimental conditions. In a separate experiment Ericksen [5] found 2.8 bits for size, 3.1 bits for hue, and 2.3 bits for brightness. Geldard has measured the channel capacity for the skin by placing vibrators on the chest region. A good observer can identify about four intensities, about five durations, and about seven locations.

One of the most active groups in this area has been the Air Force Operational Applications Laboratory. Pollack has been kind enough to furnish me with the results of their measurements for several aspects of visual displays. They made measurements for area and for the curvature, length, and direction of lines. In one set of experiments they used a very short exposure of the stimulus — 1/40 second — and then they repeated the measurements with a 5-second exposure. For area they got 2.6 bits with the short exposure and 2.7 bits with the long exposure. For the length of a line they got about 2.6 bits with the short exposure and about 3.0 bits with the long exposure. Direction, or angle of inclination, gave 2.8 bits for the short exposure and 3.3 bits for the long exposure. Curvature was apparently harder to judge. When the length of the arc was constant, the result at the short exposure duration was 2.2 bits, but when the length of the chord was constant, the result was only 1.6 bits. This last value is the lowest that anyone has measured to date. I should add, however, that these values are apt to be slightly too low because the data from all subjects were pooled before the transmitted information was computed.

Now let us see where we are. First, the channel capacity does seem to be a valid notion for describing human observers. Second, the channel capacities measured for these unidimensional variables range from 1.6 bits for curvature to 3.9 bits for positions in an interval. Although there is no question that the differences among the variables are real and meaningful, the more impressive fact to me is their considerable similarity. If I take the best estimates I can get of the channel capacities for all the stimulus variables I have mentioned, the mean is 2.6 bits and the standard deviation is only 0.6 bit. In terms of distinguishable alternatives, this mean corresponds to about 6.5 categories, one standard deviation includes from 4 to 10 categories, and the total range is from 3 to 15 categories. Considering the wide variety of different variables that have been studied, I find this to be a remarkably narrow range.

There seems to be some limitation built into us either by learning or by the design of our nervous systems, a limit that keeps our channel capacities in this general range. On the basis of the present evidence it seems safe to say that we possess a finite and rather small capacity for making such unidimensional judgments and that this capacity does not vary a great deal from one simple sensory attribute to another.

Absolute judgments of multidimensional stimuli

You may have noticed that I have been careful to say that this magical number seven applies to one-dimensional judgments. Everyday experience teaches us that we can identify accurately any one of several hundred faces, any one of several thousand words, any one of several thousand objects, etc. The story certainly would not be complete if we stopped at this point. We must have some understanding of why the one-dimensional variables we judge in the laboratory give results so far out of line with what we do constantly in our behavior outside the laboratory. A possible explanation lies in the number of independently variable attributes of the stimuli that are being judged. Objects, faces, words, and the like differ from one another in many ways, whereas the simple stimuli we have considered thus far differ from one another in only one respect.

Fortunately, there are a few data on what happens when we make absolute judgments of stimuli that differ from one another in several ways. Let us look first at the results Klemmer and Frick [13] have reported for the absolute judgment of the position of a dot in a square. In Fig. 5 we see their results. Now the channel capacity seems to have increased to 4.6 bits, which means that people can identify accurately any one of 24 positions in the square.

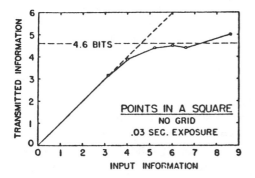

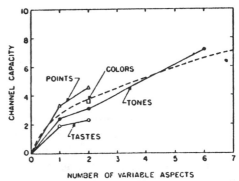

Figure 5. Data from Klemmer and Frick [13] on the channel capacity for absolute judgments of the position of a dot in a square.

Figure 6. The general form of the relation between channel capacity and the number of independently variable attributes of the stimuli.

The position of a dot in a square is clearly a two-dimensional proposition. Both its horizontal and its vertical position must be identified. Thus it seems natural to compare the 4.6-bit capacity for a square with the 3.25-bit capacity for the position of a point in an interval. The point in the square requires two judgments of the interval type. If we have a capacity of 3.25 bits for estimating intervals and we do this twice, we should get 6.5 bits as our capacity for locating points in a square. Adding the second independent dimension gives us an increase from 3.25 to 4.6, but it falls short of the perfect addition that would give 6.5 bits.

Another example is provided by Beebe-Center, Rogers, and O'Connell. When they asked people to identify both the saltiness and the sweetness of solutions containing various concentrations of salt and sucrose, they found that the channel capacity was 2.3 bits. Since the capacity for salt alone was 1.9, we might expect about 3.8 bits if the two aspects of the compound stimuli were judged independently. As with spatial locations, the second dimension adds a little to the capacity but not as much as it conceivably might.

A third example is provided by Pollack [18], who asked listeners to judge both the loudness and the pitch of pure tones. Since pitch gives 2.5 bits and loudness gives 2.3 bits, we might hope to get as much as 4.8 bits for pitch and loudness together. Pollack obtained 3.1 bits, which again indicates that the second dimension augments the channel capacity but not so much as it might.

A fourth example can be drawn from the work of Halsey and Chapanis [9] on confusions among colors of equal luminance. Although they did not analyze their results in informational terms, they estimate that there are about 11 to 15 identifiable colors, or, in our terms, about 3.6 bits. Since these colors varied in both hue and saturation, it is probably correct to regard this as a two-dimensional judgment. If we compare this with Eriksen's 3.1 bits for hue (which is a questionable comparison to draw), we again have something less than perfect addition when a second dimension is added.

It is still a long way, however, from these two-dimensional examples to the multidimensional stimuli provided by faces, words, etc. To fill this gap we have only one experiment, an auditory study done by Pollack and Ficks [19]. They managed to get six different acoustic variables that they could change: frequency, intensity, rate of interruption, on-time fraction, total duration, and spatial location. Each one of these six variables could assume any one of five different values, so altogether there were 5^6, or 15,625 different tones that they could present. The listeners made a separate rating for each one of these six dimensions. Under these conditions the transmitted information was 7.2 bits, which corresponds to about 150 different categories that could be absolutely identified without error. Now we are beginning to get up into the range that ordinary experience would lead us to expect.

Suppose that we plot these data, fragmentary as they are, and make a guess about how the channel capacity changes with the dimensionality of the stimuli. The result is given in Fig. 6. In a moment of considerable daring I sketched the dotted line to indicate roughly the trend that the data seemed to be taking.

Clearly, the addition of independently variable attributes to the stimulus increases the channel capacity, but at a decreasing rate. It is interesting to note that the channel capacity is increased even when the several variables are not independent. Eriksen [5] reports that, when size, brightness, and hue all vary together in perfect correlation, the transmitted information is 4.1 bits as compared with an average of about 2.7 bits when these attributes are varied one at a time. By confounding three attributes, Eriksen increased the dimensionality of the input without increasing the amount of input information; the result was an increase in channel capacity of about the amount that the dotted function in Fig. 6 would lead us to expect.

The point seems to be that, as we add more variables to the display, we increase the total capacity, but we decrease the accuracy for any particular variable. In other words, we can make relatively crude judgments of several things simultaneously.

We might argue that in the course of evolution those organisms were most successful that were responsive to the widest range of stimulus energies in their environment. In order to survive in a constantly fluctuating world, it was better to have a little information about a lot of things than to have a lot of information about a small segment of the environment. If a compromise was necessary, the one we seem to have made is clearly the more adaptive.

Pollack and Ficks's results are very strongly suggestive of an argument that linguists and phoneticians have been making for some time [19]. According to the linguistic analysis of the sounds of human speech, there are about eight or ten dimensions — the linguists call them *distinctive features* — that distinguish one phoneme from another. These distinctive features are usually binary, or at most ternary, in nature. For example, a binary distinction is made between vowels and consonants, a binary decision is made between oral and nasal consonants, a ternary decision is made among front, middle, and back phonemes, etc. This approach gives us quite a different picture of speech perception than we might otherwise obtain from our studies of the speech spectrum and of the ear's ability to discriminate relative differences among pure tones. I am personally much interested in this new approach [15], and I regret that there is not time to discuss it here.

It was probably with this linguistic theory in mind that Pollack and Ficks conducted a test on a set of tonal stimuli that varied in eight dimensions, but required only a binary decision on each dimension. With these tones they measured the transmitted information at 6.9 bits, or about 120 recognizable kinds of sounds. It is an intriguing question, as yet unexplored, whether one can go on adding dimensions indefinitely in this way.

In human speech there is clearly a limit to the number of dimensions that we use. In this instance, however, it is not known whether the limit is imposed by the nature of the perceptual machinery that must recognize the sounds or by the nature of the speech machinery that must produce them. Somebody will have to do the experiment to find out. There is a limit, however, at about eight or nine distinctive features in every language that has been studied, and so when we talk we must resort to still another trick for increasing our channel capacity. Language uses sequences of phonemes, so we make several judgments successively when we listen to words and sentences. That is to say, we use both simultaneous and successive discriminations in order to expand the rather rigid limits imposed by the inaccuracy of our absolute judgments of simple magnitudes.

These multidimensional judgments are strongly reminiscent of the abstraction experiment of Külpe [14]. As you may remember, Külpe showed that observers report more accurately on an attribute for which they are set than on attributes for which they are not set. For example, Chapman [4] used three different attributes and compared the results obtained when the observers were instructed before the tachistoscopic presentation with the results obtained when they were not told until after the presentation which one of the three attributes was to be reported. When the instruction was given in advance, the judgments were more accurate. When the instruction was given afterwards, the subjects presumably had to judge all three attributes in order to report on any one of them and the accuracy was correspondingly lower. This is in complete accord with the results we have just been considering, where the accuracy of judgment on each attribute decreased as more dimensions were added. The point is probably obvious, but I shall make it anyhow, that the abstraction experiments did *not* demonstrate that people can judge only one attribute at a time. They merely showed what seems quite reasonable, that people are less accurate if they must judge more than one attribute simultaneously.

Subitizing

I cannot leave this general area without mentioning, however briefly, the experiments conducted at Mount Holyoke College on discrimination of number [12]. In experiments by Kaufman, Lord, Reese, and Volkmann random patterns of dots were flashed on a screen for 1/5 of a second. Anywhere from 1 to more than 200 dots could appear in the pattern. The subject's task was to report how many dots there were.

The first point to note is that on patterns containing up to five or six dots the subjects simply did not make errors. The performance on these small numbers of dots was so different from the performance with more dots that it was given a special name. Below seven the subjects were said to *subitize;* above seven they were said to *estimate.* This is, as you will recognize, what we once optimistically called "the span of attention."

This discontinuity at seven is, of course, suggestive. Is this the same basic process that limits our unidimensional judgments to about seven categories? The generalization is tempting, but not sound in my opinion. The data on number estimates have not been analyzed in informational terms; but on the basis of the published data I would guess that the subjects transmitted something more than four bits of information about the number of dots. Using the same arguments as before, we would conclude that there are about 20 or 30 distinguishable categories of numerousness. This is considerably more information than we would expect to get from a unidimensional display. It is, as a matter of fact, very much like a two-dimensional display. Although the dimensionality of the random dot patterns is not entirely clear, these results are in the same range as Klemmer and Frick's for their two-dimensional display of dots in a square. Perhaps the two dimensions of numerousness are area and density. When the subject can subitize, area and density may not be the significant variables, but when the subject must estimate perhaps they are significant. In any event, the comparison is not so simple as it might seem at first thought.

This is one of the ways in which the magical number seven has persecuted me. Here we have two closely related kinds of experiments, both of which point to the significance of the number seven as a limit on our capacities. And yet when we examine the matter more closely, there seems to be a reasonable suspicion that it is nothing more than a coincidence.

The span of immediate memory

Let me summarize the situation in this way. There is a clear and definite limit to the accuracy with which we can identify absolutely the magnitude of a unidimensional stimulus variable. I would propose to call this limit the *span of absolute judgment,* and I maintain that for unidimensional judgments this span is usually somewhere in the neighborhood of seven. We are not completely at the mercy of this limited span, however, because we have a variety of techniques for getting around it and increasing the accuracy of our judgments. The three most important of these devices are (*a*) to make relative rather than absolute judgments; or, if that is not possible, (*b*) to increase the number of dimensions along which the stimuli can differ; or (*c*) to arrange the task in such a way that we make a sequence of several absolute judgments in a row.

The study of relative judgments is one of the oldest topics in experimental psychology, and I will not pause to review it now. The second device, increasing the dimensionality, we have just considered. It seems that by adding more dimensions and requiring crude, binary, yes-no judgments on each attribute we can extend the span of absolute judgment from seven to at least 150. Judging from our everyday behavior, the limit is probably in the thousands, if indeed there is a limit. In my opinion, we cannot go on compounding dimensions indefinitely. I suspect that there is also a *span of perceptual dimensionality* and that this span is somewhere in the neighborhood of ten, but I must add at once that there is no objective evidence to support this suspicion. This is a question sadly needing experimental exploration.

Concerning the third device, the use of successive judgments, I have quite a bit to say because this device introduces memory as the handmaiden of discrimination. And, since mnemonic processes are at least as complex as are perceptual processes, we can anticipate that their interactions will not be easily disentangled.

Suppose that we start by simply extending slightly the experimental procedure that we have been using. Up to this point we have presented a single stimulus and asked the observer to name it immediately thereafter. We can extend this procedure by requiring the observer to withhold his response until we have given him several stimuli in succession. At the end of the sequence of stimuli he then makes his response. We still have the same sort of input-output situation that is required for the measurement of transmitted information. But now we have passed from an experiment on absolute judgment to what is traditionally called an experiment on immediate memory.

Before we look at any data on this topic, I feel I must give you a word of warning to help you avoid some obvious associations that can be confusing. Everybody knows that there is a finite span of immediate memory and that for a lot of different kinds of test materials this span is about seven items in length. I have just shown you that there is a span of absolute judgment that can distinguish about seven categories and that there is a span of attention that will encompass about six objects at a glance. What is more natural than to think that all three of these spans are different aspects of a single underlying process? And that is a fundamental mistake, as I shall be at some pains to demonstrate. This mistake is one of the malicious persecutions that the magical number seven has subjected me to.

My mistake went something like this. We have seen that the invariant feature in the span of absolute judgment is the amount of information that the observer can transmit. There is a real operational similarity between the absolute judgment experiment and the immediate memory experiment. If immediate memory is like absolute judgment, then it should follow that the invariant feature in the span of immediate memory is also the amount of information that an observer can retain. If the amount of information in the span of immediate memory is a constant, then the span should be short when the individual items contain a lot of information and the span should be long when the items contain little information. For example, decimal digits are worth 3.3 bits apiece. We can recall about seven of them, for a total of 23 bits of information. Isolated English words are worth about 10 bits apiece. If the total amount of information is to remain constant at 23 bits, then we should be able to remember only two or three words chosen at random. In this way I generated a theory about how the span of immediate memory should vary as a function of the amount of information per item in the test materials.

The measurements of memory span in the literature are suggestive on this question, but not definitive. And so it was necessary to do the experiment to see. Hayes [10] tried it out with five different kinds of test materials: binary digits, decimal digits, letters of the alphabet, letters plus decimal digits, and with 1,000 monosyllabic words. The lists were read aloud at the rate of one item per second and the subjects had as much time as they needed to give their responses. A procedure described by Woodworth [20] was used to score the responses.

The results are shown by the filled circles in Fig. 7. Here the dotted line indicates what the span should have been if the amount of information in the span were constant. The solid curves represent the data. Hayes repeated the experiment using test vocabularies of different sizes but all containing only English monosyllables (open circles in Fig. 7). This more homogeneous test material did not change the picture significantly. With binary items the span is about nine and, although it drops to about five with monosyllabic English words, the difference is far less than the hypothesis of constant information would require.

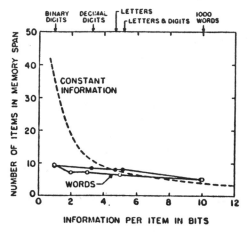

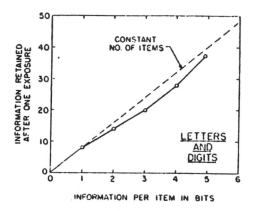

Figure 7. Data from Hayes [10] on the span of immediate memory plotted as a function of the amount of information per item in the test materials.

Figure 8. Data from Pollack [16] on the amount of information retained after one presentation plotted as a function of the amount of information per item in the test materials.

There is nothing wrong with Hayes's experiment, because Pollack [16] repeated it much more elaborately and got essentially the same result. Pollack took pains to measure the amount of information transmitted and did not rely on the traditional procedure for scoring the responses. His results are plotted in Fig. 8. Here it is clear that the amount of information transmitted is not a constant, but increases almost linearly as the amount of information per item in the input is increased.

And so the outcome is perfectly clear. In spite of the coincidence that the magical number seven appears in both places, the span of absolute judgment and the span of immediate memory are quite different kinds of limitations that are imposed on our ability to process information. Absolute judgment is limited by the amount of information. Immediate memory is limited by the number of items. In order to capture this distinction in somewhat picturesque terms, I have fallen into the custom of distinguishing between *bits* of information and *chunks* of information. Then I can say that the number of bits of information is constant for absolute judgment and the number of chunks of information is constant for immediate memory. The span of immediate memory seems to be almost independent of the number of bits per chunk, at least over the range that has been examined to date.

The contrast of the terms *bit* and *chunk* also serves to highlight the fact that we are not very definite about what constitutes a chunk of information. For example, the memory span of five words that Hayes obtained when each word was drawn at random from a set of 1,000 English monosyllables might just as appropriately have been called a memory span of 15 phonemes, since each word had about three phonemes in it. Intuitively, it is clear that the subjects were recalling five words, not 15 phonemes, but the logical distinction is not immediately apparent. We are dealing here with a process of organizing or grouping the input into familiar units or chunks, and a great deal of learning has gone into the formation of these familiar units.

Recoding

In order to speak more precisely, therefore, we must recognize the importance of grouping or organizing the input sequence into units or chunks. Since the memory span is a fixed number of chunks, we can increase the number of bits of information that it contains simply by building larger and larger chunks, each chunk containing more information than before.

A man just beginning to learn radio-telegraphic code hears each *dit* and *dah* as a separate chunk. Soon he is able to organize these sounds into letters and then he can deal with the letters as chunks. Then the letters organize themselves as words, which are still larger chunks, and he begins to hear whole phrases. I do not mean that each step is a discrete process, or that plateaus must appear in his learning curve, for surely the levels of organization are achieved at different rates and overlap each other during the learning process. I am simply pointing to the obvious fact that the dits and dahs are organized by learning into patterns and that as these larger chunks emerge the amount of message that the operator can remember increases correspondingly. In the terms I am proposing to use, the operator learns to increase the bits per chunk.

In the jargon of communication theory, this process would be called *recoding*. The input is given in a code that contains many chunks with few bits per chunk. The operator recodes the input into another code that contains fewer chunks with more bits per chunk. There are many ways to do this recoding, but probably the simplest is to group the input events, apply a new name to the group, and then remember the new name rather than the original input events.

Since I am convinced that this process is a very general and important one for psychology, I want to tell you about a demonstration experiment that should make perfectly explicit what I am talking about. This experiment was conducted by Sidney Smith and was reported by him before the Eastern Psychological Association in 1954.

Begin with the observed fact that people can repeat back eight decimal digits, but only nine binary digits. Since there is a large discrepancy in the amount of information recalled in these two cases, we suspect at once that a recoding procedure could be used to increase the span of immediate memory for binary digits. In Table 1 a method for grouping and renaming is illustrated. Along the top is a sequence of 18 binary digits, far more than any subject was able to recall after a single presentation. In the next line these same binary digits are grouped by pairs. Four possible pairs can occur: 00 is renamed 0, 01 is renamed 1, 10 is renamed 2, and 11 is renamed 3. That is to say, we recode from a base-two arithmetic to a base-four arithmetic. In the recoded sequence there are now just nine digits to remember, and this is almost within the span of immediate memory. In the next line the same sequence of binary digits is regrouped into chunks of three. There are eight possible sequences of three, so we give each sequence a new name between 0 and 7. Now we have recoded from a sequence of 18 binary digits into a sequence of 6 octal digits, and this is well within the span of immediate memory. In the last two lines the binary digits are grouped by fours and by fives and are given decimal-digit names from 0 to 15 and from 0 to 31.

Table 1
Ways of Recoding Sequences of Binary Digits

Binary Digits (Bits)		1 0 1 0 0 0 1 0 0 1 1 1 0 0 1 1 1 0							
2:1	Chunks	10	10	00	10	01	11	00	11	10
	Recoding	2	2	0	2	1	3	0	3	2
3:1	Chunks	101	000		100		111	001		110
	Recoding	5	0		4		7	1		6
4:1	Chunks	1010		0010		0111		0011		10
	Recoding	10		2		7		3		
5:1	Chunks	10100			01001			11001		110
	Recoding	20			9			25		

It is reasonably obvious that this kind of recoding increases the bits per chunk, and packages the binary sequence into a form that can be retained within the span of immediate memory. So Smith assembled 20 subjects and measured their spans for binary and octal digits. The spans were 9 for binaries and 7 for octals. Then he gave each recoding scheme to five of the subjects. They studied the recoding until they said they understood it — for about 5 or 10 minutes. Then he tested their span for binary digits again while they tried to use the recoding schemes they had studied.

The recoding schemes increased their span for binary digits in every case. But the increase was not as large as we had expected on the basis of their span for octal digits. Since the discrepancy increased as the recoding ratio increased, we reasoned that the few minutes the subjects had spent learning the recoding schemes had not been sufficient. Apparently the translation from one code to the other must be almost automatic or the subject will lose part of the next group while he is trying to remember the translation of the last group.

Since the 4:1 and 5:1 ratios require considerable study, Smith decided to imitate Ebbinghaus and do the experiment on himself. With Germanic patience he drilled himself on each recoding successively, and obtained the results shown in Fig. 9. Here the data follow along rather nicely with the results you would predict on the basis of his span for octal digits. He could remember 12 octal digits. With the 2:1 recoding, these 12 chunks were worth 24 binary digits. With the 3:1 recoding they were worth 36 binary digits. With the 4:1 and 5:1 recodings, they were worth about 40 binary digits.

It is a little dramatic to watch a person get 40 binary digits in a row and then repeat them back without error. However, if you think of this merely as a mnemonic trick for extending the memory span, you will miss the more important point that is implicit in nearly all such mnemonic devices. The point is that recoding is an extremely powerful weapon for increasing the amount of information that we can deal with. In one form or another we use recoding constantly in our daily behavior.

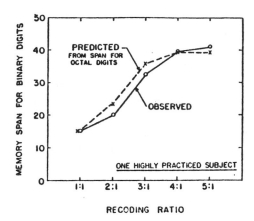

Figure 9. The span of immediate memory for binary digits is plotted as a function of the recoding procedure used. The predicted function is obtained by multiplying the span for octals by 2, 3, and 3.3 for recoding into base 4, base 8, and base 10, respectively.

In my opinion the most customary kind of recoding that we do all the time is to translate into a verbal code. When there is a story or an argument or an idea that we want to remember, we usually try to rephrase it "in our own words." When we witness some event we want to remember, we make a verbal description of the event and then remember our verbalization. Upon recall we recreate by secondary elaboration the details that seem consistent with the particular verbal recoding we happen to have made. The well-known experiment by Carmichael, Hogan, and Walter [3] on the influence that names have on the recall of visual figures is one demonstration of the process.

The inaccuracy of the testimony of eyewitnesses is well known in legal psychology, but the distortions of testimony are not random — they follow naturally from the particular recoding that the witness used, and the particular recoding he used depends upon his whole life history. Our language is tremendously useful for repackaging material into a few chunks rich in information. I suspect that imagery is a form of recoding, too, but images seem much harder to get at operationally and to study experimentally than the more symbolic kinds of recoding.

It seems probable that even memorization can be studied in these terms. The process of memorizing may be simply the formation of chunks, or groups of items that go together, until there are few enough chunks so that we can recall all the items. The work by Bousfield and Cohen [2] on the occurrence of clustering in the recall of words is especially interesting in this respect.

Summary

I have come to the end of the data that I wanted to present, so I would like now to make some summarizing remarks.

First, the span of absolute judgment and the span of immediate memory impose severe limitations on the amount of information that we are able to receive, process, and remember. By organizing the stimulus input simultaneously into several dimensions and successively into a sequence of chunks, we manage to break (or at least stretch) this informational bottleneck.

Second, the process of recoding is a very important one in human psychology and deserves much more explicit attention than it has received. In particular, the kind of linguistic recoding that people do seems to me to be the very lifeblood of the thought processes. Recoding procedures are a constant concern to clinicians, social psychologists, linguists, and anthropologists and yet, probably because recoding is less accessible to experimental manipulation than nonsense syllables or T mazes, the traditional experimental psychologist has contributed little or nothing to their analysis. Nevertheless, experimental techniques can be used, methods of recoding can be specified, behavioral indicants can be found. And I anticipate that we will find a very orderly set of relations describing what now seems an uncharted wilderness of individual differences.

Third, the concepts and measures provided by the theory of information provide a quantitative way of getting at some of these questions. The theory provides us with a yardstick for calibrating our stimulus materials and for measuring the performance of our subjects. In the interests of communication I have suppressed the technical details of information measurement and have tried to express the ideas in more familiar terms; I hope this paraphrase will not lead you to think they are not useful in research. Informational concepts have already proved valuable in the study of discrimination and of language; they promise a great deal in the study of learning and memory; and it has even been proposed that they can be useful in the study of concept formation. A lot of questions that seemed fruitless twenty or thirty years ago may now be worth another look. In fact, I feel that my story here must stop just as it begins to get really interesting.

And finally, what about the magical number seven? What about the seven wonders of the world, the seven seas, the seven deadly sins, the seven daughters of Atlas in the Pleiades, the seven ages of man, the seven levels of hell, the seven primary colors, the seven notes of the musical scale, and the seven days of the week? What about the seven-point rating scale, the seven categories for absolute judgment, the seven objects in the span of attention, and the seven digits in the span of immediate memory? For the present I propose to withhold judgment. Perhaps there is something deep and profound behind all these sevens, something just calling out for us to discover it. But I suspect that it is only a pernicious, Pythagorean coincidence.

References: Miller

1. Beebe-Center, J.G., Rogers, M.S., and O'Connell, D.N. Transmission of information about sucrose and saline solutions through the sense of taste. *J. Psychol.,* 1955, **39,** 157-160.

2. Bousfield, W.A., and Cohen, B.H. The occurrence of clustering in the recall of randomly arranged words of different frequencies-of-usage. *J. Gen. Psychol.,* 1955, **52,** 83-95.

3. Carmichael, L., Hogan, H.P., and Walter, A.A. An experimental study of the effect of language on the reproduction of visually perceived form. *J. Exp. Psychol.,* 1932, **15,** 73-86.

4. Chapman, D.W. Relative effects of determinate and indeterminate *Aufgaben. Amer. J. Psychol.,* 1932, **44,** 163-174.

5. Eriksen, C.W. Multidimensional stimulus differences and accuracy of discrimination. *USAF, WADC Tech. Rep.,* 1954, No. 54-165.

6. Eriksen, C.W., and Hake, H.W. Absolute judgments as a function of the stimulus range and the number of stimulus and response categories. *J. Exp. Psychol.,* 1955, **49,** 323-332.

7. Garner, W.R. An informational analysis of absolute judgments of loudness. *J. Exp. Psychol.,* 1953, **46,** 373-380.

8. Hake, H.W., and Garner, W.R. The effect of presenting various numbers of discrete steps on scale reading accuracy. *J. Exp. Psychol.,* 1951, **42,** 358-366.

9. Halsey, R.M., and Chapanis, A. Chromaticity-confusion contours in a complex viewing situation. *J. Opt. Soc. Amer.,* 1954, **44,** 442-454.

10. Hayes, J.R.M. Memory span for several vocabularies as a function of vocabulary size. In *Quarterly Progress Report,* Cambridge, Mass.: Acoustics Laboratory, Massachusetts Institute of Technology, Jan.-June, 1952.

11. Jakobson, R., Fant, C.G.M., and Halle, M. *Preliminaries to speech analysis.* Cambridge, Mass.: Acoustics Laboratory, Massachusetts Institute of Technology, 1952. (Tech. Rep. No. 13.)

12. Kaufman, E.L., Lord, M.W., Reese, T.W., and Volkmann, J. The discrimination of visual number. *Amer. J. Psychol.,* 1949, **62,** 498-525.

13. Klemmer, E.T., and Frick, F.C. Assimilation of information from dot and matrix patterns. *J. Exp. Psychol.,* 1953, **45,** 15-19.

14. Külpe, O. Versuche über Abstraktion. *Ber. ü. d. I Kongr. f. Exper. Psychol.,* 1904, 56-68

15. Miller, G.A., and Nicely, P.E. An analysis of perceptual confusions among some English consonants. *J. Acoust. Soc. Amer.,* 1955, **27,** 338-352.

16. Pollack, I. The assimilation of sequentially encoded information. *Amer. J. Psychol.,* 1953, **66,** 421-435.

17. Pollack, I. The information of elementary auditory displays. *J. Acoust. Soc. Amer.,* 1952, **24,** 745-749.

18. Pollack, I. The information of elementary auditory displays. II. *J. Acoust. Soc. Amer.,* 1953, **25,** 765-769.

19. Pollack, I., and Ficks, L. Information of elementary multi-dimensional auditory displays. *J. Acoust. Soc. Amer.,* 1954, **26,** 155-158.

20. Woodworth, R.S. *Experimental psychology.* New York: Holt, 1938.